Lecture Notes in Computer Science 3084

Commenced Publication in 1973
Founding and Former Series Editors:
Gerhard Goos, Juris Hartmanis, and Jan van Leeuwen

T0189288

Springer
Berlin
Heidelberg
New York
Hong Kong
London
Milan
Paris

ne Persson   Janis Stirna (Eds.)

dvanced Information ystems Engineering

h International Conference, CAiSE 2004
;a, Latvia, June 7-11, 2004
ceedings

 Springer

lume Editors

ne Persson
iversity of Skövde, School of Technology and Society
). Box 408, 541 28 Skövde, Sweden
mail: anne.persson@ida.his.se

is Stirna
yal Institute of Technology and Stockholm University
partment of Computer and Systems Sciences
RUM 100, 16440, Kista, Sweden
mail: js@dsv.su.se

orary of Congress Control Number: 2004106910

R Subject Classification (1998): H.2, H.4-5, H.3, J.1, K.4.3-4, K.6, D.2, I.2.11

SN 0302-9743
BN 3-540-22151-4 Springer-Verlag Berlin Heidelberg New York

inger-Verlag is a part of Springer Science+Business Media

ingeronline.com

Springer-Verlag Berlin Heidelberg 2004
nted in Germany

besetting: Camera-ready by author, data conversion by Olgun Computergrafik

Preface

CAiSE 2004 was the 16th in the series of International Conferences on Advanced Information Systems Engineering. In the year 2004 the conference was hosted by the Faculty of Computer Science and Information Technology, Riga Technical University, Latvia.

Since the late 1980s, the CAiSE conferences have provided a forum for the presentation and exchange of research results and practical experiences within the field of Information Systems Engineering. The conference theme of CAiSE 2004 was Knowledge and Model Driven Information Systems Engineering for Networked Organizations.

Modern businesses and IT systems are facing an ever more complex environment characterized by openness, variety, and change. Organizations are becoming less self-sufficient and increasingly dependent on business partners and other actors. These trends call for openness of business as well as IT systems, i.e. the ability to connect and interoperate with other systems. Furthermore, organizations are experiencing ever more variety in their business, in all conceivable dimensions. The different competencies required by the workforce are multiplying. In the same way, the variety in technology is overwhelming with a multitude of languages, platforms, devices, standards, and products. Moreover, organizations need to manage an environment that is constantly changing and where lead times, product life cycles, and partner relationships are shortening. The demand of having to constantly adapt IT to changing technologies and business practices has resulted in the birth of new ideas which may have a profound impact on the information systems engineering practices in future years, such as autonomic computing, component and services marketplaces and dynamically generated software.

These trends pose a number of challenges to both the operational systems and the development processes of the organization, its work practice, and its IT systems. In order to cope with increasingly complex business and IT environments, organizations need effective instruments for managing their knowledge about these environments. Essential among these instruments are models, i.e. representations of aspects of reality including the domain of work, the processes, and the context. Models come in a variety of forms, formal or informal; describing static or dynamic aspects; representing agents, processes, or resources; focusing on business or IT aspects, etc. To realize the full potential of models, there is a need for a business and technology architecture as well as a way of working that places the models firmly in the center and lets them be the driving force in analysis, design, implementation, deployment and use of systems and services. This implies developing not only new modeling languages but also new ways of developing models, which incorporate in a participatory manner all stakeholders involved.

The challenging theme of CAiSE 2004 attracted scientists from all over the world to submit their contributions. The total number of submissions was 160, out of which the program committee selected 39 top-quality papers. The resulting program reflects the fact that the topic of information systems engineering encompasses human and organizational issues as well as technical issues. In addition to the main program, 16 papers presenting emerging ideas were invited to the CAiSE Forum. The CAiSE Forum was initiated by the organizers of CAiSE 2003 in Velden as a means of stimulating scientific debate.

The success of the CAiSE conferences is shown by the large number of co-located events. CAiSE 2004 was accompanied by eleven workshops and four tutorials, which attracted a large number of participants. The tutorials were given by Scott Ambler (Canada), Brian Henderson-Sellers (Australia) and Dov Dori (Israel). In addition, the Sixth International Baltic Conference on Databases and Information Systems was co-located with CAiSE 2004.

We devote a special thanks to the members of the program committee for providing excellent reviews of the submitted papers. Their dedicated work was instrumental in putting together yet another high-quality CAiSE conference. We wish also to give special thanks to the local organizers at the Riga Technical University for their hard work and devotion, which made the conference a great success.

The CAiSE 2004 organizers would also like to thank the conference sponsors – the Latvian Council of Science, the Dati Group (Latvia), Tieto Enator (Latvia), Lattelekom (Latvia), and the SISU Foundation (Sweden).

March 2004   Anne Persson
                                                                    Janis Stirna

CAiSE 2004 Conference Organization

Advisory Committee

Janis Bubenko
The Royal Institute of Technology, Sweden
Colette Rolland
Université Paris 1 - Pantheon - Sorbonne, France
Arne Sølvberg
The Norwegian University of Science and Technology, Norway

General Chair	Program Committee Co-chairs	Organizing Chair
Janis Grundspenkis *Riga Technical University Latvia*	**Anne Persson** *University of Skövde, Sweden* **Janis Stirna** *Royal Institute of Technology, Sweden*	**Girts Vulfs** *Riga Technical University, Latvia*

Workshop Chair	Tutorials and Panel Chair	Poster Chair
Marite Kirikova *Riga Technical University, Latvia*	**Uldis Sukovskis** *Riga Information Technology Institute, Latvia*	**Janis Grabis** *Riga Technical University, Latvia*

Publicity and Communications Chair

Victoria Vinogradova
Riga Technical University, Latvia

Program Committee

Additional Referees

CAiSE 2004 Pre-conference Workshops

The Sixth International Bi-Conference Workshop on Agent-Oriented Information Systems (AOIS 2004)

Paolo Bresciani, Italy
Brian Henderson-Sellers, Australia
Graham Low, Australia

The Fifth Workshop on Business Process Modelling, Development, and Support

Ilia Bider, Sweden
Gil Regev, Switzerland
Pnina Soffer, Israel

The Doctoral Consortium on Advanced Information Systems Engineering

Xiaomeng Su, Norway
Ewald Kaluscha, Austria

The International Workshop on Data and Information Quality

Martin J. Eppler, Switzerland
Markus Helfert, Ireland
Barbara Pernici, Italy

The Third International Workshop on Data Integration over the Web (DIWeb 2004)

Zohra Bellahsène, France
Peter McBrien, UK

The Ninth CAiSE/IFIP8.1/EUNO International Workshop on Evaluation of Modeling Methods in Systems Analysis and Design (EMMSAD 2004)

John Krogstie, Norway
Terry Halpin, USA
Keng Siau, USA

The Open INTEROP Workshop on Enterprise Modelling and Ontologies for Interoperability (EMOI - INTEROP 2004)

Giuseppe Berio, Italy
Christoph Bussler, Ireland
Asunción Gómez-Pérez, Spain
Michele Missikoff, Italy
Michael Petit, Belgium
Yves Pigneur, Switzerland

The Tenth Anniversary International Workshop of Requirements Engineering: Foundations for Software Quality (REFSQ 2004)

Björn Regnell, Sweden
Erik Kamsties, Germany
Vincenzo Gervasi, Italy

Ubiquitous Mobile Information and Collaboration Systems (UMICS)

Luciano Baresi, Italy
Schahram Dustdar, Austria
Harald Gall, Switzerland
Maristella Matera, Italy

Workshop on Component Engineering Methodology (WCEM)

Peter Fettke, Germany
Peter Loos, Germany
Klaus Turowski, Germany

International Workshop on Web Information Systems Modeling (WISM 2004)

Flavius Frasincar, The Netherlands
Richard Vdovjak, The Netherlands
Geert-Jan Houben, The Netherlands
Peter Barna, The Netherlands

Table of Contents

Invited Talks

Enterprise Modelling I

Data Integration

Conceptual Modelling I

Workflows

Methodologies for Is Development

Databases

Support for Collaboration between Individuals and Organisations I

Web-Based Systems

Requirements Engineering

Ontologies

Conceptual Modeling II

Data Warehousing

Enterprise Modelling II

Support for Collaboration
between Individuals and Organisations II

Author Index

Modelling in Information Systems Engineering
When It Works and When It Doesn't

Björn E. Nilsson

anatés ab
Björnhuvud 1, SE-184 91 ÅKERSBERGA, Sweden
bjorn@pt.lu

This talk will reveal two secrets.

The first secret is that it is not due to lack of formal methods or inappropriate formalisms that roughly 50% of all implemented system functionality is thrown away even before the roll out of the systems concerned – and 70% of the rest is unused after some two years in production.

The second secret is that today, if you make a small effort, you will learn how to beat 80% of the consultants on the market when it comes to modelling processes – just by a simple twist of perspective.

The aim of this talk is to make you less easy to fool and to give some hints concerning potentially profitable research directions as well as some inspiration for further thinking. A basic assumption is that businesses as well as academia exist to create value. After some 25 years of experience in commercial modelling, this leads to some questions concerning general aims and basic paradigms in research and practice.

In my opinion, the academician has an extremely important role to play, but something seems to have gone wrong. The basic reason might be that, paradoxically, the concept of information as well as the consequences of its proper definition seems to be more or less completely disregarded in information science. Naturally, this leads to severe misconceptions concerning the relevant problems to attack. As a further consequence, academic structures often represent a real mismatch with respect to necessary interdisciplinary cooperation.

(Yes, yes, of course, there is a plethora of definitions of information.)

In my opinion, the practitioner in modelling has avoided responsibility and real influence by being too narrowly focused. Modelling as an art has often deteriorated to simple description. While simple design instruments are used analytical instruments, if they are at all known, are not. Moreover, in some cases, commercially developed methods are sometimes downright dangerous to put in the hands of the normal analyst. Finally, inviting disaster, the modeller at large has limited abilities and instruments for the necessary cooperation with management and business development representatives.

There are, however, some remedies available…..

A. Persson and J. Stirna (Eds.): CAiSE 2004, LNCS 3084, p. 1, 2004.

Aligning Organizational Performance to IT Development and Integration

Andris Laucins

Ernst&Young Baltic
11. novembra krastmala 23, Rīga, LV-1050, Latvia
andris.laucins@lv.ey.com

We are currently observing that formerly "large" information systems development and integration projects are becoming "smaller and smaller". This trend is somewhat related to key performance indictors and other business targets that are today set for top and middle management of traditional customers for such projects. Today an average business line manager of a medium size company is very much concerned about meeting personal scorecard goals that are in many cases measured by different industry specific performance indicators and in some cases purely financial ratios. Translation of typical indicators into IT development and integration project goals and objectives really makes the difference. There are very few incentives for a line manager to be involved with an IT integrator into a multiyear project involving thousands of man days and huge financial resources, thus bearing related risks. In turn there is a growing need for component based solutions that could be developed and rolled out in short lifecycles with limited resource requirements.

We are facing a similar trend in the public sector working with e-government projects. Here, as a rule, we are working for top level government or municipality officials that expect to demonstrate to the general public tangible project results every budget period or at least before the next election campaign starts. These expectations from business customers as well as government sector customers are challenging IT industry players to come up with project structures and management approaches that deliver much shorter planning-to-rollout cycles and ability to integrate components of different business solutions.

A. Persson and J. Stirna (Eds.): CAiSE 2004, LNCS 3084, p. 2, 2004.
© Springer-Verlag Berlin Heidelberg 2004

Model Driven Architectures
for Enterprise Information Systems

Judith Barrios[1] and Selmin Nurcan[2,3]

[1] Universidad de Los Andes, Facultad de Ingeniería
Escuela de Ingeniería de Sistemas, Departamento de Computación
Mérida, 5101, Venezuela
ijudith@ula.ve
[2] Université Paris 1 – Panthéon – Sorbonne, Centre de Recherche en Informatique
90, rue de Tolbiac 75634 Paris cedex 13 France
[3] IAE de Paris (Business School), Université Paris 1 - Panthéon - Sorbonne
21, rue Broca 75005 Paris France
nurcan@univ-paris1.fr
Fax : 33 - 1 53 55 27 01

Abstract. Over the past decade, continuous challenges have been made to traditional business practices. At the same time, organisations have also experienced the effects of the integration and evolution of information and communication technologies (ICT). The Enterprise Information Systems (EIS) gained a new strategic support role as enabler of automation, monitoring, analysis and co-ordination of whole business functioning, a central role in the evolution of today organisations. These rapid changing situations originate a critical need for realistic representations -called business models- of what are the current or future business situations or what should be changed as well as its potential organisational impacts. This paper characterises the strong relationship existing between Business Models and EIS Architectures in a changing environment. Our main contribution is a set of roadmaps, which highlight the relationships between business process models and the requirements of EIS. These roadmaps provide guidance during the business modelling and the information system (IS) modelling processes.

1 Introduction

The last twenty years, the evolution of Information and Communication Technologies (ICT), along with the search for management strategies that could take advantage of them, are pushing organisations into a very competitive and changing environment. Rapid market changes such as electronic commerce, deregulation, globalisation and increased competition have led to a business environment that is constantly evolving. Companies change to better satisfy customer requirements, address increasingly tough competition, improve internal processes and modify the range of products and services they offer [1]. While information systems (IS) continue to serve traditional business needs such as co-ordination of production and enhancements of services

A. Persson and J. Stirna (Eds.): CAiSE 2004, LNCS 3084, pp. 3–19, 2004.
© Springer-Verlag Berlin Heidelberg 2004

offered, a new and important role has emerged for them. ICT are thus positioned as a strategic resource that enables automation, monitoring, analysis and co-ordination to support the transformation of business processes [2].

In that sort of environment, only those organisations, which can react quickly to environment demands, are the ones that survive. That capacity of quick reaction is often due to their capacity of handling ICT in favour of the business evolution requirements. ICT and management go hand by hand in the way of reacting, adapting and implanting new ways of doing business in today dynamic environments. IS are thus not just supporting businesses; they are an integral part of them.

All these ICT and management changes have imposed serious challenges to traditional business practices. For instance, in a competitive and evolving environment, quality became a fundamental key to obtain and to keep market share [3]. Another important wave in the evolution of management strategies was the Business Process Reengineering [4], which consists of a radical remodelling of the organisation around its processes[1]. In all these management challenges, the ICT and the EIS act as facilitators of business changes implementation and standardisation.

In the field of Information Systems, the notion of "Enterprise modelling" refers to a collection of conceptual modelling techniques for describing different facets of the organisation including operational (IS), organisational (business processes, actors, flow of information etc), and teleological (purposes) considerations [5]. Existing enterprise modelling frameworks [6], [7], [8], ([9], [10], [11], [12] and [13] stress the necessity of representing and structuring enterprise knowledge taking into account all these facets in order to develop IS and IT architectures that enterprises need.

In order to take business through a well managed change process, the organisation needs to strike a balance between the technical and the social organisational levels; i.e. there must be a consolidation of the diversity of perspectives that stakeholders, managers, and IS engineers have about the business and the way organisation must change.

The work presented in this paper concerns principally the need of methods providing guidance while the transformation process takes place. We present an extension of the EKD-CMM[2] method previously presented in [14],[15], [4], [16], [17], [18], and [19]. This extension provides a clear and complete picture of what are the main activities related with the definition of IS architectures in a dynamic and evolving environment. Considering that our approach is requirements driven, we describe the way of moving from business processes to EIS architecture and from ICT requirements to business process redesign.

This paper is organised as follows. In Section 2, we present the concepts associated to our representation of an enterprise model. We made special emphasis on the relationships between business processes and IS. Section 3 presents the concepts associated to the IS architecture of an organisation. We highlight those elements that

---

[1] A set of activities which produces, from one or several inputs, an output valuable for the customer.

[2] The term EKD-CMM stands for Enterprise Knowledge Development-Change Management Method.

are more vulnerable to environment changes. This section presents also the modelling needs for those who define the IS architecture of an organisation. The guidance offering a methodological response to these needs is expressed by roadmaps that show a set of alternative ways of moving from business processes to IS architecture. Section 4 illustrates an example of path for the specification of an IS model through the conceptualisation of the enterprise process model. Finally, section 5 concludes the paper.

2 Business Modelling through EKD-CMM

As introduced before, the recent transformations in economical and ICT environments have imposed radical changes in the way business is driven nowadays. There is an increasing need for ICT support in achieving competitive business goals. Examples of this are the Enterprise Application Integration (EAI) approach, the Enterprise Resources Planning (ERP), and the e-Business [20], among the most known.

Analysing these innovative approaches, we found that they are based on a common business driver: "the urgency of adapting business to the dynamical environment demands". This adaptation must be made by taking into account not only the internal processes and ICT exigencies, but considering the reasons that caused the change process. For example, if the change is caused by a modification in business goals because of a predefined surviving strategy, then the change problem must be analysed in a top-down manner. In this case, the ICT technologies must act as a support for the decision making process and also as a solution for implementing and consolidating change in the organisation. The perspective for analysing the change process is different if the origin of change is at the IS layer, i.e. if the change process is caused by the introduction or modification of some ICT technologies. In that case, the change situation must be analysed in a bottom-up manner so the advantages for the whole business can be elicited. In this case, the ICT is a cause of the business change, thus its impacts must analysed from many perspectives. For instance, the IS Architecture, as well as the way business processes are organised and executed, may change.

These two complementary examples of the ICT role in a business transformation process aim to help us to state that the relationships between business processes and IS are the nucleus of a successful organisational change process. In other words, it does not matter what causes the change process. What it is relevant is how well the relationships between business functioning and ICT are characterised and implemented. This characterisation will allow business managers to visualise, analyse and implement business changes without neglecting the crucial effects that ICT have over business functioning and vice versa. Moreover, models facilitate understanding and communicating about the business and its support systems only if the objective of the model is well understood. For instance, if the objective is to understand the business well enough to specify supporting systems, it is not useful to model the entire business in detail. Contrary, if the aim is to innovate the business, it is necessary to provide more effort to define and/or redefine the entire business and to find improved ways of conducting it [18], [14].

2.1 A Survey of EKD-CMM Method

EKD-CMM is a method for documenting an enterprise, its objectives, business processes and support systems, helping enterprises to consciously develop schemes for implementing changes. EKD-CMM satisfies two requirements: (i) assisting enterprise knowledge modelling and (ii) guiding the enterprise modelling and the organisational transformation processes.

The EKD-CMM *enterprise knowledge modelling* component [14], [15], [21], [18], [16] recognises that it is advantageous to examine an enterprise from multiple and inter-connected perspectives. Thus, EKD-CMM models describing an enterprise are structured in three layers of concern (see Figure 1): *Enterprise Goal Model, Enterprise Process Model* and *Enterprise Information System Model*. The first two layers focus on intentional and organisational aspects of the enterprise, i.e. the organisational objectives and how these are achieved through the co-operation of enterprise actors manipulating such enterprise objects. The third layer is useful when the EKD-CMM approach is applied to define the requirements for the IS supporting the enterprise.

The result of applying EKD-CMM method is an *enterprise model*, which represents a set of operational (information systems), organisational (business processes) and intentional (business objectives) models describing several views of the organisation.

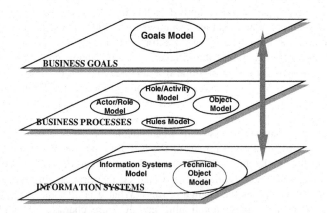

Fig. 1. EKD-CMM enterprise representation layers

From the point of view of method engineering, an enterprise model is a product [22], [23]. In fact, the product is the desired output of the design process, whereas the process keeps track of how the product has been constructed. A *Product Model* defines the set of concepts and their relationships that can be used to build a product, i.e., in our case, to build a model representing a given enterprise. The *Process Model* defines how to use the concepts defined within a Product Model. A *Process Model* and its related *Product Model* [3] are specific to a *method*. The EKD-CMM Product and Process Models, according to method engineering principles, have been previously presented in [18], [19], [24], [25] and [26].

The intention oriented modelling used in EKD-CMM provides a basis for understanding and supporting the enterprise modelling, and the managing the organisational changes. At the same time, it helps to define the supporting IS. Process guidance provided by EKD-CMM is based on the map formalism [27], which is a navigational structure in the sense that it allows the modellers to specify paths from *Start* intention to *Stop* intention. The approach suggests a dynamic construction of the most appropriate path by navigating in the map. Thus, EKD-CMM proposes several ways of working, and in this sense, it is a multi-method. In fact, using the EKD-CMM framework, one can start at any enterprise representation layer and move on to other layers, depending on the modelling and organisational situations.

The method may be used for both business engineering and IS engineering purposes, permitting: *(a) Business process reengineering*: from business processes layer to the business objectives for change [11], [14], [28], [29] and then to the business process architecture for the future; *(b) Reverse engineering*: from legacy information systems at the IS layer to the business processes layer [30], [31]; *(c) Forward engineering* or *information system design*: from business objectives to business process modelling and to the choice of the processes to be supported by the information and communication technologies (ICT) and than to the IS modelling [19]; *(d) Business process improvement*: by modelling and analysing the business processes in order to enhance them by specific modifications such as role definition or activity flow; *(e) Quality management*: by defining the business processes and quality procedures and by aligning them, ones with respect to others.

The EKD-CMM three layers framework and the associated Process Model allow us to understand, to analyse and finally to model the enterprise according to its multiple perspectives, i.e. its strategy, its structure, and its IT strategy and support systems, in a global, interrelated and guided manner.

During our previous work, we were particularly interested in the definition and modelling of the organisational change processes. To this end, we focused our attention on business processes to understand the current way of working of the enterprise (second layer in Figure 1) and reasoned on the organisational change at the intentional level [14], [28], [29]. The EKD–CMM approach has been thus successfully applied in an ESPRIT Project (ELEKTRA) aiming to discover generic knowledge about change management in the electricity supply sector for reusing it in similar settings. Two end-user applications have been considered within the project. Our conclusion at the issue of these two real life projects was that reasoning on the enterprise objectives makes easier understanding of problems and communication on essential aspects (*what* and *why* instead of *who, when, where* and *how*). Our current work focuses on the two lower layers shown in Figure 1, namely business processes

---

[3] We use capitalised initials in order to differentiate the method specific Models from the application specific models (for instance a business model) that compose the product.

and information systems in order to highlight the relationships between the enterprise process models and the specifications of the ICT systems.

2.2   EKD-CMM Product Models

A business model can act as the basis for designing the supporting software systems in an enterprise. Typically, business modelling and software modelling use different languages and concepts making integration of the two models difficult [32]. The set EKD-CMM Product Models aims to ease this integration by providing methodological tools to use a *business model* (enterprise goal model and enterprise process models) to define the supporting IS' architecture.

From the EKD-CMM perspective and experience, an important conclusion about *business models* use, is that it has a twofold goal: first, a model helps organisational members to understand what they are, what they want to be as an organisation, and how they can achieve an identified set of business goals by reorganising or (re)defining the business processes. Second, a model aims to design the IS architecture that best fits organisational needs already expressed by the business goals and their corresponding business processes.

The instantiation of the Product Model's concepts allows business modellers to build specific *business models*, which represent particular business situations. Let us suppose that the future business has been modelled from different perspectives (see [18] and [25] for details), i.e. by modelling the business goals, the actors that are responsible for the execution of the underlying business processes and the set of activities that are under the responsibility of those actors, as well as the resources involved in the execution of those activities. The resulting *business models* are instances of the Goal Model, the Actor/Role Model, the Role/Activity Model and the Business Object Model with their relationships.

2.3   EKD-CMM Process Model

A map [27] is a Process Model in which a non-deterministic ordering of intentions and strategies has been included. It is a labelled directed graph with intentions as nodes and strategies as edges between intentions. A map consists of a number of *sections* each of which is a triplet < source intention I_i, target intention I_j, strategy S_{ij}>. The map is a navigational structure that supports the dynamic selection of the intention to be achieved next and the appropriate strategy to achieve it whereas the associated guidelines help in the achievement of the selected intention.

The EKD-CMM high-level map, shown in Figure 2, contains a finite number of paths; each of them is a *EKD-CMM Process Model*. Therefore the EKD-CMM map is a *multi-model*. None of the finite set of models included in the map is recommended 'a priori'. Instead the approach suggests a dynamic construction of the actual path by navigating in the map. In this sense the approach is sensitive to the specific situations as they arise in the modelling process. The EKD-CMM multi-model allows us to express all modelling strategies that can be followed to build an enterprise model (a business model and an IS model). The formalisation used to define the EKD-CMM Process Model is intention oriented, i.e. the business owners', the business modellers' and the systems developers' modelling intentions are directly expressed by maps. This is carefully described in [24] and [25].

The experience gained during our previous work shows that the path to be followed in the map during a particular enterprise modelling project is situation-dependent. For instance, the selection of the bottom-up[4] path for one of the two end-users in the ELEKTRA project was influenced by the uncertainty regarding both the current Electricity Distribution Business Unit situation and its possible re-organisation alternatives. The application of the specific strategies forming this path was also affected by a number of situational factors including: (i) *organisational culture*; (ii) *ability to commit resources*; (iii) *social skills and consensus attitudes of participating actors*; (iv) *use of software tools* to facilitate the process execution; and (v) *familiarity with applied strategies and supporting technologies.*

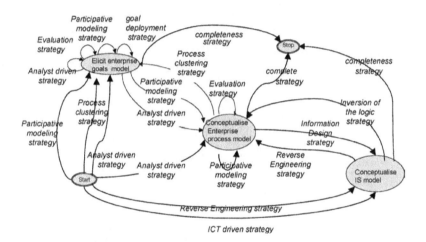

Fig. 2. EKD-CMM Roadmap

By opposition, for the second end-user a different path of the map, called top-down, was used. The map sections composing this path use mainly the participative modelling strategy. For this end-user, the future enterprise goal structure was first elicited and then future enterprise process models were conceptualised.

The EKD-CMM Process Model is shown in Figure 2 as a roadmap. Guidelines help users to choose between two alternative sections between a source process intention and a target process intention (strategy selection guidelines) or to choose be-

---

[4] So called because this part suggests first to conceptualize the current enterprise process model, then to elicit the current enterprise goal structure and finally to model alternative change scenario.

tween possible target intentions when moving from a source intention (intention selection guidelines). This will be described in Section 4. The execution of each map section is also *supported by* a guideline.

Some map sections can be defined as maps in a lower level of abstraction. For instance, the global map section <*Start, Conceptualise enterprise process model*, Analyst Driven Strategy> is defined as a local map shown in Figure 3. This means that the method knowledge embodied in the guideline supporting the execution of this map section is too complex and too rich to be described in operational terms and requires an intermediary intentional description in a lower level of abstraction.

All guidelines corresponding to the sections between the process intentions *Elicit Enterprise Goal Structure* and *Conceptualise Enterprise Business Process Model* have been developed in [18] and [24]. Our current work consists in identifying and developing the methodological guidelines associated to the map sections having the process intention *Conceptualise Information System Model* as source or as target. For instance, Figure 4 shows the local map defined to provide guidance to the global map section (see Figure 2) <*Conceptualise Enterprise Business Process Model, Conceptualise Information System Model*, IS design strategy>. The next sections concentrate in developing guidance (using local maps) for passing from the Business Process layer to the IS layer.

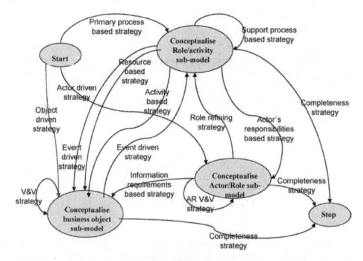

Fig. 3. Roadmap for conceptualising a *business process model* from scratch

3 The Information Systems Architecture (ISA)

The Information System Model contains not only the representation of the set of IS, but also the definition of the local and shared databases, as well as the information requirements and management indicators that should be satisfied by applications or IS.

As we explained before, the main goal of the IS architecture (ISA) is to support business processes at the operational and strategic levels. The definition of *information requirements* and *management performance indicators* is directly associated to business processes through the *Business Objects Model* (BOM) shown in Figure 1.

As stated in [33], business objects do not only provide a natural way to model the enterprise, but also guarantee a close link to the business applications. Considering that the BOM constitutes the central link between the business processes and the IS that support them, special implementation requirements must be considered when designing and distributing the enterprise databases and the software components that handle them. In order to complete the *business objects model* of the Business Process layer (BOM), the *business rules* must be linked to the *business objects model* built at the IS layer. We call the latter *technical business objects model* (TBOM). Business rules are useful for defining (i) the set of operations that should be performed over the business objects for satisfying information requirements; (ii) the conditions under which these operations should be performed. Business rules set up also what business objects attributes may change, and what are their domains of validity, when operations are performed. Finally they can set the non-functional requirements (security, accuracy, etc.). Consequently, the TBOM constitutes the heart of the ISA.

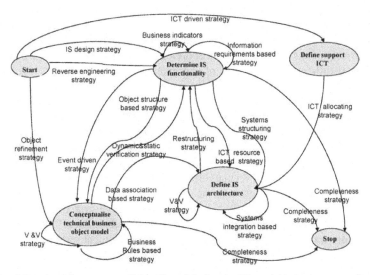

Fig. 4. Roadmap for conceptualising *IS model* after the BP model being conceptualised

An ISA comprises the set of enterprise IS, the connections and dependencies between them and the ICT required for their implementation. ICT includes hardware (PC, servers, nets, and storage, input/output devises, etc.), software (exploitation, support, development, and applications) and finally, methodological (project management, development, change control, maintenance, etc.) and technical (languages, modelling tools, etc.) artefacts. Considering the evolving environment where enterprises are immersed nowadays, the ISA may include all or part of these types of IS: legacy systems, enterprise resource planning applications (ERP), and new specific developments. The data distribution and exploitation is directly associated to each IS functionality. For completing the set of concepts associated to the enterprise IS layer, we include strategic and operational plans which define what, when and how developing, maintaining, integrating, or purchasing the systems contained in the IS architecture.

3.1   Technical Business Objects in the Information Systems Layer

At the IS layer of the EKD-CMM framework, the technical business objects model (TBOM) is defined as a refinement of the BOM, which is a sub-model of the Business Process layer (see Figure 1). The BOM must be refined and expressed according to the adopted software engineering techniques. Therefore, we determine two complementary perspectives for defining the set of business objects of an enterprise. Each perspective is associated with an enterprise representation layer: (1) the business object model (BOM), built at the business process layer, and (2) the technical business object model (TBOM) built at the IS layer.

Processes inputs and outputs, as well as business resources involved in activities drive the business process perspective. Figure 5 shows the process map associated to the BOM definition. This map provides guidance for the map section <Start, Conceptualise business objects sub-model, Object driven strategy> shown in Figure 3.

Observe that there are many ways of conceptualising business objects involved in business process executions. There are two main intentions that can be achieved in a non-deterministic manner: *Define business objects* and *Elicit business objects*. Each intention has a set of achieving strategies that may be chosen according to specific modelling situations. For instance, there are three different ways of "eliciting business objects", the *resource based* strategy; the *event based* strategy, and the *activity-based* strategy. Selecting the *activity based strategy* means that the business objects will be discovered by analysing low level activities of the business processes. Notice that, the selection of one of these strategies for achieving the *elicit business objects* intention does not eliminate the possibility of selecting the others (two strategies) for completing the knowledge associated to the business objects already elicited. The BOM at the business process layer, is expressed in conceptual terms without technical considerations, thus managers and others enterprise members can easily understand it.

The IS perspective is technology driven; i.e. technical factors such as formal languages, and graphical notations controls the modelling process. Figure 6 shows the process map associated to TBOM at the IS layer. This map provides guidance for the map section <Start, Conceptualise technical business objects model, Object refinement strategy> shown in Figure 4. Observe that the intentions associated to TBOM construction are different from those depicted at Figure 5: *Debug business objects* and *Build technical business objects model.* The associated strategies allow modellers to choose complementary ways of building and validating the TBOM.

Notice that the BOM obtained at the BP layer is here refined (see Figure 6) with respect to the software engineering and database concepts and techniques for obtaining first, the logical data model expressed according to the object oriented paradigm; and then, the object implementation model. In order to assure the complete correspondence between the resulting data model and the business information requirements and rules, the data model must be validated against the business process model built at the BP layer. Thus, the possible inconsistencies on business object representations can be corrected assuring the correspondence between the two business object models.

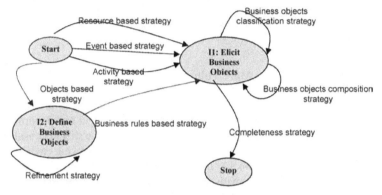

Fig. 5. Conceptualising BOM using the object driven strategy at the *BP layer*

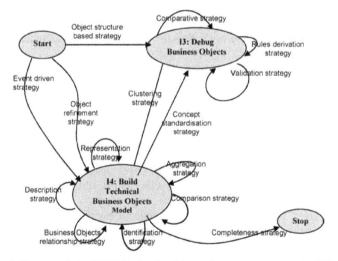

Fig. 6. Conceptualising TBOM using the object refinement strategy at the *IS layer*

3.2   The ISA and the BP Needs

It is not easy to discover what the appropriate ISA for a particular enterprise is. There are many factors that must be considered while specifying business objects, information requirements, and business processes and activities. The way an activity or a set of activities (a business process) is performed, determines if one or several IS are needed. This determines also if the business objects should be shared or not, and security, quality and access restrictions that must be included in the IS functionalities.

Therefore, the relationship between the IS layer and the BP layer goes further than the simple business objects model definition (BOM and TBOM). The way a set of IS is structured, the definition and distribution of IS responsibilities, is a consequence of the way that business processes are performed. Besides, there are many other enterprise factors such as priorities, financial and technical issues, that affect the decision of implanting a particular IS structure or another.

3.3   The BP and the IS Issues More Vulnerable to Changes

In the context of the work still done, we just considered the technical factors associated to the technologies needed for business process execution and for supporting the exchange of information between business processes. Besides, we should consider the strategic perspective of an enterprise that wish to survive in an evolving environment, and then its requirement for a flexible ISA. That way, the changes can be analysed, defined and implanted easily and with minimal business and ICT impact. From this perspective, the definition of the ISA for a business is based on:

- Business processes execution dependencies, such as inputs/outputs, support, and workflow coordination.
- Business objects owners and users, thus the set of permitted manipulations can be elicited and imposed.
- Legacy and acquired systems and their integration through an Enterprise Application (EAI) perspective.
- The kind of technology required for the execution of business processes, as well as the standardisation of some related procedures.
- The ICT available and required (restricted according to business financial possibilities) in the enterprise.

Almost all of these subjects concern with BP layer characterisation. Nevertheless, the responsibility of implementing an appropriate and flexible support for them belongs to the IS layer.

At the IS layer, the elements more vulnerable to changes are: business objects definition (operations, structure, dependence degree, and owner); IS functionalities (requirements, dependence degree, and support technology); ICT use (obsolescence, flexibility, versions, security, growth capacity); IS implantation (purchase, ERP, integration, performance improvement).

At the BP layer, the elements more vulnerable to changes are: process change (re-engineering- new way of working, TQM); standardisation requirements (business processes, procedures, methodologies); work technologies (basic, new, improved); business structure (new, restructured); organisation (actors, roles, workflow).

For concluding this section, it is important to recall that any of these changes affects the two other business representation layers (Figure 1) or it may comes from one of them. For instance, a reengineering process may be the consequence of a change in the organisational politics (goals layer). In that case, this change causes a redefinition of a set of business processes, and also a redefinition of the IS that support them.

4   How to Use the Process Maps

This section illustrates an example of path for the specification of an *IS model* through the conceptualisation of the *enterprise process model*. Our purpose is to explain how to use the process maps as methodological guidelines. In fact, those maps assist business owners, business modellers and IS modellers while specifying *business models* and *IS models*.

Enterprise modelling using EKD-CMM is an intention driven process that resolves two issues, namely, (1) how to fulfil the modelling intention according to a strategy and (2) how to select the right map section to progress. Because the next intention and strategy to achieve it are selected dynamically, *guidelines* that make available all choices open to handle a given situation are of great importance. Maps have associated guidelines [27], namely one *'Intention Selection Guideline'* per node I_{i}, except for *Stop*, one *'Strategy Selection Guideline'* per node pair $<I_{i},I_{j}>$ and one *'Intention Achievement Guideline'* per section $<I_{i},I_{j},$ $S_{ij}>$. Given an intention I_{i}, an *Intention Selection Guideline* (ISG), identifies the set of intentions $\{I_{j}\}$ that can be achieved in the next step. Given two intentions I_{i}, I_{j} and a set of possible strategies $S_{ij1}, S_{ij2},..S_{ijn}$ applicable to achieve I_{j}, the role of the *Strategy Selection Guideline (SSG)* is to guide the selection of one S_{ijk}. Finally, the execution of each section is *supported by* an IAG that provides an operational or an intentional means to fulfil a modelling intention. For the former, the IAG provides process knowledge specified by the means of operational models. For the latter, the IAG is defined as a map in a lower level of abstraction.

All ISGs and SSGs and also the IAGs providing a methodological knowledge described in an operational level are specified according to the contextual formalism developed within the ESPRIT project NATURE [34]. We just recall here that a *context* is defined as a pair *<(situation),* intention>. The kind of EKD-CMM guidelines specified above are organised into hierarchies of contexts of three types, namely *choice* (refinement of contexts), *plan* (composition of contexts) or *executable*. More details about EKD-CMM guidelines can be found in [14], [24] and [25].

Let us suppose that we are performing an enterprise modelling process in the following situation: the organisational maturity of modelling and the participative involvement are low and there is no available documentation of the business processes.

The ISG associated to the intention *Start* in the EKD-CMM map shown in Figure 2 suggests us to choice *Conceptualise enterprise process model* as next intention and to apply the IAG associated to the unique map section between these two intentions. This IAG is defined as a map, shown in Figure 3, in a lower level of abstraction.

The ISG associated to the intention *Start* in the map shown in Figure 3 provides us a choice between three intentions. Let us suppose that the modelling team has a great experience with object modelling -and less with activity modelling- and a partial documentation of the legacy systems is available. Than the ISG associated to the intention *Start* suggests us to choice *Conceptualise business objects sub-model* as next intention and to apply the IAG associated to the unique map section between these two intentions. This IAG is again defined as a map shown in Figure 5.

Let us suppose that the modelling team has a great experience with event-based object modelling techniques, for instance Remora. The ISG associated to the intention *Start* in the map of Figure 5 suggests to choice *Elicit business objects* as next intention, and the SSG associated to the couple <*Start, Elicit business objects*> suggests to select the *Event based strategy* and to apply the IAG associated the section supporting this strategy. To make short, let us suppose that navigation is terminated in the map of Figure 5 and the other sub-models of the BP layer are specified successively leading thus to end the navigation in the map of Figure 3. The specification of the *business process model* being completed, the EKD-CMM map of Figure 2 suggests us to *Conceptualise information system model* using *IS design strategy*. The IAG associated to this map section is again defined intentionally as shown in Figure 4. The map section <*Start, Conceptualise technical business objects model*, Object refinements strategy> is, in its turn, defined intentionally as shown in Figure 6. When the navigation is terminated in the map of Figure 6, modellers go back on the upper intentional level to navigate in the map of Figure 4, and finally in the map of Figure 2.

5   Conclusions and Future Work

This paper reports on the use of an intentional framework for modelling enterprise knowledge using *business models* and *IS models*. A major advantage of the proposed approach is the systematic way of dealing with enterprise modelling and organisational transformation in terms of *knowledge modelling* used with a *process guidance* framework. The experience gained during our previous work has substantiated the view that, paths of the EKD-CMM maps to be followed in a particular enterprise modelling project are very much dependent on the enactment context of the enterprise project and a number of situational factors. Including degree of formal hierarchy (few vs. many formal levels), decision structure (authoritative vs. management by objectives), company culture (collectivistic vs. individualistic), degree of distance of power (short vs. long), type of market (deregulated vs. regulated), etc. Thus, the *EKD-CMM framework* provides a systematic, nevertheless flexible, way to organise and to guide the enterprise modelling processes.

The EKD-CMM modelling framework allows us to represent an enterprise from interrelated perspectives using a three-layer model. It integrates enterprise objectives, processes and systems in a single modelling framework. The more relevant feature of our framework is that it makes explicit the link between these three modelling layers. The way the three layers model has been structured assures that business processes are at the origin of the technical business objects as well as the definitions of information requirements and management performance indicators. In consequence, they will be taken into account for the design and distribution of the software components.

The EKD-CMM requires the domain knowledge to fully understand the organisation from its multiple perspectives. Rather than trying to gain huge amounts of knowledge, a better solution seems to involve several key persons of the enterprise in the modelling process. These persons will provide organisational knowledge or will know where it may be found. Simultaneously they will become an important resource by gaining knowledge of EKD-CMM, which will be useful if the organisation desires to continue working with enterprise analysis and modelling.

Our framework contributes to define accurate decision making processes inside modern organisations, which are highly dependent of ICT. It reinforces also the ability of companies, which apply it to adopt a policy of knowledge management.

Our future work will consist to integrate in the EKD-CMM modelling framework, the ability to handle the issues listed in Section 3.3.

References

1. Jacobson I., Ericsson M. and Jacobson A. (1994) The object advantage - Business Process Reengineering with object technology, Addison-Wesley.
2. Grover, V., Fiedler, K.D. and Teng, J.T.C. (1994). Exploring the success of information technology enabled business process reengineering. *IEEE Transactions on Engineering Management*, 41:3 (August), 276-283.
3. Dumas P. and Charbonnel G. (1990). *La méthode OSSAD-Pour maîtriser les technologies de l'information - Tome 1:Principes.* Les Editions d'Organisation, Paris.
4. Hammer M. and Champy J. (1993) *Reengineering the Corporation: a Manifesto for Business Revolution,* Harper Collins Publishers, Inc., New York.
5. Bubenko, J. (1994) Enterprise Modelling. *Ingénierie des Systems d' Information*, Vol. 2, N° 6.
6. Dobson, J.S., Blyth, A.J.C., Chudge, J. and Strens, R. (1994) The ORDIT Approach to Organisational Requirements, *in 'Requirements Engineering: Social and Technical Issues'*, Academic Press, London, 87-106.
7. Van Lamsweerde, A., Darimont, R. and Massonet, P. (1995) Goal-Directed Elaboration of Requirements for a Meeting Scheduler: Problems and Lessons Learnt, RE'95, IEEE Computer Society Press, 194-203.
8. Yu, E.S.K. and Mylopoulos, J. (1996) Using Goals, Rules and Methods to Support Reasoning in Business Process Reengineering, *Intelligent Systems in Accounting, Finance and Management*, Vol. 5, 1-13.

9. Loucopoulos, P., Kavakli, V., Prekas, N., Dimitromanolaki, I. Yilmazturk, N., Rolland, C., Grosz, G., Nurcan, S., Beis, D., and Vgontzas, G. (1998) The ELEKTRA project: Enterprise Knowledge Modeling for change in the distribution unit of Public Power Corporation. 2nd IMACS Int. Conference on Circuits, Systems and Computers, Athens, Greece, 352-357.

10. Nurcan, S., Grosz, G. and Souveyet, C. (1998) Describing business processes with a guided use case approach. 10th International Conference on Advanced Information Systems Engineering (CAiSE'98), B. Pernici (ed.), Springer-Verlag, Pisa, Italy, 339-361.

11. Rolland, C., Loucopoulos, P., Grosz and G., Nurcan, S. (1998b) A framework for generic patterns dedicated to the management of change in the electricity supply industry. 9th International DEXA Conference and Workshop on Database and Expert Systems Applications (August 24-28), 907-911.

12. Loucopoulos, P., and Kavakli, V. (1995) Enterprise modeling and teleological approach to requirements engineering. *International Journal of Intelligent and Cooperative Information Systems*, Vol. 4, N° 1, 44-79.

13. Bubenko,J.A.,jr., Persson, A. and Stirna, J. (2001)
http://www.dsv.su.se/~js/ekd_user_guide.html

14. Nurcan, S., Barrios, J., Grosz, G. and Rolland, C. (1999) Change process modelling using the EKD - Change Management Method. 7th European Conference on Information Systems, ECIS'99, Copenhagen, Denmark, June 23-25, 513-529.

15. Loucopoulos, P., Kavakli, V., Prekas, N., Rolland, C., Grosz, G. and Nurcan, S. Using the EKD approach: the modeling component. *ELEKTRA project*, Athena Deliverable (March 1997).

16. Bubenko, J., and Stirna, J. (1997). EKD User Guide. ELEKTRA project, Research report, February 1997.

17. Rolland, C., Nurcan, S. and Grosz, G. (1999) Enterprise knowledge development: the process view. *Information and Management*, 36:3, September 1999.

18. Nurcan, S. and Rolland, C. (2003). A multi-method for defining the organisational change. *Journal of Information and Software Technology*, Elsevier. 45:2, 61-82.

19. Nurcan, S. and Barrios, J. (2003). Enterprise Knowledge and Information System Modelling in an Evolving Environment. The EMSISE workshop in the OOIS Conference, Geneva, Switzerland, September 2003.

20. Canfora, G., Rollo, F., and Venturi, G. (2003). Business Change in Systems Integration. Proceedings of the International Conference on Enterprise Information systems. ICEIS 2003. April 2003. Angers, France.

21. Rolland, C., Grosz, G., Nurcan, S., Yue, W. and Gnaho, C. (1998c) An electronic handbook for accessing domain specific generic patterns, *IFIP WG 8.1 Working Conference: Information Systems in the WWW environment*, July 15-17, Beijing, Chine, 89-111.

22. Odell, J. (1996) A primer to Method Engineering. *INFOSYS. The Electronic Newsletter for Information Systems.* 3:19, Massey University, New Zealand.

23. Brinkemper, J. (1996) Method Engineering: Engineering of Information Systems, Methods and Tools. *Information and Software Technology*, 38, 275-280.

24. Barrios, J. (2001) Une méthode pour la définition de l'impact organisationnel du changement. *Thèse de Doctorat de l'Université de Paris 1.*

25. Nurcan, S., Barrios, J. and Rolland, C. (2002) Une méthode pour la définition de l'impact organisationnel du changement. *Numéro Spécial de la Revue Ingénierie des Systèmes d'Information "Connaissances Métier dans l'Ingénierie des SI*, 7:4.

26. Barrios, J. and Nurcan, S. (2002) MeDIC: A Method Engineering Proposal for the Analysis and Representation of the Organisational Impact of Change. The 2002 Int. Conference on Software Engineering Research and Practice, SERP'02 - June 24-27, Las Vegas, USA.

27. Rolland, C., Prakash, N. and Benjamen A. (1999c) A Multi-Model View of Process Modelling, *Requirements Engineering Journal*, 4:4, 169-187.

28. Nurcan, S. and Rolland. C. (1999) Using EKD-CMM electronic guide book for managing change in organisations. 9th European-Japanese Conference on Information Modelling and Knowledge Bases, ECIS'99, Iwate, Japan, May 24-28, 105-123.

29. Rolland, C., Loucopoulos, P., Kavakli, V. and Nurcan S. (1999b) Intention based modelling of organisational change: an experience report. Fourth CAISE/IFIP 8.1 International Workshop on Evaluation of Modeling Methods in Systems Analysis and Design (EMMSAD'99), Heidelberg, Germany, June 14-15.

30. Kavakli, V. and Loucopoulos, P. (1998) Goal-Driven Business Process Analysis: Application in Electricity Deregulation. 10th Int. Conf. on Advanced Information Systems Engineering, B. Pernici (ed.), Springer-Verlag, Pisa, Italy, 305-324.

31. Kardasis, P. and Loucopoulos, P. (1998) Aligning Legacy Information Systems to Business Processes. 10th Int. Conf. on Advanced Information Systems Engineering (CAiSE'98), B. Pernici (ed.), Springer-Verlag, Pisa, Italy, 25-39.

32. Eriksson, H.-E. and Penker, M. (2000), *Business modeling with UML- Business patterns at work*, J. Wiley.

33. Papazoglou, M.P., van den Heuvel W.-J. (2000) Configurable business objects for building evolving enterprise models and applications, in *Business Process Management – Models Techniques and Empirical Studies*, Springer, 2000.

34. Rolland, C., Souveyet, C., Moreno, M. (1995) An approach for defining ways-of-working, *Information System Journal* 20(4), pp. 337-359.

Simple and Minimum-Cost Satisfiability
for Goal Models*

Roberto Sebastiani[1], Paolo Giorgini[1], and John Mylopoulos[2]

[1] Department of Information and Communication Technology
University of Trento, Italy
{rseba,pgiorgio}@dit.unitn.it
[2] Department of Computer Science, University of Toronto, Canada
jm@cs.toronto.edu

Abstract. Goal models have been used in Computer Science in order to represent software requirements, business objectives and design qualities. In previous
work we have presented a formal framework for reasoning with goal models, in a
qualitative or quantitative way, and we have introduced an algorithm for forward
propagating values through goal models. In this paper we focus on the qualitative
framework and we propose a technique and an implemented tool for addressing
two much more challenging problems: (1) find an initial assignment of labels
to leaf goals which satisfies a desired final status of root goals by upward value
propagation, while respecting some given constraints; and (2) find an minimum
cost assignment of labels to leaf goals which satisfies root goals. The paper also
presents preliminary experimental results on the performance of the tool using the
goal graph generated by a case study involving the Public Transportation Service
of Trentino (Italy).

1 Introduction

The concept of goal has been used in different areas of Computer Science since the early
days of the discipline. In AI, problem solving and planning systems have used the notion
of goal to describe desirable states of the world [9]. For example, a planning system might
be given the goal on(A,B) and on(B,C), which describes states where blocks A,
B, C form a stack. The planning system can then analyze the goal (e.g., by decomposing it
into two subgoals) and find suitable actions that will satisfy it. More recently, goals have
been used in Software Engineering to model early requirements [2] and non-functional
requirements [8] for a software system. For instance, an early requirement for a library
information system might be "Every book request will eventually be fulfilled", while
"The new system will be highly reliable" is an example of a non-functional requirement. Goals are also useful for knowledge management systems which focus on strategic
knowledge, e.g., "Increase profits", or "Become the largest auto manufacturer in
North America" [5]. Goal-oriented requirements engineering has received considerable attention recently, and is nicely motivated and surveyed in [12] and [11]. Given the

---

* We thank Maddalena Garzetti for sharing with us a version of her goal model for the Trentino
Public Transportation Service, and Paolo Liberatore for helping us with the Minweight solver.
The first author is sponsored by a MIUR COFIN02 project, code 2002097822_003.

criticality of requirements engineering for information system development, the formal representation and analysis of goals has become an important research problem to be addressed by the CAiSE research community.

Traditional goal analysis consists of decomposing goals into subgoals through an AND- or OR-decomposition. If goal G is AND-decomposed (respectively, OR-decomposed) into subgoals $G_1, G_2, \ldots, G_n$, then all (at least one) of the subgoals must be satisfied for the goal G to be satisfied. Given a goal model consisting of goals and AND/OR relationships among them, and a set of initial labels for some nodes of the graph (S for "satisfied", D for "denied") there is a simple label propagation algorithm that will generate labels for other nodes of the graph [10]. The propagation is carried out from subgoals towards an And/OR-decomposed. This algorithm can be used to determine if the root goals of a goal model are satisfied, given an assignment of labels for some of the leaf goals.

Unfortunately, this simple framework for modeling and analyzing goals won't work for many domains where goals can't be formally defined, and the relationships among them can't be captured by semantically well-defined relations such as AND/OR ones. For example, goals such as "Highly reliable system" have no formally defined predicate which prescribes their meaning, though one may want to define necessary conditions for such a goal to be satisfied. Moreover, such a goal may be related to other goals, such as "Thoroughly debugged system", "Thoroughly tested system" in the sense that the latter obviously contribute to the satisfaction of the former, but this contribution is partial and qualitative. In other words, if the latter goals are satisfied, they certainly contribute towards the satisfaction of the former goal, but certainly don't guarantee it. The framework will also not work in situations where there are contradictory contributions to a goal. For instance, we may want to allow for multiple decompositions of a goal G into sets of subgoals, where some decompositions suggest satisfaction of G while others suggest denial.

The objective of this paper is to present further results on a formal model for goals that can cope with qualitative relationships and inconsistencies among goals. In [4] we presented an axiomatization of a qualitative and a quantitative model for goals and proposed sound and complete algorithms for forward reasoning with such models. In particular, given a goal model and labels for some of the goals, our algorithms propagate these labels forward, towards root goals. (If the graph contain loops, this is done until a fixpoint is reached.) Figure 1 illustrates a simple example of a goal graph. The figure shows a single root goal "Protect users" that might associated with a public transit system, AND/OR decomposed several times. The figure also includes some positive qualitative contributions, e.g., "Protect driver health" contributes positively ("+" label) to the goal "Ensure driver capabilities". The algorithm proposed in [4] takes as input labels for some of the lower goals of the model and infers other labels higher up. This is accomplished through propagations from the AND/OR subgoals of a goal to the goal itself, also propagations in the forward direction for qualitative relationships. It is important to note that this algorithm supports forward reasoning only and requires no search.

This paper uses the same formal setting as [4], but addresses a different set of problems. In particular, now we want to know if there is a label assignment for leaf nodes of a

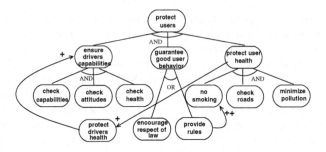

Fig. 1. A sample goal graph.

goal graph that satisfies/denies all root goals. Assuming that the satisfaction/deniability of every leaf goal may require some unit cost, we have also addressed the problem of finding a minimum cost label assignment to leaf goals that satisfies/denies all root goals of a goal graph. Both problems are solved by reducing them to the satisfiability (SAT) and minimum-cost satisfiability (minimum-cost SAT) problems for Boolean formulas.

The rest of the paper is structured as follows. Section 2 introduces the formal framework of [4], including a definition of goal graphs and the axiomatization proposed for qualitative goal models. The section also reviews SAT and minimum-cost SAT. Sectionì 3 defines the problem of (simple or minimum-cost) goal satisfiability for a goal graph, and shows how it can be reduced to a (simple and minimum-cost) SAT problem. Section 4 presents two tools named respectively GOALSOLVE and GOALMINSOLVE that solve either goal satisfiability problem. In section 5 we present experimental results on the performance of these tools using the goal graph generated by a case study involving the Public Transportation Service of Trentino (Italy).

2 Preliminaries

In this section we recall some preliminary notions which are necessary for a full comprehension of the paper. In Sections 2.1 and 2.2 we recall from [4] and extend a little the notions of goal graphs and the axiomatic representation of goal relations. In Section 2.3 we recall some basic notions about boolean satisfiability and minimum-weight boolean satisfiability.

2.1 Goal Graphs

As in [4], we consider sets of goal nodes G_i and of relations $(G_1, ..., G_n) \overset{r}{\longmapsto} G$ over them, including the $(n+1)$-ary relations *and*, *or* and the binary relations $+_S$, $-_S$, $+_D$, $-_D$, $++_S$, $--_S$, $++_D$, $--_D$, $+$, $-$, $++$, $--$. We briefly recall the intuitive meaning of these relations: $G_2 \overset{+s}{\longmapsto} G_1$ [resp. $G_2 \overset{++_S}{\longmapsto} G_1$] means that if G_2 is satisfied, then there is some [resp. a full] evidence that G_1 is satisfied, but if G_2 is denied, then nothing is said about the denial of G_1; $G_2 \overset{-s}{\longmapsto} G_1$ [resp. $G_2 \overset{--_S}{\longmapsto} G_1$] means that if G_2 is satisfied, then there is some [resp. a full] evidence that G_1 is denied, but if G_2 is denied, then nothing is said about the satisfaction of G_1. The meaning of $+_D$, $-_D$, $++_D$, $--_D$ is dual w.r.t. $+_S$, $-_S$, $++_S$, $--_S$ respectively. (By "dual" we mean that we invert satisfiability with deniability.) The relations $+$, $-$, $++$, $--$ are such that each $G_2 \overset{r}{\longmapsto} G_1$ is a shorthand for the combination of the two corresponding relationships $G_2 \overset{r_S}{\longmapsto} G_1$ and $G_2 \overset{r_D}{\longmapsto} G_1$. (We call the first kind of relations *symmetric* and the latter two *asymmetric*.)

If $(G_1, ..., G_n) \overset{r}{\longmapsto} G$ is a goal relation we call $G_1...G_n$ the *source goals* and G the *target goal* of r, and we say that r is an *incoming relation* for G and an *outcoming relation* for $G_1,...,G_n$. We call *boolean relations* the *and* and *or* relations, *partial contribution relations* the $+$ and $-$ relations and their asymmetric versions, *full contribution relations* $++$ and $--$ relations and their asymmetric versions. We call a *root goal* any goal with an incoming boolean relation and no outcoming ones, we call a *leaf goal* any goal with no incoming boolean relations.

We call a *goal graph* a pair $\langle \mathcal{G}, \mathcal{R} \rangle$ where $\mathcal{G}$ is a set of goal nodes and $\mathcal{R}$ is a set of goal relations, subject to the following restrictions:

- each goal has at most one incoming boolean relation;
- every loop contains at least one non-boolean relation arc.

In practice, a goal graph can be seen as a set of and/or trees whose nodes are connected by contribution relations arcs. Root goals are roots of and/or trees, whilst leaf goals either are leaves or nodes which are not part of them.

2.2 Axiomatization of Goal Relationships

Let $G_1, G_2, ...$ denote goal labels. We introduce four distinct predicates over goals, $FS(G)$, $FD(G)$ and $PS(G)$, $PD(G)$, meaning respectively that there is (at least) *full* evidence that goal G is satisfied and that G is denied, and that there is at least *partial* evidence that G is satisfied and that G is denied. We also use the proposition $\top$ to represent the (trivially true) statement that there is at least null evidence that the goal G is satisfied (or denied). Notice that the predicates state that there is *at least* a given level of evidence, because in a goal graph there may be multiple sources of evidence for the satisfaction/denial of a goal. We introduce a total order $FS(G) \geq PS(G) \geq \top$ and $FD(G) \geq PD(G) \geq \top$, with the intended meaning that $x \geq y$ if and only if $x \rightarrow y$. We call FS, PS, FD and PD the possible *values* for a goal.

We want to allow the deduction of *positive* ground assertions of type $FS(G)$, $FD(G)$, $PS(G)$ and $PD(G)$ over the goal constants of a goal graph. We refer to externally provided assertions as *initial conditions*. To formalize the propagation of satisfiability and deniability evidence through a goal graph $\langle \mathcal{G}, \mathcal{R} \rangle$, we introduce the axioms described in Figure 2.

(1) state that full satisfiability and deniability imply partial satisfiability and deniability respectively. For an AND relation, (2) show that the full and partial satisfiability of the target node require respectively the full and partial satisfiability of all the source nodes; for a "$+_S$" relation, (4) show that only the partial satisfiability (but not the full satisfiability) propagates through a "$+_S$" relation. Thus, an AND relation propagates the minimum satisfiability value (and the maximum deniability one), while a "$+_S$" relation propagates at most a partial satisfiability value.

$$\begin{array}{ll}
\textbf{Goal} & \textbf{Invariant Axioms} \\
G: & FS(G) \to PS(G), \quad FD(G) \to PD(G) \qquad (1) \\
\textbf{Goal relation} & \textbf{Relation Axioms}
\end{array}$$

$$(G_1, ..., G_i, ...G_n) \xmapsto{and} G: \quad (\bigwedge_i FS(G_i)) \to FS(G), \quad (\bigwedge_i PS(G_i)) \to PS(G) \qquad (2)$$

$$\bigwedge_i (FD(G_i) \to FD(G)), \quad \bigwedge_i (PD(G_i) \to PD(G)) \qquad (3)$$

$$G_2 \xmapsto{+s} G_1: \quad PS(G_2) \to PS(G_1) \qquad (4)$$

$$G_2 \xmapsto{-s} G_1: \quad PS(G_2) \to PD(G_1) \qquad (5)$$

$$G_2 \xmapsto{++s} G_1: \quad FS(G_2) \to FS(G_1), \quad PS(G_2) \to PS(G_1) \qquad (6)$$

$$G_2 \xmapsto{--s} G_1: \quad FS(G_2) \to FD(G_1), \quad PS(G_2) \to PD(G_1) \qquad (7)$$

Fig. 2. Ground axioms for the invariants and the propagation rules in the qualitative reasoning framework. The (or), $(+_D)$, $(-_D)$, $(++_D)$, $(--_D)$ cases are dual w.r.t. (and), $(+_S)$, $(-_S)$, $(++_S)$, $(--_S)$ respectively.

Let $A : (\bigwedge_{i=1}^n v_i) \to v$ be a generic relation axiom for the relation r. We call the values v_i the *prerequisites values* and v the *consequence value* of axiom A, and we say that the values v_i are the *prerequisites* for v through r and that v is the *consequence* of the values v_i through r.

We say that an atomic proposition of the form $FS(G)$, $FD(G)$, $PS(G)$ and $PD(G)$ *holds* if either it is an initial condition or it can be deduced via modus ponens from the initial conditions and the ground axioms of Figure 2. We assume conventionally that $\top$ always holds. Notice that all the formulas in our framework are propositional Horn clauses, so that deciding if a ground assertion holds not only is decidable, but also it can be decided in polynomial time.

We say that there is a *weak conflict* if $(PS(G) \wedge PD(G))$ holds, a *medium conflict* if either $(FS(G) \wedge PD(G))$ or $(PS(G) \wedge FD(G))$ hold, a *strong conflict* if $(FS(G) \wedge FD(G))$ holds, for some goal G.

2.3 SAT and Minimum-Cost SAT

Propositional satisfiability (SAT) is the problem of determining whether a boolean formula Φ admits at least one satisfying truth assignment μ to its variables A_i. In a broad sense, a SAT solver is any procedure that is able to decide such a problem. SAT is an NP-complete problem [1], so that we can reasonably assume that there does not exist any polynomial algorithm able to solve it.

In the last years we have witnessed an impressive advance in the efficiency of SAT techniques, which has brought large previously intractable problems at the reach of state-of-the-art solvers (see [13] for an overview).

The most popular SAT algorithm is DPLL [3], in its many variants, and CHAFF [7] is probably the most efficient DPLL implementation available. In its basic version, DPLL tries to find a satisfying assignment recursively by assigning, at each step, a value to a proposition. The input formula must be previously reduced in conjunctive normal form (CNF)[1]. At each step, if there exists a unit clause, DPLL assigns it to true; otherwise, it chooses a literal l and it tries to find an assignment with l set to true; if it doesn't success, it tries with l set to false. In this way, DPLL performs the deterministic choices first while postponing, as far as possible the branching step, which is the main source of exponential blow up. There are several techniques to improve the efficiency of DPLL such as, e.g., backjumping, learning, random restart (again, see [13] for an overview).

A noteworthy variant of SAT is Minimum-Weight Propositional Satisfiability (MW-SAT from now on) [6]. The boolean variables A_i occurring in Φ are given a positive integer weight w_i, and MW-SAT is the problem of determining a truth assignment μ satisfying Φ which minimizes the value

$$W(\mu) := \sum_i \{w_i \mid A_i \ is \ assigned \ \top \ by \ \mu\}, \tag{8}$$

or stating there is none. In the general case MW-SAT is Δ_2^p-complete problem[2] [6], that is, it is much harder than simple SAT. The state-of-the-art solver for MW-SAT is MINWEIGHT [6], which is based on a variant of the DPLL procedure.

3   Goal Satisfiability for Goal Graphs

In [4] we focused on the problem of the *forward propagation* of goal values and of the *detection of conflicts*. Given a goal graph, the user assigns some initial values to some goals, *input goals* from now on (typically leaf goals), then these values are forward propagated to all other goals according to the rules described in Section 2. As the goal graph may be cyclic, the process stops when a fixpoint is reached. The user then can look the final values of the goals of interest, *target goals* from now on (typically root goals), and reveal possible conflicts. The whole algorithm is linear in time as it requires no form of search.

In this paper instead we focus on the *backward search* of the possible input values leading to some desired final value, under desired constraints. The user sets the desired final values of the target goals, and the system looks for possible initial assignments to the input goals which would cause the desired final values of the target goals by forward propagation. The user may also add some desired constraints, and decide to avoid strong/medium/weak conflicts.

3.1   Input and Target Goals

The notions of "input goal" and "target goal" deserve some more comment. Goal graphs may contain cycles, so that, in principle, it is not obvious a priori which goals are target goals and which are input ones. Although in our experience the boolean relations tend to

---

[1] A boolean formula is in CNF if and only if it is in the form $\bigwedge_i \bigvee_{j_i} l_{j_i}$, l_{j_i} being literals. A disjunction $\bigvee_{j_i} l_{j_i}$ is called *clause*. A one-literal clause is called *unit clause*.

[2] Broadly speaking, Δ_2^p is the class of problems requiring a polynomial amounts of calls to a procedure solving an NP problem.

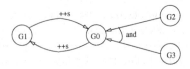

Fig. 3. The simple goal graph of Example 1.

$$FS(G) \rightarrow \begin{pmatrix} \bigwedge_i FS(G_i) & \vee & \text{If } (G_1,...,G_i,...G_n) \stackrel{and}{\longmapsto} G \\ \bigvee_i FS(G_i) & \vee & \text{If } (G_1,...,G_i,...G_n) \stackrel{or}{\longmapsto} G \\ FS(G_i) & \vee & \text{For every } R_i: G_i \stackrel{++s}{\longmapsto} G \\ FD(G_i) & & \text{For every } R_i: G_i \stackrel{--D}{\longmapsto} G \end{pmatrix} \quad FD(G) \rightarrow \begin{pmatrix} \bigvee_i FD(G_i) & \vee & \text{If } (G_1,...,G_i,...G_n) \stackrel{and}{\longmapsto} G \\ \bigwedge_i FD(G_i) & \vee & \text{If } (G_1,...,G_i,...G_n) \stackrel{or}{\longmapsto} G \\ FD(G_i) & \vee & \text{For every } R_i: G_i \stackrel{++D}{\longmapsto} G \\ FS(G_i) & & \text{For every } R_i: G_i \stackrel{--s}{\longmapsto} G \end{pmatrix} \quad (11)$$

$$PS(G) \rightarrow \begin{pmatrix} \bigwedge_i PS(G_i) & \vee & \text{If } (G_1,...,G_i,...G_n) \stackrel{and}{\longmapsto} G \\ \bigvee_i PS(G_i) & \vee & \text{If } (G_1,...,G_i,...G_n) \stackrel{or}{\longmapsto} G \\ PS(G_i) & \vee & \text{For every } R_i: G_i \stackrel{++s}{\longmapsto} G \\ PD(G_i) & \vee & \text{For every } R_i: G_i \stackrel{--D}{\longmapsto} G \\ PS(G_i) & \vee & \text{For every } R_i: G_i \stackrel{+s}{\longmapsto} G \\ PD(G_i) & & \text{For every } R_i: G_i \stackrel{-D}{\longmapsto} G \end{pmatrix} \quad PD(G) \rightarrow \begin{pmatrix} \bigvee_i PD(G_i) & \vee & \text{If } (G_1,...,G_i,...G_n) \stackrel{and}{\longmapsto} G \\ \bigwedge_i PD(G_i) & \vee & \text{If } (G_1,...,G_i,...G_n) \stackrel{or}{\longmapsto} G \\ PD(G_i) & \vee & \text{For every } R_i: G_i \stackrel{++D}{\longmapsto} G \\ PS(G_i) & \vee & \text{For every } R_i: G_i \stackrel{--s}{\longmapsto} G \\ PD(G_i) & \vee & \text{For every } R_i: G_i \stackrel{+D}{\longmapsto} G \\ PS(G_i) & & \text{For every } R_i: G_i \stackrel{-s}{\longmapsto} G \end{pmatrix} \quad (12)$$

Fig. 4. Axioms for backward propagation (G are non-input goals).

have a dominant role, so that target goals are typically roots and input goals are typically leaves, the choice is typically left to the user. Nevertheless, the choice is not completely free, as we impose that every path incoming in a target goal must be originated in an input node, that is:

for every target goal G there exists a direct acyclic subgraph (9)

(DAG) rooted in G whose leaves $G_{i_1}, ..., G_{i_k}$ are input nodes,

so that the value of G derives by forward propagation from those of $G_{i_1}, ..., G_{i_k}$. An easy-to-verify sufficient condition for (9) is that

all leaf goals are input goals[3]. (10)

Example 1. Consider the simple goal graph of Figure 3, and suppose that G_0 is the target goal and G_2 and G_3 are the input goals. (Notice that G_0 and G_1 form a loop without input goals.) If we assigned a final value $FS(G_0)$, then by backward search we could have $FS(G_1)$ and then $FS(G_0)$ again. Thus, $FS(G_0)$ could be derived by forward propagation from itself without any input value, which is a nonsense. If instead G_1 is an input goal, then by backward search we obtain $FS(G_1)$ or $FS(G_2)$ and $FS(G_3)$, which are suitable initial assignments to the input goals. Notice that $(G_2, G_3) \stackrel{and}{\longmapsto} G_0$ and $G_1 \stackrel{++s}{\longmapsto} G_0$ form a DAG rooted in G_0 whose leaves are input nodes. ◇

3.2 Basic Formalization

We want to reduce the problem of backward search for input values to that of the satisfiability (SAT) of a boolean formula Φ. The boolean variables of Φ are all the

---

[3] Recall that, by definition of goal graph, every loop contains at least one leaf goal.

values $FS(G)$, $PS(G)$, $FD(G)$, $PD(G)$ for every goal $G \in \mathcal{G}$, and Φ is written in the form:

$$\Phi := \Phi_{graph} \wedge \Phi_{outval} \wedge \Phi_{backward} \left[\wedge \, \Phi_{constraints} \wedge \Phi_{conflict} \right], \qquad (13)$$

where the conjuncts Φ_{graph}, Φ_{outval}, $\Phi_{backward}$ are explained below and the optional components $\Phi_{constraints}$, and $\Phi_{conflict}$ will be described in Section 3.4.

Encoding the Goal Graph: Φ_{graph}. The first component Φ_{graph} is the representation of the goal graph $\langle \mathcal{G}, \mathcal{R} \rangle$, given in the form:

$$\Phi_{graph} := \bigwedge_{G \in \mathcal{G}} Invar\_Ax(G) \wedge \bigwedge_{r \in \mathcal{R}} Rel\_Ax(r), \qquad (14)$$

$Invar\_Ax(G)$ being the conjunction of the invariant axioms (1) for the goal G in Figure 2 and $Rel\_Ax(r)$ being the conjunction of the relation axioms in (2)-(7) and their dual ones corresponding to the relation r. These axioms encode the forward propagation of values through the relation arcs in the goal graph.

Representing Desired Final Output Values: Φ_{outval}. The second component Φ_{outval} is a representation of the output values the user want to be assigned to the target goal. Φ_{outval} is written in the form:

$$\Phi_{outval} := \bigwedge_{G \in Target(\mathcal{G})} vs(G) \wedge \bigwedge_{G \in Target(\mathcal{G})} vd(G) \qquad (15)$$

$Target(\mathcal{G})$ being the set of target goals in $\mathcal{G}$ and $vs(G) \in \{\top, PS(G), FS(G)\}$, $vd(G) \in \{\top, PD(G), FD(G)\}$ being the maximum satisfiability and deniability values assigned by the user to the target goal G. Φ_{outval} is a conjunction of unit clauses, which force the desired output values $vs(G)$ and $vd(G)$ to be assigned to $\top$.

Encoding Backward Reasoning: $\Phi_{backward}$. The third component $\Phi_{backward}$ encodes the backward search. $\Phi_{backward}$ is written in the form:

$$\Phi_{backward} := \bigwedge_{G \in \mathcal{G}/Input(\mathcal{G})} \bigwedge_{v(G)} Backward\_Ax(v(G)) \qquad (16)$$
$$Backward\_Ax(v(G)) := v(G) \rightarrow \bigvee_{r \in Incoming(G)} Prereqs(v(G), r) \qquad (17)$$

$Input(\mathcal{G})$ being the set of input goals in $\mathcal{G}$, $Incoming(G)$ being the set of relations incoming in G, $v(G) \in \{PS(G), FS(G), PD(G), FD(G)\}$, and $Prereqs(v(G), r)$ is a formula which is true if and only if the prerequisites of $v(G)$ through r hold. The list of possible backward propagation axioms $Backward\_Ax(v(G))$ is reported in Figure 4, (11)-(12).

Suppose G is not an input goal. If $v(G)$ holds, then this value must derive from the prerequisite values of some of the incoming relations of G. $Prereqs(v(G), r)$ are exactly the conditions which must be verified to apply the corresponding relation axioms (2)-(7) and their dual ones in Figure 2.

3.3   Correctness and Completeness

The following theorem states the correctness and completeness of the approach.

Theorem 1. *Let $\langle \mathcal{G}, \mathcal{R} \rangle$ be a goal graph. Let $G_{i1}, ..., G_{ik} \in \mathcal{G}$ be the input goals verifying condition (9). Let $G_{f1}...G_{fn} \in \mathcal{G}$ be the target goals which are assigned the values $vs(G_{f1})$, $vd(G_{f1})$, ... $vs(G_{fn})$, $vd(G_{fn})$ respectively. Let $vs(G_{i1})$, $vd(G_{i1})$, ... $vs(G_{ik})$, $vd(G_{ik})$ be a set of values for the input goals.*

Then $vs(G_{f1})$, $vd(G_{f1})$, ... $vs(G_{fn})$, $vd(G_{fn})$ can be inferred from $vs(G_{i1})$, $vd(G_{i1})$, ... $vs(G_{ik})$, $vd(G_{ik})$ by means of axioms (1)-(7) if and only if there exists a truth value assignment μ satisfying (1)-(7), (11)-(12) and the values $vs(G_{i1})$, $vd(G_{i1})$, ... $vs(G_{ik})$ and $vs(G_{f1})$, $vd(G_{f1})$, ..., $vs(G_{fn})$, $vd(G_{fn})$.

Proof. **If:** Assume μ satisfies $vs(G_{i1})$, $vd(G_{i1})$, ... $vs(G_{ik})$, $vd(G_{ik})$ and $vs(G_{f1})$, $vd(G_{f1})$, ..., $vs(G_{fn})$, $vd(G_{fn})$ and all axioms (1)-(7) and (11)-(12). By condition (9), for every target goal G there exists a DAG rooted in G whose leaves are all input nodes. We reason on induction of the depth of this DAG. If G is also an input goal, then $G = G_{ik}$ for some k, so that $v(G)$ is inferred from $v(G_{ik})$ by a zero-step inference. If G is not an input goal, then there is one backward propagation axiom A in (11)-(12) in the form (17) which is satisfied by μ. As μ satisfies $v(G)$, μ satisfies $source(v(G), r)$ for some r. Thus $v(G)$ can be inferred from $source(v(G), r)$ by applying axioms (1)-(7). By induction, $source(v(G), r)$ can be inferred from $vs(G_{i1})$, $vd(G_{i1})$, ... $vs(G_{ik})$, $vd(G_{ik})$ by means of axioms (1)-(7). Therefore $v(G)$ can be inferred from $vs(G_{i1})$, $vd(G_{i1})$, ... $vs(G_{ik})$, $vd(G_{ik})$ by means of axioms (1)-(7).

Only if: from the hypothesis, $vs(G_{f1})$, $vd(G_{f1})$, ... $vs(G_{fn})$, $vd(G_{ik})$ are inferred from $vs(G_{i1})$, $vd(G_{i1})$, ... $vs(G_{ik})$, $vd(G_{ik})$ by means of axioms (1)-(7). Consider the assignment μ which assigns $\top$ to all the values which can be inferred from $vs(G_{i1})$, $vd(G_{i1})$, ... $vs(G_{ik})$, $vd(G_{ik})$ by means of axioms (1)-(7) and which assigns $\bot$ to all other values. By construction μ satisfies $vs(G_{i1})$, $vd(G_{i1})$, ... $vs(G_{ik})$, $vd(G_{ik})$ and $vs(G_{f1})$, $vd(G_{f1})$, ... $vs(G_{fn})$, $vd(G_{fn})$, and the axioms (1)-(7). Now let A be a generic instance of a backward axiom in (11)-(12), and let $v(G)$ be the atom occurring on the left side of A, before the "$\rightarrow$". G is not an input goal. If μ assigns $v(G)$ to $\bot$, then trivially μ satisfies A. If μ assigns $v(G)$ to $\top$, then, by construction of μ, $v(G)$ is inferred by means of axioms (1)-(7) from some prerequisite values which are assigned $\top$ by μ. Thus, at least one of the disjuncts on the left part of A are satisfied by μ, so that μ satisfies A. Therefore, μ satisfies all the backward propagation axioms (11)-(12).   Q.E.D.

3.4   Optional Components

We describe here the optional components $\Phi_{constraints}$ and $\Phi_{conflict}$ in (13). They allow the user to impose some constraints on the possible values of the goals or to force some desired value(s).

Adding User's Constraints and Desiderata. The first optional component $\Phi_{constraints}$ allows the user to express constraint and desiderata on goal values. $\Phi_{constraints}$ is generically written in the form:

$$\Phi_{outval} := \bigwedge_i \bigvee_j lit_{ij}, \tag{18}$$

$lit_{ij} \in \{PS(G), FS(G), PD(G), FD(G), \neg PS(G), \neg FS(G), \neg PD(G), \neg FD(G)\}$, $G \in \mathcal{G}$. A positive unit clause value is used to impose a minimum value to a goal. (E.g., "$PS(G_1)$" means "G_1 is at least partially satisfiable", but it might be totally satisfiable.) A negative unit clause value is used to prevent a value to a goal. (E.g., "$\neg FD(G_1)$" means "G_1 cannot be fully deniable", but it might be partially deniable.) A disjunction of positive values is used to state an alternative desideratum. (E.g., "$FS(G_1) \vee FS(G_2)$" means "at least one between G_1 and G_2 must be fully satisfiable".) A disjunction of negative values is used to state a mutual exclusion constraint. (E.g., "$FD(G_1) \vee FD(G_2)$" means "G_1 and G_2 cannot be both fully deniable", but they can be partially deniable.)

Preventing Conflicts. The second optional component $\Phi_{conflict}$ allows the user for looking for solutions which do not involve conflicts. Depending whether one wants to avoid (i) only the strong conflicts, (ii) the strong and medium conflicts or (iii) all conflicts, $\Phi_{conflict}$ is encoded respectively as follows:

$$\Phi_{conflict} := \bigwedge_{G \in \mathcal{G}} (\neg FS(G) \vee \neg FD(G)) \tag{19}$$

$$\Phi_{conflict} := \bigwedge_{G \in \mathcal{G}} ((\neg FS(G) \vee \neg PD(G)) \wedge (\neg PS(G) \vee \neg FD(G))) \tag{20}$$

$$\Phi_{conflict} := \bigwedge_{G \in \mathcal{G}} (\neg PS(G) \vee \neg PD(G)). \tag{21}$$

(19) states that G cannot be fully satisfiable and fully deniable; (20) states that G cannot be fully satisfiable and (fully or) partially deniable, and vice versa; (21) states that G cannot be (fully or) partially satisfiable and (fully or) partially deniable. Notice that, by Axioms (1), (21) implies (20) and that (20) implies (19).

It is easy to see that Theorem 1 extends straightforwardly to the case when we have $\Phi_{constraint}$ and $\Phi_{conflict}$ components.

4 Solving Simple and Minimum-Cost Goal Satisfiability

Consider a goal graph $\langle \mathcal{G}, \mathcal{R} \rangle$ with input goals $G_{i1}, ..., G_{ik}$ and target goals $G_{f1}, ..., G_{fn}$, and a set of desired final values $vs(G_{f1}), vd(G_{f1}), ... vs(G_{fn}), vd(G_{fn})$ to the target goals (plus possibly a set of user constraints and desiderata), and let Φ be the formula encoding the problem, as in (13).

Theorem 1 states that (i) if Φ is unsatisfiable, then no value exists to the input goals from which the desired final values derive by forward propagation (verifying the desiderata and constraints) (ii) if an assignment μ satisfying Φ exists, then the maximum values $vs(G_{i1}), vd(G_{i1}), ... vs(G_{in}), vd(G_{ik})$ which μ assigns to $\top$ are such that the desired final values derive from them by forward propagation (verifying the desiderata and constraints). This allows for reducing the problem of backward search to that of propositional satisfiability.

4.1 GOALSOLVE

We have implemented a tool, called GOALSOLVE, for the backward search of the possible input values leading to some desired final value, under desired constraints. The schema

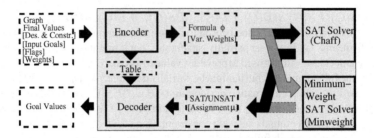

Fig. 5. Schema of GOALSOLVE (black arrows) and GOALMINSOLVE (gray arrows).

of GOALSOLVE is reported in Figure 5 (black arrows). GOALSOLVE takes as input a representation the goal graph, a list of desired final values and, optionally, a list of user desiderata and constraint and a list of goals which have to be considered as input. (The default choice is that indicated in condition (10), that is, all leaf goals are considered input goals.) The user may also activate some flags for switching on the various levels of "avoiding conflicts".

The first component of GOALSOLVE is an encoder that generates the boolean CNF formula Φ as described in Section 3, plus a correspondence table `Table` between goal values and their correspondent boolean variable. Φ is given as input to the SAT solver CHAFF [7], which returns either "UNSAT" if Φ is unsatisfiable, or "SAT" plus a satisfying assignment μ if Φ is satisfiable. Then a decoder uses `Table` to decode back the resulting assignment into the set of goal values.

4.2   GOALMINSOLVE

In general, the satisfaction/deniability value of (input) goals may have different costs. Thus we have implemented a variant of GOALSOLVE, called GOALMINSOLVE, for the search of the goal values of *minimum cost*. The schema of GOALMINSOLVE is reported in Figure 5 (gray arrows).

Unlike GOALSOLVE, GOALMINSOLVE takes as input also a list of integer weights $W(val(G))$ for the goal values. (The default choice is $W(FS(G)) = (FD(G)) = 2$ and $W(PS(G)) = (PD(G)) = 1$ if G is an input goal, $W(FS(G)) = (FD(G)) = W(PS(G)) = (PD(G)) = 0$ otherwise.) The encoder here encodes also the input weight list into a list of weights for the corresponding boolean variables of Φ. Both Φ and the list of weights are given as input to the minimum-weight SAT solver MINWEIGHT [6], which returns either "UNSAT" if Φ is unsatisfiable, or "SAT" plus a minimum-weight satisfying assignment μ if Φ is satisfiable. The decoder then works as in GOALSOLVE.

Notice that, in general, there may be plenty many satisfying assignments – up to exponentially many – corresponding so solutions for the problem. In a typical session with GOALSOLVE or GOALMINSOLVE, the user may want to work first with the "avoiding conflicts" flags, starting from the most restrictive (21) down to the least restrictive (19), until the problem admits solution. (E.g., it often the case that no solution avoiding all conflicts exists, but if one allows for weak and/or medium conflicts a solution exists.) Then, once the level of conflict avoidance is fixed, the user may want to work on refining the solution obtained, by iteratively adding positive and negative values – e.g. "$\neg FD(G_1)$", "$FS(G_2)$" – in the list of desiderata and constraints, until a satisfactory solution is found.

5   A Case Study

We consider as a case study the strategic objectives for the Public Transportation Service of the region of Trentino (Italy), we have recently analyzed for the CitiMan (Citizen Mobility Modeling and Management) project in collaboration with Centro Ricerche FIAT. As depicted in Figure 6, the main objective of the Trentino government is supply public transport service to the citizens, involving satisfy users, minimize costs per user, improve the quality of life, and protect users[4].

The objectives are further analyzed and refined using AND/OR decompositions. For instance, supply public transport service to Trentino citizen is AND-decomposed in guarantee transportation, sell tickets and manage financial budget. In turn sell tickets is AND-decomposed into decide sale strategy, decide sales strategy and avoid frauds, while the goal manage financial budget is AND-decomposed into obtain founds, manage services' costs and manage profits. Likewise, improve transportation services is OR-decomposed into improve old services and supply new services, while protect users is AND-decomposed in guarantee drivers capabilities, guarantee the user behavior, and protect user health.

The graph shows also lateral relationships among goals. For example, the goal protect user health has positive + contribution from the goal monitor pollution, while the goal minimize cost per user has two negative − contributions from goals provide comfort and improve transportation services. Asymmetric relationships are also showed; for instance, the goal satisfy users has a $++_D$ contribution from protect user and guarantee transportation, and a $+_S$ contribution from improve quality of life and again guarantee transportation.

We run a series of experiments with GOALSOLVE and GOALMINSOLVE on the goal graph in Figure 6. Both GOALSOLVE and GOALMINSOLVE have been implemented in C++ and the tests were conducted on a Dell Inspiron 8100 laptop with a Pentium III CPU and 64 MB RAM (OS: GNU/Linux, kernel 2.4.7-10). The tests were intended to demonstrate the practical effectiveness and benefits our approach, and also to check the efficiency of the tools. As for the latter aspect, in all our experiments both GOALSOLVE and GOALMINSOLVE performed in less than one second. (Of course, such performances depend on the goal model and the desiderata we want to obtain.) To provide examples, we briefly describe a few of these experiments. (We report here only the results for GOALMINSOLVE, which are more interesting.)

In a first set of experiments we imposed supply public transport services as target goal and all the leaves nodes except satisfy users and minimize cost per user as input goals, having as a desideratum the full satisfiability of the target goal. We run GOALMINSOLVE with the default settings for the weights.

Imposing the strongest conflict avoidance conditions (21) or (20), GOALMINSOLVE discovered there were no solution, whilst imposing the weakest condition (19) GOALMIN-

---

[4] The goal names are translated from Italian.

Table 1. Results of the first and the third set of experiments. (We omit the values of non-input goals and of those input goals which were not assigned any value.).

Top Goals	Exp1 S	Exp1 D	Exp3 S	Exp3 D
supply public transport service	F	P	P	P
satisfy users	P	P	P	P
improve quality of life	P		F	
minimize cost per user	P	P	P	P
protect users			F	

Input Goals	Exp1 S	Exp1 D	Exp3 S	Exp3 D
guarantee transportation	F			
obtain funds	F		P	
manage profits	F			
decide sale strategy	F			
cover services costs	F	P	P	P
invest on the services	F	P	P	P
use external funds	F		P	
use profits	P	P	P	P
increase profits	P	P	P	P
estimate services costs	F	P	P	P
evaluate alternative resources	F			
define profits to reach	F			
verify tickets	F			
estimate sale places	F			
add sale point on the path	F			
facilitate tickets purchasing	P	P	P	P
avoid traffic	P		P	
use special instruments	P	P	P	P
respect rules			F	
check driver health			F	
check drivers attitudes			F	
check drivers capabilities			F	
protect drivers health			P	
force to respect the law			P	

SOLVE found the results shown in Table 1 (Exp1). We notice the presence of conflicting values for some top and input goals. In fact, the FS value of **supply public transport service** is backward propagated down to all elements of the and tree rooted there, including **invest on the service**. This propagates a PS value to **provide comfort** and **improve transport services**, and hence a PD value to **minimize costs per user**, **satisfy users**, and hence to the target goal **supply public transport service**, generating thus a medium conflict. When we tried to eliminate only this conflict by imposing a $\neg PD$ constraint on the target goal, GOALMINSOLVE stated there was no solution anyway.

Thus, GOALMINSOLVE highlighted the fact that, with the goal graph of Figure 6, the full satisfiability of the main target goal cannot be accomplished without generating conflicts.

A second set of experiments showed that it is not possible to obtain the full satisfaction for the main goals of the Trentino Public Transportation System, namely **supply public transport service**, **satisfy users**, **improve quality of life**, and **minimize cost per user**, even admitting all kinds of conflicts. This is easily explained with the fact that both **satisfy users** and **minimize cost per user** are non-input and have no boolean, $++_S$ and $--_D$ incoming relations, so that there is no way they can be assigned a FS by forward propagation.

In a third set of experiments we have expressed as desiderata the full satisfaction for both goals **improve quality of life** and **protect users**, without saying anything about the other goal (in particular about the top goal **supply public transpiration service**). Also in this experiment it was not possible to have an assignment without conflicts, but we found a solution allowing medium conflicts (option (19)). As shown in Table 1

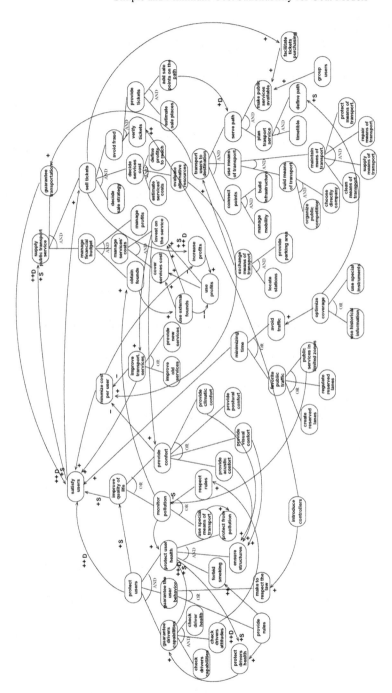

Fig. 6. The goal model for Trentino Public Transportation Service.

(Exp3), the assignment to the input goal produces conflicts to the top goals supply public transport services, satisfy users and minimize cost per user which, again, cannot be avoided.

A final set of experiments were carried out with graphs with a bigger number of nodes. The goal of the experiments was to evaluate the performance of our tool with respect to the growth of the dimension of the graphs. We generated such graphs randomly. Starting from the model of Figure 6, we generated new graphs adding randomly new goals and contribution links between goals, and thereby generating new cycles. Of course, since we were only interested on the structure of the graphs, we have not associated to them any semantics.

The results showed that also for bigger graphs (from hundred to two thousand nodes) GOALSOLVE performed in less than one second, whereas GOALMINSOLVE performed relatively well (less than five seconds) for graphs with a number of nodes less than three hundred. This suggests us that our approach can be applied in real life applications where goals models can count more than hundred goals.

6   Conclusions and Future Work

This paper introduces the problem of goal (plain/minimum-cost) satisfiability and proposed a solution by reducing goal satisfiability to the problem of (plain/minimum-cost) satisfiability for Boolean formulas. The solution has been implemented and evaluated with a case study. As illustrated by the case study, the solution makes it possible to answer questions such as "Is there a set of labels for input goals that satisfies all output (root) goals?", and if so, "Which solution is minimum cost?"

The proposed solution only works for qualitative goal models, where goals can be satisfied or denied, possibly partially. We plan to continue this research and extend these results so that they also apply to quantitative models, where one can also talk about goals being satisfied/denied with an attached probability/cost or other numerical measures.

References

1. S. A. Cook. The complexity of theorem proving procedures. In *3rd Annual ACM Symposium on the Theory of Computation*, pages 151–158, 1971.
2. A. Dardenne, A. van Lamsweerde, and S. Fickas. Goal-directed requirements acquisition. *Science of Computer Programming*, 20(1–2):3–50, 1993.
3. M. Davis, G. Logemann, and D. Loveland. A machine program for theorem proving. *Journal of the ACM*, 5(7), 1962.
4. P. Giorgini, E. Nicchiarelli, J. Mylopoulos, and R.Sebastiani. Reasoning with Goal Models. In *Proc. Int. Conference of Conceptual Modeling – ER'02*, LNCS, Tampere, Finland, October 2002. Springer.
5. R. Jarvis, G. McArthur, J. Mylopoulos, P. Rodriguez-Gianolli, and S. Zhou. Semantic Models for Knowledge Management. In *Proc. of the Second International Conference on Web Information Systems Engineering (WISE'01)*, 2001.
6. P. Liberatore. Algorithms and Experiments on Finding Minimal Models. Technical report, DIS, University of Rome "La Sapienza", December 2000. Available at http://www.dis.uniroma1.it/~liberato/mindp/

7. M. W. Moskewicz, C. F. Madigan, Y. Z., L. Zhang, and S. Malik. Chaff: Engineering an efficient SAT solver. In *Design Automation Conference*, 2001.

8. J. Mylopoulos, L. Chung, and B. Nixon. Representing and Using Non-Functional Requirements: A Process-Oriented Approach. *IEEE Transactions on Software Engineering*, 6(18):483–497, June 1992.

9. A. Newell and H. Simon. GPS: A Program that Simulates Human Thought. In E. Feigenbaum and J. Feldman, editors, *Computers and Thought*. McGraw Hill.

10. N. Nilsson. *Problem Solving Methods in Artificial Intelligence*. McGraw Hill, 1971.

11. C. Rolland. Reasoning with Goals to Engineer Requirements. In *Proceedings 5th International Conference on Enterprise Information Systems*, 2003.

12. A. v. Lamsweerde. Requirements engineering in the year 00: A research perspective. In *Proceedings 22nd International Conference on Software Engineering, Invited Paper, ACM Press*, 2000.

13. Lintao Zhang and Sharad Malik. The quest for efficient boolean satisfiability solvers. In *Proc. CAV'02*, number 2404 in LNCS, pages 17–36. Springer, 2002.

Energy Services: A Case Study in Real-World Service Configuration*

Ziv Baida[1], Jaap Gordijn[1], Hanne Sæle[2],
Andrei Z. Morch[2], and Hans Akkermans[1]

[1] Free University, FEW/Business Informatics
De Boelelaan 1081a, 1081 HV Amsterdam, The Netherlands
{ziv,gordijn,elly}@cs.vu.nl
[2] Dep. of Energy Systems, SINTEF Energy Research
7465 Trondheim, Norway
{Hanne.Saele,azm}@sintef.no

Abstract. Current eCommerce is still mainly characterized by the trading of commodity goods. Many industries offer complex compositions of goods based on customers' specifications. This is facilitated by a component-based description of goods, supported by a variety of product classification schemes, e.g., UNSPSC and eCl@ss. These focus on physical goods – wrongly referred to as *products* – rather than on services. *Services* are intangible products, for instance insurances, transportation, network connectivity, events hosting, entertainment or energy supply. Due to major differences between goods and services, product classification schemes cannot support automated service scenarios, such as a customer who wishes to define and buy a set of independent services, possibly supplied by multiple suppliers, via one website. To enable such eCommerce scenarios for services, a service ontology is required that supports a component-based structure of services. Defining a set of services is then reduced to a *configuration* task, as studied in the knowledge management literature. In this paper we use a case study from the Norwegian energy sector to describe how a component-based ontological description of services facilitates the automated design of a set of services, a so called *service bundle*.

1 Introduction

Although some e-business initiatives have failed, the massive diffusion of the Internet still opens up many new opportunities for businesses, such as in the field of online service provisioning. So far, the Internet has mainly been used as a channel for selling physical goods. It is for instance quite common that customers can configure a complex good (e.g. a PC) out of more elementary

* This work has been partially supported by the European Commission, as project No. IST-2001-33144 OBELIX (Ontology-Based ELectronic Integration of compleX products and value chains). We thank especially Nieves Peña (LABEIN, Bilbao, Spain) for useful discussions on the topic of this paper.

A. Persson and J. Stirna (Eds.): CAiSE 2004, LNCS 3084, pp. 36–50, 2004.

components and order such a good online. Examples can be found on websites of market leaders such as Dell and Cisco. Such an eCommerce scenario requires a component-based ontology of *goods*, specifically suited for *classification* (to allow customers to find goods) and *configuration* (to facilitate in composing complex goods). Examples of such supporting ontologies are UNSPSC [3] and eCl@ss [2].

Unlike physical goods, services are not supported well by these ontologies due to major differences between services and goods: their intangible nature (vs. tangible goods), customer involvement in the production process of services (vs. standard, off the shelf goods), difficulties in ensuring standard quality levels due to the important role of employees in the service process, and more [19].

However, from an economical perspective, services grow more and more in importance [4], and will be offered and deployed via the Internet increasingly. It is therefore important to extend current goods-biased classification and configuration ontologies with a service perspective. This paper proposes an ontological foundation for service configuration.

It is important to understand that our interpretation of the term *service* stems from business science, a community that has been researching the notion of services extensively already for decennia [15, 12, 23, 19, 21, 16, 8]. So, we do *not* take *web-services* publications such as [22] as our starting point; web-services take hardly a commercial/business value perspective on services, a perspective that is needed by customers and suppliers to configure valuable, complex services.

Based on service marketing and service management literature we have created a generic *service ontology* that describes services both from a supply-driven and demand-oriented perspective. We combine our business-driven conceptualization of the service sector with knowledge management research, specifically work on configuration task ontologies [13]. As a result, by using our service ontology as well as already existing configuration ontologies we can configure complex services (called a *service bundle*) out of more elementary services, possibly offered by multiple suppliers.

In the remainder of this paper we explain how the service configuration process takes place, and how it is facilitated by a service ontology. We demonstrate how we put our theory into practice by presenting a case study from the energy sector. We first present in Section 2 a top-level description of our service ontology, followed by an explanation of service terminology that underlies our work (Section 3). Subsequently, in Section 4 we explain how services can be described as components. Then, in Section 5 we introduce our case study domain, the electricity market, and we analyze potential service bundles in this market using our configuration-biased service ontology. Finally, in Section 6 we present our conclusions.

2   Service Ontology

Using the service management and marketing literature as a starting point, we have developed in earlier work a generic component-based service ontology [7, 6]. The ontology incorporates both a customer perspective and a supplier perspective on services, and it includes unique characteristics of services (compared to goods), e.g., the intangible nature of services. It allows customers to configure compound services, based on their specific requirements and expectations.

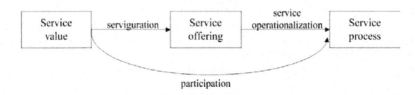

Fig. 1. Three top-level ontological distinctions to be made in a generic service ontology: the customer-value perspective, the supply-side perspective, and the joint operationalization of these viewpoints in terms of the actual service production process

On a high level of abstraction, a service ontology must embody three interrelated top-level perspectives: *service value, service offering* and *service process* (see Figure 1). The *service value* perspective describes the service from a customer's point of view in terms of a customer's needs and demands, his quality descriptors and his acceptable sacrifice, in return for obtaining the service (including price, but also intangible costs such as inconvenience costs and access time). The *service offering* perspective describes a service from a supplier's perspective; it provides a hierarchy of service components (service elements) and outcomes, as they are actually delivered by the service provider in order to satisfy customers' needs. The *service process* perspective describes how the service offering is put into operation (the *operationalization* relation in Figure 1) in terms of business processes that can be modeled using existing technologies as ebXML [1], WSFL [17] or BPEL [5]. Customers often take active part in the service production process (the *participation* relation in Figure 1).

Service configuration, or *serviguration*, is the process of defining sets of service elements (a supply-side description of services, part of the *service offering* perspective), that satisfy the customer description of his desired service (*service value* perspective). Serviguration can be split into two sub-processes: (1) transformation process between a customer description of the requested service and a supplier terminology for describing the service; and (2) defining zero or more sets of service elements that satisfy this supplier description of the requested service(s), and thus also the customer description of his requested service(s). This paper focuses on the second sub-process of the serviguration process: a task of configuring elementary services into a complex *service bundle*. It is important to understand that elements of the service offering perspective – which we model – cannot be modeled using business process modeling techniques, as the essence of value-oriented models is different from that of business process models. For a thorough explanation see [11]. Our work includes also the first sub-process of the serviguration process, a mapping task between customer requirements and available services. However, due to scope limitations, we do not discuss it in the present paper.

3   Service Terminology

In this section, we briefly review the core ontological concepts in our service ontology. For a more detailed discussion see [7, 6].

Service element represents what a supplier offers to its customers, in supplier terminology. It is what the business literature defines as *service*, a business activity (performance) of mostly intangible nature. A service element can be a composite concept; it can be decomposed to smaller service elements, as long as the smaller service elements can be offered to customers separately or by different suppliers. The business science literature discusses the notions *core service, supporting service* and *enhancing service*. A core service represents the reason for the supplier's presence on the market. For example, the core service of an insurance company is providing insurances; the core service of an airline is providing transportation. Supporting services are needed in order to enable the core service consumption. In the absence of these services, the core service consumption is no longer possible. For example room cleaning services in hotels. Enhancing services are often considered to be the elements of the service that define it and make it competitive. They increase the value of the service, or differentiate it from those of competitors [12]; the core service can nevertheless be consumed without them. An example is providing credit card holders with a "free" travel insurance. Neither supporting services nor enhancing services are offered independently of a core service. We adopt a customer-oriented definition of *core service*: a core service is not a main service that a supplier sells, but rather a main service a customer is interested in. For example, when a customer buys an airline ticket with a travel insurance, his core service is transportation, rather than insurance. However, from the insurance company's perspective, the travel insurance is a core service, since this is a core activity of that company.

Resource is either a pre-requisite for the provisioning of some service element, or the outcome (result) of a service element. We call resources *service inputs* or *service outcomes*. A resource may be the outcome of some service element, as well as the input of another service element. Very often the outcomes of a service reflect the customer benefits from a service. Resources may be of several types: *physical goods* (sometimes defined as 'those things that can be dropped on the floor'), *human resources, monetary resources, information resources* (e.g., customer information or a weather report service), *capability resources* (the ability to do something, which is of value to some actor, e.g., the ability to connect to the Internet 24x7), *experience resources* (e.g., an added value of going to Euro Disney is having fun) and *State-change resource*. The latter type requires an explanation. Services are "activities... of bringing about a desired change in – or on behalf of – the recipient of the service" [19]. Sometimes the change can be related to a property of some resource (e.g., a car's state changes in a car repair service), whereas in other services the subject of the state-change is not a resource, e.g., a passenger taking a flight undergoes a state change. In such cases the customer value of a service is a change of state: the customer *was* in Amsterdam, and now he *is* in Sydney. He pays for this change of state.

Service bundle is a set of one or more service elements that are offered together, possibly by more than one supplier. The service elements need not be related to each other; however, there will always be some logic behind the decision to bundle services. Services may be bundled because they depend on each other, to make better use of existing resources, for marketing goals, because legislation requires it and more.

4   Configuration of Services

Using the above terminology, we can describe services and service bundles in a similar way to how components and configurations are described in the knowledge systems literature. In particular, configuration is a constructive task, based on the availability of a set of predefined components, connections, and associated parameters and constraints [20, 18, 13]. We will describe service elements as components, so that a configuration process can create service bundles. Our discussion can be split into two parts: describing service elements (elementary and complex) and describing constraints on connections between service elements.

4.1   Service Element

Components, as described in the knowledge engineering literature [13, 18, 9, 10], have ports, constraints and properties. We claim that the component-based nature is inherent to services. As such, we can identify ports, constraints and properties for service elements.

Ports. Every service element has *ports* of two types: input ports and outcome ports. The provisioning of a service element requires core resources, and results in the availability of other resources. A port indicates a certain resource that is either a pre-requisite for carrying out this service element (input port), or the result of carrying out this service element (outcome port). A service element cannot be provisioned if not all required inputs are available; it results in the availability of all outcome resources. The set of all input ports, respectively all outcome ports of a service element form the element's *input interface*, respectively *outcome interface*.

Constraints. We distinguish between constraints that are internal to some service element (e.g., constraints on associated resources) and constraints on the relationships between service elements. The latter type is referred to as *functions* (see Section 4.3).

We can also identify **properties** of service elements. Some properties are generic (e.g., quality, productivity, sacrifice), whereas others are domain-specific. We found that all service properties can be described as resource properties as well. Hence, the properties of a service are expressed as the properties of its associated resources. The concept *service element* is visualized in Figure 2.

4.2   Service Bundle

A service bundle is a complex service element, that includes one or more (possibly complex) service elements. Hence, a service bundle has an input interface and

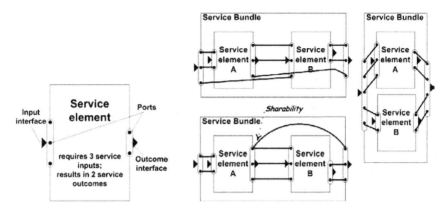

Fig. 2. Service element   **Fig. 3.** Service bundles

an outcome interface. The input interface, respectively outcome interface of a service bundle, are identical to the union of the input interfaces, respectively outcome interfaces, of all service elements included in a service bundle. Two deviations from this rule exist:

(1) when resources have the *sharability* property, they may be consumed after they had already been consumed. For example a *pricing model* is a static information resource that can be used multiple times and still be available.

(2) when resources have the *compositeness* property, multiple resources of the same type may be modeled as one resource. For instance, when two service elements are bundled, and both require a *payment* input, these two inputs can be composed into one *payment* resource. Very often the price in case of such bundling is lower than the sum of both prices.

The input interface of a service bundle must provide all inputs of all service elements that are part of this bundle, unless they are provided internally (one service element may produce an outcome that is consumed as an input by a different service element). Examples of service bundles are shown in Figure 3. Links between ports mean that one port uses a resources that another port provides.

4.3 Functions

Function is a relationship that defines dependencies between two service elements. It represents a constraint on how these service elements may or may not be bundled, rather than on the service elements themselves. A function is a formula that receives two arguments of type 'service element' (A - the *dependee*, and B - the *dependent*), and produces as output a set of possible configurations of these two inputs. We defined the following functions (with A, B as service elements) based on business science literature [12, 14, 15, 19] and on case studies:

1. **Core/enhancing (A, B):** B is an enhancing service of A (and thus A is a core service of B). Hence service A is a main service a customer is interested

in, whereas service B: (1) is not required for the provisioning of service A; and (2) adds value to A; and (3) is an optional service element, next to A; and (4) is not offered independently. If a customer wishes to consume service element A, he is presented with the option to consume also B, but he is not obliged to consume B.

Notation: $A \rightarrow_{enh} B$

Output: {A},{A,B}

2. **Core/supporting (A, B):** B is a supporting service of A (and thus A is the core service of B). In business terms it means that A cannot be provisioned without B and that B is not offered independently. Very often B will not present value as such for customers (e.g., billing services), but yet it must be provided to enable the provisioning of A. If a customer wishes to buy service A, he is obliged to consume service B as well.

Notation: $A \rightarrow_{supp} B$

Output: {A,B}

3. **Bundled (A, B):** If a customer wishes to buy service element A, he is obliged to buy also B. This is similar to the *Core/supporting* function. However, in this case B may be offered independently, and the reason for the obligatory consumption of B is different. In the case of *bundled* services, the bundling is required due to some business logic, such as cost efficiency reasons, marketing reasons, legislation and more.

Notation: $A \rightarrow_{bund} B$

Output: {A,B}

4. **OptionalBundle (A, B):** Two services A and B are offered separately, but also as an optional combination (bundle). In most cases, the bundling of two such service elements presents added value to the supplier (e.g., lower operational costs) as well as to the customer (lower price). Unlike the *core/enhancing* function, in the *optional bundle* case service B can also be offered independently of service A.

Notation: $A \rightarrow_{optBund} B$

Output: {A},{A,B}

5. **Substitute (A, B):** The benefits presented by A (in terms of service outcomes) to a customer are also presented by B (but B possibly offers more benefits). B can therefore be bought instead of A; customers can choose which one of them they prefer.

Notation: $A \rightarrow_{subst} B$

Output: {A},{B}

6. **Excluding (A, B):** If service element A is consumed, service element B may not be consumed, for example due to business reasons (A and B are competing services, and the supplier does not want to provide them together) or legislation that prohibits selling both services together.

Notation: $A \rightarrow_{excl} B$

Output: {A}

5   Case Study: Bundling Electricity Supply with Other Services

5.1   Differentiation of the Electricity Product in Norway

Electricity becomes more and more a commodity product. Competing suppliers are offering electricity to end-customers but the price per kWh is (nearly) the same. Additionally, it is delivered according to the same standard and consumed through the same electricity socket in a customer's home.

As a result, it is for electricity suppliers hard to compete with each other. Consequently, many suppliers are seeking for ways to differentiate their product. One way to do so is to add complementary and additional services such as Internet access and home comfort management. In many cases, suppliers can use existing infrastructure and/or available business processes to deploy such extra services, so bundling these services can be done with relatively modest effort. The study presented in the next sections utilizes and exemplifies our service ontology as well as existing work on configuration theory from AI, using a project we carried out for an electricity supplier in Trondheim, Norway. First, we elicit elementary service elements, their outcomes and inputs, constraints and functions. Knowing these elements, we configure *bundles* of service elements and outcomes, in effect various combinations of the outcome 'electricity' with additional outcomes.

5.2   Energy Service Elements

Multiple suppliers offer a variety of services that can be bundled with *electricity supply* in the energy sector. Some of the services are required in order to make possible the supply of electricity, while others add value or help suppliers differentiate themselves in this market. We identify the following service elements:

- **Electricity supply**; the selling of electricity to end-consumers.
- **Electricity transmission** to end-consumers. The Norwegian law forbids electricity supply and transmission to be done by the same company.
- **Heat pump** uses electricity for space heating. It provides maintained comfort with less use of electricity.
- **Energy control system** enables controlling the temperature and switching appliances on/off. It gives the customer the possibility to reduce electricity consumption and maintain a comfortable temperature.
- **Broadband (Internet) access** is offered in a limited geographic area.
- **Hot water** for room heating and tap water requires some technical infrastructure that is available in certain regions only. It provides the same functionality as heating water with electricity, but for a lower price.
- **Remote control**: web-based control of home appliances.
- **Contracting**. Many services require a contracting service element. However, the description of most services (in our case study) is quite different from that of electricity supply and transmission. Hence, we model three contracting service elements: electricity supply contracting, electricity transmission

contracting, and a generic contracting service element that all other services can use.

– **Billing** is also a service element that many other services require; it always requires some information about the contract, and results in an invoice. We model one generic billing service element.

We identified and modeled more services, e.g., ASP-services, safety check of electrical installations and more, but we do not discuss them further for the sake of brevity. In the remainder of this section we present two detailed examples of how service elements can be modeled as components. Figure 4 shows visualizations of two more such service elements.

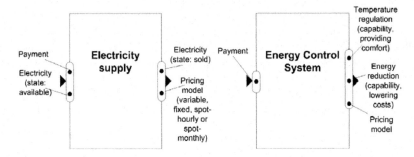

Fig. 4. Service elements: electricity supply, energy control system and contracting

Service Element: Broadband Access
Broadband Internet access is offered as an independent service (not necessarily bundled with electricity supply). The service is provided in a limited geographic region, where the required infrastructure is available.

Service Inputs:
Payment. *Type*: Monetary resource. *Compositeness*: Formula (when bundling two or more services, their payment inputs can be composed into one payment resource, based on a pricing-formula of the supplier).
Customer Information. Information about the customer, such as type of customer (household or industrial), name and address, postcode (to verify the geographic constraint of this service). *Type*: Information resource.

Service Outcomes:
Pricing Model. *Type*: Information resource. *State*: The chosen product for broadband access. Possible alternatives are *basic, regular* etc, implying differing download/upload speeds. *Sharability*: Infinite (The pricing model is determined in this service element, and then serves as input for the contracting and billing service elements. Being a static information resource, it can be consumed an infinite number of times).

Broadband Internet. *Type*: Capability resource. *State*: Available. *Productivity*: 256/128 kbps (download/upload), 512/128 kbps or 704/256 kbps. *Medium*: wireless OR fiber optics.

Service Element: Billing
Billing is a generic *supporting service element*; it is required to enable the consumption of several other service elements.

Service Inputs:
Pricing Model: *Type*: Information resource. *State*: Defined per service element.
Customer Information: Data about the consumption for the specified customer. *Type*: Information resource.

Service Outcomes:
Invoice: *Type*: Monetary resource. *Productivity:* Frequency of invoices (monthly, four times a year, yearly).

The above description of service elements is a generalization. In reality, when we model these service elements, we have multiple *broadband access* service elements, multiple *electricity supply* service elements etc, with varying values for the same resource properties. For example, instances of the *broadband access* service element exist with differing quality levels: basic, regular or luxurious.

Service Elements		Electricity supply	Contract electiricity supply	Billing	Electricity transmission	Contract electricity transmission	Heat pump	Energy Control System	Broadband access	Hot water	Remote control	Contracting
		1	2	3	4	5	6	7	8	9	10	11
Electricity supply	1	■	CS	CS	CS	-	OB	OB	OB	OB	OB	-
Contract electiricity supply	2	-	■	-	-	-	-	-	-	-	-	-
Billing	3	-	-	■	-	-	-	-	-	-	-	-
Electricity transmission	4	OB	-	CS	■	CS	-	-	-	-	-	-
Contract electricity transmission	5	-	-	-	-	■	-	-	-	-	-	-
Heat pump	6	OB	-	CS	-	-	■	-	-	-	-	CS
Energy Control System	7	OB	-	CS	-	-	-	■	-	-	OB	CS
Broadband access	8	OB	-	CS	-	-	-	-	■	-	-	CS
Hot water	9	SU	-	CS	-	-	-	-	-	■	-	CS
Remote control	10	OB	-	CS	-	-	-	BU	-	-	■	CS
Contracting	11	-	-	-	-	-	-	-	-	-	-	■

Fig. 5. Constraints on bundling services in the energy sector

5.3   Functions: Constraints on Service Bundling

Having modeled service elements in the energy sector, we can now look at dependencies between service elements. These are formulated in terms of the functions presented in Section 4.3. Together with domain experts we created a matrix of service elements, and every slot in the matrix represents the value of a function between two service elements. We use the following abbreviations: CS (Core/supporting), OB (Optional bundle), SU (Substitute), BU (Bundled). The notation '-' means that there is no function between the two associated service elements. This matrix is presented in Figure 5. It has to be read as follows: every slot defines a function *Function(row, column)*. In other words, service elements in the rows are the first argument of a function, and service elements in a column are the second argument of a function. For example: service element *electricity transmission* has an optionalBundle function with *electricity supply* and a core/supporting function with the service elements *billing* and *contract electricity transmission*. Multiple service elements naturally have a core/supporting function with *billing* and with *contracting*. Defining the set of functions (see Section 4.3) is a conceptual modeling task, mostly based on existing business science research. Instantiating the model as done in Figure 5, on the other hand, is done by mapping domain knowledge into the structures of our service ontology.

5.4   Configuring Service Bundles in the Electricity Market

A main reason behind our study of service bundles in the energy sector is to develop offerings so that our case study partner can differentiate herself from competitors. The same methodology can also be used to offer customers the possibility to define a set of services that they are interested in. In this section we analyze how services can be bundled in a scenario in which a customer is interested in electricity, as well as in broadband Internet. Similar scenarios can be created for any of the other service elements we modeled.

The input for the configuration process includes three parts:

1. A set of all available service elements, including their associated resources.
2. A set of all functions between any pair of service elements (see Figure 5).
3. A set of initial requirements. In our scenario we require the service outcomes *electricity* and *broadband Internet*. Deriving these requirements, based on a modeling of customer requirements, is facilitated by a mapping between concepts of two perspectives in our ontology: the *service value* perspective and the *service offering* perspective. As mentioned before, this process is not discussed in the present paper due to scope limitations.

The service outcomes 'electricity' and 'broadband Internet' are the results of service elements 'electricity supply' and 'broadband access' respectively. Consequently we would like to create a service bundle with these service elements.

Electricity supply has the following functions:
$electricity\_supply \rightarrow_{supp} contract\_electricity\_supply$
$electricity\_supply \rightarrow_{supp} billing$
$electricity\_supply \rightarrow_{supp} electricity\_transmission$
$electricity\_supply \rightarrow_{optBund} heat\_pump$
$electricity\_supply \rightarrow_{optBund} energy\_control\_system$

$electricity\_supply \rightarrow_{optBund} broadband\_access$

$electricity\_supply \rightarrow_{optBund} hot\_water$

$electricity\_supply \rightarrow_{optBund} remote\_control$

Consequently, any service bundle for electricity supply needs to include also instances of the service elements *contract electricity supply, billing* and *electricity transmission*, and possibly – but not necessarily – any combination of the following service elements: heat pump, energy control system, broadband access, hot water and remote control.

Broadband access has the following functions:

$broadband\_access \rightarrow_{supp} billing$

$broadband\_access \rightarrow_{supp} contracting$

$broadband\_access \rightarrow_{optBund} electricity\_supply$

Consequently, any service bundle for broadband access needs to include also instances of the service elements *billing* and *contracting*, and possibly *electricity supply*. However, since *electricity supply* is already part of our bundle, this function adds no new possibilities. Next, for every service element that we add to the bundle due to one of the above functions, we have to check recursively whether the functions of that service element pose new restrictions or add new possibilities. These service elements are: contract electricity supply, billing, electricity transmission and contracting. Three of them (contract electricity supply, billing, contracting) have no functions. But *electricity transmission* does:

$electricity\_transmission \rightarrow_{optBund} electricity\_supply$

$electricity\_transmission \rightarrow_{supp} contract\_electricity\_transmission$

$electricity\_transmission \rightarrow_{supp} billing$

The first function need not be addressed, since electricity supply *already* is part of our bundle. Both other functions are of type *core/supporting*, so their second arguments (*contract electricity transmission* and *billing*) must be added to any bundle. Since these two service elements have no functions, the recursive check of functions terminates, unless we also consider service elements that have an *optionalBundle* function with *electricity supply*. The result of this process is that any service bundle that satisfies the above mentioned requirements must include instances of the following nine service elements: (1) one instance of *electricity supply*; (2) one instance of *contract electricity supply*; (3) one instance of *electricity transmission*; (4) one instance of *contract electricity transmission*; (5) one instance of *broadband access*; (6) three instances of *billing* (for *electricity supply*, for *electricity transmission* and for *broadband access*); and (7) one instance of *contracting*.

Assuming that multiple instances exist for all these services (differing in quality levels or in other properties), the configuration process will result in a set of possible service bundles. Any such service bundle needs to include nine service elements as mentioned. An example for such a service bundle is presented in Figure 6. For clarity, we did not model how input/outcome interfaces provide the required resources to all service elements. Instead, we modeled only the three most important resources: the service input *payment* and the service outcomes *electricity* and *broadband Internet*. As can be seen, the resource *electricity* in a

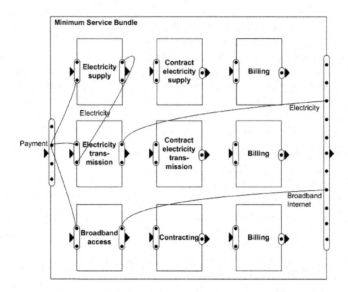

Fig. 6. A service bundle with electricity supply and broadband Internet access

certain quantity and in state *sold* is a service outcome of the service element *electricity supply*, as well as a service input of the service element *electricity transmission*. Subsequently, it is also a service outcome of the service element *electricity transmission* (and of the whole bundle), with state *transmitted*.

However, more possible service bundles exits. Instances of any of the *optionally bundled* service elements may be added to the bundle. This would require recursively adding service elements that may be required by the functions of any optional service element. For example, the service element *hot water* would require another instance of the service element *contracting*, and another instance of the service element *billing*. It is important to understand that Figure 6 is not a visualization of business processes, but a supplier description of offered services. These will be realized by business processes. There is no 1-on-1 mapping between service elements and business processes.

6   Conclusions

Services have traditionally been subject to research in business science. Discussions about services, as can be found in the business literature, are characterized by the use of natural language, which is not suitable for automated support of services. Business knowledge needs to be conceptualized and formalized as a first step towards online offering of complex service scenarios. However, scenarios in which a variety of services is offered by multiple suppliers require more than a formal description of business knowledge. For software to define sets of independent services, it is necessary to describe formally business knowledge on (1) what services are; and (2) under which circumstances services may be sold together. In other words, services need to be described as components, and their interdependencies as constraints. Our service ontology supports these two necessities through a formal conceptualization of business knowledge, based on structures from the knowledge management literature.

In this paper we have presented examples of modeling services from the energy sector, as part of a large-scale analysis of this sector. Based on our component-based description of services in the case study at hand, it seems possible to have software that configures *service bundles* that satisfy customer criteria. Currently, we are building in the EC-IST funded project OBELIX a tool that (1) allows modeling of elementary service elements and supporting constructs, and (2) configures service bundles using these elements as well as customer requirements.

The case study we have presented in this paper is part of a larger case study in the energy sector, in which we use other ontologies as well. We also investigated how the subjective customer description of services can be mapped into an objective supplier description of services; we then combined that process with the configuration of services. Among the results were new insights into the possible service bundles that are commercially viable for service suppliers, as well as feasible in the sense of interdependencies between services. Hence, our service ontology can be used not only for a customer-triggered process of configuring services, but also for an analysis of possible business scenarios.

References

1. *ebXML website*. 2003. http://www.ebXML.org
2. *eCl@ss website*. 2003. http://www.eclass.de
3. *UNSPSC website*. 2003. http://www.unspsc.net
4. An assessment of services trade and liberalization in the united states and developing economies. *World Trade Organization, Council for Trade in Services*, 31 March 2003. Document TN/S/W/12, available via
   http://www.wto.org/english/docs_e/docs_e.htm, last visited February 2004.
5. Tony Andrews, Francisco Curbera, Hitesh Dholakia, Yaron Goland, Johannes Klein, Frank Leymann, Kevin Liu, Dieter Roller, Doug Smith, Ivana Trickovic, and Sanjiva Weerawarana. *Business Process Execution Language for Web Services Version 1.1*. 2003.
   http://www-106.ibm.com/developerworks/webservices/library/ws-bpel/, last visited February 2004.
6. Z. Baida, H. Akkermans, A. Bernaras, J. Aguado, and J. Gordijn. The configurable nature of real-world services: Analysis and demonstration. In *The First International Workshop on e-services*, pages 46–56, Pittsburgh, PA, 2003. Carnegie Mellon University.
7. Z. Baida, H. Akkermans, and J. Gordijn. Serviguration: Towards online configurability of real-world services. In *Proceedings of the Fifth International Conference on Electronic Commerce (ICEC03)*, pages 111–118, Pittsburgh, PA, 2003. ACM.
8. Leonard Berry. Perspectives on the retailing of services. In Ronald W. Stampfl and Elizabeth C. Hirschman, editors, *Theory in Retailing: Traditional and Nontraditional Sources*, Chicago, 1981. American Marketing Association.

9. Pim Borst. *Construction of Engineering Ontologies for Knowledge Sharing and Reuse.* PhD thesis, Universiteit Twente, Enschede, NL, 1997.

10. W. N. Borst, J. M. Akkermans, and J. L. Top. Engineering ontologies. *International Journal of Human-Computer Studies,* 46:365–406, 1997.

11. J. Gordijn, H. Akkermans, and J. van Vliet. Business modelling is not process modelling, In: Conceptual modeling for e-business and the web (ECOMO-2000), Springer-Verlag, LNCS 1921, Salt Lake City, USA, October 9-12, 2000, pp. 40-51., 2000.

12. C. Grönroos. *Service Management and Marketing: A Customer Relationship Management Approach, 2nd edition.* John Wiley & Sons, Chichester, UK, 2000.

13. T. Gruber, G. Olsen, and J. Runkel. The configuration design ontologies and the VT elevator domain theory. *International Journal of Human-Computer Studies,* 44:569–598, 1996.

14. H. Kasper, P. van Helsdingen, and W. de Vries jr. *Service Marketing Management: An International Perspective.* John Wiley & Sons, Chichester, UK, 1999.

15. P. Kotler. *Marketing Management: Analysis, Planning, Implementation and Control, 6th edition.* Prentice Hall, Englewood Cliffs, NJ, 1988.

16. Theodore Levitt. *Your Factories in the Field: Customer Service and Service Industries,* chapter 3, in Marketing for Business Growth, pages 51–70. McGraw-Hill, New York, 1973.

17. Frank Leymann. *Web Services Flow Language (WSFL 1.0).* IBM, 2001. http://www-4.ibm.com/software/solutions/webservices/pdf/WSFL.pdf, last visited February 2004.

18. C. Löckenhoff and T. Messer. Configuration. In J. Breuker and W. Van de Velde, editors, *The CommonKADS Library for Expertise Modelling — Reusable Problem Solving Components, Chapter 9,* Amsterdam, The Netherlands, 1994. IOS Press.

19. C. Lovelock. *Services Marketing, People, Technology, Strategy, 4th edition.* Prentice Hall, Englewood Cliffs, NJ, 2001.

20. S. Mittal and F. Frayman. Towards a generic model of configuration tasks. In *Proceedings of the Eleventh International Joint Conference on Artificial Intelligence (IJCAI-89),* pages 1395–1401, San Francisco, CA, 1989. Morgan Kaufmann.

21. W. Earl Sasser, R. Paul Olsen, and D. Daryl Wyckoff. *Management of Service Operations: Text, Cases, and Readings.* Allyn & Bacon, 1978.

22. Steffen Staab, Wil van der Aalst, V. Richard Benjamins, Amit Sheth, John A. Miller, Christoph Bussler, Alexander Maedche, Dieter Fensel, and Dennis Gannon. Web services: Been there, done that? *IEEE Intelligent Systems,* 18(1):72–85, 2003.

23. V.A. Zeithaml and Mari Jo Bitner. *Services Marketing.* MGraw-Hill Companies, New York, NY, 1996.

Experimenting Data Integration with DIS@DIS

Andrea Calì, Domenico Lembo, Riccardo Rosati, and Marco Ruzzi

Dipartimento di Informatica e Sistemistica
Università di Roma "La Sapienza"
Via Salaria 113, I-00198 Roma, Italy
{cali,lembo,rosati,ruzzi}@dis.uniroma1.it

Abstract. Data integration consists in providing a uniform access to a set of heterogeneous sources through a common representation called *global schema*. In this paper we present DIS@DIS, a data integration system that adopts innovative techniques for query answering in a complex integration environment. In particular, DIS@DIS is able to deal with integrity constraints, which are used to enhance the expressiveness of the global schema. Since data at the sources may not satisfy the constraints, DIS@DIS is capable of reasoning in the presence of incomplete and inconsistent information, so as to provide consistent answers to user queries. Moreover, DIS@DIS is able to deal with both local-as-view and global-as-view approaches for the specification of the mapping between the global schema and the sources. DIS@DIS incorporates novel optimization techniques for query processing, which speed up query answering time even in the presence of complex global schemata and large amounts of data. Indeed, we show experimental results that prove the feasibility of our approach.

1 Introduction

The recent development of Information Technology has provided the availability of a huge amount of information, stored in sources that are often autonomous, heterogeneous, and both physically and logically distributed. Data integration consists in providing a uniform access to different sources; it has emerged as an important issue in the areas of distributed databases, cooperative information systems, data warehousing, and Web data management.

In data integration [17, 11, 15] the user is offered a common representation of the underlying data, called *global schema*; the user sees and queries the global schema as a single database schema, while the data integration system carries out the task of suitably querying the underlying sources and assembling the results in order to answer user queries. Integrity constraints are expressed on the global schema to enhance its expressiveness, yet the data at the sources may not satisfy such constraints.

Another crucial aspect of query processing in data integration is the specification of the relationship between the global schema and the sources, called *mapping*. Two basic approaches are possible for the mapping: the *global-as-view (GAV)*, in which elements of the global schema are associated to views over the sources, and the *local-as-view (LAV)* which requires the sources to be associated to views over the global schema [15].

A. Persson and J. Stirna (Eds.): CAiSE 2004, LNCS 3084, pp. 51–66, 2004.

In this paper we present DIS@DIS[1], a system for semantic data integration, that is capable of reasoning about integrity constraints in order to improve query answering. A significant issue here is that in DIS@DIS it is assumed that the sources are incomplete, i.e., they do not provide all information needed to answer user queries. In such a setting, due to the presence of integrity constraints, query answering amounts to reasoning about inconsistent and incomplete information, which is a difficult task. There are several data integration systems in the literature [7, 18, 12, 16, 13, 10, 2, 4]; yet, to the best of our knowledge, only IBIS [4] is able to reason about integrity constraints, though in a limited setting w.r.t. DIS@DIS. We emphasize that query processing in DIS@DIS is mostly carried out at the intensional (i.e., schema) level; in particular, DIS@DIS takes integrity constraints into account by reformulating each user query into a new one in which information about integrity constraints is encoded. Keeping most of query processing at the intensional level improves efficiency, since the size of the schema and constraints is usually much smaller than the size of the data.

The main innovative and distinguishing features of DIS@DIS are the following:

1. DIS@DIS is able to reason about a very expressive class of constraints in a relational setting, namely *key dependencies (KDs)*, *inclusion dependencies (IDs)*, which are a generalization of foreign key dependencies, and *exclusion dependencies (EDs)*, which establish disjointness between projections on relations.
2. DIS@DIS deals with incompleteness of data (violations of IDs) by reformulating user queries according to the IDs; the technique adopted, based on [6], takes advantage of novel optimization techniques.
3. DIS@DIS is capable of dealing with inconsistencies of data (violations of KDs and EDs) on the basis of a novel semantics [6], namely the *loosely-sound* semantics, that allows to obtain consistent answers from inconsistent data. DIS@DIS implements novel optimization techniques for checking the consistency of data, which is a costly step in query processing.
4. DIS@DIS is able to deal with both GAV and LAV mapping specifications. In particular, it implements a novel *ad-hoc* technique for LAV mappings, and, when only IDs and EDs are expressed over the global schema, it is able to transform a LAV system into a GAV one that is equivalent to the original w.r.t. query answering, thus allowing for the use of the techniques developed for GAV. The transformation technique extends that presented in [3], which does not directly allow for query processing and is limited to a restricted form of mapping views. Moreover, the technique of [3] works only for LAV integration systems without constraints.

In order to show the effectiveness and efficiency of the techniques implemented in DIS@DIS, we have tested the system in a real-world setting; the experimental results have shown that in practical cases DIS@DIS is able to answer queries in reasonable time, thus proving the feasibility of our approach.

The rest of the paper is organized as follows. In Section 2 we present the formal framework for data integration adopted in DIS@DIS; in Section 3 we present the query answering techniques of the system; in Section 4 we present the architecture of DIS@DIS;

---

[1] The name of the system is an acronym for *Data Integration System at the Dipartimento di Informatica e Sistemistica*.

in Section 5 we present the result of experiments that have been we have carried out on a real-world case. Section 6 concludes the paper.

2   Framework for Data Integration

In this section we present the framework for data integration adopted in DIS@DIS; such a framework is based on the relational model with integrity constraints. we assume that the reader is familiar with the basic notions of relational databases [1].

Syntax. A *relational database schema* $\mathcal{R}$ is a set of relation symbols, each with an associated *arity*, which is an integer value greater or equal than 1 that denotes the number of its attributes; to denote that a relation symbol R has arity n, we will write it as R/n. Formally, a data integration system $\mathcal{I}$ is a triple $\langle \mathcal{G}, \mathcal{S}, \mathcal{M} \rangle$, where:

1. $\mathcal{G}$ is the *global schema* expressed in the relational model with integrity constraints. Different integrity constraints are expressed over $\mathcal{G}$; in particular we have:
   (i) A set of *inclusion dependencies* Σ_I, i.e., a set of assertions of the form $R_1[\mathbf{A}] \subseteq R_2[\mathbf{B}]$, where R_1, R_2 are relations in $\mathcal{G}$, $\mathbf{A} = A_1, \ldots, A_n$ $(n \geq 0)$ is a sequence of attributes of R_1, and $\mathbf{B} = B_1, \ldots, B_n$ is a sequence of *distinct* attributes of R_2. Note that we allow repetition of attributes in the left-hand side of the inclusion[2].
   (ii) A set of *key dependencies* Σ_K, i.e., a set of assertions the form $key(R) = \mathbf{A}$, where R is a relation in $\mathcal{G}$, and $\mathbf{A} = A_1, \ldots, A_n$ is a sequence of attributes of R. We assume that at most one KD is specified for each relation.
   (iii) A set of *exclusion dependencies* Σ_E, i.e., a set of assertions of the form $R_1[\mathbf{A}] \cap R_2[\mathbf{B}] = \emptyset$, where R_1 and R_2 are relations in $\mathcal{G}$, $\mathbf{A} = A_1, \ldots, A_n$ and $\mathbf{B} = B_1, \ldots, B_n$ are sequences of attributes of R_1 and R_2, respectively.
2. $\mathcal{S}$ is the *source schema*, constituted by the schemata of the different sources. We assume that the sources are relational; considering only relational sources is not a restriction, since we may assume that sources that are not relational are suitably presented in relational form by wrappers.
3. $\mathcal{M}$ is the *mapping* between $\mathcal{G}$ and $\mathcal{S}$, specifying the relationship between the global schema and the source schema. Our framework allows for the specification of two kind of mapping: the *global-as-view (GAV)*, in which global relations are defined in terms of the sources, and the *local-as-view (LAV)*, in which, conversely, source relations are defined in terms of the global schema. We assume that views in the mapping are expressed in the language of *conjunctive queries (CQ)* [1] for LAV, and *union of conjunctive queries (UCQ)* for GAV. A UCQ of arity n is a set of conjunctive queries Q such that each $q \in Q$ has the same arity n and uses the same predicate symbol in the head. More specifically:
   (i) A GAV mapping is a set of assertions of the form $\langle R_{\mathcal{G}}, \varphi_{\mathcal{S}} \rangle$, where $R_{\mathcal{G}}/n$ is a relation of $\mathcal{G}$ and $\varphi_{\mathcal{S}}$ is a UCQ of arity n over $\mathcal{S}$.
   (ii) A LAV mapping is a set of assertions of the form $\langle R_{\mathcal{S}}, \varphi_{\mathcal{G}} \rangle$, where $R_{\mathcal{S}}/n$ is a relation of $\mathcal{S}$ and $\varphi_{\mathcal{G}}$ is a CQ of arity n over $\mathcal{G}$.

---

[2] For details about such dependencies, that have the same properties as the standard ones, we refer the reader to [1].

Now we come to queries expressed over the global schema; in our setting, we assume that such queries are expressed in the language of *union of conjunctive queries*.

Semantics. A *database instance* (or simply *database*) C for a relational schema $\mathcal{R}$ is a set of facts of the form $R(t)$ where R is a relation of arity n in $\mathcal{R}$ and t is an n-tuple of constants. We denote as R^C the set of tuples of the form $\{t \mid R(t) \in C\}$, and with Q^C the result of the evaluation of the query Q (expressed over $\mathcal{R}$) on C.

Now we come to the semantics of a data integration system $\mathcal{I} = \langle \mathcal{G}, \mathcal{S}, \mathcal{M} \rangle$. Such a semantics is defined by first considering a *source database* for $\mathcal{I}$, i.e., a database $\mathcal{D}$ for the source schema $\mathcal{S}$. We call *global database* for $\mathcal{I}$ any database for $\mathcal{G}$. Given a source database $\mathcal{D}$ for $\mathcal{I} = \langle \mathcal{G}, \mathcal{S}, \mathcal{M} \rangle$, the semantics $sem(\mathcal{I}, \mathcal{D})$ of $\mathcal{I}$ w.r.t. $\mathcal{D}$ is the set of global databases for $\mathcal{I}$ such that:

1. $\mathcal{B}$ satisfies the integrity constraints Σ_I, Σ_K and Σ_E in $\mathcal{G}$; we refer the reader to [1] for the notion of satisfaction of IDs, KDs and EDs.
2. $\mathcal{B}$ satisfies $\mathcal{M}$ w.r.t. $\mathcal{D}$. In particular,
   (i) $\mathcal{B}$ satisfies a GAV assertion $\langle R_\mathcal{G}, \varphi_\mathcal{S} \rangle$ w.r.t. $\mathcal{D}$ if $(\varphi_\mathcal{S})^\mathcal{D} \subseteq (R_\mathcal{G})^\mathcal{B}$;
   (ii) $\mathcal{B}$ satisfies a LAV assertion $\langle R_\mathcal{S}, \varphi_\mathcal{G} \rangle$ w.r.t. $\mathcal{D}$ if $(R_\mathcal{S})^\mathcal{D} \subseteq (\varphi_\mathcal{G})^\mathcal{B}$.
   Note that the above definition amounts to consider the mapping as *sound* but not necessarily complete; intuitively, for each mapping formula, the data retrievable at the sources are a *subset* of the data that satisfy the corresponding fragment of global schema. Such an assumption allows us to suitably model data incompleteness.

We now give the semantics of queries posed to a data integration system. Formally, given a source database $\mathcal{D}$ for $\mathcal{I}$ we call *certain answers* to a query q of arity n w.r.t. $\mathcal{I}$ and $\mathcal{D}$, the set $cert(q, \mathcal{I}, \mathcal{D}) = \{\bar{t} \mid \text{for each } \mathcal{B} \in sem(\mathcal{I}, \mathcal{D}), \bar{t} \in q^\mathcal{B} \}$.

3   Query Answering in DIS@DIS

In this section we present the techniques for query answering adopted in the DIS@DIS system.

The presence of integrity constraints on the global schema complicates the task of query answering; the key issue here is that in our framework it is possible that the semantics $sem(\mathcal{I}, \mathcal{D})$ of a data integration system $\mathcal{I}$ w.r.t. a source database $\mathcal{D}$ is constituted by an infinite set of databases that may have infinite size [15].

3.1   Query Answering in GAV

In order to deal with inclusion dependencies, DIS@DIS makes use of the algorithm IDrewrite [6], which is able to rewrite the user query according to the IDs expressed over the global schema. When processing a user query in the presence of IDs alone, DIS@DIS first executes IDrewrite, and then processes the obtained query as if there were no IDs; the properties of the algorithm IDrewrite ensure that the answers obtained in this way are the certain answers to the query. The execution of IDrewrite, which basically encodes the information about the IDs into the reformulated query, overcomes the violations of IDs, which are a form of *incompleteness* of the data w.r.t. the IDs.

Example 1. Consider a data integration system $\mathcal{I} = \langle \mathcal{G}, \mathcal{S}, \mathcal{M} \rangle$ with the following global schema $\mathcal{G}$:

$$\mathsf{player}(Pname, Pteam)$$
$$\mathsf{team}(Tname, Tcity)$$

The following ID is defined over $\mathcal{G}$:

$$\mathsf{player}[Pteam] \subseteq \mathsf{team}[Tname]$$

Consider a query $q(X) \leftarrow team(X, Y)$ issued by the user over $\mathcal{G}$ and asking for all team names. The rewritten query is $q'(X) \leftarrow team(X, Y) \vee player(W, X)$. Intuitively, in case of violations of the ID, instead of operating on the data, q' seeks for team names in relation team and also in the second column of player; in fact, if there are violations of the ID, there are team names appearing in player and not appearing in team.

In the presence of KDs together with IDs, the possible presence of violations, which are a form of *inconsistency* of the data w.r.t. the KDs, forces us to verify the satisfaction of KDs by the data at the sources. First of all, we have to restrict our attention to a special class of constraints, since the problem of query answering in the presence of general KDs and IDs is undecidable [5, 6]. In particular, we consider the class of *non-key-conflicting IDs (NKCIDs)*, which is a class of IDs that generalizes foreign key dependencies, together with KDs: in this case query answering is decidable [5]. Here the notion of *retrieved global database (RGDB)* comes into play; given a data integration system $\mathcal{I} = \langle \mathcal{G}, \mathcal{S}, \mathcal{M} \rangle$ and a source database $\mathcal{D}$, the retrieved global database $ret(\mathcal{I}, \mathcal{D})$ is the minimal global database w.r.t. set containment that satisfies the mapping $\mathcal{M}$ w.r.t. $\mathcal{D}$; it is obtained by evaluating, for each global relation in $\mathcal{G}$, the corresponding mapping view over $\mathcal{D}$. If the RGDB satisfies Σ_K, we can proceed as in the absence of KDs; on the contrary, a single violation of a KD leads, in the sound semantics, to a trivial case (since $sem(\mathcal{I}, \mathcal{D}) = \emptyset$, *any* tuple of the proper arity is in the answer to the query); the same holds if we add EDs on the global schema, together with NKCIDs and KDs. This property makes the sound semantics not suitable in practical cases, where we adopt the *loosely-sound* semantics [6]. In the loosely-sound semantics, the certain answers to a query are those that are in the answer to the query over all global databases which are consistent with the integrity constraints and that are obtained with a minimal repair of the violations of KDs and EDs.

Example 2. Recall Example 1, with the additional constraint

$$key(\mathsf{player}) = \{Pname\}$$

The source schema is $\{s_1/3, s_2/2, s_3/2\}$: s_1 stores name, team and age of players; s_2 stores name and city of teams, and s_3 stores name and team of players. The mapping associates to player the UCQ

$$\mathsf{player}(X, Y) \leftarrow s_1(X, Y, Z) \vee s_3(X, Y)$$

and to team the query

$$\mathsf{team}(X, Y) \leftarrow s_2(X, Y)$$

Consider a source database $\mathcal{D}$ with $(s_1)^{\mathcal{D}} = \{\langle\textit{figo}, \textit{realMadrid}, 31\rangle\}$, $(s_2)^{\mathcal{D}} = \{\langle\textit{realMadrid}, \textit{Madrid}\rangle\}$, $s_3 = \{\langle\textit{totti}, \textit{roma}\rangle, \langle\textit{figo}, \textit{cavese}\rangle\}$. The retrieved global database is as follows:

player		
figo	realMadrid
totti	roma
figo	cavese

team | realMadrid | madrid |

As for the violation of the KD, there are two ways of repairing the RGDB in a minimal way: either we eliminate the fact player(*figo*, *realMadrid*) or the fact player(*figo*, *cavese*). Violations of the ID are instead repaired by adding facts to the RGDB. We have two forms of global databases in $sem(\mathcal{I}, \mathcal{D})$:

First form: player | figo | realMadrid |
| totti | roma |

team | realMadrid | madrid |
| roma | α |

Second form: player | totti | roma |
| figo | cavese |

team | realMadrid | madrid |
| roma | α |
| cavese | β |

where α, β are constants. Considering the query $Q(X) \leftarrow \text{team}(X, Y)$, we have that the certain answers to Q under the loosely-sound semantics are $\{\langle\textit{roma}\rangle, \langle\textit{realMadrid}\rangle\}$.

We point out that DIS@DIS does not actually compute all the repairs of the RGDB, but resorts to an intensional rewriting approach: DIS@DIS first checks whether $ret(\mathcal{I}, \mathcal{D})$ satisfies the sets of KDs and EDs on $\mathcal{G}$ [3]; if this happens, it proceeds with the reformulation with **IDrewrite** and with the evaluation over the RGDB. If not, the user query is reformulated in a different query, expressed in Datalog with negation under stable model semantics [14, 8], a well-known extension of Datalog. The reformulated query is then evaluated over the RGDB by means of the deductive database system DLV [9].

When only IDs are expressed on the global schema, the consistency check is not necessary. In this case, after IDs are taken into account with the execution of **IDrewrite**, we can simply *unfold* the reformulated query; unfolding, which is the traditional technique for GAV systems without integrity constraints [15], amounts to substitute each atom in the query with the associated mapping view. Finally, the unfolded query can be evaluated over the source database.

3.2   Query Answering in LAV

Now we come to the case where the data integration system has a LAV mapping.

When the consistency check is necessary, i.e., when KDs and EDs are expressed on the global schema, the RGDB can be calculated in LAV systems as well. If the RGDB satisfies KDs and EDs, we can proceed as in the GAV case. Otherwise, we are able to do query answering in the case of violations of KDs and EDs, but this feature is not yet implemented in DIS@DIS.

---

[3] Notice that this step requires the computation of the closure of KDs and EDs w.r.t. logical implication.

When only IDs are expressed over the global schema, instead of computing the RGDB, which is a costly operation, DIS@DIS transforms the LAV system into a GAV one which is equivalent w.r.t. query answering [3]. Note that the transformation is done "at compile time", i.e. it does not depend on the queries, but it involves only the specification of the system. The transformation introduces an additional set of IDs on the global schema, which however can be treated together with the pre-existing ones; therefore, we are able to apply the same techniques as in the GAV case.

3.3   Optimizations in GAV

The experiments carried out with DIS@DIS have shown that the most costly step from a computational point of view is the generation of the RGDB (see Section 5). In the presence of a GAV mapping specification, optimizations are possible, that can actually speed up the generation of the RGDB. We have focused our attention on the GAV approach, which is used by the majority of data integration system, for example MOMIS [2] and IBIS [4].

The key point in the optimization is the loosely-sound semantics, which allows us to consider only a limited portion of the RGDB in the consistency check. In particular, we need to take into account only the tuples that can contribute to the answer and those that may conflict with such tuples. In the following, we will denote as RDGB the portion of it that is relevant to a certain query. First of all, given a user query Q, we can disregard global relations which do not appear in Q. For the remaining global relations, instead of retrieving the whole set of tuples for each one of them, we "push-down" the selections of Q, thus reducing the number of retrieved tuples. At this point, for each queried source R, if the previous selection was not performed on the key of R or on a subset of it, we need to retrieve the tuples that conflict with the ones already retrieved. This is done by selecting the tuples of R that share the same key with the ones already retrieved.

Example 3. Consider a data integration system $\mathcal{I} = \langle \mathcal{G}, \mathcal{S}, \mathcal{M} \rangle$, with $\mathcal{G} = \{R_1/1, R_2/2, R_3/2\}$, $key(R_2) = \{1\}$ and $\mathcal{S} = \{S_1/2, S_2/1, S_3/2\}$. The mapping $\mathcal{M}$ associates to R_1 the query $R_1(X) \leftarrow S_1(X, Y), S_2(Y)$, to R_2 the query $R_2(X, Y) \leftarrow S_3(X, Y)$, and to R_3 the query $R_3(X, Y) \leftarrow S_1(Y, X)$. Suppose we have the user query $Q(X) \leftarrow R_1(X), R_2(X, a)$.

To compute the retrieved global database, we can ignore R_3, since it does not appear in the body of Q. As for R_1, we have to populate it entirely, without optimizations, since there is no selection over it. For R_2 we have a selection on a non-key attribute; we first populate it with the tuples obtained by evaluating the following query over the source database: $Q_{R_2}(X_1, X_2) \leftarrow S_3(X_1, a)$, where we have pushed down the selection on R_2 in Q. After that, we still have to retrieve the tuples that are in conflict with the ones retrieved by Q_{R_2}; this is done by evaluating the query Q'_{R_2} over the source database, where Q'_{R_2} is as follows: $Q'_{R_2}(X_1, X_2) \leftarrow S_3(X_1, a), S_3(X_1, X_2)$. At this point we can proceed in the evaluation of the certain answers to Q as described in Section 3.1. The extension of R_2 is the union of the answers to Q_{R_2} and Q'_{R_2}.

4   System Architecture

In this section we present the architecture of DIS@DIS. Figure 1 shows an overall picture of the system and of its modules.

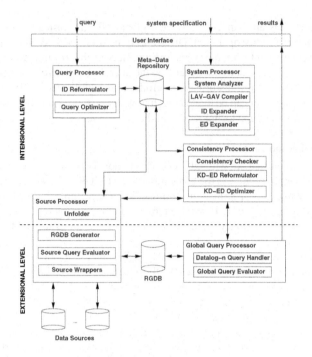

Fig. 1. Architecture of the system

In the system, the *Meta-Data Repository* stores an internal representation of the intensional information, i.e., the system specification and the user queries. Also, a *User Interface* takes care of the interaction with the system user.

The system architecture comprises five main modules:

1. the *System Processor* elaborates and reasons about the specification of the data integration system;
2. the *Query Processor* has the task of elaborating the user queries, according to IDs expressed on the global schema;
3. the *Source Processor* unfolds the query when only IDs are defined over the global schema. On the contrary, when the consistency check is necessary, it executes the reformulated query, by retrieving at the sources the data relevant for the query, and by storing such data in the RGDB. In this module, source wrappers provide a relational view of the sources (source schema $\mathcal{S}$);
4. the *Consistency Processor* is activated only when KDs or EDs are defined on the global schema. It detects the situations in which data stored in the RGDB are not consistent with the key dependencies and the exclusion dependencies and, if needed, computes a further reformulation of the query.
5. the *Global Query Processor* evaluates the reformulated query over the RGDB.

In this section we briefly describe the main components of the system.

4.1   System Processor

System Analyzer. This module verifies the properties of the data integration system. In particular: *(i)* it verifies whether the system is *non-key-conflicting*; *(ii)* based on the constraints and the mapping, it establishes whether two global relations are equivalent or contained one into the other.

LAV-GAV Compiler. The task of the LAV-GAV Compiler is to transform a specification of a LAV system into a specification of GAV system which is equivalent to the initial one w.r.t. query processing. We recall that the transformation is performed in a purely intensional fashion, and only once for any integration system specification (unless the specification changes).

ID Expander. In order to speed up the query reformulation phase, DIS@DISprocesses the IDs by computing the closure of them w.r.t. implication [1]. The computational cost of this calculation is, in the worst case, exponential in the size of the initial set of IDs; however, since this operation is to be performed only once, i.e. when the specification of a system is loaded, such an exponential blow-up is of not critical from a practical point of view. In order to further optimize the computation of the closure, indexing structures are used: their introduction allows us to avoid useless application on the implication rule. The process terminates when no new IDs can be added.

ED Expander. The ED Expander has the task of inferring new exclusion dependencies starting from the given set of EDs and IDs. Such dependencies are obtained through a recursive inference procedure that computes the closure of the initial set of EDs w.r.t. implication [1]. Such a process is necessary to efficiently deal with inconsistent data, since it reduces the computational cost of the operations performed by the Consistency Processor.

4.2   Query Processor

ID Reformulator. This module implements the algorithm IDrewrite [6], by producing a rewriting of any query posed to the system by the user.

The algorithm implemented by the ID Reformulator is actually an optimization of the procedure ID-rewrite presented in [6], which exploits the fact that the inclusion set has been previously closed by the ID Expander.

Query Optimizer. The Query Optimizer performs an optimization of the rewritten query obtained by the ID Reformulator. In particular, it can check *a priori* whether a query will not produce any result; in this case the query is immediately excluded. This module is currently under development.

4.3   Source Processor

Unfolder. This module unfolds the query produced by the ID Reformulator according to the mapping assertions, i.e., reformulates the query in terms of the source relations.

RGDB Generator. The RGDB Generator builds the RGDB from the system specification and the source data. For GAV systems, the optimized technique described in Section 3 is used. For LAV systems, the generator builds the RGDB by extracting data from the sources, and suitably adding tuples in the global relations for each extracted tuple.

Source Wrappers. Such modules provide a relational interface to data sources, which in general may be semi-structured and non-relational. Wrappers for DIS@DIS are currently under development.

4.4   Consistency Processor

Consistency Checker. The Consistency Checker analyzes the RGDB to detect the presence of violations of key and exclusion dependencies expressed over the global schema. In such a case, the KD-ED Reformulator is invoked.

KD-ED Reformulator. This module reformulates the query in order to deal with violations of KDs and EDs, under the loosely-sound semantics (see Section 3), and produces a program expressed in Datalog with negation.

KD-ED Optimizer. This module carries out the task of optimizing the rewriting produced by the KD-ED Reformulator. Indeed, it restricts the rewritten query by eliminating those parts of the query that cannot actually contribute to the answer, by checking *a priori* whether a subquery will not produce any result. This module is currently under development.

4.5   Global Query Processor

The task of this module is to evaluate the rewritten query generated by the Query Processor and the Consistency Processor over the RGDB. If the rewriting is a Datalog query with negation, then the evaluation is performed by the *Datalog-n-Query Handler*, that makes use of the Disjunctive Datalog engine DLV [9], otherwise the query is a standard union of conjunctive queries, therefore the rewriting can be evaluated by the *Global Query Evaluator*, that translates the query in SQL and then passes this query to the DBMS (currently, MySQL) that stores the RGDB.

5   Experimental Results

We have carried out experiments on the DIS@DIS system in order to test the feasibility of our approach. We have built a GAV data integration system using a set of data belonging to the information system of the University of Rome "La Sapienza"; such data contain information about students, professors and exams between 1993 and 1998. The source data come from different databases and are significantly overlapping. The source schema comprises 27 relations, while the global schema has 10 relations. Key dependencies and inclusion dependencies are expressed on the global schema; the set of dependencies is quite complex: in particular, the IDs are *cyclic*, and the semantics of the system includes global databases of infinite size.

We have deployed the DIS@DIS system, which is written in Java, on an Intel Pentium III machine, with 800 MHz processor clock frequency, equipped with 640 Mb of RAM, and with a 40 Gb hard disk drive at 7200 RPM; the machine runs the operating system Windows XP. In order to test the efficiency of our system independently of network delays, the data sources have been migrated to a local DBMS, thus avoiding delays due to remote sources. Our DBMS of choice is MySQL, which we chose for its efficiency and simplicity.

The global schema of the system we built for our experiments comprises the following relations:

student(*ID, FirstName, SecondName, CityOfResidence, Address, Telephone, HighSchoolSpecialization*)
enrollment(*StudentID, FacultyName, Year*)
exam(*Code, Description*)
professor(*FirstName, SecondName, Area*)
university(*Code, City, Name*)
master_exam_record(*StudentID, Exam, ProfFirstName, ProfSecondName, Mark, Date, CourseYear*)
bachelor_exam_record(*StudentID, ExamCode, Session, Mode, Mark*)
teaching(*Exam, ProfFirstName, ProfSecondName, AcademicYear*)
exam_plan(*Code, StudentID, PlanType, RequestDate, Status*)
exam_plan_data(*Code, ExamName, ExamType*)

We have the following constraints (KDs and IDs) over the global schema:

$$key(\text{student}) = \{1\} \qquad key(\text{exam}) = \{1\}$$
$$key(\text{professor}) = \{1, 2\} \qquad key(\text{university}) = \{1\}$$

master_exam_record$[1] \subseteq$ student$[1]$
master_exam_record$[2] \subseteq$ exam$[1]$
teaching$[1] \subseteq$ master_exam_record$[2]$
master_exam_record$[3, 4] \subseteq$ professor$[1, 2]$
professor$[1, 2] \subseteq$ teaching$[2, 3]$

bachelor_exam_record$[1] \subseteq$ student$[1]$
bachelor_exam_record$[2] \subseteq$ exam$[1]$
exam_plan$[2] \subseteq$ student$[1]$
exam_plan_data$[1] \subseteq$ exam_plan$[1]$

We have tested the system with 7 queries, which we describe below. Note that, for the sake of conciseness, we do not specify projections on the result for those queries where this choice has no consequences on the performances. The queries below are written in SQL.

(Q_1) This query returns the exams in the exam plan of the student with ID 09089903.

```
SELECT *
FROM exam_plan_data D, exam_plan P
WHERE D.code = P.code AND P.studentID = '09089903';
```

(Q_2) This query returns the exams passed by the student with ID 09089903.

```
SELECT *
FROM master_exam_record V, exam E
WHERE V.exam = E.code AND V.studentID = '09089903';
```

(Q_3) Similar to the previous one, but returns also personal data of the student.

```
SELECT *
FROM master_exam_record V, exam E, student S
WHERE V.exam = E.code AND V.studentID = S.ID
and S.ID = '09089903';
```

(Q_4) This query returns the information about students and their exam plans, for students who have as first name Federico and who have chosen the plan type T1.

```
SELECT *
FROM student S, exam_plan P
WHERE P.studentID = S.ID AND P.planType = 'T1'
  AND S.firstName = 'Federico';
```

(Q_5) This query returns the second name of professors that teach a course and whose first name is Mario. The query has been chosen to test both the algorithm IDrewrite and the optimization technique described in Section 3.3.

```
SELECT T.ProfSecondName
FROM teaching T
WHERE T.ProfFirstName = 'Mario';
```

(Q_6) This query returns the information about students with second name Rossi and the master exams they have passed.

```
SELECT *
FROM master_exam_record V, student S
WHERE V.studentID = S.ID and S.secondName = 'Rossi';
```

(Q_7) This query retrieves the information about students living in Roma and their exam plans; it was chosen to test the behaviour of the system when the number of tuples in the result is high.

```
SELECT *
FROM student S, exam_plan P, exam_plan_data D
WHERE S.ID = P.studentID AND P.code = D.code AND
  S.cityOfRresidence = 'Roma';
```

Now we come to the results we have obtained with the above queries. The optimization technique allows us to significantly reduce the number of tuples of the RGDB retrieved by the RGDB Generator, and thus the time needed for the retrieval. As a consequence, also the consistency check time is reduced, as well as the query evaluation time.

The comparison has been done between the basic optimization technique, that consists in considering only the global relations that appear in the global query, and the full optimization technique, both described in Section 3.3. The experimental data are summarized in Figure 2. The values obtained with the basic optimization are denoted as "old" in the figure.

Note that the bottleneck in query answering is the generation of the RGDB, which requires the processing of a significant quantity of data. The preprocessing of the query and its evaluation requires a time which is negligible w.r.t. the operation of retrieving the RGDB and checking the satisfaction of the constraints. The query evaluation time (in milliseconds) and the number of retrieved tuples for the different queries is reported[4] in

---

[4] We do not have bar charts here because the values would not be all readable on the same scale.

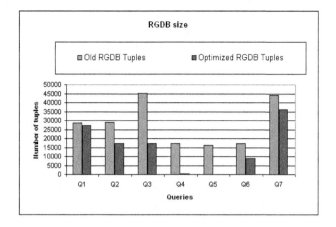

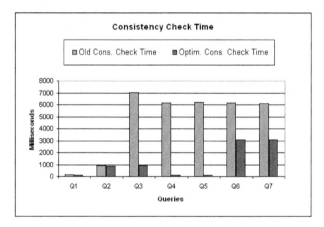

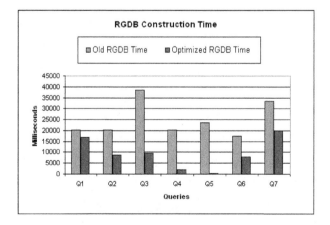

Fig. 2. Experimental results for query answering in DIS@DIS

	Q_1	Q_2	Q_3	Q_4	Q_5	Q_6	Q_7
Exec. time without optim.	181	30	70	20	10	1030	17345
Exec. time with optim.	70	20	41	10	8	746	16834

	Q_1	Q_2	Q_3	Q_4	Q_5	Q_6	Q_7
No. of tuples in the result	19	7	7	1	13	212	5119

Fig. 3. Execution time (in milliseconds) and no. of retrieved tuples for the queries considered in the experiments

Figure 3. The time needed for overall query processing, including generation of RGDB and consistency check, was acceptable in all cases.

Before concluding, we point out that there are 13 tuples in the answer to the query Q_5. This result would not have been achieved by disregarding IDs and simply evaluating the query with classical unfolding, which actually retrieves only 5 tuples. In this case, the algorithm IDrewrite rewrites Q_5 in the union of conjunctive queries reported below, whose evaluation over the RGDB produces the 15 tuples that are the certain answers to he query.

```
SELECT T.ProfSecondName
FROM teaching T
WHERE T.ProfFirstName = 'Mario';
UNION
SELECT P.SecondName
FROM professor P
WHERE P.FirstName = 'Mario';
UNION
SELECT M.ProfSecondName
FROM master_exam_record M
WHERE M.ProfFirstName = 'Mario';
```

6   Conclusions

In this paper we have presented DIS@DIS, a system for semantic data integration that implements state-of-the-art techniques for query processing under integrity constraints. To the best of our knowledge, DIS@DIS is the first system that enables query processing under constraints in both LAV and GAV specifications and that is able to deal with inconsistent data. In partiular, DIS@DIS reasons about integrity constraints expressed on the global schema, so as to provide consistent answers in the presence of incomplete and inconsistent data.

A significant issue is that DIS@DIS keeps the computation as much as possible at the intensional level. In this way, the use of computations involving data is reduced, thus improving efficiency. In fact, the size of the data is usually much larger than the size of the intensional specification of the system, and moreover source accesses typically represent a bottleneck in data integration systems. As for computations involving data, DIS@DIS exploits novel optimization techniques.

We have tested DIS@DIS on a real-world case, showing that the system is able to perform well on a large amount of data, in the presence of redundancies and inconsistencies, and under a complex set of constraints over the global schema. Response times to queries has proved to be acceptable in all tests we have carried out.

Acknowledgments

This research has been supported by the Projects INFOMIX (IST-2001-33570) and SEWASIE (IST-2001-34825) funded by the EU, and by the Project MAIS funded by MIUR (Ministero per l'Istruzione, l'Università e la Ricerca).

References

1. Serge Abiteboul, Richard Hull, and Victor Vianu. *Foundations of Databases*. Addison Wesley Publ. Co., 1995.
2. Sonia Bergamaschi, Silvana Castano, Maurizio Vincini, and Domenico Beneventano. Semantic integration of heterogeneous information sources. *Data and Knowledge Engineering*, 36(3):215–249, 2001.
3. Andrea Calì, Diego Calvanese, Giuseppe De Giacomo, and Maurizio Lenzerini. On the expressive power of data integration systems. In *Proc. of ER 2002*, 2002.
4. Andrea Calì, Diego Calvanese, Giuseppe De Giacomo, Maurizio Lenzerini, Paolo Naggar, and Fabio Vernacotola. IBIS: Semantic data integration at work. In *Proc. of CAiSE 2003*, pages 79–94, 2003.
5. Andrea Calì, Domenico Lembo, and Riccardo Rosati. On the decidability and complexity of query answering over inconsistent and incomplete databases. In *Proc. of PODS 2003*, pages 260–271, 2003.
6. Andrea Calì, Domenico Lembo, and Riccardo Rosati. Query rewriting and answering under constraints in data integration systems. In *Proc. of IJCAI 2003*, 2003.
7. Sudarshan S. Chawathe, Hector Garcia-Molina, Joachim Hammer, Kelly Ireland, Yannis Papakonstantinou, Jeffrey D. Ullman, and Jennifer Widom. The TSIMMIS project: Integration of heterogeneous information sources. In *Proc. of the 10th Meeting of the Information Processing Society of Japan (IPSJ'94)*, pages 7–18, 1994.
8. Thomas Eiter, Georg Gottlob, and Heikki Mannilla. Disjunctive Datalog. *ACM Trans. on Database Systems*, 22(3):364–418, 1997.
9. Thomas Eiter, Nicola Leone, Cristinel Mateis, Gerald Pfeifer, and Francesco Scarcello. The KR system dlv: Progress report, comparison and benchmarks. In *Proc. of KR'98*, pages 636–647, 1998.
10. Cheng Hian Goh, Stéphane Bressan, Stuart E. Madnick, and Michael D. Siegel. Context interchange: New features and formalisms for the intelligent integration of information. *ACM Trans. on Information Systems*, 17(3):270–293, 1999.
11. Alon Y. Halevy. Answering queries using views: A survey. *VLDB Journal*, 10(4):270–294, 2001.
12. Joachim Hammer, Hector Garcia-Molina, Jennifer Widom, Wilbur Labio, and Yue Zhuge. The Stanford data warehousing project. *IEEE Bull. on Data Engineering*, 18(2):41–48, 1995.
13. Matthias Jarke, Maurizio Lenzerini, Yannis Vassiliou, and Panos Vassiliadis, editors. *Fundamentals of Data Warehouses*. Springer, 1999.
14. Phokion G. Kolaitis and Christos H. Papadimitriou. Why not negation by fixpoint? *J. of Computer and System Sciences*, 43(1):125–144, 1991.

15. Maurizio Lenzerini. Data integration: A theoretical perspective. In *Proc. of PODS 2002*, pages 233–246, 2002.
16. Yannis Papakonstantinou, Hector Garcia-Molina, and Jennifer Widom. Object exchange across heterogeneous information sources. In *Proc. of ICDE'95*, pages 251–260, 1995.
17. Jeffrey D. Ullman. Information integration using logical views. In *Proc. of ICDT'97*, volume 1186 of *LNCS*, pages 19–40. Springer, 1997.
18. Jennifer Widom (ed.). Special issue on materialized views and data warehousing. *IEEE Bull. on Data Engineering*, 18(2), 1995.

Data Integration Using ID-Logic

Bert Van Nuffelen[1], Alvaro Cortés-Calabuig[1], Marc Denecker[1],
Ofer Arieli[2], and Maurice Bruynooghe[1]

[1] Department of Computer Science, Katholieke Universiteit Leuven, Belgium
{Bert.VanNuffelen,Alvaro.Cortes,Marc.Denecker,
Maurice.Bruynooghe}@cs.kuleuven.ac.be
[2] Department of Computer Science, The Academic College of Tel-Aviv, Israel
oarieli@mta.ac.il

Abstract. ID-Logic is a knowledge representation language that extends first-order logic with non-monotone inductive definitions. This paper introduces an ID-Logic based framework for database schema integration. It allows us to to uniformly represent and reason with independent source databases that contain information about a common domain, but may have different schemas. The ID-Logic theories that are obtained are called *mediator-based systems*. We show that these theories properly capture the common methods for data integration (i.e., global-as view and local-as-view with either exact or partial definitions), and apply on them a robust abductive inference technique for query answering.

1   Introduction

This work introduces a query answering system that mediates among several independent databases (sources) that contain information about a common domain, but where each source may have a different schema. These systems, called *information integration systems* (or *mediator-based systems*, see [24, 25, 31]) consist of an alphabet, called the *global schema* (representing the global information), and a structure that links the information of the sources with the global schema, such that a virtual knowledge-base in terms of the global schema is obtained. Each schema of a source, as well as the global schema, reflects its own view on the information domain. Therefore, the "intended meaning" of the different schemas should be related, and this is done by a logic theory. This requires appropriate definitions, in which the relations of one schema are expressed in terms of another. There are two common methods to define these relations: one, called *Global-as-View* (GAV) [31], expresses the relations of the global schema in terms of those of the sources. The other, called *Local-as-View* (LAV) [25], defines each source relation in terms of the relations of the global schema.

Both approaches have to deal with gaps between the amount of knowledge in the sources and in the intended global database. Even if a certain source contains a complete knowledge about its own relations, it might possess only partial information about the global relations, which means (in the LAV approach) incomplete definitions. It might happen, however, that the partial information is

A. Persson and J. Stirna (Eds.): CAiSE 2004, LNCS 3084, pp. 67–81, 2004.

complemented by other sources, so that together the sources possess complete knowledge about (part of) the intended global database. The possible relations between the amount of (extentional) knowledge contained in a source predicate and that of the (intended) global database predicates are designated in [14, 22] by different labels: a source predicate that contains a proper subset (respectively, superset) of the intended knowledge of the corresponding predicate at the global schema is labeled *open* (respectively, *closed*). A source predicate whose information is the same as that of the global one is labeled *clopen*.

In addition to its (global) schema and the mapping to the sources' schemas, a mediator-based system also defines an inference procedure that exploits the represented information in order to answer queries. Different semantics [1] have been used for query answers (in terms of the global schema): (1) According to the *certain answer* semantics a tuple [t] is an answer to a global query Q if its true in all possible instances of the global schema. (2) According to the *possible answer* semantics a tuple [t] is an answer of a query Q if [t] holds in at least one instance of the global schema. Typically, answers are computed in two phases: first, the query is rewritten in a query in terms of the source relations. Next, the sources are queried.This is needed because the sources are not materialized at the global level. Among query answering algorithms are Bucket [25], Minicon [29] and Inverse-rule [20].

We present a mediator-based system that is based on ID-Logic [15, 16], an expressive knowledge representation language. Contrary to most systems, ours explicitly distinguishes between complete and incomplete knowledge. It also allows us to formalize the knowledge expressed by the labels of [14, 22] and offers a uniform treatment of the LAV and GAV approaches (as well as a mixture of both). Query answering is implemented by abductive reasoning [19] that simplifies the construction of the transformed queries and provides informative answers when sources are temporary unavailable.

2   Preliminaries

2.1   Mediator-Based Systems

A *source database* is a structure $\langle \mathcal{L}, I \rangle$ where $\mathcal{L}$ is a first-order language and I is a database instance, *i.e.*, a set of tuples representing all true instances of the predicates of $\mathcal{L}$. It is assumed that the unique names axioms hold.

Example 1. A source describing a set of students may have the following structure: $\mathcal{S}_1 = \langle \{student(\cdot)\}, \{student(john), student(mary)\} \rangle$

Definition 1 (A mediator-based system). *A* mediator-based system $\mathfrak{G}$ *is a triple* $\langle \mathcal{L}, S, M \rangle$, *where* $\mathcal{L}$ *is a first-order language of the integrated (or global) database,* $S = \{\mathcal{S}_1, \ldots, \mathcal{S}_n\}$ *is a set of source databases, and* M *is a set of sets of formulae in* $\mathcal{L}$ *(representing the relationships between the sources and the intended global database).*

To simplify the presentation, we assume that each predicate is uniquely defined by either a source or the global schema[1]. We also assume the unique domain assumption: all involved database languages share the same domain, *i.e.*, all constants and function symbols are shared and have the same interpretation everywhere. Hence, as in the above example, the language of a database is completely determined by its *vocabulary*, i.e., its set of predicates.

Example 2. Consider the following two data-sources:
$$\mathcal{S}_1 = \langle \{student(\cdot)\}, \{student(john), student(mary)\}\rangle,$$
$$\mathcal{S}_2 = \langle \{enrolled(\cdot, \cdot)\}, \{enrolled(john, 1999), enrolled(mary, 2000)\}\rangle.$$
A possible mediator-based system $\mathfrak{G}$ for these sources is $\langle \mathcal{L}, S, M\rangle$, where
$$\mathcal{L} = \{st99(\cdot)\}, \quad S = \{\mathcal{S}_1, \mathcal{S}_2\}, \text{ and}$$
$$M = \{\{\forall\, x.st99(x) \leftarrow student(x) \wedge enrolled(x, 1999)\}\} \ ^2$$
Queries w.r.t. $\mathfrak{G}$ will be first-order formulas over $\mathcal{L}$ (*e.g.* $\exists\, x.st99(x)$).

2.2   ID-**Logic**

ID-Logic [15–18] is a knowledge representation language that extends classical first-order logic with non-monotone inductive definitions. Formally:

Definition 2 (ID-Logic). *An* ID-*Logic theory $\mathcal{T}$ based on the first-order logic language $\mathcal{L}$ is a pair ($\mathcal{D},\mathcal{F}$). $\mathcal{D}$ is a set of definitions D_i ($i = 1 \ldots n$) and $\mathcal{F}$ is a set of first-order formulas. A definition D is a set of rules of the form $p(\bar{t}) \leftarrow B$ where $p(\bar{t})$ is an atom and B is any first-order formula.*

The predicates occurring in the heads of the rules of an inductive definition D are the *defined* predicates of D. All the other predicates belong to $Open(D)$, the set of *open* predicates of D. As will be exploited in Section 3, the same predicate can be defined in different definitions. Care must be taken that different definitions are equivalent.

Definition 3 (A model of a definition[3]). *A structure M is a model of a definition D iff there exists an interpretation I of $Open(D)$ such that M is the two-valued well-founded [33] model of D that extends I. A structure M is a model of $\mathcal{D}$ iff M is a model of each $D \in \mathcal{D}$.*

Definition 4 (Formal semantics of an ID-Logic theory). *A structure M is a model of the* ID-*Logic theory $\mathcal{T} = (\mathcal{D},\mathcal{F})$ iff M is a model of $\mathcal{D}$ and satisfies all formulas of $\mathcal{F}$. The collection of all models of $\mathcal{T}$ is denoted by $Mod(\mathcal{T})$.*

Note 1 (Relation with Description Logics (DL)). Several data integration systems use DL [6] as underlying language (see, *e.g.*, [13, 14]). As shown in [32], ID-Logic can be viewed as a very expressive DL. The main differences between both are the facility to specify *inductive definitions*[4], and the computational

---

[1] If needed, a simple renaming of predicates in sources can establish this property.

[2] M expresses that $st99(x)$ is the conjunction of two relations. See Section 2.2.

[3] This is also well defined for general non-monotone inductive definitions [16].

[4] Most DL only allow transitive closure as a special case of an inductive definition.

paradigm; whereas DL systems focus on deductive query answering, ID-Logic systems also make use of abductive reasoning, *i.e.*, computing (classes of) models (explanations) that support the query.

Definition 5 (Composition of ID-Logic theories). *For two ID-Logic theories T_1 and T_2 over the same language $\mathcal{L}$, the composed theory $T_1 \circ T_2$ is an ID-Logic theory T over $\mathcal{L}$, obtained via the pairwise union of both theories:*
$$T = T_1 \circ T_2 = (\mathcal{D}_1, \mathcal{F}_1) \circ (\mathcal{D}_2, \mathcal{F}_2) = (\mathcal{D}_1 \cup \mathcal{D}_2, \mathcal{F}_1 \cup \mathcal{F}_2).$$

Proposition 1. *For two ID-Logic theories T_1 and T_2 over a language $\mathcal{L}$, it holds that $Mod(T_1 \circ T_2) = Mod(T_1) \cap Mod(T_2)$.*

2.3 Expressing Partial Knowledge

When designing mediator-based systems, the available information is often insufficient to define the ontological relations between the global database and the sources. We explain how open predicates can complete partial knowledge.

An Incomplete Set of Rules. Suppose that the set of rules $\{p(\bar{t}) \leftarrow B_i | i = 1 \ldots k\}$ only partially defines p. A complete definition can be obtained by adding a rule $p(\bar{s}) \leftarrow p^*(\bar{s})$, in which the auxiliary open predicate p^* represents all the tuples in p that are not defined by any of the bodies B_i. To ensure that the tuples in p^* do not overlap with the other tuples, the integrity constraint $\forall\, p^*(\bar{s}) \rightarrow \neg(B_1 \lor \ldots \lor B_k)$ can be added.

An Imprecise Rule. Another type of incompleteness occurs when the body of a rule $p(\bar{t}) \leftarrow B$ is overly general, *i.e.*, includes tuples not intended to be in the relation p. This can be repaired by adding to the body an auxiliary open predicate p^s that filters the extraneous tuples. The completed rule in this case is $p(\bar{t}) \leftarrow B \land p^s(\bar{t})$.

Example 3. Let $st99(\cdot)$ be defined in terms of $student(\cdot)$. The rule $st99(x) \leftarrow student(x)$ is overly general since not all students did enroll in 1999. By adding an auxiliary predicate $st99^s(\cdot)$, denoting all persons enrolled during 1999, the revised rule $st99(x) \leftarrow student(x) \land st99^s(x)$ correctly defines $st99(\cdot)$.

3   An ID-Logic Mediator-Based System

Definition 6 (An ID-Logic mediator-based system). *For a set of sources $\{S_1, \ldots, S_n\}$ and a global schema $\mathcal{L}_G$, an ID-Logic mediator-based system is a triple $\mathfrak{G} = \langle \mathcal{L}_G, S, M \rangle$, where*

- *S is a set of ID-Logic theories $\{S_1 \ldots S_n\}$ encoding the source databases.*
- *M is a set of ID-Logic theories $\{\mathcal{W}_1 \ldots \mathcal{W}_n, \mathcal{K}\}$ encoding the relationships between the sources and the intended global database:*
  - *$\mathcal{W}_i, i = 1, \ldots, n$, are source mappings for the source S_i w.r.t. $\mathcal{L}_G$,*
  - *$\mathcal{K}$ is an ID-Logic theory that describes how the information in the different sources complement each other.*

and the knowledge of the ID-Logic mediator-based system $\mathfrak{G}$ is represented by the ID-Logic theory $T = S_1 \circ \cdots \circ S_n \circ \mathcal{W}_1 \circ \cdots \circ \mathcal{W}_n \circ \mathcal{K}$.

The Sources. A source $\mathcal{S}_i = \langle \mathcal{L}_S, I \rangle$ is encoded as $S_i = (\{\{\mathcal{I}\}\}, \emptyset)$ where $\mathcal{I}$ is obtained by interpreting the database instance I as an enumeration of facts.

Example 4. The source $\mathcal{S} = \langle \{student(\cdot)\}, \{student(john), student(mary)\} \rangle$ of Example 1 is interpreted as the following ID-Logic theory:

$$S = (\{\{\ student(john).\ \ student(mary).\ \}\}, \emptyset)$$

Relating One Source with the Global Schema. This part defines the relationships between the relations of a source and of the global database. These relationships are expressed in the form of (inductive) definitions, taking into account the ontological relationships between the predicates and the actual knowledge of the source. The techniques described in Section 2.3 are used when there is a mismatch between the information in the source and in the global database.

Definition 7 (A source mapping). *A source mapping from a language $\mathcal{L}_2$ to a language $\mathcal{L}_1$ is an ID-Logic theory $\mathcal{W}$ defining the predicates of $\mathcal{L}_1$ in terms of the predicates of $\mathcal{L}_2$ and of the necessary auxiliary open predicates.*

Local-as-View (LAV) and Global-as-View (GAV) are particular instances of source mappings. For a source with vocabulary $\mathcal{L}_S$ and a global database with vocabulary $\mathcal{L}_G$, LAV (GAV) defines the predicates of $\mathcal{L}_S$ ($\mathcal{L}_G$) in terms of the predicates of $\mathcal{L}_G$ ($\mathcal{L}_S$).

Example 5. Consider the languages $\mathcal{L}_1 = \{st99(\cdot)\}$ and $\mathcal{L}_2 = \{student(\cdot)\}$, where $st99(\cdot)$ represents the students enrolled in 1999 and $student(\cdot)$ represents all the students. The possible source mappings are the following:

1. $\mathcal{W}_{1 \to 2} = (\{\{st99(x) \leftarrow student(x) \wedge student^s(x).\}\}, \emptyset)$
2. $\mathcal{W}_{2 \to 1} =$
   $(\{\{student(x) \leftarrow st99(x) \vee st99^*(x).\}\}, \{\forall\ x.st99^*(x) \to \neg st99(x).\})$

The meaning of the predicates allows only those two representations. When $\mathcal{L}_1$ is the source predicate, the first mapping is LAV and the second is GAV. Now, the auxiliary predicate $st99^*(\cdot)$ represents the students that are not known by the source, while $student^s(\cdot)$ represents the students known by the source.

Note 2 (GAV or LAV?). According to our definition GAV and LAV are equally good approaches[5]. However, as it is more natural to define abstract concepts in terms of more detailed notions, differences in abstraction levels of the source and the global languages imply that in practice one approach could be more appropriate than the other. Moreover, since the abstraction levels of the sources' languages may also be different (some of which may be more abstract than the global language and some may be less abstract than it), it makes sense to

---

[5] In the literature one finds arguments in favor of one or the other. For our representational point of view there is no difference. However, in the section on query answering, we give an argument in favor of GAV.

combine both approaches, i.e., to use GAV for the source mappings between certain sources and the global schema, and the LAV approach for the mappings between the other sources and the global schema. The fact that our framework supports such a combination may serve, therefore, as one of its advantages over other formalisms.

As noted in the introduction, special labels are sometimes used to denote the amount of knowledge a source stores (see, e.g., [14, 22]). For the sake of presentation, we show this in the context of LAV mappings between one source relation and one global relation. In the labels express a relation between a query over the source and over the global schema [14]. The following example illustrates that our use of open auxiliary predicates exactly captures the meaning of such labels. It is a variant on the world cup example, considered in [22].

closed source: The source predicate contains **more** information than the mediator predicate needs.
Consider $\mathcal{L}_G = \{st99(\cdot)\}$ and $\mathcal{L}_S = \{student(\cdot)\}$. Here, the mapping is:

$$\left(\begin{array}{l}\{\{\, student(x) \leftarrow st99(x) \vee student^*(x). \}\}\,, \\ \{\forall\, x.student^*(x) \rightarrow \neg st99(x).\,\} \end{array}\right)$$

$student^*(\cdot)$ models that there are other students than those listed by $st99(\cdot)$.

open source: The source predicate contains **less** information than the mediator predicate needs. Consider $\mathcal{L}_G = \{st99(\cdot)\}$ and $\mathcal{L}_S = \{st99male(\cdot)\}$. Now, the mapping is:

$$(\{\{\, st99male(x) \leftarrow st99(x) \wedge st99male^s(x). \}\}\,, \emptyset)$$

$st99male^s(x)$ models the unknown subset of male students.

clopen source: The source predicate has **exact** information for the mediator predicate. Consider $\mathcal{L}_G = \{st99(\cdot)\}$ and $\mathcal{L}_S = \{studentsOf1999(\cdot)\}$. The mapping is as follows:

$$(\{\{\, studentsOf1999(x) \leftarrow st99(x). \}\}\,, \emptyset)$$

Knowing What Multiple Sources Know. The last component in the composition of the ID-Logic theories, introduced in Definition 6 for representing a mediator-based system, contains an ID-Logic theory that allows the designer to formulate additional meta-knowledge about how partial information of one source (regarding a certain predicate of the global schema) is completed by data of other sources. This ID-Logic theory is denoted by $\mathcal{K}$, and as shown below, its information may be vital for a proper schema integration.

Example 6. Consider the global schema $\{student(\cdot)\}$ and the sources $\mathcal{S}_1 = \langle\{st99(\cdot)\}, \{st99(john)\}\rangle$ and $\mathcal{S}_2 = \langle\{st00(\cdot)\}, \{st00(mary)\}\rangle$ having the source mappings

$$\mathcal{W}_{1 \rightarrow G} = (\{\{student(x) \leftarrow st99(x) \vee st99^*(x).\}\}\,, \{\forall\, x.st99^*(x) \rightarrow \neg st99^{(}x).\})$$
$$\mathcal{W}_{2 \rightarrow G} = (\{\{student(x) \leftarrow st00(x) \vee st00^*(x).\}\}\,, \{\forall\, x.st00^*(x) \rightarrow \neg st00^{(}x).\})$$

Note that $\mathcal{W}_{1\rightarrow G} \circ \mathcal{W}_{2\rightarrow G}$ contains two (alternative and equivalent) definitions for the student relation. The statement that the relation $student(\cdot)$ is complete w.r.t. the set of sources $\{\mathcal{S}_1, \mathcal{S}_2\}$ can be formalized by the first-order assertion

$$\mathcal{K} = (\emptyset, \{\forall\ x. \neg(st99^*(x) \wedge st00^*(x)).\})$$

Obviously, no general rules for expressing meta-knowledge exist. It depends on the representation choices of the source mappings, the information content of the sources and the intended information content of the global database.

An Elaborated Example. We conclude this section with an elaboration of Example 2. It shows, in particular, that a certain data integration problem can be described by many different mediator-based systems.

Example 7. Consider two sources, each one has a complete knowledge about its relations. Source $\mathcal{S}_1$ stores all full-time students, and source $\mathcal{S}_2$ contains data about the year of enrollment of all students (both part-time and full-time):

$$\mathcal{S}_1 = \langle \{student(\cdot)\}, \quad \{student(john), student(mary), student(bob)\} \rangle,$$
$$\mathcal{S}_2 = \langle \{enrolled(\cdot, \cdot)\}, \{enrolled(john, 1999), enrolled(eve, 1999),$$
$$enrolled(mary, 2000), enrolled(alice, 2003)\} \rangle$$

A mediator-based system that extracts lists of full-time students enrolled at the years 1999 and 2000 looks as follows: $\mathfrak{G} = \langle \mathcal{L}_G, \{S_1, S_2\}, M \rangle$, where:

- $\mathcal{L}_G = \{st99(\cdot), st00(\cdot)\}$

- $S_1 = \left(\left\{ \left\{ \begin{array}{l} student(john). \\ student(mary). \\ student(bob). \end{array} \right\} \right\}, \emptyset \right)$

- $S_2 = \left(\left\{ \left\{ \begin{array}{l} enrolled(john, 1999). \\ enrolled(eve, 1999). \\ enrolled(mary, 2000). \\ enrolled(alice, 2003). \end{array} \right\} \right\}, \emptyset \right)$

Three possible mappings are presented below. In these mapping, we have additionally assumed that the sources contain all information about the global relations.

- The GAV approach where each source is individually related with the global schema. Here, $M = \{\mathcal{W}_{G\rightarrow 1}, \mathcal{W}_{G\rightarrow 2}, \mathcal{K}\}$, where

$$\mathcal{W}_{G\rightarrow 1} = \left(\left\{ \left\{ \begin{array}{l} st99(x) \leftarrow student(x) \wedge st99^s_{\mathcal{S}_1}(x). \\ st00(x) \leftarrow student(x) \wedge st00^s_{\mathcal{S}_1}(x). \end{array} \right\} \right\}, \emptyset \right)$$

$$\mathcal{W}_{G\rightarrow 2} = \left(\left\{ \left\{ \begin{array}{l} st99(x) \leftarrow enrolled(x, 1999) \wedge st99^s_{\mathcal{S}_2}(x). \\ st00(x) \leftarrow enrolled(x, 2000) \wedge st00^s_{\mathcal{S}_2}(x). \end{array} \right\} \right\}, \emptyset \right)$$

$$\mathcal{K} = \left(\emptyset, \left\{ \begin{array}{l} \forall\ x.st99^s_{\mathcal{S}_1}(x) \leftrightarrow enrolled(x, 1999). \\ \forall\ x.st00^s_{\mathcal{S}_1}(x) \leftrightarrow enrolled(x, 2000). \\ \forall\ x.st99^s_{\mathcal{S}_2}(x) \leftrightarrow student(x). \\ \forall\ x.st00^s_{\mathcal{S}_2}(x) \leftrightarrow student(x). \end{array} \right\} \right)$$

- An alternative GAV approach that treats the two sources as if there are one. This time, $M = \{\mathcal{W}_{G \to \{1,2\}}\}$, where:

$$\mathcal{W}_{G \to \{1,2\}} = \left(\left\{ \left\{ \begin{array}{l} st99(x) \leftarrow student(x) \land enrolled(x, 1999). \\ st00(x) \leftarrow student(x) \land enrolled(x, 2000). \end{array} \right\} \right\}, \emptyset \right)$$

- The LAV approach: $M = \{\mathcal{W}_{1 \to G}, \mathcal{W}_{2 \to G}, \mathcal{K}\}$.

$$\mathcal{W}_{1 \to G} = \left(\begin{array}{l} \{\{ student(x) \leftarrow st99(x) \lor st00(x) \lor student^*(x). \}\}, \\ \{\forall\, x.student^*(x) \rightarrow \neg(st99(x) \lor st00(x)).\} \end{array} \right)$$

$$\mathcal{W}_{2 \to G} = \left(\begin{array}{l} \left\{ \left\{ \begin{array}{l} enrolled(x,y) \leftarrow st99(x) \land y = 1999. \\ enrolled(x,y) \leftarrow st00(x) \land y = 2000. \\ enrolled(x,y) \leftarrow enrolled^*(x,y) \land (y \neq 1999 \lor y \neq 2000). \end{array} \right\} \right\}, \\ \left\{ \begin{array}{l} \forall\, x,y.enrolled^*(x,y) \rightarrow \neg(st99(x) \land y = 1999). \\ \forall\, x,y.enrolled^*(x,y) \rightarrow \neg(st00(x) \land y = 2000). \end{array} \right\} \end{array} \right)$$

$$\mathcal{K} = \left(\emptyset, \left\{ \begin{array}{l} \forall\, x.st99(x) \rightarrow student(x). \\ \forall\, x.st00(x) \rightarrow student(x). \\ \forall\, x.st99(x) \rightarrow enrolled(x, 1999). \\ \forall\, x.st00(x) \rightarrow enrolled(x, 2000). \end{array} \right\} \right)$$

According to any one of the representations above, the unique model of $\mathfrak{G}$ (restricted to $\mathcal{L}_G$) is $\{st99(john), st00(mary)\}$.

4   Query Answering

In the previous sections we have shown how to set up correctly an ID-Logic mediator-based system. This section discusses how queries can be answered with respect to such system. First, we consider the general context of ID-Logic theories and then concentrate on abductive inference as a general technique of computing answers posed to mediator-based systems. We also show that the answers generated by the abductive process are more informative than answers that are produced by other techniques.

Definition 8 (Types of queries). *Let $\mathcal{T}$ be an ID-Logic theory and $\mathcal{Q}$ a query.*

a) $\mathcal{Q}$ is skeptically true iff it is entailed by every model of $\mathcal{T}$; i.e.,

$$\mathcal{T} \models_{skep} \mathcal{Q} \quad \text{iff} \quad \text{for each model } M \text{ of } \mathcal{T} : M \models \mathcal{Q}.$$

b) $\mathcal{Q}$ is credulously true iff it is entailed by at least one model of $\mathcal{T}$; i.e.,

$$\mathcal{T} \models_{cred} \mathcal{Q} \quad \text{iff} \quad \text{there exists a model } M \text{ of } \mathcal{T} : M \models \mathcal{Q}.$$

In a mediator-based system $\mathfrak{G}$, the sources contain fixed information. Thus, answers to queries that are supported by the sources will be always skeptically true, while answers to queries for which the sources have no information might be either skeptically false or credulously true.

As mediator-based system does not materialize the knowledge of the sources in its own schema, the process of answering a global query $\mathcal{Q}$ is two-phased:

a) Compute for $\mathcal{Q}$ an equivalent (if possible) query $\mathcal{Q}_s$ expressed in terms of the source languages.
b) Query the sources with $\mathcal{Q}_s$.

Abductive Inference. Abductive reasoning is related to credulous query answering, i.e., finding a model that satisfies the query. Recall that each model of an ID-Logic theory is uniquely determined by an interpretation of the open predicates of the theory. Abductive reasoning is the inference process that constructs an explanation formula $\mathcal{E}$ in terms of the open predicates that entails the query $\mathcal{Q}$. Formally, for an ID-Logic theory $\mathcal{T}$ and a query $\mathcal{Q}$, $\mathcal{E}$ is an *abductive solution* iff $\exists\,(\mathcal{E})$ is satisfiable w.r.t. $\mathcal{T}$ and $\mathcal{T} \models \forall\,(\mathcal{E} \rightarrow \mathcal{Q})$.

Abductive reasoning for ID-Logic theories is provided by the $\mathcal{A}$system [3, 5, 23]. A preprocessing step transforms an ID-Logic theory into an equivalent ID-Logic theory consisting of one definition. Such theories correspond to abductive normal logic programs that form the input for the $\mathcal{A}$system. The open predicates of this ID-Logic theory are mapped into the abducibles in the abductive logic programming framework. We refer the reader to [19] for more details about abduction and its relation with ID-Logic.

In the case of the $\mathcal{A}$system the computed explanation formula $\mathcal{E}$ describes a class of models of $\mathcal{T}$. When $\mathcal{E}$ is **true**, the query is satisfiable w.r.t. to all models. When the $\mathcal{A}$system is unable to find an abductive solution for $\mathcal{Q}$, then $\mathcal{T} \models \forall\,(\neg\mathcal{Q})$ [6].

Answers for Queries. Consider $\mathfrak{G} = \langle \mathcal{L}_G, \{\mathcal{S}_1, \ldots, \mathcal{S}_n\}, \{\mathcal{W}_1, \ldots, \mathcal{W}_l, \mathcal{K}\}\rangle$, a mediator-based system, and $\mathcal{T}_q = \mathcal{W}_1 \circ \cdots \circ \mathcal{W}_l \circ \mathcal{K}$, the derived ID-Logic theory. This theory describes only the relationship between the languages. Then a new query $\mathcal{Q}_s$ expressed in terms of $\mathcal{L}_G$ is *derivable* from an abductive solution for the query $\mathcal{Q}$ w.r.t. $\mathcal{T}_q$. According to the mapping style, the abductive solution forms the new query $\mathcal{Q}_s$ or the basis to compute it. In GAV the open predicates are the source predicates, and thus, an abductive solution $\mathcal{E}$ is an expression in terms of the source predicates. $\mathcal{E}$ is then a representation of $\mathcal{Q}_s$. The LAV case is different: the open predicates are those of the global schema $\mathcal{L}_G$. An abductive solution $\mathcal{E}$ does not encode directly $\mathcal{Q}_s$. However, all models satisfying $\mathcal{E}$ correspond to answers for $\mathcal{Q}_s$. Hence one has to design an extra procedure to compute answers form $\mathcal{Q}_s$ out of the abductive solution for LAV mappings. In the literature one finds approaches that can form the basis for that procedure. For example, the inverse-rule algorithm for Datalog [20]. The availability of a general computational engine (an abductive solver) for GAV and the absence of such one for LAV, is in our opinion an argument in favor of GAV.

Example 8. Consider $\mathfrak{G} = \langle \{student(\cdot)\}, S, \{\mathcal{W}_{G\rightarrow\{1,2\}}\}\rangle$, a mediator-based system in which

$$S = \{\,\mathcal{S}_1 = \langle \{st99(\cdot)\}, \{st99(john)\}\rangle,\ \mathcal{S}_2 = \langle \{st00(\cdot)\}, \{st00(mary)\}\rangle\,\},$$
$$\mathcal{W}_{G\rightarrow\{1,2\}} = (\{student(x) \leftarrow st99(x) \lor st00(x) \lor student^*(x)\}, \emptyset).$$

---

[6] This is called the *duality property* of abductive systems.

Now suppose we pose the global query $\mathcal{Q} : \exists\ student(john)$ to $\mathfrak{G}$. In order to answer this query with the data from the sources, an abductive explanation for $\mathcal{Q}$ w.r.t. $\mathcal{T}_q = \mathcal{W}_{G\rightarrow\{1,2\}}$ is computed by the $\mathcal{A}$system:

$$\mathcal{Q}_s : st99(john) \vee st00(john) \vee student^*(john).$$

This explanation is exactly the expected reformulated query $\mathcal{Q}_s$. Because $\mathcal{Q}_s$ is expressed in terms of the sources and the auxiliary predicates, we can evaluate this query over the sources. When the first two predicates fail, the last one always succeeds, denoting the fact that the sources lack the knowledge to decide whether John is a student. In that case the answer is credulously true. In our case, since $\mathcal{S}_1$ contains the information that John is enrolled in 1999, it follows that he is a student. This is a skeptically true answer.

Supporting Dynamics of a Mediator-Based System. Abductive inference is particularly useful when the mediator-based system acts in a dynamic environment, i.e., the sources are dynamically added or removed. In such a situation, the produced abductive answer contains certain information that justifies the result, and helps to understand it.

Consider, for example, the following scenario: in the university restaurant one gets only a student reduction if he or she is registered in the university database as a student. When the source that contains all part-time students falls out, it might be that none of these students can get its reduction. If the mediator-based system removes each piece of knowledge from the unavailable source and it notifies the restaurant only that one of its sources is down, the restaurant is unable to grant the student reduction to all part-time students. Only when the restaurant is informed with the precise information that the list of part-time students is unavailable, it can question every person that is not recognized as a student if he or she is a part-time student.

The intended behavior is obtained by a source removal operation. Given a mediator-based system $\langle \mathcal{L}_G, \{\mathcal{S}_1, \ldots, \mathcal{S}_n\}, \{\mathcal{W}_1, \ldots, \mathcal{W}_l, \mathcal{K}\}\rangle$ and a corresponding ID-Logic theory

$$\mathcal{T} = \mathcal{S}_1 \circ \cdots \circ \mathcal{S}_n \circ \mathcal{W}_1 \circ \cdots \circ \mathcal{W}_l \circ \mathcal{K},$$

a removal of a source $\mathcal{S}_k$ $(1 \leq k \leq n)$ yields the following theory:

$$\mathcal{T}' = \mathcal{S}_1 \circ \cdots \circ \mathcal{S}_{k-1} \circ \mathcal{S}_{k+1} \circ \cdots \circ \mathcal{S}_n \circ \mathcal{W}_1 \circ \cdots \circ \mathcal{W}_l \circ \mathcal{K},$$

in which all predicates of $\mathcal{S}_k$ are open predicates[7]. Note that this update has non-monotonic characteristics, and that our framework correctly handles this. When the mediator-based system uses GAV, abductive reasoning can determine precisely the information the restaurant needs to react properly on the fall-out of the part-time student source.

---

[7] Many mediator-based systems remove all knowledge of $\mathcal{S}_k$, as shown by the first possibility in the restaurant scenario. We can simulate this by replacing the source by the empty source where all predicates are false.

Example 9 (Example 8 continued). If source $\mathcal{S}_1$ drops out, the abductive answer $\{st99(john)\}$ will have no source to be queried. The system can report to the user that in order to answer skeptically the query it is necessary to wait until $\mathcal{S}_1$ is available again, and the information $st99(john)$ can be verified.

Adding a new source is slightly more complex, because the mappings might have to be reconsidered. The amount of work in this case depends on the amount and type of information that the new source contributes. For example, a new source might require that the completeness assertions imposed in $\mathcal{K}$ must be reconsidered. In any data integration system the addition of a source requires this reconsideration. (Except when strong preconditions are imposed on the new sources.) In the worst case each mapping has to be updated. Fortunately, in most practical cases this is unlikely to happen. Moreover the modularity of ID-Logic enforces a strong locality of the changes since the changes must only be applied on the definitions that contain involved predicates.

5   Generalizations

5.1   Lifting the Unique Domain Assumption

Often two sources use different domain elements to denote the same object in the world (e.g., a client number and a social security number for the same person). By introducing an auxiliary mapping, these differences can be taken into account. Let $HU(\mathcal{L})$ denote the Herbrand Universe of the language $\mathcal{L}$.

Definition 9. *A mapping between the domains of two languages $\mathcal{L}_1$ and $\mathcal{L}_2$ is the bijection $map_{\mathcal{L}_1 \rightarrow \mathcal{L}_2} = \{map(t_1, t_2)|t_1 \in HU(\mathcal{L}_1) \text{ and } t_2 \in HU(\mathcal{L}_2)\}$. $map_{\mathcal{L}_2 \leftarrow \mathcal{L}_1}$ denotes the inverse of the mapping $map_{\mathcal{L}_1 \rightarrow \mathcal{L}_2}$* [8].

It is sufficient to define a mapping between each source and the global schema. A mapping $map(Name, ID)$ that maps names in identity numbers can be defined by the following theory: $\mathcal{W} = (\{\{st99(x) \rightarrow map(x, y) \wedge student(y).\}\}, \emptyset)$.

5.2   Reasoning with Inconsistent Knowledge

Up to now, we assumed that all information in the sources was consistent w.r.t. the intended global database, and so integrity constraints at the global level were not considered. In case that the global schema does contain such constraints, inconsistencies can arise[9]. We are aware of two approaches for handling this:

Computing repairs [3, 4, 9]: A repair is a set of atoms that must be added or retracted from the knowledge base in order to make it consistent. Repairs may advise the user about changes needed to restore consistency. In our context the repairs are computed at the level of each source.

---

[8] The mapping is the identity when both languages share the same Herbrand universe.

[9] Not to be confused with the notion of consistency in [22] where the concept is applied to conflicts that can arise when integrating complete sources.

Consistent query answering [2, 8]: This approach avoids the computation of the repairs. It transforms a query such that the answers of the transformed query are consistent w.r.t. to all repaired knowledge bases.

6 Comparison with Related Works

In the previous sections we introduced an ID-Logic mediator-based system for data integration and argued in favor of its expressive power. In this section we discuss how our work is related to some well-known existing formalisms.

GAV, LAV, and Their Combinations ([25, 29, 31]). A decade of active research in the topic of data integration has resulted in several implemented mediator-based systems. Some of them apply LAV, others are based on GAV (for a review, see [31]). Our ID-Logic framework takes into consideration both approaches, so the data integration system designer can select one or another, or work with both (see Note 2).

Generalized Methods for Data Integration. At least two extensions have been proposed to increase the expressive power of LAV and GAV paradigms.

> *GLAV approach ([21]).* This is an extension of LAV that allows to map a conjunctive query expression ϕ_G over the global schema into a conjunctive query expression ϕ_S over the sources[10]. This variant can be simulated in our framework by the introduction of an auxiliary predicate, say p, which has the view definition $\{p(\bar{t}) \leftarrow \phi_S\}$ w.r.t. the sources (ϕ_S). Using p, a LAV mapping can be constructed by $\{p(\bar{t}) \leftarrow \phi_G\}$.
>
> *Both-As-View (BAV) ([28]).* McBrien and Poulovassilis present a novel method that combines the advantages LAV and GAV in the presence of dynamic schemas. They show how LAV and GAV view definitions can be fully derived from BAV transformation sequences, and that BAV transformation sequences can be partially derived for LAV or GAV view definitions. We believe that these transformation sequences (or extensions of them) could be applied to translate BAV mapping into ID-Logic mappings.

Data Integration by Description Logics ([14]). Calvanese et al. present a general framework for data integration. Tt turns out that our framework encodes in a nice way this framework. In particular, they define labels (similar to [22]) to denote the amount of knowledge a mapping rule contributes to the global database. As shown before, this can be captured by the use of (auxiliary) open predicates.

A remarkable statement in [14] concerns the appropriateness of Description Logics for data integration. Due to the limitations on the use of variables, Description Logics are poor as query languages. Calvanese et al. argue that for the

---

[10] An equivalent extension for the GAV approach is straightforward.

data integration problem the modeling language has to be good in that respect. Since ID-Logic imposes no restriction on the use of variables, and can be regarded as a very expressive Description Logic, it is not surprising that the use of ID-Logic leads to a general approach, enclosing many of the existing approaches.

Data Integration by Abductive Methods ([10, 11]). The power of abduction for data integration has already been recognized in the COntext INterchange project, where abductive logic programs are used to represent the mappings according to the GAV approach. In the same spirit, our answering procedure is based on abductive reasoning, that may be supported by existing abductive computational tools [3].

Query Answering with Incomplete Knowledge ([1, 22, 26]). The inherent connection between incomplete knowledge and mediator-based systems has been broadly identified in the literature. Applying an expressive knowledge representation language with explicit denotation of incompleteness, a better understanding of the nature of the whole data integration problem is gained. Moreover, we argued how this knowledge can be used by the inference mechanism to compute more informative answers, for example, when a source is dropped.

Relation with Composition of Knowledge Bases. The knowledge representation origins of ID-Logic relate the data integration problem considered here with merging of knowledge bases [7, 34]. The former can be viewed as a particular case of the latter, where some knowledge bases contain actual data and others do not.

7   Conclusions and Future Work

This ID-Logic framework supports both the GAV and the LAV approaches to the data integration problem, any combination of these approaches, as well as various generalized methods (such as GLAV and BAV). Our framework provides a general method for expressing the relationships between a global schema and those of the sources. Specifically, the state of knowledge of each source w.r.t. the intended global database can be explicitly represented in the ID-Logic theories themselves. This allows to capture precisely the information of labels in [14, 22], and it clearly shows the strong relation of the data integration problem with incomplete knowledge [12], no matter which mapping approach is taken.

Since ID-Logic may be regarded as an expressive Description Logic [32], our approach generalizes all approaches that use Description Logics provided they take equal assumptions on the problem context.

For the future, we plan to implement the ID-Logic mediator-based system together with inconsistency repairing techniques, and test their behavior in realistic situations.

References

1. S. Abiteboul and O.M. Duschka. Complexity of answering queries using material-ized views. In *Proceedings of the Seventeenth ACM SIGACT-SIGMOD-SIGART Symposium on Principles of Database Systems, PODS'98*, pages 591–596, 1998.
2. M. Arenas, L. Bertossi, and J. Chomicki. Consistent query answers in inconsistent databases. In *Proc. of the Eighteenth ACM SIGMOD-SIGACT-SIGART Symp. on Principles of Database Systems, PODS'99*, pages 68–79, 1999.
3. O. Arieli, M. Denecker, B. Van Nuffelen, and M. Bruynooghe. Coherent integration of databases by abductive logic programs. Accepted to the *Journal of Artificial Intelligence Research*, 2004. See http://www.cs.kuleuven.ac.be/ dtai/.
4. O. Arieli, B. Van Nuffelen, M. Denecker, and M. Bruynooghe. Database repair by signed formulae. In *Foundations of Information and Knowledge Systems, FoIKS 2004*, pages 14–30. LNCS 2942, Springer, 2004.
5. The *A*system. Obtainable via www.cs.kuleuven.ac.be/ dtai/kt/systems-E.shtml.
6. F. Baader, D. Calvanese, D. McGuinness, D. Nardi, and P. Patel-Schneider, edi-tors. *The Description Logic Handbook. Theory, Implementation and Applications.* Cambridge University Press, 2003.
7. C. Baral, J. Minker, and S. Kraus. Combining multiple knowledge bases. *IEEE Transactions on Knowledge and Data Engineering*, 3(2):208–221, June 1991.
8. L. Bertossi, J. Chomicki, A. Cortes, and C. Gutierrez. Consistent answers from integrated data sources. In *Flexible Query Answering Systems, 5th International Conference, FQAS 2002*, pages 71–85. LNCS 2522, Springer, 2002.
9. L. Bertossi and L. Bravo. Logic programs for consistently querying data integra-tion systems. In *Proceedings of the International Joint Conference on Artificial Intelligence, IJCAI 2003*, 2003.
10. S. Bressan, C. H. Goh, K. Fynn, M. Jakobisiak, K. Hussein, H. Kon, T. Lee, S. Madnick, T. Pena, J. Qu, A. Shum, and M. Siegel. The Context Interchange mediator prototype. In *Proc. of ACM SIGMOD'97 Conf.*, pages 525–527, 1997.
11. S. Bressan, C.H. Goh, T. Lee, S.E. Madnick, and M. Siegel. A procedure for me-diation of queries to sources in disparate contexts. In *Proceedings of International Logic Programming Symposium, ILPS'97*, pages 213–227, 1997.
12. A. Calí, D. Calvanese, G. De Giacomo, and M. Lenzerini. Data integration under integrity constraints. In *Int. Conf. on Advanced Information Systems Engineering, CAiSE 2002*, pages 262–279. LNCS 2348, Springer, 2002.
13. D. Calvanese, G. De Giacomo, and M. Lenzerini. Description logics for informa-tion integration. In A. Kakas and F. Sadri, editors, *Computational Logic: Logic Programming and Beyond, Essays in Honour of Robert A. Kowalski*, pages 41–60. LNCS 2408, Springer, 2002.
14. D. Calvanese, G. De Giacomo, and M. Lenzerini. Ontology of integration and integration of ontologies. In *Working Notes of the 2001 International Description Logics Workshop (DL-2001), 2001*, CEUR Workshop Proc. 49, 2001.
15. M. Denecker. Extending classical logic with inductive definitions. In *Computational Logic - CL 2000*, pages 703–717. LNCS 1861, Springer, 2000.
16. M. Denecker, M. Bruynooghe, and V. Marek. Logic programming revisited: logic programs as inductive definitions. *ACM Transactions on Computational Logic*, 2(4):623–654, 2001.
17. M. Denecker, and E. Ternovska. Inductive Situation Calculus. In *Proc. of 9th Internation Conference on Principles of Knowledge Representation and Reasoning*, 2004, accepted.

18. M. Denecker, and E. Ternovska. A Logic of Non-Monotone Inductive Definitions and its Modularity Properties. In *Proc. of 7th International Conference on Logic Programming and Nonmonotonic Reasoning*, pages 47-60, LNCS 2923, Springer, 2004.

19. M. Denecker and A.C. Kakas. Abduction in logic programming. In *Computational Logic: Logic Programming and Beyond, Essays in Honour of Robert A. Kowalski*, pages 402–436. LNCS 2407, Springer, 2002.

20. O. Duschka, M. Genesereth, and A. Levy. Recursive query plans for data integration. In *Journal of Logic Programming*, 1:49–73, 2000.

21. S. Friedman, A. Levy and T Millstein. Navigational plans for data integration. In *Proc. 16th National Conference on AI*, pages 67-73. AAAI Press,1999.

22. G. Grahne and A. Mendelzon. Tableau techniques for querying information sources through global schemas. In *Proceedings of 7th International Conference on Database Theory, ICDT'99*, pages 332–347. LNCS 1540, Springer, 1999.

23. A.C Kakas, B. Van Nuffelen, and M. Denecker. A-system : Problem solving through abduction. In *Proc. of the Seventeenth Int. Joint Conf. on Artificial Intelligence, IJCAI 2001*, pages 591–596. 2001.

24. M. Lenzerini. Data integration: A theoretical perspective. In *Proceedings of the Twenty-first ACM SIGACT-SIGMOD-SIGART Symposium on Principles of Database Systems, PODS 2002*, pages 233–246. 2002.

25. A. Y. Levy, A. Rajaraman, and J.J. Ordille. Querying heterogeneous information sources using source descriptions. In *Int. Conf. on Very Large Data Bases, VLDB'96*, pages 251–262. Morgan Kaufmann, 1996.

26. A.Y. Levy. Obtaining complete answers from incomplete databases. In *Int. Conf. on Very Large Data Bases, VLDB'96*, pages 402–412, 1996.

27. A.Y. Levy. Logic-based techniques in data integration. In Minker, J, ed., *Logic-Based Artificial Intelligence*, Kluwer, 2000.

28. P. McBrien and A. Poulovassilis. Data integration by bi-directional schema transformation rules. In *Int. Conf. on Data Engineering, ICDE 2003*, pages 227-238. IEEE Computer Society, 2003.

29. R. Pottinger and A.Y. Levy. A scalable algorithm for answering queries using views. In *Int. Conf. on Very Large Data Bases, VLDB 2000*, pages 484–495, 2000.

30. F. Sadri, F. Toni, and I. Xanthakos. A logic-agent based system for semantic integration. In *Proceedings of 17th International Data and Information for the Coming Knowledge Millennium Conference ,CODATA 2000*, 2000.

31. J.D. Ullman. Information integration using logical views. *Theoretical Computer Science*, 239(2):189–210, 2000.

32. K. Van Belleghem, M. Denecker, and D. De Schreye. A strong correspondence between description logics and open logic programming. In *Int. Conf. on Logic Programming, ICLP'97*, pages 346–360, 1997.

33. A. Van Gelder, K.A. Ross, and J.S. Schlipf. The Well-Founded Semantics for General Logic Programs. *Journal of the ACM*, 38(3):620–650, 1991.

34. S. Verbaeten and A. Bossi. Composing complete and partial knowledge. *Journal of Functional and Logic Programming*, 2000(6):1–25, 2000.

35. I. Xanthakos. *Semantic integration of information by abduction*. Phd thesis, University of London, United Kingdom, 2003.

AutoMed: A BAV Data Integration System for Heterogeneous Data Sources

Michael Boyd, Sasivimol Kittivoravitkul, Charalambos Lazanitis,
Peter McBrien, and Nikos Rizopoulos

Dept. of Computing, Imperial College, London SW7 2AZ
{mboyd,sk297,cl201,pjm,nr600}@doc.ic.ac.uk
http://www.doc.ic.ac.uk/automed/

Abstract. This paper describes the AutoMed repository and some associated tools, which provide the first implementation of the **both as view**
(BAV) approach to data integration. Apart from being a highly expressive data integration approach, BAV in additional provides a method to
support a wide range of data modelling languages, and describes transformations between those data modelling languages. This paper documents
how BAV has been implemented in the AutoMed repository, and how
several practical problems in data integration between heterogeneous
data sources have been solved. We illustrate the implementation with
examples in the relational, ER, and semi-structured data models.

1 Introduction

The AutoMed project[1] has developed the first implementation of a data integration technique called **both-as-view** (**BAV**) [17], which subsumes the expressive
power of other published data integration techniques **global-as-view** (**GAV**),
local-as-view (**LAV**), and **global-local-as-view** (**GLAV**) [9]. BAV also distinguishes itself in being an approach which has a clear methodology for handling
a wide range of data models in the integration process, as opposed to the other
approaches that assume integration is always performed in a single common data
model.

In this paper we describe the core **repository** of the AutoMed toolkit, and
several packages that make use of this repository. Apart from giving an overview
of this freely available software product, we describe the solutions to practical
problems of using the BAV approach to integrate large schemas from heterogeneous and evolving data sources.

The paper is structured as follows. Section 2 reviews the BAV approach
and demonstrates how it models a relational data source, and introduces a new

---

[1] The AutoMed project was an British EPSRC funded research project, jointly run
by Birkbeck and Imperial Colleges, in the University of London. The Imperial College group implemented the data integration toolkit described here, with the the
exception of the query processing component based on the IQL language, which was
developed at Birkbeck College. Software and documentation are available from the
AutoMed website http://www.doc.ic.ac.uk/automed/.

A. Persson and J. Stirna (Eds.): CAiSE 2004, LNCS 3084, pp. 82–97, 2004.

model that allows BAV to handle semi-structured text file data sources. Section 3 then describes how the AutoMed system handles the BAV description of such data modelling languages and their integration. We show how to divide a large integration of data sources into a set of well defined subnetworks. Details of how we approach the transformation between modelling languages are given in Section 4, and the description of how to program higher level transformations as sequences of primitive transformations in a transformation template language are given in Section 5. Finally Section 6 addresses the problem of automating the schema matching process in the AutoMed framework.

2   BAV Data Integration

Data integration is the process of combining several data sources such that they may be queried and updated via some common interface. This requires that each **local schema** of each data source be mapped to the **global schema** of the common interface. In the GAV approach [9], this mapping is specified by writing a definition of each global schema construct as a view over local schema constructs. In LAV [9], this mapping is specified by defining each local schema construct as a view over global schema constructs. GLAV [13] is a variant of LAV that allows the head of the view definition to contain any query on the local schema.

In the BAV approach, the mapping between schemas can be described as a **pathway** of **primitive transformation** steps applied in sequence. For example, suppose we want to transform the relational schema S_3 in Fig. 2(a) into the the the global schema S_{rg} in Fig. 3(a). Using the approach described in [17], we model each table as a scheme $\langle\!\langle\text{table\_name}\rangle\!\rangle$, and each column as a scheme $\langle\!\langle\text{table\_name,column\_name,cardinality}\rangle\!\rangle$. When used in queries the cardinality of the column need not be given.

Thus, the level column in S_3 has the scheme $\langle\!\langle\text{student,level,notnull}\rangle\!\rangle$, and may be used to divide the table $\langle\!\langle\text{student}\rangle\!\rangle$ into those that belong to the undergraduate table $\langle\!\langle\text{ug}\rangle\!\rangle$, created by transformations ①–③, and those the belong to the post-graduate table $\langle\!\langle\text{pg}\rangle\!\rangle$ by transformations ④–⑥. The IQL [5] query in ① finds in the **generator** $\langle x, y\rangle \leftarrow \langle\!\langle\text{student, level}\rangle\!\rangle$ the tuples $\langle\text{'Mary', 'ug'}\rangle, \langle\text{'John', 'pg'}\rangle, \ldots$ and then the **filter** $y = \text{'ug'}$ restricts the x values returned to be only those that had 'ug' in the second argument. Other IQL queries in square brackets may be read in a similar manner. Once the specialisation tables have been created, transformation ⑦ removes the level attribute from **student**, since it may be recovered from the ug and pg tables (the IQL ++ operator appends two lists together). Finally ⑧–⑨ moves the ppt attribute from **student** to **ug**, since it only takes non-null values for undergraduate students.

$S_3 \rightarrow S_{rg}$

① addTable($\langle\!\langle\text{ug}\rangle\!\rangle, [\langle x\rangle \mid \langle x, y\rangle \leftarrow \langle\!\langle\text{student, level}\rangle\!\rangle; y = \text{'ug'}]$)

② addColumn($\langle\!\langle\text{ug, name, notnull}\rangle\!\rangle$,

$[\langle x, y\rangle \mid \langle x, y\rangle \leftarrow \langle\!\langle\text{student, name}\rangle\!\rangle; \langle x, z\rangle \leftarrow \langle\!\langle\text{student, level}\rangle\!\rangle; z = \text{'ug'}]$)

③ addPK($\langle\!\langle\text{ug\_pk, ug}, \langle\!\langle\text{ug, name}\rangle\!\rangle\rangle\!\rangle$)

④ addTable($\langle\!\langle$pg$\rangle\!\rangle$, [$\langle x\rangle$ | $\langle x, y\rangle \leftarrow \langle\!\langle$student, level$\rangle\!\rangle$; y = 'pg'])

⑤ addColumn($\langle\!\langle$pg, name, notnull$\rangle\!\rangle$,

  [$\langle x, y\rangle$ | $\langle x, y\rangle \leftarrow \langle\!\langle$student, name$\rangle\!\rangle$; $\langle x, z\rangle \leftarrow \langle\!\langle$student, level$\rangle\!\rangle$; z = 'pg'])

⑥ addPK($\langle\!\langle$pg_pk, pg, $\langle\!\langle$pg, name$\rangle\!\rangle\rangle\!\rangle$)

⑦ deleteColumn($\langle\!\langle$student, level, notnull$\rangle\!\rangle$,

  [$\langle x, y\rangle$ | $\langle x\rangle \leftarrow \langle\!\langle$ug$\rangle\!\rangle$; y = 'ug'] ++ [$\langle x, y\rangle$ | $\langle x\rangle \leftarrow \langle\!\langle$pg$\rangle\!\rangle$; y = 'pg'])

⑧ addColumn($\langle\!\langle$ug, ppt, notnull$\rangle\!\rangle$,

  [$\langle x, y\rangle$ | $\langle x\rangle \leftarrow \langle\!\langle$ug$\rangle\!\rangle$; $\langle x\rangle \leftarrow \langle\!\langle$student$\rangle\!\rangle$; $\langle x, y\rangle \leftarrow \langle\!\langle$student, ppt$\rangle\!\rangle$]

⑨ deleteColumn($\langle\!\langle$student, ppt, null$\rangle\!\rangle$, [$\langle x, y\rangle$ | $\langle x\rangle \leftarrow \langle\!\langle$student$\rangle\!\rangle$; $\langle x, y\rangle \leftarrow \langle\!\langle$ug, ppt$\rangle\!\rangle$])

Note that the transformation $S_{rg} \rightarrow S_3$ is automatically derivable from $S_3 \rightarrow S_{rg}$ by taking the inverse steps ⑨–①, formed by replacing delete for add, and replacing add for delete, in transformations ①–⑨.

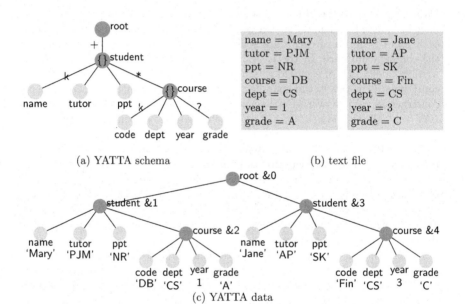

(a) YATTA schema (b) text file

(c) YATTA data

Fig. 1. S_1: Semi-structured text file of undergraduates

2.1 Handling Semi-Structured Data

The **YATTA** (YAT for transformation-based approach) is a variation of the YAT model [2] to support the handling of semistructured data in AutoMed. YATTA provides two levels of abstraction: the **schema level** where the structure of data is defined, and the **data level** where actual data is presented. Fig. 1(b) shows

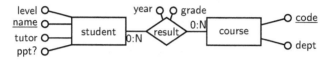

student				course		result			
name	tutor	ppt	level	code	dept	code	name	year	grade
Mary	PJM	NR	ug	DB	CS	DB	Mary	1	A
John	AP	null	pg	Fin	CS	Fin	Jane	3	C
Jane	AP	SK	ug	Geo	Maths	Fin	Fred	4	null
Fred	PJM	null	pg			Geo	Fred	4	A
						Geo	John	4	B

(a) Relational database schema and data

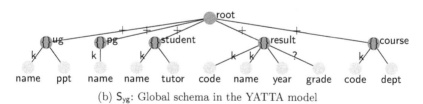

(b) ER model used to design relational database

Fig. 2. S_3: relational database covering all students

student		ug		pg	course		result			
name	tutor	name	ppt	name	code	dept	code	name	year	grade
Mary	PJM	Mary	NR	Fred	DB	CS	DB	Mary	1	A
John	AP	Jane	SK	John	Fin	CS	Fin	Jane	3	C
Jane	AP				Geo	Maths	Fin	Fred	4	null
Fred	PJM						Geo	Fred	4	A
							Geo	John	4	B

(a) S_{rg}: Global schema in the relational model

(b) S_{yg}: Global schema in the YATTA model

Fig. 3. Global Schema

a semistructured text file, containing data about the undergraduate students in Fig. 3(a), which together with a similar text file (not shown) of postgraduates, we wish to integrate with the relational schema S_{rg}. Fig. 1(a) gives a schema level YATTA model S_1 of the undergraduate text file (a similar model S_2 exists for postgraduates), and Fig 1(c) gives a data level YATTA model for that file.

In the YATTA model, schemas and data are rooted labelled trees. In a **YATTA schema**, each node is labelled by a tuple ⟨*name, type*⟩, where *name* is a string describing what a node represents and *type* is the data type of a node. Type can be either atomic *e.g.* string, integer, *etc.*, or compound *i.e.* list (marked '[]'), set (marked '{}'), or bag (marked '⟨⟩'). Each node in a **YATTA data tree** is labelled by a triple ⟨*name, type, value*⟩, where *value* is the value associated with the node. If the node is of atomic type, the value is a data value of that type. If the node is of compound type, the value is an integer identifier. Outgoing edges of list nodes are ordered from left to right; the edges of set and bag are unordered. The edges of a schema are labelled with cardinality constraints which determine the number of times corresponding edges may occur in a data tree: '∗' indicates zero or more occurrences, '+' indicates one or more occurrences, '?' indicates zero or one occurrence, and no label indicates exactly one occurrence. A 'k' is used to identify the subset of child nodes, called the key nodes, which uniquely identify the complex node with respect to its parent, all other nodes are non-key nodes, which in the schemes we identify by writing 'nk', but in the diagrams simply leave the edge unlabelled.

The YATTA model can be represented in AutoMed using two construct types. The root of the tree r is represented as a RootNode construct with scheme ⟨⟨r, t⟩⟩ where t is one of the YATTA types. A non-root node n is represented as a YattaNode construct with scheme ⟨⟨n_p, n, t, c⟩⟩ where n_p is a parent node that may be a RootNode or YattaNode, t is the type of a node and c is a cardinality constraint.

To integrate S_1 with S_{rg}, we need to transform S_1 to have the same structure as S_{rg}. Section 4 shows how derive a YATTA schema S_{yg} shown in Fig. 3(b) that is equivalent to S_{rg}. Now the task is to transform S_1 and S_2 to S_{yg}. To determine the pathway from one YATTA schema Y to another one Y' a three phase methodology is used.

The **conform phase** uses rename transformations to **conform** the schemas. In S_1, the student node matches in semantics and extent the ug node in S_{yg}, implying:

⑩ renameYattaNode(⟨⟨root, student, set, +⟩⟩, ⟨⟨root, ug, set, +⟩⟩)

The **growth phase** conducts a search over the nodes n' of Y', and for each n' not found in Y applies transformations to add n' to Y:

1. If n' is of complex type, determine if there is a query q on Y such that there is a one to one mapping between values returned by q and values associated to n'. If there is, then a new node n' is added into Y by applying a rule addYattaNode, with the special function **generateId** used on the values returned by q to generate the identifiers of the complex node. This function always returns the *same* identifier for the same input values, and *distinct* identifiers for distinct input values.

2. If n' is of simple type, determine if there is a query q on Y such that the values returned by q are equal to the values associated with n'. If there is, then a new node n' is added into Y by applying a rule addYattaNode, with q placed as the query part of the transformation.

In either case, if the query only returns some of the values of n', then we instead use extendYattaNode, with the queries set to q, Any (where Any indicates the source places no upper bound on the extent [18]), and if no query can be determined, then we use extendYattaNode with the queries Void, Any which states that there is no method to determine anything about the instances of n' in Y' from the information in Y.

For example, we would find that result node of S_{yg} does not appear in S_1, and we are able to derive *some* instances in ⑪-⑮ from S_1, since that contains the results of undergraduates. Step ⑪ generates identifiers for the new result node by finding $\langle \&0, \&1 \rangle$ and $\langle \&0, \&3 \rangle$ from $\langle r, u \rangle \leftarrow \langle\!\langle \text{root}, \text{ug} \rangle\!\rangle$, then $\langle \&1, \text{'Mary'} \rangle$ and $\langle \&3, \text{'Jane'} \rangle$ from $\langle u, n \rangle \leftarrow \langle\!\langle \langle\!\langle \text{root}, \text{ug} \rangle\!\rangle, \text{name} \rangle\!\rangle$, then $\langle \&1, \&2 \rangle$ and $\langle \&3, \&4 \rangle$ from $\langle u, c \rangle \leftarrow \langle\!\langle \langle\!\langle \text{root}, \text{ug} \rangle\!\rangle, \text{course} \rangle\!\rangle$, and finally $\langle \&2, \text{'DB'} \rangle$ and $\langle \&4, \text{'Fin'} \rangle$ from $\langle c, co \rangle \leftarrow \langle\!\langle \langle\!\langle \text{course}, \langle\!\langle \text{root}, \text{ug} \rangle\!\rangle \rangle\!\rangle, \text{code} \rangle\!\rangle$. This causes generateId to receive the lists [Mary, DB] and [Jane, Fin], and generate $\&5$ and $\&6$ as new identifiers for result. Note that the same identifiers will now be created in ⑫-⑮.

⑪ extendYattaNode($\langle\!\langle \text{root}, \text{result}, \text{set}, + \rangle\!\rangle$,
    $[\langle r, re \rangle \mid \langle r, u \rangle \leftarrow \langle\!\langle \text{root}, \text{ug} \rangle\!\rangle; \langle u, n \rangle \leftarrow \langle\!\langle \langle\!\langle \text{root}, \text{ug} \rangle\!\rangle, \text{name} \rangle\!\rangle;$
    $\langle u, c \rangle \leftarrow \langle\!\langle \langle\!\langle \text{root}, \text{ug} \rangle\!\rangle, \text{course} \rangle\!\rangle; \langle c, co \rangle \leftarrow \langle\!\langle \langle\!\langle \text{course}, \langle\!\langle \text{root}, \text{ug} \rangle\!\rangle \rangle\!\rangle, \text{code} \rangle\!\rangle;$
    $re \leftarrow [\text{generateId } [n, co]]], \text{Any})$

⑫ extendYattaNode($\langle\!\langle \langle\!\langle \text{root}, \text{result} \rangle\!\rangle, \text{code}, \text{string}, k \rangle\!\rangle$,
    $[\langle re, co \rangle \mid \langle u, n \rangle \leftarrow \langle\!\langle \langle\!\langle \text{root}, \text{ug} \rangle\!\rangle, \text{name} \rangle\!\rangle; \langle u, c \rangle \leftarrow \langle\!\langle \langle\!\langle \text{root}, \text{ug} \rangle\!\rangle, \text{course} \rangle\!\rangle;$
    $\langle c, co \rangle \leftarrow \langle\!\langle \langle\!\langle \text{course}, \langle\!\langle \text{root}, \text{ug} \rangle\!\rangle \rangle\!\rangle, \text{code} \rangle\!\rangle; re \leftarrow [\text{generateId } [n, co]]], \text{Any})$

⑬ extendYattaNode($\langle\!\langle \langle\!\langle \text{root}, \text{result} \rangle\!\rangle, \text{name}, \text{string}, k \rangle\!\rangle$,
    $[\langle re, n \rangle \mid \langle u, n \rangle \leftarrow \langle\!\langle \langle\!\langle \text{root}, \text{ug} \rangle\!\rangle, \text{name} \rangle\!\rangle; \langle u, c \rangle \leftarrow \langle\!\langle \langle\!\langle \text{root}, \text{ug} \rangle\!\rangle, \text{course} \rangle\!\rangle;$
    $\langle c, co \rangle \leftarrow \langle\!\langle \langle\!\langle \text{course}, \langle\!\langle \text{root}, \text{ug} \rangle\!\rangle \rangle\!\rangle, \text{code} \rangle\!\rangle; re \leftarrow [\text{generateId } [n, co]]], \text{Any})$

⑭ extendYattaNode($\langle\!\langle \langle\!\langle \text{root}, \text{result} \rangle\!\rangle, \text{year}, \text{integer}, nk \rangle\!\rangle$,
    $[\langle re, y \rangle \mid \langle u, n \rangle \leftarrow \langle\!\langle \langle\!\langle \text{root}, \text{ug} \rangle\!\rangle, \text{name} \rangle\!\rangle; \langle u, c \rangle \leftarrow \langle\!\langle \langle\!\langle \text{root}, \text{ug} \rangle\!\rangle, \text{course} \rangle\!\rangle;$
    $\langle c, co \rangle \leftarrow \langle\!\langle \langle\!\langle \text{course}, \langle\!\langle \text{root}, \text{ug} \rangle\!\rangle \rangle\!\rangle, \text{code} \rangle\!\rangle; \langle c, y \rangle \leftarrow \langle\!\langle \langle\!\langle \text{course}, \langle\!\langle \text{root}, \text{ug} \rangle\!\rangle \rangle\!\rangle, \text{year} \rangle\!\rangle;$
    $re \leftarrow [\text{generateId } [n, co]]], \text{Any})$

⑮ extendYattaNode($\langle\!\langle \langle\!\langle \text{root}, \text{result} \rangle\!\rangle, \text{grade}, \text{string}, ? \rangle\!\rangle$,
    $[\langle re, g \rangle \mid \langle u, n \rangle \leftarrow \langle\!\langle \langle\!\langle \text{root}, \text{ug} \rangle\!\rangle, \text{name} \rangle\!\rangle; \langle u, c \rangle \leftarrow \langle\!\langle \langle\!\langle \text{root}, \text{ug} \rangle\!\rangle, \text{course} \rangle\!\rangle;$
    $\langle c, co \rangle \leftarrow \langle\!\langle \langle\!\langle \text{course}, \langle\!\langle \text{root}, \text{ug} \rangle\!\rangle \rangle\!\rangle, \text{code} \rangle\!\rangle; \langle c, g \rangle \leftarrow \langle\!\langle \langle\!\langle \text{course}, \langle\!\langle \text{root}, \text{ug} \rangle\!\rangle \rangle\!\rangle, \text{grade} \rangle\!\rangle;$
    $re \leftarrow [\text{generateId } [n, co]]], \text{Any})$

Once the growth phase is completed, an analogous **shrinking phase** conducts a search over the nodes n of Y, and for each n not in Y', creates either a deleteYattaNode or a contractYattaNode transformation to remove n from Y.

3   The AutoMed Repository for BAV Data Integration

The AutoMed meta data repository forms a platform for other components of the AutoMed Software Architecture (Fig. 4) to be implemented upon. When a data source is wrapped, a definition of the schema for that data source is added to the repository. The schema matching tool may then be used to identify related objects in various data sources (accessing the query processor [5] to retrieve data from schema objects), and the template transformation tool used to generate transformations between the data sources. A GUI is supplied with AutoMed for

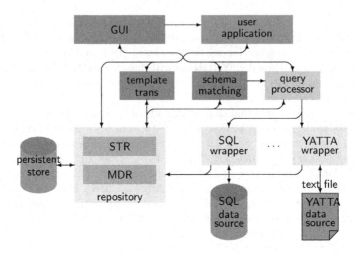

Fig. 4. AutoMed Software Architecture

these components, and it is possible for a user application to be configured to run from this GUI, and use the APIs of the various components. For example, work is in progress on using the repository in data warehousing [4].

The repository has two logical components. The **model definitions repository (MDR)** defines how a data modelling language is represented as combinations of nodes, edges and constraints in the **hypergraph data model (HDM)** [19]. It is used by AutoMed 'experts' to configure AutoMed so that it can handle a particular data modelling language. The **schema transformation repository (STR)** defines schemas in terms of the data modelling concepts in the MDR, and transformations to be specified between those schemas. Most tools and users will be concerned with editing this repository, as new databases are added to the AutoMed repository. The MDR and STR may be held in the same or separate persistent storage. The latter approach allows many AutoMed users to share a single MDR repository, which once configured, need not be updated when integrating data sources that conform to a certain set of data modelling languages.

Fig. 5 gives an overview of the key objects in the repository. The STR contains a set of descriptions of Schemas, each of which contains a set of SchemaObject instances, each of which must be based on a Construct instance that exists in the MDR. This Construct describes how the SchemaObject can be constructed in terms of strings and references to other schema objects, and the relationship of the construct to the HDM. Schemas are therefore readily translatable into HDM, and hence we have a common underlying representation of all the data modelling languages handled in AutoMed. Note that each Schema may contain SchemaObjects from more that one data modelling language. This allows AutoMed to describe the mapping between different data modelling languages. Schemas may be related to each other using instances of Transformation.

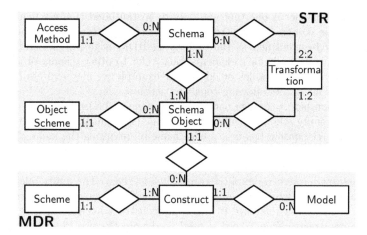

Fig. 5. Repository Schema

We now describe in detail how the MDR may be programmed to describe a modelling language, and then describe some features of the STR that allow it to manage large and evolving schema integrations.

3.1 Describing a Data Modelling Language in the MDR

In [15] a general technique was proposed for the modelling of any structured data modelling language in the HDM, which was used as the basis for the design of the MDR. The description of the Construct is made by defining elements of its scheme in the Scheme class, each instance of which must refer to a HDM node, edge or constraint, or be a textual label to use on the construct. Associating a SchemaObject to a Construct thus gives it a **type** definition. When a SchemaObject is created, and its scheme details are entered into ObjectScheme, they are checked against the corresponding Scheme of its Construct. Each modelling language construct must be classified as being one of four types: nodal, link, link-nodal, and constraint.

A **nodal** construct represents a simple list of values. Exactly one element of the construct scheme must be identified as the name of the underlying HDM node, and be of type node_name. Often a nodal construct has just this one scheme element, for example in an ER model, the construct for an entity would be defined by:

(nodal)er:entity ::= ⟨⟨(node_name)hdm_node_name⟩⟩

The brackets contain the type being used, so we read the above as stating that the entity construct in the er modelling language has a scheme that contains a single string, which is the name of the HDM node. Hence the schema objects representing entities student and course in Fig. 2(b) would have the schemes ⟨⟨student⟩⟩ and ⟨⟨course⟩⟩.

A **link** construct is one that can only be instantiated (*i.e.* a schema object of its type be constructed) by referring to other schema objects. One scheme element may be identified as the underlying HDM edge's name, and at least two of the instance scheme's elements must refer to other schema objects that have underlying HDM nodes or edges. For example we may express ER n-ary relationships using the following construct scheme:

(link)er:relationship ::= ⟨⟨(edge_name)name, (reference,2:N)er:entity_role⟩⟩
(sequence)er:entity_role ::= ⟨⟨(reference)er:entity, (string,nonkey)cardinality⟩⟩

The scheme relationship has first a edge_name representing the name of the underlying HDM edge, followed by at least two references to an entity_role construct. This 'at least two' cardinality is specified by the 2:N in the brackets; 1:1 is assumed where no explicit cardinality is given. The entity_role is a **sequence** construct, which can only appear in the definition of another construct. Its first element is a reference to the entity construct we have already defined, and the constraint element card is used to denote the use of a constraint expression in the scheme. The scheme instance for the relationship in Fig. 2(b) would be ⟨⟨result, student, 0:N, course, 0:N⟩⟩. Note that the use of nonkey in the definition of the cardinality element means that this element only has to appear in the definition of this schema object (as it appears in the first argument of a transformation) and need not appear in queries. Hence in a query one may also use the abbreviation ⟨⟨result, student, course⟩⟩ for the result relationship.

A **link-nodal** construct is a combination of a link and a node. It models a node type which cannot exist in isolation but requires another construct with which to be associated. The construct scheme must contain one string element for the name of the new HDM node, an optional name for the HDM edge name, and must contain a reference to an existing construct. For example, an ER attribute can be defined by:

(link)er:attribute ::= ⟨⟨(reference)er:attribute_target,
    (node_name)new_node_name, (constraint,nonkey)card⟩⟩
(alternation)er:attribute_target ::= ⟨⟨(reference)er:entity, (reference)er:relationship⟩⟩

The **alternation** construct allows us to define that the existing construct that this link-nodal refers to may be *either* a entity or a relationship. The last element card corresponds to a constraint expression. With this definition, the name attribute of student in Fig. 2(b) would have the scheme ⟨⟨student,name, notnull⟩⟩, and the grade attribute on result the scheme ⟨⟨⟨⟨result, student, course⟩⟩,grade,null⟩⟩.

A **constraint** construct has no extent, and must be associated with at least one other construct on which it places a constraint on its extent. For example, a subset relationship in a ER model places a restriction on two entities such that the extent of one is a subnet of the extent of another. This would be defined by:

(constraint)er:subset ::= ⟨⟨(reference)er:entity, (reference)er:entity⟩⟩

which would allow the scheme ⟨⟨student, ug⟩⟩ to exist.

3.2   Describing Schemas and Transformations in the STR

In a large data integration, there will be many schemas produced as intermediate steps in the process of mapping one data source to another. At first this would appear to make the BAV approach unworkable, since there are so many versions of schemas being kept. The AutoMed approach addresses this issue by distinguishing between **extensional** and **intensional** representations of schemas. Each data source will be represented in the AutoMed repository by describing its schema as a set of schema objects, which is the **extensional** representation of schemas. Extensional Schemas may be associated with an AccessMethod to describe the driver, username, password and URL of how a data source may be accessed via its wrapper. Transformations applied to the extensional schema produce new intensional schemas, for which the schema objects are not stored, but which can be derived when required by applying transformation rules in sequence to an extensional schema.

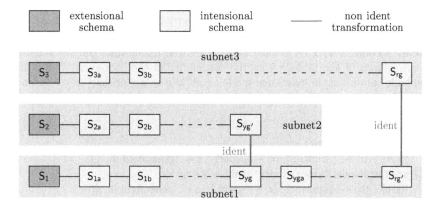

Fig. 6. Overview of Schemas held in AutoMed

Furthermore, a special transformation called **ident** is introduced, which states that two schemas have the same logical set of schema objects, but that they are derived from distinct extensional schemas. For example, in Fig. 6, the schema S_{yg} is derived from S_1, and schema $S_{yg'}$ (identical to S_{yg}) is derived from S_2. The identity of these two schemas may then be stated by adding an ident transformation between them, which query processing can use to retrieve data from alternative data sources. The YATTA model S_{yg} is then translated to its relational equivalent $S_{rg'}$ which can then be idented with the corresponding S_{rg} derived from S_3

The set of schemas connected together by transformations other than ident is called a **subnet**. By the nature of this arrangement, each subnet can exist independently of other subnets. This means that a subnet can be created, edited, connected to other subnets via ident transformations, and deleted all without changing anything in another subnet. It also allows for the schema evolution techniques in [16] to be supported. If say S_1 has been found to evolve to $S_{1'}$, then a new subnet 4 can be created for $S_{1'}$, with transformations to describe

$S_{1'} \rightarrow S_1$. Then S_1 may have its AccessMethod removed, and query processing will be directed to the new version of the data source.

4 Inter Model Transformations

A common task in data integration is to implement a **wrapper** to translate all the component schemas into a common data model. In AutoMed, this wrapping step can be formalised within the data integration methodology if the data modelling languages used for the component schemas are described in the MDR. In addition, this translation process may occur in the middle of the data integration (as illustrated by pathway $S_{yg} \rightarrow S_{rg'}$ in Fig. 6), allowing a mixture of data modelling languages to be used in a large integration.

To illustrate this process, consider the following rules that map relational constructs to YATTA constructs. First, a YATTA complex node n of set type with '*' cardinality is created under the root of the YATTA model for each table. Second, a YATTA atomic node is created under this complex node for each column of the table, where the cardinality of the column is '?' if it is a nullable column in the relational model, and 'k' if it is a primary key column in the relational model. For $S_{rg'}$, these two rules applied to the student table would generate a pathway:

$S_{rg'} \rightarrow S_{yg'}$

⑯ addYattaNode($\langle\!\langle\!\langle$root, student, set, $*\rangle\!\rangle$,

    $[\langle r, s\rangle \mid \langle n\rangle \leftarrow \langle\!\langle$student$\rangle\!\rangle; \langle r\rangle \leftarrow \langle\!\langle$root$\rangle\!\rangle; \ s \leftarrow$ [generateId $[n, r]]]$)

⑰ addYattaNode($\langle\!\langle\!\langle\!\langle$root, student$\rangle\!\rangle$, name, string, k$\rangle\!\rangle$,

    $[\langle s, n\rangle \mid \langle n\rangle \leftarrow \langle\!\langle$student$\rangle\!\rangle; \langle r\rangle \leftarrow \langle\!\langle$root$\rangle\!\rangle; \ s \leftarrow$ [generateId $[n, r]]]$)

⑱ addYattaNode($\langle\!\langle\!\langle\!\langle$root, student$\rangle\!\rangle$, tutor, string, nk$\rangle\!\rangle$,

    $[\langle s, t\rangle \mid \langle n, t\rangle \leftarrow \langle\!\langle$student, tutor$\rangle\!\rangle; \langle r\rangle \leftarrow \langle\!\langle$root$\rangle\!\rangle; \ s \leftarrow$ [generateId $[n, r]]]$)

⑲ deletePK($\langle\!\langle$student_pk, student, $\langle\!\langle$student, name$\rangle\!\rangle\rangle\!\rangle$)

⑳ deleteColumn($\langle\!\langle$student, tutor, notnull$\rangle\!\rangle$, $[\langle n, t\rangle \mid$

    $\langle s, n\rangle \leftarrow \langle\!\langle\!\langle\!\langle$root, student$\rangle\!\rangle$, name$\rangle\!\rangle; \langle s, t\rangle \leftarrow \langle\!\langle\!\langle\!\langle$root, student$\rangle\!\rangle$, tutor$\rangle\!\rangle]$)

㉑ deleteColumn($\langle\!\langle$student, name, notnull$\rangle\!\rangle$,

    $[\langle n, n\rangle \mid \langle s, n\rangle \leftarrow \langle\!\langle\!\langle\!\langle$root, student$\rangle\!\rangle$, name$\rangle\!\rangle]$)

㉒ deleteTable($\langle\!\langle$student$\rangle\!\rangle$, $[\langle n\rangle \mid \langle s, n\rangle \leftarrow \langle\!\langle\!\langle\!\langle$root, student$\rangle\!\rangle$, name$\rangle\!\rangle]$)

Note that these rules could equally well be applied in reverse as ㉒–⑯ to generate $S_{yg} \rightarrow S_{rg'}$, which would be the method used to generate the integration shown in Fig. 6. In general, translating a schema from a source to a target modelling language involves using the MDR definitions to convert constructs in the source and target language to HDM, analysing the constraint information, and building an association between the two. One common aspect of this analysis [1] is that constraint information will involve the cardinality constraints on edges in the HDM, which can be represented by just two constraint templates:

1. $N \rhd E$ states that for each value V in the extent of node N there must be at least one tuple in the extent of edge E that contains V.
2. $N \lhd E$ states that for each value V in the extent of node N there must be no more than one tuple in the extent of edge E that contains V.

Note that if neither of these constraints applies then N has 0:N occurrences in E; if $N \rhd E$ then N has 1:N occurrences in E; if $N \lhd E$ then N has 0:1 occurrences in E; and of $N \rhd E \wedge N \lhd E$ then N has 1:1 occurrences in E.

Now we are in a position to more formally analyse the relational to YATTA mapping. In the relational model, a column L of table T is represented by the scheme $\langle\langle T, L, C\rangle\rangle$. Using the methodology in Section 3.1, we model this column as a link-nodal construct, that references an existing nodal construct $\langle\langle T\rangle\rangle$ that represents table T. In the HDM, the table has node N_t, and the column has an edge E that connects N_t to node N containing the attribute value. Now C can be expressed over those HDM constructs as notnull=$N \rhd E \wedge N_t \rhd E \wedge N_t \lhd E$, and null=$N \rhd E \wedge N_t \lhd E$.

In the YATTA model, a node N is represented by the scheme $\langle\langle P, N, T, C\rangle\rangle$, which is again a link-nodal construct, that references a parent node P that may be either another YATTA node, or a root node. If in addition T indicates this is a simple type node, then we have a match between the YATTA node and the concept of a column in the relational model. In particular, the YATTA constraint C is expressed as nk=$N \rhd E \wedge N_t \rhd E \wedge N_t \lhd E$ (matching the relational constraint notnull), and ?=$N \rhd E \wedge N_t \lhd E$ (matching null).

5   Template Transformations

Schema integration in the AutoMed framework frequently relies on the reuse of specific sequences of primitive transformations. These sequences are called **composite** transformations and resemble well-known equivalences between schemas [7, 14]. For example, the equivalence between a table with a mandatory column and a table with specializations for each instance of the mandatory column is found in transformations ①–⑦ in Section 2, where the $\langle\langle$student, level$\rangle\rangle$ column is used to generate new tables $\langle\langle$ug$\rangle\rangle$ and $\langle\langle$pg$\rangle\rangle$.

To describe such equivalences between schemas, we have created a package around the AutoMed repository that enables the definition of parameterised **template** transformations [8] which are schema and data independent. For example, the parameters of the template transformation that decomposes a table to its specializations are: (a) the schema that the template transformation is going to be performed upon, (b) the existing table, (c) its mandatory column, (d) the specialization tables that are going to be added to the schema and (e) the instances of the mandatory column that correspond to the specializations. These are specified as follows:

```
INPUTS();
    OBJECT parentTable=askForObject("Existing parent table",table);
    OBJECT mandatoryColumn=askForObject("Mandatory column",column);
    OBJECT parentPrimaryKey=askForObject("Primary key of parent table",column);
    NAMELIST specializationTableNames=askForNameList("Names of specializations");
    NAMELIST descriptiveInstances=askForNameList("Values of the column ...",
        SIZEOF(specializationTableNames));
```

Note that each parameter has a description for use in a dialogue box, and optionally a Construct, which in this example ensures that the first parameter is a SchemaObject of type table and the second two parameters are of type column. After the parameters, a number of statements must be defined. In our example, since in general there are n different specialization tables to create, we require to put statements in a loop which iterate over the LIST we have specified in the INPUTS:

```
FOREACH();
    NAME specializationTableName=IN(specializationTableNames)
    NAME descriptiveInstance=IN(descriptiveInstances);
    OBJECT parentcolumn = VARIES_WITH(mandatoryColumn);
    OBJECT parent = VARIES_WITH(parentTable);
    OBJECT primaryKey = VARIES_WITH(parentPrimaryKey);
    DO();
```

This loop may contain the instructions to create each specialization table. For example, the transformations ① and ④ that create the specialization Table constructs are produced by the following template definition:

```
FUNCTION tableExtent=DEFINE_FUNCTION("[ {x} |
    {x,y} <- parentcolumn?scheme; y='@descriptiveInstance']" );
OBJECT newSpecialization=ADD(CONSTRUCT.IS(table),
    SCHEME.IS(new Object[]my(specializationTableName)), FUNCTION.IS(tableExtent));
```

Similar definitions can create the Column transformations ② and ⑤ and the PK transformations ③ and ⑥. Note that the rest of the transformations ⑧-⑨ in $S_3 \rightarrow S_{rg}$ can be produced by another template transformation that removes a column from a table and moves it down to its specialization tables.

6   Schema Matching

In all the examples seen so far, an expert user specifies the primitive transformations to be applied on the available schemas and integrate the underlying data sources. In practice, a key issue is the identification of the semantic relationships between the schema objects [6], which then imply which primitive or template transformations should be performed.

The process of discovering semantic relationships between schema objects is called **schema matching**. Most of the existing methodologies are focused on discovering equivalence relationships between schema objects [3, 10, 12], or **direct matches**, but in many cases more expressive relationships exist between schema objects, which yield **indirect matches** [11].

In our framework [21], we define five types of semantic relationships between schema objects based on the comparison of their *intentional domains*, i.e. the sets of real-world entities represented by the schema objects. These are: **equivalence, subsumption, intersection, disjointness** and **incompatibility**. Rules of the transformations that should be performed on the schemas based on the discovered semantic relationships are defined in [20].

In our example, an indirect match exists between the **disjoint** student nodes in S_1 and S_2. These nodes should be renamed in order to be distinguished, therefore transformation ⑩ renames student in S_1 to ug and an equivalent transformation renames student in S_2 to pg. These are **equivalent** to the ug and pg nodes in S_{yg} respectively, and can therefore be unified using ident transformations. Other indirect matches exist between the **intersecting** course nodes and between ug,pg and the **subsuming** student node.

In our approach to the automatic discovery of these semantic relationships, we perform a bidirectional comparison of schema objects, which has been motivated by the fact that a bidirectional comparison of the schema objects' intentional domains can be used to identify equivalence, subsumption and intersection relationships. This is depicted by the following formula:

$$d(X,Y) = \frac{|Dom_{int}(X) \cap Dom_{int}(Y)|}{|Dom_{int}(X)|},$$

where X, Y are schema objects and $|Z|$ defines the number of entities in set Z. This formula gives $d(X,Y) = d(Y,X) = 1$ when X, Y are equivalent; $d(X,Y) = 1$ and $0 < d(Y,X) < 1$ when Y subsumes X; and finally $0 < d(X,Y) < 1$ and $0 < d(Y,X) < 1$ when X, Y are intersecting. The problem with this approach is that the disjointness and incompatibility relationships cannot be distinguished, and that the *bidirectional similarity degrees* $d(X,Y), d(Y,X)$ cannot be automatically computed since a comparison of the schema objects' real-world entities is required.

We attempt to simulate the behaviour of the above formula by examining the schema objects instances and their metadata. The equivalence, subsumption and intersection relationships can still be discovered as explained previously. Now, however, the similarity degrees are fuzzier, e.g. $d(X,Y)$ and $d(Y,X)$ are unlikely to have values equal to 1 when X and Y are equivalent, but they will be above an equivalence threshold. Disjointness can also be discovered since disjoint schema objects will exhibit similarity in their instances and metadata, arising from their relationship with the same *super* schema object. Thus, disjoint pairs of schema objects will have higher similarity degrees than incompatible pairs.

This relationship discovery process is implemented by the architecture in Fig. 7, which consists of several modules that exploit different types of information to compute bidirectional similarity degrees of schema objects. Our currently implemented modules compare schema object names, instances, statistical data over the instances, data types, value ranges and lengths. There are two types of modules: **relationship identification** modules attempt to discover compatible pairs of schema objects, and **relationship clarification** modules attempt to specify the type of the semantic relationship in each compatible pair.

Initially in the schema matching process, the bidirectional similarity degrees produced by the modules are combined by the Filter, using the average aggregation strategy, to separate the compatible from the incompatible pairs of schema objects. Then, the Aggregator component combines the similarity degrees of the compatible schema objects using the product aggregation strategy and indicates

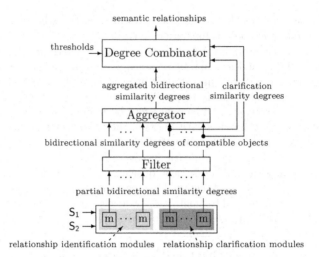

Fig. 7. Architecture of Schema Matching Tool

their semantic relationships. The output of the Aggregator becomes the input of the Degree Combinator, which based on the relationship clarification modules and the previous discussion on the values of the similarity degrees, it outputs the discovered semantic relationships. The user is then able to validate or reject these relationships and proceed to the data integration process.

7   Conclusions

This paper details the implementation of repository for BAV transformations produced by the AutoMed project, and illustrates how the AutoMed system may be used to model a number of data modelling languages, and in particular introduces the YATTA model as a method to handle semistructured text files in the BAV approach. The paper also deals with practical issues concerned with data integration, by providing a template system for defining common patterns of transformations, and a schema matching system to help automate the generation of transformations. It also introduces the notion of subnetworks into the BAV approach, which allows complex and large integrations to be divided into clearly identifiable independent units.

The AutoMed approach has the unique property that it does not insist that an entire data integration system be conducted in a single data modelling language. This gives the flexibility of integrating different domains in a modelling language suited to each domain, and then using inter-model transformations to connect between the domains.

References

1. M. Boyd and P.J. McBrien. Towards a semi-automated approach to intermodel transformations. Technical Report No. 29, AutoMed, 2004.
2. S. Cluet, C. Delobel, J. Siméon, and K. Smaga. Your mediators need data conversion! *SIGMOD Record*, 27(2):177–188, 1998.
3. A. Doan, J. Madhavan, P. Domingos, and A. Halevy. Learning to map ontologies on the Semantic Web. In *Proceedings of the World-Wide Web Conference (WWW-02)*, pages 662–673, 2002.
4. H. Fan and A. Poulovassilis. Using AutoMed metadata in data warehousing environments. In *Proc. DOLAP03*, pages 86–93, New Orleans, 2003.
5. E. Jasper, A. Poulovassilis, and L. Zamboulis. Processing IQL queries and migrating data in the AutoMed toolkit. Technical Report No. 20, AutoMed, 2003.
6. V. Kashyap and A. Sheth. Semantic and schematic similarities between database objects: a context-based approach. *VLDB Journal*, 5(4):276–304, 1996.
7. J.A. Larson, S.B. Navathe, and R. Elmasri. A theory of attribute equivalence in databases with application to schema integration. *IEEE Transactions on Software Engineering*, 15(4):449–463, April 1989.
8. C. Lazanitis. Template transformations in AutoMed. Technical Report 25, AutoMed, 2004.
9. M. Lenzerini. Data integration: A theoretical perspective. In *Proc. PODS'02*, pages 233–246. ACM, 2002.
10. W.-S. Li and C. Clifton. SEMINT: A tool for identifying attribute correspondences in heterogeneous databases using neural networks. *Data and Knowledge Engineering*, 33:49–84, 2000.
11. L.Xu and D.W. Embley. Discovering direct and indirect matches for schema elements. In *8th International Conference on Database Systems for Advanced Applications (DASFAA '03), Kyoto, Japan, March 26–28, 2003*, pages 39–46, 2003.
12. J. Madhavan, P.A. Bernstein, and E. Rahm. Generic schema matching with Cupid. In *Proc. 27th VLDB Conference*, pages 49–58, 2001.
13. J. Madhavan and A.Y. Halevy. Composing mappings among data sources. In *Proc. VLDB'03*, pages 572–583, 2003.
14. P.J. McBrien and A. Poulovassilis. A formalisation of semantic schema integration. *Information Systems*, 23(5):307–334, 1998.
15. P.J. McBrien and A. Poulovassilis. A uniform approach to inter-model transformations. In *Proc. CAiSE'99*, volume 1626 of *LNCS*, pages 333–348. Springer, 1999.
16. P.J. McBrien and A. Poulovassilis. Schema evolution in heterogeneous database architectures, a schema transformation approach. In *Advanced Information Systems Engineering, 14th International Conference CAiSE2002*, volume 2348 of *LNCS*, pages 484–499. Springer, 2002.
17. P.J. McBrien and A. Poulovassilis. Data integration by bi-directional schema transformation rules. In *Proc. ICDE'03*. IEEE, 2003.
18. P.J. McBrien and A. Poulovassilis. Defining peer-to-peer data integration using both as view rules. In *Proc. DBISP2P, at VLDB'03*, Berlin, Germany, 2003.
19. A. Poulovassilis and P.J. McBrien. A general formal framework for schema transformation. *Data and Knowledge Engineering*, 28(1):47–71, 1998.
20. N. Rizopoulos. BAV transformations on relational schemas based on semantic relationships between attributes. Technical Report 22, AutoMed, 2003.
21. N. Rizopoulos. Automatic discovery of semantic relationships between schema elements. In *Proc. of 6th ICEIS*, 2004.

Adding Agent-Oriented Concepts Derived from Gaia to Agent OPEN

Brian Henderson-Sellers, John Debenham, and Q.-N.N. Tran

University of Technology, Sydney, NSW 2007 Australia
{brian,debenham}@it.uts.edu.au, numitran@yahoo.com

Abstract. Agent OPEN offers extensions of an object-oriented methodological framework to support agent-oriented software developments. However, to date, it is incomplete. Here, we extend the Agent OPEN repository of process components to include contributions from the Gaia agent-oriented methodology. We have identified one new Task, together with six new subtasks for some pre-existing Tasks. Three extra Techniques and five new Work Products were identified and recommended to be added in order to support the Gaia approach for agent-oriented software development.

1 Introduction

In a distributed computing environment, agents are increasingly being perceived as of high potential applicability. Applying agent technology successfully in an industrial setting requires the application of an appropriate methodology "tailored" to local demands. Ensuring the methodology meets local requirements (both technical and human) can be facilitated by the use of method engineering (ME) (Kumar and Welke, 1992; Brinkkemper, 1996) or, more specifically, situated method engineering (SME) (Ter Hofstede and Verhoef, 1997). A combination of SME and agent technology is the focus of this paper.

ME and SME provide a rational approach to the construction, either fully or partially, of methods (a.k.a. methodologies) from method fragments (often called method chunks (Rolland and Prakash, 1996) or process components[1] (e.g. Firesmith and Henderson-Sellers, 2002)), typically stored in a repository. The method itself is constructed by selection of appropriate method fragments followed by their configuration in such a way as to satisfy the requirements for the method (Ralyté and Rolland, 2001) and create a meaningful overall method (Brinkkemper *et al.*, 1998).

In the object-oriented context, SME has been realized through the OPEN Process Framework (OPF) (Firesmith and Henderson-Sellers, 2002). The OPF is underpinned by a full lifecycle metamodel and contains rules for both creating and using the repository-stored process components. As part of this agent-oriented (AO) methodology-focussed project, the OPF has had some initial enhancements to include support

---

[1] We take the view that a methodology is a combination of a process and a set of products (e.g. Rolland *et al.*, 1999). Our focus here is on the process portion of a methodology and thus the words "method", "methodology" and "process" can be taken as synonyms in our discussion.

A. Persson and J. Stirna (Eds.): CAiSE 2004, LNCS 3084, pp. 98–111, 2004.

for agent concepts (Debenham and Henderson-Sellers, 2003). Thus an additional number of tasks, techniques, work products and roles has been added to the OPF repository. This paper reports on the next stage of the research: to ensure that the set of process components created in the OPF repository specifically to support agency concepts is as complete as possible. To do this, we analyze the Gaia AO methodology (Wooldridge *et al.*, 1999, 2000; Zambonelli *et al.*, 2003) in order to see what must be added to the OPF repository so that this particular AO methodology (i.e. Gaia) can be (re)created by instantiation from the elements in the OPF.

In Section 2, we outline the OPEN Process Framework as used in the context of SME and, in Section 3, we describe the basics of the Gaia methodology. In Section 4 we describe the elements of Gaia not currently supported in the OPF and which we therefore propose for addition to the OPF repository.

2 An Overview of the OPEN Process Framework

The OPEN (Object-oriented Process, Environment, and Notation) Process Framework (OPF) (Firesmith and Henderson-Sellers, 2002) combines a process metamodel and a repository of process components (Figure 1). Elements from the repository are selected and put together to form a specific process or situational method.

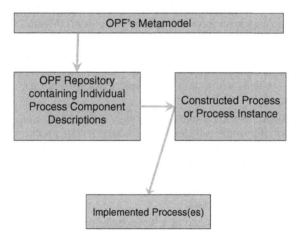

Fig. 1. The OPF defines a framework consisting of a metamodel and a repository of process components.

Process construction is accomplished using a set of OPF guidelines and rules. A major element is the use of deontic matrices, which allocate a possibility value to pairs of process elements such as Activity/Task or Producer/Work Product. Deontic values have one of five values ranging from mandatory through optional to forbidden. This gives a high degree of flexibility to the process engineer, perhaps assisted by an automated tool, who can allocate appropriate deontic values to any specific pair of process components depending upon the context i.e. the specific project, skills set of the development team etc.

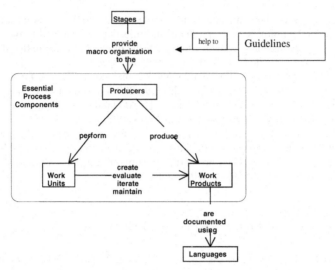

Fig. 2. The five major metaclasses of the OPF's metamodel (after Firesmith and Henderson-Sellers, 2002) © Addison-Wesley.

Underpinning the OPF framework is its full lifecycle metamodel that defines the following five main high level classes of process components (Figure 2):

Work Product: "A Work Product is anything of value that is produced during the development process" (Firesmith and Henderson-Sellers, 2002). Work Products are the result of producers (people) executing Work Units and are used either as input to other Work Units or delivered to a client. Typical examples are use case diagrams and role diagrams.

Producer: "A Producer is responsible for creating, evaluating, iterating and maintaining Work Products" (Firesmith and Henderson-Sellers, 2002). Producers play various roles within the methodology and introduce the human element (although some producers may be other software or indeed hardware). A large number of Producer and Role instances (for example, the requirements engineer and the toolsmith) are described in the OPF repository although it is a volatile set in comparison with, say, the instances of the WorkUnit metaclass.

Work Unit: A Work Unit is defined as a functionally cohesive operation that is performed by a Producer. There are three major classes of Work Unit: Activity, Task and Technique.

- Activities describe, at a high level, what needs to be undertaken. The overall software development process is often configured by the process engineer/methodologist using half a dozen or so of these Activities so they are often (but not always) the first to be identified. A typical example is the Requirements Engineering (RE) Activity.
- Tasks also focus on "what" needs to be done rather than "how" it is do be done. Tasks can be readily tracked and project managed. They are typically allocated to a small team over a period of a few days. A typical example related to the RE Activity is "Elicit requirements".

- Techniques describe the mechanism by which a Task is undertaken. They describe the "how" as compared to the "what" of Activities and Tasks. A typical RE-related Technique is storyboarding.

Language: A Language is defined as a medium for documenting a Work Product; for example; English, UML.

Stage: A Stage is defined as an identified and managed duration within the process or a point in time at which some achievement is recognized. Stages may be Phases or Cycles – examples are the Build Phase and the Development Cycle, respectively.

Each of these metaclasses has many subclasses in the detailed metamodel (see Appendix G of Firesmith and Henderson-Sellers, 2002). From each of these subclasses, one or more process component instances are generated and stored in the OPF repository (Figure 1).

Initially, the OPF repository contained about 30 predefined instances of Activity, 160 instances of Task and 200 instances of Techniques (the three main kinds of Work Unit) as well as multiple instances of Role, Stage, Language etc. Some of these are orthogonal to all others in their group and some overlap. Consequently, during process construction both association and integration strategies (Ralyté and Rolland, 2001) are needed. For example, there are several Techniques in the repository for finding objects e.g. textual analysis, use cases simulations, CRC card techniques.

Finally, when used on a specific project in real time, this is known as a process instance or "implemented process" (Figure 1). A company-customized OPEN version is then "owned" by the organization, becoming their own internal standard, while retaining compatibility with the global OPEN user community.

Since its first publication in 1997, several additions have been made to the OPF repository to enhance its support for various new technologies including additions of relevance to agent technology (Debenham and Henderson-Sellers, 2003; Henderson-Sellers et al., 2004a,b) . Here, we extend the OPF repository even further to offer additional support for agent orientation (AO) by extracting new process components from the Gaia AO methodology (Wooldridge et al., 2000; Zambonelli et al., 2003).

3   Major Elements of Gaia

Gaia views the process of multi-agent system (MAS) development as a process of *organizational design*, where the MAS is modelled as an organized society with agents playing different roles. The methodology allows a developer to move systematically from a statement of requirements to a design that is sufficiently detailed that it can be implemented directly. It supports both macro (societal) and micro (agent) aspects of MAS design, and is also neutral to both application domain and agent architecture. The newest version of Gaia (Zambonelli et al., 2003) extends the original version (Wooldridge et al., 1999; Wooldridge et al., 2000) with various organizational abstractions, enabling it to be used for the design of open MAS (which was not achievable previously). The discussion in this paper accounts for the new tasks and models presented in the newest version as well as those in the original (1999/2000) publications.

3.1 Tasks Characterizing Gaia

There are a number of tasks described in the publications on Gaia which, together, permit its use for AO systems development. These are:

- *'Identifying sub-organizations in the system':* To promote modularity, an analyst should determine whether the target system contains multiple sub-organizations that co-exist as autonomous interacting MASs.
- *'Modeling the environment':* The MAS environment is modeled as a collection of abstract computational resources, each characterized by the types of actions the agents can perform on it.
- *'Identifying roles in the system'*: Gaia models each role by its responsibilities and permissions. Responsibilities represent the role's functionality, and are divided into two types: : *liveness* and *safety*. Liveness responsibilities specify the states of affairs that an agent must bring about, while safety responsibilities are typically predicates, specifying the acceptable states of affairs that should be maintained across all states of execution.
- *'Identifying inter-role interactions'*: Gaia defines inter-role interaction protocols in terms of the essential nature and purpose of the interactions, rather than the precise ordering of particular message exchanges. Specifically, each protocol definition consists of an interaction's *purpose, initiator, responder, inputs, outputs* and *processing* (which is simply a brief textual description of the initiator's processing during interaction).
- *'Defining organizational rules':* Organizational rules (liveness or safety) are responsibilities of the agent organization as a whole.
- *'Choosing the organizational structure':* The designer needs to choose an organizational structure that provides the most appropriate topology and control regime.
- *'Identifying agent types and agent instances':* Gaia identifies agent types from roles, and agent instances from these types. Agent types are arranged in an Agent Type Hierarchy, which includes only aggregation relationships (if any) but no inheritance.
- *'Specifying services of each agent'*: A service is a single, coherent block of activity in which an agent will engage.
- *'Specifying agent acquaintances'*: This task involves identifying the communication links/pathways between agent types. It does not include defining what messages are sent or when messages are sent. The purpose of this task is simply to identify any potential communication bottlenecks and to ensure that the system is internally loosely-coupled.

3.2 Techniques Recommended by Gaia

As well as tasks, a number of specific techniques are recommended:

- *For 'Identifying sub-organizations in the system'*: Gaia suggests considering multiple sub-organizations when there are portions of the target system that exhibit behaviour specifically oriented towards the achievement of a given sub-goal, that interact loosely with other portions of the system, or that require competencies not needed in other parts of the system.

- *For 'Modeling the environment'*: GAIA does not commit to any specific modeling techniques for the specification of environmental resources.
- *For 'Identifying roles for the system'*: The process of role identification roughly goes through two phases. Firstly, the key roles in the system are identified from the "basic skills" required by the organization to achieve its goals. However, Gaia does not provide techniques for identifying these skills, or for identifying roles from these skills. The output of this phase is a Preliminary Role Model which provides informal, unelaborated descriptions of the key roles in the system. This is then refined into a fully elaborated Role Model on the basis of the organizational structure. With regard to each role's responsibilities, Gaia does not offer any explicit techniques for the identification of responsibilities, except to suggest that liveness responsibilities may follow certain patterns, being modelled in terms of *activities* and *protocols*. With regard to a role's permissions, the developer is recommended to investigate the *types* and *limits* of the information resources that an agent accesses to carry out its roles.
- *For 'Identifying inter-role interactions'*: Gaia offers no specific technique to identify interactions between roles, except for stating that each protocol description should focus on the nature/purpose of the interaction and the involved parties. No precise ordering of message exchanges needs to be defined.
- *For 'Defining organizational rules'*: Liveness organizational rules can be derived from liveness responsibilities of different roles, i.e. from the way different roles can play specific activities. Meanwhile, safety organizational rules can be related to safety responsibilities of different roles or to expressions of the environmental resources in different roles.
- *For 'Choosing the organizational structure'*: Gaia suggests selecting an organizational structure that optimizes the organizational efficiency and simplicity (e.g. balanced workload, low coordination costs) that respects the organizational rules and that reflects the structure of the real-world organization..
- *For 'Identifying agent types and instances'*: Gaia suggests a general rule of one-to-one mapping between roles and agent types. However, it also recognizes the need for grouping closely related roles to the same agent type for the purpose of convenience and efficiency. Nevertheless, Gaia recommends considering a trade-off between the coherence of an agent type and the efficiency considerations. Gaia offers no techniques for the instantiation of agent types.
- *For 'Specifying services of each agent'*: An agent's services can be derived from the list of *responsibilities* (both liveness and safety), *protocols* and *activities* of the roles that the agent encapsulates. In general, there will be at least one service associated with each protocol. Every activity identified in the agent role's responsibilities will correspond to a service, though not every service will correspond to an activity. The safety responsibility may also imply a service, defined in terms of inputs, outputs, pre- and post-conditions. The former two elements can be derived from protocol definitions in the Interaction Model, while the latter two can be revealed from the safety responsibilities of the role.
- *For 'Specifying agent acquaintances'*: The communication pathways between agent types can be directly derived from Role, Interaction and Agent Models.

3.3 Work Products Advocated by Gaia

Gaia suggests the creation of seven specific work products during AO software development:

- *Environment Model*: containing a list of resources, each associated with a symbolic name, types of actions that can be performed on it and possibly textual comments and descriptions. No specific notation is mandated.
- *Organizational Structure Model*: The designer can either adopt a formal representation scheme or a more intuitive graphical notation for the organization structure model depending on the application. Graphically, roles can simply be represented as blocks, connected by arrows to represent organizational relationships (e.g. control, peer, dependency) as shown in Figure 3.

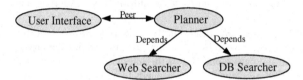

Fig. 3. Example of Gaia Organizational Structure Model.

- *Role Model*: containing a textual Role Schema for each role (Figure 4). Role responsibilities are modelled in Gaia using Fusion notation.

Role Schema:	*name of role*
Description	*short English description of the role*
Protocols and Activities	*protocols and activities in which the role plays a part*
Permissions	*"rights" associated with the role*
Responsibilities	
Liveness	*liveness responsibilities*
Safety	*safety responsibilities*

Fig. 4. Gaia's Role Model (figure 3 from Wooldridge *et al.*, 2000. With kind permission of Kluwer Academic Publishers).

- *Inter-role Interaction Model*: containing a list of definitions of inter-role interaction protocols. Each protocol definition consists of a purpose, initiator, responder, inputs, outputs and processing description.

  In the exemplar protocol definition (Figure 5), the *SearchForAnswer* protocol is initiated by the role *Planner* and involves the role *WebSearcher*. Input to the protocol is the sub-query derived from the user query.The protocol involves the *Planner* forwarding the sub-query to the *WebSearcher* to process, and results in the answer being returned by the *WebSearcher*.

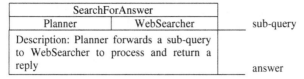

SearchForAnswer
Planner
WebSearcher
Description: Planner forwards a sub-query to WebSearcher to process and return a reply
sub-query
answer

Fig. 5. Example of Gaia Interaction Model.

- ***Agent Model***: Gaia suggests a simple diagram for the Agent Model which shows, for each agent type, the roles that map to it (Figure 6). The bottom leaf nodes correspond to roles, while other nodes represent agent types. The arrows denote mappings from roles to agent types. Agent instantiation is documented by Fusion-based annotations below the agent types (e.g. an annotation '+' means that there will be one or more agents of the type at run-time)..

UserInterfaceAgent
1
UserInterface
UserFeedback Processor
UserProfileAgent
+
UserProfile Manager
PlannerAgent
1..5
Planner
WebSearcherAgent
+
WebSearcher
DBSearcherAgent
+
DBSearcher

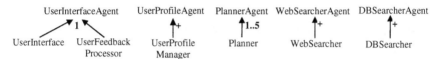

Fig. 6. Example of Gaia Agent Model.

UML Class Diagrams can be adapted for the modelling of agent types and their relationships. Major considerations are whether the association relationships between agents have a different meaning from those between objects (e.g. inter-agent associations represent communication pathways). UML also offers instanceOf relationships that can be used to model agent class instantation.

- ***Service Model***: Gaia suggests a tabular template for modelling services (Figure 6).

Service	*Inputs*	*Outputs*	*Pre-condition*	*Post-condition*
Accept user query	userQuery	awaitMessage	true	true
Create user profile	userDetails	custID, custPassword	userStatus = nil	userStatus = member

Fig. 7. Example of Gaia Service Model (for User Agent).

Currently UML does not offer a separate diagram for service modelling. However, in the AO version of the UML Class Diagram, services can be included as an internal component of an agent class (just as methods are a component of an object class).

- ***Agent Acquaintance Model***: Eliminated in Version 2 of Gaia (Zambonelli *et al.*, 2003), this information can probably best be depicted with a UML or AUML Interaction Diagram.

3.4 Stages Used in Gaia

In order to support development across the whole system lifecycle, we identify the stages (cycles and phases) advocated in Gaia:

Cycle: Gaia is iterative within each phase as well as across all phases.. This description fits the '*Iterative, Incremental, Parallel Life Cycle*' model of OPEN.

Phases: Gaia covers Analysis and Design (particularly from the statement of requirements to a design that is sufficiently detailed that it can be implemented directly). In the context of OPEN, Gaia supports '*Initiation*' and '*Construction*'.

3.5 Languages

Gaia's notation mainly comes from Fusion (Coleman *et al.,* 1994). Considering the contents of Gaia's models, UML (with necessary adaptations/extensions) can be employed as an efficient modelling language. In contrast, Gaia's design models can be implemented in any programming language.

4   Adding Support to the OPF Derived from Gaia

In this section, we outline the various Tasks, Techniques and Work Products that are proposed here as additions and modifications to the OPEN repository in order to incorporate agency concerns as identified in Gaia.

In total, only one new Task is identified, six new subtasks, three Techniques and five new Work Products are identified. These are all described in the following subsections.

4.1 Existing Support and Mapping between OPF and Gaia

4.1.1 Tasks

Roles are of high importance in Gaia (and several other AO methodologies). However, the concept of "role" has not been well supported in the object-oriented literature. Although OPEN supports role modelling more than many OO methods via its use of the "CIRT" (standing for Class, Instance, Role or Type), it does not consider "role" as a first-class concept in system analysis and design. It also does not promote the organisation-driven approach in the development of systems. Roles are covered in OPEN through the 'Construct the Object Model' Task and 'Identify CIRTs' Task. Therefore a new Task: Model agents' roles was introduced by Debenham and Henderson-Sellers (2003). Using this and the existing OPF Task: 'Map roles on to classes' adequate support is offered for both the identification of agents and their responsibilities and permissions. However, two new subtasks need to be made explicit for Task: 'Model agents' roles' (Section 4.2).

The specification of other organizational abstractions, including the MAS environment, sub-organizations, organizational rules and organizational structure, is addressed to some extent by OPF requirement engineering Tasks: 'Context modeling' and 'Analyze customer organization'. Debenham and Henderson-Sellers (2003) also introduced Tasks 'Model the agent's environment' and 'Identify system organization' that deal with MAS environmental and organizational design issues. However, due to their significance, four new subtasks need to be made explicit: subtask 'Model environmental resources' for Task 'Model the agent's environment', and subtasks 'Identify sub-organizations', 'Defining organizational rules', and 'Defining organizational structures' for Task 'Identify system organization'.

Agent interactions can be described by a variety of existing Tasks in the OPF, particularly augmented by the Agent OPEN Task: 'Determine agent interaction protocol' and Task: 'Determine agent communication protocol'. These offer similar and adequate support for the Gaian Tasks of 'Identifying inter-role interactions' and 'Specifying agent acquaintances'. Services are identified and specified using tasks (and techniques) similar to those for classes in OO developments but extended to include agents as part of the OPF CIRT.

Each of the tasks above is related to the new Task: 'Construct the agent model' (see Section 4.2) which also offers support for the Gaia task of 'Identifying agent types and agent instances'.

4.1.2 Techniques

For Gaia's 'Identifying roles for the system' techniques, OPEN offers the Technique: 'Role Modelling', which covers various aspects of role modelling, although is weak on guidance for the identification of roles.

Support for responsibility and permissions identification and modelling is found in OPEN's original Technique: 'Responsibility identification' and supplemented by the use of various user requirements Techniques such as 'CRC card modelling' and 'Scenario development'.

Techniques for inter-role interactions are found in the 'Collaboration Analysis' Technique of OPEN (Henderson-Sellers *et al.*, 1998) and the 'Reactive reasoning (ECA) rules' of Agent OPEN (Debenham and Henderson-Sellers, 2003).

OPEN offers various techniques for OO class identification/modelling (such as 'Abstract Class Identification' and 'Class Naming'). These techniques are useful but need to be oriented more towards agent classes, for example, taking into account the major differences between OO classes and agent classes - agent classes are generally more coarse-grained than OO classes (Wooldridge *et al.*, 2000) and thus the OPF Technique: 'Granularity' should be extended to account for this difference. The OPF Technique: 'Relationship modelling' may also be useful although Gaia appears to eschew the generalization and association relationships common in OO modelling languages, such as the UML (OMG, 2001).

To support Gaia's 'Specifying services of each agent', OPEN offers Technique: 'Service Identification' that can be applied (with necessary adaptations) to the specification of agents' services. Furthermore, the OPF Technique: 'Collaborations analysis' serves well to support the Gaian task of 'Specifying agent acquaintances'. Although Gaia's scope does not include the specification of communication messages between agent classes, Gaia does state that its design models should be further realized by traditional design techniques. In this case, the OPF Technique: 'Interaction modelling' provides a useful basis for modelling the communications between agent classes.

No techniques exist in the OPF to directly support the definition and modeling of system environment's resources, organizational rules and organizational structures. Therefore, these need to be added.

4.1.3 Work Products

While role models are supported within the OPF, say using UML, there is no document to capture the requirements for an individual role in terms of responsibilities and protocols. Thus the Gaia Role Schema needs to be made available through the OPF Repository (Section 4.3).

Interaction protocols in OPEN are modelled via UML Sequence Diagrams and Collaboration Diagrams. These diagrams can be readily adapted for the modelling of AO interactions by means of an Agent Protocol diagram as found in Prometheus (Padgham and Winikoff, 2002). Consequently, the Gaian template for an Interaction Model as shown in Figure 4 is probably unnecessary; however, it is added to the OPF repository for completeness. There it is renamed Protocol Schema in order to avoid confusion with UML interaction diagrams.

While the Gaia agent model is readily subsumed by UML diagrams, it is worth adding its service model as a new OPF Work Product component: the Service table.

Both the Environment Model and Organizational Structure Model can be represented as UML class diagrams. However, they should be explicitly specified as new products in the OPF repository.

4.2 New Tasks

One new Task and six subtasks are identified from Gaia tasks in Section 3.1 for inclusion in the OPF repository.

TASK NAME: Construct the agent model
Focus: Static architecture
Typical supportive techniques: Intelligent agent identification, Control architecture
Explanation: An analogue of the "object model" as the main description of the static architecture needs to be constructed. This model will show the agents, their interfaces and how they are connected both with other agents and other objects within the system being designed.

New subtasks for Task: Model agents' roles
Subtask: Model responsibilities: these include the accepted OO responsibilities (knowing, doing, enforcing) but classified in terms of liveness and safety properties.
Subtask: Model permissions: these are associated with the responsibilities allocated to each agent role.

New subtask for Task: Model the agent's environment
Subtask: Model environmental resources: these are abstract computational resources that are available to agents for sensing, effecting or consuming.

New subtasks for Task: Identifying system organization
Subtask: Identify sub-organizations: this task analyzes the target system organization to identify sub-organizations that co-exist as autonomous interacting MASs.
Subtask: Define organizational rules: focussed on modelling the responsibilities of the organization as a whole in terms of liveness and safety organizational rules.
Subtask: Define organizational structures: focussed on selecting an organizational structure that offers the most appropriate topology and control regime.

4.3 New Techniques

Three new OPF Techniques, derived from Gaia's techniques described in Section 3.2, are to be added to the OPF repository.

TECHNIQUE NAME: Environmental resources modelling
Focus: System environment
Typical tasks for which this is needed: Model the agent's environment
Technique description: Each resource should be described in terms of its symbolic name, types of actions that agents can perform on it, and if appropriate or necessary, its detailed data structure. Graphical representation of the logical/physical relationships between resources, and the specification of how and from where a resource can be accessed may be useful.
Technique usage: Identify and describe each resource in the MAS environment. The resources' details and the model's representation notation can be decided by the designer depending on the application at hand.
Deliverables: Environment model

TECHNIQUE NAME: Organizational rules specification
Focus: System organization
Typical tasks for which this is needed: Identify system organization
Technique description: Roles that affect the system organization as a whole should be described in terms of liveness and safety organizational rules. Liveness rules define how the dynamics of the organization should evolve over time, while safety rules define time-independent global invariants that the organization should respect.
Technique usage: Liveness organizational rules can be derived from liveness responsibilities of different roles, while saftety rules can relate to safety responsibilities of different roles or to expressions of the environmental resources in different roles. The definition of organizational rules is particularly necessary when the system is open.
Deliverables: Organizational rules specification

TECHNIQUE NAME: Organizational structure specification
Focus: Static architecture
Typical tasks for which this is needed: Identify system organization
Technique description: The organizational structure selected for the target system should offer the most appropriate topology and control regime. Forces affecting this choice may include: the need to achieve organizational efficiency; the need to respect organizational rules; and the need to minimize the distance from the real-world organization.
Technique usage: Together with the analysis of the above factors, the designer should exploit the existing libraries of organizational patterns. Organizational structures can be modelled either by a formal notation or a more intuitive graphical representation.
Deliverables: Organizational structure model

4.4 New Work Products

From Section 3.3, five new work products are recommended for inclusion in the OPF repository in order to support AO development using a Gaia-based approach/ philosophy.

Role schema: Textual description of each role. One schema per identified agent role. Information is displayed about the protocols, permissions and responsibilities for each agent role (Figure 3).

Protocol schema: The Gaia-based interaction model is used here to define and describe the agent protocol schema. It shows the purpose, the initiator, the responder, the inputs and outputs and the processing.

Service table: A tabular representation of each service, indicating the inputs, outputs, preconditions and postconditions for each service.

Environment Model: Specification of each resource. Typical information include the resource's name, types of actions to be performed on it, internal data structure, and textual comments.

Organizational structure model: Organizational structure is modelled using either a formal notation or a graphical representation. The model should show the topology and the control regime of the structure. Typical control relationships are control, peer and dependency.

5 Summary and Conclusions

As part of an extendive research programme to combine the benefits of method engineering and existing object-oriented frameworks (notably the OPF) to create a highly supportive methodological environment for the construction of agent-oriented information systems, we have analysed here contributions from the Gaia AO methodology. We have identified one new Task, six new subtasks (to pre-existing tasks), three new Techniques and five new Work Products, although no additional Roles or Stages were identified and no changes to the OPF metamodel were necessary.

Acknowledgements

We wish to acknowledge financial support from the University of Technology, Sydney under their Research Excellence Grants Scheme. This is Contribution number 03/27 of the Centre for Object Technology Applications and Research.

References

Brinkkemper, S., 1996, Method engineering: engineering of information systems development methods and tools, Inf. Software Technol., 38(4), 275-280.
Brinkkemper, S., Saeki, M. and Harmsen, F., 1998, Assembly techniques for method engineering. Proceedings of CAISE 1998, Springer Verlag, 381-400.

Coleman, D., Arnold, P., Bodoff, S., Dollin, C. and Gilchrist, H., 1994, Object-Oriented Development. The Fusion Method, Prentice Hall, Englewood Cliffs, NJ, USA, 313pp

Debenham, J. and Henderson-Sellers, B., 2003, Designing agent-based process systems - extending the OPEN Process Framework, Chapter VIII in Intelligent Agent Software Engineering (ed. V. Plekhanova), Idea Group Publishing, 160-190.

Firesmith, D.G. and Henderson-Sellers, B., 2002, The OPEN Process Framework. AN Introduction, Addison-Wesley, Harlow, Herts, UK

Henderson-Sellers, B., Simons, A.J.H. and Younessi, H., 1998, The OPEN Toolbox of Techniques, Addison-Wesley, UK, 426pp + CD

Henderson-Sellers, B., Giorgini, P. and Bresciani, P., 2004a, Enhancing Agent OPEN with concepts used in the Tropos methodology, Procs. ESAW'03 (Engineering Societies in the Agents World), LNCS, Springer-Verlag, Berlin (in press)

Henderson-Sellers, B., Debenham, J. and Tran, N., 2004, Incorporating the elements of the MASE methodology into Agent OPEN, Procs. ICEIS2004 (eds. I. Seruca, J. Cordeiro, S. Hammoudi and J. Filipe), INSTICC Press, Portugal (in press)

Kumar, K. and Welke, R.J., 1992, Methodology engineering: a proposal for situation-specific methodology construction, in *Challenges and Strategies for Research in Systems Development* (eds. W.W. Cotterman and J.A. Senn), J. Wiley, Chichester, 257-269

OMG, 2001, OMG: OMG Unified Modeling Language Specification, Version 1.4, September 2001, OMG document formal/01-09-68 through 80 (13 documents) [Online]. Available http://www.omg.org (2001)

Padgham, L. and Winikoff, M., 2002, Prometheus: A Methodology for Developing Intelligent Agents. In proceedings of the Third International Workshop on Agent-Oriented Software Engineering, at AAMAS'02.

Ralyté, J. and Rolland, C., 2001, An assembly process model for method engineering, in K.R. Dittrich, A. Geppert and M.C. Norrie (Eds.) Advanced Information Systems Engineering), LNCS2068, Springer, Berlin, 267-283.

Rolland, C. and Prakash, N., 1996, A proposal for context-specific method engineering, IFIP WG8.1 Conf. on Method Engineering, 191-208, Atlanta, GA, USA

Rolland, C., Prakash, N. and Benjamen, A., 1999, A multi-model view of process modelling, *Requirements Eng. J.*, **4(4),** 169-187

Ter Hofstede, A.H.M. and Verhoef, T.F., 1997, On the feasibility of situational method engineering, Information Systems, 22, 401-422

Wooldridge, M., Jennings, N.R. and Kinny, D., 1999. A Methodology for Agent-Oriented Analysis and Design. Proceedings of the 3rd International Conference on Autonomous Agents (AA'99), 69-76.

Wooldridge, M., Jennings, N.R. and Kinny, D., 2000, The Gaia methodology for agent-oriented analysis and design, J. Autonomous Agents and Multi-Agent Systems, 3, 285-312

Zambonelli, F., Jennings, N. and Wooldridge, M., 2003, Developing multiagent systems: the Gaia methodology, ACM Transaction on Software Engineering and Methodology, **12(3),** 317-370

An Ontologically Well-Founded Profile
for UML Conceptual Models

Giancarlo Guizzardi[1], Gerd Wagner[2], Nicola Guarino[3], and Marten van Sinderen[1]

[1] Centre for Telematics and Information Technology
University of Twente, Enschede, The Netherlands
guizzard@cs.utwente.nl,sinderen@ctit.utwente.nl
[2] Eindhoven University of Technology
Faculty of Technology Management, Eindhoven, The Netherlands
G.Wagner@tm.tue.nl
[3] Institute for Cognitive Science and Technology
Italian National Research Council
Laboratory for Applied Ontology, Trento, Italy
guarino@loa-cnr.it

Abstract. UML class diagrams can be used as a language for expressing a conceptual model of a domain. In a series of papers [1,2,3] we have been using the General Ontological Language (GOL) and its underlying upper level ontology, proposed in [4,5], to evaluate the ontological correctness of a conceptual UML class model and to develop guidelines for how the constructs of the UML should be used in conceptual modeling. In this paper, we focus on the UML metaconcepts of classes and objects from an ontological point of view. We use a philosophically and psychologically well-founded theory of classifiers to propose a UML profile for Ontology Representation and Conceptual Modeling. Moreover, we propose a design pattern based on this profile to target a recurrent problem in *role* modeling discussed in the literature. Finally, we demonstrate the relevance of the tools proposed by applying them to solve recurrent problems in the practice of conceptual modeling.

1 Introduction

Conceptual modeling is concerned with identifying, analyzing and describing the essential concepts and constraints of a domain with the help of a (diagrammatic) modeling language that is based on a small set of basic meta-concepts (forming a metamodel). Ontological modeling, on the other hand, is concerned with capturing the relevant entities of a domain in an ontology of that domain using an ontology specification language that is based on a small set of basic, domain-independent ontological categories (forming an upper level ontology). While conceptual modeling languages are evaluated on the basis of their successful use in (the early phases of) information systems development, ontology specification languages and their underlying upper level ontologies have to be rooted in principled philosophical theories about what kinds of things exist and what their basic relationships with each other are.

Recently, it has been proposed that UML should be used as an Ontology Representation Language [6]. Moreover, in this paper the authors argue that although UML

A. Persson and J. Stirna (Eds.): CAiSE 2004, LNCS 3084, pp. 112–126, 2004.
© Springer-Verlag Berlin Heidelberg 2004

lacks a precise definition of its formal semantics, this difficulty shall be overcome with the current developments made by the precise UML community [7]. We believe, however, that defining UML constructs only in terms of its mathematical semantics, although essential, it is not sufficient to make it a suitable ontology representation language. The position defended here is that, in order to model reality, a conceptual modeling language should be founded on formal upper-level ontologies. In other words, it should have both, formal and ontological semantics.

In a series of papers we have been employing the General Ontological Language (GOL) and its underlying upper level ontology, proposed in [4,5], to evaluate the ontological correctness of UML conceptual models and to develop guidelines that assign well-defined ontological semantics to UML modeling constructs. In [1], we have discussed the meaning of the UML metaconcepts of *classes and objects*, *power-types*, *association* and *part-whole* relations (*aggregation/composition*). The UML metaconcepts of *abstract classes* and *datatypes* are addressed in a companion paper [2]. In [3], we have employed some of the results in [1] and [2] to evaluate and improve the conceptual correctness and clarity of UML models in the area of Molecular Biology. The work presented here can be seen as a continuation of this work in which we focus on one aspect of the philosophical problem between universals and particulars (roughly, classes and instances).

Although the Class (entity type, concept) meta-construct is fundamental in conceptual modeling (being present in all major conceptual modeling languages) there is still a deficiency of methodological support for helping the user of the language deciding how to model the elements of a given domain. In practice, a set of primitives are often used to model distinctions in different types of classes (Type, Role, State, Mixin, among others). However, the choice of how the elements that denote universal properties in a domain (viz. Person, Student, Red Thing, Physical Thing, Deceased Person, Customer) should be modeled is often made in ad hoc manner. Likewise, it is the judgment of what are the admissible relations between these modeling meta-constructs. Finally, an inspection of the literature shows that there is still much debate on the meaning of these categories [8,9,10,13].

This paper proposes a philosophically and psychologically well-founded typology of classifiers, which is further used to generate a UML profile of Class types. We also propose a set of methodological guidelines that should govern the use of this profile. Moreover, we demonstrate the relevance of the tools proposed by applying them to solve recurrent problems in the practice of conceptual modeling. In particular, we address a recurrent problem in role modeling presented by Steimann in [10,11,12] and show how the techniques presented here (the profile and a design pattern based on it) account for a proposal which is philosophically better justified but requires no changes to be made in the UML meta-model.

The remaining of this article is structured as follows: Section 2 presents the theory of classifier types and its philosophical and psychological foundations. Section 3 proposes the UML profile for Class types derived from this theory along with examples of how the profile can be used to improve the conceptual quality of conceptual models. Section 4 employs the proposed modeling profile to derive a *design pattern* for the conceptual modeling of *roles*. Finally, section 5 elaborates on some conclusions and future work.

2   Towards a Theory of Classifier Types for Conceptual Modeling: Philosophical and Psychological Foundations

In [14], van Leeuwen shows an important syntactical difference in natural languages that reflects a semantical and ontological one, namely, the difference between common nouns (CNs) on one side and arbitrary general terms (adjectives, verbs, mass nouns, etc...) on the other. CNs have the singular feature that they can combine with determiners and serve as argument for predication in sentences such as:

(i) (exactly) five mice were in the kitchen last night;
(ii) the mouse which has eaten the cheese, has been in turn eaten by the cat.

In other words, if we have the patterns *(exactly) five X...* and *the Y which is Z...*, only the substitution of X,Y,Z by CNs will produce sentences which are grammatical. To see that, we can try the substitution by the adjective *Red* in the sentence (*i*): *(exactly) five red were in the kitchen last night*. A request to 'count the red in this room' cannot receive a definite answer: Should a red shirt be counted as one or should the shirt, the two sleeves, and two pockets be counted separately so that we have five reds? The problem in this case is not that one would not know how to finish the counting but that one would not know how to start since arbitrarily many subparts of a red thing are still red.

The explanation for this feature unique of CNs lies on the function that determinates (demonstratives and quantifiers) play in noun phrases, which is to determine a certain range on individuals. Both reference and quantification requires that the thing (or things) which are referred or which form the domain of quantification are determinate individuals, i.e., their conditions for *individuation* and *identity* must be determinate. In other words, if it is not determinate how to count Xs or how to identify X that is the same as Y, the sentences in the patterns (i) and (ii) do not express determinate propositions, i.e. propositions with definite truth values.

The distinction between the grammatical categories of CNs and arbitrary general terms can be explained in terms of the ontological categories of Sortal and Characterizing universals [15], which are roughly their ontological counterparts. Whilst the latter supply only a principle of application for the individuals they collect, the former supply both a principle of application and a principle of identity. A principle of application is that in accordance with which we judge whether a general term applies to a particular (e.g. whether something is a Person, a Dog, a Chair or a Student). A principle of identity supports the judgment whether two particulars are the same, i.e., in which circumstances the identity relation holds.

In [16], Macnamara, investigates the role of sortal concepts in cognition and provides a comprehensive theory for explaining the process that a child undergoes when learning proper nouns and common nouns. He proposes the following example: suppose a little boy (Tom), which is about to learn the meaning of a proper name for his puppy. When presented to the word "Spot", Tom has to decide what it refers to. One should notice that a demonstrative such as "that" will not be sufficient to determinate the bearer of the proper name? How to decide that "that" which changes all its perceptual properties is still Spot? In other words, which changes can Spot suffer and still be the same? As Macnamara (among others) shows, answers to these questions are only possible if Spot is taken to be a proper name for an individual, which is an instance of a Sortal universal. The principles of identity supplied by the Sortals are essential to judge the validity of all identity statements. For example, if for an instance of the sortal *Statue* loosing a piece will not alter the identity of the object, the same does not hold for an instance of *Lump of Clay*.

The statement that we can only make identity and quantification statements in relation to a Sortal amounts to one of the best-supported theories in the philosophy of language, namely, that the identity of an individual can only be traced in connection with a Sortal Universal, which provides a *principle of individuation* and *identity* to the particulars it collects [14,16,17,18]. The position advocated in this article affirms an equivalent stance for a theory of conceptual modeling. We defend that among the conceptual modeling counterparts of general terms (classifiers), only constructs that represent substance sortals can provide a principle of identity and individuation for its instances. As a consequence, the following principle can be postulated:

Postulate 1: Every Object in a conceptual model (CM) of the domain must be an instance of a CM-class representing a sortal.

As argued by Kripke [19], a proper name is a rigid designator, i.e. it refers to the same individual in all possible situations, factual or counterfactual. For instance, it refers to the individual Mick Jagger both now (when he is the lead singer of Rolling Stones and 60 years old) and in the past (when he was the boy Mike Philip living in Kent, England). Moreover, it refers to the same individual in counterfactual situations such as the one in which he decided to continue in the London School of Economics and has never pursued a musical career. We would like to say that the boy Mike Philip is identical with the man Mick Jagger that he latter became. However, as pointed out by Wiggins [20] and Perry [21], statements of identity only make sense if both referents are of the same type. Thus, we could not say that a certain Boy is the same Boy as a certain Man since the latter is not a Boy (and vice-versa). However, as Putnam put it, when a man x points to a boy in a picture and says "I am that boy", the pronoun "I" in question is typed not by Man but by a supertype of Man and Boy (namely, Person) which embraces x's entire existence [22]. A generalization of this idea amount to a thesis, proposed by Wiggins, named thesis D [20]: If an individual falls under two sortals in the course of its history there must be exactly one ultimate sortal of which both sortals are specializations. Griffin elaborates Wiggins' thesis D in terms of two correlated principles:

a) The Restriction Principle: if an individual falls under two distinct sortals F and F' in the course of its history then there is at least one sortal of which F and F' are both specializations.

b) The Uniqueness Principle: if an individual falls under two distinct sortals F and F' in the course of its history then there is only one *ultimate sortal* of which F and F' are both specializations. A sortal F is ultimate if there is no other sortal F' distinct from F which F specializes.

It is not the case that two incompatible principles of identity could apply to the same individual x, otherwise x would not be a viable entity (determinate particular) [14]. Imagine an individual x which is an instance of both Statue and Lump of clay. Now, the answer to the question whether loosing a piece will alter the identity of x is inde-terminate since each of the two principles of identity that x obeys imply a different answer. As a consequence, we can say that if two sortals F and F' intersect (i.e. have common individuals in their extension), the principles of identity contained in them must be equivalent. Moreover, F and F' cannot supply a principle of identity for x, since both sortals apply to x only contingently and a principle of identity must be used to identify x all possible worlds. Therefore, there must be a sortal G that supplies the principle of identity carried by F and F'. This proves the restriction principle. The uniqueness of the ultimate sortal G can be argued as follows: (i) G is a sortal, since it supplies a principle of identity for all the things in its extension; (ii) if it restricts a sortal H then, since H cannot supply an incompatible principle of identity, H either is: equivalent to G (i.e. does supply the same principle of identity) and therefore should be ultimate, or does not supply a principle of identity for the particulars in its exten-sion (see text on dispersive classifiers below). This proves the uniqueness principle. The unique ultimate sortal G that supplies the principle of identity for its instances is named a *substance sortal*.

As a consequence of the *uniqueness principle* we define a second postulate:

Postulate 2: An Object in a conceptual model of the domain cannot instantiate more than one CM-Class representing an ultimate Substance Sortal.

In the example above, the sortal Person is the *unique substance sortal* that defines the validity of the claim that Mick Jagger is the same as Mike Philip or, in other words, that Mike Philip persists through changes in height, weight, age, residence, etc., as the same individual. Person can only be the sortal that supports the proper name Mick Jagger in all possible situations because it applies necessarily to the individual re-ferred by the proper name, i.e. instances of Person cannot cease to be so without ceas-ing to exist. As a consequence, the extension of a substance sortal is world invariant. This meta-property of classifiers is named *Modal Constancy* [18] or *rigidity* [23] and is formally stated as follows:

Let W be a non-empty set of possible worlds and let $w \in W$ be a specific world. The extension function $ext_w(G)$ maps a classifier G to the set of its instances in world w. Let ext(G) be an extension function mapping to the set of instances of the classifier G that exist in all possible worlds, such that

1. $ext(G) = \bigcup_{w \in W} ext_w(G)$

and for any classifiers F and G such that F is a specialization of G and, for all $w \in W$

2. $ext_w(F) \subseteq ext_w(G)$

if G is a substance sortal then we have that

3. $ext_w(G) = ext_{w'}(G)$, for any w,w' $\in$ W and consequently,
4. $ext(G) = ext_w(G)$, for all w $\in$ W

Sortals such as Boy and Adult Man in the example above, but also Student, Employee, Caterpillar and Butterfly, Philosopher, Writer, Alive and Deceased, which possibly apply to a continuant during a certain phase of its existence, are named phased-sortal in [20]. As a consequence of the Restriction Principle we have that for every phased-sortal PS that applies to a continuant, there is a substance sortal S of which PS is a specialization.

Contrary to substance sortals, phased-sortals apply to individuals contingently and, thus, do not enjoy modal constancy. For example, for an individual John instance of Student, we can easily imagine John moving in an out of the Student type, while being the same individual, i.e. without loosing his identity. Moreover, for every instance x of Student in a world w, there is another world w' in which x is not an instance of Student. This meta-property of classifiers is named anti-rigid in [23]. Formally,

Let PS be a *phased-sortal* and S be a substance sortal restricted by PS. Let

5. $ext_w(\sim PS) = ext_w(S) / ext_w(PS)$

be the complement of the extension of PS in world w. Then for all worlds $w \in W$, there is a $w' \in W$ such that

6. $ext_w(PS) \cap ext_{w'}(\sim PS) \neq \varnothing$

Putting (2), (4) and (6) together derives another postulate:

Postulate 3: A CM-Class representing a rigid classifier cannot be a subclass a CM-Class representing an anti-rigid classifier.

To see that is the case suppose there is a rigid classifier G which specializes an anti-rigid classifier F. Let {a,b,c,d} and {a,b} be the extension of F and G in world w, respectively. By (6), there is a world w' in which $a \in ext_w(F)$ is in $ext_{w'}(\sim F)$ and thus $a \notin ext_{w'}(F)$. By (4), however, $ext_w(G) = ext_{w'}(G)$ and, by (2), $ext_{w'}(G) \subseteq ext_{w'}(F)$, ergo, $a \in ext_{w'}(F)$, which is a contradiction. We therefore conclude that there cannot be the case that a rigid classifier specializes an anti-rigid one.

If PS is a phased-sortal and S is the substance sortal specialized by PS, there is a specialization condition φ such that x is a PS iff x is a S that satisfies φ [14]. A further clarification on the different types of specialization conditions allows us to distinguish between two different types of phased-sortals which are of great importance to the practice of conceptual modeling, namely, *phases* and *roles*.

Phases (also named dynamic subclasses [13] or states [9]) constitute possible stages in the history of a substance sortal. Examples are: (a) Alive and Deceased: as possible stages of a Person; (b) Catterpillar and Butterfly of a Lepidopteran; (c) Town and Metropolis of a City; (d) Boy, Male Teenager and Adult Male of a Male Person. *Classifiers representing phases constitute a partition of the substance sortal they specialize.* For example, if <Alive, Deceased> is a *phase-partition* of a sustance sortal Person then for every world w, every Person x is either and instance of Alive or of Deceased but not of both. Moreover, if x is an instance of Alive in world *w* then there is world *w'* such that x is not an instance of Alive in *w'*, which in this case, implies that x is an instance of Deceased in *w'*.

Contrary to phases, roles do not necessarily form a partition of substance sortals. Moreover, they differ from phases in terms of the specialization condition φ. For a phase P, φ represents a condition that depends solely on intrinsic properties of P. For instance, one might say that if Mick Jagger is a Living Person then he is a Person who has the property of being alive or, if Spot is a Puppy then it is a Dog who has the property of being less than a year old. For a role R, conversely, φ depends on extrinsic (relational) properties of R. For example, one might say that if John is a Student then John is a Person who is enrolled in some educational institution or that, if Peter is a Customer then Peter is a Person who buys a Product y from a Supplier z. In other words, an entity plays a role in a certain context, demarcated by its relation with other entities. In general, we can state the following: Let R be role that specializes a sortal S (named the *allowed type* for R [9]) and $φ_r$ be a n-ary relation defined between R and the (n-1) universals on which R is *externally dependent* [23]. For instance, $φ_{enrollment} ⊆$ Student × School, $φ_{purchase-from} ⊆$ Customer × Supplier or $φ_{Marriage} ⊆$ Husband × Wife. Moreover, let the domain of a relation in world w (*Dom$_w$*) be defined as follows: $Dom_w(φ_r) = \{x \,|<x,y> ∈ ext_w(φ_r)\}$. Then for all worlds $w ∈ W$ we have that

7. $ext_w(R) ⊆ Dom_w(φ_r)$

Although Frege argued at length that "one cannot count without knowing what to count", in artificial logical languages inspired by him, natural language general terms such as CNs, adjectives and verbs are treated uniformly as predicates. For instance, if we want to represent the sentence "there are tall men", in the fregean approach of classical logic we would write $∃x (Man(x) ∧ Tall(x))$. This reading puts the count noun Man (which denotes a Sortal) on an equal logical footing with the predicate Tall. Moreover, in this formula, the variable x is interpreted into a "supposedly" universal kind Thing. So, the natural language reading of the formula should be "there are things which have the property of being a man and the property of being tall". Since, by postulate 1, all individuals must be instances of a substance sortal we must conclude that Thing is a unique universal ultimate sortal which is able to supply a principle of identity for all elements that we consider in our universe of discourse. Moreover, by postulate 2, this principle of identity must be unique. Can that be the case?

In [25], Hirsch argues that concepts such as Thing, (Entity, Element, among others) are *dispersive*, i.e. they cover many concepts with different principles of identity. For instance, in the extension of Thing we might encounter an individuals x which is a cow and an individual y which is a watch. Since the principles of identity for Cows and Watches are not the same we conclude that Thing cannot supply a principle of identity for its instances. Otherwise, x and y would obey incompatible principles of identity and, thus, would not be determinate individuals. Therefore, as defended in [14,17,18,25], dispersive concepts do not denote sortals (despite the fact that they are considered CNs in natural languages) and *therefore cannot have direct instances*. More than that, since a principle of identity supplied by a substance sortal G is inherited by all classifiers that specialize G or, to put in another way, all subtypes of G carry the principle of identity supplied by G. Thus, all subclasses of a sortal are themselves sortals, ergo,

Postulate 4: A CM-Class representing a dispersive universal cannot be a subclass of a CM-Class representing a Sortal.

3   An Ontologically Well-Founded Profile for UML Class Diagrams

The Unified Modeling Language (UML) has built-in extension mechanisms that allow one to modify the language elements to suite certain modeling needs. Extensions to the language can be performed in two different ways: (i) by specializing the UML metamodel (layer 2) to add new semantics to UML modeling elements; (ii) by changing the MOF model (layer 3) to add new elements to the UML metamodel. The former mechanism is named *lightweight extension* and the latter *heavyweight extension*. A coherent set of such extensions, defined accordingly to a specific purpose or domain, constitutes a *UML profile* [26].

In this section we propose *lightweight extension* to UML that represents finer-grained distinctions between different types of classifiers. The proposed *profile* contains a set of *stereotyped* classes (specializations of the meta-construct class) that support the design of ontologically well-founded conceptual models according to the theory proposed in section 2.

It is important to emphasize that the particular classes chosen to exemplify each of the proposed categories are used for illustration purposes only. For example, when stereotyping class *Person* as a *Kind* we are not advocating that Person should be in general considered as a kind in conceptual modeling. Conversely, the intention is to make explicit the consequences of this modeling choice. The choice itself, nonetheless, is always left to the model designer.

3.1   Kinds and Subkinds

A UML class stereotyped as a « kind » represents a *substance sortal* that *supplies* a principle of identity for its instances. Kinds can be specialized in other *rigid* sybtypes that inherit their supplied principle of identity named subkinds. For instance, if we take Person to be a kind then some of its subkinds could be Man and Woman. In general, the stereotype « subkind » can be omitted in conceptual models without loss of clarity.

Every object in a conceptual model using this profile must be an instance of a Kind, directly or indirectly (postulate 1). Moreover, it cannot be an instance of more than one ultimate Kind (postulate 2). Figure 1-a shows an excerpt of a conceptual model that violates the second postulate (extracted from the CYC[1]). Here, we assume that the kinds *Social Being* and *Group* supply different principles of identity. Moreover, it is considered that *Group* supplies an extensional principle of identity, i.e. two groups are the same iff they have the same members. This is generally incompatible with a principle supplied by *Social Being*: we can change the members of a company, football team or music band and still have the same social being. Moreover, the same group can form different social beings with different purposes. One should notice that if "The Beatles" would be an instance of both Kinds, it would not be a determinate object (an answer to the question whether it was still the same thing when Ringo Star replaced Pete Best, is both affirmative and negative!). Figure 1-b shows a version of the model of fig.1-a that obeys the constraints of this profile.

---

[1]   http://www.opencyc.org/

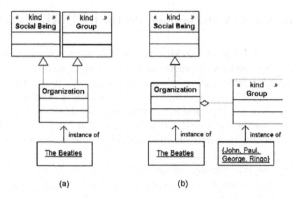

Fig. 1. (a) Example of an instance with conflicting principles of identity; (b) an ontologically correct version of the same model

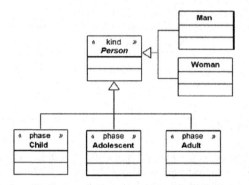

Fig. 2. Two partitions of the same kind: a subkind-partition and a phase-partition

By postulate 3 (sec.2), rigid classes cannot be supertyped by anti-rigid ones. Therefore, kinds cannot appear in conceptual models as subtypes of phases, roles (3.3), and role mixins (3.4).

3.2 Phases

UML classes stereotyped as « phase » represent the phased-sortals *phase*. Figure 2 depicts an example with the kind Person, its subkinds Man and Woman and the phases Child, Adolescent and Adult. The classes connected to one single hollow arrowhead symbol in UML (concrete syntax for the subtyping relation) define a generalization set [27]. A generalization set constitutes a partition of the class pointed by the symbol (superclass). A class with an italicized name is an abstract class, i.e. a class that cannot have direct instances.

3.3 Roles

UML classes stereotyped as « role » represent the phased-sortals *role*. Roles and Phases are anti-rigid universals and cannot appear in a conceptual model as a superclass of a Kind (postulate 3). Sometimes subtyping is wrongly used in conceptual modeling to represent alternative *allowed types* that can fulfill a role. For instance, in figure 3-a, the intention of the model is to represent that customers are either persons or organizations. Another example is shown in figure 3-b. However, in general being a customer is assumed to be a contingent property of person, i.e. there possible worlds in which a Person is not a customer but still the same person. Likewise, a participant can stop participating in a Forum without ceasing to exist. Figure 3-b contains yet another conceptual problem. In this model, a participant can take part in zero-to-many forums. It is common in Database and Object-Oriented Design to use a minimum cardinality equal to zero to express that in certain state of the system, for example, an object of type Participant is not related to any object of type Forum. However, from a conceptual viewpoint, the involvement in this relation is part of definition of the role type. In this example, the association *participation* is a specialization condition (sec.2), which is part of the content of the concept Participant, i.e. a *Participant* is a *Person* or *SIG* that takes part in a *Forum*. As a consequence of formula (7)-section 2, the following constraint must hold for classes stereotyped as « role »:

Let X be a class stereotyped as « role » and r be an association representing X's restriction condition. Then the minimum cardinality of X.r must be at least 1 (#X.r ≥1)

In section 5, in discussing some related work w.r.t. role modeling, we present a design pattern that can be used to produce ontologically correct versions for the models of figure 3-a and 3-b.

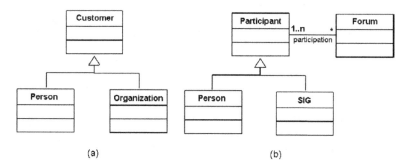

Fig. 3. (a left) and (b) Problems on modeling of roles and their *allowed types*; (b) mistaken cardinality specification for roles

3.4 Mixins

Mixins represent dispersive universals and are perceived to be of great importance in structuring conceptual models [28,29,30]. They can represent top-types such as Thing, Entity, Element (discussed in section 2) but also concepts such as *RationalEntity*, which represent an abstraction of properties that are common to different classes (fig4-a). In this case, the mixin *RationalEntity* can be judged to represent an essential property that is common to all its instances and it is itself a rigid class. We use the stereotype «category» to represent a rigid mixin that subsumes different kinds.

In contrast, some mixins are anti-rigid and represent abstractions of common properties of roles. These classes are stereotyped as «roleMixin» and represent dependent anti-rigid non-sortals. Examples of role mixins include formal roles such as *whole* and *part* and *initiatior* and *responder*. Further examples are discussed in the design pattern proposed in section 5.

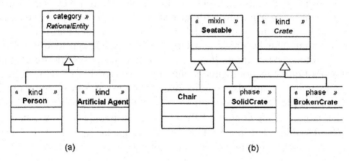

Fig. 4. (a left) Examples of categories and (b) semi-rigid mixins

Moreover, some mixins represent properties which are essential to some of its instances and accidental to others. In [23], this meta-property is named semi-rigidity (as opposed to anti-rigidity). An example is the mixin *Seatable* (fig4-b), which represents a property that can be considered essential to the kinds Chair and Stool but accidental to Crate, Paper Box or Rock. We use the stereotype « mixin » (without further qualification) to represent semi-rigid non-sortals.

Finally, by postulate 4, we have that mixins cannot appear in a conceptual model as subclasses of kinds, phases or roles. Moreover, since they cannot have direct instances, a mixin must always be depicted as an abstract class in a UML conceptual model.

Table 1 below summarizes the profile proposed in this section.

Table 1. Summary of proposed profile for different types of classifiers

Stereotype	Constraints
« kind »	supertype is **not** a member of {« subkind », « phase », « role », « roleMixin »}
« subkind »	supertype is **not** a member of {« phase », « role », « roleMixin »}
« phase »	Always defined as part of partition.
« role »	Let X be a class stereotyped as « role » and r be an association representing X's restriction condition. Then, $\#X.r \geq 1$
« category »	supertype is **not** a member of {« kind », « subkind », « phase », « role », « roleMixin »}
«roleMixin»	supertype is **not** a member of {« kind », « subkind », « phase », « role »}. Let X be a class stereotyped as « roleMixin » and r be an association representing X's restriction condition. Then, $\#X.r \geq 1$
« mixin »	supertype is **not** a member of {« kind », « subkind », « phase », « role », « roleMixin »}

4   A Design Pattern for Modeling Roles

In figure 3-a, the role *Customer* is defined as a supertype of *Person* and *Organization*. As previously mentioned, this modeling choice violates postulate 3 and produces an ontologically incorrect conceptual model. Firstly, not all persons are customers, i.e. it is not the case that the extension of *Person* is necessarily included in the extension of *Customer* (formula 2, sec.2). Moreover, an instance of *Person* is not necessarily a *Customer*. Both arguments are also valid for *Organization*.

In a series of papers [10,11,12], Steimann discusses the difficulties in specifying admissible types for Roles that can be filled by instances of disjoint types. As a conclusion, the author claims that the solution to this problem lies in the separation of role and type hierarchies which leads to a radical revision of the UML meta-model (a heavyweight extension).

In the remaining of this section we intend to show that this claim is not warranted. Moreover, we propose a *design pattern* based on the profile introduced in section 3 that can be used as an ontologically correct solution to this recurrent problem. Finally, this solution has a smaller impact to UML than the one proposed by the author, since it does not demand heavyweight extensions to the language.

In the example above, Customer has in its extension individuals that belong to different kinds and, thus, that obey different principles of identity. Customer is hence a dispersive type (a non-sortal) and, by definition, cannot supply a principle of identity for its instances. Since an (determinate) individual must obey one and only one principle of identity, every instance of Customer must be an instance of one of its subtypes (forming a partition) that carry that principle of identity. For example, we can define the sortals PrivateCustomer and CorporateCustomer as subtypes of Customer. These sortals, in turn, carry the (incompatible) principles of identity supplied by the kinds Person and Organization, respectively. In sum, if x is a Customer (abstract class) then x must be an instance of exactly one of its subtypes (e.g., PrivateCustomer) that carries the principle of identity supplied by an appropriate substance sortal (e.g., Person). Figure 5 shows how this solution can be incorporated in a conceptual modeling design pattern. In this picture the abstract class A is the role mixin that covers different role types (e.g., Customer, Participant). Classes B and C are the disjoint subclasses of A that can have direct instances, representing the sortal roles that carry the principles of identity that govern the individuals that fall in their extension. Classes D and E are the ultimate substance sortals (kinds) that supply the principles of identity carried by B and C, respectively. The association r represents the common specialization condition of B and C, which is represented in A. Finally, class F represents a type that A is *externally dependent* on.

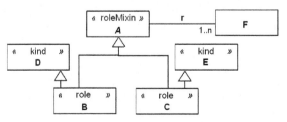

Fig. 5. A design pattern for the problem of specifying roles with multiple disjoint allowed types

An application of this pattern is illustrated in figure 6 in which it is used to produce ontologically correct versions of the models presented in figures 3-a and 3-b, respectively. In both cases, the entity the role mixin depends on, and the association representing the specialization condition are omitted for the sake of brevity.

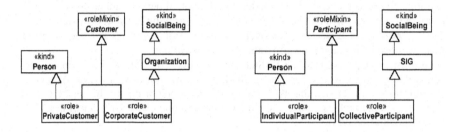

Fig. 6. Ontologically correct versions of the models of fig. 3-a and fig. 3-b obtained by the application of the Design Pattern

5   Final Considerations

The development of a well-grounded, axiomatized upper level ontology is an important step towards the definition of real-world semantics for conceptual modeling diagrammatic languages. In this paper, we use a philosophically and psychologically well-founded theory of universals to address the problem of classifiers in conceptual modeling.

The work presented in section 2 has been strongly influenced by the pioneering work of the OntoClean methodology, which proposes a number of guidelines to evaluate the conceptual correctness of generalization relationships [23,24]. Another key influence is the series of psychological claims proposed by cognitive psychologist John Macnamara in [17]. Mcnamara defends that some universals are conceptually more salient and psychologically more privileged than others and that there is a logic underlying the fact that we can understand certain propositions. A position analogous to the one defended by Chomsky, i.e., that there is a close fit between the mind's linguistic properties and properties of natural languages and, that natural languages have the properties they do because they can be recognized and manipulated by infants without the meta-linguistic support, which is available to second-language learners.

Still in section 2, we have sketched a formalization of the categories proposed by using extension sets indexed by worlds. The idea was to purposely avoid a modal logic approach with unrestricted quantification. In a subsequent article, we shall present the semantics of the proposed categories in a logic of sortals (modal logic with quantification restricted to sortal universals) in the spirit of Gupta's logic of Common Nouns [20] or Montague's systems as presented in [16].

In section 3, this theory is used in the definition of a UML profile for Ontology Representation and Conceptual Modeling. The profile comprises of: (i) a set of stereotypes representing distinctions on types of classifiers proposed by the theory (e.g., Kind, Role, Phase, Category, Mixin); (ii) Constraints on the possible relations to be established between these elements, representing the postulates of the theory. By using this profile, we were able to propose a design pattern to target a recurrent problem in *role* modeling discussed in the literature. We believe that these results contribute to the task of defining sound *engineering* tools and principles for the practice of conceptual modeling. Nevertheless, the profile should not be regarded as a final proposal. In particular, we recognize that further discussion and elaboration on the issue of role modeling is required, a topic that shall be addressed in a future paper.

Acknowledgements

This work has been supported by the Telematica Instituut in the context of the ArCo project. Part of the work has been developed during an extended visit of the first author to ISTC/LOA (Trento, Italy) and in collaboration with the OntoMed research group (Leipzig, Germany). We would like to thank Heinrich Herre, Claudio Masolo, Laure Vieu, Alessandro Oltramari, Stefano Borgo, Emanuele Botazzi, Roberta Ferrario and Luis Ferreira Pires for fruitful discussions and for providing valuable input to the issues of this article.

References

1. Guizzardi, G., Herre, H., Wagner G.: Towards Ontological Foundations for UML Conceptual Models. In Proc. of 1st Intl. Conf. on Ontologies, Databases and Applications of Semantics (ODBASE 2002), Lecture Notes in Computer Science, Springer-Verlag, Berlin, (2002)
2. Guizzardi, G., Herre, H., Wagner G.: On the General Ontological Foundations of Conceptual Modeling. In Proc. of 21st Intl. Conf. on Conceptual Modeling (ER 2002). Springer-Verlag, Berlin, Lecture Notes in Computer Science (2002)
3. Guizzardi, G., Wagner G.: Using Formal Ontologies to define Real-World Semantics for UML Conceptual Models. In 1st Workshop on Application of Ontologies to Biology, European Media Laboratory, Heidelberg, Germany (2002)
4. Degen, W., Heller B., Herre H., Smith, B.: GOL: Towards an axiomatized upper level ontology. In B. Smith and N. Guarino (eds.), Proc. of 2nd Intl. Conf. of Formal Ontologies and Information Systems (FOIS'01), Ogunquit, Maine, USA, October 2001. ACM Press (2001)
5. Heller, B., Herre, H.: Formal Ontology and Principles of GOL. Onto-Med Report No. 1/2003. Research Group Ontologies in Medicine, Univ. of Leipzig (2003)
6. Cranefield, S., Purvis M.: UML as an ontology modelling language. In Proc. of the Workshop on Intelligent Information Integration, 16th Intl. Joint Conf. on Artificial Intelligence (IJCAI 1999), Germany, Univ. of Karlsruhe (1999) 46-53
7. Evans A., France R., Lano K., Rumpe B.: Developing the UML as a formal modelling notation. In P.-A. Muller and J. Bezivin (eds.), Proc. of UML'98 Intl. Workshop, Mulhouse, France, June 3 -4, 1998, ESSAIM, Mulhouse, France (1998) 297-307
8. Evermann, J. and Wand, Y.: Towards ontologically based semantics for UML constructs. In H. Kunii, S. Jajodia, and A. Solvberg (eds.), Proc. of 20th Intl. Conf. on Conceptual Modeling (ER 2001), Lecture Notes in Computer Science, Springer (2001).
9. Odell, J., Bock, C.: A More Complete Model of Relations and their Implications: Roles. Journal of OO Programming, May, 1998, 51–54

10. Steimann, F.: On the representation of roles in object-oriented and conceptual modeling. Data & Knowledge Engineering 35:1 (2000) 83–106
11. Steimann, F.: Role = Interface: a merger of concepts. Journal of Object-Oriented Programming 14:4 (2001) 23–32
12. Steimann, F.: A radical revision of UML's role concept. In: A Evans, S Kent, B Selic (eds.), UML 2000 Proc. of the 3rd Intl. Conf., Springer (2000) 194–209
13. Wieringa, R.J. de Jonge, W., Spruit, P.A.: Using dynamic classes and role classes to model object migration. Theory and Practice of Object Systems, 1(1) (1995) 61-83
14. Van Leeuwen, J.: Individuals and sortal concepts : an essay in logical descriptive metaphysics, PhD Thesis, Univ. of Amsterdam (1991)
15. Strawson, P. F.: Individuals. An Essay in Descriptive Metaphysics. London and New York: Routledge (1959)
16. McNamara, J. A Border: Dispute, the Place of Logic in Psychology. Cambridge, M.I.T. (1986)
17. McNamara, J.: Logic and Cognition. In McNamara, J.; Reyes, G. (eds.), The Logical Foundations of Cognition, Vancouver Studies in Cognitive Science, Vol. 4 (1994)
18. Gupta, A.: The Logic of Common Nouns: an investigation in quantified modal logic. Yale University Press, New Haven (1980)
19. Kripke, S.: Naming and Necessity. Harvard University Press (1982)
20. Wiggins, D.: Sameness and Substance Renewed. Cambridge University Press (2001).
21. Perry, J.: The same F. Philosophical Review (1970)
22. Putnam H.: Logic and Psychology. In McNamara, J.; Reyes, G. (eds.), The Logical Foundations of Cognition,Vancouver Studies in Cognitive Science, Vol 4 (1994).
23. Welty, C., Guarino, N.: Supporting Ontological Analysis of Taxonomic Relationships. Data and Knowledge Engineering, 39(1), (2001) 51-74
24. Guarino, N.; Welty, C.: Evaluating Ontological Decisions with OntoClean. Communications of the ACM, 45(2) (2002)
25. Hirsch, E.: The Concept of Identity. Oxford University Press, New York, Oxford (1982).
26. Object Management Group: UML 2.0 Infrastructure Specification, Doc.# ptc/03-09-15, Sep. 2003
27. Object Management Group: UML 2.0 Superstructure Specification, Doc.# ptc/03-08-02, Aug. 2003
28. Booch, G., Rumbaugh, J., Jacobson, I.: The Unified Modeling Language User Guide. Addison-Wesley (1998)
29. Booch, G.: Object-Oriented Analysis and Design. Benjamin-Cummings (1994)
30. Hendler, J.: Enhancements for Multiple Inheritance. SIGPLAN Notices, vol.21 (10) (1986) 100-100

Measuring Expressiveness in Conceptual Modeling

Susanne Patig

Otto-von-Guericke-University of Magdeburg, PO Box 4120
D-39016 Magdeburg, Germany
susanne.patig@iti.cs.uni-magdeburg.de

Abstract. Expressiveness refers to things said in a description or sayable in a description language. It contributes to the quality of conceptual schemas and justifies the development of new modeling languages. Different notions of expressiveness exist, originating from different fields of computer science. In this paper, a framework is developed that defines different types of expressiveness, integrating the other notions. The framework contains a cardinal measure to assess the expressiveness of both descriptions and description languages.

1 Introduction: The Importance of Expressiveness

Conceptual modeling means describing reality with the help of some *description language* (*modeling language*) to create a more or less formalized *description* (*conceptual model* or *schema*). Typically, this process is characterized by offering many degrees of freedom and requiring a large number of subjective decisions. First of all, depending on the purpose of conceptual modeling, a description language must be chosen. In addition to the purpose, this choice is influenced by the preferences of the modeler. Furthermore, even if the same description language is used to model a given part of reality for the same purpose, often, alternative descriptions can be created, reflecting, for instance, subjectivity in recognizing reality or in applying the description language. Although each of the alternative descriptions may be correct, it may possess a different quality, that can influence information system design and implementation.

One of the properties that contribute to the quality of a description is expressiveness [2]. As a provisional definition, *expressiveness* (synonyms: modeling power, expressive power) refers to things said in a description or sayable in a description language. It is widely assumed that the more expressive a description language is, the more expressive its descriptions will be. Altogether, a description language must be "sufficiently expressive" for a given purpose, that is, a description language that cannot express all things required should not be chosen [20].

Apart from being an aspect of quality, expressiveness becomes important in transforming descriptions ([5], [18]). A transformation between two descriptions should preserve their expressiveness, i.e., the transformed description should be as expressive as the original one. Finally, "missing expressiveness" is often the reason to modify existing description languages [25].

In spite of its importance, the problem of expressiveness in conceptual modeling has hardly been addressed ([10], [11], [28]). Furthermore, different notions of expres-

A. Persson and J. Stirna (Eds.): CAiSE 2004, LNCS 3084, pp. 127–141, 2004.

siveness exist, originating from different fields of computer science (see section 2). It is the aim of this paper to develop a general framework that gives an explicit characterization of expressiveness and contains other notions of expressiveness as special cases (see section 3). Moreover, we propose a cardinal measure of expressiveness that is applicable when other approaches fail (see section 3). The paper concludes by applying the framework to evaluate the expressiveness of descriptions and description languages within entity-relationship modeling (see section 4).

2   Previous Research:
Expressiveness – Meaning and Measurement

Many authors assume an "intuitive" notion of expressiveness, i.e., they use the term without a definition. Their usage of the term implies that an evaluation of expressiveness is always based on some reference. Three types of *references* can be identified:

- **[Reference R1]** Modeling a *universe of discourse (UoD)* always serves a certain purpose. In conceptual modeling, the purpose either requires one to represent the UoD as completely as possible or to extract special aspects from it, e.g. dimensions and facts in multidimensional data modeling. Expressiveness is greatest when it is possible to say all the things necessary to meet a particular purpose [17], [25]. Hence, the *purpose of conceptual modeling* serves as reference to evaluate expressiveness.

- **[Reference R2]** In the field of database query languages [7] or constraint programming languages [15] expressiveness is evaluated with reference to the *set of all things sayable*, e.g., the set of all queries that can be formulated. The more that can be said absolutely, the greater expressiveness is.

- **[Reference R3]** Expressiveness is evaluated with reference to the *things said elsewhere*, i.e., in another description [5] or description language. This type of reference is employed to assess the expressiveness of planning formalisms [23], logics [18] or database schemas [19], [21]. Equivalent expressiveness is given if all the things said elsewhere can be formulated. *Schema equivalence*, which is discussed in the context of database design, establishes a special case of equivalent expressiveness.

Measuring expressiveness is typically based on sets or on mappings. Using *sets*, a description language is at least as expressive as another one:

- **[Approach S1]** if the set of its symbols contains the symbols of the other description language (implicit [25]) or

- **[Approach S2]** if the statements representable by the description language contain all the statements that can be formulated by the other one ([18], [26])

as a proper subset. In order to form sets that share elements, the symbols or statements must be translated into a common description language.

To measure expressiveness by *mappings*, every element of a certain set is assigned one and only one element of another set. In detail, mappings are established between:

- **[Approach M1]** a philosophical ontology and the symbols of a description language ([10], [11]),

- **[Approach M2]** the sets of symbols belonging to different description languages [17],

- **[Approach M3]** the sets of statements of different descriptions [1], [3], [23], [21], [19].

If a mapping is found the sets are at least equally expressive. Mappings directly translate the elements of a set into the elements of the other one.

All approaches to measure expressiveness are confronted with the purely *syntactic part* of a (description) language, which consists of symbols and their legitimate connections, and the *semantic part*, which relates syntactic expressions to structures beyond language. Semantics describes the "meaning" of syntactic expressions. By *statement* we mean a syntactic expression and its meaning.

Usually in evaluating expressiveness, syntactically different statements must be compared. Their equivalent expressiveness can be shown by syntactic transformations (schema transformation, e.g. [21],[13]). Even if such transformations can be found it must be ensured that the meaning of the statements is preserved, hence, evaluating expressiveness relates to semantics. The approaches S1, M1 and M2 to do not look at semantics in a formalized way, whereas the approaches S2 and M3 mostly use ideas from logic.

Mathematical logic provides us with means to deal with the duality of syntax and semantics. Using logics as description languages, different *descriptions*, i.e., different sets of logical formulas, are equally expressive if they have the same (formal) model [1], [21]. A *model* denotes the formal semantics of a logical description, i.e., an assignment of values to variables (*interpretation*) such that all formulas are true.

A model can be understood as a set of elements from a UoD whose properties satisfy the formulas of the logical description. From the *extensional point of view*, two models are equal if they comprise the same elements. Using first-order predicate logic to give an example, two descriptions composed of the atomic formulas `smallest_even_number(X)` and `smallest_prime_number(Y)` respectively, have the same model consisting in the natural number two (*example 1*). So, it is not possible to discriminate between both descriptions by extension. However, in line with the *intensional point of view*, the two descriptions are distinguishable by the separate characteristics they refer to [22].

We start building our framework for evaluating expressiveness from the extensional point of view. But, as example 1 indicates, the extensional point of view does not take into consideration special characteristics that must be described. Therefore, the framework also includes a cardinal measure that assesses expressiveness from the intensional point of view.

3   A Framework for Evaluating Expressiveness

The proposed framework is applicable to evaluate the expressiveness of either descriptions or description languages. To derive the framework, we assume that the intensional semantics of the descriptions, or of the symbols of the description languages, is representable by sets of logical formulas, for which (formal) models can be determined.

For the sake of simplicity, we use the term *description* in the following to refer to both descriptions and description languages. Hence, D_1 and D_2 denote separate descriptions, whose expressiveness is to be compared. The (sets of) models of the descriptions are represented by $M(D_1)$ and $M(D_2)$, respectively. Throughout this work we concentrate on minimal models. An interpretation I is called a *minimal model* of a description D if it is a model of D and if no other interpretation I' exists such that I' $\subset$ I and I' is a model of D as well [4]. The notion of minimal models is equivalent to the closed world assumption [24] because it declares that all relevant statements are contained in the (minimal) model.

Since models correspond to sets of elements, we can compare the expressiveness of different descriptions from the extensional point of view by analyzing the relationship between these sets. Any two sets are either equal or disjoint, or one set is a proper subset of the other one or they intersect. We use these types of relationships to define expressiveness from the extensional point of view (see table 1):

- **[Definition DF1]** Two descriptions D_1 and D_2 are *extensionally equally expressive* if every model of D_1 is also a model of D_2 and vice versa: $M(D_1) = M(D_2)$. This corresponds to the theoretical foundation of approach M3.

- **[Definition DF2]** A description D_1 is *extensionally more expressive* than a description D_2 *in the sense of generality* if all models of D_1 are proper supersets of the models of D_2: $M(D_1) \supset M(D_2)$. So, *generality* means an increase of extension. In other words, a larger number of elements satisfy all formulas of the description. Since only minimal models are considered, adding new formulas to descriptions is a necessary, but not a sufficient, condition for increasing expressiveness in the sense of generality. This point is addressed later on.

- **[Definition DF3]** A description D_1 is *extensionally more expressive* than a description D_2 *in the sense of precision* if all models of D_1 form proper subsets of the models of D_2: $M(D_1) \subset M(D_2)$. Hence, *precision* corresponds to a decrease in extension, i.e., there exists a smaller number of elements such that all formulas of the description have value "true". As regards precision, adding new formulas to descriptions is neither necessary nor sufficient for increasing expressiveness.

In the following cases measuring expressiveness from the extensional point of view is impossible:

- **[Definition DF4]** Two descriptions D_1 and D_2 are *comparable* concerning expressiveness if their models intersect: $M(D_1) \cap M(D_2) \neq \emptyset$.

- **[Definition DF5]** If all models of two descriptions D_1 and D_2 are disjoint, i.e., $M(D_1) \cap M(D_2) = \emptyset$, their expressiveness *cannot be compared*, since the statements of the descriptions refer to different sets of elements.

If semantics is considered, the approaches presented in section 2 mainly concentrate on equivalent expressiveness. Superior expressiveness is only proven if a description (language) subsumes another description (language) [26], [1], [3], [21]. Neither approach distinguishes between generality and precision.

The above definitions directly support two types of references for evaluating expressiveness: Definition DF1 complies with reference R3, i.e., the things said elsewhere, whereas definitions DF2 and DF3 are compatible with reference R2, which relates greater expressiveness to the possibility of saying more. To this point, reference R1, the purpose of conceptual modeling, has not been integrated into the framework.

The framework for evaluating expressiveness presented so far can be applied independent of how the models are determined. But, under certain circumstances, determining models can be computationally hard or even impossible [22]. Furthermore, focusing all attention on the models of descriptions neglects the intensional point of view and does not yield expressiveness results in case of intersecting models.

To combine the extensional and the intensional point of view within our framework (see table 1) and to include the purpose of modeling, we define **[Definition DF6]** that the *expressiveness* is greater the more that can be said for a certain purpose. The purpose of conceptual modeling is formalized with the help of a reference description RD. This allows one to derive a measure E(RD, CD) to evaluate the expressiveness of a description CD (*description of comparison*) relative to the reference description.

By *reference description* we mean a set of statements that depend on the purpose of conceptual modeling and are representable by logical formulas. The *extension* of the reference description consists of the set of elements that are a model of every formula. To comply with the extensional definitions of expressiveness given above, the reference description must satisfy the following *requirements*:

- **[Requirement RQ1]** A *first-order predicate logic* [22] is used because of the comprehensible definition of its models. In order to simplify the specification, we agree on the following:

  - The set of elements is decomposed into several distinct domains, called *sorts,* to distinguish variables by type. For each sort, we assume that we have a *binary predicate "=" for equality*, which is interpreted as equality in all models.

  - All variables are universally quantified.

  - Any variables that are not explicitly equal must be distinct.

- **[Requirement RQ2]** The set of formulas must be *consistent*, since otherwise the reference description does not posses a model [22].

- **[Requirement RQ3]** The formulas that form the reference description must be *independent* of each other, i.e., each formula is neither synonymous with, nor a logical consequence of, other formulas of the reference description. *Synonymy* is given if formulas have the same intension; this is decided by the purpose of conceptual modeling. To recall example 1 from section 2, the formulas `smallest_even_number(X)` and `smallest_prime_number(Y)` are not synonymous since the differ in intension, whereas `smallest_prime_number(Y)` and `smallest_number_above_one_and_divisible_by_one_and_itself(Z)` are. Logical consequence is defined in the usual sense [22]. Independence is required by the measure E(RD, CD) proposed. Furthermore, adding dependent formulas to a reference description changes neither its extension nor its intension and hence does not affect expressiveness. Adding an independent formula to a reference description D_1 (see table 2) alternatively:

- increases the extension of the reference description, which is equivalent to increasing expressiveness in the sense of generality from the extensional point of view (definition DF2 and description D_2, table 2),

- decreases its extension, leading to an increasing expressiveness in the sense of precision (definition DF3 and description D_3, table 2),

- leaves its extension unchanged, as in the case in example 1 from section 2.

Table 1. Extensional expressiveness – an example

	Reference Description		
	D_1	**D_2**	**D_3**
Logical Formulas	green(X)	green(X) has_thorns(Y)	green(X) has_thorns(Y) = (X, Y)
M(D_i) Real-World Semantics	all green individuals	all green individuals, all thorny individuals, all individuals that are both thorny and green	all individuals that are both thorny and green
Extensional Expressiveness		$M(D_1) \subset M(D_2)$	$M(D_1) \supset M(D_3)$
		more expressive than D_1 in the sense of	
		generality	precision

To summarize, requiring that the reference description must consist of independent formulas results in *minimal reference descriptions* for a given purpose, i.e., eliminating any of its formulas changes the intension of the reference description and thus affects the purpose.

- **[Requirement RQ4]** The reference description must consist of *literals*, i.e., atomic formulas or their negation [22]. *Atomic formulas* are constructed by combining predicate symbols and terms. Constant symbols, variable symbols or function symbols that are applied to terms constitute *terms* [22]. Literals are required because each literal represents one and only one *intension* (a characteristic or a relationship) and an extension, so its contribution to expressiveness can be easily identified. In contrast, the complex formula green(X) ∧ cactus(X) ⇒ has_ thorns(X) combines different intensions, which would be difficult to measure if only some characteristics were contained in the description whose expressiveness is evaluated.

After the reference description RD has been created, it can be compared with other descriptions CD to evaluate their expressiveness. For the description CD it must be indicated (based on the intension) whether a certain statement of the reference description is contained (1) or not (0). Table 3 summarizes the possible combinations of occurring statements; their quantities are denoted by s, t, u and v. Because minimal models are considered, statements must be contained in the reference description or in the description to be compared ($v = 0$, $s + t + u > 0$).

Table 2. Comparing descriptions

		Reference Description RD		Sum
		statement contained	statement not contained	
Description of Comparison CD	statement contained	s	t	s + t
	statement not contained	u	v = 0	u
Sum		s + u	t	s + t + u

The *cardinal measure E(RD, CD)* determines the degree of expressiveness depending on the similarity between the reference description RD and the description CD to be compared. It is derived from measuring similarity between binary vectors, e.g., by means of the Tanimoto, the Simple Matching or the Rassel-Rao coefficient [16]. Taking into account $v = 0$, these coefficients are calculated as follows:

$$E(RD, CD) = \frac{s}{s + t + u} \tag{1}$$

Expressiveness E(RD, CD) can take values between zero and one (maximum expressiveness). The expressiveness of the description that constitutes the reference description (i.e., E(RD, RD)) always amounts to one.

The measure E(RD, CD) reflects expressiveness from the intensional point of view without being in contradiction with the extensional point of view: If conceptual modeling aims at generality, then the description that is extensionally the most expressive in the sense of generality must be chosen as reference description. In that case, the reference description contains *all* statements ($t = 0$), some might be missing in the description CD ($u \geq 0$).

Furthermore, it is possible to bias E(RD, CD) towards extensional expressiveness in the sense of precision by choosing the extensionally most precise description as reference description. Because of the extensional definition of precision (definition DF3), some statements might be lacking in the reference description ($t \geq 0$). Although this seems to be somewhat counter-intuitive, remember that we require of the reference description to be minimal for a given purpose. If we want to describe only all green individuals (description D_1, table 2), any description that says more than this is less expressive, because it either weakens this statement by including more individuals than required for the purpose (description D_2 in table 2) or makes it stronger by excluding individuals that are needed for the purpose (description D_3 in table 2).

If the extensional definition of expressiveness is not appropriate because the models of two descriptions intersect (definition DF4), the intensional measure E(RD, CD) can be applied, choosing one of the descriptions as reference description. Alternatively, a special reference description can be created that contains all statements required for a certain purpose ($t = 0$). A special reference description is also able to reveal differences in the intensional expressiveness of descriptions that are extensionally equally expressive (definition DF1).

Finally, by using a special reference description, the other approaches to measure expressiveness can be integrated into our framework. In this case, the statements of the reference description refer either to a philosophical ontology (approach M1) or to the symbols of a description language (approaches S1, M2). The requirements a reference description must satisfy will help to identify unnecessary or redundant symbols ("syntactic sugar", see section 4). Furthermore, our framework provides these approaches with a semantic foundation, which has been missing so far. Table 1 summarizes the proposed framework for measuring expressiveness.

Table 3. A framework for evaluating expressiveness

The expressiveness of two descriptions D_1 and D_2 is				
equal	**greater** in the sense of		**comparable**	**not comparable**
	generality	**precision**		
	in favor of D_1			
EX $M(D_1) = M(D_2)$	$M(D_1) \supset M(D_2)$	$M(D_1) \subset M(D_2)$	$M(D_1) \cap M(D_2) \neq \varnothing$	$M(D_1) \cap M(D_2) = \varnothing$
IN	$E(RD, CD) = \dfrac{s}{s+t+u}$ $s+t+u > 0$			—
	$RD = $ purpose $t = 0, u \geq 0$	$RD = D_1$ $t = 0, u \geq 0$	$RD = D_1$ $t \geq 0, u \geq 0$	$RD = D_1$ or $RD = D_2$ $t > 0, u > 0$ alternatively: $RD = $ purpose $t = 0, u \geq 0$	

Abbreviations: D: description, M: model, EX: extensional, IN: intensional

4   Applying the Framework to Measure Expressiveness

The first example analyzes the expressiveness of different descriptions. The descriptions are given as *entity-relationship (ER)* diagrams, see table 4. Following the Chen notation [8], the ER diagram D_1 in table 4 does not show whether customers without orders may exist. On the contrary, in the ER diagrams D_2 to D_5 dotted lines indicate that customers without orders or orders without customers are allowed [12]. Taking ER diagram D_2 as an example, every order *must* be assigned *one and only* one customer, whereas each customer *may* place *several* orders.

Within our framework, evaluating expressiveness either from the extensional point of view or by applying the measure $E(RD, CD)$ is based on consistent sets of statements (table 4). Unlike in [13], we do not aim at finding transformations between the sets of statements assigned to each ER diagram. Rather, we are in line with [6], which analyze similarities between descriptors associated with schemas. In contrast to both approaches we do not derive the statements automatically from the descriptions[1] but create them manually so that they observe the requirements of the reference description.

---

[1]   This would be a mainly syntactic view and restrict the approach to a certain description language.

Table 4. The expressiveness of different descriptions

Entity Relationship Diagrams		Sets of Statements	Extensional Expressiveness
D_1	Customer —1— ‹orders› —N— Order	$= (\text{ordered}(o), c)$	--
D_2	Customer ------------‹ Order	$= (\text{ordered}(o), c)$ $\text{ordering}(\hat{c}, \hat{o})$ $\neg(\text{ordering}(\overline{c}, \overline{o}))$	$M(D_1) \subset M(D_2)$
D_3	Customer ———————‹ Order	$= (\text{ordered}(o), c)$ $\text{ordering}(\hat{c}, \hat{o})$	$M(D_1) = M(D_3)$
D_4	Customer -----------------‹ Order	$= (\text{ordered}(o), c)$ $\neg(= (\text{ordered}(\tilde{o}), \tilde{c}))$ $\text{ordering}(\hat{c}, \hat{o})$ $\neg(\text{ordering}(\overline{c}, \overline{o}))$	$M(D_1) \subset M(D_4)$ $M(D_2) \subset M(D_4)$ $M(D_3) \subset M(D_4)$ $M(D_3) \subset M(D_4)$
D_5	Customer ———————-----‹ Order	$= (\text{ordered}(o), c)$ $\neg(= (\text{ordered}(\tilde{o}), \tilde{c}))$ $\text{ordering}(\hat{c}, \hat{o})$	$M(D_1) \subset M(D_5)$

In creating the sets of atomic and independent formulas of a sorted first-order predicate logic for each ER diagram (see table 4), we use the sorts `order` ($o, \hat{o}, \overline{o}, \tilde{o}$) and `customer` ($c, \hat{c}, \overline{c}, \tilde{c}$), the variables of which are enclosed in brackets. The operation `ordered` is a mapping that assigns one and only one element of the sort `customer` to each element of the sort `order`. Furthermore, the predicate `ordering` establishes a relationship between a customer and an order.

Assessing expressiveness from the extensional point of view means analyzing the models of the sets of statements associated with the ER diagrams. The ER diagram D_1 is completely represented by the single formula `= (ordered(o), c)`, because the mathematical definition of a mapping allows both customers with several orders and customers without orders, but this is not visible from the ER diagram. However, since we concentrate on minimal models, customers without orders do not belong to the models $M(D_1)$. Therefore, the models of the ER diagrams D_1 and D_3 are identical, i.e., both descriptions are extensionally equally expressive, see table 4.

Because minimal models are considered, statements on non-existence must be included in the reference description and thus stated explicitly (similarly in [20]). So, the extensions of the descriptions increase and the models $M(D_1)$ are included as proper subsets if customers without orders (ER diagrams D_2, D_4) or orders without customers (ER diagrams D_4, D_5) are permissible. Adding `ordering`($\hat{c}$, $\hat{o}$) to a set of statements does not change its extension but introduces a new, independent intension: From the fact that each order is assigned a customer we cannot conclude that each customer has placed an order.

From the extensional point of view, ER diagram D_4 is the most expressive one in the sense of generality, whereas the ER diagrams D_1 and D_3 are extensionally equally expressive and the most expressive ones in the sense of precision. Hence, the measure

E(RD, CD) must be applied to reveal a difference in the expressiveness of the ER diagrams D_1 and D_3. If the purpose of conceptual modeling consists in creating the most precise description, the set of statements associated with ER diagram D_3 must form the reference description, as it makes it clear that neither orders without customers nor customers without orders are allowed. Since only one of the statements of the reference description D_3 is associated with ER diagram D_1, the measure E(RD, CD) = E(D_3, D_1) amounts to 0,5 (1/2), i.e., ER diagram D_3 is more expressive than ER diagram D_1 concerning precision (table 5). In measuring expressiveness in the sense of generality, the statements assigned to ER diagram D_4 form the reference description.

Table 5. Expressiveness E(RD, CD) of the ER diagrams from table 5

Description to be compared CD	Reference description RD representing		
	precision D_3	*generality* D_4	*arbitrary purpose* D_2
D_1	1/2 = 0,5	1/4 = 0,25	1/3 = 0,33
D_2	2/3 = 0,67	3/4 = 0,75	**3/3 = 1**
D_3	**2/2 = 1**	2/4 = 0,5	2/3 = 0,67
D_4	2/4 = 0,5	**4/4 = 1**	3/4 = 0,75
D_5	2/3 = 0,67	3/4 = 0,75	2/4 = 0,5

Looking at the first example, the Chen notation seems to be less expressive than other ER notations. This is examined in more detail in the second example, which treats different ER notations as different description languages. We restrict ourselves to constructs related to relationship types, since they vary strongly in terminology and symbolism. Because of their historical importance and their specific appearance, the notations proposed by Chen [8], Scheuermann et al. [27], Teorey et al. [29], ISO [14] and Barker [12] are chosen, see table 6.

In table 6, the ER notations are illustrated by a simple example: A department may have many employees, although (e.g., newly established) departments without any employee may exist. Each employee must be assigned to one and only one department. Employees may have none or several children. Each child belongs to one and only one employee. The identifier of each child contains the identifier of the employee the child belongs to.

The ER notations offer a different number of symbols to express this example. Furthermore, the names of the symbols vary, see table 6. This raises the question how many, and which, symbols are necessary to describe relationship types in general. In other words, it must be examined how expressive the five ER notations are for this purpose.

Using the proposed framework to answer this question, a reference description must be created. In this case, the statements of the reference descriptions refer to the things concerning relationship types that must be represented by the symbols of a description language. Table 7 summarizes the statements of the reference description, which will be explained in the following. To keep the logical formulas simple, the variables e and r, standing for the sorts `entity_type` and `relationship_type` respectively, are individualized by the symbol '!'. This means that '!e' and '!r' occurring in different logical formulas symbolize different variables.

Table 6. Different ER notations

Entity-Relationship Notations by Example	Symbols provided
C: Chen (1976) [8]	
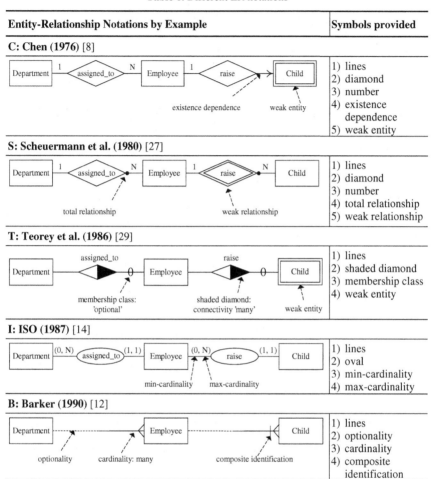	1) lines 2) diamond 3) number 4) existence dependence 5) weak entity
S: Scheuermann et al. (1980) [27]	1) lines 2) diamond 3) number 4) total relationship 5) weak relationship
T: Teorey et al. (1986) [29]	1) lines 2) shaded diamond 3) membership class 4) weak entity
I: ISO (1987) [14]	1) lines 2) oval 3) min-cardinality 4) max-cardinality
B: Barker (1990) [12]	1) lines 2) optionality 3) cardinality 4) composite identification

For the purpose of describing relationship types, the following things (intensions) must be sayable by a description language:

— Every relationship type has a *degree* [29] that specifies the number of entity types that are associated with the relationship type. This corresponds to the operation degree: relationship_type → integer. The statements in table 7 represent independent special cases in which the degree is 2 (binary, statement 1), 1 (unary, statement 2) or larger than 2 (n-ary, statement 3), respectively.

— All instances of an entity type **must** participate one time (min_participate(!e, !r, 1), statement 4) or a certain number of times (min_participate(!e, !r, N), statement 5) in the formation of instances of the relationship type. The intension of statement 4 is described by the terms *min-cardinality* [14], *total relation-*

Table 7. Expressiveness of the ER notations in describing relationship types

Reference Description		Description of Comparison									
		C		S		T		I		B	
Statements	RD	CD	Sy	CD	Sy	CD	Sy	CD	Sy	CD	Sy
1) = (degree(!r), 2)	1	1	1, 2	1	1, 2	1	1, 2	1	1, 2	1	1
2) = (degree(!r), 1)	1	1	1, 2	1	1, 2	1	1, 2	1	1, 2	1	1
3) > (degree(!r), 2)	1	1	1, 2	1	1, 2	1	1, 2	1	1, 2	0	
4) min_participate(!e, !r, 1)	1	0	4?	1	4	1	1	1	3	1	1
5) min_participate(!e, !r, N)	1	0		0		0		1	3	0	
6) max_participate(!e, !r, 1)	1	1	3	1	3	1	2	1	4	1	3
7) max_participate(!e, !r, N)	1	1	3	1	3	1	2	1	4	1	3
8) option_participate(!e, !r)	1	0		1	1	1	3	1	3	1	2
9) id_dependence(!e, !r)	1	1	4, 5	0	5?	1	4	0		1	4
E(RD, CD), RD: statements 1-9	1	6/9		7/9		8/9		8/9		7/9	
E(RD, CD), RD: statements 1-8	1	5/8		7/8		7/8		8/8		6/8	

Abbreviations: RD: binary vector of the reference description, CD: binary vector of the description of comparison, Sy: Symbols

ship [27], *mandatory membership class* [29] or simply *mandatory* [12]. In the logical formulas 4-7, the constant symbols '1' (representing 'one') and 'N' (representing 'above one') are used directly.

- All instances of an entity type participate in at most one instance of the relationship type (max_participate(!e, !r, 1), statement 6) or in more than one instance (max_participate(!e, !r, N), statement 7), respectively. These intensions are represented alternatively by *numbers* ([8], [27]), *max-cardinalities* [14], *shaded diamonds* [29] or *cardinalities* [12].

- It is possible that some instances of an entity type are not involved in instances of the relationship type (option_participate(!e, !r), statement 8). In the ER notations this is called *optional* [12] *membership class* [29] or represented by the *min-cardinality* '0' [14]. Finally, the intension of statement 8 is assumed for all relationships that are not total [27].

- The identifiers (primary keys) of the instances of a weak entity type are composed, including as a part the identifiers of those entity instances to which the weak entity instances are related (id_dependence(!e, !r), statement 9). Apart from *weak entity* ([8], [29]), this intension is named *existence dependence* [8], *weak relationship* [27] or *composite identification* [12].

Table 7 also contains the binary vector of the reference description. The binary vectors of the ER notations follow straightforwardly from the explanations above; the symbols (the numbers refer to table 6) that lead to marking a statement as contained ('1') are given. Concerning the Chen notation, the symbol for existence dependence does not seem to correspond to the intension of statement 4 because in another paper [9] a new symbol for this intension is added. Moreover, weak relationships only partly comply with the intension of statement 9, since "... [composite identification of the weak entity instances; *the author*] ... this need not always be the case" [27, p. 125].

By applying the measure E(RD, CD), it becomes obvious (see table 6) that expressiveness is not dependent on the number of special symbols a description language provides: Though it offers five symbols, the Chen notation is less expressive than the ISO notation, which uses only four symbols. This is due to the fact that the symbols 4 and 5 in the Chen notation redundantly express the intension of statement 9.

Furthermore, if we excluded statement 9 from the reference description, because the composition of identifiers is important only for database implementation and not for conceptual modeling, which deals with describing the UoD, the ISO notation would be the most expressive one.

5   Conclusion and Future Research

We have presented a framework for evaluating expressiveness in conceptual modeling. Expressiveness is discussed in different fields of computer science using different terms. The proposed framework shows that the different discussions can be integrated to define and measure expressiveness in a general and consistent manner.

In contrast to approaches concerning schema equivalence, our framework is applicable not only to descriptions but also to description languages. In both cases expressiveness may be assessed from the extensional point of view or from the intensional one, using the cardinal measure E(RD, CD). To apply the measure E(RD, CD), a reference description RD must be constructed, which must satisfy certain requirements. On the one hand, these requirements join the two different semantic views (extensional, intensional) on expressiveness. On the other hand, the requirements become important in assessing description languages. Requirement RQ3 especially, reveals that the expressiveness of a description language increases only if orthogonal symbols are added to a minimal set of orthogonal symbols. In addition, the reference description may be used as a general guideline for comparing different description languages with reference to a certain purpose, leading to criteria of comparison that are constructed in a systematic way determined by the requirements RQ1-RQ4.

As the second example indicates, in many cases there will be different description languages that are sufficiently and equally expressive for a certain purpose. Hence, choosing among description language does not depend only on their expressiveness but also on additional criteria. Such additional criteria may be how easy it is to say things by using the description language or how easily the things said can be understood. Few approaches for measuring these additional criteria have been presented so far [20], so this is a topic for future research.

Finally, the cardinal value of expressiveness we obtain by applying the measure E(RD, CD) helps to gain insight into the evolution of description languages. For instance (see the second example in section 4), the expressiveness of the first ER notation (Chen (1976)) was increased by adding symbols for the mandatory (statement 4 in table 7) or optional (statement 8 in table 7) participation of entity instances in the instances of an relationship type. Actually, the second example is a part of larger research work, which aims at discovering factors that influence the development of description languages in general. This research will be continued.

References

1. Baader, F.: A Formal Definition for the Expressive Power of Terminological Knowledge Representation Languages. Journal of Logic and Computation 6 (1996) 33-54
2. Batini, C., Ceri, S., Navathe, S.B.: Conceptual Database Design. 4th ed. Benjamin Cummings, Redwood City et al. (1992)
3. Borgida, A.: On the relative expressiveness of description logics and predicate logics. Artificial Intelligence 82 (1996) 353-367
4. Braß, S.: Vervollständigungen für Logikdatenbanken. Forschungsbericht 315. Informatik IV, Universität Dortmund (1980)
5. Cali, A., Calavese, D., De Giacomo, G., Lenzerini, M.: On the Expressive Power of Data Integration Systems. In: Spaccapietra, S., March, T.S., Kambayashi, Y. (eds.): Conceptual Modeling – ER 2002. LNCS, Vol. 2503. Springer, Berlin et al. (2002) 338-350
6. Castano, S., De Antonellis, V., Fugini, M.G., Pernici, B.: Conceptual Schema Analysis: Techniques and Applications. ACM Transactions on Database Systems 23 (1998) 286-332
7. Chandra, A.K.: Theory of Database Queries. In: Proceedings of the 7th ACM SIGACT-SIGMOD-SIGART Symposium on Principles of Database Systems. ACM Press, Austin/Texas (1988) 1-9
8. Chen, P.P.: The Entity-Relationship Model - Toward a Unified View of Data. ACM Transactions on Database Systems 1 (1976) 9-36
9. Dogac, A., Chen, P.P.: Entity-Relationship Model in the ANSI/SPARC Framework. In: Chen, P.P. (ed.): Entity-Relationship Approach to Information Modeling and Analysis. North-Holland, Amsterdam (1983) 357-374
10. Green, P., Rosemann, M.: Integrated Process Modeling: An Ontological Evaluation. Information Systems 25 (2000) 73-87
11. Gregersen, H., Jensen, C.S.: On the Ontological Expressiveness of Temporal Extensions to the Entity-Relationship Model. In: Chen, P.P. (ed.): Advances in Conceptual Modeling – ER '99. LNCS, Vol. 1727. Springer, Berlin et al. (1999) 110-121
12. Halpin, T.: Information Modeling and Relational Databases - From Conceptual Analysis to Logical Design. Morgan Kaufmann, San Francisco et al. (2001)
13. Halpin, T.A., Proper, H.A.: Database Schema Transformation & Optimization. In: Papazoglou, M.P. (ed.): OOER '95: Object-Oriented and Entity-Relationship Modeling. LNCS, Vol. 1021. Springer, Berlin et al. (1995) 191-203
14. ISO: Information processing systems - Concepts and terminology for the conceptual schema and the information base. Technical Report 9007. **Ort** (1987)
15. Jeavons, P., Cohen, D., Gyssens, M.: How to Determine the Expressive Power of Constraints. Constraints – An International Journal 4 (1999) 113-131
16. Joly, S., Le Calvé, G.: Similarity functions. In: Van Cutsem, B. (ed.): Classification and Dissimilarity Analysis. Springer, Berlin et al. (1994) 67-86
17. Kung, C.H.: An analysis of three conceptual models with time perspective. In: Olle, T.W., Sol, H.G., Tully, C.J. (eds.): Information Systems Design Methodologies: A Feature Analysis. North-Holland, Amsterdam (1983) 141-167
18. Kurtonina, N., de Rijke, M.: Expressiveness of concept expressions in first-order description logics. Artificial Intelligence 107 (1999) 303-333
19. Larson, J. A., Navathe, S. B., Elmasri, R.: A Theory of Attribute Equivalence in Databases with Application to Schema Integration. IEEE Transactions on Software Engineering 15 (1989) 449-463
20. MacKinlay, J., Genesereth, M.R.: Expressiveness and language choice. Data & Knowledge Engineering 1 (1985) 17-29
21. McBrien, P., Poulovassilis, A.: A Formalization of Semantic Schema Integration. Information Systems 23 (1998) 307-334
22. Monin, J.-F.: Understanding Formal Methods. Springer, London (2003)

23. Nebel, B.: Die Ausdrucksstärke von Planungsformalismen: Eine formale Charakterisierung. Künstliche Intelligenz 13 (1999) 12-19
24. Reiter, R.: On closed world databases. In: Gaillaire, H., Minker, J. (eds.): Logic and Data Bases. Plenum, New York (1978) 55-76
25. Sapia, C., Blaschka, M., Höfling, G., Dinter, B.: Extending the E/R Model for the Multidimensional Paradigm. In: Kambayashi, Y., Lee, D.L., Lim, E.-P., Mohania, M.K., Masunga, Y. (eds.): Advances in Database Technologies. LNCS, Vol. 1552. Springer, Berlin et al. (1999) 105-116
26. Schäuble, P., Wüthrich, B.: On the Expressive Power of Query Languages. Report 173. Department Informatik, Institut für Informationssysteme, ETH Zürich (1992)
27. Scheuermann, P., Schiffner, G., Weber, H.: Abstraction Capabilities and Invariant Properties Modelling within the Entity-Relationship Approach. In: Chen, P.P. (ed.): Entity-Relationship Approach to Systems Analysis and Design. North-Holland, Amsterdam (1980) 121-140
28. Si-Said Cherfi, S., Akoka, J., Comyn-Wattiau, I.: Conceptual Modeling Quality – From EER to UML Schemas Evolution. In: Spaccapietra, S., March, T.S., Kambayashi, Y. (eds.): Conceptual Modeling – ER 2002. LNCS, Vol. 2503. Springer, Berlin et al. (2002) 414-428
29. Teorey, T.J., Yang, D., Fry, J.P.: A Logical Design Methodology for Relational Databases Using the Extended Entity-Relationship Model. ACM Computing Surveys 18 (1986) 197-222

Design and Implementation of the YAWL System

Wil M.P. van der Aalst[1,2], Lachlan Aldred[2],
Marlon Dumas[2], and Arthur H.M. ter Hofstede[2]

[1] Department of Technology Management
Eindhoven University of Technology, The Netherlands
w.m.p.v.d.aalst@tm.tue.nl
[2] Centre for IT Innovation, Queensland University of Technology, Australia
{l.aldred,m.dumas,a.terhofstede}@qut.edu.au

Abstract. This paper describes the implementation of a system supporting YAWL (Yet Another Workflow Language). YAWL is based on a rigorous analysis of existing workflow management systems and related standards using a comprehensive set of workflow patterns. This analysis shows that contemporary workflow systems, relevant standards (e.g. XPDL, BPML, BPEL4WS), and theoretical models such as Petri nets have problems supporting essential patterns. This inspired the development of YAWL by taking Petri nets as a starting point and introducing mechanisms that provide direct support for the workflow patterns identified. As a proof of concept we have developed a workflow management system supporting YAWL. In this paper, we present the architecture and functionality of the system and zoom into the control-flow, data, and operational perspectives.

1 Introduction

In the area of workflow one is confronted with a plethora of products (commercial, free and open source) supporting languages that differ significantly in terms of concepts, constructs, and their semantics. One of the contributing factors to this problem is the lack of a commonly agreed upon formal foundation for workflow languages. Standardization efforts, e.g. XPDL [19] proposed by the WfMC, have essentially failed to gain universal acceptance and have not in any case provided such a formal basis for workflow specification. The lack of well-grounded standards in this area has induced several issues, including minimal support for migration of workflow specifications, potential for errors in specifications due to ambiguities, and lack of a reference framework for comparing the relative expressive power of different languages (though some work in this area is reported in [13]).

The workflow patterns initiative [4] aims at establishing a more structured approach to the issue of the specification of control flow dependencies in workflow languages. Based on an analysis of existing workflow management systems and applications, this initiative identified a collection of patterns corresponding to typical control flow dependencies encountered in workflow specifications, and documented ways of capturing these dependencies in existing workflow languages. These patterns have been used as a benchmark for comparing process definition languages and in tendering processes for evaluating workflow offerings. See http://www.workflowpatterns.com for extensive documentation, flash animations of each pattern, and evaluations of standards and systems.

A. Persson and J. Stirna (Eds.): CAiSE 2004, LNCS 3084, pp. 142–159, 2004.

While workflow patterns provide a pragmatic approach to control flow specification in workflows, Petri nets provide a more theoretical approach. Petri nets form a model for concurrency with a formal foundation, an associated graphical representation, and a collection of analysis techniques. These features, together with their direct support for the notion of state (required in some of the workflow patterns), make them attractive as a foundation for control flow specification in workflows. However, even though Petri nets (including higher-order Petri nets such as Colored Petri nets [12]) support a number of the identified patterns, they do not provide direct support for the cancellation patterns (in particular the cancellation of a whole case or a region), the synchronizing merge pattern (where all active threads need to be merged, and branches which cannot become active need to be ignored), and patterns dealing with multiple active instances of the same activity in the same case [2]. This realization motivated the development of YAWL [3] (Yet Another Workflow Language) which combines the insights gained from the workflow patterns with the benefits of Petri nets. It should be noted though that YAWL is not simply a set of macros defined on top of Petri nets. Its semantics is not defined in terms of Petri nets but rather in terms of a transition system.

As a language for the specification of control flow in workflows, YAWL has the benefit of being highly expressive and suitable, in the sense that it provides direct support for all the workflow patterns (except implicit termination), while the reviewed workflow languages provide direct support for only a subset of them. In addition, YAWL has a formal semantics and offers graphical representations for many of its concepts. The expressive power and formal semantics of YAWL make it an attractive candidate to be used as an intermediate language to support translations of workflows specified in different languages.

When YAWL was first proposed no implementation was available. Recently, implementation efforts have resulted in a first version of a prototype supporting YAWL. With respect to the various perspectives from which workflows can be considered (e.g. control-flow, data, resource, and operational [11]), YAWL initially focused exclusively on the control flow perspective. Since then, a novel approach for dealing with the data perspective has been designed and incorporated into the prototype. In addition, an approach has been designed (although not yet implemented) to deal with the operational perspective on the basis of a service-oriented architecture.

This paper discusses salient aspects and issues related to the design and implementation of the YAWL system, including the proposed extensions for dealing with the data and operational perspectives. In short, the main contributions of the paper are:

- A discussion of the implementation of the control flow perspective of YAWL;
- A discussion of the data perspective of YAWL and its implementation;
- A discussion of a proposal for the incorporation of the operational perspective into YAWL through the use of a service-oriented architecture.

The remainder of the paper is organized as follows. After a brief overview of related work we introduce the YAWL language. Section 4 describes the architecture of the YAWL system and motivates design decisions. Section 5 discusses the control-flow, data, and operational perspectives in more detail. Section 6 briefly discusses an example. Section 7 concludes the paper.

2 Related Work

YAWL [3] is based on a line of research grounded in Petri net theory [1, 13] and the 20 workflow patterns documented in [4]. In previous publications we have evaluated contemporary systems, languages, and standards using these patterns. An analysis of 13 commercial workflow offerings can be found in [4] while an analysis of 10 workflow languages proposed by the academic community is described in [3]. Commercial systems that have been evaluated include Ley COSA , Filenet's Visual Workflow, SUN's Forté Conductor, Lotus Domino Workflow, IBM MQSeries/Workflow, Staffware, Verve Workflow, Fujitsu's I-Flow, TIBCO InConcert, HP Changengine, SAP R/3 Workflow, Eastman, and FLOWer. Examples of academic prototypes that have been evaluated using the patterns are Meteor, Mobile [11], ADEPTflex [17], OPENflow, Mentor [20], and WASA [18]. For an analysis of UML activity diagrams in terms of (some of) the patterns, we refer to [8]. BPEL4WS, a proposed standard for web service composition, has been analyzed in [21]. Analyses of BPMI's BPML [5] and WfMC's XPDL [19] using the patterns are also available via http://www.workflowpatterns.com. In total, more than 30 languages/systems have been evaluated and these evaluations have driven the development of the YAWL language. Given that this paper focuses on the *design and implementation* of the YAWL system, we will not discuss these previous evaluations, referring the reader to the above citations.

As an open source workflow system, YAWL joins the ranks of a significant number of previous initiatives: 18 open source workflow systems are reported in [16]. Again, the distinctive feature of YAWL with respect to these systems is in the combination of its expressive power, formal foundation, and support for graphical design, complemented by its novel approach to deal with the data and the operational perspective of workflow by leveraging emerging XML and Web services technologies.

3 YAWL Language

Before describing the architecture and implementation of the YAWL system, we introduce the distinguishing features of YAWL. As indicated in the introduction, YAWL is based on Petri nets. However, to overcome the limitations of Petri nets, YAWL has been extended with features to facilitate patterns involving multiple instances, advanced synchronization patterns, and cancellation patterns. Moreover, YAWL allows for hierarchical decomposition and handles arbitrarily complex data.

Figure 1 shows the modeling elements of YAWL. At the syntactic level, YAWL extends the class of workflow nets described in [1] with multiple instances, composite tasks, OR-joins, removal of tokens, and directly connected transitions. YAWL, although being inspired by Petri nets, is a completely new language with its own semantics and specifically designed for workflow specification.

A *workflow specification* in YAWL is a set of *process definitions* which form a hierarchy. *Tasks*[1] are either *atomic tasks* or *composite tasks*. Each composite task refers to a process definition at a lower level in the hierarchy (also referred to as its decomposition). Atomic tasks form the leaves of the graph-like structure. There is one process definition

---

[1] We use the term *task* rather than *activity* to remain consistent with earlier work on workflow nets [1].

without a composite task referring to it. This process definition is named the *top level workflow* and forms the root of the graph-like structure representing the hierarchy of process definitions.

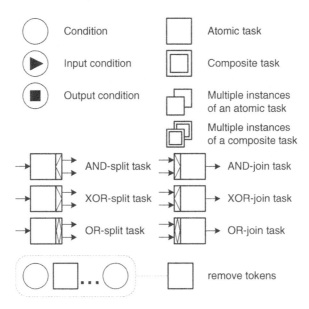

Fig. 1. Symbols used in YAWL.

Each process definition consists of *tasks* (whether composite or atomic) and *conditions* which can be interpreted as places. Each process definition has one unique *input condition* and one unique *output condition* (see Figure 1). In contrast to Petri nets, it is possible to connect 'transition-like objects' like composite and atomic tasks directly to each other without using a 'place-like object' (i.e., conditions) in-between. For the semantics this construct can be interpreted as a hidden condition, i.e., an implicit condition is added for every direct connection.

Both composite tasks and atomic tasks can have multiple instances as indicated in Figure 1. We adopt the notation described in [1] for AND/XOR-splits/joins as also shown in Figure 1. Moreover, we introduce OR-splits and OR-joins corresponding respectively to Pattern 6 (Multi choice) and Pattern 7 (Synchronizing merge) defined in [4]. Finally, Figure 1 shows that YAWL provides a notation for removing tokens from a specified region denoted by dashed rounded rectangles and lines. The enabling of the task that will perform the cancellation may or may not depend on the tokens within the region to be "canceled". In any case, the moment this task completes, all tokens in this region are removed. This notation allows for various cancellation patterns.

To illustrate YAWL we use the three examples shown in Figure 2. The first example (a) illustrates that YAWL allows for the modeling of advanced synchronization patterns. Task *register* is an 'OR-split' (Pattern 6: Multi-choice) and task *pay* is an 'OR-join' (Pattern 7: Synchronizing merge). This implies that every registration step is followed by a

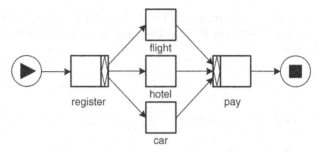

(a) After registering the request for a trip, a flight, a hotel, and/or a car are booked followed by a payment.

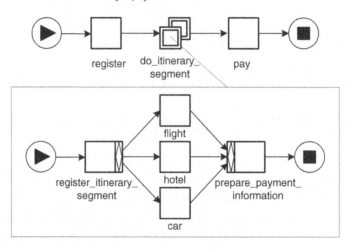

(b) A trip may consist of several legs. The sub-process is instantiated for each leg.

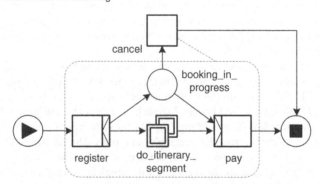

(c) Again the sub-process is instantiated for each leg but now it is possible to cancel the whole trip by removing tokens from the region indicated.

Fig. 2. Three YAWL specifications.

set of booking tasks *flight*, *hotel*, and/or *car*. It is possible that all three booking tasks are executed but it is also possible that only one or two booking tasks are executed. The YAWL OR-join synchronizes only if necessary, i.e., it will synchronize only the booking tasks that were actually selected. Note that the majority of systems do not support the Synchronizing merge (i.e., Pattern 7). A few systems support it (e.g., IBM's MQSeries Workflow, Lotus Domino Workflow, and Eastman Workflow) but restrict its application. For example, in order to simplify the implementation of the OR-join, MQSeries Workflow [10] does not support loops[2].

Figure 2(a) does not show the data aspect. The YAWL specification for this example has 10 variables ranging from the name of the customer to flight details. For the routing of the case there are three Boolean variables *want_flight*, *want_hotel*, and *want_car*. They select which of the booking tasks need to be executed.

Figure 2(b) illustrates another YAWL specification. In contrast to the first example a trip may include multiple stops, i.e., an itinerary may include multiple segments. For example, a trip may go from Amsterdam to Singapore, from Singapore to Brisbane, from Brisbane to Los Angeles, and finally from Los Angeles to Amsterdam and thus entail four itinerary segments. Each segment may include a flight (most likely) but may also include a hotel booking or a car booking (at the destination). Figure 2(b) shows that multiple segments are modeled by multiple instances of the composite task *do_itinerary_segment*. This composite task is linked to the process definition also shown in Figure 2(b). In the case of multiple instances it is possible to specify upper and lower bounds for the number of instances. It is also possible to specify a threshold for completion that is lower than the actual number of instances, i.e., the construct completes before all of its instances complete. In the example at hand this does not make sense since each segment must be booked. Another setting is available to indicate whether an instance can be added while executing other instances. In this example this would mean that while booking segments, a new segment is defined and added to the itinerary. In the specification corresponding to Figure 2(b) we assume the multiple instances to be 'static', i.e., after completing task *register* the number of instances is fixed. Again, the diagram does not show the data aspect. There are similar variables as in the first example. However, a complicating factor is that each of the instances will use private data which needs to be aggregated. We return to this in Section 5.2. For the moment, it suffices to see that YAWL indeed supports the patterns dealing with multiple instances (Patterns 12-15). Note that only few systems support multiple instances. FLOWer [6] is one of the few systems directly supporting multiple instances.

Finally we consider the YAWL specification illustrated in Figure 2(c). Again composite task *do_itinerary_segment* is decomposed into the process definition shown in Figure 2(b). Now it is however possible to withdraw bookings by executing task *cancel*. Task *cancel* is enabled if there is a token in *booking_in_progress*. If the environment decides to execute cancel, everything inside the region indicated by the dashed rectangle will be removed. In this way, YAWL provides direct support for the cancellation patterns (Patterns 19 and 20). Note that support for these patterns is typically missing or very limited in existing systems (e.g. Staffware has a cancellation concept but a cancellation can only refer to a single task and not to an arbitrary set of tasks).

---

[2] Instead of loops, MQSeries Workflow supports blocks with exit condition.

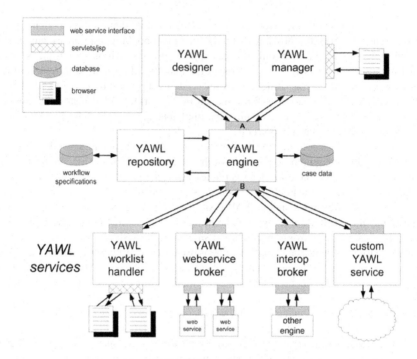

Fig. 3. YAWL architecture.

In this section we illustrated some of the features of the YAWL language. The language has an XML syntax and is specified in terms of an XML schema. See http://www.citi.qut.edu.au/yawl/ for the XML syntax of the language. In Section 5 we will show some fragments of the language. However, before going into detail, we first present the 'bigger picture' by describing the YAWL architecture.

4 YAWL Architecture

To support the YAWL language introduced in the previous section, we have developed a system using state-of-the-art technology. In this section, we describe the overall architecture of this system, which is depicted in Figure 3. Workflow specifications are designed using the *YAWL designer* and deployed into the *YAWL engine* which, after performing all necessary verifications and task registrations, stores these specifications in the *YAWL repository*, which manages a collection of "runable" workflow specifications. Once successfully deployed, workflow specifications can be instantiated through the YAWL engine, leading to workflow instances (also called cases). The engine handles the execution of these cases, i.e. based on the state of a case and its specification, the engine determines which events it should offer to the environment.

The environment of a YAWL system is composed of so-called *YAWL services*. Inspired by the "web services" paradigm, end-users, applications, and organizations are all abstracted as services in YAWL. Figure 3 shows four YAWL services: (1) *YAWL worklist handler*, (2) *YAWL web services broker*, (3) *YAWL interoperability broker*, and (4) *custom YAWL services*. The YAWL worklist handler corresponds to the classical worklist handler (also named "inbox") present in most workflow management systems. It is the component used to assign work to users of the system. Through the worklist handler users can accept work items and signal their completion. In traditional workflow systems, the worklist handler is embedded in the workflow engine. In YAWL however, it is considered to be a service decoupled from the engine. The YAWL web services broker is the glue between the engine and other web services. Note that it is unlikely that web services will be able to directly connect to the YAWL engine, since they will typically be designed for more general purposes than just interacting with a workflow engine. Similarly, it is desirable not to adapt the interface of the engine to suit specific services, otherwise, this interface will need to cater for an undetermined number of message types. Accordingly, the YAWL web services broker acts as a mediator between the YAWL engine and external web services that may be invoked by the engine to delegate tasks (e.g. delegating a "payment" task to an online payment service). The YAWL interoperability broker is a service designed to interconnect different workflow engines. For example, a task in one system could be subcontracted to another system where the task corresponds to a whole process. To illustrate that there is not a fixed set of YAWL services we included a custom YAWL service. A custom service connects the engine with an entity in the environment of the system. For example, a custom YAWL service could offer communication with mobile phones, printers, assembly robots, etc. Note that it is also possible that there are multiple services of the same type, e.g. multiple worklist handlers, web services brokers, and interoperability brokers. For example, there may exist multiple implementations of worklist handlers (e.g., customized for a specific application domain or organization) and the same worklist handler may be instantiated multiple times (e.g., one worklist handler per geographical region).

Workflow specifications are managed by the YAWL repository and workflow instances (i.e. cases) are managed by the YAWL engine. Clearly, there is also a need for a management tool that can be used to control workflow instances manually (e.g. deleting a workflow instance or a workflow specification), providing information about the state of running workflow instances, and details or aggregated data about completed instances. This is the role of the *YAWL manager*.

Figure 3 also shows the various interfaces of YAWL. The YAWL engine has two classes of interfaces: (A) interfaces capturing the interactions between the YAWL designer and the YAWL manager on the one hand, and the YAWL engine on the other; and (B) interfaces capturing the interactions between the YAWL services and the YAWL engine. Interface class (A) corresponds to Interface 1 (Process Definition tools) and Interface 5 (Administration and Monitoring tools) of the reference model of the Workflow Management Coalition (WfMC) [15]. Interface class (B) corresponds to WfMC's Interface 2-3 (Workflow Client Applications and Invoked Applications), and Interface 4 (Workflow Interoperability). Both interfaces (A and B) are implemented using a REST based architectural style [9]. For our purposes the advantages of REST over SOAP+WSDL include speed, scalability, security, and tool support. Users interact with the YAWL system through a Web browser, i.e. both the YAWL manager and the YAWL worklist handler offer HTML front-ends.

When considering the YAWL architecture there is one fundamental difference with respect to existing workflow management systems: The YAWL engine deals with control-flow and data but not explicitly with users. In addition, the engine abstracts from differences between users, applications, organizations, etc. To achieve this, the YAWL system leverages principles from service-oriented architectures: external entities either offer services or require services. In a traditional workflow management system, the engine takes care of the 'What', 'When', 'How', and 'By whom'. In YAWL, the engine takes care of the 'What' and 'When' while the YAWL services take care of the 'How' and 'By whom'. By separating these concerns it is possible to implement a highly efficient engine while allowing for customized functionality. For example, it is possible to build worklist handlers supporting specific organizations or domains, e.g., processes where a team of professionals work on the same activity at the same time. It should be noted that the architecture of YAWL is similar to the architecture envisioned in the context of web service composition languages like BPEL4WS, WSCI, BPML, etc. However, these languages typically only consider control routing and data transformations, while YAWL is not limited to these aspects and also addresses issues such as work distribution and management.

Implementation Notes. Although the current implementation of YAWL is complete in the sense that it is able to run workflow instances, it does not provide all the components and functionality described in Figure 3. The YAWL engine is fully implemented. The YAWL designer is under development and at present only supports the specification of control-flow perspective. The YAWL manager has not been implemented yet. Of the YAWL services only the YAWL worklist handler is realized, to the extent that it supports multiple users. Development is planned for an organizational model which integrates with the worklist handler. The implementation has been done in Java and uses XML-based standards such as XPath, XQuery, and XML Schema. The designer is implemented using Jgraph: an open source graphical library (http://www.jgraph.com). The YAWL engine relies on JDom (http://www.jdom.org) for evaluating XPath expressions, Saxon (http://saxon.sourceforge.net) for XQuery support, and Xerces (http://xml.apache.org/xerces-j) for XML schema support.

5 YAWL Perspectives

This section discusses three key perspectives: (1) the control-flow perspective, (2) the data perspective, and (3) the operational perspective. The first two perspectives are fully implemented and are supported by the YAWL engine. The operational perspective corresponds to the YAWL services identified in the previous section and is only partly realized.

5.1 Control-Flow Perspective

The control-flow perspective of YAWL focuses on the ordering of tasks. The building blocks offered by YAWL have been briefly discussed in Section 3 and are depicted in Figure 1. There are three features offered by YAWL not present in most workflow

Listing 1

```
1  <task id="register">
2    <name>Collect information
3      from customer</name>
4    <flowsInto>
5        <nextElementRef
6          id="flight"/>
7        <predicate>
8          /data/want_flight
9            = 'true'
10       </predicate>
11       <isDefaultFlow/>
12   </flowsInto>
13   <flowsInto>
14       <nextElementRef id="hotel"/>
15       <predicate>/data/want_hotel = 'true'</predicate>
16   </flowsInto>
17   <flowsInto>
18       <nextElementRef id="car"/>
19       <predicate>/data/want_car = 'true'</predicate>
20   </flowsInto>
21   <join code="and"/>
22   <split code="or"/>
23   <startingMappings>
24       <mapping>
25          <expression query="/data/customer"/>
26          <mapsTo>customer</mapsTo>
27       </mapping>
28   </startingMappings>
29   <completedMappings>
30       <mapping>
31          <expression query="/data/customer"/>
32          <mapsTo>customer</mapsTo>
33       </mapping>
34       <mapping>
35          <expression query="/data/want_flight"/>
36          <mapsTo>want_flight</mapsTo>
37       </mapping>
38       ....
39   </completedMappings>
40   <decomposesTo id="do_register"/>
41 </task>
```

Listing 2

```
1  <task id="pay">
2      <name>Settle payment</name>
3      <flowsInto>
4          <nextElementRef id="end"/>
5      </flowsInto>
6      <join code="or"/>
7      <split code="and"/>
8      <startingMappings>
9          ...
10     </startingMappings>
11     <decomposesTo id="pay"/>
12 </task>
```

languages: (1) the OR-join task, (2) multiple instances of a task (atomic or composite), and (3) the "remove tokens" task (i.e., cancellation of a region). Therefore, we focus on these three. Let us first focus on the realization of the OR-join. Listing 1 shows the definition of task *register* in Figure 2(a). The *name* element provides the name of the task, the three *flowsInto* elements correspond to the three outgoing arcs, the *join* element shows that the task is an AND-join[3], the *split* element shows that the task is an OR-split, the *startingMappings* element lists the input to the task, the *completedMappings* element lists the output of the task, and the *decomposesTo* element refers to the actual definition of the task (which we call its "decomposition"). Note that each *task* element refers to a *decomposition* element. The *decomposition* element can define the implementation of an atomic task or a composite task. Multiple *task* elements can refer to the same *decomposition* element to allow for reuse. Listing 2 shows the *task* element for the corresponding OR-join. Although from a syntactical point of view the OR-join is easy to realize, it is far from trivial to realize the corresponding functionality. In the classical XOR-join the flow continues after the first input. In the classical AND-join the flow waits for all inputs. The complicating factor is that the OR-join sometimes has to synchronize and sometimes not (or only partially). In the example shown in Figure 2(a) it is fairly easy to see when to synchronize, e.g., simply count the number of bookings enabled and then count back to zero for every booking that is completed. However, in a general sense this strategy does not work, because there can be multiple splits (of all types) ultimately linking to an OR-join. The semantics adopted by YAWL is that an OR-join waits until no more inputs can arrive at the join. To make sure that the semantics are well defined, i.e., have a fix-point, we exclude other OR-joins as indicated in [3]. See [14] for a more elaborate discussion on the topic. As far as we know, YAWL is the first engine implementing this strategy without adding additional constraints such as excluding loops, etc. From a performance point of view, the OR-join is quite expensive (the system needs to calculate all possible futures from the current state). To improve performance, the OR-join condition could be evaluated only if strictly necessary.

A second feature which distinguishes YAWL from many existing languages is the ability to have multiple instances of atomic/composite tasks. Figure 2(b) shows an example of this. The composite task *do_itinerary_segment* has additional elements to control the number of instances (*minimum*, *maximum*, *threshold*, and *creation mode*) and elements to control the data flow. Again the syntax is fairly straightforward but the realization in the YAWL engine is not. Note that multiple instances can be nested arbitrarily deep and it becomes quite difficult to separate and synchronize instances.

A third feature worth noting is the cancellation of a region, i.e., removing tokens from selected parts of the specification. In Figure 2(c) task *cancel* contains four *removesTokens* elements to empty the part of the specification shown. The cancellation functionality is easy to realize in the engine. The biggest challenge is to allow for an easy way to indicate a region in the YAWL designer. At this point in time we are experimenting with various interaction mechanisms to allow for a generic yet intuitive way to demarcate such regions. Condition *booking_in_process* in Figure 2(c) also illustrates that YAWL supports the Deferred choice pattern. Note that the decision to cancel is made by the external entity executing task *cancel*, and not by the workflow engine. In traditional workflow systems, such "deferred" or "environment-driven" choices are not possible: all decisions are made by evaluating system data. YAWL's XOR-split and OR-split constructs operate likewise. The notion of deferred choice has been adopted by new languages like BPEL (see *pick* construct in [7]) and BPML (see *choice* construct in [5]).

---

[3] This is not relevant in this example since there is only one incoming arc.

5.2   Data Perspective

Although the initial focus of YAWL was on control flow, it has been extended to offer full support for the data perspective. It is possible to define data elements and use them for conditional routing, for the creation of multiple instances, for exchanging information with the environment, etc. Most of the existing workflow management systems use a propriety language for dealing with data. YAWL is one of the few languages that completely relies on XML-based standards like XPath and XQuery.

Listing 3

```
1 <rootNet id="make_trip">
2   <localVariable
3     name="customer">
4       <type>xs:string</type>
5       <initialValue>
6       Type name of customer
7       </initialValue>
8   </localVariable>
9   <localVariable name=
10    "payment_account_number">
11      <type>xs:string</type>
12  </localVariable>
13  ...
14  <localVariable name=
15    "want_flight">
16      <type>xs:boolean</type>
17  </localVariable>
18  <localVariable name=
19    "want_hotel">
20      <type>xs:boolean</type>
21  </localVariable>
22  <localVariable name=
23    "want_car">
24      <type>xs:boolean</type>
25  </localVariable>
26  <localVariable name=
27    "flightDetails">
28      <type>xs:string</type>
29  </localVariable>
30  ...
```

Listing 4

```
1 <decomposition id="do_register"
2   xsi:type=
3   "YAWLServiceClientType">
4     <inputParam name="customer">
5       <type>xs:string</type>
6     </inputParam>
7     <outputExpression query=
8       "/data/customer"/>
9     <outputExpression query=
10      "/data/start_date"/>
11    ...
12    <outputExpression query=
13      "/data/want_flight"/>
14    ...
15    <outputParam name=
16      "customer">
17        <type>xs:string</type>
18    </outputParam>
19    <outputParam name=
20      "start_date">
21        <type>xs:dateTime</type>
22    </outputParam>
23    ...
24    <outputParam name=
25      "want_flight">
26        <type>xs:boolean</type>
27    </outputParam>
28    ...
29 </decomposition>
```

Listing 3 shows the declaration of variables for the example shown in Figure 2(a). Using the element *localVariable* it is possible to add typed variables to the top-level workflow. For example, lines 2-7 define the variable for storing the name of the customer. The type of this variable is *string* and an initial value is defined. Each decomposition of a task into a workflow may also have *localVariable* elements. Variables at the higher level can be passed onto the lower level. Listing 4 shows the decomposition of task *register* referred to in Figure 2(a). As shown in lines 4-6 of Listing 4, there is an input parameter named *customer*. Task *register* maps data residing at the higher level onto this input parameter at the lower level (i.e., in the decomposition) as shown in lines 23-28 of Listing 1. After completing the task, data at the lower level is passed on to the higher level. For example, lines 24-27 of Listing 4 declare the parameter *want_flight*. Lines 12-13 of Listing 4 are executed to produce a data result. After completing the decomposition, this result is mapped onto the variable *want_flight* at the higher level (see lines 35-36 of Listing 1). Note that the expression shown in line 35 of Listing 1 and the expression shown in lines 12-13 of Listing 4 is an XQuery expression to access a node. However, arbitrarily complex transformations are permitted here, using the full expressive power of XQuery. Moreover, parameters may be optional or mandatory.

If a task is an OR-split or XOR-split, *predicate* elements are used to specify Boolean expressions. Lines 7-10, line 15, and line 19 in Listing 1 specify the output conditions of task *register* (one for each outgoing arc). In the case of an OR-split or XOR-split, there is always a default indicated by the element *isDefaultFlow* (cf. line 11 in Listing 1). If all predicates evaluate to false, this arc is chosen, thereby acting like an "otherwise" branch. In the example of Figure 2(a), at least one of the three booking tasks should be executed. To ensure this, a flight is booked if none of the predicates evaluates to true. To allow the possibility that none of the three booking tasks is executed, one should add an arc directly from task *register* to either *pay* or the output condition. This would then be set to be the default arc. For an XOR-split each *predicate* needs to have an *ordering* attribute that is used in case multiple predicates evaluate to true. If predicates are not mutually exclusive, the one with the lowest number that evaluates to true is selected.

From the viewpoint of data, the handling of multiple instances is far from trivial. Consider for example Figure 2(b), the subprocess is executed for each segment of the itinerary and thus there is data for each segment (destination, start_ date, flight_ details, etc.). The number of instances created but also the maximum, minimum, and threshold may all depend on data. Data at the higher level needs to be split over the instances and after completion of the instances aggregated to data elements at the higher level. Again XQuery is used to map data from the higher level to the lower level and vice versa.

5.3 Operational Perspective

As discussed in Section 4, the YAWL engine interacts with its environment by means of a collection of "YAWL services", which are responsible for handling the operational and the resource perspectives of workflow specifications, as well as for supporting communication between different YAWL engines. A deployment of the YAWL system is expected to include a number of pre-built YAWL services. The YAWL worklist handler, web service broker, and interoperability broker mentioned in Section 4 are examples of such pre-built services. Importantly, all YAWL services are required to implement a common interface. This interface is REST based [9], hence it must be able to generate, and interpret several classes of XML messages. This interface defines messages for:

– Atomic task decomposition management: registering and un-registering atomic task decompositions into YAWL services.
– Atomic task instance management: creating task instances, notifying the start and completion (whether successful or not) of task instances, canceling task instances, and probing the status of a task instance.

- Workflow instance management: creating, monitoring, and interacting with work-flow instances.
- YAWL services connection management: registering and un-registering YAWL services, reporting and probing the availability of YAWL services.

When a new YAWL workflow specification is deployed, the YAWL engine registers each of the atomic task decompositions included in this specification, with at least one YAWL service. Each task decomposition indicates the YAWL service(s) with which it has to be registered. In the setting of the travel preparation example, one possible scenario is that the tasks *register, flight*, and *hotel* are to be registered with the worklist service, while the task *pay* is to be registered with the YAWL web services broker (e.g. the payment is handled by an external payment service). If these registrations are successful, the YAWL engine is then able to create instances of these tasks. Unsuccessful task registrations lead to errors and the YAWL engine reports back these errors to the YAWL designer or the YAWL manager. The deployment of a workflow specification is only considered to be successful if all the registrations of task decompositions in the specification, are successful. Otherwise, the deployment is aborted and any registered task decompositions are unregistered.

As a minimum, a task decomposition specifies the task's input and output data types, and an identifier stating which YAWL service to invoke. It may specify other information depending on the nature of the YAWL service with which the task will be registered. *In the case of tasks that are registered with a worklist service*, the task decomposition must specify a query over an organizational model to extract which role(s) are able to execute instances of this task. *In the case of a web service broker*, built to invoke web services based on WSDL+SOAP, the task decomposition must include:

1. A WSDL interface and SOAP binding of the web service *WS* that the broker must invoke when dispatching an instance of this task.
2. A mapping between the task management operations of the YAWL services interface and the operations in the interface of *WS*. Using this information, the web service broker can exploit the functionality provided by the Web Services Invocation Framework (http://ws.apache.org/wsif) in order to interact with *WS*.

In the setting of the travel preparation workflow, and assuming that the task *pay* is delegated to a payment service (say *PS*), the decomposition of this task must provide the WSDL interface and binding for *PS*, and a table indicating that for example:

- Operation *CreateTaskInstance* of the common YAWL services interface is mapped to operation *InitiateOnlinePayment* of *PS*.
- Operation *OnlinePaymentInitiated* of *PS* maps to operation *TaskStarted* of the YAWL services interface.
- Operation *OnlinePaymentCompleted* of *PS* maps to operation *TaskCompleted* of the YAWL services interface.
- Operation *CancelTask* of the common YAWL services interface maps to operation *CancelPayment* of *PS*.

These mappings should also specify how the input data of one operation maps to the input data of the other operation, and same for the output data.

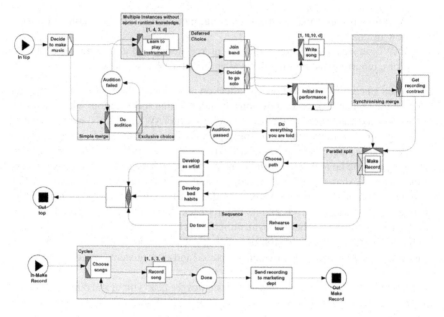

Fig. 4. Example of a YAWL process.

To be registered with a YAWL interoperability broker service, a task decomposition *TD* must specify: (i) the identifier of the YAWL engine to which instances of this task will be delegated; (ii) the name of the YAWL specification to be instantiated when an instance of the task is created; (iii) a mapping between the input data of the *CreateTaskInstance* operation and the input data of the process to be instantiated; and (iv) a similar mapping for the output data. When an instance of *TD* is created, the interoperability broker creates an instance of the designated process in a possibly remote YAWL engine (using the workflow instance management operations of the YAWL services interfaces). When this workflow instance completes, the interoperability broker collects the output data, converts them using the mapping given when the task decomposition was registered, and returns them to the YAWL engine that triggered the instantiation of *TD*. Note that this process interoperability model assumes that no communication occurs between the creation and completion of a process instance. It is envisaged that the YAWL system will be extended to support communication between running process instances.

6   Example and On-Line Demonstration

This section illustrates the current implementation of YAWL using a small example that can be downloaded and run from the YAWL site http://www.citi.qut.edu.au/yawl/. Figure 4 shows the life-cycle of a musician from the viewpoint of a record company. The goal of this playful example is not to show a realistic business scenario but an easy to understand example showing the main concepts. The top-level process

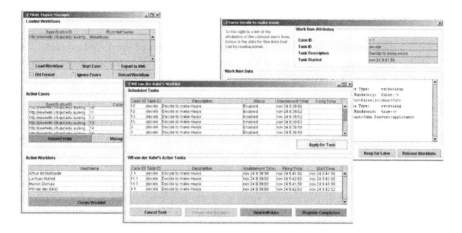

Fig. 5. Screenshots of the current YAWL manager, worklist handler, and a data entry form.

starts with a choice between doing an audition or first learning to play an instrument (Pattern 4: Exclusive choice). The musician can learn multiple instruments in parallel (Pattern 15: Multiple instances without a priori runtime knowledge) followed by the decision to join a band or to go solo (Pattern 16: Deferred choice). In both cases, multiple songs may be written (again Pattern 15) and/or a live performance is given after which the musician gets a contract (Pattern 6: Multi-choice/Pattern 7: Synchronizing merge). The audition can fail and, if so, the musician tries again or continues learning to play instruments (Pattern 5: Simple merge/Pattern 16: Deferred choice/Pattern 10: Arbitrary cycles). Eventually the musician ends up making a record. This is modeled by a composite task (Make Record) containing a multiple instance task for recording songs and a loop if re-recording is necessary (see lower-level process in Figure 4). The subprocess uses Pattern 5: Simple merge, Pattern 16: Deferred choice, and Pattern 15: Multiple instances without a priori runtime knowledge. After completing the subprocess a sequence is executed, in parallel with a choice being made, followed by a synchronization (Pattern 2: Parallel split/Pattern 16: Deferred choice/Pattern 1: Sequence/Pattern 7: Synchronizing merge) thus completing the YAWL specification.

Figure 4 does not show the data perspective (which is specified separately). The data perspective of this workflow specification states that musicians have a name, songs have a title, etc. Additionally, in the case of the composite task *Make Record*, the data perspective specifies the effective parameters that will be passed to the lower level process (e.g. an expression for retrieving the actual name and other properties of a given song).

Figure 5 shows some screenshots of the tool while executing several instances of the YAWL specification of Figure 4. The worklist of 'Wil van der Aalst' is shown in the bottom window. The left window shows the current YAWL manager containing the active workflows, active cases, and users. The right window shows an interface to enter data. This is still rather primitive. Future versions of YAWL are expected to support interactive forms.

7   Conclusion

In this paper we presented the design and implementation of the YAWL system. The YAWL system fully supports the YAWL language which is based on an analysis of more than 30 workflow systems, languages and standards. The expressiveness of YAWL leads to challenging implementation problems such as dealing with multiple instances, advanced synchronization mechanisms, and cancellation capabilities. We consider the current version of YAWL as a proof of concept for the language introduced in [3]. In our opinion any proposed language should be supported by at least a running prototype in addition to a formal definition [3]. Too many standards and languages have been proposed which turn out to have semantic problems.

At this point in time we are implementing the architecture shown in Figure 3. As indicated in Section 4, the current version of the implementation provides the basic functionality of a workflow system, but not all the components of the architecture have been realized. One of the most challenging issues is to fine-tune the definition of the interactions between the engine and the YAWL services. Other directions for future effort include testing the language and system against complex application scenarios and studying the possibility of using YAWL as an intermediate language to facilitate the development of mappings between various business process execution languages.

Both the executable and sources of YAWL can be downloaded from http://www.citi.qut.edu.au/yawl. YAWL is an open source initiative and therefore welcomes contributions from third parties which could range from dedicated YAWL services to alternative graphical editors or even alternative implementations of the engine itself.

Acknowledgments

The authors wish to thank Lindsay Bradford, David Edmond, Nick Russell, Eric Verbeek, and Moe Wynn for their contributions to the YAWL effort. This work is partly funded by an ARC Discovery Grant "Expressiveness Comparison and Interchange Facilitation between Business Process Execution Languages".

References

1. W.M.P. van der Aalst. The Application of Petri Nets to Workflow Management. *The Journal of Circuits, Systems and Computers*, 8(1):21–66, 1998.
2. W.M.P. van der Aalst and A.H.M. ter Hofstede. Workflow Patterns: On the Expressive Power of (Petri-net-based) Workflow Languages. In K. Jensen, editor, *Proceedings of the Fourth Workshop on the Practical Use of Coloured Petri Nets and CPN Tools (CPN 2002)*, volume 560 of *DAIMI*, pages 1–20, Aarhus, Denmark, August 2002. University of Aarhus.
3. W.M.P. van der Aalst and A.H.M. ter Hofstede. YAWL: Yet Another Workflow Language. Accepted for publication in *Information Systems*, and also available as QUT Technical report, FIT-TR-2003-04, Queensland University of Technology, Brisbane, 2003.
4. W.M.P. van der Aalst, A.H.M. ter Hofstede, B. Kiepuszewski, and A.P. Barros. Workflow Patterns. *Distributed and Parallel Databases*, 14(1):5–51, 2003.
5. A. Arkin et al. Business Process Modeling Language (BPML), Version 1.0, 2002.

6. Pallas Athena. *Flower User Manual*. Pallas Athena BV, Apeldoorn, The Netherlands, 2002.
7. F. Curbera, Y. Goland, J. Klein, F. Leymann, D. Roller, S. Thatte, and S. Weerawarana. Business Process Execution Language for Web Services, Version 1.0. Standards proposal by BEA Systems, International Business Machines Corporation, and Microsoft Corporation, 2002.
8. M. Dumas and A.H.M. ter Hofstede. UML activity diagrams as a workflow specification language. In M. Gogolla and C. Kobryn, editors, *Proc. of the 4th Int. Conference on the Unified Modeling Language (UML01)*, volume 2185 of *LNCS*, pages 76–90, Toronto, Canada, October 2001. Springer Verlag.
9. R. Fielding. *Architectural Styles and the Design of Network-based Software Architectures*. PhD thesis, University of Califormia, Irvine, USA, 2000.
10. IBM. *IBM MQSeries Workflow - Getting Started With Buildtime*. IBM Deutschland Entwicklung GmbH, Boeblingen, Germany, 1999.
11. S. Jablonski and C. Bussler. *Workflow Management: Modeling Concepts, Architecture, and Implementation*. International Thomson Computer Press, London, UK, 1996.
12. K. Jensen. *Coloured Petri Nets. Basic Concepts, Analysis Methods and Practical Use*. EATCS monographs on Theoretical Computer Science. Springer-Verlag, Berlin, 1992.
13. B. Kiepuszewski, A.H.M. ter Hofstede, and W.M.P. van der Aalst. Fundamentals of Control Flow in Workflows. *Acta Informatica*, 39(3):143–209, 2003.
14. E. Kindler. On the Semantics of EPCs: A Framework for Resolving the Vicious Circle (Extended Abstract). In M. Nüttgens and F.J. Rump, editors, *Proceedings of the GI-Workshop EPK 2003: Business Process Management using EPCs*, pages 7–18, Bamberg, Germany, October 2003. Gesellschaft für Informatik, Bonn.
15. P. Lawrence, editor. *Workflow Handbook 1997, Workflow Management Coalition*. John Wiley and Sons, New York, 1997.
16. Open Source Workflow Engines Written in Java (maintained by Carlos E. Perez). http://www.manageability.org/blog/stuff/workflow_in_java.
17. M. Reichert and P. Dadam. ADEPTflex: Supporting Dynamic Changes of Workflow without Loosing Control. *Journal of Intelligent Information Systems*, 10(2):93–129, 1998.
18. G. Vossen and M. Weske. The WASA2 Object-Oriented Workflow Management System. In A. Delis, C. Faloutsos, and S. Ghandeharizadeh, editors, *SIGMOD 1999, Proceedings ACM SIGMOD International Conference on Management of Data, June 1-3, 1999, Philadelphia, Pennsylvania, USA*, pages 587–589. ACM Press, 1999.
19. WFMC. Workflow Management Coalition Workflow Standard: Workflow Process Definition Interface – XML Process Definition Language (XPDL) (WFMC-TC-1025). Technical report, Workflow Management Coalition, Lighthouse Point, Florida, USA, 2002.
20. D. Wodtke, J. Weissenfels, G. Weikum, and A.K. Dittrich. The Mentor Project: Steps Toward Enterprise-Wide Workflow Management. In *Proceedings of the Twelfth International Conference on Data Engineering, February 26 - March 1, 1996, New Orleans, Louisiana*. IEEE Computer Society, 1996.
21. P. Wohed, W.M.P. van der Aalst, M. Dumas, and A.H.M. ter Hofstede. Analysis of Web Services Composition Languages: The Case of BPEL4WS. In I.Y. Song, S.W. Liddle, T.W. Ling, and P. Scheuermann, editors, *22nd International Conference on Conceptual Modeling (ER 2003)*, volume 2813 of *Lecture Notes in Computer Science*, pages 200–215. Springer-Verlag, Berlin, 2003.

MT-Flow – An Environment for Workflow-Supported Model Transformations in MDA

Jernej Kovse and Theo Härder

Department of Computer Science
Kaiserslautern University of Technology
P.O. Box 3049, D-67653 Kaiserslautern, Germany
{kovse,haerder}@informatik.uni-kl.de

Abstract. Specification of systems in a software product line (product-line members) is often supported by domain-specific languages (DSLs) that provide powerful language abstractions for selecting the features of the desired system. In this paper, we show that efficient composition of system specifications (which, in our case, are expressed as models) is also possible using (i) a domain-specific workflow model that guides the composition and (ii) a set of domain-specific templates for model transformations. We illustrate the entire approach on a product line for versioning systems, define a metamodel for workflow models and postulate a measure for estimating the benefits of the proposed approach.

1 Problem Formulation

Generative software development approaches, extensively outlined by Czarnecki and Eisenecker [6], represent a key enabling technology for *software product lines*, which have recently gained tremendous attention both from research and industry. According to Clements and Northrop [4], a *software product line* is a set of software-intensive systems sharing a common, managed set of features that satisfy the needs of a particular market segment. However, each member from this set will still possess an amount of unique functionality. A common example is to have a software product line for systems that control the performance of truck engines. Such a product line is supported by Cummins Engine Inc. [4,5], the world's largest manufacturer of commercial diesel engines above 50 horsepower. Engine types manufactured by the company come with different characteristics: engines may range from 50 to more than 3500 horsepower, have 4 to 18 cylinders, and operate with a variety of fuel systems, air-handling systems, and sensors. The software (with typical size of 130 KSLOC) that controls the engine's performance to produce an optimum mix of power, fuel consumption and emissions, has to be fully optimized for the characteristics of the engine. In cases like this one, companies will try to take advantage of the commonalities among the products in the product line to avoid developing the software for each product from scratch. A possible way to achieve this is to employ a *generator* that, once desired properties of the product are described, takes advantage of *a shared code framework* and *generation templates* to automatically produce the software that corresponds to this product.

A. Persson and J. Stirna (Eds.): CAiSE 2004, LNCS 3084, pp. 160–174, 2004.

Customers that want to buy a software system embraced in a product line have to be given a possibility to clearly describe the system they want. This process is also called *ordering*, since a formal *specification* (*order*) that describes the configuration of features to be included in the system has to be devised. Ideally, this order will serve as an input to a generator that will automatically assemble the system. In the context of product line engineering, a lot of research has been done on *domain-specific languages* (*DSLs*), which can be used to support the ordering process - a program in a DSL is considered a formal specification for the system embraced in the product line. As mentioned by Czarnecki and Eisenecker [6], DSLs are highly specialized, problem-oriented languages as they restrain from using *language elements* (*abstractions*) that are irrelevant for the domain of the product line.

As a main advantage of DSLs we recognize small specification size: Since the abstractions they support are highly specialized for the domain of the product line, the desired system can be specified very briefly and the formal specification (the DSL program) can easily be analyzed and discussed among developers. However, DSLs also come with many drawbacks. First, a separate DSL with the associated parser for DSL programs has to be developed for each product line. In case a DSL is graphical, it will require a specialized editor for devising DSL programs (specifications). Finally, each DSL requires a *dedicated generator* that understands the semantics of DSL abstractions to map them onto the implementation. Approaches like Intentional Programming (IP) [23] employ metaprogramming techniques to support accelerated development of environments for editing, compiling (generating), and debugging domain-specific programs.

In this paper, we claim that, although widely recognized, DSLs are not the only convenient way for ordering products from a software product line. Our *MT-Flow (Model Transformation workFLOWs)* approach proposes that, instead of devising a product order in form of a DSL program, such an order can as well be expressed in a general-purpose specification language, such as Executable UML [12]. MT-Flow uses a *workflow model* to guide the user through a series of *system configuration steps*. On each of these steps, the user selects the features of the system he wants to order. The process is similar to configuring mass-customized products (e.g. cars, kitchen settings, or computers) in the case of non-software product lines.

At the end of each configuration step, MT-Flow *transforms* the current state of the model, so that the decisions the user has made can be immediately observed in a modeling tool. The user selects system features within a graphic interface, which is substantially different from DSL programming, where the user first has to learn the syntax and semantics of the DSL. Another common problem when using DSLs is assuring that a DSL program represents a semantically correct specification. This is difficult until the program is completed, since there may be parts of the program the user yet attempts to write, but at some intermediate programming stage the absence of these parts appears as a correctness violation. This is not possible in our approach, because the workflow model required by MT-Flow determines the paths in which the specification is allowed to evolve: The *flow of control* among the steps prevents an incompatible selection of features and thereby assures that the choices made in the individual steps will always lead to a semantically correct specification. MT-Flow is a generic approach, meaning that its application is not limited to a single product line: The workflow model is *defined externally* and merely interpreted by MT-Flow (MT-Flow acts as a workflow engine). This means that various software product lines described using a general purpose modeling language based on the MOF Model [15] can be supported by simply exchanging the workflow model.

The rest of this paper is organized as follows. Sect. 2 will put the problem in the context of the OMG's Model Driven Architecture (MDA). A motivating example that illustrates the application of MT-Flow is given in Sect. 3. Sect. 4 defines a metamodel for MT-Flow's workflow models and illustrates the use of transformation templates. In Sect. 5, we define a measure to estimate the benefits of our approach. Sect. 6 gives an overview of related work. Finally, our results are summarized in Sect. 7, which also outlines some ideas for the future work.

2   Relation of the Problem to OMG MDA

OMG's *Model Driven Architecture* (MDA) [14] is an exciting approach to developing software systems: First, the *specification of a system* is expressed in form of a *model* in a selected *modeling language*. Afterwards, a *generator* maps this model to the *implementation of the system* on a particular execution platform.

As identified by Frankel [7], developers have four different options when choosing the modeling language for the specification. These options are best illustrated in terms of the OMG's four layer metadata architecture (Fig. 1).

- *Approach 1: Using unadorned (standardized) modeling languages.* In this case, the modeling language is an existing standardized OMG modeling language, such as UML or CWM.
- *Approach 2: Using lightweight language extensions.* Some modeling languages allow developers to define new language constructs *using the language itself*. The most prominent example of this approach are *UML profiles*, which are a built-in extensibility mechanism of the UML language. A UML profile will typically define many *stereotypes*, which are used by developers to *brand* elements in their models. In this way, an element attains supplementary semantics in addition to the semantics defined by its type in the UML Metamodel.

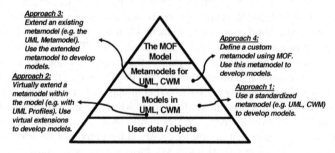

Fig. 1. Choosing the modeling language for the specification

- *Approach 3: Using heavyweight language extensions.* As an alternative to *Approach 2*, new language constructs can also be introduced by extending the metamodel of the modeling language. For example, the UML Metamodel can be enriched with additional types that we connect to the standardized metamodel types by means of generalization and associations.
- *Approach 4: Creating new modeling languages.* When applying *Approaches 2 and 3*, developers will sometimes feel burdened with the types defined by the metamodel of the language (e.g., the UML Metamodel), because the types may not be significant for their problem domain. The problem with *Approaches 2 and 3* is that in both cases, the extensions of the modeling language occur in an *additive* fashion only – the existing language constructs, i.e. types from the metamodel, cannot be modified or deleted. For such problem domains, developers can choose to define an entirely new modeling language from scratch. The metamodel for the new language will be defined in terms of the MOF Model, which is an OMG-standardized meta-metamodel used for defining different metamodels.

It is our observation that the new constructs defined in *Approaches 2, 3,* and *4* actually represent the use of a domain-specific modeling language. Recent approaches like DSL-DIA [11] aim at easy development of custom generators that understand new modeling languages defined using *Approach 4*. Except for *Approach 2*, where the use of a UML profile is largely supported by UML modeling tools, *Approaches 3* and *4* require a special modeling environment. Many *Computer-Aided Method Engineering (CAME)* approaches [22], like MetaEdit+ [13], involve automatic production of problem-oriented modeling environments to be used for new modeling languages.

By MT-Flow, we show that *problem-oriented modeling* (which is supported by domain-specific modeling constructs in *Approaches 2, 3,* and *4*) is equally possible in *Approach 1*, provided there exists a set of *domain-specific model transformation templates* (used to produce *concrete transformations*) and an associated *domain-specific workflow model* that guides their application. Since the specification is expressed using a widely accepted (standardized) general-purpose modeling language, such as UML, the problem of finding an appropriate model-based generator that will map the model to the implementation or a model-based virtual machine capable of executing the model is eliminated. For example, MC-2020 and MC-3020 [19] are available compilers capable of mapping Executable UML models to C++ and C code, while the design and implementation of a virtual machine for UML is discussed by Riehle et al. [20].

Concrete transformations produced by MT-Flow from transformation templates to transform the model can clearly be categorized as PIM-to-PIM transformations mentioned by the MDA specification document [14]. These transformations enhance or filter a model without needing any platform-dependent information. The design of a PIM-to-PIM transformation does not prove very economical in case a transformation will be used in the design of a single system only. Instead (and this is the goal of MT-Flow's transformation templates) we want to capture recurring model enhancement or filtering patterns that can be reused when modeling many systems. General *design patterns* (that do not introduce new semantics to the modeled system, but improve its *architecture*), such as those proposed by Gamma et al. [8] can be found even for very dislike systems. However, specialized patterns (these are the ones we are interested in) that sequentially introduce new semantics to the model can be defined only for systems with a controlled set of common and variable features, i.e., when the systems constitute a product line.

In MT-Flow we choose *differential model exchange* supported by OMG XMI [16] for expressing concrete transformations. In this approach, also referred to by the specification document [16] as *model merging*, a difference between two models is seen as a transformation that takes the old model to the new model. The transformation is described by four tags used for expressing differences: `XMI.difference` (the parent element), `XMI.delete`, `XMI.add`, and `XMI.replace`. MT-Flow is not bound on using the UML as the modeling language, since differential model exchange is supported for any MOF-based metamodel [16].

3   Motivating Example: A Product Line for Versioning Systems

We choose a *product line for versioning systems* as a motivating example for MT-Flow. Why do we treat versioning systems as a product line? Each versioning system possesses a unique *information model* [2], i.e., type definitions for objects and relationships to be stored and versioned (e.g., as evident from the following example, an information model used for a project management application defines object types like *Task*, *ProjectOffer*, and *Employee*).

Next, we may want to refine the information model with the following definitions.

*   Which object types support versioning? An object type that supports versioning provides a method *createSuccessor* (for deriving a successor to an object version) and a method *freeze* (for freezing an object version).
*   Which relationship type ends are *floating*? Floating relationship ends implement the behavior needed for *versioned relationships*. In case a given *project offer, p,* possesses a reference to a *task, t,* and *t* is versioned, a floating relationship end at *t* contains a user-managed subset of all versions of *t*. This subset is called a *candidate version collection* and may have a *pinned version*, which is the default version to be returned in case the client does not want to select a version from the collection manually. Maintaining floating relationship ends implies performance impedance so the user may choose to omit this feature for some relationship types.
*   How do object and version management operations like *new, copy, createSuccessor, freeze, checkout/checkin* propagate across the relationships? A detailed coverage of operation propagation is given by Rumbaugh [21].
*   What are the *workspace types* and how do these relate to regular object types? A workspace acts as a container for regular objects. However, only one version of an object may be attached to a workspace at a time. For this reason, a workspace acts as a single-version view to objects stored in the versioning system.

Many commercial versioning systems are implemented *generically* – this means that a large part of their implementation does not need to change for each user-defined information model. For example, a generic system can define a single database table for storing relationships (of every possible relationship type) and a single table for storing versioning information (like information on a predecessor version for a given version). Both tables are present for every installed information model, while tables for object types are specific for a given information model. A *fully generative approach* (like the one supported by MT-Flow), on the other hand, allows the user a fine-grained specification of desired features in an information model that will also contain user decisions on floating relationship ends, operation propagation, workspace type definitions, etc. In this case, each information model (i.e., the specification) can be mapped to a distinct, completely generated and thus optimized implementation of a versioning system. The following sections will illustrate how MT-Flow supports the development of an information model in Executable UML for a simple versioning system.

3.1 Step A: Define an Object Type

In this step, the user defines an object type. This includes the definition of a name for the object type and the attributes with the corresponding primitive data types. The interface shown by MT-Flow for this purpose is illustrated in Fig. 2. We use this interface to define the object type *Task*. MT-Flow will fill an existing transformation template with these definitions. As a result, a concrete transformation is expressed using XMI differential tags. The transformation adds a new UML class *Task* (see Fig. 2) with its attributes to the current model (we assume we begin with an empty model in each specification). In addition, an *objId* that identifies an object within the versioning system and a *globalId* that identifies a particular *object version* within the versioning system are added. *Step A* can be repeated many times to add additional object types. We repeat the step to add object types *ProjectOffer* and *Employee*. The final model obtained in this way is illustrated in Fig. 2.

3.2 Step B: Define Which Objects Are Versioned

In this step, the user specifies which object types support versioning. As an additional feature, he may choose to limit the allowed number of successors to a version. We carry out *Step B* twice to make *Task* and *ProjectOffer* versionable. Concrete transformations will add a *verID* (a unique identifier of a version within a version tree) to the classes, a reflexive association for linking a version to its successors, a *createSuccessor* operation, and a *freeze* operation. The semantics of these operations is expressed using the model elements of the *UML Action Semantics* package, which can have many possible

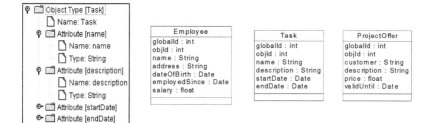

Fig. 2. Adding a new object type

syntax renderings in so-called *action languages*. For this reason, actions appear as text in diagrams. In the model, however, they are represented as instances of modeling constructs defined by the Action Semantics package, and can therefore be manipulated using XMI's differential elements. In Fig. 3, showing the result of making the class *Task* versionable, we use the Object Action Language (OAL), proposed by Mellor and

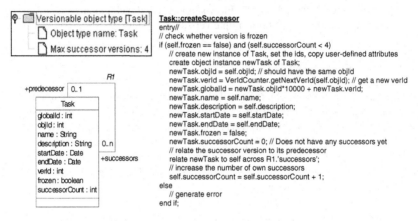

Task::createSuccessor
```
entry//
// check whether version is frozen
if (self.frozen == false) and (self.successorCount < 4)
    // create new instance of Task, set the ids, copy user-defined attributes
    create object instance newTask of Task;
    newTask.objId = self.objId; // should have the same objId
    newTask.verId = VerIdCounter.getNextVerId(self.objId); // get a new verId
    newTask.globalId = newTask.objId*10000 + newTask.verId;
    newTask.name = self.name;
    newTask.description = self.description;
    newTask.startDate = self.startDate;
    newTask.endDate = self.endDate;
    newTask.frozen = false;
    newTask.successorCount = 0; // Does not have any successors yet
    // relate the successor version to its predecessor
    relate newTask to self across R1.'successors';
    // increase the number of own successors
    self.successorCount = self.successorCount + 1;
else
    // generate error
end if;
```

Fig. 3. Making an object type versionable

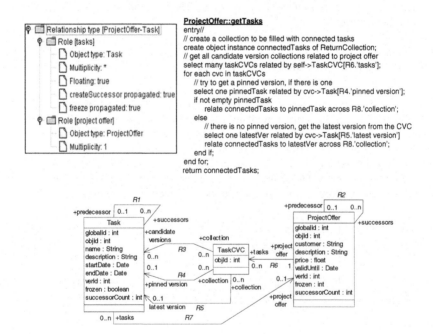

ProjectOffer::getTasks
```
entry//
// create a collection to be filled with connected tasks
create object instance connectedTasks of ReturnCollection;
// get all candidate version collections related to project offer
select many taskCVCs related by self->TaskCVC[R6.'tasks'];
for each cvc in taskCVCs
    // try to get a pinned version, if there is one
    select one pinnedTask related by cvc->Task[R4.'pinned version'];
    if not empty pinnedTask
        relate connectedTasks to pinnedTask across R8.'collection';
    else
        // there is no pinned version, get the latest version from the CVC
        select one latestVer related by cvc->Task[R5.'latest version']
        relate connectedTasks to latestVer across R8.'collection';
    end if;
end for;
return connectedTasks;
```

Fig. 4. Defining a relationship type

Balcer [12] for specifying the *createSuccessor* operation. Class definitions made in *Step A* are carried as data flows into *Step B*: This makes it impossible to define a non-existing object type as versionable. The specified constraint that limits the number of successor versions gets integrated into the procedure's actions.

3.3 Step C: Define Relationship Types

In *Step C*, we define relationship types. This includes the definition of *role names, multiplicities*, indication of *floating relationship ends* and *operation propagation* properties. In the example in Fig. 4, we define a relationship type *ProjectOffer-Task* with a floating relationship end for *tasks*. Creating a successor to a *project offer* version creates successors to related pinned *task* versions and freezing a *project offer* version freezes the pinned *task* versions (this behavior requires a refinement of *createSuccessor* and *freeze* operations that have been added to the model in *Step B*.) Partial results of the concrete transformation are illustrated in Fig. 4, which shows the class *TaskCVC* used for maintaining candidate version collections for *tasks* and the procedure *getTasks* that retrieves *tasks* connected to a *project offer*.

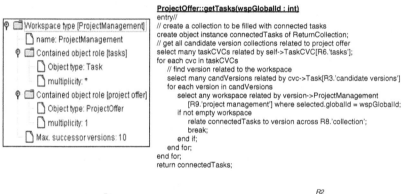

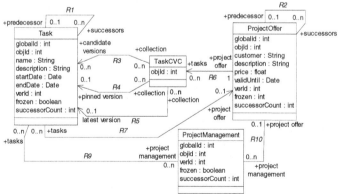

Fig. 5. Defining a workspace type

3.4 Step D: Define Workspace Types

In this step, the user defines workspace types. Each workspace type may be connected to regular object types using *attachment relationship types*. Traversal of a relationship is sensitive to the *globalId* of the workspace submitted to the navigation operation - only objects that are attached to this workspace can be reached across the relationship. Fig. 5 illustrates a definition of a workspace type *project management* that can attach one *project offer* and many *tasks* (but always only one version of each of them). The concrete transformation adds a class for the workspace type, the attachment relationship types and an operation for workspace-sensitive relationship traversal.

4 MT-Flow Templates and Workflow Models

Template-based approaches have become popular for dynamic generation of documents (like source code, tests, or documentation) that exhibit a common generic structure, but need to be instantiated many times with user-defined input values (a familiar example are *JavaServer Pages* that act as templates for HTML). Nearly all template-based approaches work in the same way. First, a template with integrated *control flow statements* that can repeat (or omit) some parts of the template is written. Second, a template engine replaces *placeholders* in a template with user-defined values (stored in a *context*) while executing the control flow. The template engine used in MT-Flow to generate concrete transformations expressed in XMI is *Velocity* [1]. An excerpt from the template used for *Step A* is illustrated in Fig. 6 (the '*$*'-signs represent references to values in the context).

MT-Flow's *workflow models* are acyclic directed graphs in which a node (called *configuration step*) represent (i) a specification of user-defined values, (ii) a production of concrete transformations from transformation templates, and (iii) an application of concrete transformations to the current model. The edges represent the flow of control and data among the steps. The *flow of control* defines the order in which configuration steps

```
...
<XMI.difference>
    <XMI.add href="currentModel.xmi|p1">
        <UML:Class xmi.id = '$Class.mId' name = '$Class.name' visibility = 'public'
            isSpecification = 'false' isRoot = 'false' isLeaf = 'false' isAbstract = 'false' isActive = 'false'>
            <UML:Classifier.feature>
            #foreach( $item in $ClassAttributes )
                <UML:Attribute xmi.id = '$item.mId' name = '$item.name' visibility = 'private'
                    isSpecification = 'false' ownerScope = 'instance'>
                    <UML:StructuralFeature.type>
                        <UML:DataType xmi.idref = '$item.typeMId'/>
                    </UML:StructuralFeature.type>
                </UML:Attribute>
            #end
            </UML:Classifier.feature>
        </UML:Class>
    </XMI.add>
</XMI.difference>
...
```

Fig. 6. Transformation template for *Step A*

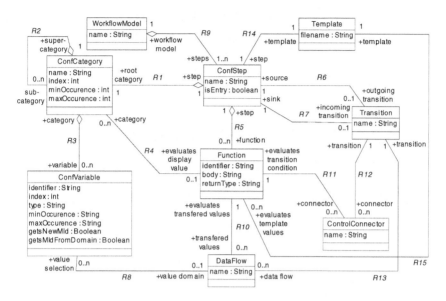

Fig. 7. Metamodel for MT-Flow's workflow models

are executed. The *flow of data* allows the exchange of configuration values among the steps. A *metamodel* for MT-Flow's workflow models is shown in Fig. 7.

A workflow model consist of many configuration steps, where one of the steps is marked as *entry*, denoting the beginning of execution. Each step defines a *root configuration category*, which may be subdivided into many *sub-categories*. A category may contain *configuration variables*, which take user values that will be used for producing a concrete transformation. These values are always of primitive types. Examples of categories and variables are illustrated throughout Figs. 2-5 (e.g., in Fig. 2, *Object type* is a category and *Name* is a variable). Categories and variables are indexed, which prescribes their ordering in the user interface. A configuration variable may be bound on one *data flow* received from the preceding configuration step (many data flows can be carried by a single transition). Such a data flow is then a set of values that are allowed to be selected for the variable (i.e., it defines the variable's domain). MT-Flow does not treat variables as scalars, but rather as *value wrappers*. A value wrapper consists of two components: a *value* (which is user-defined), and an *element identifier* associated with this value. Model elements need to provide unique identities so that succeeding model transformations can manipulate elements introduced by preceding model transformations. These identities can be created by MT-Flow automatically (using the setting *ConfVariable.getsNewMId*) or automatically adopted from a value wrapper in the value domain carried by a data flow (using the setting *ConfVariable.getsMIdFromDomain*).

There is a set of *functions* that can be associated with each step in a workflow model. These functions do not have side-effects and thus never change the state of value wrappers. They are specified in MT-Flow's own language that supports easy scrolling through configuration categories and evaluation of arithmetic and string manipulation expressions. There is no global *"memory"* context for the workflow model, i.e., a function is allowed to access only (i) configuration variables, (ii) other functions defined in the same step and (iii) incoming data flows. There are four scenarios in which MT-flow's functions are used:

- *Evaluating a display value for a configuration category* (association *R4* in Fig. 7). A category can automatically display a value obtained as a function result, e.g., the category *Workspace type* in Fig. 5 automatically displays the value of its variable *name* in square brackets.
- *Evaluating value wrappers for a data flow* (association *R10* in Fig. 7). Each data flow is associated with a function that *returns a collection* of value wrappers to be carried by the data flow. These functions prepare values for domains used in the succeeding step.
- *Evaluating transition conditions* (association *R11* in Fig. 7). Each *control connector* is associated with exactly one function that returns a boolean value. An outgoing transition will be allowed only when all control connectors for the transition evaluate to *true* for the current configuration step. These functions imply the *allowed paths* in the workflow model that will be followed depending on the values of configuration variables. In this way, transition conditions implement *composition rules* (also known as *hard constraints*) for feature interdependencies [6], i.e., what features imply other features in the configuration. For example, in Fig. 4, only versionable object types can be selected for floating relationship ends in *Step C*. In case this constraint is violated, the transition to *Step D* will be prevented.
- *Evaluating values for a template* (association *R15* in Fig. 7). These functions abstract computation and string manipulation from the templates. The values they return can be accessed as variables in the template engine's *context* (see [1] for more information on the context) and are thus easily accessible from the templates.

5   Evaluation

We associate MT-Flow with a measure to estimate the benefits of automated model transformations. We *postulate* this measure as useful based on our experience with the product line for versioning systems, but have not observed its performance on a large set of various product lines yet.

The measure $XEPR_S(i)$ *(XMI Element Production Rate for a given system i)* is defined as

$$XEPR_s(i) = \frac{x(i)}{v(i)} \tag{1}$$

where $x(i)$ is the number of XMI elements present in the final model and $v(i)$ is the number of configuration value definitions and selections made by the user when configuring the system.

According to Czarnecki and Eisenecker [6], the structure of product-line members should not be treated as a configurability aspect of the product line. In other words, we should separate *concept instantiations* (e.g., definition of a new object type, relationship type, or workspace type) from *concept configurations* (e.g., definition of whether a relationship end is floating). If this was not the case, for example, one could define a versioning system with a large number of object types in *Step A* and easily arrive at a large $XEPR_S(i)$ value. Therefore, we define $XEPR_{SN}(i)$ as a normalization of the $XEPR_S(i)$ value using the count of concept instantiations $c(i)$ (for our product line for the versioning systems, this is the count of object types, attributes, relationship types, and workspace types defined for the system):

$$XEPR_{SN}(i) = \frac{XEPR_S(i)}{c(i)} \tag{2}$$

The *XEPR value for the product line (XEPR$_{PL}$)* is the average $XEPR_{SN}(i)$ value for n representative systems embraced in the product line.

$$XEPR_{PL} = \frac{\sum_{i=1}^{n} XEPR_{SN}(i)}{n} \tag{3}$$

The $XEPR_{PL}$ value for our example product line for versioning systems is 41,2.

Remark: $XEPR_{PL}$ is a *productivity measure*, since it compares the size of the final model with the user's effort for configuring the system. Its pitfall is that it assumes that in a manual modeling process, a manual insertion of every model element is associated with roughly the same effort. In our observation, this is not the case: Especially statements in action languages usually introduce a very large number of model elements (see examples in [15]) in proportion to the actual effort for defining a statement. A simple solution to this problem would be to assign weights to diverse model elements (based on practical experience with modeling efforts) and compute $x(i)$ in $XEPR_S(i)$ as a weighted sum.

6   Related Work

Peltier et al. [18] present *MTRANS*, which is an XSLT-based framework for model transformations. A special *rule-based language* is supported for describing the effect of transformations. Programs in this language get compiled into an XSLT transformation, which is used to map an input model expressed in XMI to an output model (also expressed in XMI). The idea is not described in the context of software product lines. Dependencies among sequentially applied transformations cannot be controlled.

There is a clear distinction among *specification refinement* approaches like *evolving algebras* (later renamed to *abstract state machines*) [9] or *especs* [17] and MT-Flow. Refinement approaches start with an abstract specification of a system which already includes key definitions of what the system does, but leaves out how it does this. For example, the initial specification may state that *sorting* is required, but the *definite sorting algorithm* is chosen in the succeeding refinements. *SPECWARE* [24] is an example of a system supporting such *specification morphisms*. In MT-Flow, on the other hand, *new* structural and behavioral semantics can appear in the existing specification in each step. For this reason, the specification is not considered complete (even not on some abstract level) until the last configuration step has been performed. In this aspect, MT-Flow resembles approaches that support consecutive application of predefined patterns to automatically assemble the final application. An example of such an approach is *GREN*, described by Braga and Masiero [3]. The authors observe that when *instantiating software frameworks* to build concrete systems, the knowledge about flexible (variable) framework parts (also called the *hot spots*) is required. This problem is tightly related to software product lines, because most system families can be implemented using frameworks [6]. The authors propose a solution that relies on the sequential application of *patterns*, which is guided by a wizard and is allowed to follow only predefined paths. The allowed paths are described by associating different patterns in a formal model (the authors define a metamodel for such model). Concrete user-defined values for a selected pattern are not observed in a transition to the next pattern, as it is the case in MT-Flow. A direct relation to software product lines is not given, although the authors observe that in order for the approach to be successful, patterns have to be domain-specific.

7   Conclusion and Future Work

This paper presented MT-Flow, our approach for automatic construction of system specifications (expressed as models) within a software product line. The construction takes place by producing concrete model transformations from transformation templates and sequentially applying them to the current specification. The process is guided by MT-Flow's workflow model. In this way, we prove that defining a set of *domain-specific model transformation templates* and a *domain-specific workflow model* for modeling concrete systems from the product line represents a viable alternative to domain-specific languages for system configuration. We illustrated our approach on a product line for versioning systems. Based on our experience with this product line, we postulated a measure for estimating the benefits of MT-Flow for system configuration.

Our future work will be focused on the following areas.

- *Performance of the postulated measure*. We want to observe the performance of the measure postulated in Sect. 5 on a large set of software product lines. Our primary goal is to compare the obtained $XEPR_{PL}$ values to the effort of developing models manually (i.e. without MT-Flow).

- *Mining MT-Flow's transformation templates and workflow models*. Many companies sell a set of systems that actually belong to a software product line, without having a proper support for consistently specifying and afterwards generating individual systems on a basis of common architecture. We will try to prove that, with some human assistance, existing models of these systems (which have usually been developed from scratch) can be mined to obtain MT-Flow's transformation templates and the workflow model. In this way, MT-Flow can be used for developing further systems from the product line.

- *Relation to domain analysis.* At the moment, MT-Flow provides no direct relation to domain analysis approaches, like FODA (feature-oriented domain analysis) [10], which seem to be very important for analysis and understanding of variability within a product line. We will try to explore this relation and support it in the implementation of MT-Flow.

References

1. The Apache Jakarta Project: Velocity, http://jakarta.apache.org/velocity/
2. Bernstein, P.A.: Repositories and Object-Oriented Databases, SIGMOD Record 27:1 (1998), 34-46
3. Braga, R.T.V., Masiero, P.C.: Building a Wizard for Framework Instantiation Based on a Pattern Language, in: Proc. OOIS 2003, Geneva, Sept. 2003, 95-106.
4. Clements, P., Northrop, L.: Software Product Lines: Practices and Patterns, Addison-Wesley, 2002
5. Cummins Inc., http://www.cummins.com/
6. Czarnecki, K., Eisenecker, U.W.: Generative Programming: Methods, Tools, and Applications, Addison-Wesley, 2000
7. Frankel, D.: Model Driven Architecture: Applying MDA to Enterprise Computing, Wiley Publishing, 2003
8. Gamma, E., Helm, R., Johnson, R.E.: Design Patterns, Addison-Wesley, 1997
9. Gurevich, Y.: Evolving Algebra 1993: Lipari Guide, in: Specification and Validation Methods, Oxford University Press, 1995, 9-36
10. Kang, K., Cohen, S., Hess, J., Nowak, W., Peterson, S.: Feature-Oriented Domain Analysis (FODA) Feasibility Study, Tech. Report CMU/SEI-90-TR-21, Carnegie Mellon University, 1990
11. Kovse, J., Härder, T.: DSL-DIA - An Environment for Domain-Specific Languages for Database-Intensive Applications, in: Proc. OOIS'03, Geneva, Sept. 2003, 304-310
12. Mellor, S.J., Balcer, M.J.: Executable UML: A Foundation for Model-Driven Architecture, Addison-Wesley, 2002
13. MetaCase: MetaEdit+ Product Website, http://www.metacase.com/mep/
14. OMG: Model Driven Architecture (MDA) - A Technical Perspective, July 2001
15. OMG: Unified Modeling Language Specification, Version 1.5, Mar. 2003
16. OMG: XML Metadata Interchange Specification, Version 1.2, Jan. 2002
17. Pavlovic, D., Smith, D.R.: Composition and Refinement of Behavioral Specifications, Technical Report KES.U.01.6, Kestrel Institute, July 2001
18. Peltier, M., Bézivin, J., Guillaume, G.: MTRANS: A General Framework, Based on XSLT, for Model Transformations, Proc. workshop WTUMP 2001, Genova, Apr. 2001
19. Project Technology, Inc.: BridgePoint Development Suite, MC-2020 and MC-3020 Model Compilers, http://www.projtech.com/prods/index.html
20. Riehle, D., Fraleigh, S., Bucka-Lassen, D., Omorogbe, N.: The Architecture of a UML Virtual Machine, in: Proc. OOPSLA'01, Tampa, Oct. 2001, 327-341
21. Rumbaugh, J.E.: Controlling Propagation of Operations Using Attributes on Relations, in. Proc. OOPSLA'88, San Diego, Sept. 1988, 285-296
22. Saeki, M.: Toward Automated Method Engineering: Supporting Method Assembly in CAME, presentation at EMSISE'03 workshop, Geneva, Sept. 2003.

23. Simonyi, C.: The Death of Computer Languages, the Birth of Intentional Programming, Tech. Report MSR-TR-95-52, Microsoft Research, Sept. 1995
24. Srinivas, Y.V., Jullig, R.: Specware(tm): Formal Support for Composing Software, in: Proc. MPC'95, Irsee, July 1995.

Multiple Instantiation
in a Dynamic Workflow Environment

Adnene Guabtni and François Charoy

LORIA - INRIA - CNRS (UMR 7503) BP 239
F-54506 Vandouvre-lès-Nancy Cedex, France
{guabtni,charoy}@loria.fr

Abstract. Business processes often requires to execute a task multiple time in series or in parallel. In some workflow management systems this possibility is already supported and called "multiple instantiation". Usually the term "iteration" is used to define multiple executions in series. Nevertheless, the existing solutions impose many constraints for workflow designers and decrease flexibility. Almost all of them use new operators to represent multiple instances that are integrated in the workflow as any other workflow basic operators. This way of representation encumbers and complicates the workflow so that it's unreadable for the end user. In this article, we propose a new way of defining multiple instantiations in a workflow without using exotic operators, nor complicating the workflow itself. Our approach is based on defining sets of tasks in a dynamic workflow process. Each set contains activities that must be executed multiple times. Each set is governed by constraints making it possible to supervise the multiple executions. These sets can be nested or even overlap. We use two types of sets in this work: "parallel instance's set" for those activities that are executed multiple times in parallel. And the second type is "iterative instance's set" for those that are executed multiple times in sequence. The number of instantiations to do and the condition to iterate could be evaluated at run-time. In this paper, we also show on a real process executed in an experience how this model could have been used to ease its definition.

1 Introduction

A lot of work has been done recently on the definition of business process models for different purposes. Most of these models provide the ability to define processes using XML schemas and are based more or less on the same concepts of nodes (activities), edges (dependencies between activities) and synchronization condition. However, as it has been precisely described in [9], these models do not support well multiple instantiation of group of activities or even of single activities. Multiple instantiation means the ability to repeat several time the execution of a group of activities, either in sequence, or in parallel. Different patterns for multiple instantiation have been identified in [9], [7] and [1] and these patterns have been explicitly defined as petri net models in [10]. Workflow management systems must provide practical possibilities to realize them. Current workflow

A. Persson and J. Stirna (Eds.): CAiSE 2004, LNCS 3084, pp. 175–188, 2004.

management systems adopt very different strategies to model these patterns. It can be by introducing new operators, using sub processes or defining complex model structures. However, most of them are far from providing a simple solution to apply multiple instantiation patterns.

Executing multiple times a set of activities, in parallel or in sequence is very common. Review processes, development processes, quality assurance processes are typical cases where the number of iterations or the number of execution depends on the number of people involved, the number of object produced or some other criteria defined on the state of the objects. A workflow management system must be able to model such repetition and even to allow evolution of the parts of the process that are executed multiple times.

In this paper we present an evolution that we can apply to any model because of its generality. We choose the most basic model that gives us a simple workflow with no added constructors than the edges of control.

The first part of the paper will describe the motivation for this work and recall the multiple instantiation patterns that can be found in the process modelling literature. The second part will describe how these patterns can be implemented in current workflow management systems. The third part will describe our proposal as an extension of a simple process model with a "set oriented" multiple instantiation definition. We will then present briefly how it has been implemented in the Bonita WFMS in order to support cooperative process management.

2   Motivation and Related Work

Multiple execution of group of activities is a pattern that can be found in a lot of cooperative processes. These executions are common in such cases:

- a piece of work is split up and distributed between a group of people (writing chapters of a book, coding modules)
- a piece of work has to be done by all the people with some role (review chapters of a book, testing)
- a piece of work has to be repeated until it reaches a certain level of quality (quality assurance, testing, review/editing process)

Different multiple instantiation patterns have been precisely analysed in [9],[7] and [1]. Here, we will consider the one described in [9] because it is a generalized description. These patterns are numbered from 10 to 15 in this paper.

- 10 is arbitrary cycles or loops. Modelling loops directly in a workflow is still considered as an issue even if some systems provide some way to do it.
- 11 is implicit termination. A sub process is terminated if nothing else is to be done. Most workflow engines require a final node to specify termination of a sub process.
- 12 is multiple instantiation without synchronization. Several instances of the same activity are executed. They are not synchronized. This is supported by most workflow systems

- 13 is multiple instantiation with a priori design time knowledge. An activity has to be executed multiple times and the number of instances is known at design time.
- 14 is multiple instances with a priori runtime knowledge. An activity has to be executed multiple times and the number of instances is known at run time before they are started.
- 15 is multiple instantiation without a priori runtime knowledge. The number of instances to create depends on the execution of the instances themselves. New instances have to be created while other are still executing.

3   Multiple Instantiation and Current Workflow Models

Many workflow management systems supports some of the patterns above. The possibilities of each one of some known workflow management systems are presented in [9]. In these workflow management systems, many solutions are used. The most prevalent of them is the use of the "merge" operator. Figure 1 illustrates the use of this operator to express multiple instantiation. The number of instances can be computed before the instantiation or computed while the instantiation is working as the pattern 15. The example concerns the multiple instantiation of just one activity. When we want to use this kind of solutions to express multiple instantiation of a set of activities, we have a constraint. This constraint inflicts that the group of activities must be sequentially connected. This is a hard constraint that decreases possibilities.

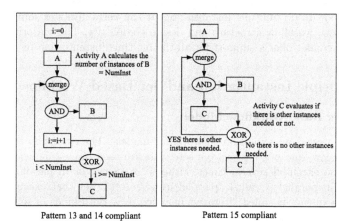

Fig. 1. Multiple instantiation using the "Merge" operator

Another kind of solution is the use of the "Bundle" operator. This solution is implemented in the FlowMark 2.3 language. The "Bundle" operator receives the number of instances of the activity it is related to and takes care of its instantiation. After that, the "Bundle" operator waits the end of all these instances to hands off the activities that follow. Figure 2 illustrate the typical use of the "Bundle" operator in a workflow process. This solution has a disadvantage: the operator involves only one activity so that we cannot express the multiple instantiation of a group of activities.

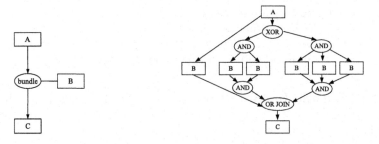

Fig. 2. Multiple instantiation using the "Bundle" operator

Fig. 3. Multiple instantiation using the XOR SPLIT, AND JOIN and OR JOIN operators

The workflow management systems that don't have direct support of multiple instantiation are required to use a combination of XOR SPLIT, AND JOIN and OR JOIN to do it. Figure 3 illustrates this case. We can see the complexity of the workflow process after expressing multiple instantiation. This solution supposes that the number of instances is limited to a maximum number. There is also no support for pattern 15 with this solution.

Most of all the workflow management systems are based on new operators introduction to do multiple instantiation. It can certainly offer some solutions but increase workflow structure and design complexity. The majority of these attempts cannot offer a support for all the multiple instantiation patterns.

4   Multiple Instantiation and Set Based Workflow Model

4.1   The Basic Workflow Model

Here we present an extension to workflow models. The extension firms up by adding a new kind of construction: sets. Sets are used to contain activities that have to be executed several times, either in sequence or in parallel. Set that executes in parallel is called "parallel instance set". Set that executes several times in sequence is called "iterative instance set". Both kinds of sets will have different kind of constraints for their definition and different behaviours for their execution. Sets can be nested or overlapped with certain conditions. This is what we present in the following sections.

This approach can be applied to any workflow model provided that the model allows dynamic creation of activities at runtime. Many works have been made on dynamic changes on workflow in [5], [4], [6], [2] and [5]. The Bonita workflow model offers these possibilities so that we chosen it to implement our set based model. This model is based on the work published in [2] concerning flexibility in workflow systems and implement the anticipation of execution of activities described in [3]. Bonita model is based on a workflow model without separated process schema and instances of the schema. Our model consists of just instances. This simplifies the use of dynamic changes as the schema and the instance are the same thing.

4.2   Multiple Instantiation Sets

A multiple instantiation set of activities has a state that can be INITIAL, ACTIVE or FINISHED.

- INITIAL: All the activities of the set are in initial state (not yet executed).
- ACTIVE: At least one of the activities of the set is started.
- FINISHED: All the activities of the set have finished their execution.

There is two types of multiple instantiation sets: parallel and iterative. Each one of these two types has also some other properties and some constraints to apply on their activities.

Parallel Instance Set. Parallel instantiation deals with patterns 12 to 15 in [8]. It is a solution to execute many times the same set of activities in parallel.

The goal of parallel instance sets is to provide an answer to the problem of activities that have to be executed several times. This execution can be made in parallel. The number of times they have to be executed is not necessarily known at the beginning of the process. This is described in [8] as patterns 14 and 15.

Parallel instance set has a special property defined as:

- A function to compute the number of times it has to be executed. This function will return the number of people belonging to a role or the value of some data produced by a preceding activity.

There is no constraints on the parallel instance set of activities. Any activity that has not been yet started can be selected to participate in a parallel instance set. This allows a very simple definition of this kind of sets.

Iterative Instance Set. The goal of iterative instance sets is to allow the repetition of a their activities until some condition is evaluated to true. This is the way to model iterations in Bonita, as cycles are not allowed.

Iterative instance set matches Pattern 10 and 11 in [8]. Iteration means that we want to specify that the given set of activities must be repeated a number of times until a given condition is true. Cycles are an issue in WFMS because of race condition. In our proposal, we overcome this issue by re-instantiating activities as long as it is needed. Thus iteration is not the re-execution of a set of activities but the successive execution of copies of these activities. This has an impact on the way data are managed and imply specific constraints that will be described here.

Iterative instance set has two special properties defined as:

- A function to evaluate if a new iteration is needed or not. This function will be called each time an iteration is finished.
- A subset of break activities belonging to the iterative instance set. A break activity incarnates a new iteration's control type. Without break activities, the termination condition is checked when all the activities of the set are terminated (implicit termination). When a break activity is finished it forces the checking of the iteration condition even when other activities are executing or still not started. if the condition allows a new iteration, a new instance of each activity of the set is created and the new iterative instance set of activities can start. The new set of activities and the old one continue their executions independently of each other. Break activities allow a kind of overlapping in iteration levels.

The only structural constraints for such a set is that there should not be a path starting from an activity of the set, going to an activity out of the set and going back to an activity of the set.

Life Cycle of Multiple Instance Sets. The life cycle of multiple instance sets is illustrated in figure 4. The state diagram depends on two conditions:

Fig. 4. State diagram of a set

- **Activating condition:** The state of the set is turned on ACTIVE when at least one of its activities is ready to start.
- **Finishing condition for parallel instance sets:** The parallel instance set state is turned on FINISHED when all of its activities are finished or cancelled.
- **Finishing condition for iterative instance sets:** There is two ways for an iterative instance set to become in FINISHED state:
  • The first is when all of its activities are finished or cancelled.
  • The second is when there is at least one activity in the set that is a break activity that becomes FINISHED.

Execution of a Parallel Instance Set. As soon as an activity of the parallel instance set is ready to execute, the set is activated. This means that the number of instances is computed and that activities of the set are copied to get as many instance as needed by this result. Thus the process evolves dynamically. New activities are created, new edge are created between activities. Activities created when activating a parallel instance set are exactly the same as the activities belonging to the set except that they are marked as being clones and that they don't belong to their original set.

Edges going out of the set are also replicated. They have different origin and leads to the destination node of the original edge. This node will be a merge

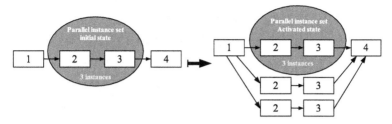

Fig. 5. A parallel instance set execution

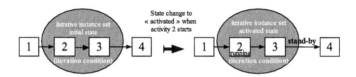

Fig. 6. Iterative instance set activation

point for the copies of the set so that the job of merging data (the different versions of the same work) is processed by this node. Figure 5 illustrates an example of activation of a parallel instance set.

Execution of an Iterative Instance Set. The iterative instance set is activated when one of the activities of the set is activated. All edges going outside the set are turned standby as described in figure 6. The standby state of an edge makes this one blocked to that state while it is not unblocked by turning it to standard state. While an edge is in standby state, activities following it cannot start.

Then, activities of the set are executed following the usual execution strategy. Once, the last activity of the set or a break activity is terminated, the iteration condition of the set is evaluated. If true, the set is re-instantiated as described in figure 7. The new copy of the set is declared as iterative instance set with the same iteration condition. The edges going outside the original set are turned to standard state so that they don't block the execution of following activities. But new copies of these edges are turned to standby state accordingly to the activation of the new iterative instance set. These new edges follow the blocking of execution of following activities.

At the final iteration, the outgoing edges are turned to standard state and there is no new instances of these edges. All the outgoing edges of all the instances of the set are in standard state and the activities that follow the set can start their execution.

4.3   Relationships between Sets

Sets can be nested or even overlap. The activation and replication process is straightforward. The rules for activation of the set remain unchanged. This is due to the dynamism of the model when any activity or set exists by itself.

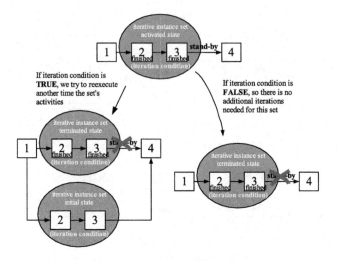

Fig. 7. Iterative instance set finishing

When activating a parallel instance set that contains other sets (parallel or iterative), these ones are also duplicated following the same scheme of cloning. A copy of a set contains the copy of activities of the original set.

When activating a parallel instance set that overlaps other sets (parallel or iterative), for each activity of the set that is also part of another overlapped set, the copies of this activity are also part of the same overlapped set (no need to copy the overlapped sets).

Figure 8 illustrate the case where a parallel instance set containing other sets and also overlapping other sets is activated.

The same approach is considered when finishing an iterative instance set that nest or overlap other sets.

Priority in Case of Concurrent Activations. Suppose the case of figure 9 where a parallel instance set and an iterative one overlap. If activity 1 is ready to start, we must decide which set will be activated first. If the parallel one is activated first, the iterative set will grow by adding the new instances of activity 1. After that the iterations will concern 4 activities. On another side, if the iterative set is activated first, there will exist an edge between the instances of activity 1 and activity 2 that is in standby state. This will paralyse the parallel instance set that will not be able to finish while iterations are not finished.

These two possibilities define an ambiguity that must be resolved by a rule: When there is two possible set activations at the same time concerning parallel and iterative instance sets, we assume that the parallel one is activated first. In the case of sets that are just parallel there is no problem of priority because the final effect is the same while activating at any arrangement.

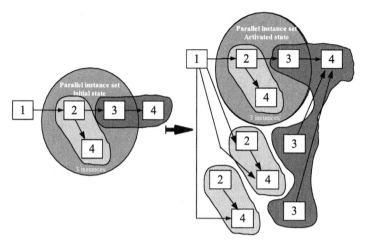

Fig. 8. Activation of a parallel instance set with nested and overlapped sets

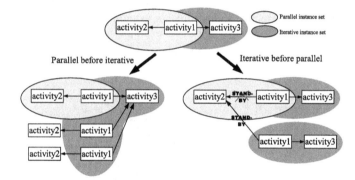

Fig. 9. Ambiguity in concurrent overlapped heterogeneous sets activations

5   Multiple Instance Sets and Workflow Patterns

The entire workflow patterns that we have presented in the introduction of this paper can be easily described as multiple instance sets like following:

- **Pattern 10**: The arbitrary cycles or loops pattern is simply mapped to iterative instance sets. The benefit is the simple definition of the set of activities and the iteration condition. This condition can be a logical formula concerning process objects states.
- **Pattern 11**: Implicit termination is implicitly used in the changing state system of sets. When all activities of a set are terminated or cancelled this set is finished.
- **Pattern 12**: Multiple instantiation without synchronization is the simple case of a parallel instance set. If there is an edge going out of the set, the

activity that this edge is going to is considered as a synchronization activity. To do a multiple instantiation without synchronization we simply don't add outgoing edges to the set.

– **Pattern 13**: Multiple instantiation with a priori design time knowledge can be simply mapped to parallel instance sets. We have there a generalized solution. Any set of activities can be instantiated multiple times. The only information to provide is a function able to calculate the number of instances that have to be created. In the case of design time knowledge, the function is simply a constant corresponding to the known number of instances.

– **Pattern 14**: Multiple instantiation with a priori runtime knowledge is also mapped to parallel instance sets. The function calculating the number of instances can calculate this number at activation time. This number can depends on any variable or property of the process. Another way is to authorize other activities to modify this function at runtime.

– **Pattern 15**: Multiple instantiation without a priori runtime knowledge is a special pattern that is generally not supported by classical workflow management systems. Multiple instance sets can offer a new solution. Oddly we don't use parallel instance sets but we use iterative instance set containing break activities. Figure 10 illustrates an example of using iterative instance sets to implement pattern 15. In this example, activity A calculates if the

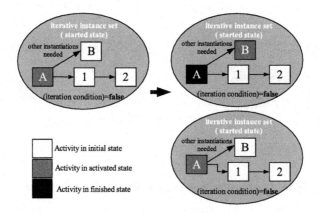

Fig. 10. The implementation of the pattern 15 based on iterative instance sets

already made instantiations (iterations) of that set are sufficient or not (instantiation time calculation). If other instantiations are needed activity B is activated. Activity B is a break activity so that when finished a new instance of the set is created. At the same time, activity 1 (the real first activity of the multiple instantiation set) is activated and the execution of the set continues normally. The next iteration that runs in parallel to the previous one applies the same mechanism until the evaluation of need of other instances is false. At the end of the execution of each copy of the set, the state of this one is tuned on finished and the condition evaluating the need of other iterations is always null so that the finish of a set doesn't engender other iterations. This special use of iterative instance sets proves that parallel and iterative instance sets are complementary.

6   The Operette Process: Application of Set Based Multiple Instantiation

The *operette* process is an experimental process that has been executed between three classes in a school. Its goal was to produce a web site about the Opera of Nancy. This process was followed by the classes but without coordination support. This was a problem since it was difficult for each class to know what has currently been done in the other classes and what remained to be done. Adding process support to these kinds of experiments appeared as a strong requirement.

A simple process was defined at the beginning of the project, to coordinate the different classes. It describes the different steps that have to be accomplished in order to complete the project. The teachers at the very beginning of the experiment defined this process. Some of these steps had to be executed by teachers themselves, by the classes as a group or by selected group of children. This first process was designed without worry about multiple executions and is illustrated in figure 11.

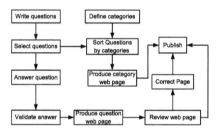

Fig. 11. The Operette process

6.1   Definition of the Operette Process Based on Multiple Instantiation Sets

The operette process can be defined using different kinds of sets, with different kinds of criteria for multiple instantiation (parallel or iterative). Some groups of activities have to be executed by a class, by a group of children, by teachers, for each question or each category. This information is not known at the beginning. Some activities have to be iterated until an acceptable state has been reached. This is the case before publishing the web site. Pages are corrected and reviewed until they are correct. Figure 12 describes the different sets that could have been defined for the process and the criteria used for multiple instantiation.

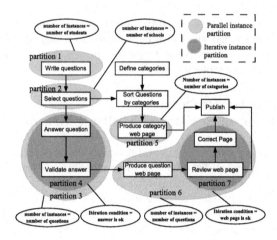

Fig. 12. The operette process with sets

Upon execution, the new activities are created and synchronized as defined by the model. We can see clearly the use of parallel instance sets with execution time knowledge of iteration number. That's the case of the set III where the number of questions is unknown at design time. Moreover, this set contains an iterative instance set. Across this example, specifying the sets is quite simple and specifying the original workflow is clearer.

7 Implementation over the BONITA Model

The implementation of our set based model has been made on the Bonita WFMS as an update to support sets. Bonita is a Dynamic Cooperative Workflow Management System implemented on a J2EE platform and is an ObjectWeb project. The Bonita workflow model is dynamic and flexible. Processes are not instantiated from a process definition but directly created by users and executed. Users can create a new process from scratch by adding activities and edges between activities. They can specify properties of activities. An activity can become executable as soon as it has been created. Process creation can also be done by reusing other existing processes. A process can be imported into a running process. In this case a copy of all the activities edges and properties is done in the target process. The user can then make the modifications he needs to adapt it. Starting a new process can be done by cloning an existing process to avoid starting the definition from scratch. As we don't expect that cooperative processes are executed so many time and that they often require adaptation to meet each project needed, we think that this way to define process avoid the complicated programming stage of process definition. Moreover, the definition of a cooperative process is often done by analogy to processes that have been executed in the past with some adaptation. This provides a very flexible way to create processes, to adapt them, to change them or combine them on the fly.

The current definition of the Bonita model provides flexible definition and flexible execution of processes. The flexible definition is achieved by allowing changes to occur at any time during execution of the process. The only and main constraint is that an activity definition cannot change once it has been started. Other constraints are structural. For instance a cycle cannot exists between activities. Flexible execution is achieved by a dynamic management of the activity state and by allowing anticipation of execution of activities. An activity may be started even if all the conditions for its execution are not fulfilled.

Scripts can be associated to activity state changes in order to automate certain parts of the process and these scripts are called Hooks. The execution of a hook can interact with the workflow process and can for example create, modify or remove other entities in the workflow. A hook can be assigned to be executed before or after the start or the end of an activity. Bonita workflow model has been implemented and integrated with different kinds of extended transaction models to allow object sharing between activities and to support concurrent long running activities.

All these properties allow the possibility to extend the bonita model to support multiple instantiation sets. The internal work of sets in Bonita is defined as EJB. The update of Bonita has been simple because the use of sets is independent of the workflow engine behaviour. The most important update to do is located on the activity state manager because the set activation is the result of an activity activation. There is two possibilities to do this change. The first is an update of the internal engine that controls activity states so that each time an activity starts, all the sets containing this activity are activated as needed in the model. The second possibility is the use of Hooks. A hook can be associated to all the activities of the process with a "before start" activation. This hook activates all the sets containing the activity as needed in the model.

We have chosen temporarily the engine update to implement that and to make tests on the sets uses but we are now integrating the solution based on hooks. The current solution uses the Jboss web application server but a newer implementation based on hooks and using the Jonas web application server is currently developed. All the files of the Bonita project are located on the ObjectWeb consortium web page (http://objectweb.org).

8   Conclusion and Perspectives

Specifying set of activities that have to be executed an unknown number of times, in sequence or in parallel is a challenge in process models. The use of control structures from traditional or parallel programming language is not adapted to the specific needs and usages of business or cooperative processes. Additional operators that have been added in other workflow models are difficult to manage and lead to complex structure to express simple things. In the Bonita model, creating an iterative or parallel instance set does not change the general intuitive structure of the process. Process execution is at the same time a mean of control, of automation and of awareness. Changing properties directly on objects or set of objects affects the behaviour of the whole system. The interface provided with the implementation allows monitoring dynamically the evolution of the process.

The solution based on sets provides a simple way to define parallel or iterative multiple instantiations. Sets of activities can be selected with practically no constraints so that we can choose dispersed activities in the workflow. In other workflow models, group of activities to multi-instantiate must be sequentially connected or simply just one activity can be instantiated multiple times. The set based workflow structure is easier to understand by the end user. The main strength of sets model is that it allows the implementation of the entire multiple instantiation patterns defined in [9]. Moreover, set based multiple instantiation allows nested and overlapped sets that is a very useful new possibility in some cases.

Now we are planning to integrate this work in a software development platform that involves data synchronization services. This platform is the Libre-Source platform and our next challenge is to integrate the control flow functions of bonita and data flow facilities of the platform. At the same time we are planning to develop an advanced transaction manager probably based on the same approach.

References

1. M. Dumas and A. ter Hofstede. Uml activity diagrams as a workflow specification language. *In Proc. of the International Conference on the Unified Modeling Language (UML). Toronto, Canada, October 2001. Springer Verlag.*, 2001.
2. D. Grigori. *Eléments de flexibilité des systèmes de workflow pour la définition et l'exécution de procédés coopératifs.* PhD thesis, Université Henri Poincaré - Nancy1, Ecole doctorale IAEM Lorraine, Paris, novembre 2001.
3. Daniela Grigori, François Charoy, and Claude Godart. Anticipation to enhance flexibility of workflow execution. In *DEXA 2001*, number 2113, pages 264–273. LNCS, 2001.
4. Manfred Reichert and Peter Dadam. A framework for dynamic changes in workflow management systems. In *DEXA Workshop*, pages 42–48, 1997.
5. W.M.P. van der Aalst. How to handle dynamic change and capture management information, 1999.
6. W.M.P. van der Aalst and T. Basten. Inheritance of workflows: an approach to tackling problems related to change. *Theoretical Computer Science*, 270(1–2):125–203, 2002.
7. W.M.P. van der Aalst, A.H.M. ter Hofstede, B. Kiepuszewski, and A.P. Barros. Advanced workflow patterns. In O. Etzion en P. Scheuermann, editor, *7th International Conference on Cooperative Information Systems (CoopIS 2000)*, volume 1901 of *Lecture Notes in Computer Science*, pages 18–29. Springer-Verlag, Berlin, 2000.
8. W.M.P. van der Aalst, A.H.M. ter Hofstede, B. Kiepuszewski, and A.P. Barros. Workflow patterns. *BETA Working Paper Series, WP 47, Eindhoven University of Technology, Eindhoven*, 2000.
9. W.M.P. van der Aalst, A.H.M. ter Hofstede, B. Kiepuszewski, and A.P. Barros. Workflow patterns. *Distributed and Parallel Databases*, 14(3):pages 5–51, 2003.
10. Jiantao Zhou, Meilin Shi, and Xinming Ye. On pattern-based modeling for multiple instances of activities in workflows. *In International Workshop on Grid and Cooperative Computing, Hainan*, pages pages 723–736, December 2002.

Method Components – Rationale Revealed

Kai Wistrand and Fredrik Karlsson

Research Network VITS
Dept. of Informatics (ESI), Methodology Exploration Lab
Örebro University, SE-701 82 Örebro, Sweden
{kwd,fkn}@esi.oru.se

Abstract. The configuration of systems engineering methods is a challenging task. As a method engineer it is essential to have conceptual constructs capable of reducing the burden of details during method configuration and thus make it possible to create a balance between precision and cost. In this paper we present the method component construct, which seems fruitful for method configuration and meta method development. Furthermore, by introducing an internal and an external view of this construct we can hide details of the method component during configuration work and connect method components to each other through use of interfaces expressing goals realized by the method components. The proposed concept and views can also be used in the process of developing tool-support for method configuration.

1 Introduction

The current popularity of rigorous 'off-the-shelf' development methods and processes, such as the Rational Unified Process (RUP) [1], gives system engineers a plethora of tools to work with during projects. The flip side of this coin is the immense number of possible tasks to perform during a project. Accordingly, this increases the need for method configuration (MC) since no single project could possibly use such a method as a whole [2].

MC is a specific kind of method engineering (ME) [3] and is possible to relate to other approaches for ME including Odell [4], Harmsen [5] and Ralyté et al. [6]. Ralyté et al. [6] present three strategies, Assembly-based, Extension-based and Paradigm-based with different points of departures. MC takes its starting point in one specific systems engineering method (SEM), a base method, which is tailored to fit the needs of a specific project. This seems valid since most practitians rarely are familiar with more than one method [7]. Hence, the Extension-based strategy is the strategy that shares most characteristics with MC. However, this strategy, at least as presented in Ralyté et al. [6], has certain limitations. As the label of this strategy suggests it focuses on the extension of SEMs. However, extension is only one possibility when dealing with MC. In many situations it is equally important to restrict the base method when transforming it into a situational SEM [2].

The need to support restriction, addition as well as exchange operators is essential based on the three scenarios that can be found when discussing MC [8]:

A. Persson and J. Stirna (Eds.): CAiSE 2004, LNCS 3084, pp. 189–201, 2004.

(a)   Selecting parts from the base method based on their articulated goals.

(b)   Integrating parts from other SEMs when relevant alternatives are miss-
       ing in the base method (i.e. when the method engineer's intentions can-
       not be realized through application of the base method alone).

(c)   Developing new parts in cases when (b) is not applicable.

Consequently, a toolbox is needed to support a method engineer who has the task
of achieving more agility in a base method. In order to facilitate the three scenarios
above, each SEM should be possible to represent in modules, which are possible to
omit, add, or exchange. Such a toolbox must at the same time take advantage of the
stability, which exists in the usage of a base method as the starting point for configuration work. Concretely, such a toolbox is about a conceptual framework, a meta-
method and tool support for MC.

Röstlinger and Goldkuhl [9] present a component based view on SEMs, with an intention of combining flexibility with stability. The basic idea with method components is to use a rather high layer of abstraction and structure the component's content
based on internal dependencies. Thus, such a construct would ease the method engineer's burden of details and enable the possibility to balance precision and cost. However, the full potential of the described concept is not explored and no advice is given
regarding how this construct can be operationalized in tool-support or in meta-
methods for MC of SEMs. This leads to a need for useful conceptual constructs to
facilitate the method engineer's task of configuring, customising and adapting methods as well as the task of communicating the results. Methods as such reflect rationality as they prescribe social action founded in arguments, perceptions, and target states
[10]. Subsequently we propose method components founded in theories on method
rationale [11, 12] in order to render the possibilities to achieve situations where rationality resonance [13] can occur. These are situations where method users fully
understand the method's inherent rationale in relation to their own rationale and the
current situation. However modeling a SEM's rationale is a non-trivial task as discussed in Ågerfalk and Wistrand [14] who conclude that a framework with a suitable
balance of precision and cost is needed. In this paper our ambition is to give method
engineers, working with a single base method, a simplified, useful construct, which
can help them to hide irrelevant details when performing MC work based on a SEM's
rationale and strike a balance between precision and cost.

The paper is organized in five sections. The following section is a discussion about
our research method and how the method component construct is empirically
grounded. The third section presents the idea of method components, and introduces
two views of the construct. The method component construct is then used in an illus-
trative example in section four. The last part contains a conclusion and implications
on further research.

2   Research Method

The process of developing the method component construct can be characterized as
action research following the recommendations of Baskerville and Wood-Harper [15].
This research strategy captures the possibility to involve competent practitioners in
the design efforts and the elaboration of our conceptual construct as well as actual

MC work. Apart from the actual development of the method component construct, much of our attention has been given to different SEMs. We have treated them as an empirical base and used them intensively during the gradual refinement of the method component concept. During this process we have performed tests on SEMs in two different industrial settings and used the feedback as input for redesign. We have chosen RUP as the primary base method for two reasons: its domination in market share among off-the-shelf methods and the fact that it can be called a rigorous SEM.

Data has been collected through the use of field notes and voice recordings from workshops over a period of two years and range from observations of method configuration work to the development of a meta method for method configuration. The analytical development work has been carried out within two different but overlapping intellectual spheres: an academic sphere and an industrial sphere. These two spheres overlap in a space of conceptualization and interpretation, shared by the practitioners and academic researchers involved in an ambition to create constructive solutions [16].

3 Method Components

Every design has its advantages and drawbacks, and since the method component is a design, evaluation criteria are central. During the empirical work with the method component construct we have elicited five criteria together with the three scenarios for MC. Our criteria are empirically grounded in a method engineer's needs.

Furthermore, the support of MC work could be formalized to different extents ranging from general guidelines, meta methods, to Computer Aided Method Engineering (CAME) support. The latter is of vital importance when considering that the industrial sphere does not adapt new methods or constructs to a large extent because vital tool support is often missing [17]. Even with a meta method for MC, it is still a challenging task to perform MC, and tool support is often required. Since the method component construct is founded in a vision to construct tool support for method configuration it has to fit into future implementation constraints, and this constitutes a sixth criterion.

The six criteria that have been important beacons when designing the method component concept are:

- *Self-contained*: It must be possible to treat the method component as a self-contained part of a SEM with regard to the guidelines that describe the deliverable and the process of producing such a deliverable. This way a method component can be modeled out from a rigorous base method or act as a building block when constructing new methods or during method integration.
- *Internal consistency and coherency:* The method component must be perceivable as an internally consistent and coherent entity. Another way to put it is to say that the construct should be stable over time and without lose ends. As a result the method component will be perceivable as meaningful. The principle is an ambition to create congruence amongst method components and homogeneity in SEMs. Otherwise the scenarios could result in fragmentation of the situational SEM.
- *Rationality:* Actions are performed and prescribed for reasons. Thus a method component must have an identified target state, a purpose for its existence. We term this the internal goal achievement of the method component.

- *Connectivity:* To support our scenarios the method components must be possible to connect with each other. Each method component, selected as part of the situational SEM, should contribute to a chain of goal achievements adding to the overall goal of the specific project. Thus each method component has to share its results through an interface. We choose to view this aspect as the method component's external goal achievement.
- *Applicability:* It should be possible to map the method component construct onto any existing SEM in order to truly support each of our three scenarios.
- *Implementability:* The construct should be possible to implement in a CAME-tool for method configuration. Thus the constructed interface between method components has to be standardized and possible to extend in order to support the need for different versions of interface specifications. Since we focus on how to improve the method component as a conceptual construct it is not within the scope of this paper to show how this improved method component neither can nor should be implemented in a CAME-tool.

3.1   Two Views of a Method Component

In order to incorporate the criteria discussed in the previous sections, we choose the following working definition of a method component:

Definition 1: A Method Component is a self-contained part of a system engineering method expressing the process of transforming one or several artifacts into a defined target artifact and the rationale for such a transformation.

Based on the self-contained and the connectivity criteria we propose two conceptual views of method components in order to express the rationale of SEMs. Firstly, we elaborate on a detailed view of the method component concept called the internal view. Secondly, we discuss how this internal view can be used for hiding details during MC work and aligning with the thought of the black-box which is central for the component concept. This second view we term the external view. The meta models are represented using UML [18].

3.1.1   The Internal View
Our first conceptual model, in Fig. 1. The Method Component Construct (The Internal View), directly corresponds to the suggested self-contained criterion. It addresses what a method engineer needs to know about a method component to regard it as independent, which is important for all three MC scenarios in order to facilitate a coherent suppression or extension of method components. This view is generated through application of a goal intrinsic perspective, i.e. by only focusing on the hands-on results produced when following actions in order to produce a certain artifact to fulfill certain goals.

Each method component consists of method elements and their goals, which are anchored in the values of the method creator. A method element in turn is an abstraction of the constituents of a method. Several definitions of the concept of method can be found [e.g. 19, 20, 21], and there seems to be a common understanding about at least three interrelated parts: actions, concepts, and notation. Each action tells project

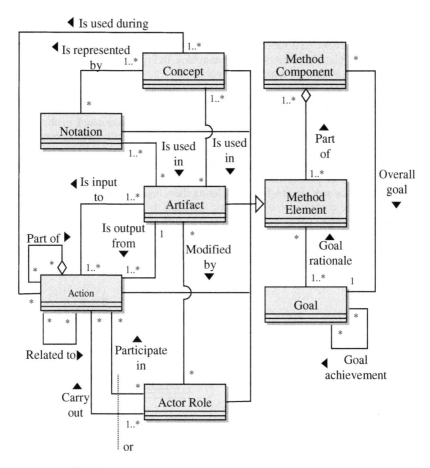

Fig. 1. The Method Component Construct (The Internal View)

members what tasks to perform during a project. During these actions a set of concepts is needed to describe the project's problem domain, a domain that is captured and represented using notation. Accordingly, these are central when representing SEMs as method components (the applicability criterion) and are therefore found as specializations of the method element concept.

However, a SEM consists of both a product and a process model [5]. Actions are the central constituents of the process model, but their results are found as artifacts in the product model. Artifacts are both inputs and as outputs from actions in the SEMs; hence the concept of artifacts plays an equally important role in our method component construct as actions. Furthermore, project members who have different roles during the project carry out these actions and produce these artifacts. Therefore, the actor role concept is the fifth method element we have identified.

The method elements are anchored in the method creator's value base through the use of goals. Accordingly, each method element has at least one goal, which contributes to the component goal rationale. Furthermore, the sub-rationales of the method elements can be related to each other in hierarchies. In Figure 1. it is referred to as the internal goal achievement of a method component.

3.1.2 The External View

The proposed criterion of connectivity is deliberately not addressed in the model above. The purpose of that model is to illustrate how one single method component expresses its rationale needed *somewhere* in a development process. Connectivity, on the other hand, addresses issues concerning how method components are related to each other in a development situation. Figure 2 illustrates how the method component construct should be perceived when considering them being parts of a SEM and hence responding to the criterion of connectivity. Through the external view we focus on how a specific method component contributes to a chain of goal achievements, sharing its rationale through an interface and adding to the overall goal of a specific development situation. A situational SEM is an aggregate of selected method components from a SEM, which contribute to the overall goal of a project.

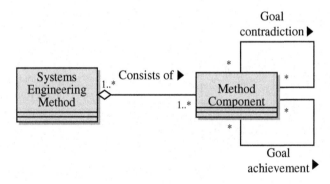

Fig. 2. The Method Component Construct (The External View)

Hence it is desirable to eliminate any goal contradictions that might exist in a set of method components that constitute a SEM.

Both the internal and the external views are possible starting points for addressing issues raised by MC-scenario (a), selecting method components from the base method based on their articulated goals, and (b) integrating method components from other SEMs when relevant alternatives are missing in the base method (i.e. when the method engineer's intentions cannot be realized through application of the base method alone). Ultimately it depends on the method engineer's prior knowledge and understanding of the base method and its method component's rationale. Our empirical observations indicate that the line of argumentation of the skilled method engineer, performing MC, has its foundation in the external view and the SEM's product model, i.e. its artifacts. Only MC-scenario (c) constructing new method components in cases when (b) is not applicable, demands that attention is given to the internal view since a newly constructed method component must respond to the criteria outlined above. This implies that the construction process should yield an independent, internally consistent and coherent method component, expressing the overall goal of the method component. MC-scenario (c) also implies that attention will be given to the external view since the new method component ultimately was created to be incorporated in a base method.

3.1.3   The Interface and Content of a Method Component

The component concept as such has connotations. The reusable aspect is one, which we have addressed when discussing method components as self-contained. Encapsulation or black-box are aspects that exist in the same domain, emphasizing the importance of information hiding [22]. How a task is executed is not interesting for an external viewer of a component. A user of a component is primarily interested in the results offered by the component and the required inputs needed to achieve these results.

A method component construct could have the same effect on MC work, if we emulate encapsulation. The black-box feeling could be created through transforming the interface and content concepts for the SEM domain. Based on our conceptual model (see Figure 1), discussed in the previous section, the results are expressed through the method component's deliverable. Furthermore, the method component's requirements can be expressed through its input artifacts. Thus we choose to define a method component's interface as the method component's overall goal and artifacts. The latter are classified as prerequisite (input) or outcome (deliverable). Our use of the term prerequisite should not be interpreted as strict prerequisites, that is a must. We treat methods as heuristic procedures or heurithms [23] and consequently prerequisites should be treated as recommended inputs. However, a method component needs to have at least one input. Otherwise, the method component will not have any meaningful input if it is not a method component that starts a new focal area which is later intertwined with the results from other method components.

The content part of a method component contains the remaining method elements presented in our detailed conceptual model (see Fig. 1. The Method Component Construct (The Internal View)): action, actor role, concept and notation. These four types of elements are only interesting when the method engineer already has chosen the method component according to MC-scenario (a) or (b), or during the construction of a new method component (MC-scenario (c)). For example, when suppressing a method component during MC (MC-scenario (a)), only the overall goal and the outcome are in focus for the analysis.

4   Application of the Method Component

The applicability criterion can only be evaluated during usage of the method component construct. An extensive coverage of different SEMs falls outside the scope of this paper. As an example we have chosen to apply the method component on the RUP, since it fulfils the criteria for a rigorous standard SEM. In the example below we have used the method component construct to elicit a meaningful reusable asset from the RUP. We have focused on creating a Business Use Case Model Component and one can argue that the choice is somewhat arbitrary. However, the importance lies in that this application is performed on a rigorous SEM, which means that the method elements are intertwined with each other and have to be separated for clarity. Furthermore, we illustrate the external view through an additional example where the connection between the Business Use Case Model Component and a Business Use Case Component is addressed. The latter component is only illustrated through its interface.

4.1   The Business Use Case Model Component

The presentation of the Business Use Case Model Component is structured into two sections. In the first section we discuss the method component's interface and in the second we present the method component's remaining content that is not part of the interface. Thus we use the notion of the black-box where a method engineer could concentrate on the interface during method configuration.

4.1.1   The Business Use Case Model Component Interface

The list in Table 1 is structured in two columns, the first contains the artifacts, and the second the artifacts' roles in the method component. As discussed in Section 3.1.3 an artifact can act either as prerequisite or outcome. The point of departure for our analysis is the method component's outcome. Only one artifact is found as outcome, which follows from our view on a meaningful part of a SEM (see Section 3.1.1). In order to deliver this outcome the Business Use Case Model Component has six prerequisites: Business Modeling Guidelines, Stakeholder Requests, Glossary, Vision, Business Actor, and Business Use Case.

Table 1. Method Component Interface: Artifact List

Artifact	Artifact Role
Business Modeling Guidelines	Prerequisite
Stakeholder Requests	Prerequisite
Glossary	Prerequisite
Vision	Prerequisite
Business Actor	Prerequisite
Business Use Case	Prerequisite
Business Use Case Model	Outcome

The method component's rationale is the range of goals specified in the method component. Goals constitute a complex structure and can be identified or reconstructed for each method element. We choose to focus on the goals related to the deliverable, to illustrate the goals of the method component's outcome. Table 2 contains two columns; the left contains the identification numbers of the goals, and the right the goal descriptions themselves. We have identified three goals for the resulting artifact of the Business Use Case Model Component by tracing the goal rationale for that particular method element. Furthermore, we have summarized these goals into an overall goal that is used for the method component. The business use case model is used to understand the business context for the future information system, to identify which tasks in the business context are appropriate to automate, and is essential for planning and following up activities in the project. The values behind these goals have deliberately been left out in order to achieve an acceptable balance between precision and cost [14].

Table 2. Method Component Interface: Goal List

Goal Number	Goal Description
(0) Overall	To agree upon the business context in order to plan and follow up subsequent software development
1	To agree that you understand the business context before you continue developing the system
2	To identify architecturally significant behavior that should be automated
3	To plan and follow up on the business modeling effort and subsequent software development

4.1.2   The Business Use Case Model Component Content

The remaining content of the method component contains the actions needed to accomplish the deliverable of the method component. Furthermore we find the actor roles who carry out these actions in this part of the method component description. In our Business Use Case Model Component, we find two activities in the RUP that have the business use case model artifact as a deliverable. These two activities are Find Business Actors and Use Cases and Structure the Business Use-Case Model. When working with a rigorous SEM the self-contained criterion is non-trivial to apply. The two activities we discuss have several deliverables, and that is not in line with our specification of a method component having only one. Thus, we have elicited which steps of the activities that are related to the method component's outcome.

Table 3 illustrates the result from our analysis. The table is split into two columns; the left contains activities gathered from the RUP, and the right contains the chosen steps that are related to the method component's outcome. The activity Find Business Actors and Use Cases have nine steps in the original method description. From this set we have chosen a smaller set of five steps that are suggested as necessary to build a business use case model and a sixth step where a business use case model is evaluated. Thus this subset is based on the goal rationale of these actions and whether or not the goals of these actions contribute to the goals of the output artifact, that is the overall goal of the method component.

The second activity, Structure the Business Use-Case Model, contains five steps, which is equal to the number of steps prescribed in the RUP. These steps are not atomic with regard to their deliverables, since their results are reworked artifacts of the business use case model, the business actors and the business use cases. The solution is to let these steps reoccur in the consequential Business Actor Component and the Business Use Case Component. Accordingly these steps will be considered as parts of all three components, otherwise it is not possible to consider them independent. This is a trade-off between the redundancy problem and the problem of a self-contained method component.

The artifacts found in the method component's interface decide which set of concepts and notation to use. Hence it is possible to elaborate a list of concepts and belonging notation that are possible to apply during use of the method component. The business use case concept in the RUP is one example, and it is stereotyped using UML notation. This concept is important in the business use case artifact as well as in the business use case model artifact.

Table 3. Method Component Execution: Actions

Action	Step
Find Business Actors and Use Cases	Develop an Outline of the Workflow of Business Use Cases
	Describe How Business Actors and Use Cases Interact
	Package Business Use-Cases and Actors
	Present the Business Use-Case Model in Use-Case Diagrams
	Develop a Survey of the Business Use-Case Model
	Evaluate Your Results
Structure the Business Use-Case Model	Establish Include-Relationships Between Business Use Cases
	Establish Extend-Relationships Between Business Use Cases
	Establish Generalizations Between Business Use Cases
	Establish Generalizations Between Business Actors
	Evaluate Your Results

Finally, we have to consider the actor role associated with this method component. According to the RUP the Business-Process Analyst is responsible for the Business Use Case Model and should therefore be included in the method component. Furthermore, we can identify two stakeholders, customer and end user that are important during work with the method component's outcome. Consequently, they are included in the Business Use Case Model Component's content part.

4.2   Connection of Method Components

Connecting method components concerns the external view of the method component construct. We have chosen to illustrate the usage of the method component with MC-scenario (a), discussed in section 4.1. Thus a demarcated external view of two method components in the RUP is found in Fig. 3 below. The method components are illustrated, exposing their interfaces. To the left we find the Business Use Case Component and to the right the Business Use Case Model Component. The latter takes the deliverable from the former as input (the figure is simplified since the Business Use Case Model Component takes several other deliverables as input, see Table 1). Furthermore, to complete the interface we present the overall goal of each component.

Consider a development situation where the business context as a problem domain is straightforward. A method engineer in such a situation might find the overall goal expressed by the business use case model of lesser or no importance since the goal is already fulfilled (an agreement about the business context has already been made). Subsequently, the Business Use Case Model Component is suppressed from the situational SEM. This means that the steps elicited in Table 3 will not be part of the situational SEM if they are not found in any other used method components. For example, the step Develop a Survey of the Business Use Case Model will not be performed.

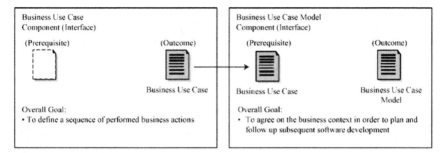

Fig. 3. Two Method Components from the External View

In an opposite, complex, development situation the Business Use Case Model Component might be found important. In such a situation it might not be possible to grasp the business' intended function without such a model. Since the Business Use Case Model Component has the artifact Business Use Case as a prerequisite the Business Use Case Component should not be suppressed. Such a MC action would mean breaking the prerequisite of the Business Use Case Model Component, and in this case a prerequisite that is considered important for producing the Business Use Case Model.

5   Conclusions and Implications for Future Research

In this paper we have presented the method component concept. It has been proven useful to balance precision and cost when performing method configuration (MC) work based on a systems engineering method's (SEM) rationale. This construct is founded in three identified MC-scenarios for method configuration and empirical results in two different settings. Furthermore during the empirical work with the method component construct we have elicited six criteria for this design. These are: self-contained, internal consistency and coherency, rationality, connectivity, applicability, and implementability.

We have presented how these criteria have been incorporated in the design of a construct that eases the burden of method engineers during MC work. The self-contained and connectivity criteria have shaped the construct into two views: the internal view and the external view of a method component. The former focuses on what makes the method component self-contained and operationalized through a set of method elements and their goals. These elements are based on both the product and the process model of the method concept, in order to satisfy the need to describe both the deliverable of a demarcated part of a SEM and the guidelines to produce this deliverable. The selection of method element types is anchored in common definitions of the method construct. The external view has proved useful when focusing on how a method component's deliverable can contribute to a development process as a whole, without discussing its details. Furthermore, the rationale criterion is operationalized as the method component's contribution to goal achievement in the external view; by focusing on the overall goal of a method component, the method engineers can estimate whether a specific method component can deliver what is needed or desired.

Furthermore, through the rationale dimension of SEMs we can align with the line of thought of skilled method engineers working with rigorous SEMs such as the Rational Unified Process (RUP). It was not within the scope of this paper to exhaustively address the applicability criterion, however some applicability of these ideas was tested in a small example using a Business Use Case Model Component from the RUP.

In this paper we have not explicitly discussed the sixth criterion, implementability, which we identified during our empirical work with the method component construct. Of course, this paper could be seen as one step along the path of developing a tool support for MC. On this path the conceptual construct is part of the specification for such a tool. This is one reason why we have modeled the method component construct using UML class diagrams. When considering a CAME-tool supporting MC based on the SEM's rationale we can use the two views to hide the content of method components. Thus the method engineer can focus on a SEM's rationale in the external view, which would yield a comprehensible picture of the situation without cluttering it with details. Development and testing of this tool is currently underway.

References

1. P. Kruchten. *The Rational Unified Process: An Introduction.* Addison-Wesley, Reading, MA (1999)
2. B. Fitzgerald, N.L. Russo and T. O'Kane. Software Development Method Tailoring at Motorola. *Communications of the ACM,* 46 4 (2003)
3. F. Karlsson. *Meta-Method for Method Configuration: A Rational Unified Process Case.* Licentiate Thesis, Linköping University, Linköping (2002)
4. J.J. Odell. A Primer to Method Engineering *Method Engineering: Principles of method construction and tool support (IFIP TC8, WG8.7/8.2 Working conference on method engineering),* Atlanta, USA (1996)
5. A.F. Harmsen. *Situational Method Engineering.* Doctoral Dissertation, Moret Ernst & Young Management Consultants, Utrecht, The Netherlands (1997)
6. J. Ralyté, R. Deneckère and C. Rolland. Towards a Generic Model for Situational Method Engineering. M.M. Johann Eder ed. *Advanced Information Systems Engineering, 15th International Conference, CAiSE 2003,* Klagenfurt, Austria (2003)
7. B. Fitzgerald, N.L. Russo and T. O'Kane. Software Development Method Tailoring at Motorola. *Communications of the ACM,* 46 4 (2003)
8. P.J. Ågerfalk, K. Wistrand, F. Karlsson, G. Börjesson, M. Elmberg and K. Möller. Flexible Processes and Method Configuration: Outline of a Joint Industry-Academia Research Project *Proceedings of the 5th International Conference on Enterprise Information Systems (ICEIS 2003)* (2003)
9. A. Röstlinger and G. Goldkuhl. *Generisk Flexibilitet - På Väg Mot En Komponentbaserad Metodsyn.* Research Report in Swedish, Dept. of Computer and Information Science, Linköping University (1994)
10. H. Klein and R. Hirschheim. Rationality Concepts in Information Systems Development Methodologies. *Accounting, Management and Information Technologies,* 1 2 (1991) 157-187
11. H. Oinas-Kukkonen. Method Rationale in Method Engineering and Use. In S.e.a. Brinkkemper ed. *Method Engineering - Principles of Method Construction and Tool Support,* Chapman & Hall, New York, USA (1996) 87-93
12. M. Rossi, J.-P. Tolvanen, B. Ramesh, K. Lyytinen and J. Kaipala. Method Rationale in Method Engineering *Proceedings of the 33rd Hawaii International Conference on System Sciences (HICSS-33),* IEEE Computer Society Press (2000)

13. E. Stolterman. The Paradox of Information Systems Methods: Public and Private Rationality. in *Proceeding of British Computer Society 5th Annual Conference on Methodologies*, Lancaster, England (1997)
14. P.J. Ågerfalk and K. Wistrand. Systems Development Method Rationale: A Conceptual Framework for Analysis *Proceedings of the 5th International Conference on Enterprise Information Systems (ICEIS 2003)* (2003)
15. R. Baskerville and A. Wood-Harper. A Critical Perspective on Action Research as a Method for Information Systems Reasearch. *Journal of Information Technology*, 11 (1996)
16. P. Järvinen. *On Research Methods*. Opinpajan kirja, Tampere (2001)
17. H. Kaindl, S. Brinkkemper, J. Bubenko, Jr, B. Farbey, S.J. Greenspan, C.L. Heitmeyer, J.C.S.d.P. Leite, N.R. Mead, J. Mylopoulos and J. Siddiqi. Requirements Engineering and Technology Transfer: Obstacles, Incentives and Improvement Agenda. *Requirements Engineering*, 7 3 (2002) 113–123
18. G. Booch, J. Rumbaugh and I. Jacobson. *The Unified Modeling Language User Guide*. Addison-Wesley, Harlow, UK (1999)
19. S. Brinkkemper. Method Engineering: Engineering of Information Systems Development Methods and Tools. *Information and Software Technology*, 38 4 (1996) 275–280
20. P.B. Checkland. *Systems Thinking, Systems Practice*. Wiley, Chichester (1981)
21. J. Rumbaugh. *What Is a Method?*, Rational Software, Inc. (1995)
22. A.W. Brown and K.C. Wallnau. Engineering of Component-Based Systems. In A.W. Brown ed. *Component-Based Engineering, Selected Papers from the Software Engineering Institute*, IEEE Computer Society Press, Los Alamitos, CA, USA (1996)
23. B. Langefors. *Essays on Infology: Summing up and Planning for the Future*. Studentlitteratur, Lund (1995)

Towards a Meta-tool for Change-Centric Method Engineering: A Typology of Generic Operators

Jolita Ralyté[1], Colette Rolland[2], and Rébecca Deneckère[2]

[1] CUI, University of Geneva, Rue de Général Dufour, 24, CH-1211 Genève 4, Switzerland
ralyte@cui.unige.ch
[2] CRI, University of Paris 1 – Sorbonne, 90 Rue de Tolbiac, 75013 Paris, France
{rolland,denecker}@univ-paris1.fr

Abstract. The work presented in this paper considers how Method Engineering (ME) helps in method changes that are required by Information Systems (IS) changes. In fact, ME provides different approaches allowing to construct situation-specific methods by adapting, extending, improving existing methods or by assembling method components. All these approaches use a set of operations to realize these method changes. Our objective in this paper is to provide a meta-tool for change-centric ME which takes the form of a typology of generic ME operators. The operators for each specific ME approach are instantiated from the generic ones. The paper illustrates and discusses the instantiation of the generic typology for two assembly-based ME approaches.

1 Introduction

In order to survive in a more and more competitive environment, *organizations undergo frequent changes* that imply to adapt, enhance, reform, evolve, merge, interoperate their supporting Information Systems (IS). There are many different kinds of *IS change* and many circumstances for change such as business change, technology progress, ERP installation, company merge/take-over, globalization, standardization of practices across branches of a company etc. Each of them requires specific methods to handle change. Thus, as a consequence of the need for IS change, engineering methods shall themselves adapt to new circumstances of IS evolution. In other words, IS change implies *method change*.

The position taken in this paper is that *Method Engineering* (ME) can help to respond to this need. ME is the 'discipline to study engineering techniques for constructing, assessing, evaluating and managing methods and to study educational techniques for teaching and training method users' [27]. We see ME at two levels of abstraction: the *method level* and the *method meta-level*. The *former* refers to the construction of new change-centric methods using ME techniques. This leads to the development of methods supporting different kinds of evolution such as IS improvement, expansion, transformation as well as methods tailored to emerging application domains such as e-commerce, web services, mobile IS, etc. The *latter* seeks to provide generic ME tools and techniques to support ME at the method level. Processes/Algorithms to support 'on the fly' construction of situation-specific methods is an example of such meta-technique. Typologies of ME approaches or techniques are another example.

A. Persson and J. Stirna (Eds.): CAiSE 2004, LNCS 3084, pp. 202–218, 2004.
© Springer-Verlag Berlin Heidelberg 2004

Our concern in this paper is to provide a meta-tool for change-centric method engineering which takes the form of a set of *ME operators*. Indeed, at the core of every ME process there is a set of operations to be carried out on the components of the method(s) involved in the ME activity. As these components are mainly Product and Process Models (PPMs), these operations can be formalized as *operators* applicable to the various elements of PPMs. These operators are generic in the sense that they are not dependent of a specific ME approach. On the contrary, they can be *instantiated* in every specific ME approach.

In order to ease the use of generic operators in a given ME approach, we provide in the paper a framework, the *operator-driven ME framework,* to deal with the meta and method levels and to generate operators for any specific ME approach from the generic ones. The usefulness of such a typology of operators is manifolds. It offers a means to easily generate a complete set of operators for a specific ME approach and to base the ME approach on a theoretically sound ground. Such a formalisation is especially required in the case of a corresponding CAME tool creation. Moreover, it offers a possibility to develop mixed ME approaches to deal with a combination of ME situations. This will be achieved by combining operators of different ME types.

The remainder of this paper is as follows: section 2 proposes a typology of ME approaches, which is used for the definition of the generic ME operators presented in section 3. In section 4 we illustrate how the generic typology of ME operators can be instantiated in order to obtain operators for a specific ME approach. Finally, section 5 draws some conclusions and discussions about our future work.

2   Typology of Method Engineering Approaches

A large number of Method Engineering approaches have been proposed in the literature. These approaches provide guidance for the creation of a new method [11, 20, 21] and for the adaptation of an existing method to some conditions of change [30] or to a specific project situation [6, 7, 10]. A literature survey [4, 5, 8, 25, 29] complemented by our own experience [18] leads us to classify these approaches according to four types of method engineering that we referred to as *Ad-Hoc, Paradigm-Based, Extension-Based* and *Assembly-Based*, respectively.

Ad-Hoc approaches deal with the construction of a new method 'from scratch'. There are different reasons that can initiate a decision to construct a new method. The appearance of a new application domain that is not yet supported by a specific method is one example, experience capitalisation serving as the start point for a new method construction is another example.

Paradigm-Based ME [17] uses some initial paradigm model or meta-model as a baseline As-Is model which is instantiated [5], abstracted [18] or adapted [30] according to the current ME objective to develop the new To-Be model.

Extension-Based ME proposes different kinds of extension that can be realised on an existing method. Their objective is to enhance a method with new concepts and properties [3]. For example, a static method such the one for construction E/R schemas can be extended to deal more systematically with the representation of time through a calendar of time points, intervals etc. and temporal aspects such as the histories of entities.

Assembly-Based ME proposes to construct new methods or to enhance existing ones by reusing parts of other methods. The core concept in these approaches is one of reusable *method component* [28] also called *method chunk* [16, 22], *method fragment* [2, 7, 14, 26] or *method block* [12]. An Assembly-Based method construction consists in defining method requirements for a current situation, selecting method components satisfying this situation and assembling them. Association and integration are two kinds of assembly that can be applied on the selected method components [15]. Association concerns assembly of method components with different purposes and objectives, whereas integration deals with overlapping method components having the same or similar objective but providing different manners to satisfy it.

3   Towards Generic Operators for Method Engineering

3.1   Role of Operators in Method Engineering

Each ME approach proposes a specific method engineering process which uses a specific set of method construction operators. The objective of this work is to propose a generic typology of ME operators which should ease the definition of a set of specific operators for every specific ME approach while guaranteeing their completeness and correctness. Fig. 1 presents our *operator-driven ME framework* where specific ME operators are generated from the generic ones.

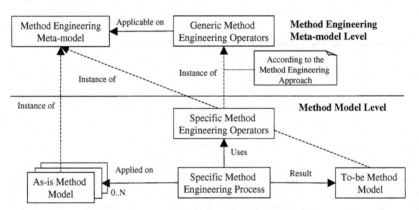

Fig. 1. Operator-driven Method Engineering Framework

The generic ME operators are applicable to generic elements that compose any model involved in a ME activity. To achieve this, it is necessary to abstract from the specificity of a given model and generalize model elements, their relationships as well as relationships between different models. Meta-modelling is known as a means to do so. Thus, in order to build the typology of generic ME operators, we first developed a *meta-model* for ME, i.e. a model of models. This meta-model is presented in the following section.

Following our framework (Fig. 1), a set of specific operators is instantiated from the generic ones according to the selected ME approach. These operators are then applied by the specific ME process to transform one or several As-Is model(s) into a To-Be model. In Paradigm-Based ME there is only one To-Be model whereas in Assembly-Based and Extension-Based ME two or more As-Is models are used to produce the resulting To-Be model. Ad-Hoc method construction starts with no As-Is model at all. To sum up, there are some advantages of using a generic typology of ME operators:

1. The generic typology serves as a guide to define the specific typology: the latter is just an instance of the former;
2. The completeness of the specific typology is subsumed by the completeness of the generic typology;
3. Specific typologies are consistent with each other as they are generated from the same mould: this is important when several sub-typologies are used in the same ME approach or several different ME approaches are combined together [17].

3.2 The Meta-model for Defining Generic ME Operators

In Fig. 2 we propose a meta-model which has been designed to highlight characteristics of models involved in a ME activity and therefore to permit to identify the fundamental construction and transformation operations which can be executed on a model. As shown is this figure, every model is made of *Elements*. Every element has a *Name* and is characterised by a set of *Properties*. In the E/R model for example, *Entity type*, *Attribute* and *Relationship type* as well as the *Is-A* relationship are *elements*. *Domain* is a *property* of *Attribute*. Fig. 2 shows that an element *is-a* another element, i.e. might inherit some of its properties from another element.

Elements are classified into *Simple* and *Compound* ones. *Compound elements* are composed from fine-grained ones whereas *Simple Elements* are not decomposable. For example, in the E/R model an *Entity type* is a compound element made of *Attributes*, which are simple elements.

As the same element can be part of different models, the concept of *ModelElement* represents the link of an element and the model it belongs to. For example, the concept of *Scenario* exists in the *L'Ecritoire* model [23] and the *Use Case* model [9]. In the integration process of these two models [19] we need to know the origin of the *Scenario* that we are manipulating. The concept of *ModelElement* is also necessary to model the relationships between elements of different models. These relationships are represented in Fig. 2: an element from one model can represent an *Abstraction-of* an element in another model; the link *Instance-of* represents the fact that an element can be obtained by instantiating an element of another model; moreover, elements from different models can be connected in order to assemble or extend models. Three connection types are defined in the meta-model: *Association*, *Composition* and *Is-a*. Finally, any model is a compound element which can be reduced to the *root* element.

3.3 The Typology of the Generic ME Operators

The meta-model (Fig. 2) identifies elements (*Element*) in models and relationships between elements *(ModelElement)* belonging to different models. Both of them can be subject to change in a method engineering activity. This allowed us to identify a

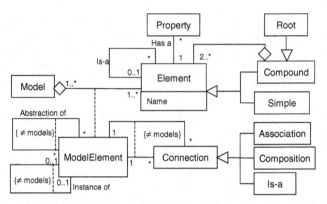

Fig. 2. Meta-model for Method Engineering

set of *ME operators*, which are listed and briefly described in Table 1. In synthesis, we can say that ME operators cover three major types of change: *naming* changes, *element* changes and *structural* changes.

- *Naming changes* are defined with the *Rename* operator. Naming is dealing with hyponyms, synonyms and the like.
- *Element changes* affect elements and are circumscribed to the elements themselves: adding an *attribute* to an *entity type* is an example of such localised change. Table 1 proposes three operators to specify element changes, namely *Modify*, *Give* and *Withdraw*.
- *Structural changes* are the most important as they correspond to a modification of the set of elements that compose the model. There are two types of structural changes:
  - *Inner changes* which affect elements of one single given model: there are eleven operators to specify structural changes (Table 1): *Add*, *Remove*, *Merge*, *Split*, *Replace*, *Retype*, *Generalise*, *Specialise*, *AddComponent*, *MoveComponent* and *RemoveComponent*. For example, merging two steps of an As-Is process model in the To-Be process model is an example of such inner structural change.
  - *Inter-model changes* which consists in establishing connections between elements of different models. Table 1 identify six of them: *ConnectViaSpecialisation*, *ConnectViaGeneralisation*, *ConnectViaMerge*, *ConnectViaComposition*, *ConnectViaDecomposition* and *ConnectVia-Association*. For example, defining a set of *Ordered Requirements Chunks* of the *L'Ecritoire* RE method [23] as a specialization of the *Use Case* Concept of the *Use case Model* [9] is an example of inter-model connection.

4   Instantiation of the Generic ME Operators for Assembly-Based ME

This section illustrates the framework and the use of our generic operators to define the collection of operators relevant for a specific ME case. We consider two assem-

Table 1. Generic ME operators

Object	Operator	Description
Element	*Rename*	Change the name of an element.
	Add	Add a new element in the model.
	Remove	Remove an element from the model.
	Merge	Two separate elements become one element.
	Split	An element is decomposed into two elements.
	Replace	An element is replaced by a different one.
	Generalize	An element is created as a generalization of two elements.
	Specialize	Specialise an element into two sub-elements.
Com-pound	AddComponent	Add a component into an element.
	RemoveComponent	Remove a component from a compound element.
	MoveComponent	A component is repositioned in the structure of a compound.
Property	*Give*	Add a property to an element.
	Withdraw	Remove a property from an element.
	Modify	Change a property in an element.
	Retype	Change the type of an element.
Model Element	Instantiate	Instantiate an As-Is model element into To-Be model element.
	Abstract	Create a To-Be model element as an abstraction of an As-Is model element.
	ConnectVia Specialization	Define an element from one model as a specialization of an element from another model. An is-a link is created between these two elements.
	ConnectVia Generalization	Generalize two elements from different As-Is models into a super-element in the To-Be model.
	ConnectVia Composition	Create a compound element in the To-Be model containing as components elements from two different As-Is models.
	ConnectVia Decomposition	Define an element as a component of an element from another model.
	ConnectVia Association	Add an association link in the To-Be model between two elements from different As-Is models.
	ConnectViaMerge	Two similar elements from different As-Is models become one element in the To-Be model.

bly-based ME approaches: (a) the *assembly by association* proposed by Brinkkemper et al. in [2] and (b) the *assembly by integration* proposed by Ralyté et al. in [19]. In both cases product and process models of the selected method chunks/fragments must be assembled. Therefore, we will first, define the corresponding meta-models and then, instantiate the generic typology of operators in line with the elements of these meta-models and illustrate them with examples.

4.1   Operators for Product Models Assembly

In both ME examples considered in this section, the product models of the method fragments/chunks to assemble are expressed by using class diagrams. Fig. 3 presents the meta-model of the *Object Model* as instance of the ME meta-model (Fig. 2). As shown in this figure, the *Object Model* is composed of *Classes*, which are *compound elements* composed of *Attributes*. A *Class* is connected with one or several other classes via *Association*, *Composition* or *Is-a* links. As an *Association* can have attributes, it is also a compound element whereas the *Composition* or *Is-a* links are *simple* ones. An *Attribute* has a *property* named *Domain* and an *Association* has two properties *SourceMultiplicity* and *TargetMultiplicity*.

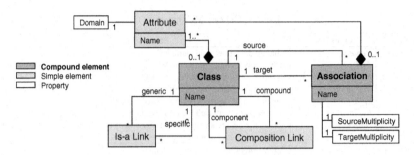

Fig. 3. Meta-model of the Object Model

Table 2 summarizes the operators that are relevant for each of the elements defined in the meta-model (Fig. 3). The name of a specific operator is obtained by concatenation of the name of the generic operator and the name of the corresponding element. Due to space constraint, some names have been shortened. 'N/A' means not applicable.

Table 2. Operators for the Object Models Assembly

Generic Operator	Operators for object models assembly				
	Class	Attribute	Association	Composition	Is-a
Rename	RenameClass	RenameAttribute	RenameAssoc	N/A	N/A
Add	AddClass	N/A	AddAssociation	AddComp	AddIsa
Remove	RemoveClass	N/A	RemoveAssoc	RemoveComp	ReIsa
Merge	MergeClass	MergeAttribute	N/A	N/A	N/A
Split	SplitClass	SplitAttribute	N/A	N/A	N/A
Replace	ReplaceClass	ReplaceAttribute	N/A	N/A	N/A
Generalize	GeneralClass	N/A	N/A	N/A	N/A
Specialize	SpecializeClass	N/A	N/A	N/A	N/A
AddComponent	N/A	AddClassAttr, *	N/A	N/A	N/A
RemoveComponent	N/A	RemoveClAtt, *	N/A	N/A	N/A
MoveComponent	N/A	MoveClAttr, *	N/A	N/A	N/A
Give	N/A	GiveDomain	GiveMultiplicity	N/A	N/A
Withdraw	N/A	With.Domain	WithdrawMultipl	N/A	N/A
Modify	N/A	ModifyDomain	ModifyMultipl	N/A	N/A
Retype	RetypeClass	RetypeAttribute	RetypeAssociation	RetypeComp	RtIsa
***CVSpecialization*	CVSpecClass	N/A	N/A	N/A	N/A
CVGeneralization	CVGenerClass	N/A	N/A	N/A	N/A
CVComposition	CVCompClass	N/A	N/A	N/A	N/A
CVDecomposition	CVDecompClass	N/A	N/A	N/A	N/A
CVAssociation	CVAssocClass	N/A	N/A	N/A	N/A
CVMerge	CVMergeClass	N/A	N/A	N/A	N/A
*: AddAssociationAttribute, RemoveAssociationAttribute, MoveAssociationAttribute, **CV: ConnectVia,					

Let us briefly comment the table before entering in the detailed analysis of both ME approaches. According to [15, 19], the *integration* of two object models is based on establishing connections between similar classes. Two similar classes from different As-Is models can be *merged* into a new one in the To-Be model. They can also *be connected* via is-a or composition link and finally, a new *generalised class can be created* in the To-Be model in order to relate them. Therefore, the operators which serve for the integration of two object models are *ConnectViaMerge, Connect-ViaSpecialisation, ConnectViaGeneralisation, ConnectViaComposition, ConnectViaDecomposition*. The simple association between similar classes is not applicable here. On the contrary, the operator *ConnectViaAssociation* is the core connection operator in the assembly by association [2]. The *Instantiate* and *Abstract* operators are not applicable in the assembly-based ME as the As-Is and To-Be models are at the same levels of abstraction.

Product Models Assembly by Association. According to [2], the assembly by association of two product fragments is based on the three following operations: (1) Addition of new objects, (2) Addition of new associations, (3) Addition of new attributes. Besides, this approach provides a set of rules that should be satisfied during the assembly process. For instance, at least one concept and/or association should connect two method fragments to be assembled, is an example of a rule. There are no concepts which have the same name and which have different occurrences in a method description, is another example of a rule.

It can be seen that the required operations can be realised by applying the operators *AddClass, ConnectViaAssociationOfClasses, AddClassAttribute* and *AddAssociationAttribute*. These operators are formalised as follows:

ConnectViaAssociationOfClasses. This operator connects two classes from different As-Is models with a new association in the To-Be model.

CnnectViaAssociationOfClasses: $Class^2 \rightarrow$ Association
CnnectViaAssociationOfClasses(C_1, C_2) = A.source (C_1) $\wedge$ A.target (C_2) | A$\in$ Association, $C_1 \subset OM_1$, $C_2 \subset OM_2$, (OM_1, OM_2) $\in$ Object Model

Let us exemplify the association of the two following method fragments *Statechart* and *Object model* as considered in [2]. The behaviour of each *Class* is specified by a set of *States*. An association *Has* is added between these two classes in order to connect them:
CnnectViaAssociationOfClasses(Class, State) = Has.source(Class) $\wedge$ Has. target(State) | State $\subset$ Statechart, Class $\subset$ Object Model.

AddClass. This operator can be applied to add a new class in the To-Be model to make possible the connection between As-Is models.
AddClass: Object Model $\rightarrow$ Class
AddClass(OM) = C | C $\subset$ OM, C $\in$ Class

For example, the *Transaction* element in the *Statechart* fragment has a post condition that refers to an *Attribute* which is an element of the *Object Model* fragment. As a consequence, a new class *PostCondition* should be added in the To-Be model in order to connect the *Transition* and *Attribute* classes:
AddClass(Objectchart) = PostCondition | PostCondition $\subset$ Oojectchart.

AddClassAttribute and ***AddAssociationAttribute*** allow to add attributes in the To-Be method fragment to the classes and associations created as connectors of the As-Is method fragments.

AddClassAttribute: Class → Class.Attribute
AddClassAttribute(C) = C.At | At∈ Attribute
AddAssociationAttribute: Association → Association.Attribute
AddAssociationAttribute(A) = A.At | At∈ Attribute

According to the example shown in [2], the attribute *Is-hidden* should be added to the association *Is-annotated-with*:

AddAssociationAttribute(Is-annotated-with) = Is-annotated-with.Is-hidden

As shown in Table 2, there are other operators that support methods assembly in addition to the four presented above. It seems to us that these operators are relevant, in particular to tailor some As-Is fragments to the special needs of the assembly process and also to refine the obtained To-Be fragment if necessary. As an illustration let us consider again the previous *Postcondition* case: we could directly associate these two classes using the *ConnectviaAssociationofClasses* and then, retype this association into the class *Postcondition* by applying the operator *RetypeAssociation*.

RetypeAssociation. This operator transforms an association A, connecting two classes C_1 et C_2, into a new class C. Besides, two new associations are added in order to connect the class C with the classes C_1 et C_2.

RetypeAssociation: Association, $Class^2$ → Class, $Association^2$
RetypeAssociation(A, C_1, C_2) = C ∧ A_1.source(C_1) ∧ A_1.target (C) ∧ A_2.source(C) ∧ A_2.target (C_2) | (A_1, A_2) ∈ Association, C ∈ Class

In order to satisfy the assembly rules mentioned above, it might be necessary to modify the names of some classes before the assembly of the method fragments.

RenameClass. The operator *RenameClass* allows to give a new name to a class:

RenameClass: Class → String
RenameClass(C) = C.name(N) | N∈ String

For sake of space it is not possible to illustrate the use of each of the operators for method assembly proposed in Table 2, but a systematic study convinced us that they are useful in method assembly by association.

Product Models Assembly by Integration. To illustrate operators for the assembly by integration, we consider the approach proposed in [19]. According to this approach, the assembly process consists in identifying common elements in product and process models of some selected method chunks and in merging and/or connecting them. This might require some terminology adjustments of model elements before their integration. Elements of product and process models of the selected methods need to be unified based on their similarities, abstracting away their differences and eliminating ambiguities. The integration of two product models which we consider in this section requires to identify similar classes. For example, [15] illustrates the integration of the *Use case* model [9] and the *L'Ecritoire* model [23]. The class *Actor* in the *Use case* model and the class *Agent* in the *L'Ecritoire* model have the same semantic. Therefore, one of these two classes must be renamed prior their merge. In our example *Actor* is renamed into *Agent*.

RenameClass(Actor) = Name(Agent)

MergeClass. When two classes C_1 and C_2 from different As-is models are merged into a new class C in the To-Be model, the class C replaces C_1 and C_2 in any association having initially C_1 or C_2 as source class or target class.

MergeClass: Class^2, {Association}^{2} → Class

MergeClass(C_1, C_2, {A^s_i, A^t_j}) = [∀ i, A^s_i.source(C)] ∧ [∀ j, A^t_j.target(C)] | C_1 ⊂ OM_1, C_2 ⊂ OM_2, C ⊂ OM, C ∈ Class, (OM, OM_1, OM_2) ∈ Object Model

Therefore, the *Actor ($Actor_{UC}$)* from the *Use case* model and *Agent* (renamed into *Actor*) *($Actor_E$)* from *L'Ecritoire* are merged into a new class *Actor*. Two associations, *Executes* and *Supports*, between the classes $Actor_{UC}$ and *Use case* are preserved by replacing $Actor_{UC}$ by *Actor*. Similarly, in the associations *From* and *To* between the classes *Action* and $Actor_E$ in the *L'Ecritoire*, the $Actor_E$ is replaced by *Actor:*

MergeClass($Actor_{UC}$, $Actor_E$, Executes.source($Actor_{UC}$), Supports.source($Actor_{UC}$), From.target($Actor_E$), To.target($Actor_E$)) = Actor ∧ Executes.source(Actor) ∧ Supports.source(Actor) ∧ From.target(Actor) ∧ To.target(Actor)

The operators as *ConnectViaSpecializationClass*, *ConnectViaGeneralizationClass*, *ConnectViaCompositionClass*, *ConnectViaDecompositionClass* are also useful in the assembly by integration. They allow to connect classes that have a similar semantic but different structures and cannot be directly merged. For example, the *Goal* concept exists in both the *Use Case* and *L'Ecritoire* models, but it is defined as an attribute named *Objective* in the class *Use Case* of the first model and as a class in the second one. In order to connect these two concepts we need to transform first the attribute *Objective* into a class in the *Use Case* model. The original approach [19] uses the *Objectify* operator to do that. This operator is formalised here by the *RetypeAttribute* operator.

RetypeAttribute. An attribute of a class C_1 is transformed into a new class C_2 which is associated to the class C_1 with new association.

RetypeAttribute: Class.Attribute → Class, Association
RetypeAttribute(C_1.At) = C_2 ∧ A.source(C_1) ∧ A.target(C_2) | C_2 ∈ Class, A ∈ Association

RetypeAttribute(Use Case. Objective) = Goal ∧ Has.source(Use Case) ∧ Has.target(Goal).

Even after retyping, the merge is not possible because the *Goal* of the *L'Ecritoire* has a specific structure whereas the goal of the *Use Case* model is an informal statement. The solution is to rename (a) the *Goal* of the *Use Case* model into *Informal Goal* and (b) the *Goal* of the *L'Ecritoire* into *Formal Goal* and to connect them via generalisation into the class *Goal*.

ConnectViaGeneralizationClass. Two classes from different As-Is models are generalized into a generic class in the To-Be model. Two is-a links are created between the specific classes and the generic one.

ConnectViaGeneralisationClass: $Class^2 \rightarrow Class$, $Is\text{-}a^2$

ConnectViaGeneralisationClass$(C_1, C_2) = C \wedge [Is\text{-}a.generic(C) \wedge Is\text{-}a.specific(C_1)]$
$\wedge [Is\text{-}a.generic(C) \wedge Is\text{-}a.specific(C_2)] \mid C \in Class$

ConnectViaGeneralisationClass(Informal Goal, Formal Goal) = Goal ∧ [Is-a.generic(Goal) ∧ Is-a.specific(Informal Goal)] ∧ [Is-a.generic(Goal) ∧ Is-a.specific(Formal)].

4.2 Operators for Process Models Assembly

In this section we use the generic typology of operators to generate specific ME operators to assemble process models in (a) the case of assembly by association and (b) the case of assembly by integration. Different kinds of process models can be used to express the process dimension of a method fragment/chunk. It can be a simple ordered list of operations, a more structured activity diagram or a complex multi-strategy model expressed through a directed graph structure. The definition of operators for process models assembly depends on the type of the process models used by the As-Is methods. For example, the approach for assembly by association [2] uses an activity diagram to model process fragments whereas the approach for assembly by integration proposes to integrate process maps [24] (directed graphs of intentions and strategies). In both cases, before generating operators we need to define first the corresponding meta-models.

Process Models Assembly by Association. Fig. 4 presents the meta-model for the *Activity diagram* as instance of the ME meta-model (Fig. 2).

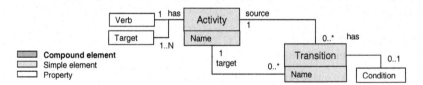

Fig. 4. Meta-model for an Activity Diagram

As shown in this figure, an activity diagram is represented by set of *Activities*, which are *simple elements. Transitions* define in which order activities are realised by specifying for each transition the source activity and the target one. Each *Activity* has two *Properties*: a *Verb*, which represents the operation to realise, and a *Target*, which represents the resulting product elements. *Condition* is a property of a *Transition*. Table 3 shows the operators related to the core Activity diagram elements.

In the example dealing with the assembly of *Statechart* and *Object Model* fragments [2], the authors use two core operations: (1) addition of new transitions and (2) addition of new activities. A new transition can be added only to connect the activities from different fragments as well as a new activity can be added only if a new class was added during the corresponding product fragments assembly. These two operations can be formalised with the operators *AddActivity, AddTransition* and *ConnectViaAssociationOfActivities*.

Table 3. Operators for the Activity-driven Process Models Assembly

Generic Operator	Operators for activity-driven process models assembly	
	Activity	Transition
Rename	RenameActivity	RenameTransition
Add	AddActivity	AddTransition
Remove	RemoveActivity	RemoveTransition
Merge	MergeActivity	MergeTransition
Split	SplitActivity	SplitTransition
Replace	ReplaceActivity	ReplaceTransition
Give	GiveVerb, GiveTarget	GiveCondition
Withdraw	WithdrawVerb, WithdrawTarget	WithdrawCondition
Modify	ModifyVerb, ModifyTarget	ModifyCondition
ConnectViaAssociation	ConnectViaAssociationOfActivities	N/A
ConnectViaMerge	ConnectViaMergeOfActivities	N/A

ConnectViaAssociationOfActivities. A new transition connects two activities from form different As-Is models. The source activity must produce the product element(s) required as input product by the target activity.

ConnectViaAssociationOfActivities: Activity^2 → Transition
ConnectViaAssociationOfActivities (A_1, A_2) = T.source(A_1) ∧ T.target(A_2) | T∈ Transition, $A_1 ⊂ AD_1$, $A_2 ⊂ AD_2$, (AD_1, AD_2) ∈ Activity Diagram

For example, the list of classes obtained by executing the *Object Model* construction activity *O1: Identify Objects and Classes* provides an input for the *Statechart* construction activity *S1: Identify States*. Therefore, these two activities can be connected with a new transition called *Input*:

ConnectViaAssociationOfActivities (O1, S1) = Input.source(O1) ∧ Input.target(S1).

Again, this example illustrates only partially the use of operators listed in Table 3. However, operators such as *Merge, Split, Replace, Remove* applied to both *Activity* and *Transition* are obviously useful. Similarly, the need for renaming an activity of the As-Is fragment in the To-Be fragment is meaningful. Finally, *Give, Withdraw* and *Modify* make sense to change the properties of an As-Is *Activity* or *Transition* in the corresponding To-Be fragment. For instance, a condition for the transition between two activities can be modified and the verb designating an activity can be different in the To-Be fragment compared to what it was in the As-Is model.

Process Models Assembly by Integration. According to the assembly by integration proposed in [19, 15], the process models integration consists in integrating process maps [24]. Fig. 5 represents the map meta-model as instance of the ME meta-model (Fig. 2).

As shown in Fig. 5, a *Map* is a collection of *Sections*. A section is a *compound element* aggregating two types of *Intentions*, the *Source Intention* and the *Target Intention*, and a *Strategy*.

An *Intention* is a goal that can be achieved by the performance of an activity (automated/semi-automated or manual). For example, *Elicit a goal* is an intention in the *L'Ecritoire* requirements elicitation process; *Write a scenario* is another intention. There are two special intentions *Start* and *Stop* that allow to begin and to end the progression in the map, respectively. An intention is a *simple element* expressed following a linguistic approach proposed by [13] as a clause with a *verb* and a *target*. It can also have several *parameters*, where each parameter plays a different role with respect to the verb.

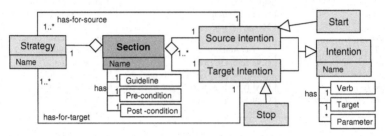

Fig. 5. Map meta-model

A *Strategy* is an approach, a manner to achieve an intention. For example, *By using goal template* is a strategy to achieve the intention *Elicit a goal* proposed in the *L'Ecritoire* approach. A strategy is a *simple element*.

A *Section* is a triplet <*Source Intention, Target Intention, Strategy*>. The arrangement of he sections in a map forms a labelled directed graph with *Intentions* as nodes and *Strategies* as edges. Pre- and Post-conditions of each section specify the progression flows in the map. Each section provides a *Guideline* indicating how to achieve the target intention following the strategy given the source intention has been achieved.

Table 4 proposes the list of operators for maps integration. Only 11 operators have been instantiated from 20 potential ones (Table 5). In fact, some of generic operators do not make sense in the maps integration process. For example, the *Generalize* and *Specialize* operators cannot be instantiated as there are no is-a relationships between intentions, strategies or sections in the map. The three missing operators, namely *AddComponent*, *RemoveComponent* and *MoveComponent* have not been introduced, as it does not make sense to apply them to the *Section* element the structure of which is immutable. The integration of two maps can be done only by merging similar intentions or sections. As a consequence, only the *ConnectViaMerge* operator was instantiated. It is impossible to merge two strategies belonging to different maps.

The example of integration [19] of the *Use Case* and *L'Ecritoire* maps starts with the identification of similar intentions and their merge. The intention I_{UCI}: *Elicit Use Case* in the Use Case model and the intention I_{EI}: *Elicit Goal* in L'Ecritoire have the same semantic: in both cases it means 'to elicit a users goal'. Moreover, the *Goal* concept was defined in the Use Case model during the product models integration illustrated above and allows us to unify the terminology of the two maps. In [19] this was done intuitively by renaming the intention I_{UCI}: *Elicit Use Case* into I_{UCI}: *Elicit Goal*. The generic typology of ME operators allows us to formalise this kind of change in a more precise way: each property of an intention has a proper *Modify* operator: *ModifyVerb*, *ModifyTarget* and *ModifyParametter*. In this example, we need to apply the *ModifyTarget* operator.

ModifyTarget. The value of the intention property *Target* is replaced by a new one. This new value must represent an element of the corresponding product model.

ModifyTarget: Intention $\rightarrow$ String
ModifyTarget(I) = I.target(N) | N$\in$ String

ModifyTarget(I_{UCl}:Elicit Use Case) = I_{UCl}.target(Goal)

Table 4. Operators for Maps Integration

Generic Opera-tor	Operators for Maps integration		
	Intention	Strategy	Section
Rename	RenameIntention	RenameStrategy	RenameSection
Add	AddIntention	AddStrategy	AddSection
Remove	RemoveIntention	RemoveStrategy	RemoveSection
Merge	MergeIntention	MergeStrategy	MergeSection
Split	SplitIntention	SplitStrategy	SplitSection
Replace	ReplaceIntention	N/A	N/A
Give	GiveVerb, GiveTarget GiveParameters	N/A	GivePreCond, GivePostCond, GiveGuideline
Withdraw	WithdrawVerb, WdrTarget WithdrawParamerters	N/A	WithdrawPreCondition WdrPostCond, WdrGuideline
Modify	ModifyVerb, ModifyTarget ModifyParameters	N/A	ModifyPreCond, ModifPost-Cond ModifyGuideline
Retype	RetypeIntention	RetypeStrategy	N/A
ConnectViaMerge	CVMergeIntentions	N/A	ConnectViaMergeSections

ConnectViaMergeIntentions. This operator allows to integrate two maps by merging their similar intentions. When two intentions I_1 and I_2 are merged, the intention I replaces I_1 and I_2 in any section having initially I_1 or I_2 as source intention or target intention.

ConnectViaMergeIntentions: Intention^2, {Strategy}^{2} $\rightarrow$ Intention

ConnectViaMergeIntentions(I_1, I_2, {St^s_i}, {St^t_j}) = [$\forall$ i, St^s_i.has-for-source(I_r)] $\wedge$
[$\forall$ j, St^t_j.has-for-target(I_r)] | $I_r \in$ Intention, $I_1 \subset M_1$, $I_2 \subset M_2$, (M_1, M_2) $\in$ Map

In order to merge the intentions I_{UCl}: *Elicit a Goal* and I_{El}: *Elicit a Goal* we must know in which sections of their corresponding maps they are involved. As shown in Fig. 6, there are three sections in the Use Case map containing the intention I_{UCl} whereas the intention I_{El} is involved in four sections in the L'Ecritoire map. The intention I_l:*Elicit a Goal* replaces I_{UCl} and I_{El} in all these sections.

ConnectViaMergeIntentions(I_{UCl}, I_{El}, St_{UC1}, St_{UC2}, St_{UC3}, St_{E1}, St_{E2}, St_{E3}, St_{E4}) =
St_{UC1}.target(I_l) $\wedge$ St_{UC2}.source(I_l) $\wedge$ St_{UC3}.source(I_l) $\wedge$ St_{E1}.target(I_l) $\wedge$ St_{E2}.source(I_l) $\wedge$
St_{E2}.target(I_l) $\wedge$ St_{E3}.source(I_l) $\wedge$ St_{E4}.source(I_l).

In the same manner the *Start* and *Stop* intentions of both maps are merged. Other operators such as *AddStrategy* and *RemoveStrategy* are needed in order to improve the final *To-Be* map. For example, the integration of the Use Case and L'Ecritoire maps allows to improve the scenario writing process which is rather poor in the first model by rich guidelines provided by second one. It appears that the original Use Case strategy supporting scenario writing became obsolete and should be removed from the final integrated map.

To conclude on the assembly by integration, a systematic comparison of operators identified in [19] and those generated from the typology of generic ones shows that (a) we missed useful operators in the former and (b) the systematic definition provided by the latter avoid 'ad-hoc' and not fundamentally justified assembly types. The so-called *Objectify* operator mentioned above is an example of (b); *Give, Withdraw and Modify* applied to intention and section are examples of (a).

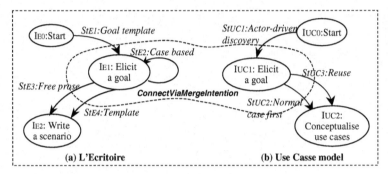

Fig. 6. Example of integration of L'Ecritoire and Use Case maps

5 Conclusion

In this paper we provided a formal ground for tool-supported ME in the form of a set of generic ME operators. The production of these operators is based on a ME meta-model that was especially defined for this purpose and a classification of ME approaches issued from a literature survey. The set of operators allows to understand in a cohesive and consistent way which operations constitute the basis of method construction and method transformation. The set of generic operators considerably eases the generation of the specific set of operators required in a given ME approach.

Our future preoccupation is to facilitate even more the process of generating specific operators from the generic ones by introducing sub-typologies, each being relevant for a ME class of approaches. Table 5 shows our first view on this. For sake of space the figure shows the operators which are different depending of the class of approaches. It can be noticed that the differences relate to *ModelElements*. We indeed think that all operators related to *Element* are relevant irrespective of the ME class.

The generic typology seems to capture all interesting types of method engineering operations. However, the problem to consider next is the validation of its completeness and correctness. According to Banerjee [1], a set of operators is considered to be complete if it subsumes every possible schema evolution; it is correct if the execution of any operator does not result in an incorrect schema. By analogy, in order to prove the completeness of the generic ME operators typology we need to identify a minimal set of operators whereas the correctness of a set of specific operators required to define a set of model invariants. For example, to ensure the correctness of the operators for maps integration, we need to define what a *correct* map is. This is achieved by

Table 5. Sub-typologies of ME operators

Object	Operator	From Scr.	Paradigm-Based			Exten-sion	Assembly	
			Instan.	Abstr.	Adapt.		Assoc.	Integr.
Model Ele- ment	*Instantiate*		+					
	Abstract			+				
	ConnectViaSpecialisation					+		+
	ConnectViaGeneralisation.					+		+
	ConnectViaComposition.					+		+
	ConnectViaDecomositionp					+		+
	ConnectViaAssociation					+	+	
	ConnectViaMerge							+

adding a set of conditions called invariants to the structural definition of a map. An invariant must hold in any quiescent state of a map, that is, before and after any execution of an operator to one or several As-Is map(s) resulting in a new state of the To-Be map.

Finally, the generic ME operators will serve to the development of a CAME tool supporting different ME approaches.

References

1. Banerjee, J., Kim, W., Kim, H.-J., Korth, H. F. Semantics and Implementation of Schema Evolution in Object Oriented Databases. *Proceedings. of the ACM-SIGMOD Annual Conference*, pp. 311--322, San Francisco, CA, 1987.
2. Brinkkemper S., Saeki, M., Harmsen, F. Assembly Techniques for Method Engineering. *Proceedings of the 10th International Conference CAiSE'98*. Pisa, Italy, 1998.
3. Deneckere, R. Using Meta-patterns to Construct Patterns. *Proc. of the Conference on Object-Oriented Information Systems, OOIS'2002*, Springer, France, 2002.
4. Grundy, J.C., Venable, J.R. Towards an Integrated Environment for Method Engineering. In *Challenges and Strategies for Research in Systems Development*. W.W. Cotterman and J.A. Senn (Eds.). John Wiley & Sons. Chichester. pp. 45-62, 1996.
5. Gupta, D., Prakash, N. Engineering Methods from Method Requirements Specifications. *Requirements Engineering Journal*, Vol.6, pp.135-160, 2001.
6. Harmsen A.F., Brinkkemper, S., Oei, H. Situational Method Engineering for Information System Projects. *In Olle T.W. and A.A. Verrijn Stuart (Eds.), Mathods and Associated Tools for the Information Systems Life Cycle*, Proceedings of the IFIP WG8.1 Working Conference CRIS'94, pp. 169-194, North-Holland, Amsterdam, 1994.
7. Harmsen, A.F. *Situational Method Engineering. Moret Ernst & Young*, 1997.
8. Heym, M., Osterle, H. Computer-aided methodology engineering. *Information and Software Technology*, Vol. 35 (6/7), June/July, pp. 345-354, 1993.
9. Jacobson I., Christenson, M., Jonsson, P., Oevergaard, G. Object Oriented Software Engineering: a Use Case Driven Approach. *Addison-Wesley*, 1992.
10. Kumar, K., Welke, R.J. Method Engineering, A Proposal for Situation-specific Methodology Construction. *In Systems Analysis and Design: A Research Agenda*, Cotterman and Senn (eds), Wiley, pp257-268, 1992.
11. Prakash, N., Bhatia, M. P. S. Generic Models for Engineering Methods of Diverse Domains. *Proceedings of CAISE'02*, Toronto, Canada, LNCS 2348, pp. 612., 2002.
12. Prakash, N. Towards a formal definition of methods. *RE Journal*, 2 (1), 1997.

13. Prat, N. Goal formalisation and classification for requirements engineering. In: Proceedings of the REFSQ'97, Barcelona, 1997.
14. Punter H.T., Lemmen, K. The MEMA model : Towards a new approach for Method Engineering. *Information and Software Technology*, 38(4), pp.295-305, 1996.
15. Ralyté, J., Rolland, C. An Assembly Process Model for Method Engineering. *Proceedings of the 13th CAISE'01*, Interlaken, Switzerland, 2001.
16. Ralyté, J., Rolland, C. An approach for method reengineering. *Proceedings of the 20th ER2001*, Yokohama, Japan, LNCS 2224, Springer, pp.471-484, 2001.
17. Ralyté, J., Deneckère, R., Rolland, C. Towards a Generic Model for Situational Method Engineering. *Proceedings of the 15th International Conference CAISE'03*, Klagenfurt/Velden, Austria, LNCS 2681, Springer, pp. 95-110, 2003.
18. Ralyté, J., Rolland, C., Ben Ayed, M. An Approach for Evolution Driven Method Engineering. To be published in *Information Modeling Methods and Methodologies*. J. Krogstie, T. Halpin, K. Siau (Eds.), Idea Group, Inc., USA, 2003.
19. Ralyté J., Rolland, C., Plihon, V. Method Enhancement by Scenario Based Techniques. *Proc. of the 11th Conference CAISE'99*, Heidelberg, Germany, 1999.
20. Rolland, C., Plihon, V. Using generic chunks to generate process models fragments. *Proceedings of 2nd IEEE International Conference on Requirements Engineering*, ICRE'96, Colorado Spring, 1996.
21. Rolland, C., Prakash, N. A proposal for context-specific method engineering. *Proceedings of the IFIP WG 8.1 Conference on Method Engineering,* Chapman and Hall, pp 191-208, Atlanta, Gerorgie, USA, 1996.
22. Rolland, C., Plihon, V., Ralyté, J. Specifying the reuse context of Scenario Method Chunks. *Proceedings of the 10th International Conference CAISE'98*, Pisa, Italy, 1998.
23. Rolland, C., Souveyet, C., Salinesi, C. Guiding Goal Modelling using Scenarios, IEEE Transactions on Software Engineering, 24(12): 1055-1071, 1998.
24. Rolland, C., Prakash, N., Benjamen, A. A Multi-Model View of Process Modelling. *Requirements Engineering Journal*, Vol. 4 (4), pp169-187, 1999.
25. Rossi, M., Tolvanen, J-P., Ramesh, B., Lyytinen, K., Kaipala, J. Method Rationale in Method Engineering. Proceedings of the 33rd Hawaii International Conference on Systems Sciences, 2000.
26. Saeki, M. Embeding metrics into Information Systems Development methods: An Application of method Engineering Technique. *Proceedings of the 15th International Conference CAISE'03, Velden, Austria, LNCS 2681, Springer,* pp. 374-389, 2003.
27. Saeki, M. Toward Automated Method Engineering: Supporting Method Assembly in CAME. Invited talk in the Int. Workshop on Engineering Methods to Support Information Systems Evolution (EMSISE'03), http://cui.unige.ch/db-research/EMSISE03/ , 2003.
28. Song, X. Systematic Integration of Design Methods. *IEEE Software*, 1997.
29. Tolvanen, J-P., Rossi, M. & Liu H., Method Engineering : Current research directions and implications for future research. In *Method Engineering: Principles of method construction and tool support*. S. Brinkkemper, K. Lyytinen, R.J. Welke (Eds.), Proceedings of the IFIP TC8 WG8.1/8.2. Atlanta, USA, pp. 296-317, 1996.
30. Tolvanen, J.-P. Incremental Mehtod Engineering with Modeling Tools: Theoretical Principles and Empirical Evidence. *PhD Dissertation. University of Jyväskylä, Finland*, 1998.

Two-Hemisphere Model Driven Approach: Engineering Based Software Development

Oksana Nikiforova and Marite Kirikova

Institute of Applied Computer Systems, Riga Technical University
1 Kalku, Riga, LV-1658, Latvia
{ivasiuta,marite}@cs.rtu.lv

Abstract. Several model driven approaches are currently used and developed, namely, generic model driven approaches, agile model driven approaches, business process model driven approaches, etc. This paper proposes the model driven approach, which is based on a two-hemisphere model. The two-hemisphere model integrates application and problem domain issues. The model utilizes automatic model transformations, but in the same time allows room for input of tacit knowledge. It is a practice-oriented approach which ties together methods of business process modeling, object oriented, and model transformation approaches in order to support cognitive needs of requirements holders and object oriented software developers, and provide framework for explicit and transparent representation of mutually related business and software development knowledge. It utilizes tacit knowledge of stakeholders (including software designers), but in the same time reflects this knowledge in explicit and automatically reconfigurable models that form the basis for automatic code generation.

1   Introduction

"Agile" is one of the most popular words in current software development practice. Agile software development methods, agile modeling, etc are attracting more and more interest and attention. However the ultimate goal of the agility is not just software development, - it is business agility [1], [2] that is to be achieved by organizations to survive in a rapidly changing turbulent environment. The role of information technology and information systems in supporting business agility is well understood [1], [3], [4]. One of the most debated promises to support business agility is the Model Driven Architecture [4] that aims at automatic model transformation from a platform independent application domain model into platform specific design and implementation models [5]. The approach is developed by the Objects Modeling Group and is based on the UML [6] (object oriented) application domain model. However this approach does not address the question of how to develop such an UML platform independent model, which would meet business needs and would be ease adaptable to the changes of those needs. Therefore there is room for the claim that a sophisticated application domain model is not needed, i.e., that the agile model at this level is barely good enough [7]. This thesis is backed up by the practical as-

A. Persson and J. Stirna (Eds.): CAiSE 2004, LNCS 3084, pp. 219–233, 2004.
© Springer-Verlag Berlin Heidelberg 2004

sumption that tacit models that are close to the reality are better than sophisticated explicit models that are far from the reality. The claim reflects the main problem of contemporary object oriented approaches: an attempt to gather requirements on the bases of use case descriptions without automatically tracking relationships between use cases and without automatically analyzing their consistency. Automatic checking of correspondence between application model and problem domain model also is not supported.

Several model driven approaches are currently used and developed, namely, generic model driven approaches, agile model driven approaches, business process model driven approaches, etc. With respect to the model that drives the software development process we may distinguish between the art based model driven approaches (driven mainly by tacit or mental models) and the engineering based ones, which are driven by externalized explicit models. This paper proposes a model driven approach, which is based on an explicit two-hemisphere model. The purpose of the paper is to demonstrate that sophisticated models are not an obstacle in software development and that engineering based approaches can well support business agility. The two-hemisphere model integrates application and problem domain issues. The model utilizes automatic model transformations, but in the same time allows room for input of tacit knowledge. It is a practice-oriented approach which ties together methods of business process modeling, object oriented, and model transformation approaches in order to support cognitive needs of requirements holders and object oriented software developers, and provide framework for explicit and transparent representation of mutually related business and software development knowledge. It utilizes tacit knowledge of stakeholders (including software designers), but at the same time reflects this knowledge in explicit and automatically reconfigurable models that form the basis for automatic code generation.

The paper is structured as follows. In Section 2 we analyze several model driven software development approaches. Section 3 introduces the two-hemisphere model driven approach and discusses its applicability from business, software development, and cognitive perspectives. Section 4 briefly illustrates some model transformations utilized in the two-hemisphere model driven approach.

2   Software Development Driven by Particular Models

The notion Model Driven Approaches [8] has become popular only recently, however, all approaches are model driven. The question is only what type of model drives the approach. Is it a tacit mental model of the designer or a particular explicit model represented using particular formal notations that are supposed to be understood by all participants of software development team. In this section we discuss briefly the following software development approaches:
- Traditional object oriented approach (TOO)
- Generic model driven approach (GMD)
- Agile model driven approach (AMD)
- Business process model driven a approach (BPMD)
- Two-hemisphere model driven approach (2HMD)

Differences between approaches are graphically illustrated in Fig. 1. The fully explicit model here is depicted by filled rectangle, semi explicit model (some aspects of systems are represented by explicit representations, while other aspects are presented only in tacit mental models) are shown by non-filled rectangles, and fully or mainly tacit models (non essential proportion of explicit representations may be present) are represented by cloud like notation. Differences between approaches are analyzed from the point of view of model transformations, "the heart and the soul" of model driven approaches [5]. Formal (automatic transformations) between models at different levels of abstraction are denoted by continuous line arrows, but mental and manual transformations by dotted line arrows.

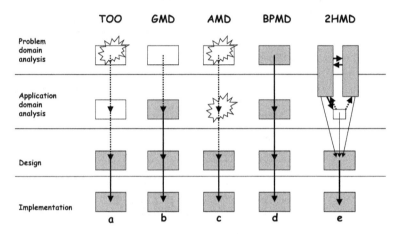

Fig. 1. Level of exploration in model driven approaches

2.1 Traditional Object Oriented (TOO) Approach

The TOO approaches [10-16] the problem domain is considered as a black box by describing a number of aspects of the system [17]. Primarily, designers' tacit knowledge acquired during application domain analysis drives the traditional object-oriented approach (Fig. 1. a). Thus it is an approach, which is based on art rather than engineering, despite sophisticated modeling techniques used in lower levels of abstraction.

Modeling efforts in TOO usually start with the identification of *use-cases* (Fig.2.) for the software to be developed. A use-case reflects interactions between the system to be built and the actor (an outside object in a particular role) that has a particular purpose of using the system. Each interaction starts with an event directed from the actor to the system and proceeds through a series of events between the actor, the system, and possibly other actors, until the interaction initiated by the original event reaches its logical conclusion. The sequence of interactions can be specified in words or by one or more prototypical scenarios, which then are to be translated into the elements of an *interaction diagram*. The interaction diagrams are created for each use-case and show the sequence of message passing during certain use-case realization. The *class diagram* shows an overall structure of the software system and encapsulates the responsibility of each class. The *component diagram* represents the realization of classes into a particular programming language. Therefore during the design stage the target software system is organized into components, based on the knowledge gained in the analysis stage. As a result the *design model* is developed that further *may be automatically translated* into a particular programming language, and thus serve as a basis for software system's implementation [17].

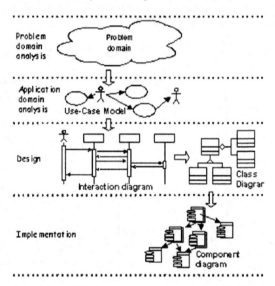

Fig. 2. UML diagrams to be built during traditional object-oriented software development

The TOO approach is usually based on a quite rigid requirements specification, which is developed on the basis of use-cases and problem domain analysis. Knowledge in higher levels of abstraction is documented, however, the form of documentation – use-cases, does not permit one to check consistency of requirements and does not show their relationship to the problem domain explicitly. This leads to major problems in change management of traditional object oriented projects.

2.2 Generative Model Driven (GMD) Approach

The GMD approach (Fig. 1. b) "is based on the idea that people will use very sophisticated modeling tools to create very sophisticated models that they can automatically transform with the tools to reflect the realities of various deployment platforms" [7]. One of such approaches is Object Management Group's Model Driven Architecture [8]. Formal transformation here starts from platform independent application domain model represented in UML. This model is transformed into platform specific design models, and further the code is generated from the platform specific model [18]. The main gain here is higher flexibility that can be obtained by shorter time needed for software design and implementation, because automatic transformation is possible not only from the design level models into the implementation, but already from application domain models into the design level models. Therefore the GMD approach indirectly addresses business agility better than the TOO approach [4].

Opponents of the Model Driven Architecture call GMD "a great theory - as was the idea that the world is flat" [7]. And, indeed, the application domain class model [5], [19], which should conform to all problem domain requirements and incorporate all details necessary for platform specific design model generation, is extremely complicated and may be understood only by experts in object oriented software development. This is a weakness of the approach, because there is no possibility to prove the application domain level model's conformance to user requirements neither formally nor mentally.

2.3 Agile Model Driven (AMD) Approach

The AMD approach [20] uses formal model transformation from design level into implementation level, like the TOO approach, but it relies on simpler formalized models and highly elaborated tacit models in upper levels of abstraction. Some arguments as to why the AMD approach is viewed as more effective than the generative model driven approach are as follows [7]: (1) every software system has both a user interface on the front end and the database on the back end, yet UML still does not address these issues; (2) in many cases people do not have the modeling skills in UML and (3) the tool support is still not sufficient for proper handling of UML models, i.e., vendors claim support for a standard, but then implement their own version of it for competitive reasons.

The main claim of users of the AMD approach against the TOO approach is that it is more reasonable to spend time for acquiring proper tacit knowledge about user requirements than spend time for developing specifications and models that are formal but hard to understand and change. The AMD approach is based on the art (tacit knowledge) of highly qualified systems developers in upper, problem and application, domains and may utilize engineering for translation of design level models into implementation (Fig. 1. c).

2.4 Business Process Model Driven (BPMD) Approach

Engineering can be applied already at the problem domain level. One way how this can be achieved is through the use of appropriate business process modeling methods and tools. If a detailed enough business process model is developed, it automatically may be translated into application level UML model [21]. We call such approach a business process model driven approach (Fig. 1. d). Theoretically, such an approach directly supports business agility, because the only thing that is to be changed to obtain new software code is the business model. However the approach requires high business process modeling skills with respect to both problem and application domain levels, because the problem domain business process model should include the details necessary for application domain model generation. Thus business process model becomes a complicated multilevel system where automated processes are clearly identified and their expected behavior represented. The BPMD approach has high potential feasibility because business process redesign and improvement is one of the methods used by many organizations to achieve or preserve their competitive advantages [18], [22], [23].

2.5   Two-Hemisphere Model Driven (2HMD) Approach

The 2HMD approach [9] may be considered as a version of business process model driven approach. The approach addresses the following issues currently relevant in software development:

- Business process models usually are developed in a comparatively high level of abstraction and rarely pin down all details needed for software development
- Diagrams preferred by business team differs from those preferred by software developers

Therefore the 2HMD approach utilizes the problem domain conceptual model and the application level use-case diagram in addition to the business process diagram for driving the software development process. It is based on sophisticated models, but it enables the generation of simpler models from the sophisticated ones in order to support development of stakeholders' tacit knowledge. Hypothetically, the transformation from two-hemisphere model (or just from one of its constituents – the business process model) into platform independent application level model is possible (Fig. 1e). However, this paper describes a softer version of 2HMD approach where stakeholders' tacit knowledge, if needed, may be added down to the design level. The approach is applicable for software development teams that possess conventional business process modeling and UML tools. The 2HMD approach is described in detail in Section 3.

3   The 2HMD Approach in Detail

Cognitive psychology [24] proposes that the human brain consists of two hemispheres, one of which is responsible for logic and another one for concepts. Harmonic interrelated functioning of both hemispheres is a precondition of an adequate human behavior. A metaphor of two hemispheres may be applied to software development process because this process is based on investigation of two fundamental things: business and application domain logic (processes) and business and application domain concepts.

Some recent surveys show that about 83% of companies are engaged in business process improvement and redesign [18]. This implies that many companies are common with business process modeling techniques [18] or at least they employ particular business process description frameworks [22]. On the other hand practice of software development shows that functional requirements can be derived from problem domain task descriptions even about 7 times faster than if trying to elicit them directly from users [25]. Both facts mentioned above and existence of many commercial business modeling tools (such as GRADE [26], ARIS [27], etc.) are a strong motivation to base software development on the business process model rather than on any other soft or hard models.

However, business process diagrams developed by business analysts rarely show all details necessary for software development, as well as in many cases, do not reflect the "to be" business situation. Therefore formal transformation of business process model into the application model, design model, and implementation is not possible, and software developers shall step in and try to acquire software requirements. They usually interview business managers and then create UML diagrams, typically beginning with use-case and class diagrams. Business managers may be forced to review those diagrams, that can be frustrating for them, because use-case and class diagrams do not reflect the business perspective very well [18].

The 2HMD approach (Fig. 3) addresses this problem by use of two interrelated models at problem domain level, namely, the business process model and the conceptual model, which are related to the use-case model at the application domain level.

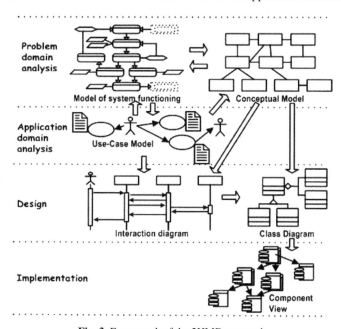

Fig. 3. Framework of the 2HMD approach

A notation of the business process model, which reflects functional perspectives of the problem and application domains, is optional, however, it must reflect the following components of business processes [28]: external entities (processes); sub-processes (the number of levels of decomposition is not restricted); performers; information flows; triggering conditions, and information (data) stores. Use-cases are tied to the business process model and can be derived from it. The conceptual model is used in parallel with business process model to cross-examine software developers understanding of problem and application domain models. Use-cases are always either generated from the business process model or reflected in the business process models, i.e., they "depart" from the business process model for discussions with respect to software development details, prototyping, etc., and, when details are known, manually return back to the business process model together with the details [29]. Current functional requirements always are present in the business process model, that helps to maintain their consistency [29]. As a result sophisticated models are used without disturbing software developers' and business managers' natural ways of thinking [9].

Relevance of particular models of 2HMD framework with respect to business modeling, object oriented software development, and model transformation is shown in Table 1.

Table 1. Use of problem domain and application domain models in 2HMD approach

Perspective	Business process model	Conceptual model	Use case model
Business modeling	Knowledge organized in business oriented terms Requirements can be derived faster from task descriptions than if asked directly from users Appropriate business modeling tools exist	May be used for checking adequacy of developers knowledge	Convenient for discussing requirements in detail
Object oriented software development	Enables consistency check of use cases	Developers usually build tacit and explicit conceptual models that reflect their current knowledge	Main tool for requirements gathering and understanding
Model transformation	At a particular stage the process model may be automatically transformed into implementation (see Section 2.4)	May be (at least partly) derived from business process model If organized as class diagram may (hypothetically) mirror business process model	May be automatically generated from business process model

Initial version of the 2HMD approach was proposed in [17], where the general framework for object oriented software development had been discussed and it's application for driving school's software development had been demonstrated. The current version of the approach supports semi-formal model transformation from problem and application domain into design and implementation. By semi-formal, we mean a transformation of part of elements of one model into the subset of elements of another model. Transformation is fully formal if all elements of the target model can be obtained from the source model. The 2HMD approach utilizes two formal (automatic) transformations: (1) from a business process model into an use-case diagram, and (2) from a design level model into implementation. All semiformal and formal transformations are illustrated in Fig.4.

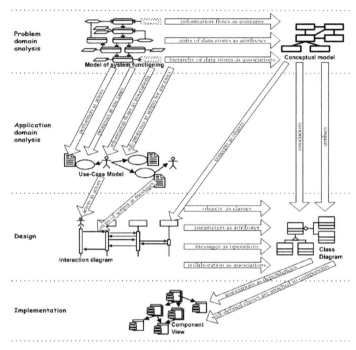

Fig. 4. Formal and semi-formal transformations in 2HMD approach

Semiformal transformation from the business process model into the problem domain conceptual model. As mentioned above, the conceptual model reflects tacit knowledge of software developers in an explicit diagram, i.e., software developers build it. However, part of a conceptual model can be generated automatically. Real-world classes relevant to the problem domain and their relationships are presented in the conceptual model. The conceptual model shows the things that exist in the problem domain and their relations to other things. The notational conventions of the business process diagram give a possibility to identify concepts by analyzing all the data stores in the diagram [17]. Data stores from the business process model can be transformed into the concepts of the conceptual model. The same refers to the units of data stores as well as information flows. Automatic transformation possibilities of other business process model elements into conceptual model are under the investigation. The automatically generated part of conceptual model may be compared to the manually constructed model to ensure consistency between the business process model and developers knowledge.

Formal transformation from the business process model into use-cases is possible, if processes to be performed by software system are identified in the business process model [29]. Processes to be performed by software system become use-cases in the use-case model, performers of related processes become actors in the use-case model, and scenarios for realization of use-cases may be defined by decompositions of business processes (sub-processes) corresponding to the use-cases [17].

The interaction diagram is developed by *semiformal transformation from the use-case model and the conceptual* model. Interaction diagram for each use-case is based on its realization scenario (or sequence of sub-processes). Appropriate interacting objects are extracted from the conceptual model. Alternatively, the transformation directly from the business process model could be provided, because the use-case model and part of the conceptual model are generated from the business process diagram. However, in the case where semi-formal transformations dominate over formal ones and human intelligence is involved at different levels of abstraction, simpler transparent transformations are more preferable than sophisticated ones.

The class diagram is based on the conceptual model and is formed according to information in the interaction diagram. It is obtained by *semiformal transformations from the interaction diagram and the conceptual model*. The class diagram here is already a structure of a software application and contains only those classes, whose objects interact during the use-case realization [17]. *Formal transformation from Class diagram into software code* may be utilized.

In overall, the 2HMD approach is engineering based, because only those use cases, which are automatically generated from the business process model are used for further transformations. This allows maintaining consistency between the requirements. On the other hand possibility to generate use cases automatically fastens software development process and support business agility. In the next section some of transformations mentioned in this section are described in more detail.

4   Application Case: An Administration of Driving School

Administration of the driving school [17] is used as a problem domain to illustrate how the 2HMD approach may be applied. This section shows main steps, which were made during software development for administration of the driving school.

Problem domain analysis: The simplified version of the business process for the driving school is reflected in Fig. 4. The driving school has several classrooms in several locations. The director of driving school assigns learning sessions for new groups based on a predefined schedule. The driving school already has a teaching staff, which consists of instructors having a car and teachers. When the applicant comes to driving school, the administrator of the school offers him a list of available groups for learning and helps to select the most appropriate group location and time schedule. After at least three applicants were assigned for learning in a particular group the start date of learning is defined, the teacher for the group is assigned and the instructor for every pupil in the group is attached. Each group is registered at the Road Traffic Safety Directorate (RTSD).

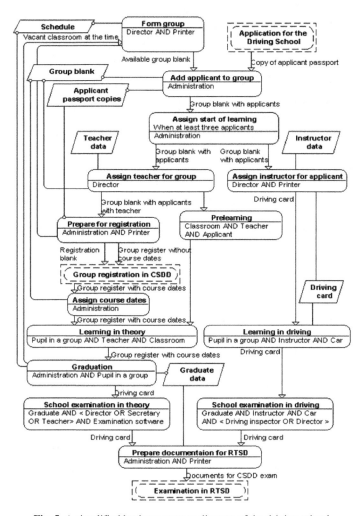

Fig. 5. A simplified business process diagram of the driving school

The diagram in Fig. 4 is a result of business process modelling done by the developer in straight collaboration with the user, and using a particular business-modelling tool – GRADE [26]. Identification of real-world classes relevant to the software system and their relationships is done during conceptual modelling. The conceptual model shows the things that exist in the driving school problem domain and their relations to other things. It is expressed in terms of classes. The notational conventions of the business process diagram give a possibility to identify concepts also by analysing all data stores in this diagram. Data stores are represented as concepts in the conceptual model Fig. 6.

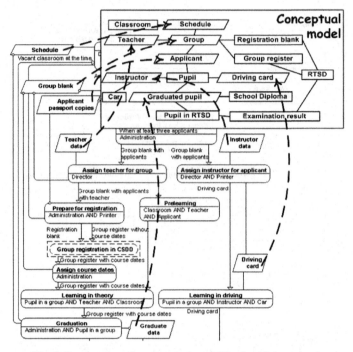

Fig. 6. Construction of a conceptual model for the driving school

Concepts coming from the business process diagram at the highest level of abstraction are indicated as parallelograms. Concepts identified by analysis of sub-process defined during business process modelling – as rectangles. The hierarchical structure of data stores in the business process model gives a possibility to detect potential relationships between system concepts. Data stores are characterized by a set of attributes, which are useful for definition of class structure.

Application Domain Analysis: Looking for processes in business process model (Fig. 5) that can be automated, and potential actors to implement use-cases is a basis for building the use-case diagram (Fig. 7). Analysis of the business process identifies the boundary of the software system and helps to decide, which processes refer to the software system. Those processes are presented as use-cases of software system required and their performers are presented as external actors that perform defined use-cases. The use-case diagram shows how driving school's actors use the software system.

Design and Implementation: The business process model developed, the use-case diagram generated and the conceptual model built are used for the further system model refinement during the steps of design and implementation according to the framework described in the previous section.

The interaction diagram may be partly generated from the use-cases and the conceptual model, or, alternatively, obtained directly from the business process diagram

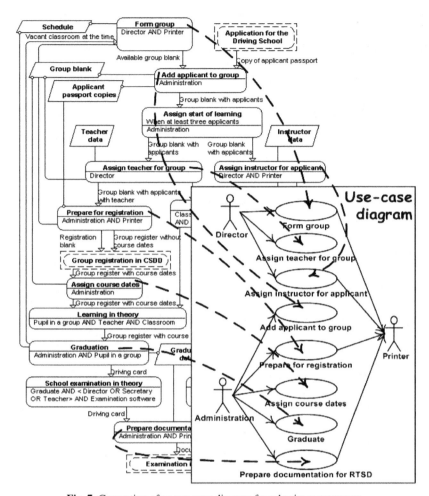

Fig. 7. Generation of an use-case diagram from business processes

as shown in Fig. 8 where generation of an interaction diagram for the use-case "Form group" is shown. As far as scenarios for realization of use-cases may be defined by decompositions of business processes (sub-processes) corresponding to the use-cases, sub-process diagrams serve for construction of object interaction. Information flows in sub-process diagrams help to find objects in message passing, and sub-processes are redefined as a messages passed between objects. The class diagram is constructed based on the information about object interaction and refines the structure of the conceptual model. Further implementation of the design model by components is based on traditional object-oriented approach.

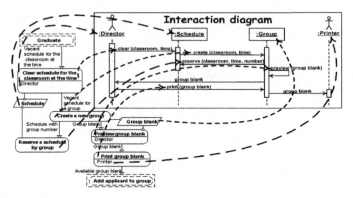

Fig. 8. Generation of a sequence diagram from a sub-process model

5 Conclusion

Today software systems should be built in a way they can support business agility. Therefore software development projects must deal with more complex and massive problem domain knowledge than years ago. This, in turn, requires processing problem domain knowledge more in the style of engineering than in the style of art. We analyzed several approaches of object oriented software development to identify the main differences in handling problem domain knowledge. Only the BPMD approach and the 2HMD approach use engineering at the problem domain level. The BPMD approach requires complete and consistent business process knowledge in the very beginning of the project. The 2HMD approach illustrates how sophisticated models and engineering based software development may be applied even in situations when complete business process knowledge is not provided at the beginning of the project and the most advanced experimental software development tools are not applied.

References

1. Sherrat M. Aligning costs with revenues, Financial Executive, October 2003, pp.59-62.
2. C.K. Prahalad, M.S. Krishnan, & Venkat Ramaswamy, The Essence Of Business Agility: Available at http://www.optimizemag.com/issue/011/leadership.htm
3. Meeting the agility challenge: Increasing business agility through adaptive IT infrastructure, Hewlett-Packard, 2002.
4. Witkop St. Driving business agility with Model Driven Architecture, EDS, 2003.
5. Sendall Sh. And Kozaczunski W. Model transformation: The heart and soul of Model Driven Software development, *IEEE Software*, September/October 2003, pp. 42-45.
6. "UML Specification. Ver.1.3", available at http://www.rational.com
7. Ambler Sc. W. Agile Model Driven development is good enough, *IEEE Software*, September/October 2003, pp.71-73.

8. MDA Guide Version 1.0.1, June 2003, available at http://www.omg.org/docs/omg/03-06-01.pdf
9. Nikiforova O., Kirikova M. *"Enabling Problem Domain Knowledge Transformation during Object Oriented Software Development"*, Conference of Information System Development, ISD'2003, Melbourne, Australia, 25-27 August 2003
10. Jacobson I., Booch G., Rumbaugh J. *The Unified Software Development Process*, Addison-Wesley, 1999.
11. Larman Cr. Applying UML and Patterns: An Introduction to Object-oriented Analysis and Design, Prentice Hall PTR, 1998
12. Leffingwell D. & Widrig D. Managing Software Requirements: A Unified approach, Addison-Wesley, 2000
13. Martin J. & Odell J. *Object-oriented Methods: A Foundation*, Prentice Hall, 1995
14. Mathiassen L., Munk-Madsen A., Nielsen P. A. & Stage J. *Object-oriented Analysis & Design*, Marko Publishing House, 2000
15. Quatrany T. *Visual Modeling with Rational Rose 2000 and UML* (2nd ed.) Addison-Wesley, 2000
16. Rumbaugh J. Models Through the Development Process, *Journal of Object-oriented Programming*, May 1997, Vol. 10, No 2, pp. 5-8, 14.
17. Nikiforova O. "General Framework for Object-Oriented Software Development Process", Scientific Proceedings of Riga Technical University, Series – Computer Science. Applied Computer Systems, 13 vol., 2002.
18. Harmon P. *Business Process Change: A Manager's Guide to Improving, Redesigning, and Automating Processes, Morgan Kaufmann Publishers, 2003*
19. Atkinson C. and Kuhne Th. Model Driven Development: A Metamodelling foundation, in IEEE Software, September/October 2003.
20. The Impact of Agile Processes on Requirements Engineering, Advanced Development Methods, Inc. 2000, available at: http://www.agilealliance.com/
21. ArcStyler MDA-Business Transformer Modeling Style Guide for ARIS, Interactive Objects, 2002.
22. Bruce A. and Kutnick D. *Building Operational Excellence: IT People and Process Best Practices*, Intell Press, 2002.
23. *Organizing Business Knowledge:* The MIT *Process Handbook* (Th. W. Malone, K. Crowston, and G.A. Herman Eds.), MIT Press, 2003
24. Anderson, J.R.: *Cognitive Psychology and Its Implications*, W.H. Freeman and Company, New York, 1995.
25. Lausen S. Task descriptions as functional requirements, IEEE Software, March/April, 2003.
26. GRADE tools, GRADE Development Group, web-site -http://www.gradetools.com/
27. ARIS Toolset Available at: http://www.ids-scheer.com/
28. Kirikova M. "Modelling the boundaries of workspace: A business process perspective", *Information Modelling and Knowledge Bases XIII*, H.Kangassalo, H.Jaakkola, E. Kawaguchi, T. Welzer (eds.), IOS Press, Ohmsha, Amsterdam, Berlin, Oxford, Tokyo, Washington, DC, 2002, pp. 266-278.
29. Kirikova M. "Business Modelling and Use Cases in Requirements Engineering", *Information Modelling and Knowledge Bases XII*, H.Jaakkola, H.Kangassalo E. Kawaguchi (eds.), IOS Press, Ohmsha, Amsterdam, Berlin, Oxford, Tokyo, Washington, DC, 2001, pp. 410-420.

Secure Databases: An Analysis of Clark-Wilson Model in a Database Environment

Xiaocheng Ge[1], Fiona Polack[1], and Régine Laleau[2,*]

[1] Department of Computer Science, University of York
York, YO10 5DD, UK
{xchge,fiona}@cs.york.ac.uk
Fax: +44 1904 432767
[2] Research Laboratory LACL, IUT Fontainebleau, Université Paris 12
Route forestière Hurtault 77300 Fontainebleau, France
laleau@univ-paris12.fr

Abstract. Information systems are vulnerable to accidental or malicious attacks. Security models for commercial computer systems exist, but information systems security is often ignored or added at or after implementation. The paper explores common security models, and their relevance to databases. It demonstrates how security-relevant concepts can be extracted during a conventional database development.

Keywords: Databases, security models, access control, data integrity, development methods

1 Introduction

This paper considers security models for information systems (ISs); the work is part of ongoing research into a development process for commercial databases that incorporates security. The research objective is to incorporate, in a formally verifiable way, the fundamental requirements of commercial security. For simplicity, we assume a target implementation of a relational DBMS and SQL3[13].

This section introduces key security concepts, outlines the overall research plan, and summarises existing security models. Section 2 explores the Clark-Wilson security model in the context of ISs. Section 3 looks at designing for security with a conventional database development and SQL3 implementation. The case study is necessarily brief, and does not cover the formal verification of the security content, or conventional verification techniques such as normalisation. Section 4 compares our approach to existing work, whilst section 5 presents our conclusions in the context of our ongoing research.

1.1 Background of Database Security

ISs are important to the modern society. Information stored in databases is a valuable resource that enables an organisation to operate effectively. Modern

---

* Prof. Laleau's contribution is supported by an EPSRC visiting fellowship, grant 006R02664.

A. Persson and J. Stirna (Eds.): CAiSE 2004, LNCS 3084, pp. 234–247, 2004.

organisations are so dependent on the proper functioning of their ISs that corruption or loss of data has serious consequences.

Database security is concerned with ensuring the *confidentiality (or secrecy)*, *integrity*, and *availability* of stored data. *Confidentiality* is the protection of data from unauthorised disclosure either by direct retrieval or by indirect logical inference; it also concerns the possibility that information may be disclosed by legitimate users acting as an information channel, passing secret information to unauthorised users. *Integrity* requires data to be protected from invalid modification, insertion or deletion. Integrity constraints are rules that define the correct states of a database, and maintain correctness under operation. *Availability* ensures that data is available to authorised users. Availability is very closely related to integrity because service denial may cause or be caused by integrity violations.

Database security is not an isolated problem; it is affected by other components of a system, such as the operating system (OS). The security requirements of a system are specified by means of a security policy and enforced by security mechanisms. For databases, [21, 5, 20] classify the secure database requirements.

Our research focuses on database integrity, and those aspects of confidentiality that relate to data protection, namely access control. Of the following security requirements, which are the minimum that need to be supported by the IS, the first relates directly to integrity; the other two relate to confidentiality.

1. *Integrity, Consistency.* Semantic integrity constraints are rules defining the correct states of the system during operation; they exist to protect against malicious or accidental modification of data, and ensure the logical consistency of data. Rules can be defined on the static state of the database, or on transitions (as conditions to be verified before data is modified).
2. *Identification, Authentication, Audit.* Before accessing a system, every user is identified and authenticated, both for the audit trail and for access permission. Auditing is the process of examining all security relevant events.
3. *Authorisation (access control).* Authorisation applies a set of rules that defines who has what type of access to which information. Access control policies govern the disclosure and modification of information.

In the context of requirement engineering, security aspects should not be afterthoughts of database design process. We cannot simply *'firewall* databases, because firewalls cannot do anything against invalid modification by authorised users. We need an IS development method that incorporates security aspects.

1.2   Secure Database Design Process

Our design process (Figure 1) extends a conventional database design process[10] with security; it includes a formalisation (referred to as OAZIS), to support verification of the integrity of state and operations.

The first step, **requirements collection and analysis**, documents users' data and functional requirements (ie required transactions). There are three types of security requirement: logical, physical and organisational. We concentrate on logical requirements, derived by analysis of threats and risks.

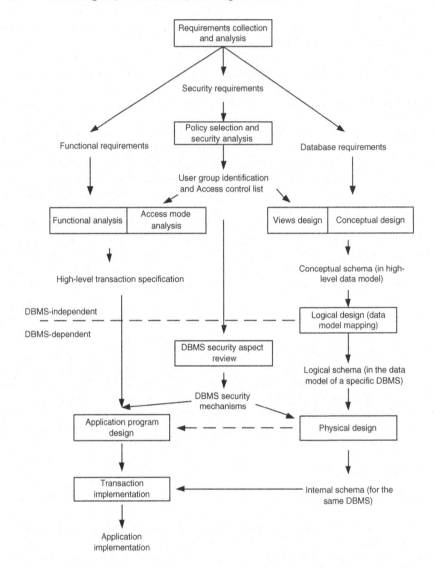

Fig. 1. The development process of OAZIS method

The logical security requirements are the basis for **security analysis and policy selection**. This step is crucial. The security policy determines the access mode for each subject (or role) on each object (data, operations). The permissions of each user role are specified, and the access control list determined.

Once requirements have been analysed, **functional analysis** and **conceptual design** produce a conceptual schema, a concise description of data types, relationships, and constraints. Sub-schemas are identified to aid the expression of security constraints and access control. Basic data operations (create, delete, and update) are used to specify transactions – both the user-required functional transactions and those relating to the chosen security policy. The results of these steps need to be verified against the security requirements, so development iterates between conceptual modelling and model verification.

Logical design translates the conceptual model into a logical model for a specific DBMS. Analysis of the security features in the conceptual model establishes which security requirements can be achieved by OS and DBMS security mechanisms, or by specific security packages, resulting in a logical security model. If any security requirements in the conceptual model cannot be addressed using available mechanisms, the developer should design further specific mechanisms.

Finally, **physical design** implements the internal database structures, including security mechanisms. Application programmes are coded for those parts of transactions that cannot be implemented directly on the chosen DBMS.

1.3   Literature of Security Models

There are many security policies and models in the literature, relevant to various environments. In a military environment, confidentiality is critical – all classified information shall be protected from unauthorised disclosure or declassification – so models focus on mandatory classification. For example, Bell-LaPadula [3] and its derivatives describe models for confidentiality, whilst Biba [4] defines a similar level-oriented integrity model. In the commercial environment, the goal is to prevent fraud and errors – no user, even if authorised, should be able to modify data in an invalid way – so models focus on integrity enforcement and authorisation mechanisms to prevent illegal modification. The seminal work is Clark-Wilson's integrity model.

Policies and models are implemented by security mechanisms, which can be either *discretionary* or *mandatory*. *Discretionary* models include mechanisms for granting and delegating access permissions by (some) system users. *Mandatory* security is built-in and cannot be changed by system users. These models govern information access on the basis of classifications of subject and object[1].

For our commercial security requirements, the Clark-Wilson model results in a conceptual security model that is defined by identification of,

- data items for which security enforcement is crucial (CDIs);
- transformation procedures (TPs) that can access data;
- user roles, in terms of authorisation to use particular TPs.

The access control is specified as an access triple, $< user, tp, data >$, stating that a *user* has permission to execute *tp* on *data*. Implementation is usually discretionary, but there is no fundamental reason why a Clark-Wilson triple could not be implemented as a mandatory security mechanism.

---

[1] A subject is a person or application that actively accesses data/processes; objects are passive data or processes stored in the IS. For military systems, the implementation of mandatory security mechanisms is described in the U.S. Department of Defence Trusted Computer System Evaluation Criteria (the Orange Book) [9].

To enforce basic access control and integrity mechanisms, Clark-Wilson identifies two principal mechanisms. The **well-formed transaction** preserves data integrity and prevents users from arbitrarily manipulating data. **Separation of duty** dictates that each critical operation comprises two or more subparts, each of which has to be executed by a different user role. Our research is concerned with how these mechanisms can be established during the database design process.

2   Clark-Wilson and Information Systems

The Clark-Wilson security model derives from commercial data processing practices. It is based on time-tested business methods; thus it represents a real-world approach, rather than an academic exercise. Furthermore, the Clark-Wilson model can be used to evaluate the security of a complete system, rather than just the subject-object accesses [11]. The focus on data integrity and well-formed transactions makes it particularly attractive for database systems.

2.1   The Clark-Wilson Model

In 1987, Clark and Wilson proposed their commercial security model [6]. It can be used for systems where integrity is enforced across both the OS and the application. Clark-Wilson was extended to cover separation of duty in 1993 [1].

Clark-Wilson is not the first approach to model the integrity aspect of security. Biba [4] defined an integrity model based on the security classifications of subjects and objects, using *integrity level* for classification. Later, Lipner [17] tried to describe integrity using the Bell-LaPadula model. In his model, a list of users is attached to transactions and data separately, to ensure that data can only be manipulated by certified transactions. These are all *lattice* models, with security verification based on the mathematical theory of lattices and relations. For IS, they are inadequate as they do not restrict data manipulation to programs that implement well-formed transactions.

In Clark-Wilson, each datum in the system is classified as either a *constrained data item* (CDI) or an *unconstrained data item* (UDI). CDIs must be protected, whilst UDIs are conventional data objects whose integrity is not assured under the model. No datum can be in both classes:

$$Data = CDI \cup UDI \wedge CDI \cap UDI = \varnothing$$

Operations on CDIs are performed by TPs and *integrity verification procedures* (IVPs)[2]. IVPs ensure that all CDIs conform to some application-specific model of integrity. TPs change the state of the set of CDIs.

Appendix A lists Clark-Wilson rules for certification, enforcement, and separation of duty. *Enforcement rules* specify security requirements that should be

---

[2] Although it is tempting to think of a TP as a user transaction, the analogy is unsound, as we will see later.

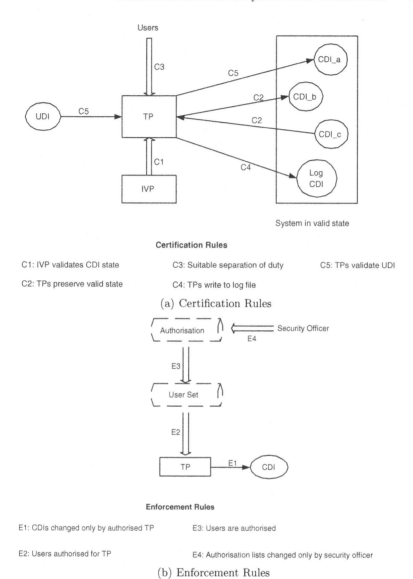

Fig. 2. Certification and Enforcement Rules of the Clark-Wilson Model

supported by the protection mechanisms in the underlying system. *Certification rules* specify security requirements that the application system should uphold.

Figure 2 (derived from [6]) shows how these rules apply to data management. UDIs represent data that exists outside the secure system. Certification rules ensure that such data is properly validated on entry to the system – for example, rule C5 requires that well-formed TPs that convert UDIs to CDIs perform only the complete, certified transformations; rules C1 and C2 require that CDIs conform to the IVPs on entry and under subsequent transformations. Rule C4 requires the logging of all transactions, as is normal for databases – though database logging is for rollback, whilst Clark-Wilson logging is for audit; rule C3 requires appropriate separation of duties. Since data can only be entered in accordance with the certification rules, for the systems in which we are interested, it follows that all data in the database are CDIs. The enforcement rules prevent modification of CDIs in ways that contravene the IVPs. Rules E2 to E4 relate to TP authorisation of access, whilst remaining rules ensure that only well-formed, certified TPs can be used to modify CDIs.

2.2   Applying Clark-Wilson Using a DBMS

Conventional DBMSs support many of the Clark-Wilson mechanisms for access authorisation and control. However, implementations based on standard SQL require some compromises. SQL3 access control mechanisms are primarily on data not transactions, so the access-control triples cannot be directly or fully implemented for user transactions. Inspiration for implementation mechanisms comes from Lee [16] and Shockley [23], who independently developed an implementation of the Clark-Wilson model, using the Biba model categories and trust subjects to interpret access triple authorisations at the data level.

Figure 3 shows a classical DBMS and the related OS and programming functions. The fundamental database principle, that data can only be accessed via the DBMS, is assumed, and the DBMS provides authorisation checking, transaction and data management and logging. The OS authentication also applies as normal and can be extended at the DBMS interface, for example with extra access rules. We now consider how these concepts can be related to the Clark-Wilson rule-application in Figure 2.

First, we consider validation of UDIs. In figure 3, the application object, outside the DBMS box, represents a UDI. Following rule C5, the application object is processed by an application program, invoking integrity enforcement procedures such as procedure preconditions or an integrity contract. During execution, connection to the DBMS server is established, and the user who is executing the application program is authenticated by DBMS-level authorisation. If authentication succeeds, then a database transaction takes over, applying its own checks on data integrity via the DBMS integrity enforcement. The transaction is logged, part in the DBMS transaction log and part by the OS (rule C4).

Secondly, we review the implementation of the enforcement rules on CDIs. At login, users are checked by OS authentication; they can then access either application programs or database transactions according to the relevant access rules (rule E3). Under rule E4, access permissions can only be modified by a specific user role (security officer). Enforcement rule application is strongest if as much processing as possible takes place under the control of DBMS access rules. This is the case with *Stored Procedures* (supported by, for instance, ORACLE[19], IBM DB2[12], and Microsoft SQL server [18]) and DBMS programming facilities such

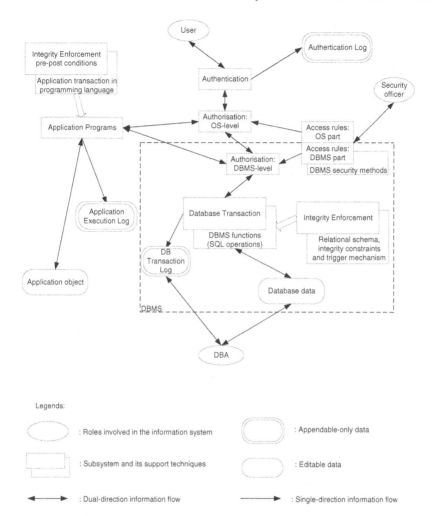

Fig. 3. DBMS classical architecture

as Oracle's PL/SQL. For complex algorithms, library procedures, graphics, and access to other systems, it is necessary to use program code managed by the OS; each time a CDI is exported to an embedding program, it reverts to UDI status.

A typical database transaction is made up of a number of separate TPs, some of which convert UDIs into DBMS CDIs, and some of which update CDIs. Transactions must also implement IVPs. Most database transactions (and their associated access control) must therefore conform to the Clark-Wilson rules. Access triples grant access to whole TPs. However, most SQL authorisation mechanisms are defined on data and simple commands using the **GRANT** statement (coupled with views):

GRANT   *list of privileges*
ON   *data object*
TO   *list of users*
[WITH GRANT OPTION]

Access is given **TO** specified users and roles, **ON** specified data structures. The access can be via any of the basic commands listed in the **GRANT** statement. The basic commands are **SELECT, DELETE, INSERT, UPDATE, REFERENCES, TRIGGER** and **EXECUTE**. One side-effect of SQL access control is to reduce the likelihood that transactions commit. For instance, consider transaction T:

```
BEGIN T
  SELECT * FROM X;
  DELETE FROM X WHERE ...;
COMMIT T
```

On table X, role U has permission for **SELECT** and **DELETE**, whilst role V has only **SELECT** permission. If U executes T there is no problem, provided that integrity constraints are not violated. If, however, V executes T, the transaction always aborts. Here, a solution would be to implement T as a stored procedure, and grant **EXECUTE** permission on T only to U. This is not a general solution, as some transactions cannot be defined as stored procedures.

Application programs are beyond the scope of SQL access control, and can violate confidentiality. For example, if transaction T had additional program commands to store or pass on the value of X.*, the values stored in X would be available to users who might not have **SELECT** access to X.

A final problem with SQL authorisation is **WITH GRANT OPTION**. Although this is a popular concept, as it allows distributed management of authorisations, it contradicts Clark-Wilson rule E4.

Our development process addresses these limitations by considering security mechanisms during design, as well as at implementation. Our eventual goal is to use a formal language to specify both the security policy and the functional requirements, and to check their mutual consistency. We can derive implementations that meet the specification, using SQL integrity and access control, stored procedures, and application code.

3   Designing for Security: A Case Study

We now illustrate some aspects of our process. Our research shows that,

- access triples, TPs and separation of duty can be analysed in use case models;
- data details can be checked via class models, extended for modelling ISs to include the constraints needed to enforce data integrity;
- well-formedness can be designed in to transactions, checked using interaction diagrams, and implemented by the usual embedded SQL approaches;
- IVPs can be modelled as operation preconditions, event guards etc; these can be implemented in SQL constraint and trigger statements.

The scenario is a system for processing university examination papers.

Each academic year, thousands of students sit examinations. The papers have to be set by the lecturer, then checked by an Exam Board (EB). Students' scripts are marked by lecturers. Marks are checked and entered by administrators. The examination, processing and marks achieved are reviewed by EB, which has authority to modify marks. Finally, students are given access to their marks and degree grades.

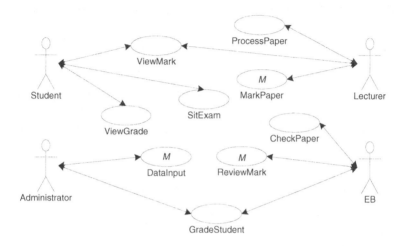

Fig. 4. Use cases of the examination management system

Figure 4 shows use cases for the system. Because of the characteristics of UML use case diagrams, each link between an actor and a use case presents an access triple in form of $< actor, usecase, data >$ – that is, each use case represents a TP. The implementation must enforce rule E3, that only programs that implement an access triple can be executed on the data.

Each use case models the processing of data into a valid final state (rule C2). For example, *Mark*, is accessed and modified by each of the use cases labelled *M*. The link between the actor **Administrator** and use case **DataInput** generates the access triple $< Administrator, DataInput, Mark >$; the implementation must check the integrity rules on *Mark* before it becomes a CDI in the database.

In order to make sure that the design meets the separation of duty requirement (rule C3), we can list all the access triples relating to the modification of each CDI. For the data item *Mark*, these are:

$$< Lecturer, MarkPaper, Mark >$$
$$< EB, ReviewMarks, Mark >$$
$$< Administrator, DataInput, Mark >$$

Three different roles are involved in processing *Mark* before a student can access it – separation of duty is preserved, at least at the conceptual level.

The conceptual model class diagram, defining structural integrity, is not illustrated here. In our approach, data constraints are expressed in a suitably formal language (UML recommends OCL; we use Z; elsewhere, we also recommend B [22]). Transactions are specified using UML interaction diagrams, with well-formedness checked by ensuring that structural integrity is maintained; we can also translate the models to a formal language for analysis. Rule C1 says that all IVPs must properly ensure that all CDIs are in a valid state when an IVP is executed – the modelled constraints effectively specify Clark-Wilson IVPs.

IVPs exist for all three mark-processing transactions (some related to the wider organisation):

- the lecturer's marking must conform to published marking criteria;
- at entry, values are checked against data domains and other constraints;
- the EB checks human aspects of the examining system – illness, academic misconduct, exam irregularities – and adjusts marks accordingly, but within the data constraints, plus time constraints imposed by the university.

Part of the IVP controlling data input relates to the constraint that the value of *Mark* must be an integer on the university mark scale, 0 and 100. In SQL, we can implement this either as a **CHECK** statement, or as a **TRIGGER**:

```
CREATE TRIGGER EnforceMark BEFORE INSERT
    ON achievement
    REFERENCING NEW ROW AS new
BEGIN
    IF new.mark > 100 THEN ROLLBACK
    ELSE COMMIT
END IF
```

A well-formed transaction combines such clauses and TPs, enforcing integrity.

4 Related Work

The main recent work on designing secure systems is *UMLsec* [14, 15], an extension of UML to include standard security requirements for critical systems, targeted at general security-critical systems design. UMLsec extends use case diagrams, activity diagrams, class diagrams, sequence diagrams, statechart diagrams, and deployment diagrams. It covers a wide area of information security, providing a rich set of security semantic in UML diagrams.

Like UML, the UMLsec graphical notation can be used with any development process, but does not directly represent IS characteristics such as keys and transactions. UMLsec's philosophy is based on the lattice models' multi-level security classification; Clark-Wilson is not level-oriented, and separation of duty is outside the scope of UMLsec. We cannot use UMLsec as the basis for our development process.

In terms of the application of security models to IS, Cuppens et al [8, 7] reviewed applicable models, and have formally specified, in deontic logic, rules and obligations for database confidentiality, integrity and availability. Prolog implementation is used to check rules for contradiction. Cuppens' work is more extensive than ours, and expresses many of the security aspects covered by the Clark-Wilson rules. However, publications do not address the completeness or consistency of the formal security models. Implementation of security mechanisms does not relate to commercial DBMSs and SQL, focusing instead on object-oriented databases with a novel prolog-based query language.

5   Conclusion

In this paper, we summarise support for the Clark-Wilson security model in a conventional DBMS context, and an approach to database design that builds security requirements into the design.

The discussion of security models suggests that the Clark-Wilson focus on well-formed transactions makes it appropriate for ISs. Indeed, the main disadvantage normally cited for Clark-Wilson, that the IVPs and associated techniques are not easy to implement in real computer systems [2], is largely overcome in the database context. For relational database, some integrity constraints are inherent in the theory (entity and referential integrity); others can be stated as static constraints using SQL. Some dynamic integrity constraints can be implemented using the SQL3 triggers, and others can be stated in code. These enforce the integrity of CDIs accessed and modification by TPs.

Although conventional DBMSs have most of the security features needed to implement the Clark-Wilson rules, access triples are not fully supported; a combination of OS and DBMS facilities is required. A verification of security can be achieved by calculating the overall data accesses of the implemented transactions and ensuring that these match triples constructed in design for each required transaction.

The case study extract presents part of an approach for building security requirements into the development process. The conventional conceptual models used for ISs specification and design provide the basis for expressing, checking and implementing the necessary security features. Work is ongoing on the detail of the development process, incorporating the formal analysis of system integrity, and dynamic TP/IVP enforcement of integrity by transactions.

The ability to map designed security features to the SQL concepts supported by current DBMSs is also critical to the success of our approach. The case study shows just one aspect of this – the derivation of a trigger to enforce a simple data constraint. We are devising template translations from our conceptual and formal models to SQL, and are working on a prototype of a tool that can express formally-verified integrity rules as appropriate SQL constraints and triggers.

References

1. M. Abrams, E. Amoroso, L. LaPadula, T. Lunt, and J. Williams. Report of an integrity research study group. *Computers and Security*, 12:679–689, 1993.
2. E. Amoroso. *Fundamentals of Computer Security Technology*. Prentice Hall, 1994.
3. D. E. Bell and L. J. LaPadula. Secure computer systems: Mathematical foundations and model. Technical Report MTR 2547 v2, MITRE Corporation, 1973.
4. K. J. Biba. Integrity constraints for secure computer systems. Technical Report EST TR-76-372, Hanscom AFB, 1977.
5. S. Castano, M. Fugini, G. Martella, and P. Samarati. *Database Security*. Addison-Wesley, 1994.
6. D. D. Clark and D. R. Wilson. A comparison of commercial and military computer security policies. In *IEEE Symposium on Security and Privacy*, pages 184–194, Oakland, April 1987.
7. F. Cuppens. *Modélisation formelle de la sécurité des systèmes d'informations*. Habilitation, Paul Sabatier University, Toulouse, France, 2000.
8. F. Cuppens and C. Saurel. A logical formalization of integrity policies for database management systems. In S. Jajodia, W. List, G. W. McGregor, and L. Strous, editors, *Integrity and Internal Control in Information Systems*. Kluwer, 1998.
9. DOD. TCSEC: Trusted computer system evaluation criteria. Technical Report 5200.28-STD, U.S. Department of Defense, 1985.
10. R. Elmasri and S. B. Navathe. *Fundamentals of Database Systems*. Benjamin Commings, 2nd edition, 1994.
11. S. N. Foley. The specification and implementation of "commercial" security requirements including dynamic segregation of duties. In *4th ACM Conf. on Computer and Communications Security*, pages 125–134. ACM Press, April 1997.
12. IBM. DB2 universal database: SQL reference, release 7. IBM Corporation, 2000.
13. ISO. International standard – SQL. Technical report, ISO/IEC 9075-1, 1999.
14. J. Jürjens. Towards development of secure systems using UML. In *FASE 2001, Genova, Italy*, volume 2029 of *LNCS*, pages 187–201. Springer Verlag, April 2001.
15. J. Jürjens. UMLsec: Extending UML for secure systems development. In *UML 2002, Dresden, Germany*, volume 2460 of *LNCS*, pages 412–425. Springer Verlag, Sept-Oct 2002.
16. T. M. P. Lee. Using mandatory integrity to enforce "commercial" security. In *IEEE Symposium on Security and Privacy*, pages 140–146, Oakland, April 1988.
17. S. B. Lipner. Non-discretionary controls for commercial applications. In *IEEE Symposium on Security and Privacy*, pages 2–10, Oakland, May 1982.
18. Microsoft. SQL server, version 7.0. Microsoft Corporation, 1999.
19. Oracle. Oracle8i SQL reference, release 8.1.6. Oracle Corporation, 1999.
20. G. Pernul, W. Winiwarter, and A. Min Tjoa. The entity-relationship model for multilevel security. In *Int. Conf. on Conceptual Modeling / the Entity Relationship Approach*, pages 166–177, 1993.
21. C. P. Pfleeger and S. L. Pfleeger. *Security in Computing*. Prentice Hall, 3rd edition, 2003.
22. F. Polack and R. Laleau. A rigorous metamodel for UML static conceptual modelling of information systems. In *CAiSE 2001, Interlaken, Switzerland*, volume 2068 of *LNCS*, pages 402–416. Springer Verlag, June 2001.
23. W. R. Shockley. Implementing the Clark/Wilson integrity policy using current technology. In *11th National Computer Security Conference*, pages 29–37, Baltimore, October 1988.

A   Clark-Wilson Certification Enforcement, and Separation of Duty Rules

The following rules are directly quoted from [6]:

C1: All IVPs must properly ensure that all CDIs are in a valid state at the time the IVP is run.

C2: All TPs must be certified to be valid. That is, they must take a CDI to a valid final state, given that it is in a valid state to begin with. For each TP, and each set of CDIs that it may manipulate, the security officer must specify a "relation", which defines that execution. A relation is thus of the form: $(TP_i, (CDI_a, CDI_b, CDI_c, \ldots))$, where the list of CDIs defines a particular set of arguments for which the TP has been certified.

E1: The system must maintain the list of relations specified in rule C2, and must ensure that the only manipulation of any CDI is by a TP, where the TP is operating on the CDI as specified in some relation.

E2: The system must maintain a list of relations of the form:

$$(UserID, TP_i, (CDI_a, CDI_b, CDI_c, \ldots))$$

which relates a user, a TP and the data objects that TP may reference on behalf of that user. It must ensure that only executions described in one of the relations are performed.

C3: The list of relations in E2 must be certified to meet the separation of duty requirement.

E3: The system must authenticate the identity of each user attempting to execute a TP.

C4: All TPs must be certified to write to an append-only CDI (the log) all information necessary to permit the nature of the operation to be reconstructed.

C5: Any TP that takes a UDI as an input value must be certified to perform only valid transformations, or else no transformations, for any possible value of the UDI. The transformation should take the input from a UDI to a CDI, or the UDI is rejected.

E4: Only the agent permitted to certify entities may change the list of such entities associated with other entities: specifically, those associated with a TP. An agent that can certify an entity may not have any execute rights with respect to that entity.

The following rules are from [1]:

SP1: User roles should be administered by two different agents: one agent assigns roles to users, but is constrained by information in the system that defines the roles. The other agent can define roles.

SP2: The use of so-called "primary CDIs" is recommended to support separation of duty. Primary CDIs have values that require corroboration by two or more different users. A primary CDI should change only as a result of the last TP in an enabling sequence.

SP3: To apply integrity to mechanisms that implement integrity, access triples can be protected from unauthorised modification by storing them in *CDI-triples* and restricting access to the *Triple Manager* by a role assignment. Similarly, TPs and IVPs can be protect from unauthorised modification by assigning roles and including TP/IVP management TPs in appropriate access rights.

Optimizing DOM Programs on XML Views over Existing Relational Databases

Atsuyuki Morishima[1] and Akira Kojima[2]

[1] Research Center for Knowledge Communities, University of Tsukuba
amorishima@acm.org
[2] Graduate School of Engineering, Shibaura Institute of Technology
m103197@sic.shibaura-it.ac.jp

Abstract. Since XML has become the de-facto standard for data interchange through the Internet, more and more application programs to process XML data are being developed. On the other hand, a huge amount of existing data is stored in relational databases. We developed a system that allows XML application programs using DOM APIs to take as input relational data through their XML views. A key issue is optimization. We developed an optimization technique having a training mechanism for efficient execution of the programs. This paper presents the system's architecture, the optimization technique, and preliminary experimental results showing that the proposed technique can achieve dramatic performance improvements.

1 Introduction

Since XML has become the de-facto standard for data interchange through the Internet, more and more application programs to process XML data are being developed. On the other hand, a huge amount of existing data is stored in relational databases. One possible reason is that XML is a *data format* while the relational database provides a *data model* and facilities for efficient data management. In order to connect the two different worlds, how to process *XML views* of databases has been a crucial research topic.

An XML view is *virtual*, if the system materializes a part of the XML view only when an application consumes the part. In other words, it materializes only a required part of the data on demand. The virtual XML view approach has the following two advantages compared to full materialization of XML views: First, it is *scalable*. It does not require a huge amount of additional memory or storage to keep the entire XML data at a time. In general, the data stored in the underlying databases can be huge in size, and full materialization of XML views are impractical in such cases. Moreover, application programs may not need the entire XML data but only a small portion of it. Second, we do not have to worry about the freshness of data and can assume that the obtained data are always up-to-date. The approach is especially effective in situations where the target databases are autonomously managed and actively updated.

A. Persson and J. Stirna (Eds.): CAiSE 2004, LNCS 3084, pp. 248–262, 2004.
© Springer-Verlag Berlin Heidelberg 2004

Technically, the (virtual) XML view approach has to translate operations of XML data into that of underlying databases. Previous works [2][5] developed techniques to translate declarative XML queries, such as XQuery queries, into SQL queries.

We focus on the problems of how to allow XML application programs using DOM [8] API (shortly, *DOM Programs*) to take as input relational data through their XML views and how to optimize them. Since both XQuery-like declarative queries and DOM-style operations are major ways for XML processing, frameworks to allow DOM programs to process XML views have huge benefits. In particular, if we got such a framework, any existing application program to process XML data through DOM API could process any data stored in relational databases without the source code changed. We do not have to redevelop nor rewrite such application programs in order to process the data in databases. This is a significant advantage, especially when one of the important concerns is the software development cost.

An important technical problem of XML view approaches is *optimization*, since naive translation of XML operations into SQL queries can lead to inefficient executions. Efficient evaluation of XML views of relational data have been discussed in situations where XML operations are written in XQuery-style declarative query languages [2][5].

However, it is a non-trivial task to develop optimization techniques to work with DOM programs; A typical DOM program contains a large number of DOM operations scattered over the code. A naive execution framework, in which one SQL query is generated and executed for each DOM operation, is obviously inefficient, since it requires a large number of SQL query submissions. One might consider methods to compose more than one DOM operations into one SQL query. The DOM operations, however, are interleaved with other code written in ordinary, procedural programming languages, such as java, and the control of executions does not depend on the DOM operations only. This makes it difficult to apply normal optimization techniques for declarative queries to the problem.

This paper proposes an optimization framework for DOM operations, interleaved with procedural programming language codes, to deal with XML views of relational data. The underlying idea is to observe executions of DOM programs in order to find efficient *SQL generation rules* for later executions of the programs. The SQL generation rules are used to construct a fewer number of SQL queries having the same effects with less execution costs compared to the naive SQL generation method.

Figure 1 shows the architecture of our system. First, the user has to give to the system a *view query* to define an XML view of relational data stored in the relational database. Then, ordinary DOM programs whose inputs are XML data can be applied to the relational data. Note that the XML view is *not* materialized. Instead, results of DOM operations are computed by SQL queries on demand. The rule repository stores SQL generation rules, which describe *when and what SQL queries to generate and execute*. In the first execution, every DOM operation is translated into one SQL query, as explained in Section 2. During

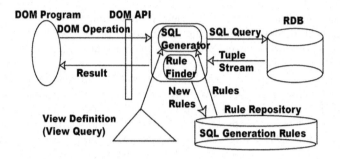

Fig. 1. Architecture

the execution, the rule generator tries to find SQL generation rules for efficient evaluation and stores them in the rule repository. The SQL generation rules are used in later executions.

An interesting issue in the approach is how to find SQL generation rules. A feature of our proposed method is that it provides a simple and efficient algorithm to find SQL generation rules. It is efficient both in time and required spaces.

The contributions of the paper are as follows: (1) We propose a general framework for applying XML application programs using DOM API to existing relational databases. (2) We explain an efficient algorithm to find SQL generation rules that are used for efficient executions of the DOM programs. (3) We give the results of our preliminary experiments, which show that the SQL generation rules can dramatically reduce execution costs.

Related Work. SilkRoute [2] and Xperanto [5] are well-known systems that publish XML data from relational databases. They provide mechanisms to construct *XML views* over relations and allow declarative XQuery-style queries against the views. Our system adopts the same mechanism as the SilkRoute's to define XML views, but allows any procedural program using DOM operations to access the XML views. The difference is essential and requires new optimization techniques.

To the best of our knowledge, ROLEX [1] is the only system that realizes DOM operations of XML views of relational data. ROLEX is different from our system in that it is designed to use a main-memory database system. The focus is mainly on utilization of data management facilities, such as concurrency control and recovery features, of the main-memory database system. In contrast, our system is designed to give an easy way to apply latest programs using XML-technologies to ubiquitous, possibly legacy data stored in relational databases. For optimization, ROLEX introduces a navigational profile to represent the probability of the application navigating along edges in the DOM tree. Our SQL generation rules provide a finer granularity control of SQL generation, which is driven by the status of running DOM programs.

DBDOM [7] is a persistent DOM implementation that uses RDBMs to store XML data. DBDOM defines a fixed database schema and cannot work as a bridge between DOM programs and existing relational data. So our system and DBDOM have completely different purposes.

2   Motivating Example

We motivate the problem of generating efficient SQL queries for DOM operations with an example. We use TPC-H benchmark database [6], which contains information on parts, the suppliers of those parts, customers, and their orders. Figure 2 shows a part of its database schema.

> Supplier(suppkey, name, addr, nationkey)
> Nation(nationkey, name, regionkey)
> Region(regionkey, name)
> PartSupp(partkey, suppkey, availqty)
> Part(partkey, name, brand, size)

Fig. 2. Part of TPC-H database schema

XML Views of Relational Data. We assume that the information in the relational database is exported in the XML format determined by the schema in Figure 3. Each **supplier** element contains a **suppinfo** and a list of the supplier's **parts**. Each **suppinfo** contains the supplier's **name**, its **nation**, and the **region** to which it belongs. Each **part** element contains its **name**.

Fig. 3. Schema of XML view over the database

We use RXL [2] to define the XML view. Figure 4 shows the RXL view query mapping the relational data to XML data conforming to the schema in Figure 3. RXL's semantics is simple: As in SQL, *tuple variables* specified in the **from** clauses iterate over tuples of tables. For example, tuple variable $s iterates over the **Supplier** table. The **where** clause has conditions over these variables. For example, **$s.nationkey = $n.nationkey** is a join condition. The **construct** clause specifies an XML fragment to output. If a binding to the tuple variables specified in the **for** clause satisfies the condition in the **where** clause, the fragment in the **construct** clause is generated. The **construct** clause can

```
from Supplier $s
construct
  <supplier> <suppinfo><name>$s.name</name>
    { from Nation $n
      where $s.nationkey = $n.nationkey
      construct
        <nation>$n.name</nation>
        { from Region $r
          where $n.regionkey = $r.regionkey
          construct <region>$r.name</region> }
    }</suppinfo>
    { from PartSupp $ps, Part $p
      where $s.suppkey = $ps.suppkey,
            $ps.partkey = $p.partkey
      construct
        <part> <name>$p.name</name> </part> }
  </supplier>
```

Fig. 4. RXL view of TPC-H database

contain nested sub-queries surrounded by block boundaries "{" and "}". For example, there are three sub-queries in Figure 4.

Given an XML element specified in a `construct` clause, it is easy to construct an SQL query that computes instances of the given element; An XML element in a `construct` clause is generated for each tuple of the result of *joins* of relations in its `from` clause and that of superqueries. For example, instances of `<name>` and `<nation>` elements are generated for each tuple of the following queries' results:

```
select $s.suppkey, $s.name
from Supplier $s
```

```
select $s.suppkey, $n.nationkey, $n.name
from Supplier $s, Nation $n
where $s.nationkey=$n.nationkey
```

This is best summarized by a tree structure called *viewtree* [2] (Figure 5). In the viewtree, we associate to each node a unique identifier based on Dewey Decimal Encoding[3]. For example, nodes with identifiers $N1.x$ are children of the node N1. Each viewtree node is also associated with a *query* to compute instances of the XML element represented by the viewtree node. For example, $q(N1.1.2)$ specifies how to compute instances of `<nation>` element represented by N1.1.2; For each tuple in the result of Supplier $s \bowtie$ Nation $n[1]$, one `<nation>` instance is generated. *Key attributes* to identify each such tuple (e.g. `$s.suppkey`) is annotated to each viewtree node. Some of nodes have additional attributes for element values (e.g. `$s.name`). In the following, we call an XML element instance an *XML node*.

Formally, each (computed) XML node is represented by pair $(n, \bar{k})$, where n is a viewtree node identifier and $\bar{k}$ is a sequence of values of the key attributes as-

---
[1] We omit join conditions for simplicity.

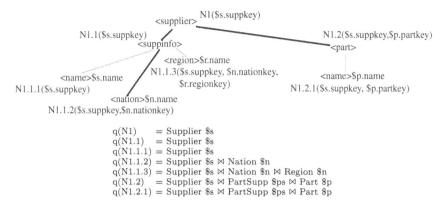

$$q(N1)   = \text{Supplier } \$s$$
$$q(N1.1)   = \text{Supplier } \$s$$
$$q(N1.1.1) = \text{Supplier } \$s$$
$$q(N1.1.2) = \text{Supplier } \$s \bowtie \text{Nation } \$n$$
$$q(N1.1.3) = \text{Supplier } \$s \bowtie \text{Nation } \$n \bowtie \text{Region } \$r$$
$$q(N1.2)   = \text{Supplier } \$s \bowtie \text{PartSupp } \$ps \bowtie \text{Part } \$p$$
$$q(N1.2.1) = \text{Supplier } \$s \bowtie \text{PartSupp } \$ps \bowtie \text{Part } \$p$$

Fig. 5. Viewtree $\mathcal{T}_1$ (Bold lines represent $\mathcal{T}_1'$)

sociated with viewtree node n. The tag associated to XML node $(n, \bar{k})$ is the tag associated to n in the viewtree. The parent-child relationship among XML nodes are defined as follows: $(n_1, \bar{k}_1)$ is a child of $(n_0, \bar{k}_0)$ if n_1 is a child of n_0 in the viewtree, and the values in $\bar{k}_1$ has the same values for the same attributes in $\bar{k}_0$. For example, XML node (N1.1.2, [$s.suppkey=#s1, $n.nationkey=#UK]) is a child of (N1.1, [$s.suppkey=#s1]).

DOM Operations on XML Views. The DOM (Document Object Model) is a programming API for documents [8]. Intuitively, it models a document instance as an object (node) tree that reflects the structure of the document. We use the program in Figure 6 (Ignore superscripts for a while) as a running example. The program takes as input an XML document, which is given by file name v (Line 2), traverses the document's element hierarchy in the depth-first order (Line 4, Lines 7-14), and outputs each element's tag name and content (Line 10-11). Typically, a DOM operation takes an XML node and returns one or more XML nodes. In the program, getFirstChild method (Line 8) returns the first child of the given XML node. Assume that the method is applied to an XML node (N1.1, [suppkey=#s2]). Then, the SQL query to compute the result can be obtained by adding selection condition $s.suppkey=#s2 to the query for the viewtree node N1.1.1:

```
select $s.suppkey, $s.name
from Supplier $s
where $s.suppkey=#s2
```

Another example is the getNextSibling method (Line 9), which returns the next sibling in the tree structure of XML instance nodes. Assume that the result of the previous getFirstChild method is (N1.1.1, [suppkey=#s2]) and we apply the getNextSibling method to the result. Since the viewtree node identifier of the current XML node is N1.1.1, we need the query of N1.1.2:

```
1. void main() {
2.     Document doc= new Document(v) (id1);
3.     Node root=doc.getDocumentElement()(id2);
4.     show(root)
5. }
6.
7. void show(Node node) {
8.     for (Node n=node.getFirstChild()(id3); n!=null;
9.                 n=n.getNextSibling()(id4)) {
10.        System.out.println(n.getNodeName()(id5));
11.        System.out.println(n.getNodevalue()(id6));
12.        show(n);
13.     }
14. }
```

Fig. 6. Fragment of DOM program $\mathcal{P}_1$

```
select $s.suppkey, $n.nationkey, $n.name
from Supplier $s, Nation $n
where $s.nationkey=$n.nationkey
      and $s.suppkey=#s2
```

Assume that we apply the getNextSibling method to (N1.2, [suppkey=#s2, partkey=#p3]). In this case, the siblings are computed by the same query, since one <supplier> may have more <part>s (See Figure 3). The system submits the following query:

```
select $s.suppkey, $s.partkey,
from Supplier $s, $PartSupp $ps, Part $p
where $s.suppkey=$ps.suppkey,
      $ps.partkey=$p.partkey,
      $s.suppkey=#s2
order by $suppkey, $s.partkey
```

and retrieves the next tuple of the tuple satisfying the condition $s.partkey=#p3. Note that the **order by** clause is used to enforce a fixed order among siblings; The siblings are sorted by key attributes.

Generating SQL queries in this way is simple but inefficient, since the system has to submit the same number of SQL queries as DOM operations. We call the SQL generation schema above the *naive SQL generation*.

2.1   Sorted Outer Union Plans and Introduction of ADO Labels

But what if the execution of DOM operations follows a particular order? A simple example is a program that traverses XML nodes in the depth-first order. In this case, *sorted outer-union* plans [5] are effective. A sorted outer-union plan is a particular form of SQL query to compute XML query results on XML views of relational databases. Intuitively, the query result is a relation that corresponds to an *unnested* form of the result XML document, where each tuple corresponds to one instance of XML element or path. We use a variation of sorted outer-union plans here.

```
1. select * from (
2. select 1 as L1, $s.suppkey, N as L2, N, N as L3, N, N                    // N1
3. from Supplier $s
4. union
5. select 1 as L1, $s.suppkey, 1 as L2, N, N as L3, N, N                    // N1.1
6. from Supplier $s
7. union
8. select 1 as L1, $s.suppkey, 1 as L2, N, 2 as L3, $n.nationkey, $n.name // N1.1.2
9. from Supplier $s, Nation $n
10. where $s.nationkey=$n.nationkey
11. union
12. select 1 as L1, $s.suppkey, 2 as L2, $p.partkey, N as L3, N, N        // N1.2
13. from Supplier $s, $PartSupp $ps, Part $p
14. where $s.suppkey=$ps.suppkey, $ps.partkey=$p.partkey,
15. )
16. order by L1, $suppkey, L2, $p.partkey, L3, $n.nationkey
```

Fig. 7. Sorted outer union plan for $\mathcal{T}_1'$

To explain our sorted outer-union plans, we use XML view $\mathcal{T}_1'$ that is a subtree of XML view $\mathcal{T}_1$. In Figure 5, $\mathcal{T}_1'$ is represented by the bold lines. Figure 7 is an outer-union plan SQL query for a depth-first traversal of the XML view. Here, N means a null value. The query is a naive implementation of the outer-union plan. More sophisticated implementations are given in [5] [2]. In the result of the SQL query, each tuple corresponds to one instance of an XML element. In each tuple, XML element instance $(n, \bar{k})$ is encoded as follows: (1) Viewtree node identifier $n = \text{N } l_1.l_2.\ldots.l_n$ is decomposed and stored in the attributes $L1$, $L2, \ldots$, and Ln. (2) key values in $\bar{k}$ are stored in their corresponding attributes.

The **order by** clause sorts the tuples by $L1$, key attributes for the root node in the viewtree (i.e., $s.suppkey. We use $k_{(1,i)}$ to denote the attributes), $L2$, key attributes that appear for the first time in the viewtree nodes at level 2 (i.e., $p.partkey. $k_{(2,i)}$), etc. The tuple order is compatible with the the depth-first traversal of the XML view of the relational data (Figure 8), and traversal in the depth-first order is achieved by executing the query and reading the tuples in a sequential way. In other words, if we assign to each node label "$l_1, k_{(1,1)}, \ldots, k_{(1,n_1)}, l_2, k_{(2,1)}, \ldots, k_{(2,n_2)}, l_3, k_{(3,1)}, \ldots,$", and define the *lexicographic order* on the labels, the labels *encodes* structural relationship among XML nodes. We call the framework the *Augmented Dewey Order Encoding* here and name each such label an *ADO label*. Note that given an ADO label for an XML node, we can easily extract the viewtree node identifier $l_1.\ldots.l_n$ whose query computed the XML node. As explained later, our proposed method utilizes the characteristic of the encoding framework.

The sorted outer-union plan is much more efficient compared to the naive SQL generation for the program $\mathcal{P}_1$: The query is executed only once, and the tuples in the query result all contribute to the DOM operations' results. In contrast, as explained in Section 2, these are not true in the naive SQL generation. In general, sorted outer union plans are effective when the program is something like the depth-first traversal (details are explained in Section 3).

2.2   Problem and Our Approach

It is not a trivial task, however, to extract such "effective" patterns from the program source code. There are so many different ways to implement the same

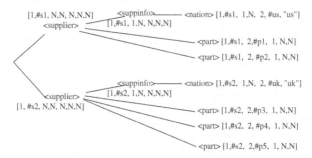

Fig. 8. Structure of an XML instance and ADO labels

```
 1. void show(Node node) {
 2.    if (node!=null) {
 3.       System.out.println(node.getNodeName());
 4.       System.out.println(node.getNodevalue());
 5.    }
 6.    Node n1=node.getFirstChild();
 7.    show(n1);
 8.    Node n2 node=n1.getNextSibling();
 9.    show(n2);
10.    }
11. }
```

Fig. 9. Another DOM program

functions in programs. For example, the program in Figure 6 and the one in Figure 9 output the same results if their input XML data is a binary tree. In the extreme case, a program may *hard-wire* the complete structure of XML instance. In addition, it is not always true that a program has a *perfect* pattern like the depth-first-order example above. For example, a program that traverses XML data in the depth-first order but skips over a small number of XML nodes, should be efficiently supported by the same outer-union plan query. Considering these, we choose not to analyze the program source code, nor to match pre-defined patterns with the code. Instead, we developed a technique that observes program executions to find better SQL generation rules. The rules found are used for later executions of the program with different data. This is explained in detail in the following section.

3 Optimization Technique

3.1 How the Rule Finder Works

The rule finder (Figure 1) takes as input a stream of DOM operation results. Formally, it takes pairs $(\langle id, a \rangle, l)$ where id is an *operation identifier* associated with each DOM operation in the program (See Figure 6) and a is a collection of *parameter values* of the operation. l is an ADO label (i.e., a tuple representing an XML node instance) that is the result of the operation's execution. To make it possible for the system to take ADO labels even in the first execution, attributes for viewtree node identifiers, such as L1 and L2, are incorporated into SQL queries for the naive SQL generation.

Each such pair is given to the rule finder every time when an operation having *id* with parameter values *a* is executed and the returned answer is an XML node whose ADO label is *l*. The stream is used to find SQL generation rules.

In later executions of the program, the SQL generator uses the stored rules to make more efficient SQL queries having the same effects with the program and the XML view definition. The rule finder keeps trying to find other new rules because one execution of a program does not necessarily go through every possible execution patterns of the program. A key issue in the architecture is how to find SQL generation rule quickly so that the system can take advantages of the latest findings as soon as possible.

3.2   SQL Generation Rules

Let $\mathcal{T}$ be a given viewtree and $\mathcal{P}$ be a prgram. An SQL Generation Rule (shortly, a *rule*) over $\mathcal{T}$ and $\mathcal{P}$ has the form of $p \rightarrow t$. Here, p is a sequence of pairs $\langle id_i, a_i \rangle$ where id_i is an *operation identifier* and a_i is a collection of *parameter values* of the operation. In a_i, *obj* is used as a special parameter whose value is the object to which a method is applied.

In each rule, t is either $\mathcal{T}$ or a contraction of $\mathcal{T}$. A contraction of a tree is a result of contracting the tree by removing some of the nodes [4]. Unlike subtrees, a contraction can contain nodes that are not adjacent to each other in the original tree. The following (R_1) is a rule over $\mathcal{T}_1$ in Figure 5 and $\mathcal{P}_1$ in Figure 6:

$$R_1 : [\langle id1, \phi \rangle, \langle id2, [obj = \mathtt{N1}] \rangle] \rightarrow \mathcal{T}_1.$$

R_1 says that if operation $id2$ (Line 3, Figure 6) is applied to an XML node having viewtree node identifier $\mathtt{N1}$, following an execution of operation $id1$ (Line 2), an outer-union plan SQL query for $\mathcal{T}_1$, similar to the one in Figure 7, should be generated and executed.

Note that parameter values in a_i do not contain XML node instance $(n, \bar{k})$ but contain viewtree node identifier n (e.g., $\mathtt{N1}$) only. This is because a pattern containing particular XML nodes is too strong in the sense that it cannot match the data even if values in the relational data are slightly changed.

The rule above is a special case where parameter values for methods contain no value other than XML node and $\mathcal{T}$ is the original viewtree itself. Let $\mathcal{P}_4$ be a DOM program[2] that contains operations with $id8$ and $id9$ and the latter operation is $\mathtt{a.getElementsByTagName(x)}$. The following is a more general example of a rule over $\mathcal{T}_1$ and program $\mathcal{P}_4$:

$$R_2 : [\langle id8, [obj = \mathtt{N1.2}] \rangle, \langle id9, [obj = \mathtt{N1}, par1 = \text{"part"}] \rangle] \rightarrow \mathcal{T}_2$$

where $\mathcal{T}_2$ (Figure 10) is a contraction of $\mathcal{T}_1$ and $\mathtt{"part"}$ is a value of $\mathtt{x}$ observed when the system executes the operation with $id9$. The rule says that if the pattern matches the stream observed in the execution, an outer-union plan SQL query for $\mathcal{T}_2$ should be generated and executed.

---

[2] The entire code of $\mathcal{P}_4$ is omitted here.

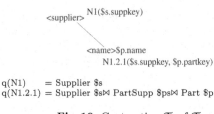

q(N1)   = Supplier \$s
q(N1.2.1) = Supplier \$s⋈ PartSupp \$ps⋈ Part \$p

Fig. 10. Contraction $\mathcal{T}_2$ of $\mathcal{T}_1$

3.3   Using Generation Rules

If the system knows an SQL generation rule $p \to t$ where $p = [\langle id_1, a_1 \rangle, \langle id_2, a_2 \rangle]$, the rule is used in the following way: First, the system watches an execution of the DOM program and takes as input the stream of pairs $(\langle id, a \rangle, l)$ from the execution. If p matches a subsequence of the stream, the system generates an outer union plan SQL query q for t, and adds selection conditions to q to avoid computing too many unnecessary tuples according to the types of operations. For example, if the operation id_2 is `getFirstChild`, conditions are added as explained in Section 2.

Then, the query q is submitted to the RDBMS, and subsequent DOM operations consume the tuples from its result, without submitting other SQL queries. How to choose necessary tuples from the result depends on types of DOM operations. For example, `getFirstChild` operation selects the tuples having ADO Labels compatible with the ADO label of its parent. This is done in a similar way as explained in Section 2. If the system cannot find necessary tuples in the result stream, the system returns to its normal job; it submits one SQL query to the RDBMS for each DOM operation while searching for subsequences of the stream that matches rules.

3.4   Observing Executions to Find Rules

As mentioned, a point of our method is that it gives a simple and efficient mechanism to find rules. The basic idea is to use ADO labels to (1) search the tuple stream for sequences of XML nodes that can be computed by outer-union plans and (2) to efficiently construct SQL generation rules. Compatibility with outer-union plans can be easily decided by checking if ADO labels of successive XML nodes follow the lexicographic order defined on ADO labels. Efficient construction of rules is realized by utilizing the fact that we can easily extract from ADO labels the information on the viewtree nodes who computed XML nodes.

Figure 11 is an algorithm to find rules each of which has a sequence p of length two. In other words, each rule generated by the algorithm has the form $[\langle id_1, a_1 \rangle, \langle id_2, a_2 \rangle] \to t$, like R_1 and R_2. Its input is a stream of pairs $(\langle id, a \rangle, l)$ (Line 4). The output is a set of rules, which is generated in turn (Line 15).

In the algorithm's execution, two successive pairs are kept in $(\langle id', a' \rangle, l')$ (Line 19) and $(\langle id, a \rangle, l)$. Variable t (Lines 1, 8, 11, and 15) represents a contraction of $\mathcal{T}$ for a rule. In t, each contraction is encoded as a set of viewtree nodes;

```
 1. t={};
 2. inOrder=false; // true when the input follows the order
 3. <id', a'>=<nil, []>; l'=infinite;
 4. for each (<id, a>, l) in the Input Stream {
 5.     if (l' < l) {
 6.         if (!inOrder) {
 7.             inOrder=true;
 8.             t.add(l'.getViewTreeNodeID());
 9.             <id_2, a_2>=<id', a'>;
10.         }
11.         t.add(l.getViewTreeNodeID());
12.     } else {
13.         if (inOrder) {
14.             inOrder=false;
15.             outputRule( [<id_1, a_1>, <id_2,a_2>]->t );
16.             t={};
17.         } else <id_1, a_1>=<id', a'>;
18.     }
19.     <id', a'>=<id, a>; l'=l;
20. }
```

Fig. 11. Algorihtm for finding rules

For example, $t = \{N1, N1.2.1\}$ represents a contraction with two nodes $N1$ and $N1.2.1$ (Figure 10).

Basically, what the algorithm does is just to compare ADO labels of two successive XML nodes (DOM operation results) (Line 5), and as long as the labels follow the lexicographic order, the algorithm adds viewtree nodes to t (Lines 8 and 11). The initial values of $(\langle id', a' \rangle, l')$ is $(\langle nil, [] \rangle, infinite)$ (Line 3), where $infinite$ is a special label that is greater than any other labels. If the algorithm finds a label on the stream not following the lexicographical order, it decides that the remaining DOM operation results should be computed by other SQL queries, outputs the rule constructed so far (Line 15), and resets t for the next rule (line 16).

Note that some DOM operations, such as getElementsByTagName(), return a list of XML nodes. For such operations, we use a special value 0 for l, where comparison predicates (like $<$) to compare 0 and any other value always return true. In other words, the algorithm ignores the nodes in the list at that time. But the nodes affect the rule generation process anyway, since sooner or later each such node should be extracted from the list, by using other methods like item().

The algorithm is quite efficient with time complexity $O(S)$ and space complexity $O(V)$, where S is the size of the input stream and V is the size of the viewtree.

4   Preliminary Experiments

This section shows the results of our preliminary experiments. The purpose is to examine the impact of using outer-union plan queries to process DOM operations.

The experiments were run using the following configuration: We use the TPC-H benchmark databases (with different scale factors) managed by the PostgreSQL 7.3.2. The XML view query used is the one shown in Figure 5. The database server has Pentium-4 1.5GHz CPU and 512MB memory. The operating system is Linux RH 8.0. A DOM-compliant library that implements our proposed algorithm was run on the same database server.

First, we executed program P_1 (Figure 6) on the XML view with different sizes of databases. This is an ideal situation where all the DOM operations constitute a depth-first traversal of the entire XML data. One outer-union plan SQL query is generated. The result is shown in Figure 12 (left). The horizontal axis is the number of XML nodes contained by the XML view of each entire database. P_1 generates all of the XML nodes in the depth-first order. The dotted line represents the execution time after SQL generation rules are found. As we can seen, the outer-union plan *dramatically* improves the performance.

Next, we executed a more realistic program P_3 that retrieves some XML nodes from the XML view and traverses subelements of each retrieved XML nodes in turn (Figure 13). This is a typical fragment of a DOM program we can see in practical situations. Interestingly, the system generates only one SQL query, corresponding to viewtree nodes N1.1, N1.1.1, N1.1.2, and N1.1.3 in Figure 5. This is because the result tuple stream is consistent with the lexicographic order defined on ADO labels. The result is shown in Figure 12 (right). P_3 is faster than P_1 since it retrieves and traverses a limited number of XML nodes. The size of database having 1,000,000 (virtual) XML nodes is about 405MB.

Finally, to show that our approach is scalable, we applied the optimized P_3 to larger databases with the TPC-H scale factors 0.5 and 1, which means the sizes of databases are about 500MB and 1GB, respectively. The result is shown in Figure 14. We found that after SQL generation rules are obtained, both P_1 and P_3 run in linear time. In addition, as Figure 14 shows, P_3 with SQL generation rules takes only 3.3 sec. for query evaluation even with 1GB database. It is possible that we can make the total execution time further smaller by considering other factors than SQL query evaluation, but it is beyond the scope of the paper.

Note that our approach requires only a *small and constant memory space*, even if application programs traverse the entire XML data. Applying DOM operations to (virtual) XML views is effective for large database since the system materializes only a required part of the data on demand. In contrast, usual DOM libraries would not work with a huge XML data since it requires the entire XML data to be materialized at a time.

5   Conclusion and Future Work

This paper proposed a system that allows XML application programs using the DOM API to take as input existing relational data. The proposed system has a practical impact because a huge amount of data still remains in relational databases, while more and more XML application programs are being developed. The key issue is an *optimization framework* for DOM operations, interleaved with ordinary programming language codes, to deal with XML views of relational data. Our proposed optimization framework has a training mechanism

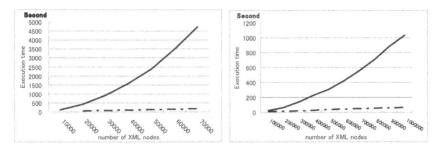

Fig. 12. Experimental results

```
1. void main() {
2.    Document doc= new Document(v);
3.    NodeList a=doc.getElementsByTagName("suppinfo");
4.    Node b=null;
5.    for (int i=0; (b=a.item(i))!=null; i++) { show(b); }
6. }
```

Fig. 13. The main program of $\mathcal{P}_3$ (show function is given in Figure 6)

Size	Total Time(sec)	Query Execution Time(sec)
500MB	77.4	1.7
1GB	154.7	3.3

Fig. 14. Results for large databases

to find SQL generation rules for efficient executions of the programs. We developed an algorithm to efficiently find such SQL generation rules. Our preliminary experiments showed that our approach is promising and scalable.

Future work includes development of algorithms to find more sophisticated SQL generation rules. We believe incremental evolution of rules is possible when we apply machine learning techniques to our approach. Another interesting issue is development of a *just-in-time* optimization mechanism to allow SQL generation rules to be applied during the same program execution as soon as they are found. Also, supporting updates is important, although the view update problem is known to be difficult in general.

Acknowledgments

We would like to thank Prof. Seiichi Komiya of Shibaura Institute of Technology for discussions, and we thank the reviewers for their detailed comments and suggestions. This research was partially supported by the Ministry of Education, Culture, Sports, Science, and Technology, Grant-in-Aid for Young Scientists (B) (15700108).

References

1. P. Bohannon, S. Ganguly, H. F. Korth, P. P. S. Narayan, P. Shenoy: Optimizing View Queries in ROLEX to Support Navigable Result Trees. Proc. VLDB 2002, 119-130, 2002.
2. M. F. Fernandez, Y. Kadiyska, D. Suciu, A. Morishima, WC Tan. SilkRoute: A Framework for Publishing Relational Data in XML. ACM Trans. Database Syst. 27(4): 438-493, 2002.
3. Online Computer Library Center. Introduction to Dewey Decimal Classification. http://www.oclc.org/oclc/fp/about/about_the_ddc.htm
4. M. Atallah (ed). Algorithms and Theory of Computation Handbook, CRC Press, 1998.
5. J. Shanmugasundaram, E. Shekita, R. Barr, M. Carey, B. Lindsay, H. Pirahesh, B. Reinwald: Efficiently publishing relational data as XML documents. VLDB Journal 10(2-3): 133-154, 2001.
6. Transaction Processing Performance Council. TPC-H (Decision Support for Ad Hoc Queries) http://www.tpc.org
7. DBDOM Home Page. http://dbdom.sourceforge.net
8. W3C. Document Object Model (DOM). http://www.w3.org/DOM/

Formulating a General Standards Life Cycle

Eva Söderström

School of Humanities and Informatics, University of Skövde
Box 408, 541 28 Skövde, Sweden
eva.soderstrom@ida.his.se

Abstract. Standards-related literature within business-to-business (B2B) covers many separate areas. Examples are enabling technology, development processes for standards in formal, semi-formal and informal fora, base standards (XML and EDI) extensions and evolvement, intellectual property rights, etc, etc. In computer science literature, the term life cycle is usually used to denote the previously mentioned phases for a product or process, from "birth to death". They are useful for understanding various phenomena and how these relate to their respective environments such as to stakeholders. However, the standards life cycles is only rarely discussed in literature. This paper examines seven existing life cycle models for standards and standardisation, and shows where extensions to the current approaches are needed. The result is a general standards life cycle model, which may serve as the basis for discussion and to identify perspectives for both standards research and standards practice to consider.

1 Introduction

This is not intended to be "yet another paper" describing how much e-business and Internet technology has changed the business world in terms of globality, competitiveness, and inter-operation. Instead, such utterances are an underlying foundation for the paper. The focus is instead placed on the use of standards in inter-organisational co-operation and communication, primarily within Business-to-Business (B2B). Using a general definition, a standard is a document that provides guidelines or characteristics for activities or their results [1]. Standards exist anywhere in our everyday life, in all kinds of products and processes. Often, we use them without paying much regard to them as being standards, e.g. electrical outlets. Since B2B is the scope for this paper, the general definition of a standard can be further detailed. A *B2B standard* includes guidelines for how communication and information sent between organisations should be structured and managed. This definition is two-fold, or rather comprises a range of possible standardisation roles in communication. Firstly, it concerns message content for documents sent and received during communication. Secondly, it concerns how the communication process should be structured (see Figure 1). One example of a document-centric standard is XML Common Business Library (xCBL[1]), which is a set of XML building blocks and a document framework for creating XML documents for e-commerce. Examples of

---

[1] The xCBL homepage is available at: www.xcbl.org

A. Persson and J. Stirna (Eds.): CAiSE 2004, LNCS 3084, pp. 263–275, 2004.
© Springer-Verlag Berlin Heidelberg 2004

more process-centric standards are RosettaNet[2] and electronic business XML (ebXML[3]), which aim at enabling exchange of electronic business information via global processes and an infrastructure respectively.

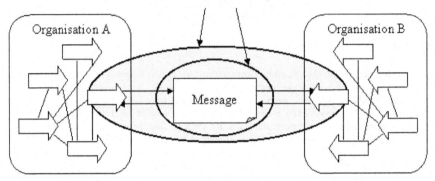

Fig. 1. The role of standards in organisational communication

Standards-related literature covers areas such as enabling technology, development processes for standards in formal, semi-formal and informal fora, base standards (XML and EDI), intellectual property rights, etc. B2B standards evolvement, however, is not as frequently discussed, i.e. what the different stages or phases in their life cycle are. Focus is instead placed on one or a few of the sub-phases such as development. The goal of this paper is to elevate the perspective to a more general level and to formulate a draft life cycle for B2B standards. Existing life cycles will be reviewed and merged into a general one. The merged life cycle model will be used to identify weaknesses in current approaches, to allow for extensions to be suggested.

2 Standards-Related Life Cycles

Standards are becoming a natural part of organisations' daily lives. In B2B, there are numerous transactions occurring either between an organisation and its suppliers and/or an organisation and its customers [2]. Like any other system, process, or product, a standard passes through certain phases and activities during its "life", or existence. The life of something, in this case a standard, can be defined as:

> "The term of existence, activity, or effectiveness of something inanimate" [3]

Looking up the term "life cycle" in dictionaries, it is usually defined from a biological perspective as a (continuous) sequence of changes undergone by an organism

---

[2] The RosettaNet homepage is available at: www.rosettanet.org
[3] The ebXML homepage is available at: www.ebxml.org

[3; 4]. In computer science literature, the term life cycle is usually used to denote the previously mentioned phases for a product or process, from "birth to death". They are useful for understanding various phenomena and how these relate to their respective environments such as to stakeholders. Unfortunately, most life cycles in literature are not described in detail. In the remainder of this chapter, two different approaches to life cycles will be described and compared. The largest cluster concerns life cycles that directly relate to various parts of standards and standardisation (section 2.1). There are also similarities and comparisons made to the product life cycle (section 2.2).

2.1 Life Cycles with Direct Relation to Standardisation

In literature, seven versions of life cycles have been identified that directly relate to standards. Most of these focus on the first life cycle phases and on the activity of standards development.

The most referenced life cycle model was created by *Cargill* [5], and was also described in Burrows [6]. It is a five phase model consisting of: initial requirements, base standards development, profiles/product development, testing, and user implementation feedback. To our knowledge, this is the only life cycle model that explicitly relates phases and stakeholders: Initial requirements may come from sources like standards software organisations, various standards developers and from users. Both development phases may involve software organisations, developers, users and service providers. The fourth phase is performed by either software organisations or testing organisations (a kind of service provider). The final stage consists of feedback from users. The model's strength is its inclusion of stakeholders and an attempt to look beyond development. Its weakness is that it does not manage to broaden the horizon well enough. The focus is still on standards development.

The second model is described in *Köller et al* [7], and consists of four phases: definition, implementation, certification and installation and usage. The definition phase includes standards creation, and phase two is implementation of standards-compliant software. Step three refers to certification of that the software complies with the standard, and phase four means installation and usage of the software in question. Strengths with the model are firstly that it identifies the software certification activity, which not many life cycle models do. Secondly, it mentions the *use* of the standards-based software. However, the model may be confusing in the similarity between the implementation and installation and use phases. It seems that implementation refers to creation of software based on a standard, while installation refers to putting the software to use in real user organisations. However, this is not further described in the model, and is hence our interpretation.

The next model is described by *Ollner* [8], and focuses on standards development. The cycle is repetitive, with three main phases simply called pre-standardisation, standardisation and post-standardisation. In pre-standardisation, new developments and market requirements arise, which create a need and basis for standardisation. The standardisation phase includes all activities in creating a standard, e.g. co-ordination and adaptation of sizes and dimensions, specification of function requirements, variety reduction and development of unambiguous testing methods. There are three subphases here (see figure 2): preparation, publication and implementation of standards.

The resulting standard may in post-standardisation be the basis for developing, designing, producing, procuring and marketing products. Ollner does not explicitly
relate the life cycle to stakeholders, but claims that standardisation experts should co-
operate with users. One strength of the model is its elaboration of the development (or
standardisation) phase. Another strength is the claim that existing standards must be
revised when they no longer measure up to practical requirements, e.g. due to technical developments. The model's major weaknesses lie in its failure to capture phases
beyond development.

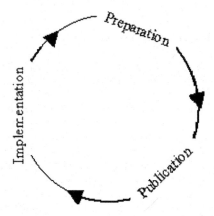

Fig. 2. Cycle for standardisation work (after [8], p.17)

Our next life cycle model is also focused on standards development, with particular
reference to development within single companies. According to *de Vries* [9], input to
life cycle processes is needs for a company standard. The phases (or processes) are:
prioritising, standards development and revision, standards introduction, and standards distribution. The result is a company standard, which also is the focus of standards implementation. Feedback from e.g. implementation may result in new needs,
which starts the cycle all over again. Besides the included phases, de Vries also identifies external factors that may have an influence on the development cycle: policy
process, funding process, human relations management, and facility management.
These are all part of the company as a whole, and constitute the strength of this
model. The weakness is the same as for the previous model, i.e. failure to capture
more that the standards development activities.

Weiss and Spring [10] provide the next life cycle model with three phases: development, distribution and implementation. During development, unambiguous and
public specifications are created. The exact contents and requirements of this phase
varies depending on whether the standard is anticipatory or responsive, i.e. preceeding
or following technology developments (see also section 2.2). The distribution phase
consists of getting the standard out to users and software organisations. This includes
both making the standard known by name and enabling users and software organisations to acquire extensive knowledge about standards in order to use them effectively
and efficiently. Finally, implementation involves creating products conforming to the
standard, and testing the software's conformance to the same. However, implementa-

tion concerns product development and testing, not implementation in user organisations. The major strength of the model is the identification of the distribution aspect of standards development. The weaknesses are the same as with previous life cycle models, the standards development focus, but the naming of the implementation phase is unfortunate in not being descriptive for what the phase actually includes.

The "development weakness" applies to the next model as well. *Egyedi* [11] describes standardisation stages as being: planning, negotiation, and implementation. In planning, priorities for standardisation are determined. Negotiation concerns reaching consensus, e.g. as in formal committee standardisation. Implementation refers to how standards are implemented. Egyedi does not describe the phases in more detail, which is a weakness. It is furthermore noteworthy that Egyedi uses the term standardisation to refer to what we call standards development. Thus, the model's strength lies in its elaboration of the development phase, in particular in explicitly mentioning the negotiation activity.

Finally, *Hanseth and Braa* [12] provide us with a four-phase model: conception, definition, implementation, and use. Conception corresponds to identifying the need for a standard, while definition refers to creating the standard with its contents, scope etc. Implementation is creating products that are based on the standard, while use includes diffusion, adoption and actual use of the software. Hanseth and Braa mention the phases as part of describing a standardisation case study, and hence not specifically as being part of a life cycle. This is our interpretation. The strengths of the interpreted model are that it mentions activities like adoption, diffusion and use, meaning that it raises the horizon somewhat from development. Its weaknesses, like with some previously identified models, is that it does not successfully accomplishes the task.

2.2 Product Life Cycles

In the previous section, [10] touched upon relating life cycles for standards with life cycles of products. The authors mentioned standards that either precede or follow technology developments. In this field, [13] and [14] describe the product life cycle in a similar fashion (see figure 3). Standards can be anticipatory, participatory/enabling, and responsive. Anticipatory standards come before a product or technology has been widely accepted, or even before the product/technology exists. Participatory standards are developed, tested and used interactively with both developers and users. Responsive standards follow the emergence and acceptance of a product/technology, as a way to distill scientific information into useful products [13].

This description merely shows if standards come in before or after a technology/product has been produced. The product life cycle as such can be described in two ways. The first consists of five phases [15]: design, production, operation, support, and disposal. The second consists of five different phases [16]: innovation, improvement, maturity, substitution and obsolescence. [16] elaborates his division of life cycle phases by illustrating them in conjunction with market penetration. Market penetration grows the most during the improvement phase, is generally high during maturity, and decreases the most during the substitution phase. Merging the explanation of the product/technology life cycle with how standards relate to the cycle, we can show a more detailed picture of how standards fit into the product/technology life cycle (see figure 4).

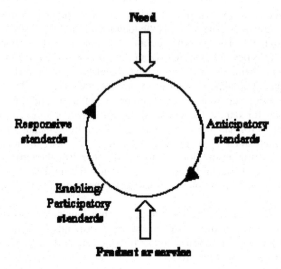

Fig. 3. Standardisation position in the product cycle (from [13], fig. 4 and [14], fig. 1)

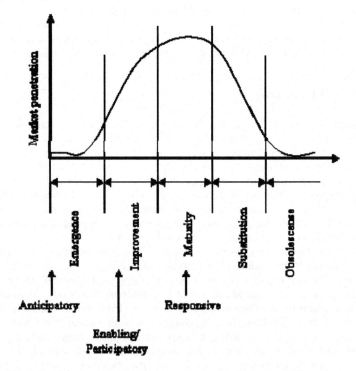

Fig. 4. Detailing how standards relate to the product/technology life cycle

Anticipatory standards precede the first phase, emergence, since they do come before the actual technology. Enabling/participatory standards are developed in parallel to technology developments, placing them during the improvement phase. Finally, responsive standards come into play during the maturity phase, since they emerge after the technology has been developed, but before its substitution and obsolescence.

3   Comparing the Standards-Related Life Cycles

Having presented and described existing standards-related life cycles, this chapter will compare the life cycles, and extract a general model from the descriptions. The merger is made firstly to illustrate the differences and similarities between the approaches, and secondly use the model as a basis to point out where further additions are needed (see chapter 4). The comparison in table 1 shows that there are both significant differences and significant similarities between the current life cycle approaches. All approaches have one phase in common, the development phase. The naming differs for this phase, though: develop, define, standardise, and negotiate. Depending on how [10] is interpreted, distribute can also be used. Regardless of the name, the phase includes the creation of the standards specifications, which are the essence of standards.

Before development starts, there must be an initiation phase, during which the idea of the standard is born based on needs or estimations. This applies whether the standard-to-be is anticipatory, participative/enabling or responsive. As with standards development, there are different names for the phase, e.g. initiate, pre-standardise, need, plan and conception. The common denominator suggests that the phase includes preparations for the standards development process. Needs may stem from market requirements, technology developments or from the organisation itself. It may also include setting the standard's scope and defining how the following development process should be performed. Five out of the seven life cycles in table 1, include an initial phase. Thus, the first phase is regarded as rather important. It is possible that the two life cycle models that do not include the initial phase implicitly include them in their standards development phase, or regard it as in input to standardisation activities. We believe it is important to distinguish initiation from development for several reasons. Firstly, a first look into the claimed standardisation need may not result in any further actions, if the need is determined to cost more than the return of the investment would be. Secondly, the preparations made set the conditions for coming standards development activities, and thus clearly affect the standard's final structure, content and application area.

Three out of the seven life cycle models include a sub-phase where products are created based on one or more standards. Two of them [5/6 and Weiss & Spring] include testing of the products before they are implemented in user organisations (denoted by a * in table 1). Weiss and Spring's [10] implementation phase was placed in the product development column since it by its own definition deals with product creation and not user implementation. Product development may be viewed as part of the remaining four life cycles as well, in either standards development or in implementation. However, we believe it should be a separate phase since it not necessarily is the way in which organisations implement standards. In other words, software products are not a necessary requirement for standards implementations, even though it is the most common approach.

Table 1. Comparing standards-related life cycles

Cargill/ Burrows	Initiate	Develop standards	Develop products*	Implement		Feedback
Köller et al		Define		Implement*/ install	Use	
Ollner	Prestand.	Stand.	Poststand.			
De Vries	Need	Develop		Implement		Feedback
Weiss & Spring		Develop/ distribute	Implement*			
Egyedi	Plan	Negotiate		Implement		
Hanseth & Braa	Conception	Define		Implement	Use	

Five out of seven life cycles include an implementation phase, where standards and/or standards-based products are implemented in organisations. The explanation for the phase's absence in the two remaining life cycles may be that these are only focused on standards development, with its preparation and conclusion. For example, [8] describes how standards may be used for a variety of things once they are created. This phase still ended up in the product development column since one example is that products may be created. Still, it is evident that this particular life cycle does not focus on anything but standardisation. As with two of the product development phases, there is an asterix in the implementation column as well. Testing can this be done in two ways here, one for testing products when they are developed, and one for testing actual implementations of standards and/or products in organisations. Since testing can be a part of different activities, we chose not to include it as a separate activity in the table. We will, however, get back to testing in section 4.1 when discussing extensions to the life cycle model.

When moving one column to the right, the number of life cycle models covering use decreases sharply. Only two models include the actual use of standards and related products. However, neither of the two proceeds to describe what "use" actually includes. [7] only specify it by use of standards-based software, which as we described earlier is no definite pre-requisite for using standards. Clearly, further research is needed into how standards are used in practice, and not just how they ought to be used in theory.

The situation is the same when moving to the right-most column of table 1. Here, feedback refers to users giving feedback to developers of products or standards of what they think about the standard: what works, what does not, which problems have been experienced and so on. The feedback creates one of the possible inputs for evolving standards, and is thus an important separate phase. Today, most standards development organisations are open to, and even encourage, user participation in their development activities. However, open participation does not mean free participation, and few users therefore have the financial resources required, nor the time for that matter.

Looking at table 1, each column makes up a phase in standards life cycles. Figure 5 provides a graphical model of a result. To summarise, the process starts by an initiation phase where the idea is born and general conditions for coming activities are set. Based on conditions from the initial phase, the actual work with developing standards specification is started. After completion of the specifications, the cycle can proceed in two ways: by product development before implementation, or directly to implementation. After implementation, the standard and/or standards-based products are used in organisations' daily work, and feedback may be sent back to developer organisations as a basis for improvement.

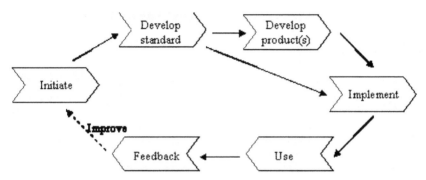

Fig. 5. Generalised life cycle model for standards

In standards-related literature, life cycles for the most part concern the standards development process alone. This means that the life cycle focus stops after implementation. As figure 6 shows, there is more to the life cycle than development, its prerequisites and consequences. As Cargill [5] puts it, issues that are important to other stakeholders, primarily users are not taken into consideration. Hence, there is also more to the life cycle than figure 5 shows. The next chapter will discuss possible extensions to this model.

4   Adding Phases to the Standards Life Cycle

The previous chapter presented and compared a number of life cycle models for standards and standardisation. The resulting generalised model of the standards life cycle does, however, have weaknesses. There are several activities that should be an explicit part of the model, namely: testing, education, maintenance and termination (figure 6).

Each additional phase will be motivated and described in sub-sections of this chapter, with facts and motivations.

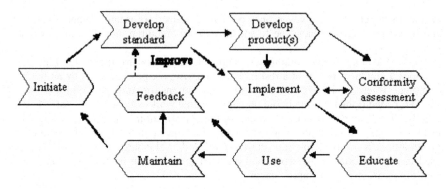

Fig. 6. The general standards life cycle model extended

4.1 Conformity Assessment

The first phase, conformity assessment (CA), has partly been mentioned by a couple of life cycle models in the terms of testing. Since there are different occasions where CA can be applied, e.g. after completion of a standards-based product or after implementing a standard or a standards-based product, we did not include it in the generalised life cycle model. Another reason was that besides differences in occasions, there are also differing techniques for performing CA. Examples are [18]:

- *Testing*: may consist of activities such as calibration and measurement, and is the basic technique for product certification.
- *Inspection*: examination of products, materials, installations, plants, processes, work procedures and services, for e.g. quality and fitness for use.
- *Certification*: a first, second or third party gives written assurance that a product, service, system, process or material conforms to specific requirements.
- *Accreditation*: how an authoritative body gives formal recognition that a body or person is competent to carry out specific tasks.

First, second and third parties refer to by whom the assessment is made, and applies to CA as a whole. First-party is performed by the supplier, second-party by the customer of the supplier, and third-party by an independent assessment body. There is a fourth alternative, the supplier itself giving some written assurance of meeting the standard. CA is an important phase, since it helps guide e.g. users in determining whether or not their product/implementation meets the set requirements, and software organisations in determining that their products work as specified in the standard and that they are inter-operable with other standards-based products.

4.2 Education

In a previous study, the lack of knowledge in user organisations has been recognised by standards developers as a problem [2]. Users do not know how standards work, what they can do for them, or how they work. Instead, they outsource their standards management to e.g. consultancy firms. This may be a problem if the consultancy firms cancels the contract or goes out of business. Furthermore, without knowledge about standards, users have fewer chances of affecting the standards development process. It should be noted that users are willing to learn. The Korean Integrated Forum on Electronic Commerce (ECIF) conducted a study in year 2002, where they concluded that 64,5% of their study respondents were willing to learn more about standards [19]. In particular, the subjects for education were said to be application methodology, implementation and application case studies, benefits for adopting standards, standards specifications and information about support solutions. According to de Vries, standardisation education should disclose the standardisation phenomenon to students in a way that students can get accustomed with standardisation, get knowledge about it and be equipped to use this knowledge in practice [9]. What, how, why and who are four important questions to ask. Education is an important matter if standards and their related products should be used efficiently and effectively. It should therefore be part of the life cycle.

4.3 Maintenance

Maintenance in the standards community is a forgotten subject. Nevertheless, it is important. Often, technology for using standards, particularly with the early technology such as Electronic Data Interchange – EDI, has required substantial financial investments. Therefore, when new standards or versions of them, as well as new technology, are introduced, many organisations cannot afford to simply throw their existing systems out. As any other technology or system investment, maintenance is needed to keep the standard/system operating as intended, e.g. to monitor and improve quality and productivity [19]. This phase should therefore be made explicit, in particular since it for so long has been neglected. In the end, it is the standards users that pay for changes in the standard.

4.4 Termination

The fourth and final extension suggestion is to explicitly include a phase for termination of standards. There are occasions when standards are determined to be obsolete, and are taken out of use. Such occasions should be explicitly noted, in particular if the decision to terminate them has international consequences. By consequences, we here mean if standards that are international are terminated, the phase must be co-ordinated and communicated world-wide. If not, there is a risk that some use the standard while others, perhaps their partners, have ceased to use them. Standards may also be put out of use by a single company or group of companies that may not be on an international level. Still, there may be consequences for the company environment. For example, if we speak of communication standards, any connection a company has with suppliers and/or customers will be affected by a change in or removal of a standard.

5 Conclusions

The focus of this paper was to cover the existing gap in standards literature and sketch out a first general life cycle model for standards, with particular focus on B2B standards. However, much of what is discussed applies on a more general standards level as well. We lifted the focus from standards development to a more general view of how standards evolve during their existence. Seven existing models for standards life cycles were examined and compared. The resulting general model showed weaknesses in current approaches. Four additional phases were suggested and merged into an extended life cycle model. Life cycle models are useful for understanding standards and how they relate to their environments. One example is how activities in one phase may affect activities in other phases. How education is performed may for example affect how standards are used. Different stakeholders may also have varying interests in different phases. Standards users may have an interest in affecting the contents of a standard, and which kind of education they may have access to in subsequent phases, as well as how standards and systems should be maintained. A life cycle view may thus serve as a basis for discussion. As an example, maintenance has so far been a missing perspective in standards research and perhaps also in practice. The life cycle model can therefore point to important aspects of standards to consider, both for standards users, developers, software organisations and so on.

Acknowledgements

The author wishes to thank the Knowledge Foundation for sponsoring the research project, as well as colleagues for spurring interesting and fruitful discussions.

References

1. ISO-IEC (1996), *ISO-IEC Guide 2:1996(E/F/R)*, ISO/IEC, Switzerland 1996
2. Söderström, E. and Petterson, A. (2003), Adoption of B2B standards, In Jardim-Goncalves et al. (eds.) *Concurrent Engineering: Enhanced Interoperable Systems*, A.A.Balkema Publishers, Lisse, Netherlands, 2003, pp.343-350
3. Webster's (1996), *Webster's Encyclopedic Unabridged Dictionary of the English Language*, Gramercy Books, Random House Value Publishing, Inc.
4. OROD (2003), *Open Resources On-Line Dictionary*, http://www.openresources.com/cgi-bin/dict, Open Resources on the web, as is: 2003-10-28
5. Cargill, C. (1995), A Five-Segment Model for Standardization, in Kahin and Abbate (eds.), *Standards Policy for Information Infrastructure*, MIT Press, Cambridge, MA, USA, pp.79-99
6. Burrows, J. (1999), *Information Technology standards in a changing world: the role of the users*, Computer Standards & Interfaces, pp.323-331, Elsevier Science B.V.
7. Köller, J., Jarke, M., and Schoop, M. (2003), Towards a standardization process for component-based architectures, In Jardim-Goncalves et al (eds.), *Concurrent Engineering: The Vision for the Future Generation in Research and Applications*, Balkema Publishers, Lisse, Portugal, 2003, pp.359-367
8. Ollner, J. (1988), *The Company and Standardization*, 3rd edition, Swedish Standards Institution, Stockholm, Sweden
9. de Vries, H. (2002), *Standardisation education*, ERIM report series: Research in Management, Ref no.ERS-2002-82-ORG, Rotterdam, the Netherlands

10. Weiss, M. and Spring, M. (2000), Selected Intellectual Property Issues in Standardization, in Jakobs, K. (ed.), *Information Technology Standards and Standardization: A Global Perspective*, IDEA Group Publishing, USA, pp.63-79
11. Egyedi, T. (2000), Institutional Dilemma in ICT Standardization: Coordinating the diffusion of technology?, in Jakobs, K. (ed.), *Information Technology Standards and Standardization: A Global Perspective*, IDEA Group Publishing, USA, pp.48-62
12. Hanseth, O. and Braa, K. (1999), Hunting for the treasure at the end of the rainbow: standardising corporate IT infrastructure, in Ngwenyama et al (eds.), *New Information Technologies in Organizational Processes: Field Studies and Theoretical Reflections on the Future of Work*, Kluwer Academic Publishers, chapter 9
13. Baskin, E., Krechmer, K. and Sherif, M. (1998), The six dimensions of standards: Contribution towards a theory of standardization, In Lefebvre et al (eds), *Management of Technology, Sustainable Development and Eco-Efficiency*, Elsevier Press, Amsterdam, 1998
14. Sherif (2003a), When is Standardization slow?, International Journal of IT Standards & Standardization Research, 1(1), Jan.-Mar. 2003, IDEA Group Publishing, pp.19-32
15. Ishikawa, Y. (2003), Concurrent Engineering: Part 1: Business requirements, life cycle activity, key agenda for success and challenge with ISO standards, in Cha et al (eds), *Concurrent Engineering: The Vision for the Future Generation in Research and Applications*, Balkema Publishers, Lisse, Portugal, 2003, pp.523-532
16. Sherif, M. (2003b), Technology Substitution and Standardization in Telecommunication Services, in Egyedi et al (eds.), *Proceedings of the 3rd IEEE Conference on Standardization and Innovation in Information Technology*, IEEE, October 22-24, 2003, Delft University of Technology, the Netherlands, pp.241-252
17. ISO (2003), *How conformity assessment works*, available at: http://www.iso.org/iso/en/comms-markets/conformity/iso+conformity-02.html, as is: June 2, 2003
18. ECIF (2002), *2002 Survey of Demands for E-Business Standardization in Korea*, Integrated Forum on Electronic Commerce (ECIF), December 30, 2002
19. Fasolino, A., Natale, D., Poli, A., and Quaranta, A. (2000), Metrics in the development and maintenance of software: an application in a large scale environment, *Journal of Software Maintenance: Research and Practice*, 12 (2000), pp.343-355

Applicability of ERP Systems
for Knowledge Management
in the Context of Quality Management

Imandra Galandere-Zile

Department of Systems Theory and Design, Riga Technical University
1 Kalku, Riga, LV-1658, Latvia
ImandraGZ@delfi.lv

Abstract. Today technological advances are frequently affecting all aspects of a typical organization. One of such aspects is organisational quality management. As work environment changes dramatically, the need for appropriate business systems to support the new working conditions arises. The assumption behind this paper is that quality management oriented knowledge management system would be a proper mean for enchasing effectiveness of an organisation. The goal of the paper is to analyse direct and indirect support of different ERP modules and technologies to knowledge and quality management in order to identify which ERP solutions and technologies could be used in quality management oriented knowledge management system.

1 Introduction

Today's dynamic and turbulent environment makes it difficult for organisations to operate successfully and maintain competitive advantage. Therefore, organizations are looking for new solutions and possibilities for improvement of existing systems in order to achieve and/or maintain their competitiveness.

Rapid environmental changes challenge existing organisational quality management systems by requesting agile quality strategies and innovative quality solutions. Such requirements hardly can be met by traditional quality information systems, because managing in rapidly changing environment requires knowledge (not just information) based solutions. In the same time particular knowledge management oriented properties are presented by several information systems solutions, e.g., particular solutions incorporated in ERP systems.

This paper presents a part of the research on the development of quality management oriented knowledge management system [1]. Quality management oriented knowledge management system is a knowledge management system that is designed to enhance the effectiveness of quality management system and thus contribute to the overall welfare of the organisation. The goal of the paper is to analyse direct and indirect support of different ERP modules and technologies to knowledge and quality management in order to identify which ERP solutions and technologies could be used in quality oriented knowledge management system. Research method is analytical, i.e. the conclusions are derived on the basis of feature analysis of ERP systems compo-

A. Persson and J. Stirna (Eds.): CAiSE 2004, LNCS 3084, pp. 276–289, 2004.
© Springer-Verlag Berlin Heidelberg 2004

nents. The research relies on a wide variety of information sources in order to identify the current situation in the research areas. In general, organizational information systems can provide a part of knowledge management systems infrastructure and components. Here, in particular, the potential contribution of ERP systems to quality management oriented knowledge management system is analysed.

ERP are comprehensive, packaged software solutions that seek to integrate the complete range of business processes and functions in order to present a holistic view of the business from a single information and information technology architecture. It provides seamless integration of all information flowing through a company, such as financial, accounting, human resources, supply chain, and customer information [2]. ERP combines all the information of an organization together into a single, integrated software program that converges on a single database so that the various departments can share information and communicate with each other more easily [3]. Once the data are input at one system, they immediately become available throughout all systems, which deliver a consistent management interface. ERP packages are usually upgraded on a regular basis to adopt new technology, further improve the productivity with advanced work process, streamline and standardize work process, and yet bring more data consistency and integrity across all modules, so the management can benefit from prompt real-time processing to provide information for decisions [4]. Many large organisations worldwide have already adopted ERP, and increasingly small- and medium - sized enterprises also are finding it cost effective and competitively advantageous to follow the example of large organisations [5].

Impact of ERP systems modules and technologies on knowledge management in the context of quality management is threefold: (1) ERP systems provide knowledge management oriented modules that may be used in quality management, (2) ERP systems incorporate technologies applicable for knowledge management systems, and (3) ERP systems have quality management oriented modules that can be included as an information sources in the quality management oriented knowledge management system of the organisation.

This paper investigates the field that has not been broadly researched yet. Although the interaction and intersection between ERP and knowledge management, and the ways, in which the knowledge management initiatives can help to facilitate the processes of implementation and maintenance of ERP systems, are extensively investigated [2, 5, 6, 7, 8, 9, 10], by authors knowledge, ERP systems in the context of their application to knowledge management have not been thoroughly analysed. Therefore, the goal of the paper is to analyse the ERP systems in order to identify the ERP modules and technologies that support knowledge management, as well as to determine whether it is possible to apply these solutions and technologies to quality management to enhance effectiveness of an organisation. The ERP systems are chosen as representatives of information system in general because of their wide application in organisations and their high competitive capacity within the information systems' market. No specific criteria were used to choose particular ERP systems for analysis. However, principles of popularity and diversity were taken as bases for ERP systems selection. Therefore the most advanced and popular ERP systems (e.g. SAP, Baan, Oracle, and PeopleSoft) that are oriented to large organizations and international corporations, as well as such ERP systems as Microsoft Navision and Great Plains, that are focused on the segment of small- and medium- sized enterprises, where included in the list of systems to be investigated. The paper presents data about specific ERP systems, as well as provides summaries of all the analysed ERP systems where the specific features of each ERP system are not reflected.

The paper is organised as follows. The relationship between knowledge management and information systems is analysed, potential contribution of ERP systems to knowledge management is discussed, and the basic knowledge management oriented technologies offered by ERP systems are identified in Section 2. The short overview of the area of quality management is presented and ERP systems potential support for quality management is discussed in Section 3. These two sections set the background for the analysis of potential ERP systems support for quality management oriented knowledge management system that is presented in Section 4. Brief conclusions and directions of intended future work are given in Section 5.

2   ERP Systems Support for Knowledge Management

This section is focused on the relationship between knowledge management and information systems, discusses potential contribution of ERP systems to knowledge management, and identifies the basic knowledge management oriented technologies offered by ERP systems.

2.1 Knowledge Management and Information Systems

The resent trends in the organisational development have demonstrated the importance of knowledge management. Knowledge management is systematic, precise, and deliberative process of knowledge creation, retrieval and utilization. The aim of knowledge management is to maximise efficiency of activities related to knowledge as well as benefits acquired from this knowledge. Knowledge management is improving the ways the organisations are doing the business. Knowledge management systems have been applied in different areas of organisational performance. There are knowledge management systems for strategic planning, marketing, manufacturing, finances and human resources management [11].

In order to transform knowledge into a valuable organisational asset, knowledge, experience, and expertise must be formalised, distributed, shared, and applied. Effective management of knowledge requires hybrid solutions involving both people and technology. Therefore it is very important to determine the technology for storing the knowledge, persuade employees to contribute to the repository, create a structure for holding the knowledge.

Past management information systems basically used the computer as a means of providing information to solve recurring operational problems Today, there is a need for new types of systems that focuses on discovering knowledge that responds to the changing environment. By increasing capabilities of decision makers, information systems that support knowledge management initiatives improve the chances that an organization will achieve its goals.

Past and current management information systems that influenced today's knowledge management systems indirectly are integrated management information systems, real-time management information systems, and distributed management information systems. Mostly these systems focus on processing a company's critical applications

– applications without which the business could not continue its operation [12]. These systems are integral part in building company's knowledge management system.

Information systems that support information flow are one essential component in knowledge management system. Information systems create good virtual environment for knowledge management. One type of such information systems is ERP systems.

2.2 Potential Contribution of ERP Systems to Knowledge Management

Some academic research has been done in the area of ERP systems' application to knowledge management within the organisations. However, important claims in this regard are emerging from the practitioner literature [2]. For example, articles debate the effectiveness or ineffectiveness of ERP systems in extracting usable information from the underlying organisational data [13], the role of ERP systems as organisational "knowledge libraries" [14], or the addition of ERP modules that incorporate groupware and decision support systems [15]. In order to find out how ERP systems can support knowledge management, such ERP systems [16, 17, 18, 19, 20, 21, 22] as SAP, Baan, Oracle, PeopleSoft, Microsoft Navision, and Great Plains are analysed.

ERP purports to support all business functions of an enterprise. High functionality is one of the main differentiators of ERP. The main features of ERP are provided business solutions, which support the core processes of the business and administrative functionality. In addition to these general business functions, ERP often supports industry specific functions like student administration at universities or high volume warehousing transactions for retailers etc [5]. However, further in this section only those ERP solutions that support knowledge management will be discussed.

The results of the detailed analysis of ERP systems with respect to ERP systems potential support to knowledge management are identified and summarized in Table 1. The first column of the table presents ERP solutions that support knowledge management. The second column describes potential contribution of ERP systems to knowledge management.

Table 1. Potential contribution of ERP systems to knowledge management

ERP solutions	Potential contribution of ERP systems to knowledge management
Enterprise Portal (EP)	Enable users to: • Access any type of content via intelligent search functionality, publish-and-subscribe methods, or simple browsing, • Efficiently manage, classify, and search content, • Control the publishing cycle, using online collaboration and editorial workflow capabilities, • Integrate information with transactions, • Search internal and external sources and identify subject-matter experts. In addition, offers: • Web-based authoring that simplifies publishing processes with online editing, discussion forums, and automatic document version control, • Feedback, discussion, and annotation functions that make it easy to interact with content owners, experts, and other resources.

Table 1. (continued)

ERP solutions	Potential contribution of ERP systems to knowledge management
Customer Relationship Management (CRM)	• Optimises customer knowledge across the enterprise, • Consolidates key customer information from multiple touch-points to provide an understanding of the "cost to serve" each customer or prospect.
Supply Chain Management (SCM)	• Delivers the tools company need to increase cooperation with its partners and manage its total supply chain to achieve better business performance, • Ensures efficient, reliable, and timely information exchange throughout the extended enterprise. To help achieve this, ERP leverages core capabilities in the areas of integration, information, and collaboration, • Offers to optimise company's internal processes and use e-commerce to work more closely with customers and suppliers.
Product Lifecycle Management (PLM)	A comprehensive, Internet-enabled solution that: • Spans the complete lifecycle of a product, • Captures product information at any relevant stage in the lifecycle, and • Can help ensure that every department is working with the right information.
Electronic Document Management (EDM)	• Can be used to transfer data in document information records between the ERP internal system and the external system, • Support such functions as creating, changing, and displaying a document information record.
File Management (FM)	Offers the right architecture for file and content management: • Provides versioning, integrated workflow and approval processing that make teams more efficient, • Allows to consolidate hundreds or even thousands of file servers into a single, secure, scalable file service, • Offers to find the necessary information easily and fast with the help of integrated search tools.
Business Flows (BF)	Collection of application components designed to enable end-to-end business processes, that: • Automate the critical business processes utilized to support a complete business strategy for managing operations, customers, suppliers, partners, and employees, • Help to improve current business processes using best practices built into the product, streamline and efficiently manage the flow of transactions and information etc.
Services Management	Solution empowers to take advantage of the knowledge that company possesses. It allows to: • Access complete histories of clients, projects, and contracts, • Scrutinize operations, competitors, and employees, • Look at the whole picture, or scrutinize the details, and • Create online discussion forums and virtual chat rooms, • Capture, distribute, and exploit information.

Table 1. (continued)

ERP solutions	Potential contribution of ERP systems to knowledge management
Solution for Public Sector	• Seamlessly integrate data from various sources to help public sector organisations to understand better the interrelationships of tactical activities and strategic goals, • Creates knowledge libraries to handle structured and unstructured information in a wide variety of formats and supports e-learning scenarios.
Business Intelligence Suite (BIS) or Analytics	Helps: • Deliver actionable information to management at all levels, • Managers make the right decisions, close the gap between intent and execution, • Transform data into meaningful, valuable information.
E-Learning	An enterprise learning management system, that: • Provides a complete infrastructure for organizations to manage, deliver, and track training participation of employees, customers, and partners in both e-learning and classroom based environments, • Ensures quicker time-to-market for product training and consistent delivery of information, knowledge and training across the enterprise.
Workflow Management System (WMS)	• Helps an organisation acquire, store, and catalogue content of organizational knowledge.
Collaboration Suite	• Leverages a relational database to offer a secure, reliable and scalable way to simplify business communications and consolidate information, • Provides users with access to integrated email, voicemail, calendaring, file sharing, search capabilities and web conferencing.
Web Conferencing	• Enables individuals and groups to meet on-line to collaborate, share presentations, applications or their entire desktop.
E-commerce Series	• Offers seamless integration between e-commerce solution and business management system, • Ensuring accuracy of information across all systems, helping company serve its customers better, and improving decision making at all levels.
HelpDesk	Provides a collaborative framework for streamlining help desk operations. It delivers: • Powerful tools that automate the support of information technology systems and • Facilities to sustain company's global enterprise infrastructure smoothly and cost-effectively. With HelpDesk, company can: • Achieve a complete view of the employee, allowing the agent to determine quickly and easily the correct solution to the employee's query or issue, • Determine the best resolution to a problem with a robust search engine delivering solutions weighted, ranked, or scored by accuracy, • Recognize the most appropriate solution to a case with visual icon identification, • Access a central repository of diagnostic tools such as troubleshooting scripts, problem-solving techniques, and agent-recommended solutions, and • Leverage self-service to allow workers to create cases and search the knowledge base for efficient problem resolution, etc.

Thorough analysis of the ERP systems shows that ERP systems support many knowledge management functions and encourage knowledge management initiative in an organisation. According to R. Maier's system-centric classification of knowledge management systems functions [23], ERP systems at least in some extent support the following knowledge management functions:

- Knowledge search,
- Knowledge presentation,
- Knowledge publication, structuring and linking,
- Knowledge acquisition,
- Knowledge communication and cooperation,
- Computer-based training.

2.3 Basic Knowledge Management Oriented Technologies Offered by ERP Systems

During the analysis of the ERP systems the ERP built-in technologies that support knowledge management were also identified. The following knowledge management oriented technologies [24, 25] were identified in ERP systems:

- *Intranet technologies.* Intranets and Extranets are technologies that can be used to build a knowledge management system. The unified surface and access to various sources of information make this technology perfect for acquiring and sharing knowledge throughout a company [24].
- *Groupware.* Groupware is a substantial technology that is used for knowledge management. Groupware offers a platform for communication, collaboration, and coordination. It allows users to interact with both people and databases [12].
- *Information retrieval tools.* Information retrieval offers a solution to tasks from text searches to the automatic categorization and summation of documents.
- *Data warehousing.* Data warehousing is the assembling of selected, filtered, and structured data from a variety of sources into one coherent assembly for the purpose of being able to find meaningful relationships within the data [26 by 27]. Connections that are not readily apparent can be uncovered with the use of data mining and on-line analytical processing (OLAP). These techniques are part of data analysis.
- *Data analysis.* Pattern recognition and classification and forecasting are the techniques used for data analysis. Data analysis is a possible method for generating new knowledge.
- *Agent technologies.* Software agents based on the essentials of artificial intelligence enable the user to search independently for information according to a personal profile and to use various sources and other agents.
- *Computer based training.* It is interactive instructional experience between a computer and a learner in which the computer provides the majority of the stimulus and the learner responds, resulting in progress toward increased skills or knowledge [28]. This technology is also used to pass on knowledge to colleagues.

The results of the ERP systems analysis with respect to utilized technologies are summarized in Table 2. The first column of the table presents the basic ERP built-in technologies that support knowledge management. The other columns encompass the analysed ERP systems. The notation "X" identifies the ERP systems that support particular knowledge management technologies.

Table 2. The basic knowledge management oriented technologies offered by ERP systems

KM technologies offered by ERP	SAP Business Suite	Oracle E-business Suite	IBaan Solution Portfolio	PeopleSoft Product Lines	Microsoft Navision	Microsoft Great Plains
Intranet technologies	X	X	X	X	X	X
Groupware	X	X	X	X	X	X
Information retrieval tools	X	X	X	X	X	X
Data warehousing	X	X	X	X	X	X
Data analysis	X	X	X		X	X
Agent technologies[1]	X	X				
Computer based training	X	X		X		

3   ERP Systems' Support for Quality Management

This section presents a short overview of the area of quality management and discusses how ERP systems can support quality management.

3.1   Quality Management

Organisations implement quality management systems to enhance customers' satisfaction and to improve the effectiveness of the organisations. Quality management is a management approach of an organisation, centred on quality, based on the participation of all the involved parties, and aiming at long-term profitability through customer satisfaction. Quality management system may be defined as an assembly of components, such as the organisational structure, responsibilities, procedures, processes and resources for implementing quality management [29]. Quality management system should apply to and interact with all activities of the organisation. One of the main tasks of a quality management system is to support employees and managers of an organisation by information that is relevant for effective decision-making concerning operational and strategic issues of an organisation. In ERP systems this support is supposed to be provided by quality management subsystem.

---

[1]   As the strict borders of the agent technologies do not exist, it is difficult to detect the intelligent agent functions of ERP systems from the descriptions of the systems.

However, many areas exist that indirectly influence quality management initiatives- starting from the strategy definition, ending with the detailed technical aspects, that will support effective implementation and maintenance of quality management system. Therefore it is essential to identify all possible approaches and technologies of ERP systems that can promote quality management initiatives in organisations.

3.2 Contribution of ERP Systems to Quality Management

In order to identify potential ERP support for quality management whole spectrum of ERP solutions was analysed. Many ERP systems have quality management module as a subsystem that directly supports quality management activities. Nevertheless also performance measurement principles and human resources management solutions that indirectly influence quality management activities are widely supported by ERP systems.

The results of detailed analysis of ERP solutions that potentially can support quality management are reflected in Table 3. The first column of the table comprises those ERP solutions that support quality management. The second column presents in detail how particular ERP solutions can support quality management.

Table 3. Contribution of ERP systems to quality management

ERP solutions	Contribution of ERP systems to quality management
Quality Management (QM) solutions	Quality management solutions of the most advanced ERP systems provide two types of functions: 1. Cross application functions that are incorporated in such modules as Materials Management, Production, Sales & Distribution and Cost Accounting. They fulfil the following tasks: • Manage quality information for materials, vendors, and manufacturers, • Request quality certificates and monitor their receipt, • Manage problems using quality notifications and process complaints against vendors, • Integrate inspection planning and work scheduling, • Handle in-process inspection during production at freely defined inspection points, • Confirm quality and quantity information for manufacturing orders, • Monitor production quality with the help of control charts and determines process capability scores, • Manage customer-related quality information, • Settle appraisal and nonconformity costs, • and many others. 2. Internal functions of the solutions, that are meant for the following tasks of quality planning, inspection and control: • Manage master data for quality planning, • Support inspection planning, • Provide inspection results in the form of characteristic values, defect data, and texts, • Support flexible reporting with the user-defined reports, • Record the nature of the problem and the problem analysis.

Table 3. (continued)

ERP solutions	Contribution of ERP systems to quality management
Enterprise Performance Management (EPM) solutions	• Delivers real-time business insight to drive faster, smarter decisions and superior business performance, • Rapidly align company's strategic goals with tactical execution to help to gain better control of company's daily operations. It allows to react quickly to any unexpected changes in business conditions and improve the predictability of company's results, • Employees can continuously track and measure their own performance against objectives, allowing to increase accountability within an organisation, • With a full suite of analytic applications to plan, measure and adjust in real time, EPM helps to drive operational excellence within an organisation, • Help managers at all levels of a company understand the factors that affect performance, determine the level of performance that is required, and identify actions they can take to improve results.
Human Resources Management (HRM) solutions	HRM is a discipline that drives operating performance and creates value, enterprise–wide. It helps companies to improve the speed and cost-effectiveness with which company performs key human resources processes while enabling managers and executives to make better and more timely decisions. HRM solutions help to: • Provide a flexible central repository of employee information for improved personnel management, • Manage and streamline human resources business processes - from recruitment to retirement, • Manage workforce information for analytic reporting and analysis, • Deploy self-service across the enterprise, to speed transactions and improve productivity, • Align company's workforce with goals and objectives, to drive business performance, and • Implement and track meaningful benefit programs etc.

4 ERP Systems' Support for Quality Management Oriented Knowledge Management System

Potential ERP systems' support for quality management oriented knowledge management system is threefold (Figure 1):

1. particular knowledge management oriented technologies offered by ERP systems can be used in knowledge management system;
2. the following ERP modules/ solutions are a direct information source of quality management oriented knowledge management system:
   - quality management,
   - enterprise performance management, and
   - human resources management;
3. particular knowledge management oriented ERP solutions may be incorporated in the quality management oriented knowledge management system.

Figure 1 presents ERP systems' support for quality management oriented knowledge management system. ERP solutions that support knowledge management are located in box on the left side of the figure. ERP solutions that support quality management are presented in the box on the right side of the figure. The arrows from one solution to another denote support relationship between the solutions.

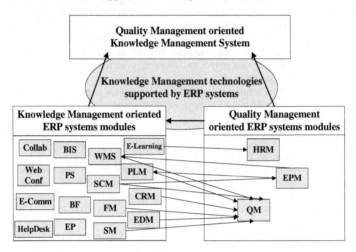

Fig. 1. ERP systems' support for quality management oriented knowledge management system

Notations:

EP - Enterprise Portal
CRM - Customer Relationship Management
SCM - Supply Chain Management
PLM - Product Lifecycle Management
EDM - Electronic Document Management
FM - File Management
BF - Business Flows
WMS – Workflow Management Systems
BIS - Business Intelligence Suite

SM - Services Management
PS - Solution for Public Sector
Collab - Collaboration Suite
Web Conf - Web Conferencing
E-Comm - E-commerce series
QM – Quality Management
EPM – Enterprise Performance Management
HRM – Human Resources Management

The results of detailed analysis of ERP systems' support for quality management oriented knowledge management system are identified and summarized in Table 4. The first column of the table comprises those knowledge management oriented ERP solutions that support quality management. The second column presents in detail how particular ERP subsystems can support quality management.

As shown above in this section, ERP systems successfully can be applied to facilitate quality management initiatives and may form a part of quality management oriented knowledge management system.

Table 4. ERP systems' support for quality management oriented knowledge management system

ERP solutions	ERP systems' support for quality management oriented knowledge management system
Customer Relationship Management (CRM)	A keystone of the quality management that helps customer-driven organisations to stimulate customer satisfaction and improve profitability. CRM can help: • Excel in anticipating and meeting unique customer requirements to increase customer intimacy, • Maximize sales efficiency, order accuracy and standardization, • Minimize service costs to optimise operational performance, • Accelerate commercialisation of ideas and utilize customer feedback to develop leading-edge products, and • Optimise customer knowledge across the enterprise.
Supply Chain Management (SCM)	SCM helps a company to control business-critical processes and streamline process cycle. Thereby company can provide superior customer service that keeps them coming back. SCM can help: • Link business processes across the extended supply chain by sharing detailed, real-time information, • Achieve the best combination of price, product quality, lead-time, and service, • Provide critical business intelligence at all levels in an organisation, including strategic, tactical and operational.
Electronic Document Management (EDM)	• Can be used to transfer data in document information records between the company's ERP system and the external system, • Such functions are supported as creating, changing, and displaying a document information record.
File Management (FM)	• Provides versioning, integrated workflow and approval processing that make teams more efficient.
Service Management (SM)	• Total solution for organisational profitability and customer satisfaction, • Makes it profitable for company to deliver superior customer service by allowing to meet and exceed customer expectations and ensuring customer loyalty, • The combination of a complete service management solution with other business management capabilities helps company manage all aspects of its operations.
Product Lifecycle Management (PLM)	Comprehensive, Internet-enabled solution that can help companies reduce costs, increase quality and speed time-to-market. It: • Spans the complete lifecycle of a product, • Captures product information at any relevant stage in the lifecycle and can help ensure that every department is working with the right information.
E-Learning	• With E-Learning an organisation can approach learning strategically and improve enterprise performance. • Provides a complete infrastructure for organisations to manage, deliver, and track training participation of employees, customers, and partners in both e-learning and classroom based environments, • Ensures quicker time-to-market for product training and consistent delivery of information, knowledge and training across the enterprise.
Workflow Management System	• The business processes of a company contain a large part of knowledge. Workflow is used to help an organization acquire, store, and catalogue content.

5 Conclusions and Future Work

The paper addresses applicability of ERP systems for knowledge management in the context of quality management. It fills the gap in academic research in the area of ERP systems' applicability to knowledge management and quality management within the organizations. Several ERP systems were analysed in order to find out how ERP systems can support knowledge and quality management.

The main conclusions derived from the analysis of several aspects of ERP systems are the following:

- ERP systems can facilitate knowledge management because of the following reasons:
  - ERP systems (by their functions and technologies) fit into the classification of technologies, tools and systems that support knowledge management;
  - several ERP systems' built-in technologies meet demands of knowledge management systems;
  - ERP systems support many knowledge management functions and encourage knowledge management initiative in an organisation.

- ERP systems and knowledge management oriented technologies offered by ERP systems can support quality management:
  - the quality management solutions are encompassed in the most of the ERP systems;
  - the quality management solutions offered by ERP systems have encompassed many principles of knowledge management;
  - ERP solutions oriented to knowledge management provide indirect support for quality management initiatives.

The results of this research will be used to analyse dependency relationships between quality management oriented knowledge management system and organisational information system in general.

References

1. Galandere-Zile, I., Application of knowledge management elements for quality management systems, 11th International Conference on Information Systems Development, Riga, Latvia, 2002, pp.15-25.
2. Baskerville, R., Pawlowski, S., and McLean, W., Enterprise Resources Planning and Organizational Knowledge: Patterns of Convergence and Divergence, pp.396-406.
3. ERP-2, The ABCs of ERP by Christopher Koch,
   http://www.cio.com/research/erp/edit/erpbasics.html
4. ERP-1, Enterprise Resource Planning Research center, http://www.cio.com/research/erp/
5. Klaus, H., Rosemann, M., and Gable, G.G., What is ERP?, Information Systems Frontiers (2:2), Kluwer Academic Publisher, Boston, Manufactured in the Netherlands, 2000, pp.141-147.
6. Sage, A.P and Rouse, W.B, Information Systems Frontiers in Knowledge Management, Information Systems Frontiers (1:3), Kluwer Academic Publisher, Boston, Manufactured in the Netherlands, 2000, pp.205-209.

7. Pan, S.L, Huang, J.C., Newell, S., and Cheung, A.W.K., Knowledge Integration as a Key Problem in an ERP Implementation, 22nd International Conference on Information Systems, 2001, pp.321-327.
8. Sousa, R.D., Enterprise Systems Extended Use, 8th Americas Conference on Information Systems, 2002, pp.2580-2585.
9. Klaus, H. and Gable, G.G., Senior Managers' Understandings of Knowledge Management in the Context of Enterprise Systems, pp.981-987.
10. Sieber, M.M., A Recurring Improvisational Methodology for Change Management in ERP Implementation.
11. Galandere-Zile I., Vanags J., Kirikova M. Towards knowledge management system for quality management: Improving effectivity of organisations, 5th International Baltic Conference on Databases and Information Systems, Tallin, Estonia, 2002.
12. R.J.Thierauf, Knowledge Management Systems for Business, Quorum Books, 1999.
13. Webb.D., Business Intelligence Tools Help Iron Out the Wrinkles, Computing Canada (25:5), 1999, p.19.
14. Michel, R., Model Citizens, Manufacturing Systems (16:2), 1998, pp.29-44.
15. Michel, R., Groupware and ERP, Manufacturing Systems (16:10), 1998, p.18.
16. Packaged ERP Suites, http://erp.ittoolbox.com/nav/t.asp?t=420&p=420&h1=420
17. SAP Solutions, http://www.mysap.com/
18. Oracle, http://www.oracle.com/
19. Baan, http://www.baan.com/
20. Microsoft Business Solutions - Great Plains, http://www.microsoft.com/businessSolutions/Great%20Plains/default.mspx
21. Microsoft Business Solutions - Navision, http://www.microsoft.com/businessSolutions/Navision/default.mspx
22. PeopleSoft, http://www.peoplesoft.com/
23. Maier, R., Knowledge Management Systems: Information and Communication Technologies for Knowledge Management, Springer – Verlag Berlin, Heidelberg, 2002.
24. Mertins, K., Heisig, P., and Vorbeck, J. (Eds.), Knowledge Management: Best Practices in Europe, Springer, Heilderberg, 2001.
25. Galandere-Zile I., Zaharova S., The Role of Information Technologies in Effective Knowledge Management, In Scientific Proceedings of Riga Technical University: Applied Computer Systems, 8th volume, Riga Technical University, 2001, pp.101-107.
26. T.Kanti Srikantaiah, Michael, E.D.Koenig, Knowledge Management for the Information Professionals, American Society for Information Science, 1999.
27. Darling, Charles B. 1997., "Datamining for the Masses", Datamation 43, no.2 (February): p.52-55.
28. KnowledgeNet, Dictionary of Terms, http://www.knowledgenet.com/helpdesk/dictionary/index.jsp
29. Oakland, J.S., Total Quality Management: The Route to Improver Performance, Second Edition, Butterworth – Heinemann Ltd, Oxford, 1993.

Model-Driven Web Service Development

Karim Baïna[1,4], Boualem Benatallah[1], Fabio Casati[2], and Farouk Toumani[3]

[1] CSE, UNSW, Sydney NSW 2052, Australia
{kbaina,boualem}@cse.unsw.edu.au
[2] Hewlett-Packard Laboratories, Palo Alto, CA, 94304, USA
casati@hpl.hp.com
[3] LIMOS, Campus des Cezeaux, BP 125, 63173 Aubiere, France
ftoumani@isima.fr
[4] ENSIAS, B.P. 713 Agdal, Rabat, Morocco
baina@ensias.ma

Abstract. Web services are emerging as a promising technology for the effective automation of inter-organizational interactions. However, despite the growing interest, several issues still need to be addressed to provide Web services with benefits similar to what traditional middleware brings to intra-organizational application integration. In this paper, we present a framework that supports the model-driven development of Web services. Specifically, we show how, starting from the external specifications of a Web service (e.g., interface and protocol specifications), we can support the generation of extensible service implementation templates as well as of complete (executable) service specifications, thereby considerably simplifying the service development work.

Keywords: Web services, Web service conversation, Web service composition, model-driven generation.

1 Introduction

Web services, and more in general service-oriented architectures (SOAs), are emerging as the technologies and architectures of choice for implementing distributed systems and performing application integration within and across companies' boundaries. The basic principles of SOAs consist in modularizing functions and exposing them as services, that are typically specified using (de jure or de facto) standard languages and interoperate through standard protocols.

Modern SOAs have two important characteristics that are relevant to the topics discussed in this paper. The first is that service descriptions are more detailed with respect to what happened in conventional middleware. This is because clients and services are typically developed by separate teams, possibly even by different companies, and service descriptions are all what client developers have to understand to know how the service behaves. In particular, a trend that is gathering momentum is that of including, as part of the service description, not only the service interface, but also the *business protocol* supported by the service, i.e., the specification of which message exchange sequences are supported by the service, for example expressed in terms of constraints on the order

A. Persson and J. Stirna (Eds.): CAiSE 2004, LNCS 3084, pp. 290–306, 2004.

in which service operations should be invoked. In the following, we use the term *external specification* to refer to the combination of the interface and business protocol specifications, that define the externally visible behavior of a service.

The second characteristic is that when services are described and interact in a standardized manner, the task of developing complex services by composing other (basic or composite) services is considerably simplified with respect to conventional middleware, where composition technologies (such as workflow technology) where available but failed to become widely adopted, mostly due to the heterogeneity of the services to be combined and therefore to the difficulty in developing composite services. Indeed, as SOA-related technologies mature, service composition is expected to play a bigger and bigger role in service development [1, 10].

Today, most Web services platform provide support for bottom-up design, especially in terms of taking existing code (e.g., Java classes) and deriving WSDL interface specifications for it. Analogously, support for top-down design is in terms of taking service interface specifications and generating Java (or otherwise) interfaces. While these are useful tools, they do not take into account protocol specifications and in particular they do not facilitate the development of services that are *compliant* with a certain protocol specification (i.e., whose execution is in accordance with the specified external behavior). This task is left to the developer, who must implement the protocol management logic and verify that each service implementation behaves as declared in the external specifications, which is a very time consuming activity.

This paper presents a framework that aims at addressing this issue, by supporting the model-driven design of Web services. We specifically focus on top-down design of composite services that, as stressed above, is likely to become a key activity in Web services development due to the increased adoption of protocol and composition languages and technologies. In this area, we provide two main contributions, corresponding to two different approaches that may be taken in top-down design. First, we show how, starting from the external specifications, it is possible to generate a *skeleton* of a composite service (also called *service composition template*) that is compliant with the service specification. Designers can then extend this skeleton with business logic, thereby completing the specification of the service up to the point where detailed, executable service specifications are obtained, typically in the form of a process definition. As an alternative approach, instead of generating and extending the composition skeleton (that deals with the service as a whole), the designer may wish to start the development by separately defining the composition logic for each operation[1]. The proposed framework also supports this case, by combining the specification of the operation implementations with the external specifications to produce a more complete, executable specifications of a service that not only implements the service operations as specified, but also takes care of maintaining the conversation state in a way that is compliant with the business protocol specifications,

---

[1] As we will see, this is possible only if the service operations are independent, aside from the constraints defined by the protocol.

by generating the appropriate logic and combining it with the operation implementation logic. Thanks to this automated code generation, service development is considerably simplified and protocol compliance is ensured, thereby reducing the time and effort needed to generate correct service implementations. We believe that as business protocols become widely adopted, such a framework will be an important part of any Web service development environment.

As a concrete example, we will show how the proposed framework can automatically generate BPEL specifications [3] starting from protocol specifications expressed in the Self-Serv service description and composition models [5].

The remainder of this paper is organized as follows: Section 2 briefly oveviews the conversation model and main constructs of BPEL. Section 3 discusses the generation of service implementation skeletons from external service specifications. Section 4, discusses an alternative approach which allows the generation of more complete executable specifications from service composition and conversation models. In Section 5, we discuss related work, give some concluding remarks, and outline future research directions.

2   Concept Definitions

This section briefly describes the service conversation model we use for the external specifications of services and summarizes the main constructs of BPEL.

2.1   Service Conversation Model: An Overview

In this section, we briefly describe the protocol definition model and language we use in this paper. The reason for selecting this specific model is because it has been proven to support the definition of many commonly needed protocols, and because it is fairly rich and complex, thereby enabling us to treat the problem in its generality. Briefly stated, a *conversation* is a sequence of message exchanges that can occur between a client and a service as part of the invocation of a Web service. This exchange occurs according to a *business protocol* (also called *conversation protocol* in the following), i.e., a specification of the set of correct and accepted conversations.

Following our previous work [5], we choose to specify the conversation model of a Web service as an extended state machine, where states denote the different logical stages in which a service could be in its interaction with a client, while transitions among states occur (mostly, but not only) as a result of operation invocations. Figure 1 presents an example of a simplified conversation model supported by the Web portal of a bookseller. States are labeled with a logical name, such as BookFound, BookOrdered. Transitions are labeled with events corresponding to operation invocations, such as Login or OrderBook.

Furthermore, transitions are extended beyond the traditional state machine model to capture abstractions that are necessary to model Web service conversations, including *activation* and *completion* patterns. Activation patterns describe the triggering features of a transition (e.g., when the transition should occur).

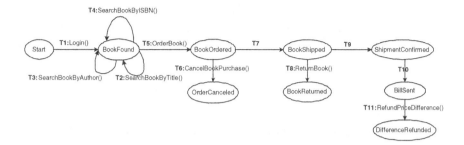

Fig. 1. Sample of an **eBookShop** service conversation protocol

Completion patterns describe the implications and the effect of a transition from requester perspective (e.g., whether requesters can cancel an operation and what is the cancellation fee).

Activation Abstractions. In the extended state machine model, besides the fact that a transition is activated by invoking an operation, an activation property specifies an *activation mode, activation event* and *pre-conditions*. The activation mode indicates whether the triggering of the transition is explicit (mode="user") or implicit (mode="provider"). When the activation mode is explicit, the transition is activated by explicitly invoking a service operation. When the activation mode is implicit, the transition will occur automatically after the occurrence of a temporal event. A pre-condition is a triple (O-condition, U-condition, and T-condition), where:

- ○ An O-condition specifies conditions on service objects (i.e., service request parameters);
- ○ A U-condition specifies conditions on requester profiles. It is used to specify the fact that an operation can be invoked only by certain users (e.g., an operation is only available to "premium" customers);
- ○ A T-condition specifies temporal constraints to allow the description of timed transitions (e.g., a transition can occur only within a certain time period).

We adopt XPath as a language to express queries and conditions. The definitions of temporal constraints use XPath time functions (e.g., current-time) and some predefined time functions in our model. In the remainder, begin(t) (resp., end(t)) denotes the beginning (resp., termination) date of the last invocation of the transition T within the same conversation instance. The conversation model features the following temporal predicates:

- ○ M-invoke prescribes when an implicit transition must be automatically fired;
- ○ C-invoke prescribes a deadline or a time window within which a transition can be fired.

M-invoke is used to specify temporal events. C-invoke is used to specify temporal pre-conditions of a transition. Formally, a temporal constraint is specified as either Pred(boolop,d), where Pred may be M-invoke, or C-invoke. boolop is a comparison operator (e.g., =, <, >) and d is either an absolute date time or a relative date time (e.g., begin(t)). The constraint M-invoke(boolop,d) is only authorized for implicit transitions and means that the transition is automatically fired when the condition current-time boolop d is evaluated to true. Here, current-time denotes the system time. The constraint C-invoke(boolop,d) means that the transition can be triggered only if the condition current-time boolop d is evaluated to true.

Table 1 illustrates temporal conditions of eBookShop conversation protocol. For instance, the table shows that the operation associated to transition T_6 can only be invoked within 7 days after the completion of T_5 (i.e. $begin(T_6) < end(T_5)+7$). The transition T_9 will be automatically performed 30 days after the completion of the transition T_7 (i.e. $begin(T_9) >= end(T_7)+30$).

Table 1. eBookShop Conversation time properties

Transition	T-condition
$T_1 \ldots T_5$	true
T_6	C-invoke($<, end(T_5)+7$)
T_7	M-invoke($>=, end(T_5)+7$)
T_8	C-invoke($<, end(T_7)+30$)
T_9	M-invoke($>=, end(T_7)+30$)
T_{10}	M-invoke($>=, end(T_9)+2$)
T_{11}	C-invoke($<, end(T_{10})+10$)

Completion Abstractions. The completion property of a transition specifies the *effect* of a transition. With regard to this property, we distinguish the following types of transitions[2]

- Effect-less denotes a transition which has no permanent effect from the client's perspective. Canceling this kind of transition does not require the execution of any particular operation. For example, the transition T2, carried out during the execution of the operation SearchBookByTitle(), does not have any permanent effect, as far as the client is concerned;

- Compensatable denotes a transition which has an effect that can be undone by explicitly invoking a compensation operation. A compensatable transition is characterized by giving the name of the corresponding compensation transition and its cancellation cost. Consider, for instance, the transition T7. The effect of this transition consists of transferring money from the client bank account to the provider account. However, the effect of this transition can be (partially) undone (i.e., the client can be refunded) if the client

---

[2] Other types of transactional properties are identified but not presented here due to space limitations. The interested reader is referred to [4] for details.

decides to return the purchased items (operation ReturnBook()). The transition T8:CancelBookPurchase() can be used to compensate the transition T5:OrderBook();

○ Definite denotes a transition whose transactional effects are permanent (i.e., are not compensatable). For example, after the delivery of the purchased items, the eBookShop.com service remains in the state BookShipped during 30 days, corresponding to the period of time where the user can, under certain conditions, return the purchased items (operation ReturnBook). After this period of time, the transition cannot be undone. This abstraction is conveyed by labeling the transition T9, for instance, as a definite transition.

2.2 Overview of BPEL

BPEL (Business Process Execution language) [3] is an XML-based language intended to specify processes that involve operations provided by one or several Web services. It can be used to define *executable* and *abstract processes*. An *abstract process* defines a set of message exchanges between a Web service and a client of the Web service, without revealing the Web service's internal business logic. An *executable process* defines the service business logic based on a number of constituent *activities*, the *partners* involved in these activities, the *messages* exchanged between partners, and *exception handling* procedures.

An *activity* in a BPEL process is either *primitive* or *structured*. The types of primitive activity are: `invoke`, to invoke a web service operation; `receive`, to wait for a message from an external source; `reply`, to reply to an external source message; `wait`, to remain idle for a given time period; `assign`, to copy data from one variable to another; `throw`, to raise exception errors; and `empty`, to do nothing. Structured activities are defined using the following control flow constructs: `sequence`, for representing sequential order between activities; `switch`, for execution conditional routing; `while`, for loop iteration; `pick`, for non-deterministic choices based on events; `flow`, for parallel execution routing; and `scope`, for grouping activities to be treated by the same fault-handler and possibly within a given transactional context.

Given a set of activities contained within the same flow block, control `links`, allow the definition of dependencies between two activities. The target activity of a control link may only start when the source activity has ended.

3   Generating Implementation Skeletons from External Service Specifications

Now that the basic conversation concepts have been introduced, we show how external service specifications can be used to generate internal specifications, that is, executable business logic. The basic idea consists in generating a service implementation skeleton starting from the service interface (specified for instance in a WSDL document) and from a protocol specified with the model described above. The skeleton includes code that maintains the conversation state and checks whether messages are received and sent in accordance with coordination protocol definitions, returning an error to the client if a message is not compliant. It has constructs for receiving service invocation messages, detecting transition activation events (such as explicit operation invocations or temporal events for implicit transitions), triggering transitions, and ensuring that the implications and effects of transitions are performed in accordance with the defined coordination protocol. In a nutshell, the skeleton implements what we call *conversation management logic*.

The skeleton does not include any service-specific business logic, i.e., it does not include information on how the individual operations are implemented. Operation invocations appear as black boxes in the skeleton, and it is up to the service developer to extend the skeleton by refining the implementation of each of the operations. The benefits of the model-driven generation is that developers "simply" focus on implementing the internal business logic. The code for managing the conversation state and verifying compliance of messages with conversations is automatically generated, thereby considerably simplifying the development.

The remainder of this section describes how the different aspects of a protocol translate into a service skeleton. Although we will focus on the concepts behind this mapping, we endow these concepts with examples based on the use of the protocol model introduced earlier and of BPEL as service implementation language. The presentation revolves around the three logical steps of the transformation: first, we show how each transition is mapped into a process skeleton (called *transition skeleton*). Then, we show how each state is mapped into a state skeleton, which combines the skeletons of the transition in output to that state. Finally, once we have defined how individual states and transitions are mapped, we show how the state skeletons are linked together into an overall process skeleton, based on the overall graph topology of the statechart.

In BPEL terms, we follow the generation approach depicted in Figure 2(a): A service protocol is transformed into a BPEL *flow* of activities (the state skeletons, Figure 2(b)). To preserve and enforce the overall conversation model, that is, to enforce the semantic of the whole protocol, state skeletons are linked together using BPEL links.

3.1   Mapping Transitions

Transitions in the protocol definition are mapped into transition skeletons that 1) check that the preconditions are met (generating a fault message in response otherwise), 2) execute the operation implementation logic (which will have to be specified by the designer), and 3) return a reply to the client, by sending a message corresponding to the operation output parameters.

Each time a transition t is activated from a state S where t is allowed, the corresponding skeleton of t evaluates the transition preconditions (T-condition, U-condition and O-condition in case of explicit transitions or U-condition and O-condition in case of implicit transitions). If all the conditions are true, then the skeleton proceeds by executing the operation implementation logic of the operation associated to t, and the result is returned via a <reply> activity to the

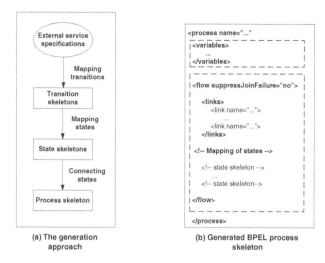

(a) The generation
approach

(b) Generated BPEL process
skeleton

Fig. 2. Process skeleton generation

client. The definition of the data flow, and specifically of which process variables flow into the receive activity (i.e., how the return values are determined), is to be done by the designer as it is part of the internal business logic, not part of the external specifications. If the preconditions are evaluated to false, an error message is returned to the client by an automatically generated (i.e. `<reply>`) activity that returns a fault. As we will see later when discussing state skeletons, if such conditions are false then the transition is still active (it has not been triggered, and therefore the conversation has not changed its state), and therefore we will need a looping mechanism to get back to the point where the transition can be triggered (e.g., by new operation invocations). We will discuss in the following how to map the fact that the transition is waiting for an operation invocation (or for a time interval to elapse) in order to be triggered, as the appropriate mapping for this depends not only on the transition, but on the characteristics of the state to which the transition belongs, as shown later in this section.

Furthermore, in the case of a compensatable transition, a skeleton of a compensation handler is generated in order to implement the compensation activity of the transition. More precisely, a transaction begin/end block is transformed into a `<scope></scope>` BPEL block. If a transaction t is compensatable, its compensation transition, say t_c, is transformed into `<compensate>` BPEL construct. The skeleton of the compensatable transition t will contain a `<compensationHandler>` that will be executed if t is compensated, and that of the transition t_c will contain a `<compensate>` construct that will be used to compensate t.

Finally, it is worth noting that transition activation patterns (e.g., explicit invocation message or temporal events) are not considered during mapping of transitions but are dealt with during mapping of states. As explained in the next section, the reason of this choice is that the constructs generated to implement a transition activation patterns depend on the type of the state (e.g., a state with one or multiple output transitions). As a consequence of this choice, the generated transition skeletons are very similar for both implicit and explicit transitions.

3.2 Mapping States

This section shows how each state is mapped into a state skeleton by combining the skeletons of the transitions in output to the state.

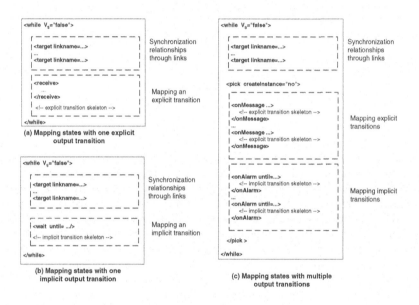

Fig. 3. States skeletons

First, assume that a state S has only one output transition t_o, and that t_o is explicit. In this case, we want to express the semantics that when the conversation is in state S, the transition is active and therefore the corresponding skeleton must be waiting for an operation invocation (i.e., for an incoming message to arrive). In BPEL, this means that the generated state skeleton will include a `<receive>` activity followed by the transition skeleton of t_o (Figure 3 (a)). If t_o is implicit, then this means that the protocol semantics waits for a certain period to elapse before triggering the transition. This is expressed by introducing a delay node, represented by a `<wait>` activity followed by the implicit skeleton of t_o (Figure 3 (b)).

Consider now the general case in which a state S of a service protocol has n output transitions t_1, t_2, t_n, mapped into transition skeletons $sk_1, sk_2, \ldots sk_n$.

Then, since these transitions are in output to the same state, they are all active at the same time. Furthermore, only one at a time can be processed, since as one transition is triggered then the conversation changes state and therefore the other transitions need to be disabled. To enforce this semantic in BPEL, we place the activities $sk_1, sk_2, \ldots sk_n$ into a `pick` construct, that has as one `onMessage` statement for each explicit transition, corresponding to the operation input message for that transition, and one `onAlarm` statement for each implicit transition, corresponding to the M-invoke condition for that transition (c.f., figure 3(c)). Then, the remainder of the skeletons is placed into an activity which is invoked if the event (i.e., message or alarm) occur. The semantics of the pick is such that only one branch of the pick is executed, i.e., only one event is processed. This is what we want, as when an event is received, then it is processed and the conversation changes state, so that operation invocations corresponding to other transitions in output from the same state are not processed.

There is an exception to this rule in the case in which the invocation fails due to the fact that the activation condition is false. To cater for this case, the pick activities are inserted into a `while` construct where a state variable, noted V_S for the state S, that controls the loop is set to true at the start of the loop, and set to false if any of the activation conditions for the invoked operations are false (Figure 3).

We observe also that the reason for handling the simplified case (state with only one output transition) differently, although the general case cover the simplified one as well, is because in simple cases it is possible to generate simpler skeleton, that are easier to interpret for the developer and therefore easier to extend with proprietary business logic.

3.3   Handling Connections among State Skeletons

We now show how state skeletons can be linked together to express the semantics of the statecharts. This is the final step of this generation process. Due to space constraints, this section only gives an overview of the concepts used to handle connections among state skeletons, omitting some implementation details, which are often specifics of this or that implementation language (e.g., for BPEL these include handling dead path elimination or the handling of loops in the statechart with an acyclic flow language). We begin the description by showing how state skeletons are linked together in the general case (i.e., states with multiple input/output transitions). Basically, this amounts to linking together the different pick activities (along with their enclosing while loop), as shown in Figure 3(c)). This is done as follows: all while loops are inserted into a higher level `flow` statement. The dependencies among the states are modeled by links. Each state skeleton (i.e., each while loop) will have as many outgoing links as there are states connected in output, each going to the while skeleton corresponding to one of the output states. Each outgoing link is endowed with a link `transitionCondition`, automatically inserted by the mapper, that identifies whether the flow should move to that state (i.e., should activate the while loop). The condition is based on variables, also automatically defined by the mapper, that are set to true depending on which branch of the pick activity is executed, that is, depending on which transition has been followed and therefore on which state the conversation should go to. Note that the variables are set only of the invocation succeed, that is, only if the transition is actually followed. Note also that if a state has multiple incoming transition, then it will have multiple incoming links, which is consistent with the semantics of the protocol as a state is entered as any one of the input transition occurs.

Handling Special Cases. There are some special cases that require specific treatments as they are not supported by the general approach described above. For example, in BPEL, self-transitions (i.e., transitions that end up in the same state) cannot be handled explicitly because BPEL do not support cyclic process graphs (e.g., in BPEL, links must not create a control cycle). However, such transitions can be handled using a condition in the while loop of a state, similarly to the case of invocation failures described in the previous section. Therefore, in case of self-transitions, the state variable V_S that controls the loop is set to `false` even when the transition is executed correctly, thereby enabling a self-transition to return to its starting state after a successful execution of its associated operation.

Also note that, just like for state skeletons, simplifications with respect to the general approach described above can be made for statecharts with simpler topologies. For example, if we have a linear statechart (each state has one input and one output transition), then the linkage among state skeletons can be achieved by wrapping state skeletons into a `sequence` constructs. Again, these simplifications are dependent on the details of the selected execution language.

4   Generating Service Operation Implementation Logic

4.1   Concepts

Instead of generating the composition skeleton and then extending it with operation implementation logic, the developer may take an alternative approach and start by first defining the implementation logic for each operation, and by then having the CASE tool generate BPEL (or otherwise) specifications that combine conversation management logic (the skeleton) with the specified operation implementation logic, up to the point executable specifications are generated.

This approach has advantages and limitations. On the plus side, it provides independence from the execution language (i.e., the one generated by the CASE tool and ultimately executed by the service composition engine). In fact, in the approach described in the previous section, the developer specifies the operation implementation logic in BPEL (by extending the skeleton). Instead, if the executable code is automatically generated, developers can use different languages to specify how each operation is implemented, independently of what language is supported by the composition engine. For example, they could use statecharts, Petri nets, activity diagrams, or BPEL. It will be up to the tool to then translate these specifications into BPEL (or into whatever execution language is selected). As CASE tools evolve, we expect that they will be able to provide more and more flexibility in terms of support for a variety of operation specification languages (the ones developers use to specify the operation implementation) and for a variety of executable languages, to be able to generate specifications for several composition engines.

This approach is however not applicable in the general case, and this is why we discuss it separately. In fact, there are cases in which it is not possible to specify the implementation of the different operations independently of each other. As an example, assume that a service interface includes operations *getCredit-CardNumber()*, *getExpirationDate()*, and *getName()*. The service implementer would like to specify that once both a credit card number, an expiration date, and a name have been entered, then operation *verifyCredentials()*, offered by an internal application or by a third party, is invoked. In this case, the implementation logic for these three operations would consists of waiting until they have all been invoked (in workflow terminology, this implies the presence of an and-join), and then call the *verifyCredentials()* service. The operations can still be separately implemented, for example by having the three operation implementations set variables once they are completed as well as check variables (to verify if the other two operations have been executed as well) before invoking the verification service. However, this may result in a cumbersome design, that gets overly complex as the level of interactions among operation increases.

This being said, we expect most of the operation implementations to be functionally independent (i.e., to share state information and data, but to be such that the business logic can be independently specified)[3]. After all, this is what is done when services are implemented in Java. Therefore, we believe that providing users with the opportunity of separately specifying implementation logic for each operation - in a language of their liking - and of then automatically generating executable specifications will turn out to be a very useful and widely applicable functionality.

As a final comment before showing a concrete example of how this automated generation achieved in our prototype system for a given specification and a given execution language, we stress that hybrid approaches are also possible. In fact, the operation specification language can be at different levels of abstractions. If the specifications are so detailed to be executable, then the CASE tool will directly generate executable specifications from the combination of protocol descriptions and operation specifications. Otherwise, if specification are at a higher level (e.g., they only contain the operations to be invoked and their execution dependencies, but not the data dependencies or how data is transferred from one operation invocation to the next), then the output of the CASE tool will still need to be refined, although the refinement is simpler as more can be done by the tool. This also enables a flexible mechanism for separating roles during development: for example, an operation can be fully implemented by a developer. In this case, a low-level operation specification language can be used. Otherwise, an architect may first want to define the operation implementation at a high level, to

---

[3] Our framework, as well as the prototype implementation, allows for context to be shared among the different operation implementation logic specified by the user.

then let a developer fill in the details (including the inevitable platform-specific details). In this case, a high-level language will be best as operation specification language.

4.2   A Sample Mapping: From Self-Serv to BPEL

We now present a concrete example of the generation of the operation implementation logic starting from the operation specification. Specifically, we will use as example the languages supported by our prototype implementation, developed within the Self-Serv system [5]. As execution language, we use BPEL. As operation specification language, Self-Serv supports a variation of statecharts.

For ease of presentation, we abstract from the details of the Self-Serv specification model, and present a simplified version here. In particular, we assume that an interface operation O can be implemented in terms of invocation of operation o_x offered by service s_y (denoted by the syntax $O \equiv s_y.o_x$). In this case, we call the operation O a *singleton* operation. Otherwise, operation O can be *structured*, and consist of the parallel or sequential invocation of other operations O_i and O_j. Sequential invocation of two operations O_i and O_j is denoted by the syntax O_i ; O_j, while parallel execution is denoted by $O_i \parallel O_j$. In turn, operations O_i and O_j can also be structured and be further decomposed, until elementary operations, corresponding to invocations of actual operations offered by a service interface, are reached. Examples of operation composition, and their corresponding pictorial representations based on the statechart model of Self-Serv, are shown in figure 4.

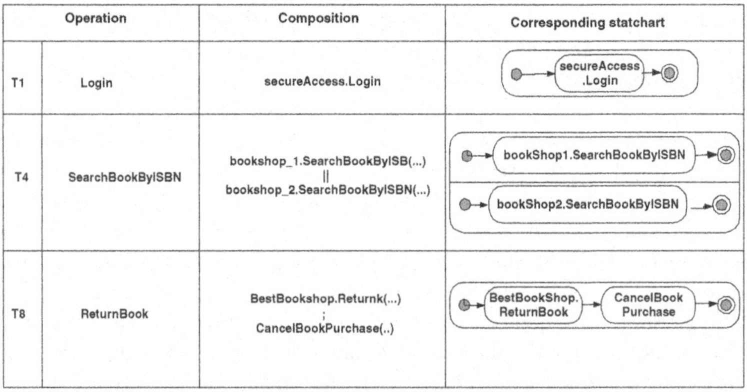

	Operation	Composition	Corresponding statchart
T1	Login	secureAccess.Login	secureAccess .Login
T4	SearchBookByISBN	bookshop_1.SearchBookByISB(...) || bookshop_2.SearchBookByISBN(...)	bookShop1.SearchBookByISBN bookShop2.SearchBookByISBN
T8	ReturnBook	BestBookshop.Returnk(...) ; CancelBookPurchase(..)	BestBookShop. ReturnBook — CancelBook Purchase

Fig. 4. Operation implementation logic of 3 eBookShop service transitions

We now describe how the BPEL implementation skeleton is generated starting from the external specification and the operation implementation specification both expressed with the Self-Serv model. Note that we are still generating skeletons (although more complete than the ones of the previous section) since in this case the operation specification language is at a high abstraction level.

Table 2 presents rules used to generate the BPEL code of an operation given its specification. Moreover, in case the specified operation is associated to a compensatable transition, the generation rules describe how the implementation logic of the corresponding compensating operations is generated.

Table 2. Composition Model generation rules to BPEL

Entity	Method	BPEL construct
Internal	invoke	`<!-- empty implementation logic -->`
	compensation	`<!-- empty compensation logic -->`
Singleton	invoke	`<invoke partner="Si" operation="opj" ../>`
$S_i.op_j$	compensation	op_j is related to a **Definite** or **Effect-less** transition in S_i protocol
		`<!-- empty compensation logic -->`
		op_j is related to a **Compensatable** transition in S_i protocol
		`<invoke partner="Si" operation="opjc" ../>`
Serial	invoke	`<sequence>`
$OP_j; OP_k$		`    <!-- generating operation implementation logic of OPj -->`
		`    <!-- generating operation implementation logic of OPk -->`
		`</sequence>`
	compensation	`<sequence>`
		`    <!-- generating OPk compensation logic -->`
		`    <!-- generating OPj compensation logic -->`
		`</sequence>`
Parallel	invoke	`<flow>`
$OP_j \| OP_k$		`    <!-- generating operation implementation logic of OPj -->`
		`    <!-- generating operation implementation logic of OPk -->`
		`</flow>`
	compensation	`<flow>`
		`    <!-- generating OPj compensation logic -->`
		`    <!-- generating OPk compensation logic -->`
		`</flow>`

As the table shows, if an interface operation op associated to a transition t is a singleton operation, then the corresponding BPEL skeleton will include an `<invoke ../>` activity to invoke the related operation op_j of the service S_i (see table 2). If t is compensatable, the compensating operation of op, say op_c, can be inferred automatically, but only if $S_i.op_j$ is compensatable according to the conversation protocol of the service S_i. In this case, the `<compensationHandler>` of BPEL skeleton of t will contain an `<invoke ../>` activity to invoke the compensating operation of op_j.

If an operation op consists of serial composition $OPj; OPk$, the corresponding BPEL skeleton will contain a `<sequence></sequence>` block of the operations OPj, OPk. The generation of the implementation logic of the operation op is performed through a recursive analysis of its serial component operations. If the operation op is associated to a compensatable transition t, then `<compensationHandler>` of t will contain a `<sequence></sequence>` block of compensation operations of the component operations of *op*. The compensation operations should appear in the opposite order of the corresponding operations of the composition sequence. Note that since the operation in the `<sequence></sequence>` block can be structured, this has to be recursed until elementary operations are found, at which point the compensating operation of the invoked operation is determined from the protocol specifications of the invoked services.

Finally, if an *op* is **parallel** operation, the corresponding BPEL skeleton will contain a `<flow></flow>` block of the component operations. If the operation *op* is associate to compensatable transition t, then the `<compensationHandler>` `<flow></flow>` block of the BEPL skeleton of t will contain a the corresponding compensation operations the component operations of *op*.

5   Discussion

The work presented in this paper discusses issues related to web service conversation models and model-driven service development. With regard to first aspect, several efforts that recognize the need for extending existing service description languages to cater for constraints such the valid sequence of service invocations [7]. These include work done in standardisation efforts such as BPEL, WSCL (www.w3.org/TR/wscl10) and WSCI (www.w3.org/TR/wsci). Our work makes complementary contributions to the efforts mentioned above by endowing service descriptions with abstractions such as temporal constraints, implications and effects of service invocations.

With regard to the second aspect, it should be noted that model driven development of applications is a well established practice [8]. However, in terms of managing the Web service development lifecycle, technology is still in the early stages. We believe that the level of automation can be substantially increased with respect to what is available today, especially in terms of factorizing into the middleware those chores common to the development of many Web services. The approach proposed here has several advantages with respect to previous art, including early formal analysis and consistency checking of system functionalities, refinement and code generation. For example, the work proposed in [2] features generation rules from UML activity diagrams to BPEL processes. The work presented in [9] focuses on generating executable process descriptions from UML process models. The contribution of our work is specializing the model driven approach to web service conversation and composition models. As mentioned before, our approach focuses on specifying service composition models along with the conversation definitions and generating the executable specifications of a service that not only implements the service operations as specified, but also guarantees of conformance of the service implementation with the conversation specification.

The framework presented in this paper has been implemented in a prototype, built as an extension of the Self-Serv service development platform [6]. In particular, the prototype implements the generative approach where conversation models are specified using an extended state machine model as proposed in [4], composition models are specified using statecharts, and executable processes are described using BPEL. Through the tool, users can visually edit service conversations and composition models and automatically generate the BPEL skeletons, which can then be extended by the developers and eventually executed using BPEL execution engine such as the IBM's BPWS4J (www.alphaworks.ibm.com/tech/bpws4j).

This model-driven development framework is one of the components of a broader CASE tool, partially implemented, that manages the entire service development lifecycle. In fact, we envision a model driven service development framework where various service functionalities such as composition logic, conversation management, trust negotiation, security, and exception handling are specified using high level notations. Based on these notations, effective automation of various aspects of service development activities will become a reality (e.g., formal analysis and validation of service composition models, generation of service composition skeletons, generation of conversation models and trust negotiation policies of composite services, etc). The development of this kind of framework and its supporting infrastructure is clearly a complex endeavor, likely to require further progress both in terms of research and of standardization. Our early results related to other parts of the model-driven generation approach, such as the details of the conversation model and the security/trust negotiation models can be found in [4, 11].

Our ongoing work involves the generation of conversation models starting from the composition model. Another line of research and development is related to the identification of what should be generated as part of the specification of the (composite) service and what should be instead embedded into the middleware. For example, the automatic generation of conversation management logic can be handled in two ways: one has been proposed in this paper, and involves the automatic generation of the service specification. Another approach consists in developing a separate middleware component, that we call *conversation controller*, which is separate from the service implementation: it sits in between clients and services and enforces protocol compliance, by maintaining the conversation state and verifying that each operation invocation is in accordance with the conversation state and protocol definition. The two approaches have pros and cons. Having a middleware component is useful in that it hides complexity from the developer and manages protocols automatically, and can also provide such features as logging, monitoring, and analysis. It is also more robust to changes, as protocol evolution can be handled independently from changes to the detailed service specification. On the other hand, this approach requires yet another middleware component, which by the way is not available yet. Although not supported by the current prototype, the approach proposed here is anyway applicable to both scenarios, as the generation of the conversation management logic described in Section 3 can be used to feed specifications to the conversation management middleware instead of resulting in extensible process skeletons. This requires modifications to the tool that are conceptually relatively simple although implementation intensive. The benefits in terms of independence of the specific conversation management language supported by the tool would remain the same.

In summary we believe that, once the research and development work on the aspects described above has been completed, this approach will result in a comprehensive platform that can substantially reduce the service development effort and therefore foster the widespread adoption of Web service technology and of service-oriented architectures.

References

1. G. Alonso, F. Casati, H. Kuno, and V. Machiraju. *Web Services Concepts, Architectures and Applications*. Data-Centric Systems and Applications. Springer Verlag, 2004.
2. J. Amsden, T. Gardner, C. Griffin, and S. Iyenger. *Draft UML 1.4 Profile for Automated Business Processes with a mapping to BPEL 1.0.* http://dwdemos.dfw.ibm.com/wstk/common/wstkdoc/services/demos/uml2bpel/docs/UMLProfileForBusinessProcesses1.1.pdf, June 9, 2003.
3. BEA, IBM, Microsoft, SAP, and Siebel. *Business Process Execution Language for Web Services (BPEL)*. http://www-106.ibm.com/developerworks/library/ws-bpel/, May 5 2003.
4. B. Benatallah, F. Casati, and F. Toumani. Web Service Conversation Modeling: Cornerstone for e-Business Automation. *IEEE Internet Computing*, 7(6), 2003.
5. B. Benatallah, F. Casati, F. Toumani, and R. Hamadi. Conceptual Modeling of Web Service Conversations. *CAiSE'2003*, 449–467, Klagenfurt, Austria. Springer.
6. B. Benatallah, Q. Z. Sheng, and M. Dumas. The Self-Serv Environment for Web Services Composition. *IEEE Internet Computing*, 7(1), January-February 2003.
7. J. Koehler, R. Hauser, S. Kapoor, F. Y. Wu, and S. Kumaran. A Model-Driven Transformation Method. In *Procs of EDOC 2003*, Brisbane, Australia, Sept. 2003.
8. S. Mellor, A. N. Clark, and T. Futagami. Special Issue on Model-Driven Development. *IEEE Software*, 20(5), 2003.
9. E. D. Nitto, L. Lavazza, M. Schiavon, E. Tracanella, and M. Trombetta. Deriving Executable Process Descriptions from UML . In IEEE *ICSE'2002*, Orlando, USA.
10. M. P. Papazoglou and D. Georgakopoulos. Special issue on service oriented computing. *Commun. ACM*, 46(10):24–28, 2003.
11. H. Skogsrud, B. Benatallah, and F. Casati. Model-Driven Trust Negotiation for Web Services. *IEEE Internet Computing*, 7(6), 2003.

A Combined Runtime Environment
and Web-Based Development Environment
for Web Application Engineering

Martijn van Berkum[1], Sjaak Brinkkemper[2], and Arthur Meyer[1]

[1] <GX>, Toernooiveld 225, Nijmegen, The Netherlands
{mvberkum,arthurm}@gx.nl
http://www.gx.nl/
[2] Institute of Information and Computing Sciences
Utrecht University, The Netherlands
s.brinkkemper@cs.uu.nl
http://www.cs.uu.nl/people/sjaak

Abstract. In the last 5 years, server side application server technology became very popular. The two most popular, .NET and J2EE have a large mindshare in the commercial world. Application servers have raised the productivity of server side web developers. In this paper we give a short overview of the history of application servers, and try to answer the question: what options or features would raise the productivity even more? While building commercial websites at <GX>, we found out that that a combined web-based development environment and persistent runtime environment raised our productivity, even compared to .NET or J2EE environments. In this paper we describe such a system built at <GX>, which we called a WRDE (Web-based Runtime and Development Environment), and show the strength and weaknesses of this approach.

1 Introduction

The evolution of systems to build websites can be viewed in a few steps. In the first step, web servers were very simple and followed a simple client/server model. In the second step, more complex operations were done by spawning an external process for every request, and the connection between this external process and the web server was standardized. The third step was to enable generic components inside the web server itself. The fourth step was making use of this generic component to forward requests to an external application server. The next section describes those steps in more depth and will give some drawbacks of the current existing application servers. We propose some new features which would make server side development easier and more productive.

1.1 Evolution to Web Application Servers

During the first days when the Internet, and especially the web, became mainstream, web servers were seen as a new and simple kind of servers, just like mail servers and

A. Persson and J. Stirna (Eds.): CAiSE 2004, LNCS 3084, pp. 307–321, 2004.

ftp servers. These systems did not need a lot of customization, the only thing they needed to do was deliver files to a client, which then rendered it to show it in a browser. The development environment for websites was therefore quit simple; a text editor to create HTML files and an ftp server to put those files on the server where the web server resided.

After a while, people needed ways to create more dynamic page, for example to place the current time on a page. At first this was done by changing the web server itself, but soon after that a standardized way to create dynamic pages was invented; CGI-BIN, which stands for Common Gateway Interface. For every request for a dynamic page, the web server just starts up a new process on the server. The web server returned the output of this process to the client.

This idea has a drawback; for every dynamic request the web server has to spawn a process, which takes a lot of CPU power. A better way is to add a component inside the web server itself, which is running al the time. There is no generic name for this, in the Apache web server it is called a module, in Microsoft IIS an 'ISAPI' (Internet Server API) and in the Netscape web server it is called NSAPI (NetScape API). Developers can create a module (most of the time written in C or C++, using common development environments) that will run inside the web server process.

The disadvantage of this approach was that when the module crashed, the whole web server crashed. To solve this problem, a new architecture was invented. In this architecture, most of the dynamic web application logic is placed in a separate process, and a small module inside the web server acts as a proxy and forwards any (dynamic) requests to the other process. This has several advantages; the process is more loosely coupled with the web server, and can be implemented several times, to spread the load. Such an application is called an application server, a separate process from the web server. Developers that want to enhance the web server create an application inside those application servers. Common characteristics of these environments are:

- Used for dynamic website
- Tools for deployment, security, session managers are included
- Tools for performance, like automated load balancing and persistent session are part of the environment
- The main purpose is generating ASCII/Unicode, most of the time HTML of XML
- The target for an application server is a web browser or any other HTTP compliant client
- Build for usage in HTTP sessions

The two most popular and competing application server standards are .NET and J2EE. During the last five years both application server standards evolved a lot. Important components in these application servers are:

- Code is running inside a virtual machine. This virtual machine is called a Common Language Runtime in .NET and the Java Virtual Machine in Java.
- A template engine to generate HTML or XML easily, and a visual environment to generate web pages on a higher level (Java Server Pages and Java Server Faces in Java, ASP.NET and Web Forms in .NET).
- A persistent layer which makes the translation between relational databases and the objects in the application environment itself (Enterprise Java Beans in J2EE, not yet standardized in .NET).

These kind of application server also has a lot of tools and libraries to help the developer, for example to parse XML, transaction management tools, mail libraries, tools to send and retrieve messages and build message queues and libraries to send Internet e-mail. See the references for URL's that give a broader overview of these technologies [1][2].

1.2 Drawbacks of Current Web Application Servers

Server-side application servers are powerful. Despite that power, based on the experience of building commercial websites we built during the last 5 years some drawbacks of these application servers became apparent. All drawbacks have immediate impact on development productivity. We have identified the following four drawbacks:

1. *Lack of transparent persistency.* The environment is object oriented, yet objects created inside a virtual machine are never persistent, which means that every object has to be created again when restarting the virtual machine. The problem with this is that the developer has to come up with his own persistence engine to store the objects. Ideally, the developer should not be doing anything to gain persistency, and the underlying virtual machine takes care of the persistence of objects. Such a persistency is also called orthogonal persistency [9]. For larger data-objects some facilities exists, like Enterprise JavaBeans in J2EE, but they are never transparent and a developer has to do lot of administrative work to take care of the persistence, like creating the right configuration files in XML or keeping in mind some of the constraints of the custom persistence layer.

2. *Minimal redeployment is not a design goal.* When a change has to be made in a system, a redeployment of the application inside the application server is needed, which means that the application is not reachable for a short time. This also means that the code-run-test-debug cycle of a developer is taking a lot of time. Changing anything at runtime is hard and gives a lot of complications. An application server should have as a design goal minimization of redeployments, so a developer can focus on solving problems, not on redeployments.

3. *No testing during deployment.* Although you can set up a staging environment to test new code, it is never really possible to simulate the real environment, with thousands of visitors and all kinds of connections with backend systems. The proof is in the pudding with high-traffic websites. Current application servers do not support debugging, testing and changing code at runtime very well, not only because of the application server itself, but also because the underlying language and virtual machine does not support it.

4. *Separated development and runtime environment.* The development environment itself is a separate application, almost always client based. The runtime environment and the development environment are strictly separated. While this can be a good thing, during testing it is very easy for developers to work inside the runtime environment to see the effect of changes immediately. By separating the environments, for every change in the source code a redeployment of the compiled code is needed, which can take a lot of time. To compensate for this, several of the J2EE and .NET development environments like Eclipse and Visual Studio .NET include

an application server or servlet engine, making it possible to test the application in much the same way that one uses a traditional development environment for C++ or Java programs. But even so, these are still two separate environments.

While the current server-side application server systems are very useful and used a lot in commercial and non-commercial environments, we state that they miss three essential features, which makes developing in a web environment much more productive:

1. A runtime environment that takes care of the persistence of objects in the system, completely transparent for the developer
2. The possibility to change everything on runtime, even object type definitions and source code.
3. The development environment is completely web based, which means everything can be done using a web browser.

Such a system can be called a Web-based Runtime and Development Environment (WRDE).

1.3   Related Work in Web Application Engineering

Given the current emerging role of web applications in e-commerce worldwide, there is an abundance of research activity going on in this area. Among others, two main streams can be identified that are relevant to our work: web-service oriented computing, and design of web applications. Based on the W3C and OASIS standardization of web-service technology (e.g. UDDI, WSDL, SOAP, ebXML, WSRP) numerous approaches have been proposed for the composition of complex business applications based on generated or created web-services (see for example Papazoglou, 2003 [13], and Fraterneli, 1999 [14]). Goal oriented design of web applications was suggested in (Liu, 2002 [16]), where a variant of Use Case Maps were combined with a Goal-oriented Requirements Language to model the scenarios of interaction with a web application. In (Garcia, 2002 [17]) an agent based architecture for an e-commerce site was presented to facilitate intermediary operation in complex inter-enterprise business transactions. A powerful modeling language for web sites, called WebML, has been developed by the group of Ceri and Fraternali of the Politecnico di Milano. The accompanying WebRatio case tool enables specifying and generating complete web applications (Ceri, 2002 [15]).

1.4   Overview of the Paper

In the following chapter we will explain the SiteWorks system, in which all of the above characteristics are realized. After explaining the actual implementation of such a system, we will go more deeply into the three characteristic features in chapter 3. In chapter 4 we will give examples of usages of this system in a real world environment. Chapter 5 will give a conclusion and further research possibilities.

2   SiteWorks

2.1   Explanation and Infrastructure of SiteWorks

SiteWorks is built on top of the J2EE architecture, but is itself a virtual machine in which applications are running. It needs an external relational database to store its data in. See figure 1 for the infrastructure SiteWorks needs to get it running.

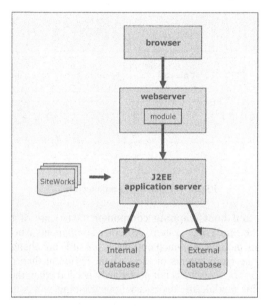

Fig. 1. The SiteWorks infrastructure

The browser is always the interface for the user of the system. When a user requests a page, the browser makes a request to the web server. The web server checks if the page asked for is a special page. If so, the request is forwarded to a module inside the web server (depending on the type of web server, it is called ISAPI, NSAPI or module). This module is very lightweight and simple forwards the request to a separate servlet engine. Servlets are a part of the J2EE specification, and as such, the servlet engine is a part of a J2EE compliant application server. The servlet engine is running inside a Java Virtual Machine and is waiting for requests.

The servlet engine is an application server, and SiteWorks is one of the applications running inside the server. To store internal data, SiteWorks uses an internal database, which can be a SQL 92 compliant relational database. SiteWorks can also connect to other databases to integrate that data in the web solution. SiteWorks also depends on a few third party libraries like JDBC database drivers or XML parsers.

2.2   SiteWorks Internal Architecture

See figure 2 for the SiteWorks architecture. SiteWorks consists of the following components:

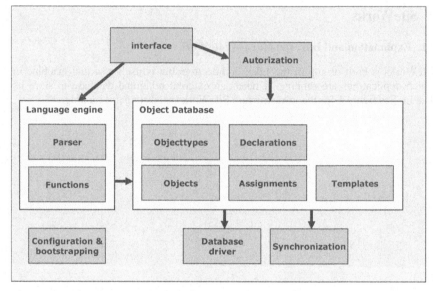

Fig. 2. The SiteWorks architecture

The **configuration and bootstrapping component** takes care of the configuration needed to boot up the SiteWorks system. All other components can retrieve configuration items from this module. As much options as possible are changeable at runtime, as that was one of the requirements of the system. Different than regular J2EE and .NET application servers, a restart is not necessarily needed when the configuration is changed. Also, in this module the necessary bootstrapping procedures are executed. As configuration is partly stored in objects which are not retrieved yet, this is a crucial part.

SiteWorks has a **generic interface** that has two functions; it is a standardized web based user interface for developers (see figure 3) and it is a controller for incoming request. In the user interface for the developer he or she can browse and change the object type definitions, the object population, templates, connections with the database(s), configuration options, user and groups, permissions and maintenance options. All user interface interaction is based on web technology. Developers use a web browser to access and change the system. This interface is also available on live, deployed environments. The controller functionality takes care of incoming requests, for example by checking authorization levels in the authorization module and forwarding the request to the parser.

The **authorization layer** in the SiteWorks system has 3 concepts for authorization and security: users, groups and permissions. Users can be in one or more groups. Groups have permissions. Depending on these permissions users in a group can change or browse through certain object types and have access right to the development environment. The users and groups can also be used when making new web applications with SiteWorks, as users and groups are objects itself, and can be manipulated as any other object.

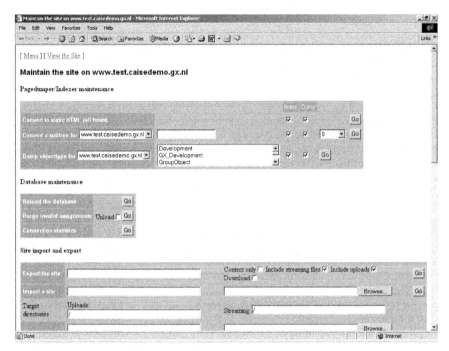

Fig. 3. The SiteWorks user interface

The **object database** is the core of SiteWorks. Five main entities represent this core:

- Object Types are the equivalent of classes in object oriented languages. They have a unique name as an identifier, and have 1 or more declarations.
- Declarations are the attributes of an object type. The combination object type with the name of a declaration is unique. A declaration has at least a name, a type and a constraint (1, 1 or more, uniqueness etc).
- Objects are instances of an object type. Objects are identified by a unique number.
- Assignments always belong to an object and are the filled-in declarations of the object type it belongs to. The combination of object, declaration and order number makes them unique.
- Templates are presentation and logical templates to present and manipulate the objects. A template always has a name. The combination of the template with an object type is unique, therefore the name of the template needs to be unique for all templates of that object type.

For example, in SiteWorks you can create (by configuring) an Object Type 'page' with a declaration title and another declaration paragraph. After creating it, you can create instances of this object type, which contain the actual title and text of that page itself. Next to it you can create templates, for example a 'show' template to present the page to visitors, and an 'edit' template to change the page.

Persistence and storage of the object database in the relational database is done automatically and transparent for the developer. The five entities can be introspected, changed, created and deleted on runtime, using the web interface.

The **script engine** consists of two parts; a parser and a library. The parser parses the templates belonging to the object types and executes it. The language used is arbitrary; in SiteWorks a custom language is used. In theory, it is possible to use almost any object oriented language or object oriented capable language, especially scripting languages, as they need to be executed and compiled on runtime. The language needs to be object oriented, because the language needs to be able to manipulate the object database. A good example of such a language would be JavaScript. The library contains all kinds of functions available for the developer, for example file manipulation or external database access.

To store the data from the object database and to access other databases, SiteWorks has a **database connectivity** layer, which makes it possible to use different kind of relational databases. This module is used by the object database for storage of the objects, and by the library for external database access. The database connectivity layer also contains functionality like connection pooling. The configuration of the database connection can be changed on runtime. For performance reasons, all data of the object database is cached in memory, and only when changing objects or object types, data is written to the database. This also means that access to the internal database for other applications is prohibited, as there is no way to know for SiteWorks when the database is changed.

Web applications need to be able to scale. As the amount of visitors to a website is hardly predictable, it is a necessity that a SiteWorks engine, including SiteWorks applications, can be installed multiple times, to spread the load and create redundancy. This poses a problem, because when the SiteWorks engines all need to do the same, they need access to the same objects. Every object is loaded in the memory of the various SiteWorks engines, and therefore exists multiple times. The **synchronization module** solves this problem by interconnecting the SiteWorks engines. When an object is changed, the change is stored in the internal database. Then, the SiteWorks engine that changed the object give the other SiteWorks engines a signal that an object has been changed. The other SiteWorks engines then retrieve the new data of the object from the internal database. To make use of this functionality, it is a requirement that all SiteWorks engines use the same internal database. This is similar to other approaches (Koch, 1990 [3]).

2.3 Application Engineering

There are two ways for a developer to use SiteWorks as a development environment; the first option is to install a J2EE environment on the local machine and deploy the SiteWorks applications in it. SiteWorks needs a database, which needs to be installed locally or centralized. The advantage of this solution is that developers work in their own environment. Templates and other objects inside the system are automatically synchronized with files on the hard disk, which makes it possible to use configuration management tools, text editors and the browser interface next to each other. The second option is to set up a centralized installation. All developers use their browser to make changes in the system. Because everyone works on the same code base, this is very fast way of working. However it can lead to unexpected and confusing errors, for when one developer introduces a bug, all other developers may run into it, or worse, will notice it immediately. The last scenario is best used when the development team is very small, and is not used very much at <GX>.

When the application built in SiteWorks is deployed, and changes need to be introduced, there is a three-way approach. Developers work locally on the source code base, making changes and committing the changes to the configuration management tool. When done, the changes are deployed on a test and acceptation server. Customers and end-users can test and accept the changes on this server. When they accept it, the changes are deployed on the live server, where they are tested once again. When changes in the SiteWorks system itself are made, the J2EE environment needs to be restarted. Applications inside SiteWorks can almost always be deployed without restarting, further reducing downtime of the live environment.

3   Implementing the WRDE

In section 1.2, we proposed that incorporating the WRDE concept in application servers would make developers much more productive. SiteWorks is a prototype of a system that uses these ideas. It's important to note that these design goals were a few of many design goals for SiteWorks. SiteWorks gives us a very good idea of the power of an application server using the WRDE concepts. The next paragraphs evaluate the WRDE concepts in SiteWorks.

3.1   Persistent Runtime

The main characteristic of the SiteWorks system is the built in transparent persistency. Persistency is not unique to SiteWorks. During the past few years numerous attempts are made to introduce persistence in the J2EE, .NET and other development and runtime environments (see reference for URL's with persistency tools for Java [4]). These attempts can be divided in two categories; the first is to create object-relational mappings and the second is to introduce transparent persistency.

Almost all persistence tools are based on object-relational mapping paradigm. When using those tools, a relational database and objects in the virtual machine are mapped to each other. When a change in an object is made, it is stored in the database, and the other way around, a change in the database implies a change in the corresponding objects. However, a problem is that object orientation and relational model are different paradigms, which do not fit at all times. Also, a lot of configuration or code generation is necessary to implement those mappings, which hamper development progress (Hou, 2002. A performance improvement by using caching is almost always a problem as a relational database can be changed without notice for the virtual machine. The objects inside the virtual machine need a signal to know they are stale, which isn't something a relational database provides, although research for it has been done (Machani, 1996 [5]).

The transparent persistency approach is not to think in terms of a relational database, but just to take care of the storage of the objects somewhere, not necessarily in a relational database. Prevayler ([6]) is an open source persistency handler that uses this approach, without a database. Developers can define normal classes and create normal objects in Java, storage is handled by the Prevayler engine. When the Java Virtual Machine is restarted, the Prevayler engine reloads all the previous created objects. Because no connection with an external database and SQL manipulation is needed, the performance can be very fast. All objects need to be kept in memory though, which can create scalability problems for very large datasets.

SiteWorks is also using the second approach, but instead of building a persistent framework on top of the virtual machine, it implements the persistence inside the SiteWorks virtual machine.

This transparent persistency inside the SiteWorks engine itself is also known as orthogonal persistency, which cannot only be used in virtual machines, but also in operating systems (Dearle, 1994 [7]). A system like this is called a Persistent Object System or, when the system is more aimed at purely storing objects, a Persistent Object Store (Brown, 1988 [8]).

Attempts are made to do this in the Java Virtual Machine (Atkinson, 1996 [9]and 1998 [10]), but the Java Virtual Machine is not designed for such an environment. Java is a strongly typed compiled language. When changing a class, instances of this class need to change accordingly, but those instances are not available until the virtual machine is started. This causes a lot of problems to keep the object population compatible with the classes.

SiteWorks takes a different approach. Object type definitions can only be changed when the virtual machine itself is running. When an object type is changed, the objects belonging to this object type are changed accordingly and immediately. The developer will immediately see what the consequences are. Furthermore, as every change is atomic to the system, SiteWorks can change the instances belonging to the changed object type following strict defined rules, known by the developer. Because of the strict separation of the development and runtime environment for languages in Java and .NET, this is very hard to do in these languages. A developer can change all classes at once, which creates migration problems for the object population.

The main advantage of the transparent persistency in SiteWorks is the productivity gain for developers. They do not have to think about object persistence and can focus on the business problem, not on infrastructural problems like storage.

3.2   Development in a Runtime Environment

The second characteristic of the SiteWorks system is that development takes place inside the running Virtual Machine. Almost all popular languages have a strict separation between the development environment and the runtime environment. In Site-Works, the developer can change templates, object types and objects while the engine is running. This approach makes it much easier to change object types, because the underlying engine can change instances of the object type immediately. Templates can be changed while a system is running, without the need to restart. By using the SiteWorks environment, the object population can be introspected and changed. This is especially useful when debugging, either in a test environment or on a deployed SiteWorks system.

A similar approach is tried with the Java Virtual Machine. Using classloaders and a special debug mode, it is possible to change classes ([11]) in a running Java Virtual Machine. When a class is replaced, problems occur when instances of the class already exist and the new class has new or changed field declarations. Also, non-literal field declarations that point to other classes can be a problem. Because a developer can change the whole class at once, the virtual machine will have to create a migration strategy for the 'old' objects. SiteWorks was designed from the ground up with these requirements in mind. As was said in paragraph 3.1, because the developer changes object types in the running environment one at the time, the changes are atomic, and the behavior of the system when making such a change can be strictly defined.

Advantages of this approach are the immediate visible effect of changes in templates, object types and objects, direct manipulation possible of the core entities and less restarting of the SiteWorks system necessary.

3.3 Web-Based Development

The third characteristic of SiteWorks is a fully web enabled user interface. This has two advantages. First, during development, a web browser is all that a developer needs, access to the development environment is very easy and can be done from almost any workstation with an Internet connection. This makes the development cycle a lot more efficient. When the system is deployed, developers can inspect and change the system using a web browser. Secondly, a clean separation between developers and system engineers is achieved. System engineers set up the system, engineers work on the application itself.

Admittedly, it does have some disadvantages too; because source code is centralized, configuration management tools can not be used as almost all of them are file based. Configuration and version management needs to be implemented in the system itself. Alternatively, developers may run a SiteWorks system locally. However, the advantage of separation of system engineering and development is then lost, the developer needs to know how to set up a SiteWorks system.

4 Usage of the WRDE

4.1 WebManager

The most prominent application built in SiteWorks is the content management and portal software WebManager. See figure 4 for screenshots.

In the left screenshot, the editor environment of WebManager is shown. Editors can manipulate content, layout and structure of the website, place functionalities on web pages etc. The left screenshot shows the resulting page. During the last 5 years about 100 WebManager installations are deployed, for large commercial companies like Planet Internet (largest Dutch ISP), Ajax, Mercedes and KPN (see appendix for the site addresses). It is also used by several Netherlands municipalities to implement their e-government initiative. WebManager itself consists of several components, like content management, interaction management, connectivity management and workflow (see figure 5). They are built in SiteWorks, but have several hooks to Java and other environments, to accommodate and leverage those platforms.

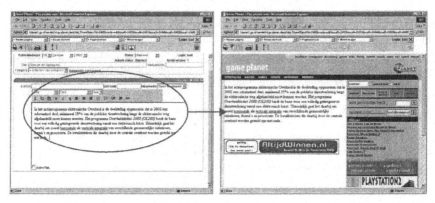

Fig. 4. A web application (right) engineered with WebManager (left)

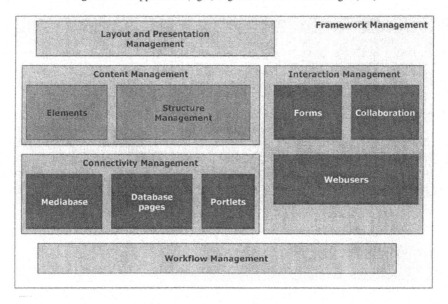

Fig. 5. The WebManager architecture

4.2 Support System & Systems Maintenance Manager

Using SiteWorks, a support system has been built for our support department at
<GX>. With it, our support engineers can administrate problem reports, so called
tickets, with accompanying knowledge and actions. Customers can log in on our
extranet and can see the outstanding tickets, and the status they have. The system
makes extensive use of the build in authorization module, and stores all data in Site-
Works objects. Because the developers do not need to care about the storage, we can
adapt the system very fast, for example to give customers more options.

SiteWorks is also used for maintaining our installed base. This system keeps track of which version of WebManager runs where, what logins are, what customer logins and passwords are, how to get to the installed system. It also has connections with the support system, which is running in a separate SiteWorks installation. Because the system is web based, everyone can access the information very easily. This system also makes use of the build in authorization module, to prevent employees from viewing sensitive data.

5 Conclusions and Further Research

In this paper we stated that by letting developers using a WRDE, major productivity gains can be achieved. Evidence from various websites deployments supports this claim, especially with regard to the functionality and speed of development. The WRDE SiteWorks provides an important step forward in current web application engineering tools with transparent persistency handling, development in a runtime environment, and web based development tools. Customer reports and extremely high-availability rates of major sites in the Netherlands support the innovative directions in web technology.

We admit that we in the current stage we can only support the productivity gains in a qualitative manner. Therefore, further research is necessary to support this with more quantitative analysis, for example, by letting two development teams built the same functional application on different application server frameworks. Also, a serious challenge emerges when two populations of objects need to be merged (for example a development environment and a deployment environment). Object types and templates have a unique name and are merged accordingly. This is much harder for nameless objects.

We are currently working on several improvement of the SiteWorks system. For example, the development environment is now separate from the template system. Ideally, the development environment is built using those templates. The same can be done for the function library, as many functions inside the library can be accomplished using templates and special objects. These changes in the system could give a clearer and pure view of what exactly a WRDE is.

In the nearby future we hope to report on our current research program.

Acknowledgements

The authors wish to thank Arnoud Verdwaald and Mark Machielsen of <GX>, and their colleagues at Utrecht University, The Netherlands for their contributions and feedback on the SiteWorks system and on earlier versions of this paper.

References

1. An overview of the J2EE architecture: http://java.sun.com/j2ee/overview3.html
2. An overview of the .NET architecture:
   http://msdn.microsoft.com/netframework/technologyinfo/overview/default.aspx
3. Bett Koch, Tracy Schunke, Alan Dearle, Francis Vaughan, Chris Marlin, Ruth Fazakerley, Chris Barter (1990), Cache coherency and storage management in a persistent object system. Proceedings of the Fourth International Workshop on Persistent Object Systems, pages 99--109, Martha's Vineyard, MA (USA)
4. Overviews of Object Relational mapping and persistency tools available for Java. http://c2.com/cgi/wiki?ObjectRelationalToolComparison and http://www.cetus-links.org/oo_db_java.html
5. Salah-Eddine Machani (1996). Events in an Active Object-Relational Database System http://www.masi.uvsq.fr/rapports/1996/
6. Prevayler, a fast, transparent persistence, fault tolerant and load balancing architecture for Java objects. http://www.prevayler.org/
7. Alan Dearle, Rex di Bona, James Farrow, Frans Henskens, Anders Lindstrom, John Rosenberg, Francis Vaughan (1994). Grasshopper: An Orthogonally Persistent Operating System, Computing Systems volume 7, number 3, 289-312
8. A.L. Brown (1988). Persistent Object Stores, Ph.D thesis, University of St. Andrews, http://www-fide.dcs.stand. ac.uk/Info/Papers4.html#thesis
9. M.P. Atkinson, L. Daynès, M.J. Jordan, T. Printezis, S. Spence (dec 1996). An Orthogonally Persistent Java, ACM SIGMOD Record, 25, 4, pp68-75.
10. Malcolm Atkinson, Mick Jordan (1998), Providing Orthogonal Persistence for Java, Lecture Notes in Computer Science, volume 1445, page 383
11. Hotswap options in the Java Platform Debugger Architecture: http://java.sun.com/j2se/1.4.1/docs/guide/jpda/enhancements.html#hotswap
12. Daqing Hou, H. James Hoover, Eleni Stroulia (may 2002). Supporting the Deployment of Object-Oriented Frameworks, Proceedings of the 14th International Conference CaiSE 2002, LNCS 2348, Springer Verlag, page 151-166
13. Mike P. Papazoglou (2003), Web Services and Business Transactions. World Wide Web vol. 6, nr. 1, pp. 49-91.
14. P. Fraterneli (1999), Tools and approaches for developing data-intensive web applications: a survey, ACM Computing Surveys, vol. 31, nr. 3, pp. 227 – 263.
15. Stefano Ceri, Piero Fraternali, Aldo Bongio, Marco Brambilla, Sara Comai, Maristella Matera (2002), Designing Data-Intensive Web Applications. Morgan Kaufmann
16. L. Liu, E. Yu, Designing Web-Based Systems in Social Context: A Goal and Scenario Based Approach, 14th International Conference on Advanced Information Systems Engineering (CAiSE'02), Toronto, May 27-31, 2002. LNCS 2348 Springer Verlag. pp. 37-51.
17. F.J. Garcia, A.B. Gil, N. Moreno, B. Curto (2002), A web-based e-commerce facilitator intermediary for small and medium enterprises: a b2b/b2c hybrid proposal. In: Proceedings of the 3rd Int. Conf. EC-Web 2002. LNCS 2455, Springer Verlag.

Appendix – Websites Running on the SiteWorks System

- Ajax – A consumer oriented fan site of the famous Dutch football club: http://www.ajax.nl/
- KPN Breedbandportal – A consumer broadband site commercialized by KPN: http://breedbandportal.kpn.com/

- Planet Technologies – The web portal of the largest ISP in the Netherlands: http://www.planet.nl/
- Daimler Chrysler Nederland – Consumer oriented website for their main brand Mercedes: http://www.mercedes-benz.nl/
- Gemeente Maastricht – Municipality Maastricht website: http://www.maastricht.nl/
- Gemeenten Vlissingen – Municipalities Vlissingen website: http://www.vlissingen.nl/
- Unicef Nederland – Consumer site for Unicef the Netherlands: http://www.unicef.nl/

Enabling Personalized Composition
and Adaptive Provisioning of Web Services

Quan Z. Sheng[1], Boualem Benatallah[1], Zakaria Maamar[2],
Marlon Dumas[3], and Anne H.H. Ngu[4]

[1] School of Computer Science and Engineering
The University of New South Wales, Sydney, Australia
[2] College of Information Systems
Zayed University, Dubai, U.A.E
[3] Centre for Information Technology Innovation
Queensland University of Technology, Brisbane, Australia
[4] Department of Computer Science
Texas State University, San Marcos, Texas, USA

Abstract. The proliferation of interconnected computing devices is fostering the emergence of environments where Web services made available to mobile users are a commodity. Unfortunately, inherent limitations of mobile devices still hinder the seamless access to Web services, and their use in supporting complex user activities. In this paper, we describe the design and implementation of a distributed, adaptive, and context-aware framework for personalized service composition and provisioning adapted to mobile users. Users specify their preferences by annotating existing process templates, leading to personalized service-based processes. To cater for the possibility of low bandwidth communication channels and frequent disconnections, an execution model is proposed whereby the responsibility of orchestrating personalized processes is spread across the participating services and user agents. In addition, the execution model is adaptive in the sense that the runtime environment is able to detect exceptions and react to them according to a set of rules.

1 Introduction

Web services are self-describing, open components that support programmatic access to Web accessible data sources and applications. Web services are also poised to become accessible from mobile devices [1], as the proliferation of such devices (e.g., laptops, PDAs, 3G mobile phones) and the deployment of more sophisticated wireless communication infrastructures (e.g., GPRS and UMTS), are empowering the Web with the ability to deliver data and functionality to mobile users. For example, business travelers now expect to be able to access their corporate servers, enterprise portals, e-mail, and other collaboration services while on the move.

However, several obstacles still hinder the seamless provisioning of Web services in wireless environments. Indeed, current Web service provisioning tech-

A. Persson and J. Stirna (Eds.): CAiSE 2004, LNCS 3084, pp. 322–337, 2004.

niques are inappropriate because of the distinguishing features and inherent limitations of wireless environments such as low throughput and poor connectivity of wireless networks, limited computing resources, and frequent disconnections of mobile devices. In addition, the variability in computing resources, display terminal, and communication channel require intelligent support for personalized and timely delivery of relevant data to users [2]. Examples of issues that need to be addressed in order to make the service-oriented computing paradigm of real benefit to mobile users include:

- **Personalized composition of services.** Like their non-mobile counterparts (i.e., stationary users), mobile users also require an integrated access to relevant services. Indeed, the provision of Web services for mobile users tends to be *time* and *location* sensitive, meaning that the mobile users might need to invoke particular services in a certain period and/or a certain place. For example, a student will need the class assistant service only when she is attending a class. Service selection, composition, and orchestration should take in consideration the context of the service provisioning environment (e.g., CPU, bandwidth, state of the user) and the user preferences.
- **Limited resources and wide heterogeneity of mobile devices.** Mobile devices normally posses limited battery power and input capabilities. Therefore, mobile devices are better suited as *passive listeners* (e.g., receiving the service results) than as active tools for service invocation (e.g., searching for the service and sending the request) [3]. Furthermore, the provisioning of services should consider the location of the user. The Web services near her current location should be selected or only the highly customized content should be delivered (e.g., the closest restaurant).
- **Robust service execution.** Numerous situations could prevent a smooth execution of Web services in wireless environments. Indeed, obstacles can range from the dynamic nature of the Web services such as changes of Quality of Service (QoS) to the characteristics of mobile devices like frequent disconnections. We believe that services should be *self-managed* to support their adaptive execution over the Internet. To facilitate the robust execution of services, it is necessary to provide the capabilities for detecting the exceptions at run-time so that appropriate actions can be promptly taken.

The aforementioned challenges call for novel approaches to support dynamic and adaptive Web service provisioning in wireless environments. As a contribution toward this aim, this paper presents the design and implementation of *PCAP*: a framework for **P**ersonalized **C**omposition and **A**daptive **P**rovisioning of Web services. This framework provides a distributed, adaptive, and context-aware infrastructure for personalized composite service provisioning, which takes into account the needs of mobile users. The salient features of PCAP are:

- A personalized composite service specification infrastructure. Using this infrastructure, users specify their needs by reusing and adjusting existing process templates, rather than building their own services from scratch. Users locate process templates and annotate them with contextual information (e.g., execution time/place), thereby defining *personal composite services.*

- A self-managed and adaptive service orchestration model. Participating services and a user agent, a component that acts on behalf of the user, collaborate with each other for the smooth execution of the personalized composite services and interact with the user when and where she decides to do so, achieving the goal of "performing the right task at the right time and at the right place". The knowledge that the participating services and the user agent require is generated based on the context information, the data/control dependencies, and the user preferences. The model is complemented by the fact that user agents and services are able to adapt to runtime exceptions (e.g., service failures) according to exception handling rules.

Section 2 presents the personalized composite service model. Section 3 describes an orchestration model for the distributed execution of personalized composite services, as well as the dynamic exception handling. The PCAP system architecture and its implementation are described in Section 4. Finally, Section 5 provides some concluding remarks.

2   Definition of Personal Composite Services

In this section, we first introduce the modeling of process templates and then describe the configuration of personal composite services.

2.1   Process Templates

Process templates are reusable business process skeletons that are devised to reach particular goals. For example, a class assistant template enables students to manage their class activities by composing multiple services like question posting and consultation booking. We specify process templates with statecharts [4]. It should be noted that the process templates developed in the context of statecharts can be adapted to other process definition languages such as BPEL4WS.

A statechart is made up of states and transitions. The transitions of a statechart are labeled with events, conditions, and assignment operations over process variables. States can be *basic* or *compound*. A basic state (also called *task* in the rest of the paper) corresponds to the execution of a service (which we call a *component service*) or of a member in a *Web service community*. A service community is a collection of Web services with a common functionality but different non-functional properties such as different providers and different QoS parameters. When a community receives a request to execute an operation, the request is delegated to one of its current members based on a selection strategy [5]. Compound states contain one or several statecharts within them. An example will be given in Section 2.3.

In process templates, a task t has a set of input and output parameters. We denote the input (resp., output) as Θ_i (resp., Θ_o) where $\Theta_i(t) = \{i_1, i_2, \ldots, i_m\}$

and $\Theta_o(t) = \{o_1, o_2, \ldots, o_k\}$. The value of a task's input parameter may be:
i) requested from user during task execution, ii) obtained from the user's profile,
or iii) obtained as an output of another task. For the first case the following
expression is used: i_j:=USER. For the other cases, they are expressed as queries:
i_j:=Q_j. Queries vary from simple to complex, depending on the application
domain and users' needs, and can be expressed using languages like XPath.

In our approach, values that users supply as input parameters are handled
differently from the values obtained from user profiles. Indeed, because mobile
devices are resource-constrained, values that can be obtained from user profiles
should not be requested from users. However, in a process template specification,
the template provider only indicates for which input parameters users have to
supply a value. It is the responsibility of the user to specify, during the configuration phase, if the value will be provided manually or derived from her profile.

Similarly, the value of a task's output parameter may be: i) sent to other
tasks as input parameters, and/or ii) sent to a user in case she wants to know
the execution result of the task. Symbol $\rightsquigarrow$ is used to denote the delivery of
output parameters. For instance, $o_j \rightsquigarrow \{$USER$\}$ means the value of o_j should be
sent to the user. Note that the value of an output parameter can be submitted to
multiple places (e.g., to a task and the user as well). Similar to input parameters,
the provider of a process template does not decide which output parameters need
to be returned.

2.2 Configuration of Personal Composite Services

Personalization implies making adjustment according to user preferences. Three
kinds of user preferences are associated for each process template's task:

- *execution constraints* are divided into *temporal* and *spatial* constraints, which
  respectively indicate *when* and *where* the user wants to see a task executed,
- *data supply and delivery preferences* are related to supplying values to the
  input parameters and delivering values of output parameters of the task, and
- *execution policies* are related to the preferences on service selection (for communities) and service migration during the execution of a task.

Temporal and Spatial Constraints. We denote the temporal and spatial
constraints of a task t as $\Theta_t(t)$ and $\Theta_s(t)$ respectively. Formally, a temporal
constraint is specified as TMP(op, tm), where op is a comparison operator (e.g.,
$=$, $\leq$, and between) and tm is either an absolute time, a relative time (e.g.,
termination time of a task), or a time interval in the form of [tm_1, tm_2]. TMP(op,
tm) means that the task can be triggered only if the condition ct op tm is
evaluated to true. Here, ct denotes the system time. For the sake of simplicity,
we assume that all temporal values are expressed at the same level of granularity.

Similarly, Θ_s is a spatial constraint specified as SPL(1), meaning that the task
can be fired only when the condition cl IS l is evaluated to true. cl denotes the
current location of the user, and l is a physical location. A location l_1 is
considered the same as another location l_2 if the distance between two points of

l_1 and l_2 does not exceed a certain value. We assume that all spatial values are expressed at the same level of granularity.

It should be noted that the temporal (resp., spatial) constraint can be empty, meaning that the corresponding task can be executed at anytime (resp., at anywhere). We also assume that the user's (mobile device) location is collected periodically by our system. In fact, with the advances in positioning technologies such as assisted-GPS (A-GPS) [6], we believe that obtaining mobile users location does not represent an issue anymore.

Data Supply and Delivery Preferences. As stated before, the values of some input parameters of a task can be obtained from a user's profile. The user proceeds in two steps: i) identify which input parameter values can be derived from her profile, and ii) supply the location of the profile and the corresponding attribute names. Similarly, for the output parameters of a task, a user may specify which parameter values need to be delivered to her.

Execution Policies. The execution policies include the *service selection policy* and the *service migration policy*. For a specific task, users can specify how to select a service for this task. The service can be a fixed one (the task always uses this service), or can be selected from a specific service community or a public directory (e.g., UDDI) based on certain criteria (e.g., location of the mobile user). Furthermore, users can specify whether to migrate the services to their mobile devices (e.g., if mobile devices have enough computing resources) or to the sites near the users current location for the execution. Our works on service selection and migration are described elsewhere [7, 8].

2.3 An Example

The example introduced here is inspired by two recent ubiquitous computing applications: UIUC's Gaia [9] and, to a greater extent, UCSD's ActiveClass [10]. ActiveClass is a novel computing application for enhancing participation of students and professors in the classrooms via wireless mobile devices such as PDAs. ActiveClass provides several distinct features including: i) students are encouraged to ask questions anonymously without exposing themselves to the class, thereby avoiding the problems associated with the traditional practice of *raise-hand-up* asking where those students who are diffident are unlikely to ask any questions; ii) professors are able to choose the questions which are worth to be answered; and iii) students can vote the questions asked by other students, which helps the professors to identify the questions of most concern.

Figure 1 is the statechart of a simplified `classAssistant` process template that helps students manage their class activities. In this template, an attendance reminder notifies students about the time and place of the lecture. During the lecture, when a student wants to ask a question, she first browses the questions asked by other students using her PDA. Then she decides either to vote for an already posted question (if her question was already asked by someone else) or

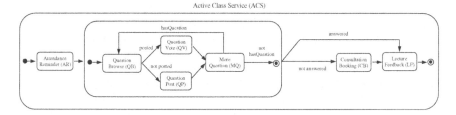

Fig. 1. classAssistant process template

Table 1. Data dependencies of the **classAssistant** process template (see Figure 1)

Task	Input Parameters & dependencies	Output Parameters & dependencies
AR	string subjectID:=doc(PROFILE)/subject1, string studentID:=doc(PROFILE)/studentid, integer remindTime:=USER	string lectureTime↝{USER}, string lecturePlace↝{USER}, string subjectID↝{QB, QV, QP, CB, LF} string studentID↝{CB}, string professor↝{CB}
QB	string subjectID=doc(rcv(QB))/subjectID,	XMLDoc questions↝{USER}
QV	string subjectID=doc(rcv(QV))/subjectID, string questionID:=USER	XMLDoc voteDetails↝{USER}
QP	string subjectID=doc(rcv(QP))/subjectID, string question:=USER	XMLDoc postDetails↝{USER},
MQ	boolean newQuestion:=USER	
CB	Date preferredDate:=USER, string subjectID=doc(rcv(CB))/subjectID, string professor=doc(rcv(CB))/professor string studentID=doc(rcv(CB))/studentID	Date consultationDate, XMLDoc consultationDetails↝{USER}
LF	string subjectID=doc(rcv(LF))/subjectID, string comments:=USER	XMLDoc commentDetails↝{USER}

to post her question (if no one has asked a similar question). The student may ask several questions during the lecture. After the class, a consultation booking is performed if not all of her questions are answered. In both cases, feedback for the lecture is provided by the student.

Now, assume a student, Andrew, is interested in using the **classAssistant** process template. First, Andrew has to personalize this template by indicating his preferences for each task. For instance, because the lecture will be held from 9am to 11am at **Quad01A**, Andrew sets the temporal and spatial constraints of tasks **QB**, **QV**, **QP**, and **MQ** to be **TMP(between, [9:00 01/01/04, 11:00 01/01/04])** and **SPL(Quad01A)** respectively.

Table 1 describes the input and output parameters of the personal composite service. To describe the data supply and delivery preferences, the following additional notations are used:

- **USER** denotes an end user (e.g., a student), while **PROFILE** denotes the XML document where the user's profile is stored,
- **doc(rcv(CB))/professor** is an XPath query and **rcv(CB)** stands for the XML document that includes the outputs of other tasks received by **CB**. Attribute **professor** is extracted using this query.

The values of some input parameters are supplied by the user. For instance, in order to give lecture feedback (task **LF**), Andrew must input his comments (e.g., comments). On the other hand, the value of input parameter subjectID of QB can be derived from the value of output parameter subjectID of AR, which in fact, is also used to provide the values of the same input parameter of other tasks (i.e., QV, QP, CB, and LF). Further, Andrew specifies that the input parameter studentID and subjectID of task AR will be derived from his profile. Andrew also would like to receive the detailed result (e.g., postDetails) of each task. It should be noted that there are six conditions in the statechart transitions. Conditions are modeled as boolean variables, whose values are provided by the user at runtime.

3   Personal Composite Service Orchestration

During the execution of a composite service, the involved component services need to coordinate with each other and with the client device in order to ensure that the business logic of the composite service is enforced. This process is often termed *orchestration*. Existing orchestration models [11, 12] assume that the connection between the central scheduler and the component services is continuously available, and that it has the same characteristics (e.g., bandwidth, reliability) as a connection between two component services. This assumption is not valid in the case of personal composite services, where executions are initiated and followed up by, and specifically for, a given (possibly mobile) client. Accordingly, we advocate that in order to achieve robust and smooth execution of personal composite services in mobile environments, these composite services should be *self-orchestrating*: they should be able to coordinate their actions in an autonomous way, without having to continuously synchronize with the client, which could lead to idle periods and timeouts due to disconnections.

In our approach, *self-orchestration* is achieved by encoding the interactions between services in the form of *control tuples* which are placed in and retrieved from *tuple spaces*. The tuple space model has its origins in the Linda [13] language for distributed programming and is recognized as an attractive model for managing interactions among loosely coupled entities in wireless environments [2]. Tuple spaces have the advantage of providing direct support for *pull-based asynchronous interactions* in which the "sender" (e.g. the client device) and the "receiver" (e.g. a component service) are separated in both space and time. This enables mobile users to disconnect at any time, and re-synchronize with the underlying infrastructure upon reconnection.

3.1   Control Tuples and Compound Transitions

In this section, we define two concepts used in the rest of the paper: *control tuple* and *compound transition*.

Definition 1. *A control tuple is a rule of the form Event-Condition-Action (E[C]A) where:*

- E *is a conjunction of execution events. The conjunction of two events e_1 and e_2 is denoted as $e_1 \wedge e_2$ and the semantics is that if an occurrence of e_1 and an occurrence of e_2 are registered in any order, then an occurrence of $e_1 \wedge e_2$ is generated.*
- C *is a conjunction of conditions on execution states including event parameter values and service information (e.g., inputs and outputs of tasks).*
- A *is a sequence of execution actions $a_1; a_2; \ldots; a_n$. The actions are executed in the order specified by the sequence. Some selected events and actions supported in our approach are given in Table 2.* □

As discussed earlier, a statechart can have compound states and therefore, there can be multiple direct and indirect ways of transitioning from a given basic state to another one. In other words, when exiting a given state, there are a number of transitions that can be taken, some of which are simple (e.g., the transition between QV and MQ in Figure 1) and others are compound (e.g., the transition between MQ and LF). Hence, in order to determine how to route control-flow notifications and data items between basic states, we need to introduce a concept of *compound transition*.

Definition 2. *A compound transition CT is a sequence of transitions tr_1, tr_2, ..., tr_n belonging to a given statechart, such that:*

- *source$(tr_1)^1$ is a basic state,*
- *target(tr_n) is a basic state, and*
- *for all i in [1..n-1], either target(tr_i) is the final state of a region belonging to the compound state source(tr_{i+1}), or source(tr_{i+1}) is the initial state of a region belonging to the compound state target(tr_i).* □

3.2 Service Orchestration Tuples in PCAP

In this section, we present four types of control tuples used to coordinate personal composite service executions in PCAP, namely *precondition tuples*, *postprocessing tuples*, *context awareness tuples*, and *exception handling tuples*.

Precondition and Postprocessing Tuples. Determining when should a given task be activated during the execution of a personal composite service requires answering the following questions: i) what are the *preconditions* for executing this task? and ii) once an execution of this task is completed, which entities (e.g., other tasks or the user agent) need to be notified of this completion? The knowledge needed to determine the moment(s) of activation of a task during an execution of a personal composite service can therefore be captured by two sets: i) a set of *preconditions* to be checked before the task is executed; and ii) a set of so-called *postprocessing actions* capturing which other tasks may need to be notified when the execution of a given task is completed. Below, we provide formal definitions of the concepts of precondition and postprocessing of a task.

---

[1] Here, source(tr) denotes the source state of transition tr, while target(tr) denotes the target state of tr.

Table 2. Selected events and actions supported in PCAP

○ Events and Descriptions
entered(location *l*): the user has entered the location *l*.
disconnected(device *d*): the device *d* has disconnected. For example, the user's mobile device may be switched off or can not be reached in an uncovered area.
unpresentable(serviceResult *r*, **device** *d*): the service result *r* is evaluated to be unpresentable in the user's device *d* due to the limited capabilities of the device.
QoSDegraded(service *s*, **QoS** *q*): the QoS *q* of service *s* has deteriorated. For example, the execution time of the service becomes longer.
○ Actions and Descriptions
notify(task *t*): send a notification of completion to task *t*.
transform(serviceResult *r*, **tranformService** *s*, **device** *d*): transform service result *r* using the transformation service *s* according to the capabilities of the user's device *d*.
informNewLocation(location *newL*, **serviceSet** *SC*): inform the location *newL* of a user to the relevant Web services *SC*.
reassign(service *s*): delegate the invocation of a service to service *s*.

Definition 3. *The precondition of task t of a personal composite service S is a set of control tuples such that:*

- E *is a conjunction of events of the form* ready($\Theta_i(t)$) *and* completed(t') *where t' is a task for which there exists a compound transition CT such that source(CT)=t' and target(CT)=t. The event* completed(t') *is raised when a notification of completion is received from the controller of t'.*
- C *is a conjunction of temporal and spatial constraints of t, $\Theta_t(t)$ and $\Theta_s(t)$. If t does not have any constraint,* C *is interpreted as* true.
- A *is an execution action* execute(t), *which invokes the task t.* □

In Andrew's classAssistant service (see Section 2), the precondition of CB is expressed as: {ready(Θ_i(CB))∧completed(MQ)[TMP($\geq$, 11:10 01/01/04)]execute(CB)}, where Θ_i(CB) is the set of the input parameters of task CB. This tuple indicates that when all the values of input parameters of CB are available and MQ is finished, if current time is later than 11:10 01/01/04, the invocation of CB will start. Note that Andrew did not specify a spatial constraint for CB.

Definition 4. *The postprocessing of t of S is a set of control tuples such that:*

- E *is an event of the form* completed(t). *The event is generated when the execution of task t is completed.*
- *There exists a compound transition CT where source(CT)=t and target(CT)=t'.*
- C *is Cond(CT), which is the conjunction of the conditions labeling transitions of CT (i.e., tr_1, tr_2, ..., tr_n), expressed as $c_1 \wedge c_2 \wedge \cdots \wedge c_n$, where c_i is the condition labeling transition tr_i.*
- A *is a set of actions of the form* notify(t') *and* sendResult(o, r), *where o is an output parameter whose value needs to be delivered to a receiver r, which could be the user or another task of S.* □

In the example, the postprocessing of task QP is: {completed(QP)[true]notify(MQ);sendResult(postDetails, Andrew)}. This tuple indicates that when the execution of QP is completed, task MQ should be notified of this completion and the value of output parameter postDetails should be sent to Andrew.

The concepts of precondition and postprocessing of a task as defined above possess two advantageous features. Firstly, the knowledge (i.e., precondition and postprocessing) of the execution of a task is expressed in the form of tuples, which provide the possibility to store and operate the knowledge using powerful coordination models such as tuple spaces. Life cycle information can be associated with tuples, indicating how long a tuple should be made available in the tuple space. Thus, the potential overhead of tuple space can be avoided because the tuples will be removed automatically when they expire. Secondly, the design of precondition and postprocessing tuples considers both the control flow and data dependencies of the personal composite services. In particular, when the execution of a task is completed, only the output parameters whose values are needed by other entities (e.g., the user or other tasks of the composite services) are dispatched.

Context Awareness Tuples. There are two major pieces of context information relevant for the execution of personal composite services: *current time* and user's *current location*. It is assumed that the current time is known by all the entities participating in execution (i.e., derived from their system clock). The user's location, on the other hand, is only known and maintained by the *user agent*: a component whose role is to facilitate the orchestration of personal composite services on behalf of mobile users. In order to achieve context awareness, and in particular, to take into account the above two pieces of context information, control tuples encoding context awareness rules are placed in the user agent's tuple space at the beginning and during the composite service execution. For example, the following control tuple can be placed in the user agent's tuple space to capture the fact that when the user agent detects that the user enters a given location, this location needs to be communicated to the services participating in a personal composite service execution: entered($newL$)[true]informNewLocation($newL$, SC), where $newL$ is the new location of the mobile user and SC is the set of involved Web services.

Exception Handling Tuples. There are numerous situations that could prevent a smooth execution of a personal composite service. Indeed, obstacles are multiple, ranging from the dynamic nature of the Web to the reduced capabilities of mobile devices. To support adaptive execution of personal composite services over the Internet, services should be *pro-active*: they should be capable of adapting themselves in reaction to run-time exceptions.

We distinguish two levels of exceptions: *user level* and *service level*. The user level exceptions are due to the characteristics of mobile devices (e.g., display size) or changes of the personal composite services launched by users. A mobile device can be disconnected due to discharged battery, alignment of antennas, or lack of coverage area. As a result, service results can not be delivered to the user. Further, a service result may not be able to be displayed on a mobile device because of lack of appropriate facilities (e.g., device cannot display graphics). Other exceptions at the user level are changes of personal composite services. For example, Andrew may want to change his preferences on a specific task (e.g., spatial constraint of QB, QV, and QP) because the lecture room is rescheduled (e.g., the lecture will be held at Quad01C instead of Quad01A).

During a service execution, different exceptions can occur. In particular, the selected Web service that executes a task of a personal composite service may become unavailable because it is overloaded or its respective server is down. The QoS parameters[2] of a service may be changed (e.g., the service provider increased the execution price). For a specific task of a personal composite service, some new Web services with better QoS may become available.

An *exception handling tuple* acts as an instruction to execute actions if specific *exception events* occur and specific conditions hold. Exception events are generated in response to changes of service execution states. Examples of such events are: mobile device disconnection, services failure, and violation of QoS constraints. The following is an example of exception handling tuples:

- arrived(a)∧unpresentable(r,d)[true]transform(r,TS,d), where TS is a transformation service and a is the user agent. Note that the description of transformation services is outside the scope of this paper for space reasons. This rule, specified by the user, indicates that if the result r of a service can not be displayed in the user's current device d, the result will be sent to service TS for adaptation before being forwarded to d.

3.3   Control Tuples Generation

The creation of control tuples of a personal composite service occurs at various stages. First, the process template designer defines control tuples at design time to capture failure handling policies (see Section 3.2) and other behavior which cannot be personalized by the user. The tuples created in this way are injected into the control tuple spaces of the relevant entities (e.g., component services, service communities) before the process template is made available to users. Later, when a process template is personalized and the resulting personal composite service is executed, the user agent automatically generates and injects control tuples (i.e., precondition and postprocessing tuples) from the preferences specified by the user and the information encoded in the process template. Finally, once the personalized service is being executed, the user agent keeps adding tuples into the tuple spaces of the participating services, according to the information that it receives from the user, and the tuples (e.g., context awareness tuples) that exist in its own tuple space (a user agent has its own tuple space).

The generation of precondition and postprocessing tuples of each task of a personal composite service is complex and challenging because the information encoded in the statechart (e.g., control flow and data dependencies) of the personal composite service needs to be extracted and analyzed. In what follows,

---

[2] Detailed description of QoS parameters can be found in [8].

we therefore describe the algorithms for the generation of postprocessing and precondition tuples.

The algorithm for generating postprocessing tuples (namely PostProc) for a task takes as input a task t, and produces a set of postprocessing tuples. The algorithm analyses the data dependencies of the output parameters (OD) and the outgoing transitions of t (TR). From OD, a set of actions is created indicating which outputs should be delivered to which receivers. The postprocessing set of t is the union of the postprocessing tuples associated to TR.

The postprocessing tuples for each outgoing transition of a task are generated by a function named PostProcT, which takes as input a transition tr, and returns a set of postprocessing tuples including the postprocessing actions associated with this transition. Various cases exist. When tr leads to a basic state (say t'), the tuple completed(source(tr))[c]notify(t') is created, meaning that after the execution of the task is completed, if the condition c is true, a notification must be sent to t'. If tr points to a compound state, one postprocessing tuple is generated for each initial transition of this compound state. Finally, if tr points to a final state of a compound state, the outgoing transitions of this compound state are considered in turn, and one or several postprocessing tuples are produced for each of them.

Similarly, the algorithm for generating precondition tuples of a task (namely PreCond) relies on the personalized attributes of the task (e.g., temporal and spatial constraints, input parameters), and control flows associated with the task. The task's *incoming* transitions are analyzed and the precondition is generated for each incoming transition of the task. For space reasons, we omit the description of the algorithm.

4   Implementing PCAP

In this section, we overview the status of the PCAP prototype implementation. The prototype architecture (see Figure 2) consists of a *user agent*, a *process manager*, and a *pool of services*, all implemented in Java. Below, we describe the implementation of the process definition environment (also called the process manager) for specifying and managing process templates, and a set of pre-built classes that act as a middleware for enabling the self-orchestration of personal composite services.

4.1   Process Definition Environment

The process definition environment consists of a set of integrated tools that allow template providers to create process templates: *templates/service discovery engine* and *process template builder*. The process template builder assists template providers in defining the new templates and editing the existing ones. A template definition is edited through a visual interface. The template builder offers an editor for describing a statechart diagram of a process template (an extension of our previous work in [14]).

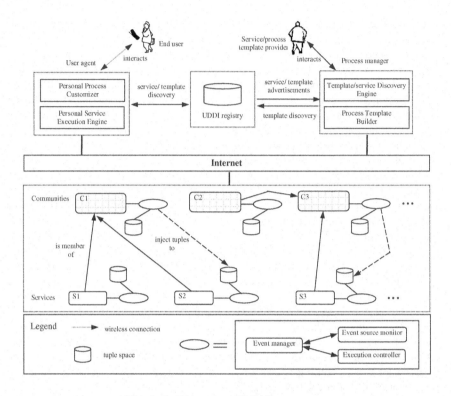

Fig. 2. Architecture of PCAP prototype

The template/service discovery engine facilitates the advertisement and location of processes and services. In the implementation, the Universal Description, Discovery and Integration (UDDI) is used as process/service template repository. Web service providers can also register their services to the discovery engine. The Web Service Description Language (WSDL) is used to specify Web services.

4.2   Pre-built Classes

For any user (resp., service) wishing to participate in our platform, the user (resp., the administrator of the service) needs to download and install a set of pre-built class, namely the *user agent* (resp., the *task controller*), the *event manager*, and the *event source monitor*.

User Agent. User agents are used for specifying and executing personal composite services. A user agent consists of a *personal process customizer*, and an *execution engine*. The process customizer generates personal services for users by customizing process templates based on user preferences. It provides an interface for the mobile user, implemented using Pocket PC Emulator. Currently, kXML 2 (http://kxml.enhydra.org), an open source designed to run in an

MIDP (Mobile Information Device Profile) environment (e.g., PalmOS), is used to parse XML documents on mobile devices. The personalized service is then translated into an XML document for subsequent analysis and processing by the execution engine. The user agent maintains the user profile. An interface is also provided for the mobile user to create and modify her profile information.

The execution engine provides a method called `deploy()` that is responsible for generating control tuples of each task of a personal composite service, using the approach presented in Section 3. The control tuples are then uploaded into the tuple spaces of the corresponding selected Web services, as well as into the tuple space of the user agent (not shown in the architecture).

Task Controller. The functionalities of a task controller are realized by a pre-built Java class, called `Controller`. This class provides services with capabilities to participate in service management including exception handling. It provides a method called `coordinate()` for receiving messages, managing service instances (i.e., creating and deleting instances), registering events to the event manager, triggering actions, tracing service invocations, and communicating with other controllers. There is one controller class per service. The controller relies on the control tuple space of the associated service to manage service activities. Each tuple space is represented using a local XML repository. Controllers monitor and control service activities by creating and reading tuples of their associated space as well as injecting (uploading) tuples in spaces associated to their peers.

Event Manager and Event Source Monitor. The event manager and the event source monitor are attached to a service or the user agent. The event source monitor detects the modifications of the *event sources*. For example, the event source of the event `entered` is the mobile user's current location. The event manager fires and distributes the events. These two components are mapped into classes called `eventManager` and `eventSourceMonitor` respectively. The `eventManager` provides methods for receiving messages, including subscribing messages from controllers and event source information from `eventSourceMonitor`, and notifying the fired events to the subscribed controllers. In particular, the class `eventManager` implements a process that runs continuously, listening to incoming messages. The messages are either `subscribe` or `monitor`. The former are the messages for subscribing to events, while the latter are the messages notifying the detected event source information. When the `eventManager` receives a message, it first examines the identifier of the message and proceeds as follows: i) if it is a subscribing message, extracts the controller and the subscribed event, then add the controller to the array of the event, which maintains all the subscribers of this event, ii) if it is a monitor message, extract the event source information and fire the corresponding event.

5   Conclusion

In this paper, we have presented the design and implementation of PCAP, a framework of enabling personalized composition and adaptive provisioning of

Web services. While much of the work on Web services has focused on low-level standards for publishing, discovering, and provisioning Web services in wired environments and for the benefit of stationary users, we deemed appropriate to put forward novel solutions and alternatives for the benefit of mobile users. Main contributions of PCAP include: i) personalized composition of Web services by considering users' preferences (e.g., temporal and spatial constraints), ii) distributed execution of personal composite services that is coordinated by tuple space based orchestration model, and iii) run-time exceptions handling.

So far, we have implemented a prototype that realizes the specification and execution of personal composite services. This implementation effort has served to validate the viability of the proposed approach. Ongoing work includes assessing the performance and scalability of PCAP. Another direction for future work is to add more flexibility to PCAP (beyond its exception handling capability) by supporting runtime modifications to the schema of a personal composite service (e.g., removing a task).

References

1. Chen, Y., Petrie, C.: Ubiquitous Mobile Computing. IEEE Internet Computing **7** (2003) 16–17
2. Mascolo, C., Capra, L., Emmerich, W.: Mobile Computing Middleware (A Survey). In: Advanced Lectures on Networking (NETWORKING 2002), Pisa, Italy (2002)
3. Burcea, I., Jacobsen, H.A.: L-ToPSS-Push-oriented Location Based Services. In: Proc. of the 4th VLDB Workshop on Technologies for E-Services (VLDB-TES03), Berlin, Germany (2003)
4. Harel, D., Naamad, A.: The STATEMATE semantics of statecharts. ACM Transactions on Software Engineering and Methodology **5** (1996) 293–333
5. Benatallah, B., Sheng, Q.Z., Dumas, M.: The Self-Serv Environment for Web Services Composition. IEEE Internet Computing **7** (2003) 40–48
6. Giaglis, G., Kourouthanasis, P., Tsamakos, A.: Towards a Classification Network for Mobile Location Services. In Mennecke, B., Strader, T., eds.: Mobile Commerce: Technology, Theory, and Applications. Idea Group Publishing (2002)
7. Maamar, Z., Sheng, Q.Z., Benatallah, B.: On Composite Web Services Provisioning in an Environment of Fixed and Mobile Computing Resources. Information Technology and Management Journal, Special Issue on Workflow and e-Business, Kluwer Academic Publishers (forthcoming) **5** (2004)
8. Zeng, L., Benatallah, B., Dumas, M., Kalagnanam, J., Sheng, Q.Z.: Quality Driven Web Services Composition. In: Proc. of the 12th International World Wide Web Conference (WWW'03), Budapest, Hungary (2003)
9. Roman, M., Hess, C., Cerqueira, R., Ranganathan, A., Campbell, R.H., Nahrstedt, K.: A Middleware Infrastructure for Active Spaces. IEEE Pervasive Computing **1** (2002) 74–83
10. Griswold, W.G., Boyer, R., Brown, S.W., Truong, T.: A Component Architecture for an Extensible, Highly Integrated Context-Aware Computing Infrastructure. In: Proc. of the 25th International Conference on Software Engineering, Oregon, Portland (2003)

11. Schuster, H., Georgakopoulos, D., Cichocki, A., Baker, D.: Modeling and composing service-based and reference process-based multi-enterprise processes. In: Proc. of the 12th Int. Conference on Advanced Information Systems Engineering (CAiSE'00), Stockholm, Sweden, Springer Verlag (2000)
12. Casati, F., Shan, M.C.: Dynamic and adaptive composition of e-services. Information Systems **26** (2001) 143–162
13. Ahuja, S., Carriero, N., Gelernter, D.: Linda and Friends. Computer **19** (1986) 26–34
14. Sheng, Q.Z., Benatallah, B., Dumas, M., Mak, E.: SELF-SERV: A Platform for Rapid Composition of Web Services in a Peer-to-Peer Environment. In: Proc. of the 28th Very Large DataBase Conference (VLDB'02), Hong Kong, China (2002)

A Systematic Approach to Express IS Evolution Requirements Using Gap Modelling and Similarity Modelling Techniques

Camille Salinesi, Anne Etien, and Iyad Zoukar

CRI - Université Paris 1, 90, rue de Tolbiac, 75013 Paris, France
camille@univ-paris1.fr
{anne.etien,iyad.zoukar}@malix.univ-paris1.fr

Abstract. Gaps and similarities are two important concepts used in Information System (IS) projects that deal with the evolution issue. The idea in using these concepts is to analyse what changes or what remains similar between two situations, typically the changed situation and the new one, rather than just describing the new situation. Although in the industry, the daily practice consists in expressing evolution requirements with gaps and similarities, little attention has been paid in research to better systematically define these two kinds of concepts so as to better support the expression of evolution requirements. This paper proposes an approach that combines meta-modelling with generic typologies of gap operators and similarity predicates. Our purpose is not to define yet another requirement modelling language. On the contrary, the two generic typologies can be adapted to existing modelling language such as Use Cases, I* and KAOS goal models, Goal/Strategy maps, Entity-Relationship diagrams, and Workflow models.

1 Introduction

In nowadays business competitive world, organizations have recognized the need for more agility in the development of their Information Systems (IS). Indeed, it is not anymore enough to have a system that fulfils the needs of a business. Now, it is necessary that systems evolution matches the evolution of businesses. [Salinesi03a] [Salinesi04].

According to [Jarke94], a system evolution can be designed as the movement from a situation to a new one. Traditionally, these situations are (as shown in Fig. 1) respectively captured in *As-Is* models and *To-Be* models. In many academic approaches, the evolution requirements are expressed by only specifying the To-Be. Our experience in several industrial projects showed us that, on the contrary, evolution requirements were initially captured relatively to the As-Is (even when this one is implicit and not specified), then the To-Be models are specified (if necessary from scratch). In this approach, the change process is an As-Is to To-Be movement for which requirements can be expressed as gaps and similarities relative to As-Is models. In [Salinesi03a], we demonstrated that this framework can be adapted to four different classes of IS evolution projects, namely: direct change propagation, customisation from a product family, adaptation of a baseline product and component assembly.

A. Persson and J. Stirna (Eds.): CAiSE 2004, LNCS 3084, pp. 338–352, 2004.

- In *direct change propagation*, the issue is to propagate the change requirements from the business level to the system functionality level. Change requirements are expressed as gaps with the As-Is [Salinesi03a].
- In *customisation from a product family*, the issue is to match the initial vision of the business (defined in As-Wished models) with models of the functionality capability of the product family (defined in Might-Be models) to specify the To-Be on the business and on the system functionality levels. The requirements for these To-Be models are expressed as similarities with the As-Wished and with the Might-Be [Zoukar04a] [Zoukar04b].
- In the case of *adaptation of a baseline product*, the issue is to find how the To-Be should differ from the As-Wished (on the business level) and the Is-Baseline (on the system functionality level) to obtain a correct adaptation of the baseline product. The required differences are specified under the form of gaps [Rolland04].

In *component assembly*, the change process consists in retrieving from a collection of COTS those that match the organization needs (defined in As-Wished business models (BMs)), and assembling them to obtain the To-Be situation. In this complex process, the matching requirements are expressed as similarities between the As-Wished BMs and the Might-Be models of the system functionality (SFMs). The requirements for component adaptation and assembly are expressed as gaps with the initial Might-Be [Rolland01b].

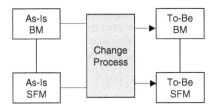

Fig. 1. Methodological framework for IS evolution

Despite the diversity of engineering processes dealing with these four classes of IS evolution projects, our experiences led us to identify two common underlying strategies. One is based on gaps, and the other is based on similarities. Intuitively, our proposal is to express IS evolution requirements with:

- gaps as operators that express transformations of As-Is models into the To-Be models, and
- similarities specify through predicates what the As-Is (or Might-Be) and To-Be (or As-Wished) should have in common.

Our languages of gaps and similarities are defined as two generic typologies of gap operators and similarity predicates. A number of gaps operators and similarity predicates were discovered within industrial projects. To achieve genericity and completeness, the typologies were specified so that the gap operators and similarity predicate would apply on the elements and structures of a generic meta model. This generic meta-model can be instantiated by any specific meta-model such as Use Case, Entity Relationship, etc.. As gap operators and similarity predicates relate to the generic meta-model, the specific elements and structures identified for a specific meta-model can be easily transposed onto specific gap operators and specific similarity predicates.

This allows us to express gaps and similarities in a specific way whichever language are required in the IS evolution project to specify the As-Is, As-Wished, Is-Baseline, Might-Be or To-Be models. The language formed by our two typologies can then be used to express evolution requirements; there is no assumption whether or not expressing these requirements necessitates the existence of the As-Is, As-Wished or Might-Be models. Our experience showed that this language is richer and more allows more precise specification of evolution requirements than the languages that are intuitively used in practice or developed in academy without a reference meta-model.

The rest of the paper is structured as follows: section 2 details the approach adopted to develop our generic typologies of similarity predicates and gap operators. The two resulting languages are respectively described in section 3 and 4. An example of application with goal/strategy maps, E/R diagrams and workflow models is presented in Section 5. Sections 6 and 7 discuss respectively related works and the future works in our research agenda.

2 Approach Taken to Develop the Typologies of Gap and Similarity

Gaps and similarities are the two central concepts needed to express requirements in an IS evolution project. There are different kinds of gaps, different kinds of similarities, and those can be defined to express requirements related to different kinds of models. Therefore, we adopted a systematic approach aiming to (i) identify a list of gap operators and similarity predicates that would be as complete as possible, and (ii) provide the means to adapt the identified gap operators and similarity predicates to the project situation.

2.1 General Overview

The general overview of our approach is presented in Fig. 2. As the figure shows, gaps (represented by the symbol Δ) and similarities (represented by the symbol $\equiv$) are specified at the modelling level. Gaps and similarities are relative; hence they can relate to various models (As-Is BM, As-Is SFM, As-Wished BM, Might-Be SFM, etc). These models can be specified using different meta models such as Use Case, E/R, Workflow, Business Process, Goal hierarchy, etc. In a concrete project, it is for instance possible to express a number of change requirements using gaps predicates, then build the To-Be models, then forecast the value/cost ratio of the change requirements in reference to the future business and system.

The link between models and meta-models is an instantiation link. This means that any element in a model instantiates an element in a meta-model. Similarly, we believe that any requirement expressed as a gap or as a similarity on the modelling level should be an instance of some concept formalised on the meta-model level. We call the different kinds of meta-models "specific meta models" (as they all have their specificities), and the typologies of gap operators and similarity predicates that correspond to them "specific typologies". The link between the specific typologies and the specific meta-models shows that any specific typology of gap operators or specific typology of similarity predicates applies on a specific meta-model.

Rather than defining as many typologies of gap operators and similarity predicates as there are of specific meta-models, our approach proposes to take a larger generic view. A generic meta-model level is thus used on top of the specific meta-model level. This generic meta-model level contains a unique generic meta-model on top of the specific meta-models, and a generic typology of gap operators and of similarity predicates on top of the specific typologies.

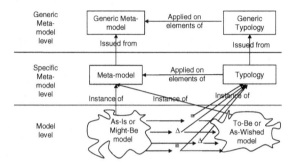

Fig. 2. Overview of the approach for defining the typologies

Let us take the example of a hotel room booking system specified with a Use Case Model. Similarities could be used to express which Use Case, and which part of the Use Cases have a similar equivalent in the Use Case Models defined for a number of software packages available for the hotel business. These similarities instantiate the specific typology of similarity predicates developed for Use Cases. This typology contains predicates such as "Two actors have the same name" or "the attributes of a Use Case include those of another Use Case", etc. These predicates shall be used to express requirements such as: (i) the actors in a Use Case have the same name as those identified by the legacy system, and (ii) a component of the software package can be selected if its attribute values are included in the attributes values defined for one of the Use Cases that define the legacy system.

Similarly, the specific typology of gap operators contains the operator "Add Use Case", "Change Origin of Use Case-Actor Association", or "Merge Actors". This allow to express requirements such as: (1) add a "cancel booking after booking date" Use Case in the Use Case Model of a booking system, or (2) merge the "salesman" and "receptionist" actors into a unique "front-desk" actor to simplify the organisation of sales in the hotel.

As these examples show it, specifying gaps and similarities to express requirements is not difficult once the specific typologies of gap operators and similarity predicates are known. However, defining these typologies from the generic typologies requires knowing how the specific meta-model at hand specialises the generic meta-model.

2.2   Generic Meta-model

The generic meta-model is not a 'universal' meta-model that would aim at specifying any concept in any method. On the contrary, its purpose is only to make explicit the main elements and structures of method parts that can be specified in a product meta-model [Rolland02]. We developed this meta-model based on a long experience of meta-modelling and meta-meta-modelling [Grosz97] [Plihon96] [Si-Said99] [Ralité01]. The generic meta-model shown in Fig. 3 with the UML notation stipulates that any that can be represented graphically model is composed of a collection of elements with properties.

Elements have a name and have properties. For example, a Use Case Model, a Use Case, an Actor, or a Scenario are different elements of the Use Case meta-model. The various attributes of Use Cases are as many properties that directly relate to the Use Case element. Elements are also classified into two pairs of sub-groups. First, a distinction is made between simple elements and compound elements. Second, elements are classified into link and not link.

Compound elements are composed of elements. Those can at their turn be simple or compound, and thus several levels of composition can be defined. For example, a Use Case Model is composed of Use Cases, which are at their turn composed of scenario descriptions, etc. Let us notice that any model or diagram is composed of elements. There are models in which one element always appears. This is for example the case of the system boundary in a Use Case model, or for the Object class in a class inheritance diagram. These elements are classified as *Root*.

Link Elements are connectors between pairs of elements. Every link can be oriented. Therefore, one of the linked elements plays the role of *Source* and the other of *Target*. For example, the "extends" relationship and the uses relationships are link elements of the Use Case meta-model.

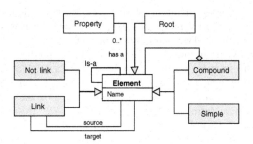

Fig. 3. Generic meta-model for defining the gap and the similarity typologies

The systematic definition of generic gap operators and generic similarity predicates directly results of the structure of the generic meta-model. For example, (i) adding or removing elements in the composition of a compound element are gaps, and (ii) having the same collection of components is a similarity that typically relate to compound elements. The two typologies were therefore developed by: first, looking for gap operators and similarity predicates in the literature, then, by systematically generalising them by applying them on all parts of the generic meta-model.

3   Generic Typology of Similarity Predicates

The generic meta-model indicates that any meta-model is composed of elements with properties. Besides, the structure of a meta-model is shown through element composition and through links between elements. Based on this, the generic typology of similarity predicates emphasises that given a pair of elements, (i) their properties can be similar, and (ii) their structure can be similar. As Fig. 4 shows, there are thus two classes of similarities, intrinsic similarities and structural similarities.

A pair of elements has an *intrinsic* similarity if they have similar properties. Element properties can be considered similar if they have a close semantics. In the first place, intrinsic similarity relates to synonymy. However, hyponymy (or the other way round hyperonymy) are also semantic relationships that can be used to define intrinsic similarities.

Structural similarity deals with (i) the composition of elements, and (ii) their organisation within models. There are thus two classes of structural similarity: compositional similarity, and relational similarity. Contrary to intrinsic similarity that only involves the two compared elements, structural similarities also imply comparisons between other elements that are related to the two compared ones. As shown in Fig. 4 by the aggregation link from structural similarity class to the similarity class, a structural similarity is a complex one and involves other similarities. For example, two elements have the "same components in a composition" if each component in one element has a semantically "same" counterpart in the composition of the other element.

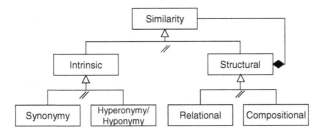

Fig. 4. Generic typology of similarity predicates (main categories)

Thirty-three similarity predicates composing the generic typology have been identified so far and are listed in table 1. These were classified in the four aforementioned classes and are defined as follows:

(i) *Synonymy*:

- Two elements have a synonym type if their types are equal or have a common super-type (they are then cousins). This is, for example, respectively the case of two goals in map models, or two actors in Use Case models.
- There are different degrees of possible resemblances between the properties of a pair of elements: two elements have the *same property* when their properties have exactly the same name and the same meaning (for example two extension conditions in two different Use Case models); they have *alike properties* when their properties are identified with different words but have the same meaning (for example two classes that specify the same business object in two different ERP modules); or they have a *resembling property* when the properties have different names and values, but they still have a close meaning (like for example a standard business object in two different ERPs).

(ii) *Hyponymy/Hyperonymy* relates two elements when the meaning of the one subsumes/is subsumed by the meaning of the other. As with synonymy, hyponymy/hyperonymy similarity can be defined on the type and on the properties of elements:

- with respect to type, hyponymy/hyperonymy relates to a *father/son* relationship between the types of the involved elements.
- With respect to properties, two elements are in a hyponymy/hyperonymy relationship if the properties of the ones *includes/extends* the properties of the other. This is for instance the case when the attributes of one class are included (or have a similar counterpart) in the collection of attributes of another class.

(iii) *Relational* similarities are defined between link elements that are connected to similar source/targets, or between elements that are related to the rest of their models through similar links. As table 1 shows, there are different kinds of relational structure similarity predicates. These include (without being restricted to): *same number of links* (when two elements are source/target of the same number of links), *same number of links entering in a node* (when two elements are source of the same number of links), *same number of links outgoing from a node* (idem, the other way round), *same/alike/resembling source, target, or source and target* (when two links have similar extremities), *same depth* (same max distance between nodes and leaves of the trees they belong to) or *same height* (same max distance between nodes and the root of the trees they belong to).

(iv) *Compositional* similarities deal with compound elements that are similar in their composition, and with elements that belong to similar compositions. Table 1 quotes a number of compositional structure similarity predicates: *same cardinality of a component* (when two compound elements have the same number of components), *same / alike / resembling components in a composition* (when the compositions of two compound elements are comparable), *same/alike/resembling common component in a composition* (when part of the compositions are comparable), *etc.*

Table 1. Generic typology of similarity predicates (details)

Synonymy	Hyperonymy Hyponymy	Relational	Compositional
Type	Type	Same number of links	Same cardinality of a component
Equal type	Father type	Same links number entering in a node	Same/Alike/Resembling components in a composition
Cousin type	Son type	Same links number outgoing from a node	Same/Alike/Resembling common component in a composition
		Same/Alike/Resembling source	Part of Same/Alike/Resembling compound
Property	Property	Same/Alike/Resembling target	
Same property	Includes property	Same/Alike/Resembling source & target	
Alike property	Extends property	Same depth	
Resembling property		Same height	

4   Generic Typology of Gap Operators

We propose to define gaps operators under the form of change operations made on models. There are different kinds of such operations: adding elements, removing them, changing their definition, replacing them by others, etc. Fourteen operators have been identified and defined on the generic level, i.e. to apply on the generic

Table 2. Meta-model elements and related operators

Element	Link	Compound	Property	Root
Rename	ChangeOrigin	AddComponent	Give	Add
Merge		RemoveComponent	Withdraw	Remove
Split		MoveComponent	Modify	
Replace				
Retype				

meta-model. Each operator identifies a type of change that can be performed on an element or a property of the As-Is model. Table 2 sums up the *generic gap typology* composed of 14 operators that we identified on *Element* or *Property*.

The operators have been classified according to the part of the generic meta-model on which they apply. The five operators that can be applied on an element can also be applied on any of the element specification (i.e. Link Element, Not Link Element, Compound Element and Simple Element). The *Rename* operator changes the name of the element in the To-Be model. Two separate As-Is elements become one in the To-Be model when the *Merge* is applied on them. For example, two Use Cases can be merged into one to indicate that from now on, the corresponding services shall be provided by the system within a single transaction. In the opposite, the *Split* operator decomposes one As-Is element into two To-Be elements. For example, a Use Case UC1 can be split into UC2 and UC3. This can occur when the user requires to be able to use independently the service defined in UC2 and UC3, and initially defined as part of UC1. It may be necessary to replace an As-Is element by a different To-Be one with the *Replace* operator. The *Retype* operator allows to change in the To-Be model the type of an As-Is element.

All the other operators can only be applied on one type of element: the *ChangeOrigin* operator only applies on Link elements in order to change the sources or targets of links. The changeOrigin operator can for instance be used to specify that the initiator actor of a Use Case has changed. The *AddComponent* operator is used when a component is added in the To-Be. In the opposite, a component can be removed with the *RemoveComponent* operator.

Three operators were also defined to specify when it is the properties of elements that change: the *Give* operator allows to add a property to the To-Be element. This operator is for example used when a new invariant predicate is attached to a Use Case. In the opposite the *Withdraw* operator removes an As-Is property in the To-Be element. Finally, the *Modify* operator changes the property of the To-Be element.

Finally, two operators can be applied on Root elements: Add, that allows to create a model by introducing the Root, and the other way round, the Remove operator when the model is destroyed. Typically, the system boundary is the first element to be added; and the last element that should be removed when a Use Case model is created or destroyed. Each gap operator at the specific meta-model level is defined with parameters to specify on which element it is applied.

5   Example of Application

This section illustrates the ability of our approach to adapt to different contexts. The example taken is that of an IS evolution project in which goal/strategy maps [Rolland99] [Rolland01a], E/R diagrams [Chen76], and workflow diagrams [Casati96] are used. The application domain is the one of hotel room booking [Salinesi03b]. In this example, a hotel chain initially uses a system to handle room booking in a centralised way. A project is undertaken to change the hotel booking business process in order to improve competitiveness.

In the current situation, the products offered by the hotel chain are independently designed in the system in a flat list which is augmented each time a new product is designed. Once products are in the list, they are used to create booking contracts. Any product of this list can be removed when it terminates its lifecycle. As shows the goal/strategy map extract on top of Fig. 5, there are two strategies available to achieve booking contracts management goal in the current situation: on the spot (i.e. at the hotel), and with a third party (e.g. at the city's tourist office or in an agency). The contract management process ends up either by cancellation of the contract, or by consumption of the associated product by the consumer.

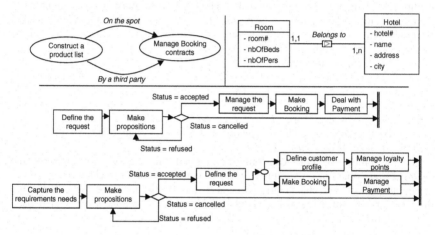

Fig. 5. Extracts of the three As-Is models; goal/strategy map (top left); E/R (top right); workflow (bottom)

A number of evolutions were required. Three major evolutions can be highlighted: (1) From now on, the system should be customer-centric; (2) It should be possible to propose complex products (such as packages including tourist activities) to customers; (3) The sales channels have to be diversified.

Each of the three following sub-sections shows how specific typologies of gap operators and similarity predicates are defined then used to express evolution requirements with each of the three modelling techniques used in the project.

Two different ways have been chosen to manage these evolutions: (i) by modification of the legacy to create an 'in-house' To-Be (ii) by introducing COTS. These two approaches are simultaneous described in following sub-sections; the first one is based on gaps whereas the second one uses similarities.

5.1 Expressing Goal/Strategy Maps Evolution Requirements

A goal/strategy *map* is an oriented graph which nodes are *goals* and edges *strategies*, i.e. ways to achieve a goal. Instantiating the generic meta-model shows that goal/strategy maps are compound elements that contain "sections". Every section in a map is itself a triplet composed of two goals and a strategy. One goal plays the role of source and should be achieved for the section to be undertaken. The other goal is the target i.e. the section aims at achieving. Strategy is a link between goals that defines way to reach the target goal from the source goal. Goals are simple/not link elements which main property is the goal statement structure [Ralyté01]. As shown in [Rolland04], this allows to define specific operators for each kind of elements in goal/strategy maps.

For example, the diversification of sales channels calls for a change on the As-Is goal/strategy map (Fig.5) in which the As-Is system only proposes to achieve the "Manage Booking contracts" goal with two strategies: *on the spot* and *by a third party.* adding a third strategy. The *AddStrategy(with web site, Attract People, Manage Customer relationship)* gap operator can for example be used to express this requirement. It is a specialisation of the *AddComponent* gap operator.

Another decision could be to use a hotel management software package (e.g. such as Orchestra, WebHotel or Betisoft). Fig. 6 shows the intended business goals and strategies and the facilities provided by one of these COTS. The COTS models have a number of structural and intrinsic similarities with the As-Wished models, namely: (i) the two goals "Attract people" and "Attract potential clients" are synonymous, and have alike properties, and (ii) the COTS strategy of "Promotion" is labelled as a hyperonym of the strategy "By keeping customer's loyalty" that was initially wished. It is therefore decided to acquire the COTS and implement it in the new system.

Fig. 6. Extracts of As-Wished (left hand) and COTS (right hand) goal/strategy maps

5.2 Required Evolutions with Respect to the WIDE Workflow Model

The contracting process is currently achieved as described in the WIDE workflow model in Fig. 5. Fig. 7 shows two other workflow models, one which is the wished target defined by the stakeholders, and the other which is the one supported by the selected COTS.

In the WIDE meta model [Casati96], a *Workflow Schema* is a graph which nodes are *Tasks* and edges *Connectors*. Connectors are links between tasks that define the order in which they must be executed. Besides, a set of *Variables* with values (that can be a default value) is associated with any Workflow schema. A *Task* is a unit of work. Every Task has a *ConditionFonction* specifying the conditions that need to be

satisfied before the task can be executed. A *Null Task* is a task that immediately finishes after it starts (no work is done); it is introduced only as a conceptual device to
define the semantics of a workflow schema. For example, an empty schema is defined
as containing a null task. A *Connector* defines a link of precedence / succession between tasks. There are different kinds of connectors: fork, and join.

The requirements for the new organisation have been initially defined as follows:
the system should be customer centric. It is thus decided to *rename* the first task "Define the request" into "Capture customer needs". Stakeholders also decided to enforce
customer loyalty. Two tasks should be *added* for this purpose: (i) "Define Customer
profile" that will allow the hotel consortium to make personalised offers to clients;
and (ii) "Manage loyalty points" that specifies that each time the client buy a product,
it receives loyalty points. Finally, the task "Deal with payment" is *replaced* by "Manage payment". Indeed, the payment can not only be made with credit card, cash, personal cheques etc. as before, but henceforth also with loyalty points.

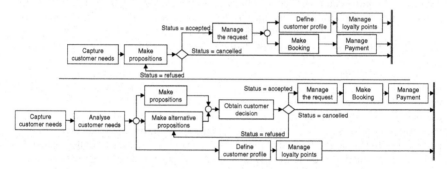

Fig. 7. Parts of the As-Wished model (top) and the Might-Be model (bottom) concerning the
products in the catalogue

A number of the facilities can also be implemented by adapting the COTS that was
considered in the previous section. Indeed, the COTS Might-Be model has the *same*
decision function as the As-Wished discussed above. Besides, a number of the tasks it
supports have the *same properties as* the ones that were initially wished, e.g. "manage
the request" and "manage loyalty points". Compositional and relational similarities
can be easily detected too. All the facilities offered by the COTS and specified in the
Might-Be are adopted as fulfilling the requirements that were initially wished. Therefore, the decision that is made is to keep all these facilities. This requirement for the
To-Be is therefore specified under the form of similarities with the COTS-supported
workflow.

5.3   Evolution Requirements with Respect to the E/R Models

One of the important required evolutions was to replace the flat product list with a
collection of complex product definitions. It is decided that contract should now include all the hotel facilities such as for instance tennis, swimming pool, amphitheatre
and meeting rooms, Internet connections. In terms of gaps with the As-Is E/R model,

the evolution requirements are thus to: *AddEntity(Activity), AddEntity(Option), AddRelationship(Proposes, Hotel, Activity), AddRole(<Proposes, Hotel, Activity>), AddRelationship(Offers, Hotel, Option), AddRole(<Offers, Hotel, Option>), AddAttribute(Activity, activity#), AddAttribute(Activity, activityName)*. These gaps directly instantiate the specific typology of gap operators developed for the E/R meta-model. The E/R model resulting from these evolution requirements can be designed as shown in Fig. 8.

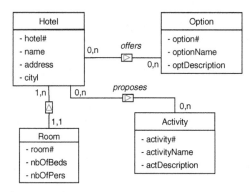

Fig. 8. Extract of the To-Be model with the products catalogue

Fig. 9 shows an E/R model of the COTS. A number of structural similarities are necessary to confirm that the COTS matches the wished requirements. For example we can notice that there are type and property synonymies concerning each entity of the To-Be model with their counterpart in the Might-Be model. The "same common component in a composition" structural compositional similarity allows to show that the part of the To-Be is included in the Might-Be model.

These structural and intrinsic similarities between the two models help the requirement engineer to master the matching process in order to establish the COTS customisation tables. In addition, we can notice that the E/R model of the COTS is richer than the To-Be.

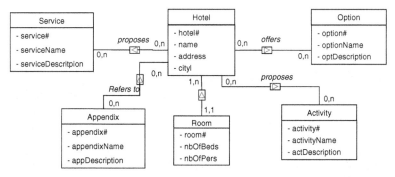

Fig. 9. Parts of the Might-Be model concerning the products in the catalogue

6   Related Works

Handling IS evolution is an important issue in both the academic world and in industry; as show for example the IWPSE series of workshop [IWPSE]. The literature proposes different approaches to manage IS evolution. Some approaches deal with the propagation of change on the system implementation using a maintenance or a correction point of view. For example, [Breche96] defines a typology of operators to make the class instances migrate from the old system to the new one. [Sadiq00] and [Bandinelli93] propose similar approaches, respectively with a workflow meta-model and a software process meta-model. Our approach differs from those in that we adopt a requirement-driven point of view [Rolland04], whereas the aforementioned approaches rather focus on technical aspects such as system implementation or instance.

Several typologies of gap operators or similarity predicates were already proposed to maintain the consistency and the validity of models [Breche96], [Bandinelli93] [Deruelle99], [Ralyté01]. However, each of these typologies is only defined for one specific meta-model. In our approach, we propose a generic typology of gap operators and a generic typology of similarity predicates that can be specialised for any meta-model, as we showed with 3 different examples of application and in [Etien03].

Similarity measurement is also a topic of interest in different areas of IS engineering and Requirements Engineering. For example, [Castano92] proposes to evaluate components reusability through conceptual schema. [Jilani97] used similarity measures to select best-fit components. Similarity metrics for heterogeneous database schema analysis were introduced by [Bianco99]. Our similarity approach is inspired by [Castano92] and [Bianco99]. It could be compared to that of [Ralyté01], except that we are not defining similarities between meta-models but between models, and except the fact that the purpose is not just to find which element looks like another, but also to specify evolution requirements according to which there should be similarities between a future situation and an old one. Similarity measurement can also be automated (e.g. see [NattOchDag01]). Such techniques could be used to guide the matching between COTS and As-Wished models, but manual work is still needed to transform the matching results into proper evolution requirements.

7   Conclusions

The example of the hotel room booking system shows how to use the gap modelling and similarity modelling to express requirements in a context of IS evolution. Applying this approach on three different meta-models does not demonstrate that the approach is generic. However, combined with the fact that we already used this approach in the context of several different industrial projects ([Zoukar04a], [Rolland04], [Salinesi02a], [Salinesi02b]) we believe it is sufficient to show that this approach is indeed *usable* in different methodological contexts, and *scalable* to real-world projects. Our approach to deal with scalability is to abstract As-Is, As-Wished, Might-Be and To-Be using goal models, then drive the analysis in a top-down way. As shown in the aforementioned experience reports, this helps to undertake the analysis in a synthetic way, prune uninteresting parts of the business and of the system functionalities, then concentrate on those parts of the business that are the most likely to change or with respect to which stability is crucial. Our approach is however not applicable in any IS evolution project. For instance it shouldn't be used in project in which the foreseen change has a revolutionary impact on the IS and on its business environment (i.e. there should be only a limited amount of evolutions).

Further evaluations of our approach are however needed to substantiate our claim. Besides to being generic, we expect that the evolution requirements language that is constituted by our typology of gap operators and by our typology of similarity predicates has also a number of other qualities such as completeness, exhaustiveness, minimality, concision, and coherence. We have already empirically evaluated the gap typology according these criteria [Etien03]. However, we believe further experiments are needed, e.g. to evaluate the efficiency of expressing evolution requirements using our approach, and to compare it with other approaches in real project situations.

Another important issue is the one of guiding the elicitation of evolution requirements and checking their correctness. We are currently developing three process models. One is to elicit compliance requirements ensuring an adequate transition to the new system when business evolution requirements have already been specified [Salinesi03b]. The second one is being developed for an ERP project at the French national railway company. It aims at guiding the elicitation of ERP requirements [Zoukar04a] [Zoukar04b] so as to ensure maximum fitness of the ERP implementation with the new organisation of the business that the ERP project makes itself evolve. The process model was developed in a project with a French company of the automotive industry and guides adaptation of a baseline product [Rolland04]. We would like to develop in the near future a process model for the fourth kind of project that our methodological framework lead us to identify (namely component assembly), and to look for an integrated multi-way-of-working process model [Plihon96] [Grosz97] [Ralyté01] that could be adapted to any project situation. We believe that one of the salient characteristic of these process models might be that evolution requirements are not independent from each other. Clusters of change requirements and inter-requirements dependency links are concept that we are considering in our current research project to complete our approach.

References

[Bandinelli93] Bandinelli, S., et al. *Software Process Model Evolution in the SPADE Environment*. IEEE Transactions on Software Engineering, 19(12) pp.1128-1144, (1993).

[Bianco99] Bianco G. *A Markov Random Field Approach for Querying and Reconciling Heterogeneous Databases*. Proc. DEXA'99, Pisa, Italy, September 1999.

[Breche96] Breche P. *Advances Primitives for Changing Schemas of Object Databases*, Proc. CAiSE'96, Springer Verlag (pub), Heraklion, Greece, 1996.

[Casati96] Casati, F., Ceri, S., Pernici, B., Pozzi, G. *Workflow Evolution*. Proc. Of 15th Int. Conf. On Conceptual Modeling (ER'96), Cottbus, Germany, pp. 438-455 (1996)

[Castano92] Castano S. De Antonellis V. Zonta B. *Classifying and Reusing Conceptual Components*. Procs. of ER'92, pp. 121-138, Karlsruhe, 1992.

[Chen76] P. Chen. *The Entity-Relation Model - Towards Unified View of Data*. ACM Transactions on Database System, 1(1):9-36, March 1976.

[Deruelle99] Deruelle, L., et al. *Local and Federated Database Schemas Evolution An Impact Propagation Model*. Proc. DEXA'99, pages 902-911, Italy, September 1999.

[Etien03] Etien, A., Salinesi, C. *Towards a Systematic Definition of Requirements for Software Evolution: A Case-study Driven Investigation.* Proc of EMMSAD'03, Austria, 2003.

[Grosz97] G. Grosz, et al. *Modelling and Engineering the Requirements Engineering Process: An Overview of the NATURE Approach.* Requirements Engineering Journal, (2), 1997.

[IWPSE] IWPSE International Workshop on the Principles of Software Evolution

[Jarke94] Jarke, M., Pohl, K. *Requirements Engineering in 2001: Managing a Changing Reality.* IEEE Software Engineering Journal, pp. 257-266. November 1994.

[Jilani97] Jilani L.L. Mili R. Mili A.. *Approximate Component Retrieval: An Academic Exercise or a Practical Concern?.* Procs. (WISR8), Columbus, Ohio, March 1997.

[Plihon96] Plihon V. *Un environnement pour l'ingénierie des méthodes.* PhD Thesis, University of Paris1 Panthéon-Sorbonne, 1996

[Ralyté01] Ralyté J. *Ingénierie des méthodes à base de composants*, PhD Thesis, University of Paris1 Panthéon-Sorbonne, January 2001.

[NattOchDag01] Natt och Dag J. *Evaluating Automated Support for Requirements Similarity Analysis in Market-driven Development.* Procs. REFSQ'01, Switzerland, 2001.

[Rolland99] Rolland C., Prakash N., Benjamen A. *A Multi-Model View of process Modelling*, Requirements Engineering Journal, Vol 4, pp 169-187, 1999.

[Rolland01a] Rolland C., Prakash N. *Matching ERP System Functionality to Customer Requirements*, Proceedings of RE'01, Canada, pp. 66-75, 2001.

[Rolland01b] Rolland C. *Requirements Engineering for COTS based Systems.* XXVII Latin American Conference on Informatics (CLEI'2001), Merida, Venezuela. September, 2001.

[Rolland02] Rolland C. *A Comprehensive view of Method Engineering* Invited talk, PromoteIT2002, Knowledge Foundation Symposium, Skovde, Sweden, April 2002.

[Rolland04] Rolland, C., Salinesi, C., Etien, A. *Eliciting Gaps in Requirements Change.* Requirement Engineering Journal Vol. 9, pp1-15, 2004

[Sadiq00] Sadiq, S. Handling *Dynamic Schema Change in Process Models.* Australian Database Conference, Canberra, Australia, 2000.

[Salinesi02a] Salinesi, C., et al. *A Method to Analyse Changes in the Realisation of Business Intentions and Strategies for Information System Adaptation.* Proc. EDOC'02, Sept. 2002.

[Salinesi02b] Salinesi, C., Wäyrynen J.: A Methodological Framework for Understanding IS Adaptation through Enterprise Change. Proceedings of OOIS'02, France, September 2002

[Salinesi03a] Salinesi, C., Rolland, C.: *Fitting Business Models to Systems Functionality Exploring the Fitness Relationship.* Proceedings of CAiSE'03, Velden, Austria, 2003.

[Salinesi03b] C. Salinesi, A. Etien, *Compliance Gaps: a Requirements Elicitation Approach in the Context of System Evolution*, Proceedings of the OOIS'03, Switzerland, Sept. 2003.

[Salinesi04] Salinesi C. et al *Goal / Strategy Maps - Methods, Techniques and Tools to Specify Requirements in Different Evolutionary Contexts.* Proc. INCOSE'04, France, June 2004.

[Si-Said99] Si Said S. *Proposition pour la modélisation et le guidage des processus d'analyse des systèmes d'information.* University of Paris1 Panthéon-Sorbonne, February 1999.

[Zoukar04a] Zoukar I., Salinesi C. *Engineering the Fitness Relationship between an ERP and the Supply Chain Process at SNCF.* Proc. IRMA'04, USA, May 2004.

[Zoukar04b] Zoukar I., Salinesi C. *Matching ERP Functionalities with the Logistic Requirements of French Railway.* Proc. ICEIS'04, Portugal, April 2004.

How Requirements Specification Quality Depends on Tools: A Case Study

Raimundas Matulevičius

Dept. of Computer and Information Science, Norwegian Univ. of Science and Technology
Sem Sælands vei 7-9, NO-7491 Trondheim, Norway
raimunda@idi.ntnu.no

Abstract. Requirements specification is a complex activity, where the automated support by the requirements engineering (RE) tools plays an important role. However, the surveys report that the mainstream practice relies on office and modelling tools rather than the targeted RE-tools. This work performs a case study, where two requirements specification processes are analyzed. In order to prepare a requirements document, standard office and modelling tools are used in the first case. In the second case, requirements specification is executed by the means of the RE-tools. Finally, the quality of both requirements documents is compared and evaluated by their qualitative properties. The results indicate that the targeted RE-tools provide better support for the RE process than the standard office and modelling facilities. The requirements document prepared using the targeted RE-tools, is substantially of better quality. The work findings suggest the RE-tool features which could be improved for the qualitative automated support of the RE process.

1 Introduction

Requirements engineering (RE) process concerns real world goals, functions, and constraints of software systems. It is also a relationship between these factors and a precise specification of software behaviour [36]. RE is a complex activity, where the adequate automated process support plays an important role for the process success [11, 12, 16]. However, most of the requirements engineers will hardly heard of or used the RE-tools [10, 28]. Instead, they tend to use the generic office, drawing and modelling tools. One might wonder if the targeted RE-tools are useful, as the vendors claim.

This work investigates the issue by performing a case study where two alternative requirements specifications for the same system are developed. The standard office, modelling, and communication tools are used in the first case, and the targeted RE-tools are applied in the second. The paper addresses the following questions:

1) What software tools do provide a qualitative support for the RE process?
2) Do the RE-tools provide facilities to create better-quality requirements specification than office and modelling tools?

A. Persson and J. Stirna (Eds.): CAiSE 2004, LNCS 3084, pp. 353–367, 2004.

The RE process is evaluated by the means of an evaluation framework [24]. The requirements documents produced in both cases, are considered by the qualitative requirement document properties [5]. The evaluations indicate the better RE process support and the higher quality of the requirements document in the case, where the RE-tools are applied. The work concludes with the suggestions, how to improve the RE-tool functionality, that they would provide the proper support for RE.

The paper is structured as follows: section 2 analyzes the background and related work. Section 3 describes the research design. First, the research questions are formulated, next, the problem definition, tools, the evaluation of the RE process and the requirements document are considered. Finally, the potential validity threats are analyzed. Section 4 discusses the lessons learned and provides conclusions of the study.

2 Background

The term "requirements specification" is used in two ways in the literature. It defines:
- the *process* undertaken to specify requirements. It is considered as the RE activity [16, 23, 29], which deals with the *understandability* at the certain time moment.
- the *document*, which contains a complete description of *what* the system should do without describing *how* it should do it [5, 8, 18].

In order to avoid confusion, "requirements specification" will by used only about the process in this work, while the document will be called "requirements document".

2.1 RE Process

The RE process is characterized as a network of activities, like elicitation, specification, and validation [7, 16, 21]. Activities are customized by choosing the appropriate techniques to the specific applications. RE is described as smoothly evolutionary and cumulative process. However, in [27], RE is characterized by occasional "crisis" points where the requirements model is reconceptualised, restructured, and simplified.

An evaluation framework [24] describes the RE process along three orthogonal dimensions [29] – representation, agreement and specification. The framework features (figure 1) correspond to the functional requirements categories, which are expanded with the lists of activities [17, 19, 22], which describe the RE process.

The *representation* dimension deals with the degree of formality, where requirements are described using informal, semiformal and formal languages. It is important to keep the traceability between different representations.

The *agreement* dimension deals with the degree of agreement among project participants. It is important to ensure communication among the project participants. The rationale leads to agreement about the requirements model.

The *specification* dimension deals with the degree of requirements understandability, and it should be supported by the documentation and reports. The knowledge gathered in the projects should be possible to reuse. The existing standards should be applied in order to ensure the quality level of requirements specification.

While the evaluation framework [24] is originally developed to evaluate the RE tools, it mainly decomposes RE into various activities and tasks, and can thus be used also to evaluate the RE process.

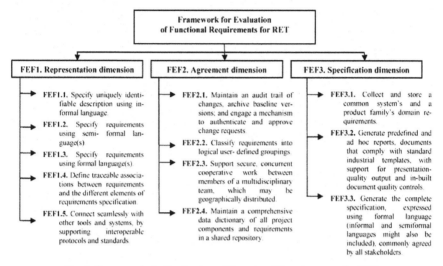

Fig. 1. Framework for Evaluation of Functional Requirements for RET

2.2 Metrics of Requirements Document

The literature [3, 5, 8, 14, 20, 26] defines metric taxonomies for the requirements documents. Usually, the desirable properties are completeness, consistency, correctness, traceability, understandability, verifiability, and maintainability. Whether the requirements are documented in formal or natural language, each requirement should be individually countable, it should be consistent with all other requirements, and carry any annotations in use by the program [3]. Conventions used to specify requirements should be consistent for all specifications within a given level and a traceability matrix should exist for each specification. To increase the accuracy of data collection, it is recommended to store requirements document electronically in a form that permits individual requirements to be identified and traced to requirements in higher or lower specification level.

Davis *et al.* [5] describes the comprehensive list of the qualitative properties for the requirements document. Furthermore [17], the requirements document quality is considered in respect with the goals and means of the semiotic quality framework, which divides the quality into physical, empirical, syntactic, pragmatic, semantic, perceived semantic, and social.

The qualitative property which addresses the physical quality is that a requirements document should be *electronically stored. Reusability* of a requirements document could be considered through the physical representation. But it also influences other quality types, such as semantic (domains for actual reuse), and syntactic (level of formality reuse). Empirical quality is understood as the ergonomic representation of the requirements model and it considers *understantability* and *concision* of a requirements document. The goal of syntactic quality is syntactic correctness. Syntactic quality is not precisely stated in [5], although, some semantic qualitative properties could be reduced to analyze the syntactic quality. Most of the properties concern semantic quality, which has the goals of feasible validity and completeness. Goal of the pragmatic quality is comprehension and it analyses if a requirements document is *executable* (*interpretable* or *prototypable*), *organized* and *cross-referenced*. Qualitative properties for empirical, semantic, and pragmatic qualities are defined in table 1. Social quality is dealing with the agreement about requirements document. This quality type is not analyzed in [5]. However, the importance of the argumentation tool support through the requirements specification is mentioned in [17].

2.3 Related Work

RE process is characterized by the correctness, completeness, non-ambiguity and traceability metrics in [1], and RequisitePro helps to manage the complexity. The study concludes that the technical and non-technical actors should be involved in requirements specification, which should be supported by quality standards [8].

In [5] an experiment compares the guidelines for the use cases. Elsewhere, [33] investigates the effects of using entity-based and object-oriented modelling. The work concludes that conceptual models are more effective than logical, and that the mapping from conceptual to logical models is more effective by using the object-oriented methods than entity-based methods.

The case study [15] explores how well the RE methods are applicable in an environment, and how efficient the activities to produce a requirements document are. The results show that the formal methods are time consuming to apply. Hierarchical models lead to better understandability. But the formal methods contribute with better quality of requirements documents.

The purpose of this study is to investigate if the quality of requirements specification depends on the tools. The findings suggest features for improving the automated RE process support in order to produce the qualitative requirements document.

3   Research Design

The study design is shown in fig. 2. The research questions and the problem description will be provided first. The study consists of two cases. The office and modelling tools are used in case A. In case B the RE-tools are adopted. Both cases are evaluated with the evaluation framework [24]. The requirements documents quality is compared by the qualitative properties of the requirements document [5].

Table 1. Qualitative property definitions

Qua lity	Qualitative properties	Property Definitions
Em-pirical	understandable	A reader with a minimum explanation easily comprehends all classes.
	concise	A requirements document is short as possible without affecting any other quality of it.
Semantic	complete	A requirements document possess the following four features: 1) Everything that the software is supposed to do is included in the document. 2) Definitions of the responses of the software to all realizable classes of input data in all realizable classes of situations are included. 3) All pages are numbered, all figures and tables are numbered, named, and referenced; all terms and units of measure are provided; and all referenced material and sections are presented. 4) No section is marked "to be determined".
	correct	Every requirement represents something required of the system to be built.
	internally consistent	No subset of individual requirements stated therein conflicts.
	external consistency	No requirement stated therein requirements document conflicts with any already base-lined project documentation.
	precise	Numeric quantities are used whenever possible and appropriate levels of precision are used for all numeric quantities.
	traced	The origin of each requirement is clear.
	annotated by relative importance	A reader can easily determine which requirements are the most important.
	annotated by relative stability	A reader can easily determine which requirements are most likely to change.
	annotated by version	A reader can easily determine which requirements will be satisfied in which version of the product.
	traceable	A requirements document is written in a manner that facilitates the referencing of each individual statement.
	verifiable	There exists a finite cost effective technique that can be used to verify that every requirement is satisfied by the system to be built.
	achievable	There exists at least one system design and implementation that correctly implements all the requirements stated in the requirements document.
	design-independent	There exists more than one system design and implementation that correctly implements all the requirements stated in the requirements document.
	at right level of detail	It is described how the requirements document is being used.
	unambiguous	Every requirement stated therein has only one possible interpretation.
	modifiable	A requirements document structure and style are such that any changes can be made easily, completely and consistently.
	not redundant	The same requirement is not stated more than once.
Pragmatic	executable (interpret-able, prototypable)	There exists a software tool, capable of inputting the requirements document and providing a dynamic behavioural model.
	organized	A requirements document contents are arranged so that readers can easily locate information, and logical relationships among adjacent sections are apparent.
	cross-referenced	Cross-references are used in the requirements document to relate sections containing requirements to other sections.

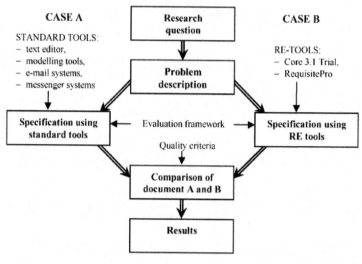

Fig. 2. Research design

3.1 Research Questions

RE could be performed using various software tools. The tool combination does not provide adequate quality for the RE process, and many RE activities are done manually. The targeted RE-tools could be a solution. The RE-tools tend to improve the quality by suggesting the means to perform RE activities in a more efficient way than manual. The first research question is

1) What software tools do provide a qualitative support for the RE process?
The automated support for the requirements documentation is recognized in [11, 12, 16], however, the mainstream of RE practice relies on the office and modelling tools rather than the targeted RE-tools. This leads to the second research question:

2) Do the targeted RE-tools provide facilities to create better-quality requirements documents than standard editing and modelling tools?

3.2 Problem Definition

The requirements document was created for MEIS (Model Evaluation of the Information System), which is used during the course taken by the third year students in Norwegian University of Science and Technology. The system registers two types of users: students and student assistants. Students submit the solutions to the system. Student assistants evaluate the solutions and form the reviewer groups from the students. Next step is the review process. The reviews are done according to the semiotic quality framework [22]. If the reviews are essentially different, the student assistant rejects them, and the reviewer group should provide the new evaluations. If the evaluations are accepted, they are sent to the student who delivered the solution.

Two different sets of requirements were specified in both cases. The number of the requirements was almost the same. Approximately the same amount of time was spent to elicit them. Case A produced the requirements document, which described how:
- students should upload the solution to the system;
- student assistants should accept or reject the solution;
- if the solution is accepted, student assistants should form the reviewer groups;
- reviewers should evaluate solutions;
- students and student assistants should print reports about the solution evaluation.

In case B the functionality was improved with additional features:
- student assistants should provide comments about the solution and evaluation;
- student assistants should disband reviewer groups;
- student assistants should accept or reject evaluations;
- student assistants should provide comments to the evaluations;
- student assistants should print the report about the whole student's performance during the semester.

3.3 Tools in Case A

Standard office tools (MS word and excel), modelling tools (Rational Rose and RML editor), graphical packages (MS paint), and communication tools (ICQ, MSN messengers, and e-mail systems) were used in case A. IEEE std. 830-1998 [8] recommendation was adapted to the requirements document.

RML editor [34] facilitated in creation of the conceptual model of the problem. Rational Rose [31] was used to describe behavioural model and to prepare the use case diagrams for the individual requirements.

The participants chose the communication tools according to their experience. In order to support the communication ICQ and MSN messengers were used. The e-mail correspondence helped in distributing the requirements document for the participant consideration.

3.4 Tools in Case B

In Case B two RE-tools - CORE [2] and RequisitePro [32], were applied. The engineer created traceability between requirements, functional and design models in CORE [2]. CORE was used to create the requirements model as ER (entity-relationships) diagrams and FFBD (Functional Flow Block Diagrams). The tool does not support traceability between the elements on the same abstraction level and does not have discussion facilities.

The traceability between requirements on the same abstraction level was created with RequisitePro [32], which dynamically links the requirements in Word documents to the information stored in a database. The rationale of requirements model was kept as the discussions over the requirements model in the RequisitePro database.

3.5   RE Process Comparison

Comparison of the RE process is performed by the means of the evaluation framework [24], which separates RE process into representation, agreement and specification dimensions. The feature evaluations in the tables 2, 3, and 4 mean: *Yes* – the feature is supported. *No* – the feature is not supported. *Partly* – the support is not adequate.

3.5.1   Comparison along the Representation Dimension

Comparison of the cases A and B along the representation dimension is shown in table 1. In case A the engineers chose the modelling perspectives, what they prefer. The requirements are represented in natural and reference modelling languages, state transition diagrams, the set theory notations, use case templates and use case diagrams. In case B the requirements engineers were dependent on the modelling perspective, supported by the RE-tool. The system description was prepared with CORE, using structured natural language, ER and FFBD diagrams.

In case A, requirements traceability was maintained manually. In case B the RE-tools provided different traceability: CORE supported hierarchical relationships between elements; RequisitePro maintained child-parent and peer-to-peer relationships.

The data exchange between the tools lets to use different modelling languages. In case A the representations screenshots were prepared with MS paint. In case B the connection between the RE-tools and the text editors was provided. However, the information transfer between CORE and RequisitePro was done using the text editor.

3.5.2   Comparison along the Agreement Dimension

Comparison of the cases A and B along the agreement dimension is shown in table 2. The agreement about the requirements was achieved in face-to-face meetings in both cases. The requirements rationale was registered as the sequence of e-mail correspondence in case A. In case B, RequisitePro maintained discussions over the requirements model. In both cases, the rationale helped to reach understanding about requirements.

In case A the requirements document versions were registered. The RE-tools registered the requirements revision history in case B. Both cases organized requirements according to the functional behaviour. Requirements views, traceability matrixes in RequisitePro helped to check requirements consistency.

Neither case A nor case B suggested the work for the geographically distributed teams. The requirements document was distributed using e-mails in case A. In case B, the RE-tools suggested possibilities to access the databases through the local organizational intranet. The maintenance of term dictionary is poor both in case A and B.

3.5.3   Comparison along the Specification Dimension

Comparison of the cases along the specification dimension is shown in table 3. In case A copy-paste functionality could be used for reuse. In case B RequisitePro suggested the functionality to import related information from the existing projects.

Table 2. Comparison along the representation dimension

Frame-work feature	Case A		Case B	
	Evaluation	Comments	Evaluation	Comments
FEF1.1.	YES	Natural language, Use Case templates.	YES	Structured natural language.
FEF1.2.	YES	State transition Use Case and RML diagrams.	YES	ER, and FFBD diagrams in CORE. Association with Rational Rose in RequisitePro (not used in project)
FEF1.3.	PARTLY	Set theory notations, prepared manually.	NO	RE-tools do not support formal requirements representation.
FEF1.4.	PARTLY	Hypertext links defined manually.	YES	Hierarchical traceability in CORE. Peer-to-peer, parent-child, traceability in RequisitePro.
FEF1.5.	NO	Performed manually by creating representation screen-shots.	PARTLY	Requirements import/export from/to the text documents. No correspondence between RE-tools.

Table 3. Comparison along the agreement dimension

Framework feature	Case A		Case B	
	Evaluation	Comments	Evaluation	Comments
FEF2.1.	PARTLY	Rationale as the e-mail correspondence. Difficult to maintain version control.	YES	Rationale is created as RequisitePro discussions. Requirements access and revision registration.
FEF2.2.	PARTLY	Requirements are sorted according to the functionality.	YES	Requirements are sorted and filtered according to the functionality and properties.
FEF2.3.	NO	No cooperative work for the distributed teams.	PARTLY	No cooperative work for the distributed teams. Access of databases through intranet.
FEF2.4.	NO	Data and term dictionaries were maintained manually.	NO	Term dictionaries were created manually in the database. Help was provided to the skilled users.

Requirements reports could be prepared manually in case A. The RE-tools suggested a variety of viewpoints in case B. It is possible to print semiformal requirements representations in CORE. RequisitePro prepars the requirements views, traceability matrixes, change history and discussion reports.

Requirements standards lead to requirements understandability. In case A IEEE std. 830-1988 was adapted manually to the requirements document. In case B, the requirements document was prepared using CORE wizard. The defined template could be reused for other projects, too.

Table 4. Comparison along the specification dimension.

Framework feature	Case A		Case B	
	Evaluation	Comments	Evaluation	Comments
FEF3.1.	NO	The reuse is manual by copy-paste functionality.	PARTLY	Reuse of information from o the projects in RequisitePro.
FEF3.2.	NO	Reports could be generated manually.	YES	Reports of views, discussion, representations, traceability.
FEF3.3.	YES	The IEEE std. 830-1998 was adapted by the requirements engineer.	YES	Organizational standard, created according to the RE-tool wizard.

3.6 Comparison of Requirements Documents

The requirements documents quality is evaluated by four researchers. The evaluator interests include conceptual modelling, requirements engineering, traceability and design of requirements repositories. The evaluators were not involved in the requirements document development, but they were familiar with the MEIS. Some evaluators were asked to perform double-cross evaluation of both requirements documents.

1. Please evaluate the understandability of the

	5	4	3	2	1	0
tables	o	o	o	o	o	o
diagrams						
singular requirements statements	o	o	o	o	o	o
whole requirements specification	o	o	o	o	o	o

4. Please evaluate specification annotations.

	5	4	3	2	1	0
annotating by importance	o	o	o	o	o	o
annotating by relevant stability	o	o	o	o	o	o
annotating by version	o	o	o	o	o	o

5. Please evaluate the third feature of specification completeness.

	5	4	3	2	1	0
page numeration	o	o	o	o	o	o
diagram titles	o	o	o	o	o	o
table titles	o	o	o	o	o	o
referenced material	o	o	o	o	o	o
all important terms	o	o	o	o	o	o
all important units	o	o	o	o	o	o
all needed concepts	o	o	o	o	o	o
all needed relationships between separate parts	o	o	o	o	o	o

Fig. 3. Fragment of the questionnaire to evaluate the requirements document

3.6.1 Document Evaluation Method

The questionnaire (fig 3.) describes the requirements document quality according to the semiotic quality framework [17] and the qualitative properties [5]. The qualitative properties are divided to the requirement document characteristics. For example, to evaluate the document consistency, the requirements behaviour representation, terms, and requirements properties were considered. The evaluators had to perform 39 characteristic evaluations in the scale of 5 to 0 (5 – best, 0 – worst evaluation).

Table 5. Comparison of the qualitative properties of the requirements documents. A – qualitative property of the requirement document in case A is higher; B – qualitative property of the requirement document in case B is higher; = - qualitative property of both requirements documents is equal; I – indirect assumptions about the qualitative property

Quality type	Qualitative property	Evaluation results	Discussion
Physical	Electronically stored	I	Both documents are stored electronically. Indirect assumption is that the evaluation is equal.
	Reusable	I	Both documents could be reused by "copy-paste" functionality. RequisitePro suggests the requirements extraction from the projects.
Empirical	Understand-able	B	3 (out of 4) characteristics describe requirements document of case B more understandable.
	Concise	I	The document in case B is longer than in case A (60 page in comparison to 43), but the evaluation shows better its quality.
Syntactic		=	The findings indicate syntactic correctness equal. The reason could be because both case have syntactic error prevention and detection means.
Semantic, Perceived semantic	Complete	B	9 evaluations indicate higher completeness of the requirements document produced in case B. They include better definition of terms, units, and concepts, relationships, style of referenced material. 6 characteristics evaluated better for case A, concern numeration pages, figures, paragraphs and requirements.
	Consistent	B	Consistency was evaluated by consideration consistency of described system behaviour, terms and requirements definitions.
	Precision	A	Adequacy number of numeric qualities and level of precision was evaluated.
	Traced	B	The origin of separate requirements, the possibility to make design and implementation according to the requirements document were evaluated.
	Traceable	B	
	Achievable	B	
	Design inde-pendent	B	
	Annotated	B	Annotation level according to element importance, relevant stability and version was considered.
	At the right level of for-mality	B	Level of the document formality was evaluated for separate requirements and the whole requirements model.
	Unambiguous	=	Level of ambiguity was evaluated.
Pragmatic	Cross-referenced	A	Level cross referencing was evaluated.
	Organized	B	Level organization was evaluated.
Social			Level of agreement about the requirement model is investigated through RE process.

Not evaluated features are *verifiable*, *executable*, *interpretable*, and *prototypable*, because they are domain, design and implementation oriented, and *modifiable*, *correct*, and *not redundant*, because they are dependent on the skills of the evaluators.

3.6.2 Results of Requirements Documents Evaluation

The results indicate that 25 (out of 39) characteristics of the requirements documents are evaluated higher in case B than in case A. 12 characteristics are found better in the requirements specification produced in case A. And 2 characteristics are evaluated equally. Table 5 shows the discussions of the evaluated characteristics and the qualitative properties after analysis of the characteristics of requirements documents.

3.7 Threats to Validity

The following possible threats to the validity of this study have been identified:
- The case study is executed in the university. But the case study examines the real problem - the system used to manage student exercises.
- The evaluation framework [24], applied to compare the RE process, is originally created to evaluate the functionality of the RE-tools. However, the literature study did not suggest an evaluation method for RE process. The evaluation framework [24] is chosen for comparison, because it addresses the major quality types and it is produced in respect to the RE activities and process.
- The subjective choice of the modelling and RE-tools. The software tools in both cases are chosen according to the participant experience and availability of the tools. RML editor and Rational Rose are used for the teaching purposes. Both CORE and RequisitePro got one of the highest scores in the tool evaluation [24].
- Most, if not all, of the quality properties are subjective [35]. But the evaluators provided comments on the requirements documents according the qualitative properties. The comments are used to improve the requirements documents.
- Participants provided subjective evaluations. The individuals interpret the quality according to their experience. Nevertheless, peer-to-peer method is used in order to collect as objective opinion about the requirements documents as possible.
- The case study and evaluation design are prepared by the same researcher. However, different participants were involved into the specification process, and the study contributes towards the objective evaluation results.
- The feasibly better requirements specification support and requirements document in case B could be because of the learning effect. The engineer was already familiar with the problem domain in case B. But both requirements specifications pay emphasis on the different requirements. Even more, the engineer was not familiar with the RE-tools. It results feasibly equal learning efforts in both cases.

The last threat suggests the settings for the similar case study with a higher number of participants and with the specification development in parallel in order to avoid the learning effect.

4 Conclusions and Lessons Learned

Two requirements specifications, which differ in the use of the engineering tools, are considered in this case study. In the first case the office and modelling tools are applied, in the second the RE-tools are used. The RE process is analyzed by the means of the evaluation framework [24]. Four experts investigate the quality of the requirements documents according to the qualitative properties [5].

The work findings suggest the management of the requirements specification by the means of the RE-tools, instead of the general tools. The results suggest that the RE-tool vendors should emphasize and support their products to the industrial and academic environments, that the requirements engineers would propagate the use of the RE tools in the companies. The findings also challenge to engineer the quick and inexpensive RE-tool acquisition method according to the environmental settings. Furthermore, the case study findings show the improvements for the RE-tools:

- Improve facilities for the geographically distributed collaborative work. Collaborative work contributes for improvement of requirements analysis, negotiation and strategic planning [6, 30].
- Improve user training on modelling languages and methods. The tool tutorials present only main functions without consideration of the modelling perspective. The RE-tools are meant for experienced users [10, 16, 24], who are familiar with the tool supported modelling language. However, the RE-tools should help both experienced and not skilled users.
- Improve RE support by the ad-hoc functionality. Although the RE tools suggest the basic functionality for the RE activities, they: 1) lack ad hoc functionality [27], 2) do not provide the pre-configuration to organizational needs [10], 3) act as CASE tools [13], 4) lack "how to do" scenarios.
- Provide means to create formal representation. None of the RE-tools represent requirements formally. Formal model contributes with operational semantics, and leads to the executable and interpretable requirements document [5].
- Improve information interchange among software tools. The support of different modelling facilities under the same environment would ensure the information control, understandability and flexibility of a requirements document.
- Improve the reuse of the requirements. The RE-tools, however, support reuse of syntactic aspects. Semantic and pragmatic viewpoints are addressed through the engineer. Maintenance of repositories would allow the reuse of requirements specification at different levels of formality through various projects.
- Support standard requirements documentation. Vendors of RE-tools claim that their products support international standards. However, the RE-tools support standards, defined within the organization. The tools should provide guidelines of standard applicability.
- Provide requirements numeration schemes. RE-tools should suggest guidelines for the uniquely identifiable requirement numeration according to semantic dependency to requirements group and domain. The functionality would improve the precision, completeness and cross reference of a requirements document.

The presented requirements specification process is feasible small and thus might be not representative for the larger information system development, where the automated support is most heavily needed. This suggests the investigation of requirements specification under the industrial settings, and involving a bigger number of participants as a future work.

Acknowledgment

The author would like to thank Guttorm Sindre for discussions and feedback concerning drafts of this paper.

References

1. Bayias P. P.: The Requirements Engineering Process of ΟΑΣΗΣ: An Industrial Case Study. Joint 7th European Software Engineering Conference and 7th ACM SIGSOFT Symposium on the Foundations of Software Engineering (ESEC/FSE), Toulouse, France, 1999
2. CORE: A Guided Tour. Release 3.0. 1 2.2000, URL: http://www.vtcorp.com/productline.html
3. Costello R. J., Liu D. B.: Metrics for Requirements Engineering. System Software, 29, (1995), 39-63.
4. Cox, K., Phalp, K.T., Shepperd, M.: Comparing Use Case Writing Guidelines. 7th Int. Workshop on Requirements Engineering: Foundation for Software Quality, REFSQ'01, 2001, Interlaken, Switzerland, 101-112.
5. Davis A. M, Overmeyer S., Jordan K., Caruso., Dandashi F., Dinh A., Kincaid A., Ledeboer G., Reynolds G., Sitaram P., Ta P., Theofanos A.: Identifying and Measuring Quality in a Software Requirements Specification. Proceedings of the First International Software Metrics Symposium, (1993) 141-152.
6. Damian D. E., Eberlein A., Shaw M. L. G. Gaines B. R. An Exploratory Study of facilitation in Distributed Requirements Engineering. Requirements Engineering, 8 (2003), 23-41.
7. Ferdinandi, P. L.: A Requirements Pattern. Succeeding in the Internet Economy. Addison-Wesley, (2002).
8. IEEE Recommended Practice for Software Requirements Specification, IEEE Std 830-1993 (Revision of IEEE Std 830-1998), (1994).
9. ISO/IEC 9126: Information Technology – Software Product Evaluation - Quality Characteristics and Guide Lines for their Use. ISO/IEC IS 9126, Geneva, Switzerland, (1991).
10. James L.: What Wrong with Requirements Management Tools, Requirements Engineering, 1, (1996), 190-194
11. Harrison W., Ossher H., Tarr P.: Software Engineering Tools and Environments: a Roadmap. In: Finkelstein A. (eds.): The Future of Software Engineering. ACM Press (2000).
12. Kaindl H., Brinkkemper S., Bubenko Jr. J., Farbey B., Greenspan S. J., Heitmeyer C. L., do Prado Leite J. C. S., Mead N. R., Mylopoulos J., Siddiqi: Requirements Engineering and Technology Transfer: Obstacles, Incentives, and Improvement Agenda. Requirements Engineering, 7 (2002), 113-123.
13. Kelly S., Lyytinen K., Rossi M.: MetaEdit+ A Fully Configuarable Multi-User and Multi-Tool CASE and CAME Environment. In: Constantopoulos P., Mylopoulos J., Vassiliou Y. (eds.): Advances Information System Engineering, 8th International Conference, CAiSE'96, Heraklion, Crete, Greece, May 20-24, 1996, 1-21.
14. Khwaja A. R., Urban J. E.: A Synthesis of Evaluation Criteria for Software Specifications and Specification Techniques. Journal of Software Engineering and Knowledge Engineering, 15 (5), 2002, pp 581-599

15. von Knethen A., Kamsties E., Reussner R., Bunse C., Shen B.: A Comparative Study with Industrial Requirements Engineering Methods. Software and Systems Engineering. 3, 1998.
16. Kotonya G., Sommerville I.: Requirements Engineering: Process and Techniques. Wiley, (1998).
17. Krogstie J.: A Semiotic Approach to Quality in Requirements Specifications. Proceedings IFIP 8.1 Working Conference on Organizational Semiotics, (2001).
18. Kulak D., Guiney E.: Use Cases: Requirements in Context. Addison-Weslay (1998).
19. Lang M., Duggan J.: A Tool to Support Collaborative Software Requirements Management. Requirement Engineering 6 (2001) 161-172
20. Lausen, S.: Software Requirements. Styles and Techniques. Addison-Wesley, (2002).
21. Leffingwell D., Widrig D.: Managing Software Requirements. A Unified Approach. Addison-Wesley, (2000)
22. Lindland O.I., Sindre G., Sølvberg A.: Understanding Quality in Conceptual Modelling. IEEE Software 11, 2 (1994) 42-49.
23. Loucopoulos P., Karakostas V.: System Requirements Engineering. McGraw-Hill, (1995).
24. Matulevičius, R.: Validating an Evaluation Framework for Requirement Engineering Tools. Proceedings of the 8th CAiSE/IFIP8.1 International Workshop on Evaluation of Modeling Methods in Systems Analysis and Design (EMMSAD'03), (2003) 84-93.
25. McCall J. A., Richards P. K., Walters G. F.: Factors in Software Quality. Rome Air Development Center, (1977).
26. Mora M. M.: Requirements Metrics. An Initial Literature Survey on Measurement Approaches for Requirement Specifications. Kaiserslautern, 2003.
27. Nguyen L., Swatman P. A.: Managing the Requirements Engineering Process, Requirements Engineering. 8 (2003), 55-68.
28. Nikula, U., J. Sajaniemi, J., Kälviäinen H.: A State-of-the-Practice Survey on Requirements Engineering in Small- and Medium-Sized Enterprises. TBRC Research Report 1, Telecom Business Research Center Lappeenranta, Lappeenranta University of Technology, (2000).
29. Pohl K.: The Three Dimensions of Requirements Engineering: a Framework and its Applications. Information systems, 19 (3), (1994) 243-258.
30. Regnell, B., Host M., Natt och Dag J., Hjelm T.: Visualization of Agreement and Satisfaction in Distributed Prioritization of Market Requirements. Proceedings of the 6th International Workshop on Requirements Engineering – Foundation for Software Quality, REFSQ2000, Sweden, 2000.
31. Rational Rose: URL: http://www.rational.com/
32. RequisitePro: Rational RequisitePro v2002. Evaluators Guide with a Requirements Management Overview. URL: http://www.rational.com/
33. Sinha A. P., Vessey I.: An Empirical Investigation of Entity-based and Object-oriented Data Modeling: a Development Life Cycle Approach. Proceedings of the 20th International Conference on Information Systems, Charlotte, North Carolina, USA, (1999), 229-244.
34. Sølvberg A: Data and What They Refer To. In: Chen P., Akoka J., Kangassalo H., and Thalheim B. (eds.): Conceptual Modeling: Current Issues and Future Trends. LNCS 1565, Springer Verlag, (1999).
35. Wilson W. M., Rosenberg L., H., Hyatt L.: Automated Quality Analysis of Natural Language Requirement Specification. Fourteen Annual Pacific Northwest Software Quality Conference, October, 1996.
36. Zave, P.: Classification of Research Efforts in Requirements Engineering. ACM Computing Surveys, 29(4), (1997), 5-32.

Model-Driven Requirements Engineering: Synchronising Models in an Air Traffic Management Case Study

Neil A.M. Maiden[1], Sara V. Jones[1], Sharon Manning[1],
John Greenwood[2], and L. Renou[3]

[1] Centre for Human-Computer Interaction Design, City University, London
[2] National Air Traffic Services, London, UK
[3] Sofreavia/CENA, Paris, France

Abstract. Different modelling techniques from different disciplines are needed to model complex socio-technical systems and their requirements. This paper describes the application of RESCUE, a process that integrates 4 modelling techniques to model and analyse stakeholder requirements for DMAN, a system for scheduling and managing the departure of aircraft from major European airports. It describes how human activity, use case and *i** modelling were applied and integrated using synchronisation checks to model requirements on DMAN. Synchronisation checks applied at predefined stages in RESCUE revealed omissions and potential inconsistencies in the models and stakeholder requirements that, in turn, led to improvements to the models and resulting specification. The paper ends with implications for requirements model integration, and describes future work to extend and apply RESCUE.

1 Introduction

Complex socio-technical systems such as air traffic management (ATM) – in which people depend on computer systems to do their work – need to be analysed from different perspectives. To do this we need to employ different modelling techniques in synchronised ways to analyse a future system and its requirements from all necessary perspectives. Research provides us with different system and requirements modelling techniques (e.g. Yu & Mylopoulos 1994, De Landtsheer et al. 2003, Hall et al. 2002, Rumbaugh et al. 1998). However, further research is needed to synchronise them when modelling complex socio-technical systems.

In particular, research must overcome 2 major challenges. Firstly, we need to be scale existing techniques to model and analyse large systems in which people computer systems interact. Whilst some techniques such as the Rational Unified Process (RUP) and UML are used to model large systems, more research-based techniques such as *i** have yet to be used extensively to model large socio-technical systems. The RUP was developed to model software systems, and lacks representations for early requirements and techniques for reasoning about complex systems boundaries and work allocation that *i** offers. Secondly, given the divergent purposes for which these techniques were originally developed, we need to be able to synchronise them to detect possible requirements omissions, inconsistencies and conflicts. One problem is

A. Persson and J. Stirna (Eds.): CAiSE 2004, LNCS 3084, pp. 368–383, 2004.
© Springer-Verlag Berlin Heidelberg 2004

that established requirements techniques have emerged from single disciplines – use cases from software engineering and task analysis from human-computer interaction are two obvious examples. Safety-critical socio-technical systems such as ATM demand rigorous analyses of controller work, software systems that support this controller work, and the complex interactions between the controllers, the air traffic and the software systems. To do this we need new processes that synchronise and analyse models from the relevant disciplines. This paper presents one such process, RESCUE, and describes its application to a large and computerised ATM system project.

Previously, academic researchers worked with Eurocontrol to design and implement RESCUE, an innovative process to determine stakeholder requirements for systems that will provide computerised assistance to air traffic controllers. RESCUE was successfully applied to determine the requirements for CORA-2, a complex socio-technical system in which controllers work with a computerised system to resolve conflicts between aircraft on a collision path (Mavin & Maiden 2003). The first half of this paper reports the application of a new version of RESCUE to model the requirements for DMAN, a socio-technical system for scheduling and managing the departure of aircraft from major European airports such as Heathrow and Charles de Gaulle. A requirements team that included engineers from UK and French air traffic service providers modelled the DMAN system and requirements using techniques including human activity modelling (Vicenze 1999), $i*$ (Yu & Mylopoulos 1994), and use cases (Cockburn 2000). The second half of the paper reports the use and effectiveness of RESCUE synchronisation checks for cross-referencing and integrating these different model types during the RESCUE process.

The remainder of this paper is in 5 sections. Section 2 describes related research. Sections 3 and 4 outline the RESCUE process and describe its synchronisation checks. Section 5 reports the application of RESCUE to DMAN with emphasis on data about the effectiveness of the synchronisation checks. The paper ends with discussion and future research and applications.

2 Related Work

RESCUE draws together and extends work from different sources. Several authors, including Cockburn (2000), have extended use case techniques with structured templates. Our work adopts these best-practice extensions to use cases, but also adds several use case attributes that inform scenario generation from use cases reported in Mavin & Maiden (2003).

The $i*$ method for agent-oriented requirements engineering is well documented (e.g. Yu & Mylopoulos 1994). More recently, researchers have been reporting examples that demonstrate $i*$'s applicability for handling non-functional issues such as security and privacy applied to healthcare systems (Liu et al. 2003). Whilst the reported examples demonstrate $i*$'s potentially scaleability, most models have been developed by the research team. In contrast, RESCUE requires other engineers to produce $i*$ models for the large socio-technical systems, thus providing additional data about the usability and effectiveness of the method on industrial case studies.

Other researchers have integrated the $i*$ goal modelling approach implemented in RESCUE with use case approaches. Santander & Castro (2002) present guidelines for automatically deriving use case models from $i*$ system models, and Liu & Yu (2001) integrate goal modelling with the GRL with use case maps to refine scenarios into architectural designs with goal-based rationale. Our work in RESCUE is similar to the latter work but exploits $i*$ models to scope use case models, specify use cases and inform scenario walkthroughs rather than derive architectures per se.

Detecting and reasoning across models during early requirements work has received little attention, especially for socio-technical systems (Nuseibeh et al. 2003). Leveson et al. (2000) describe a safety and human-centred approach that integrates human factors and systems engineering work. Although similar in spirit to RESCUE, their approach includes safety hazard analysis and verification that were outside RESCUE's scope, and covers the full development cycle.

3   The RESCUE Process

The RESCUE (Requirements Engineering with Scenarios for User-Centred Engineering) process was developed by multi-disciplinary researchers (Maiden et al. 2003). It supports a concurrent engineering process in which different modelling and analysis processes take place in parallel. The concurrent processes are structured into 4 streams shown in Figure 1.

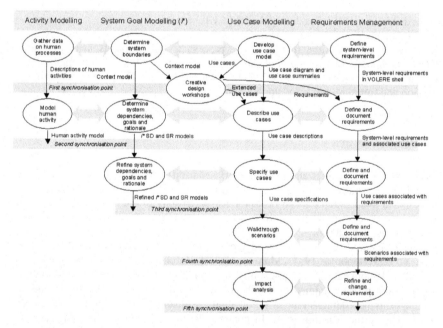

Fig. 1. The RESCUE process structure – activity modeling ends after the synchronization stage at stage 2, system modeling after the synchronization stage at stage 3, and scenario-driven walkthroughs and modeling requirements after synchronization checks at stage 5.

Each stream has a unique and specific purpose in the specification of a socio-technical system:

1. Human activity modelling provides an understanding of how people work, in order to baseline possible changes to it (Vicente 1999);
2. System modelling enables the team to model the future system boundaries, actor dependencies and most important system goals (Yu & Mylopoulos 1994);
3. Use case modelling and scenario-driven walkthroughs enable the team to communicate more effectively with stakeholders and acquire complete, precise and testable requirements from them (Sutcliffe et al. 1998);
4. Managing requirements enables the team to handle the outcomes of the other 3 streams effectively as well as impose quality checks on all aspects of the requirements document (Robertson & Robertson 1999).

Sub-processes during these 4 streams are co-ordinated using 5 synchronisation stages that provide the project team with different perspectives with which to analyse system boundaries, goals and scenarios. These stages are implemented as synchronisation checks described later in the paper that are applied to the models at each stage. The next sections describe each of the 4 streams in more detail.

3.1 Human Activity Modelling

In this RESCUE stream the project team develops an understanding of the current socio-technical system to inform specification of a future system. Activity modelling focuses on the human users of the technical system, in line with the principle of human-centred automation (ICAO 1994). To do this the project team must first understand the controllers' current work – its individual cognitive and non-cognitive components and social and co-operative elements - to specify the technical systems that can better support that work. Introducing artefacts, tools or procedures into the work domain changes the way in which people work and process information. It also brings about changes in the cooperative, and possibly organisational structures that are related to the new system. The stream consists of two sub-processes – gathering data about and modelling the human activity. Figure 2 describes 2 actions that make up one human activity description – how runway controllers at Heathrow give line-up clearance to aircraft. Different aspects of the model are linked to the scenario as a whole or each action, thus providing a structured but flexible description of current work practices.

One key concept in an activity model is goals - the desired states of the system. Goals may be: (i) high-level functional goals relating to the system as a whole, or local goals relating to particular tasks; (ii) individual goals, relating to single actors, or collective goals, relating to teams of actors; (iii) prescribed goals or non-prescribed goals. Other aspects to describe in a model include human actors - people involved in system; resources – means that are available to actors to achieve their goals, for example flight strips and information about a flight; resource management strategies – how actors achieve their goals with the resources available, for example writing down flight information on the flight strips; constraints - environmental properties that affect decisions, for example the size on the flight strip bay, which limits the number of strips to work with; actions - undertaken by actors to solve problems or achieve goals; contextual features – situational factors that influence decision-making, for example

Goals: Decision made to when the next aircraft can line up, Pilot given line-up clearance, Strip positioned correctly in the bay, LVP or MDI procedures adhered to, if in effect
1.   Departure/Air controller decides which aircraft can next line up and when   Resources - strip   Physical actions - touch strip, look at airfield, aircraft, holding point and runway, move to look out of window   Cognitive actions - read strip information, validate visually, recognise aircraft and match with strip, recognise when it is appropriate to give line up clearance, formulate aircraft line up clearance sequence, understand current airspace, runway and capacity situation
2.   Runway ATCo calls Pilot and gives line up clearance   Resources - strip, radio, headset   Physical actions - touch strip, flick radio transmission switch, look aircraft, runway and holding point, move to look out of window   Communication - talk to pilot, issue clearance, provide information   Cognitive actions - read strip information, validate visually,

Fig. 2. Part of the DMAN Human Activity Model.

priorities are given to incoming aircraft. Data describing these concepts is structured into the activity descriptions such as the one presented in Figure 2.

3.2   System Modelling

In this RESCUE stream the project team models the future system's actors (humans and otherwise), dependencies between these actors and how these actors achieve their goals, in order to explore the boundaries, architecture and most important goals of the socio-technical system. RESCUE adopts the established *i** approach (Yu & Mylopoulos 1994) but extends it to model complex technical and social systems, establish different types of system boundaries, and derive requirements. *i** is an approach originally developed to model information systems composed of heterogeneous actors with different, often-competing goals that nonetheless depend on each other to undertake their tasks and achieve these goals – like the complex socio-technical systems found in ATM.

The systems modelling stream requires 3 analyses to produce 3 models. The first is a context diagram, similar to the REVEAL process (Praxis 2001) but extended to show different candidate boundaries based on different types of adjacent actors (Robertson & Robertson 1999). The result is an extended context model with typed actors that provides a starting point for *i** system modelling.

The second model is the *i** Strategic Dependency (SD) model, which describes a network of dependency relationships among actors identified in the context model (Yu & Mylopoulos 1994). Figure 3 shows a draft SD model for the DMAN system. It specifies other systems that either depend on or are depended on by DMAN (e.g. TACT and A-SMGCS), and human roles that depend on DMAN to do their work (e.g. Runway ATCO and Departure Clearance ATCO). For example, the SD model specifies that *DMAN depends on TACT to achieve the goal CTOT and slot messages updated*, and *A-SMGCS depends on DMAN to undertake the task update taxi time estimates*. Likewise, *DMAN depends on the Tower Departure Sequencer ATCo to have the departure sequence manual update*, and the *Departure Clearance ATCo depends on DMAN to achieve the soft goal workload not increased*.

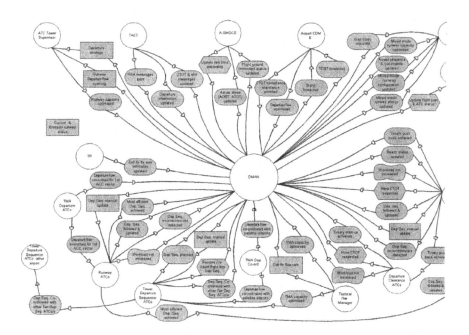

RESCUE provokes the team to ask important questions about systems boundaries by re-expressing them in terms of the goal dependencies between actors on either side of a boundary. Actors with goals that the team will seek to test for compliance are, by definition, part of the new system. Such re-expression also leads to more effective requirements specification by referring to named actors that will be tested for compliance (e.g. "The *controller* using DMAN shall have access to the departure sequence"). It also suggests a first-cut architecture and functional allocation for the socio-technical system by defining which actors undertake which tasks.

The second type of *i** model is the Strategic Rationale (SR) model, which provides an intentional description of how each actor achieves its goals and soft goals. In the SR model for DMAN's human Runway ATCO actor, this actor undertakes one major task – *control flight around the runway* – that is decomposed into other tasks such as *issue line-up clearance* and *issue take-off clearance*. The former task can be further decomposed into sub-tasks and sub-goals which, if undertaken and achieved, contribute negatively to the achievement of an important soft goal – that *workload should not be increased*. Furthermore, to do the *issue line-up clearance* task, the Runway ATCO depends on the resource *flight information* from the electronic flight strip.

This stream provides key inputs to the managing requirements and scenario-driven walkthroughs. Goals and soft goals in *i** SR models become requirements in the managing requirements stream. Context and *i** models define the system boundaries essential for use case modelling and authoring. The *i** SR models define goal and task structures that suggest skeletal use case descriptions to refine the scenario-driven walkthroughs stream.

3.3 Scenario-Driven Walkthroughs

In this RESCUE stream the team writes use cases then generates and walks through rich scenarios to discover and acquire stakeholder requirements that are complete, precise and testable. It uses the research-based ART-SCENE environment, which supports the automatic generation of scenarios from use case descriptions and systematic scenario walkthroughs to discover, acquire and describe requirements. The ART-SCENE environment was successfully to discover requirements for the CORA-2 system (Mavin & Maiden 2003). In this paper we focus on 2 out of the 5 sub-processes.

The first sub-process is use case modelling (Jacobson et al. 2000) that we have extended to model and investigate different system boundaries identified in the context model. The outcome is a use case model with use cases and short descriptions that are inputs into use case authoring. The DMAN use case diagram specifies human actor roles and their associations with 13 use cases and one abstract use case.

In the second sub-process the team writes detailed use case descriptions using the structured templates derived from use case best practice (e.g. Cockburn 2000). To write each description the team draw on outputs from the other streams – activity models, *i** strategic rationale models, stakeholder requirements, and innovative design ideas from the creativity workshops. Once each use case description is complete and agreed with the relevant stakeholders, the team produce a use case specification from it, and parameterise it to generate scenarios automatically from each description. Part of a use case description is shown in Figure 4.

	UC9 Change the Runway Spacing Strategy
Date	16 October 2003
Source	Stage 1 Document
Actors	ATC Tower Supervisor, Tower Departure Sequencer ATCO, TMA Departure Co-ordinator, AMAN, Tower Departure Sequencer ATCO (other airports), ATC Tower Supervisor (other airports), Tactical Flow Manager.
Problem Statement (now)	Integrate runway spacing strategy into departure planning process
Triggering Event	An imbalance between arrival and departure delay is predicted
Assumptions	We assume that the runway spacing is defined by the number of take off and landing per hour for each runway.
Successful End States	A time to implement new runway spacing is agreed by ATC Tower Supervisor and TMA Departure Coordinator. The DMAN departure sequence takes into account the change in runway allocation.
Unsuccessful End States	DMAN departure plan does not allow for runway spacing change at the correct time.
Normal Course	1. The ATC Tower Supervisor looks at the predicted arrival delays in AMAN
	2. The ATC Tower Supervisor looks at the predicted departure delays in DMAN
	3. The ATC Tower Supervisor considers the predicted arrival and departure delays
	4. The ATC Tower Supervisor decides that a different spacing strategy would be preferable.
	5. Abstract Use Case 14(the ATC Tower Supervisor performs "What-Ifs" with DMAN)
	6. The ATC Tower Supervisor contacts the TMA Departure Coordinator by telephone
	7. The ATC Tower Supervisor states the proposed new runway spacing strategy.
	8. The TMA Departure Coordinator agrees the new spacing strategy.
	9. AMAN re-plans arrivals taking into account the new runway configuration
	10. AMAN notifies DMAN that the re-planning of arrivals is complete
	11. CALL UC6 (DMAN Updates the Departure Sequence) for this airport.

Fig. 4. Part of a draft DMAN use case description for UC9: Change the runway spacing strategy.

3.4 Managing Requirements

In this fourth RESCUE stream the project team documents, manages and analyses requirements generated from the other 3 streams – automation and process requirements emerging from human activity modelling, system actor goals and soft goals from *i** system modelling, and requirements arising from scenario walkthroughs.

Each requirement is documented using the VOLERE shell (Robertson & Robertson 1999), a requirement-attribute structure that guides the team to make each requirement testable according to its type. Use cases and scenarios are essential to making requirements testable. Each new requirement is specified either for the whole system, one or more use cases of that system, or one or more actions in a use case. This RESCUE requirement structure links requirements to and places them in use cases and use case actions "in context", thus making it much easier to a write a measurable fit criterion for each requirement. RESCUE requirements are documented using IBM Rational's Requisite Pro. Outputs from other streams, such as use case, context and *i** models, are also included in the document.

4 Synchronisation Checking

Work and deliverables from RESCUE's 4 streams are coordinated at 5 key synchronisation points at the end of RESCUE's 5 stages, implemented as one or more workshops with deliverables to be signed off by stakeholder representatives:

1. The **boundaries** point, where the team establishes first-cut system boundaries and undertakes creative thinking to investigate these boundaries;
2. The **work allocation** point, where the team allocate functions between actors according to boundaries, and describe interaction and dependencies between these actors;
3. The **generation** point, where required actor goals, tasks and resources are elaborated and modelled, and scenarios are generated;
4. The **coverage** point, where stakeholders have walked through scenarios discover and express all requirements so that they are testable;
5. The **consequences** point, where stakeholders undertake walkthroughs of the scenarios and system models to explore impacts of implementing the system as specified on its environment.

The synchronisation checks applied at these 5 points are designed using a RESCUE meta-model of human activity, use case and *i** modelling concepts constructed specifically to design the synchronisation checks. It is shown in simplified form in Figure 5 – the thicker horizontal lines define the baseline concept mappings across the different models used in RESCUE.

In simple terms, the meta-model maps actor goals in human activity models to requirements in use case descriptions and *i** goals and soft goals. Likewise, human activities map to use cases, and human actions to use case actions that involve human actors in use cases and tasks undertaken by human actors in *i** models. Human activity resources map to *i** resources and objects manipulated in use case actions, and actors in all 3 types of model are mapped. The complete meta-model is more refined. Types and attributes are applied to constrain possible mappings, for example use case descriptions and *i** models describe system actors, however only human actors in these models can be mapped to actors in human activity models.

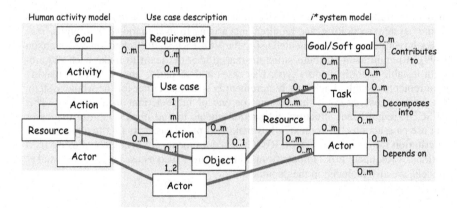

Fig. 5. RESCUE concept meta-model as a UML class diagram showing mappings between constructs in the 3 model types.

This paper reports the application of synchronisation checks at the first 2 stages. At Stage 1, data about human activities and the extended context model are used to check the completeness and correctness of the use case model. Use case summaries are used to check system-level requirements. Checks are:

Check 1.1	Every major human activity (e.g. applying resolutions) should correspond to one or more use cases in the use case model.
Check 1.2	Every actor identified in human activity modelling is a candidate actor for the context model.
Check 1.3	Every adjacent actor (at levels 2, 3 or 4 of the context model) that communicates directly with the technical system (level 1 in the context model) should appear as an actor in the use case diagram.
Check 1.4	The system boundary in the use case diagram should be the same as the boundary between levels 1 and 2 in the context model.
Check 1.5	Services and functions related to use cases in the use case model should map to system level requirements, i.e. high-level functional and non-functional requirements, in the requirement database.

At Stage 2, most cross checking is done in order to bring the human activity and first-cut *i** models to bear on the development of correct and complete use case descriptions. Checks are:

Check 2.1	Actors, resources, goals, actions and resource management strategies identified in activity modelling should be represented in the *i** SD and SR models as appropriate.
Check 2.2	Actors, resources, goals, actions, differences due to variations, and differences due to contextual features in the activity models should appear in relevant use case descriptions.
Check 2.3	Goals identified in the activity models should be reflected in the system and use case-level requirements in the requirement database
Check 2.4	All external actors in the *i** SD model should correspond to actors in the use case descriptions.
Check 2.5.1	Each low level task (i.e. each task that is not decomposed into further lower-level tasks) undertaken by an actor in the *i** SR model, should correspond to one or more actions in a use case description.

Check 2.5.2	Each resource used in, or produced from, a task in the $i*$ SR model should be described in a use case description.
Check 2.5.3	Ensure that dependencies modelled in the $i*$ models are respected in the use case descriptions, in particular: • For goal and soft goal dependencies, the dependee must first produce whatever is needed for the depender to achieve the goal or soft goal; • For resource dependencies, the dependee must first produce the resource that the depender needs in order for the depender to be able to use it; • For task dependencies, the dependee must first make available whatever the depender needs in order for the depender to be able to do the task, perhaps via communication.
Check 2.6	All goals and soft-goals to be achieved by the future system according to the $i*$ SR model should be specified in the system requirements specification and stored in the requirements database.
Check 2.7	All requirements associated with a use case in the use case template should be expressed in the system requirements specification and stored in the requirements database.

These synchronisation checks were applied in first 2 stages of DMAN, as described in the remainder of this paper.

5 DMAN Case Study

The RESCUE process was applied to specify the operational requirements for DMAN, Eurocontrol's new system for scheduling and managing departures from major European airports. DMAN is a complex socio-technical system involving a range of human actors including tower controllers and aircraft pilots, interacting with other computer-based systems related to both airport and air movements, and supporting aircraft movement from push back from the gate to take off from the runway. The project was led by the UK's National Air Traffic Services (NATS) and involved participants from Centre d'Etudes de la Navigation Aerienne (CENA) and City University's RESCUE experts. The DMAN team was composed of 2 systems engineers employed by NATS and CENA and one RESCUE team member from City. It also worked with 4 UK and 4 French air traffic controllers who were seconded to the project, other NATS and CENA engineers, and software engineering academics. At the beginning of the project the City experts trained 5 NATS and CENA engineers, including the 2 in the DMAN team, in the RESCUE process using presentations and exercises. There were two days training on $i*$ system modelling, two days on use cases, scenarios and requirements management, and one day on human activity modelling.

The project started in February 2003 and was timetabled to take 9 months to produce DMAN's operational requirements document. Stages 2 and 3 were completed in September 2003, with stage 4 scenario walkthroughs taking place in October and November 2003. Stage 2 deliverables included a human activity model describing how UK controllers at Heathrow currently manage the departure of aircraft, a DMAN use case model and use case descriptions, system-level requirements, and some $i*$ SD and SR models for DMAN. The human activity model was divided into 15 scenarios describing controller work, reported in a 50-page deliverable. The use case model contained 8 actors and 15 use cases. Each use case contained, on average, 13 normal course actions and 3 variations to the normal course behaviour. The majority of these use case actions were human actions or actions involving interaction with DMAN and other computer-based systems, rather than system actions. The $i*$ SD model specified 15 actors with 46 dependencies between these 15 actors. The SR model was more complex, with a total of 103 model elements describing 7 of the 15 actors defined in the SD model.

Stage 2 RESCUE deliverables were developed in parallel based on signed off deliverables from stage 1 of the RESCUE process by staff with the relevant available resources and expertise. The human activity model was developed primarily by City staff, the use case model and descriptions by NATS staff, and the $i*$ models by CENA staff. Throughout stage 2 all staff had access to intermediate versions of the models under development elsewhere in the project. Therefore, synchronisation checks were needed at the end of stage 2 to detect omissions, ambiguities and inconsistencies in the requirements models that arose in spite of regular communication between partners.

The RESCUE stage 2 synchronisation checks were described in the previous section. In DMAN, the checks were applied by the RESCUE quality gatekeeper, one member of City staff responsible for maintaining the DMAN requirements repository and validating inputs to it. The synchronisation checks took the gatekeeper approximately 8 days of full-time work to apply. Results were documented using pre-designed tables with issues and action lists that were reported to DMAN team members to resolve.

5.1 Results from the Synchronisation Checks

Table 1 summarises the number of checks applied, issues arising, and actions resulting from the checks. Furthermore check 2.0, which verifies that the $i*$ SR model is consistent with its originating SD model, led to 19 additional issues to be resolved – mostly SD elements and dependency links that were missing from the SR model. Likewise, other within-stream checks, such as verifying all use case descriptions against the originating use case model were undertaken. In the remainder of this paper we focus on the more interesting results arising from the model synchronisation checks across the streams.

Table 1 shows that the synchronisation checks generated very different numbers and types of issue and actions for the team to resolve. Three checks – 1.3, 2.4 and 2.5.3 - generated nearly 92% of all identified issues. In contrast, Checks 1.5, 2.3 2.6 and 2.7 were not applied due to the model-driven approach adopted by the DMAN team – rather than establish VOLERE requirements at the same time as the models, the team chose to derive such requirements from the models at the end of stage 3, hence there were no requirements in the data base to check against. Check 2.1 was also not applied in Stage 2 due to lack of resources. The check verifies the human activity and $i*$ models – given the importance of scenarios in RESCUE, resources were focused on verifying the use case descriptions against other models.

Synchronisation with the human activity model was verified using checks 1.1, 1.2 and 2.2. Check 1.1 revealed 3 current human activities that were not included in a DMAN use case – subsequent analysis revealed that these activities were not part of the DMAN socio-technical system, and no model changes were needed, and the ra-

Table 1. Quantitative summary of synchronisation checks applied to RESCUE models arising from stages 1 and 2.

Check ID	Total issues arising	Issues and actions for RESCUE models
Check 1.1	3	Activities without use cases, no action required.
Check 1.2	4	Actors missing from context model, no action required.
Check 1.3	21	Missing actors and actor links in use case model, incorrect actor naming, needs changes.
Check 1.4	0	No issues arising between context and use case model.
Check 1.5	0	No system-level requirements.
Check 2.1	-	Not applied yet – reason explained in text.
Check 2.2	1	Ambiguity detected, needs changes.
Check 2.3	0	No use case-level requirements.
Check 2.4	37	Omitted actors from use case descriptions, needs changes.
Check 2.5.1	5	Omissions from use case descriptions, needs changes.
Check 2.5.2	0	All resources included.
Check 2.5.3	55	Ambiguities needing clarification, missing use case elements, dependencies between use cases discovered, use case decomposition needed, action ordering wrong, missing non-functional requirements, needs changes.
Check 2.6	0	No use case-level requirements.
Check 2.7	0	No use case-level requirements.

tionale for this was documented. Likewise, check 1.3 revealed that 4 human actor roles missing from the context model were no longer roles in the new DMAN system, and no changes were made to the model. Check 2.2 verified whether contextual features in the human activity model had been included in the use case descriptions, and one issue arose. The activity model revealed the importance of removing flights completely from the departure sequence – activities without responding use cases and actions in the use case description. The issue led to a pending change to the use case model.

Check 1.3, verifying that actors in the context model are also specified in the use case model, revealed 21 issues to synchronise. Of these 21 issues, 2 were discrepancies in actor names, 13 were missing links between the actor and the use case, and 6 actors were missing from the use case diagram. A pattern emerged. All but one of the missing actors were external software systems (e.g. FDPS and A-SMGCS) while the missing links were with human actors such as Ground ATCO. This was because of a decision to simplify the stage 1 use case model to only show primary rather than secondary actors on the use case diagram. One consequence from this decision is the result of check 2.4, which identified 37 actors that were missing from the use case descriptions. During the retrospective interview, the NATS systems engineer reported that use case descriptions provided effective mechanisms for describing detailed interaction, but at the expense of structure (*"it's always hard to see both the wood and the trees"*). New mechanisms to show the overall structure of an individual use case were needed.

Checks 2.5.1 to 2.5.3 verified the use case descriptions against the *i** models. Check 2.5.2 revealed no missing resources from the use case descriptions. Check 2.5.1 identified 5 SR model tasks undertaken by actors that are not described in any use case description. The tasks *Departure Clearance ATCO, Ground ATCO and Runway all respect the CTOT, the Runway ATCO issues takeoff clearance*, and *Tower Departure Sequencer ATCO gets discrepancy between capacity and departure de-*

mand lacked corresponding actions in the use cases, suggesting omissions and further actions to synchronise the use case descriptions and *i** models.

Check 2.5.3, which investigates whether use case descriptions respect *i** model dependencies, revealed 55 important issues to resolve in the RESCUE models. Furthermore, only 14 of the total of 69 checks did not raise an issue, suggesting that check 2.5.3 is more useful to apply than other checks. Table 2 describes the different types of issues and their frequency of occurrence that arose from applying check 2.5.3.

Table 2. Total instance of different types of result arising from applying Check 2.5.3.

Types of issues arising from application of Check 2.5.3	Total instances of occurrence
Checks resulting in no issue or change	14
Potential ambiguities requiring clarification and resolution	18
Actors and/or actors missing from use case description	17
Important dependencies between use cases discovered	6
Other elements missing from use case description	5
Error or inconsistent data in the use case description	2
Use case and use case description missing	2
Soft goals or non-functional requirements missing from use case	2
General ambiguity identified in the use case	1
Potential decomposition of a use case and its description needed	1
Actions in use case description in the wrong order	1

Most of the 18 potential ambiguities arose from *i** dependencies that require a specific ordering of actions both within and across use cases. Each ambiguity gave rise to a potential inconsistency that might arise due to un-stated assumption about the DMAN system. For example, the *i** models specified that the Ground ATCo depends on DMAN to undertake the task *Check MOBT (measured off-block time)*, and *DMAN must update the MOBT*. Use case UC3 specifies 2 actions: (2) *The Ground ATCO looks for the flight information on the DMAN display*: (3) *The Ground ATCO checks that the status of the flight in DMAN is 'OK to Push'*. The two dependencies are true if we assume that MOBT information is provided by DMAN and is included in the check undertaken by the ATCO. The resulting action was to establish and document the underlying domain assumption and, where necessary, change one or more of the models.

The check also revealed 17 cases of actor actions missing from the use case descriptions. For example, the *i** models specified that the R*unway ATCO (an actor in many use cases) depends on the Tower Departure Sequencer (TDS) ATCO to have the departure sequence followed and updated*, which in turn depends on the *TDS ATCO planning the departure sequence*. However, no actions in which the TDS ATCO plans the departure sequence are specified in the use case descriptions. Other use case elements were also missing, for example, the *i** models specified that *DMAN depends on the Ground ATCO to achieve the goal of ready status updated*, which in turn depends on the *Ground ATCO doing the task forward ready status*, but no actions corresponding to the task were specified in the use case descriptions. In 2 cases, these dependencies revealed a possible missing use case – *an actor uses DMAN to evaluate capacity and demand*.

Finally, the check revealed potentially important dependencies between use cases that were not explicitly identified beforehand. Again, consider one of the simpler examples. The *i** models specified that the *TMA Departure ATCO depends on the Runway ATCO to do the task control flight after takeoff* (referred to here as task T1), which in turn depends on the *Runway ATCO doing the task transfer flight to TMA Departure ATCO* (referred to as task T2). Task T1 maps to action-7 in UC7, and task T2 maps to action-6 in UC13. This reveals an implied dependency between UC7 and UC13, and that action-6 in UC13 shall happen before action-7 in UC7. From this and 5 other similar dependencies, we have produced a simple model showing previously un-stated dependencies between DMAN use cases that have important implications for the timing and order of actor behaviour in the future DMAN system.

Further application of synchronisation check 2.5.3 was restricted because 23 dependencies between *i** SR actor models could not be checked due to incomplete elaboration of *i** SR models for all actors.

5.2 Case Study Conclusions

The DMAN requirements process enabled us to investigate and report the effectiveness of RESCUE and some of its model synchronisation checks on a real and complex project. Several key findings emerge. Systems engineers with the pre-requisite training are able to apply advanced modelling techniques such as *i** to model complex socio-technical systems, and these models do provide new and useful insights. In spite of this success, further method engineering work is needed to support the development of scaleable *i** models. For example, constructing a single SR models specifying all actors and their dependencies is very difficult due to number and nature of these dependencies.

In the use case descriptions, the systems engineers provided more specification of human actor behaviour rather than system actor behaviour, perhaps due to the focus of socio-technical systems in RESCUE. Furthermore, to our surprise, very few system-level requirement statements were specified in the first 2 stages – instead the engineers were satisfied to develop and agree requirements models in the form of use case descriptions and *i** models from which approximately 220 requirement statements have subsequently been derived.

The RESCUE synchronisation checks required resources to apply, due primarily to the degree of human interpretation of the models needed. Furthermore, some synchronisation checks were more effective than others at revealing insights into the DMAN specification. Synchronisation checks often resulted in further knowledge elicitation and document (specification of the 'world' in REVEAL terms) to resolve potential model ambiguities. Finally, synchronisation checks appeared to fall into 2 basic types: (i) synchronisation of models based on their first-order properties often related to naming conventions (e.g. check 1.3), and: (ii) synchronisation of models based on their derived properties, such as in check 2.5.3, which leads to in-depth verification of the use case descriptions using *i** actor and element dependencies. These latter types of checks appear to be more useful to the engineers.

6 Discussions and Future Work

This paper describes intermediate results from an industrial case study that applied and integrated established and research requirements modelling techniques to a complex socio-technical system in air traffic management. It reports 2 major innovations:

1. New requirements modelling techniques namely *i**, with simple process extensions, can be applied effectively to model socio-technical systems;
2. The analysis of these models combined in the RESCUE stream and synchronisation structure shown in Figure 1 revealed important insights that are unlikely to have been obtained using other modelling techniques.

Most research-based requirements engineering techniques have been developed in isolation. Our results, although preliminary, suggest that there are benefits from extending current and designing future techniques to integrate with established ones. Conceptual meta-models, such as the RESCUE meta-model in Figure 8, provide one foundation for model synchronisation, but more research in method engineering is needed to design integrated techniques for process guidance (which models to develop in what order), model synchronisation (which checks to do when) and model integration (when is one integrated model preferable to several different models). A good example of method integration emerging from the DMAN experience is the use case dependency model generated as a result of applying check 2.5.3.

This DMAN case study also has implications for the multi-disciplinary requirements and design teams advocated by other authors (e.g. Viller & Sommerville 1999 for the ATM domain). The DMAN team was composed of engineers with systems and software rather than human factors backgrounds, and yet adequate training and methodology enabled the production of human activity models that effectively underpinned the development and analysis of the system models and were praised by the client.

Future research will refine and formalise the specification of the synchronisation checks, with a view towards introducing software tool support for model synchronisation. Given the need for human interpretation, we believe that software tools will be limited to detecting and ranking candidate issues in pairs of models – issues that engineers with considerable domain expertise will still have to resolve. In this sense, we view our work as different to ongoing research of viewpoints (e.g. Nuseibeh et al. 2003) and inconsistency management (e.g. Nentwich et al. 2003)., that is increasing formal specification of system requirements and automation of development processes. The advantage of RESCUE here is that it implements existing and tried-and-tested modelling techniques, limited between-model synchronisation based on simple concept meta-models and types, and guided synchronisation strategies for engineers to adopt.

Acknowledgements

The authors acknowledge the support from Eurocontrol, NATS and Sofeavia/CENA in the DMAN project.

References

Cockburn A., 2000, 'Writing Effective Use Cases', Addison-Wesley Pearson Education.

De Landtsheer R., Letier E. & van Laamsweerde A., 2003, 'Deriving Tabular Event-Based Specifications from Goal-Oriented Requirements Models', Proceedings 11th IEEE International Conference on Requirements Engineering, IEEE Computer Society Press, 200-210.

Hall J., Jackson M., Laney R., Nuseibeh B. & Rapanotti L., 2002, 'Relating Software Requirements and Architectures using Problem Frames', Proceedings 10th International Joint Conference on Requirements Engineering, IEEE Computer Society Press, 137-144.

ICAO, 1994, 'Human Factors in CNS/ATM systems. The development of human-centred automation and advanced technology in future aviation systems' ICAO Circular 249-AN/149.

Jacobson I., Booch G. & Rumbaugh J., 2000, 'The Unified Software Development Process', Addison-Wesley.

Leveson N, de Villepin M., Srinivasan J., Daouk M., Neogi N., Bachelder E, Bellingham J., Pilon N. & Flynn G., 2001, 'A Safety and Human-Centred Approach to Developing New Air Traffic Management Tools', Proceedings Fourth USA/Europe Air Traffic Management R&D Seminar.

Liu L., Yu E. & Mylopoulos J., 2003, 'Security and Privacy Requirements Analysis within a Social Setting', Proceedings 11th IEEE International Conference on Requirements Engineering, IEEE Computer Society Press, 151-161.

Liu L. & Yu E., 2001, 'From Requirements to Architectural Design – Using Goals and Scenarios', Proceedings first STRAW workshop, 22-30.

Maiden N. & Gizikis A., 2001, 'Where Do Requirements Come From?", IEEE Software September/October 2001 18(4), 10-12.

Maiden N.A.M., Jones S.V. & Flynn M., 2003, 'Innovative Requirements Engineering Applied to ATM', Proceedings ATM (Air Traffic Management) 2003, Budapest, June 23-27 2003.

Mavin A. & Maiden N.A.M., 2003, 'Determining Socio-Technical Systems Requirements: Experiences with Generating and Walking Through Scenarios', Proceedings 11th International Conference on Requirements Engineering, IEEE Computer Society Press, 213-222.

Nentwich C., Emmerich W. & Finkelstein A.C.W, 2003, 'Flexible Consistency Checking', ACM Transactions on Software Engineering and Methodology 12(1), 28-63.

Nuseibeh B., Kramer J., & Finkelstein A.C.W., 2003, 'Viewpoints: Meaningful Relationships are Difficult', Proceedings 25th IEEE International Conference on Software Engineering, IEEE Computer Society Press, 676-681.

Praxis, 2001, 'REVEAL: A Keystone of Modern Systems Engineering', White Paper Reference S.P0544.19.1, Praxis Critical Systems Limited, July 2001.

Robertson S. & Robertson J., 1999, 'Mastering the Requirements Process', Addison-Wesley.

Rumbaugh J., Jacobson I. & Booch G., 1998, 'The Unified Modelling Language Reference Manual', Addison-Wesley.

Santander V. & Castro J, 2002, 'Deriving Use Cases from Organisational Modeling', Proceedings IEEE Joint International Conference on Requirements Engineering (RE'02), IEEE Computer Society Press, 32-39.

Sutcliffe A.G., Maiden N.A.M., Minocha S. & Manuel D., 1998, 'Supporting Scenario-Based Requirements Engineering', IEEE Transactions on Software Engineering, 24(12), 1072-1088.

Vicente, K., Cognitive work analysis, Lawrence Erlbaum Associates, 1999.

Viller S. & Sommerville I., 1999, 'Social Analysis in the Requirements Engineering Process: from Ethnography to Method', Proceedings 4th IEEE International Symposium on Requirements Engineering, IEEE Computer Society Press, 6.13.

Yu E. & Mylopoulos J.M., 1994, 'Understanding "Why" in Software Process Modelling, Analysis and Design', Proceedings, 16th International Conference on Software Engineering, IEEE Computer Society Press, 159-168.

Facing Document-Provider Heterogeneity in Knowledge Portals*

Jon Iturrioz, Oscar Díaz, and Sergio F. Anzuola

The EKIN group
Department of Languages and Computer Systems
University of the Basque Country
{jipitsaj,jipdiago}@si.ehu.es, jibfeans@sc.ehu.es

Abstract. Knowledge portals aim at facilitating the location, sharing and dissemination of information by sitting ontologies at the core of the system. For heterogeneous environments where content-providers are free to deliver the content in any format, mechanisms are required that extract and lift these content sources onto a common ontology model. This paper focuses on document providers where diversity stems from either the metadata vocabulary or the metadata location mechanism used. The ontology repository should be isolated from this heterogeneity. To this end, a rule-based approach is presented where rules encapsulate the specificities of each provider. The paper presents a working system where *JENA, WebDAV,* and *QuickRules* realise the knowledge portal, the resource repository and the rule component, respectively. Rules are given for *PDF, WORD* and *OpenOffice* resources.

1 Introduction

Knowledge portals *"exploit an ontology for achieving a conceptual foundation for all their functionalities, i.e. information integration as well as information selection and presentation, are glued together by a conceptual model"* [9]. In the same way that a database is characterised by its schema, a knowledge portal is distinguished by its ontology. While traditional databases take data structures out of the applications, a knowledge portal extracts knowledge out of the applications that hereafter, rely on the portal for knowledge obtention (i.e. inference capabilities are externalised to the portal).

An ontology (i.e. *"an agreement about a shared, formal, explicit and partial account of a conceptualisation"* [21]) is "populated" by metadata that describe the "portal resources" (e.g. HTML pages, documents, images, etc) that stand for instances of the ontology. The resource providers can be numerous, heterogeneous and evolve as time goes by. Document processors are a case in point. The new crop of document processors (e.g. editors, workflow, content managers) are metadata-aware. Each proc-

---

* This work was partially supported by the Spanish Science and Technology Ministry (MCYT) and European Social Funds (FEDER) under contract TIC2002-01442. It also benefits of funding from la "Consejería de Ciencia y Tecnología" de la Junta de la Comunidad de Castilla La Mancha (PCB-02-001).

A. Persson and J. Stirna (Eds.): CAiSE 2004, LNCS 3084, pp. 384–397, 2004.

essor takes the document as input, processes it, and potentially, attaches, either manually or automatically, some metadata.

The issue is how to keep consistent the document collection with its ontology model counterpart. A mechanism is needed that punctually reflects operations on the document to its ontology counterpart so that portal users can obtain an ontologically valid view of this resource. And this extractive operation is processor-dependant since, for instance, a Word document and a PDF document have different mechanisms to support metadata.

Specifically, document-processors difer on both the metadata vocabulary and the metadata location. As for the vocabularies, the PDF world is promoting the *Extensible Metadata Platform* (XMP) [5]. XMP metadata defines a core set of metadata properties that are relevant for a wide range of applications including all of Adobe's authoring and publishing products. On the other hand, *OpenOffice* [3] has a different set of metadata which also overlaps (but does not totally coincides) with *Dublin Core* [2]. Hence, the first issue is to harmonize the vocabularies coming from different document processors.

It should be note that most previous works focus on how to characterize Web resources (e.g. an HTML page) along a given ontology, i.e. how to obtain the ontology description after the content/layout of the HTML page [17,8,16,11]. By contrast, this work assumes that such a characterisation is somehow attached to the resource, and the issue is how to cope with the diversity of the formats used for document storage.

As for metadata location, it refers to how metadata is attached to the subject document (i.e. the resource). Currently, there are two alternatives. One option is to keep the metadata embedded in the document itself, and hence, metadata appears as part of the resource data stream (e.g. this is the PDF option using XMP [5]). A special API is then used to extract this metadata. This has the advantage that the metadata stays with the application data file, even if the file is moved. The downside is that the API is dependent on the editor you use to generate the data file. By contrast, other option is to store the metadata in a separate file which is associated by convention with the source document. *OpenOffice* is a case in point. This works universally, but has the disadvantage that the metadata can be lost in a processing step if the metadata file is not kept together with the data file.

Both metadata vocabularies and metadata location, are two source of variations whose variants are far from being settle down, i.e. ontology standards, processors and resource formats are all evolving rapidly.

To isolate the ontology layer for the heterogeneity and evolvable nature of content providers, this paper presents a rule-based propagation mechanism. The rule paradigm has proved to facilitate the building of systems that are easy to adapt to evolving requirements. Their self-contained, isolated and decoupled nature, allows rules to be easily enlarged, removed or updated. The use of this reactive architecture accounts for the separate evolution of each layer (i.e. the ontology, and the content providers that populate the ontology) as well as the smooth inclusion of new document processors as time goes by.

As a proof of concepts, this paper presents an implementation. The knowledge portal[1], the resource repository, and the rule manager are three independent components.

---

[1] For the aim of this paper, the knowledge portal is restricted to a repository for RDF expressions.

Which have been realised through *JENA* [12], *WebDAV* [1], and *QuickRules* [20] were used to support the knowledge portal, the resource repository and the rule component, respectively.

The rest of the paper is organized as follows. Section 2 outlines the architecture. Section 3, 4 and 5 presents the *ontology* component, the *resourceCollection* component and the *ruleManager* component, respectively. Rules are presented in section 6. Finally, conclusions are given.

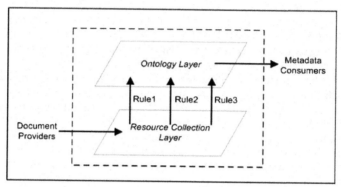

Fig. 1. A two-layers architecture.

2 The Architecture

The DOGMA initiative [18] is promoting a formal ontology engineering framework that generally consists of a three-layer architecture comprising (i) the heterogeneous data sources, (ii) the wrappers that lift these data sources onto a common ontology model, (iii) the integration modules (mediators in the dynamic case) that reconcile the varying semantics of the different data sources, and (iv) the consumers of the ontology.

This architecture is also basically followed in this work where data sources are restricted to document providers, the ontology model is RDF, and where wrapping and mediator concerns are realised as rules (see figure 1).

The idea is to sit an ontology layer on top of the collection of documents. The structure of the ontology (and, in the future, the inference power of the ontology formalism) facilitates a more dynamic and powerful location and navigation of the underlying document collection. This enables automated processing of the resources regardless of both its origin (i.e. the editor used to create it) or its use (i.e. whether they are used for presentation matters by a content manager, or for defining the document flow in a Lotus-like application). The main endeavor of this work is then to keep the *RDF* model consistent with the underlying document repository.

To this end, an architecture is introduced with three components namely, the *ontology* component, which is realised using the JENA API [12], the *resourceCollection* component, which is supported by *WebDAV* [1], and the *ruleManager* component, which is implemented using *QuickRules* [20], respectively. The dependencies between these components is depicted in figure 2. Next sections present the concrete realisation.

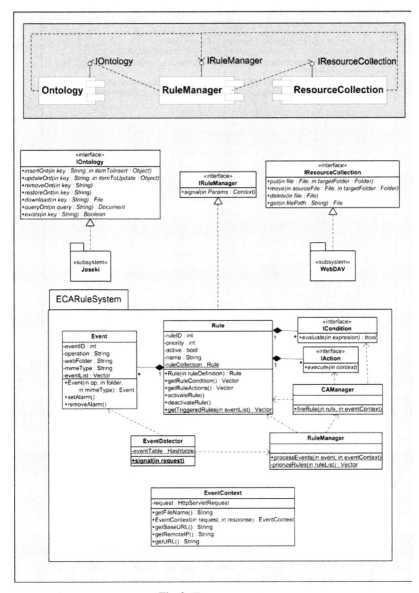

Fig. 2. The components.

3   The *Ontology* Component

The World Wide Web has introduced the Resource Description Framework (RDF) [7], in an attempt to produce a standard language for *machine-understandable* descriptions of resources on the Web.

```xml
<?xml version="1.0" encoding="ISO-8859-15"?>
<rdf:RDF xmlns:dc="http://purl.org/dc/elements/1.1/"
         xmlns:rdf="http://www.w3.org/1999/02/22-rdf-syntax-ns#"
         xmlns:dce="http://www.atarix.org/dcExtension#">
    <rdf:Description rdf:about="http://www.vldb.org/03mdde/03mdde.sxw">
        <dc:title>Facing content-provider heterogeneity in Knowledge Portals</dc:title>
        <dc:description>
            Ontology languages are being proposed to provide machine-understandable
            descriptions of resources that permit easy location of these resource.
        </dc:description>
        <dce:creator>Sergio Fernández</dce:creator>
        <dc:language>en-US</dc:language>
        <dc:date>2003-05-21T17:41:00</dc:date>
        <dc:subject>Ontology</dc:subject>
        <dc:subject>Document Engineering</dc:subject>
        <dc:creator>Jon Iturrioz</dc:creator>
        <dc:creator>Oscar Díaz</dc:creator>
        <dc:creator>Sergio Fernández</dc:creator>
        <dce:table-count>0</dce:table-count>
        <dce:image-count>3</dce:image-count>
        <dce:object-count>0</dce:object-count>
        <dce:page-count>10</dce:page-count>
        <dce:paragraph-count>304</dce:paragraph-count>
        <dce:word-count>1905</dce:word-count>
        <dce:character-count>14613</dce:character-count>
        <dc:format>texto/sxw</dc:format>
        <dce:submissionDate>2003-06-10T00:00:00</dce:submissionDate>
        <dce:workshop>CAISE'04</dce:workshop>
        <dce:retrievedBy>158.227.111.111</dce:retrievedBy>
        <dce:consultedBy>158.227.111.112</dce:consultedBy>
    </rdf:Description>
</rdf:RDF>
```

Fig. 3. *RDF* representation of the resource *http://www.atarix.org/04Caise.sxw.*

To describe a resource in terms of RDF, three things are required: a data model, a schema, and the statement itself using XML syntax. The RDF data model is expressed using directed labeled graphs which identify the properties and property values that qualify the resource. Next, a schema needs to be defined or existing schemas must be identified. Schemas provide the RDF type system. The properties could be expressed using appropriate existing vocabularies (e.g. Dublin Core) that can be complemented with properties specific to the application at hand. Finally, a specific resource can be described along the lines of the schemas. Here, *rdf/xml* is used for this purpose.

This paper considers a very simple ontology with a single class. This class describe resources along distinct properties (see figure 3). Properties can be:

- attributive, if they kept basic properties of the resource. To this end, the *Dublin Core* vocabulary is used. In figure 3, these attributes come from 'dc' namespace.
- relational, if they provide links to other resources. Here, relational properties are not extracted from the document but obtained through inference rules. For instance, the property *<relatedTo>* can be inferred if two documents share at least an author. This problem is not addressed here.
- operational, if they are related with operations the document has undergone, and therefore, no related with the content of the document. For instance, *OpenOffice* provides the *"editing-cycles"* metadata that specifies the number of editing cycles the document has been through while in the realm of *OpenOffice*. As you move away from editing to other kind of processing, the corresponding software can en-

rich the document with additional operational metadata. For instance, if the *"submission-date"* needs to be kept, this data can not be recorded by the document editor but registered by the repository manager when the document enters the repository. In figure 3, the "dce" namespace is used for this extended vocabulary.

RDF descriptions are kept in JOSEKI [13]. Broadly speaking, JOSEKI is a DBMS for RDF data models that support a SQL-like language to query the data model. The Data Manipulation Language follows the JENA API [12], a *de facto* standard for insertion, deletion and updates of data models. This API is abstracted into the *Iontology* interface (see figure 2) with the aim of decoupling the system for the specific DBMS used to store the RDF descriptions. This permits to change either the ontology standard (e.g. OWL [22]) or the ontology repository without affecting the rest of the system.

4   The resourceCollection Component

The *Iresource* interface offers the signatures for inserting (PUT), renaming (MOVE), deleting (DELETE) and retrieving (GET) documents (see figure 2). This interface is realized using a *WebDAV* implementation.

WebDAV is an extension of *HTTP* that aims to provide a standard infrastructure for asynchronous, collaborative, authoring across the Internet. The *WebDAV* extensions support the use of *HTTP* for interoperable publishing of variety of content, providing a common interface to many types of repositories, and making the Web analogous to a large-grain, network-accessible file system [23].

WebDAV is also metadata aware. That is, it permits to collect (operational) metadata about the document being placed in the repository. These metadata, called "properties" in *WebDAV*, roughly correspond to the parameters of the *httpRequest* object which is generated when the document is transported to the repository. This information includes the IP of the user agent which generates the petition, or the date when the petition was issued. This is known as the *eventContext*.

5   The *ruleManager* Component

The heterogeneity of metadata as well as the impossibility to foreseen in advance the range of processors to be addressed, make us choose a rule-based approach. Event-condition-action rules (ECA rules) or triggers have long been available in Database Management Systems (DBMSs) to perform a wide range of tasks [19], including change propagations between tables.

In a DBMS setting, rules are tightly coupled with the "resource repository" (i.e. the database). This is not the case in this setting. Here, the RDF resource repository (i.e. JENA) and the document repository (i.e. WebDAV) are two different components. In this scenario, the rule manager needs to capture events coming from either component, and acts appropriately on the other component. This accounts for a loose coupling between both component.

Moreover, the self-contained nature of rules allows to encapsulate within a rule the specificities of a document editor. In this way, we cope with the heterogeneity of both metadata vocabulary and metadata location. A rule addresses the idiosyncrasies of a single document editor. Accordingly, introducing/deleting a format (e.g. *ppt*) is traced back to a single rule. If an existing editor changes the format of its metadata vocabulary/location in a new version (e.g. WORD), the impact of the change is isolated in the corresponding rule. This facilitates the evolution and maintenance of the system.

The *ruleManager* component provides the *Irule* interface with a single operation, *SIGNAL*, (see figure 2(c)), and utilizes both the *Iontology* interface and the *Iresource* interface. Basically, the component captures signals coming from the *resourceCollection* component, and reacts by invoking operations on the *ontology* components.

Implementation wise, the *Irule* interface is realized through the class diagram depicted in figure 2. The following classes are included:

- *EventDetector*, whose duty is to capture the signals. It implements the *SIGNAL* operation.
- *RuleManager*, which is the class responsible for obtaining the rules triggered by the event being signaled, for priorizing them, and for dispatching them in the priority order.
- *CAManager*, which is responsible for evaluating the rule's condition. This class is implemented using the *QuickRules* system [20] which provides an expressive condition language.
- *Rule*. The elements of an ECA rule are, not surprisingly, an event, a condition and an action. The event part of a rule describes a happening to which the rule may be able to respond. The condition part examines the context in which the event has taken place. Finally, the action describes the task to be carried out by the rule if the relevant event has taken place and the condition has evaluated to true. Besides, each rule has a name, a priority and a Boolean tag to indicate whether the rule is enabled or not.

Some rule examples are presented in the next section.

6   Some Rule Examples

This section illustrates how the *ontology* component can be isolated from the heterogeneity of the content providers through the use of rules. These rules are triggered by events produced by the *resourceCollection* component, and act on the *ontology* component. More specifically:

- *the event* is signaled by the *resourceCollection* component. Hence, the event corresponds to an insertion (PUT), renaming (MOVE), deletion (DELETE) or retrieving (GET) of a document. These events abstract away from the concrete classes that realise the component. In this case, these operations have a *WebDAV* counterpart, though *WebDAV* can be substituted for other repository without affecting the rules. The event is parameterized by an *eventContext* object. In this case, this object holds the *activeFolder*, i.e. the *WebDAV* folder where the document is placed, or the *mimeType*, which holds a regular expression on the files names (e.g. "*.ps" refers to those files with *Postscript* extension). The *activeFolder* can provide properties about the resource. For instance, by placing a document on the folder VLDB, the value of a *conference* property can be obtained. Broadly speaking, the *eventContext* object mirrors the *HttpServletRequest* object.

– *the condition* is a predicate on the state of the context where the rule is fired. This context includes both the resource repository and the RDF descriptions.

– *the action* processes the resource, and propagates relevant metadata to the ontology layer. Hence, the action duties include retrieving the metadata, solving metadata mismatches between the terms used by the document editor and the terms of the ontology, and finally, adding the new RDF description. Most of these aspects are processor-dependent.

Next subsections provide examples for *OpenOffice, WORD* and *PDF*. The heterogeneity in the location and metadata model vindicates the use of the rule approach.

6.1 Rules for *OpenOffice*

Location Model. *OpenOffice* [3][2] uses XML as the storage format. Specifically, when storing an *OpenOffice* document on disk, an *OpenOffice*-compliant software creates a ZIP file which comprises four subdocuments, namely: *meta.xml*, which keeps the document meta information, *styles.xml*, which records the styles used in the document, *content.xml*, the content as such, and *setting.xml* which corresponds to application-specific settings, such as the window size or printer information. These four documents are delivered as a single ZIP file.

Metadata Model. Figure 4 shows an example of the metadata generated by *OpenOffice* when editing a manuscript similar to this one. Some tag examples follow: *<generator>* which corresponds to the document processor being used to generate the content, *<title>* which corresponds to the title of the document, *<editing-cycles>* which indicates the number of times the document has been edited, *<creator>* that specifies the name of the person who last modified the document, etc. Besides, these automatically-generated tags, the user can introduce up to four specific metadata. In this example, the authors of the manuscript have been added as *<user-defined>* metadata.

Extractive Process. When the user moves an *OpenOffice* document to the *WebDAV* repository, a rule is triggered that lifts this document onto the common ontology model. Specifically, the components of the rule are defined as follows:

---

[2] OpenOffice is an OASIS initiative to decouple content from how this content is processed. Today most of documents are stored within binary formats, which means they are worthless without the applications that created them. Worse, there is not guarantee, given today's undocumented, proprietary formats, that these documents will be readable even five years from now. Besides, that binary format prevents applications others than the creators from re-using these documents for their own means, and jeopardizes document portability and interoperability.

392 Jon Iturrioz, Oscar Díaz, and Sergio F. Anzuola

```xml
<?xml version="1.0" encoding="UTF-8"?>
<!DOCTYPE office:document-meta PUBLIC "-//OpenOffice.org//DTD OfficeDocument 1.0//EN" "office.dtd">
<office:document-meta xmlns:office="http://openoffice.org/2000/office"
                      xmlns:xlink="http://www.w3.org/1999/xlink"
                      xmlns:dc="http://purl.org/dc/elements/1.1/"
                      xmlns:meta="http://openoffice.org/2000/meta"
                      office:version="1.0">
    <office:meta>
        <meta:generator>OpenOffice.org 1.0.3 (Win32)</meta:generator>
        <dc:title>Facing content-provider heterogeneity in Knowledge Portals</dc:title>
        <dc:description>
            Ontology languages are being proposed to provide machine-understandable
            descriptions of resources that permit easy location of these resource.
        </dc:description>
        <meta:creation-date>2003-05-21T17:41:00</meta:creation-date>
        <dc:creator>Ekin Member</dc:creator>
        <dc:date>2003-07-28T18:52:54</dc:date>
        <meta:keywords>
            <meta:keyword>Webdav</meta:keyword>
            <meta:keyword>RDF</meta:keyword>
            <meta:keyword>Document Engineering</meta:keyword>
        </meta:keywords>
        <dc:language>en-US</dc:language>
        <meta:editing-cycles>15</meta:editing-cycles>
        <meta:editing-duration>PT2H20M45S</meta:editing-duration>
        <meta:user-defined meta:name="Authors">
            Jon Iturrioz, Oscar Díaz, Sergio Fernández
        </meta:user-defined>
        <meta:user-defined meta:name="Info 2"/>
        <meta:user-defined meta:name="Info 3"/>
        <meta:user-defined meta:name="Info 4"/>
        <meta:document-statistic meta:table-count="0" meta:image-count="3" meta:object-count="0"
                                 meta:page-count="10" meta:paragraph-count="304"
                                 meta:word-count="1905" meta:character-count="14613"/>
    </office:meta>
</office:document-meta>
```

Fig. 4. *OpenOffice.* The content and the metadata of the document are placed in two different files. The figure shows the one holding metadata.

- an event, that can be described by the triplet *<PUT, *, "*.sxw">*. This triplet indicates that the event happens as a result of introducing a new document in *WebDAV* regardless of the folder. However, the extension of the document must be *"sxw"* (i.e. that is, an *OpenOffice* document) for the rule to be fired.
- a condition, that verifies that there exists no document with the same title in the repository -since the title is used as key. The JOSEKI's API is used for this purpose. Specifically, the *exists* operation takes a *key* as an input, and returns a boolean which indicates whether a resource with this key exists or not.
- an action, that updates the RDF model to reflect this insertion. This implies to:

1. extract the metadata from the document to an XML intermediate document,
2. map the *OpenOffice* metadata model to the canonical ontology model defined in RDF,
3. append additional data obtained from *WebDAV* (e.g. the *<submitted_date>* property),
4. introduce the new RDF description.

The concrete code follows:

```
//Extract and normalize metadata from document
zipFilePath = eventContext.getFileName( )
xmlDoc = OpenOfficeExtraction.extract (zipFilePath)
//Transform to the RDF description
rdfDocument = RDFTransform.processXML(xmlDoc, zipFilePath)
//Introduce the new resource description into the RDF model
joseki.insertOnt ( zipFilePath, rdfDocument)
```

6.2   Rules for WORD 2003

Location Mode. *Microsoft Office Word 2003* widely embrace XML. Specifically, this new release introduces the *"Save as XML"* command that produces an XML-compliant counterpart of the traditional, proprietary Word-format files [4]. These XML files are produced according with the *WordML* schema, a *XML Schema* that is designed to mirror the information found in traditional *.doc* files. The root element of a *WordML* document is always *w:wordDocument*. This element contains several other elements that represent the complete *Word* document structure, including properties, fonts, lists, styles, and the actual document body that contains sections and paragraphs. Figure 5 gives an example.

Metadata Model. For the purpose of this work, we focus on the element *<o:DocumentProperties>* (see figure 5). This element contains the document properties available for all *Microsoft Office* documents such as title, author, last author, creation date, last saved date and so on. Notice that this element is from a different namespace that *WordML* since it applies to all *Microsoft Office* documents, and then, it will be shared across *Office* XML vocabularies (e.g. *ExcelML*). This greatly facilitates our job as the homogenization of the metadata is at least already achieved for *Microsoft Office* resources.

Moreover, a WordML document also holds a <docPr> element that contains Word-specific properties for the given document. So far, these properties are mainly related with style-like issues (e.g. view and zoom settings, existence of a template). However, nothing prevents the user from using this element to keep content-related metadata. Indeed, annotation mechanisms such as those described in [14,10] can be used to obtain metadata from the document content. When the document is saved, "the annotator" attaches the corresponding metadata to the *<docPr>* element.

Extractive Process. When the user moves a *"Word.xml"* document to the *WebDAV* repository, a rule is triggered that lifts this document onto the common ontology model. Specifically, the components of the rule are defined as follows:

- an event, that can be described by the triplet *<PUT, *, "*.xml">*. This triplet indicates that the event happens as a result of introducing a new document in *WebDAV* regardless of the folder. The extension of the document must be *"xml"*. However, this is not enough to ensure that this document comes from a *Word* processor. An additional verification needs to be done in the rule's condition.

```
<?xml version="1.0" encoding="UTF-8" standalone="yes"?>
<?mso-application progid="Word.Document"?>
<w:wordDocument xmlns:w="http://schemas.microsoft.com/office/word/2003/wordml"
    xmlns:o="urn:schemas-microsoft-com:office:office">
    <o:DocumentProperties>
        <o:Title>Facing content-provider heterogeneity in Knowledge Portals</o:Title>
        <o:Author>Sergio F. Anzuola</o:Author>
        <o:LastAuthor>Jon Iturrioz</o:LastAuthor>
        <o:Revision>2</o:Revision>
        <o:TotalTime>1</o:TotalTime>
        <o:Created>2003-08-14T12:44:00Z</o:Created>
        <o:LastSaved>2003-08-14T12:44:00Z</o:LastSaved>
        <o:Pages>1</o:Pages>
        <o:Words>10</o:Words>
        <o:Characters>59</o:Characters>
        <o:Company>Ekin Group</o:Company>
        <o:Lines>1</o:Lines>
        <o:Paragraphs>1</o:Paragraphs>
        <o:CharactersWithSpaces>68</o:CharactersWithSpaces>
        <o:Version>11.5329</o:Version>
    </o:DocumentProperties>
    <w:fonts>
        <!-- fonts used in document -->
    </w:fonts>
    <w:styles>
        <!-- named styles used in document -->
    </w:styles>
    <w:docPr>
        <!-- Word-specific document properties -->
    </w:docPr>
    <w:body>
        <!-- document content -->
    </w:body>
</w:wordDocument>
```

Fig. 5. *WordML*. Both the content and metadata of the document are located in the same XML file.

- a condition, that first checks that the *".xml"* document has been produced with a Word editor and hence, follows the WordML schema. To this end, the condition checks the existence of a processing instruction in the *".xml"* document: *<? mso-application progid= "Word.Document" ? >*. Next, and similar to the previous rule, the condition verifies that there exists no document with the same title in the repository.
- an action, that updates the RDF model to reflect this insertion. This implies to:

1. extract the metadata from the *WordML* document (i.e. the *DocumentProperties* element),
2. map the Word-proprietary metadata model to the canonical ontology model defined in RDF,
3. append additional data obtained from *WebDAV* (e.g. the *<submitted_date>* property),
4. introduce the new RDF description in the ontology model.

The code is similar to rule 6.2.

```
<rdf:RDF xmlns:rdf="http://www.w3.org/1999/02/22-rdf-syntax-ns#" xmlns:iX="http://ns.adobe.com/iX/1.0/">
    <rdf:Description about="" xmlns="http://ns.adobe.com/pdf/1.3/" xmlns:pdf="http://ns.adobe.com/pdf/1.3/">
        <pdf:CreationDate>2003-11-28T09:43:08Z</pdf:CreationDate>
        <pdf:ModDate>2003-11-28T09:43:08Z</pdf:ModDate>
        <pdf:Producer>Acrobat Distiller 5.0 (Windows)</pdf:Producer>
        <pdf:Author>Sergio F. Anzuola</pdf:Author>
        <pdf:Creator>PScript5.dll Version 5.2</pdf:Creator>
        <pdf:Title>
            Facing content-provider heterogeneity in Knowledge Portals
        </pdf:Title>
        <pdf:Subject>
            Ontology languages are being proposed to provide machine-understandable
            descriptions of resources that permit easy location of these resource.
        </pdf:Subject>
        <pdf:Keywords>Ontology, Document Engineering</pdf:Keywords>
    </rdf:Description>
    <rdf:Description about="" xmlns="http://ns.adobe.com/xap/1.0/" xmlns:xap="http://ns.adobe.com/xap/1.0/">
        <xap:CreateDate>2003-11-28T09:43:08Z</xap:CreateDate>
        <xap:ModifyDate>2003-11-28T09:43:08Z</xap:ModifyDate>
        <xap:Author>Sergio F. Anzuola</xap:Author>
        <xap:MetadataDate>2003-11-28T09:43:08Z</xap:MetadataDate>
        <xap:Title>
            <rdf:Alt>
                <rdf:li xml:lang="x-default">
                    Facing content-provider heterogeneity in Knowledge Portals
                </rdf:li>
            </rdf:Alt>
        </xap:Title>
        <xap:Description>
            <rdf:Alt>
                <rdf:li xml:lang="x-default">
                    Ontology languages are being proposed to provide machine-understandable
                    descriptions of resources that permit easy location of these resource.
                </rdf:li>
            </rdf:Alt>
        </xap:Description>
    </rdf:Description>
    <rdf:Description about="" xmlns="http://purl.org/dc/elements/1.1/" xmlns:dc="http://purl.org/dc/elements/1.1/">
        <dc:creator>Sergio F. Anzuola</dc:creator>
        <dc:title>
            Facing content-provider heterogeneity in Knowledge Portals
        </dc:title>
        <dc:description>
            Ontology languages are being proposed to provide machine-understandable
            descriptions of resources that permit easy location of these resource.
        </dc:description>
    </rdf:Description>
</rdf:RDF>
```

Fig. 6. *PDF.* Both the content and metadata of the document are placed in the same BINARY file.

6.3 Rules for PDF

Location Model. PDF stores the document's content in a binary file using a native format, and uses *Adobe Extensible Metadata Platform* (XMP) [5] to embed the document's metadata into the very same file. Metadata extractors retrieve the document's metadata through a XMP's API (for a concrete realisation, see [15]). It is important to note that XMP can be applied to any binary file other than PDF (e.g. JPEG).

Medatada Model. The metadata stored in PDF documents can be split into three sections (see figure 6). First, a section dedicated to PDF standard properties. A second section that holds *Adobe XAP* digital asset metatadata. This is an initiative to find a common ground to describe digital resources [6]. Finally, a last section that captures *DublinCore*-compliant properties. As shown in figure 6, these three views overlap for some properties that are replicated in the three sections though using different annotation vocabularies.

Extractive Process. In this case, the rule's parts include:

- an event, described by <PUT,*,"*.pdf">. This event happens when introducing a *PDF* file in the *WebDAV* repository,
- a condition, that checks out the document's title is unique,
- an action, that introduce a new RDF instance that correspond to this new resource. This is similar to the previous cases. The difference stems from the metadata being obtained through the XMP's API. Specifically, this work uses the *Java XMP Parser* found at *http://www.kegel-mediendesign.de/XmpUtil/*.

7 Conclusions

As new tools require/provide metadata about the resources they process, it becomes paramount to facilitate the sharing of metadata among heterogeneous tools. This paper introduced an architecture which is characterized by (1), an ontology layer that provides a canonical model for resource metadata, and (2), a rule component for achieving a metadata "synchronization" between the ontology layer and the resource layer. The use of this reactive architecture accounts for the separate evolution of each layer as well as the inclusion of new document processors as time goes by.

As a proof of concept, this work outlines an implementation using *WebDAV*, *JOSEKI* and *QuickRules* as the supporting technologies, and *OpenOffice*, *WORD* and *PDF* as the content types.

Our next work addresses how to embed annotation tools into document processors so that metadata can be automatically obtained at the time the document is saved.

References

1. IETF WEBDAV Working Group Home Page, 2002.
   http: //www.ics.uci.edu/ ejw/authoring
2. Dublin Core Metadata Initiative, 2003. http://dublincore.org
3. OpenOffice.org 1.0: The Open Source Office Suite, 2003. http: //www.openoffice.org
4. Aaron Skonnard. The XML Files: XML in Microsoft Office Word 2003 – MSDN Magazine, November 2003.
   http: //msdn.microsoft.com/msdnmag/issues/03/11/XMLFiles/default.aspx.
5. Adobe.XMP Extensible Metadata Platform, 2002.
   http://partners.adobe.com/asn/ developer/xmp/pdf/ MetadataFramework.pdf
6. Andrew Salop. XAP, a Digital Asset Metadata Architecture Utilizing XML and RDF, 2001. http: //www.gca.org/papers/xmleurope2001/papers/html/sid-03-9b.html
7. W3C: World Wide Web Consortium. Resource Description Framework (RDF)/W3C Semantic Web Activity, 2003. www.w3.org/RDF
8. Valter Crescenzi, Giansalvatore Mecca, and Paolo Merialdo. Roadrunner: Towards automatic data extraction from large web sites. In *Proceedings of 27th International Conference on Very Large Data Bases*, pages 109–118, 2001.

9. Daniel Oberle and Peter Spyns. The knowledge portal "ontoweb". *STAR Lab Technical Report*, 2003.
10. S. Handschuh and S. Staab. Authoring and annotation of web pages in cream. In *The Eleventh International World Wide Web Conference (WWW2002), Honolulu, Hawaii, USA*, pages 462–473, 2002.
11. Alberto Pan, Juan Raposo, Manuel Álvarez, Justo Hidalgo and Ángel Viña. Semi-automatic wrapper generation for commercial web sources. In Colette Rolland, Sjaak Brinkkemper, and Motoshi Saeki, editors, *Engineering Information Systems in the Internet Context (EISIC)*, volume 231 of *IFIP Conference Proceedings*, pages 265–283. Kluwer, September 2002.
12. HP. jena, 2003. http: //www.hpl.hp.com/semweb/jena.htm
13. HP. Joseki, 2003. http: //www.joseki.org
14. Jose Kahan and Marja-Ritta Koivunen. Annotea: an open RDF infrastructure for shared web annotations. In *World Wide Web*, pages 623–632, 2001.
15. Knud Kegel. Java XMP parserl, 2003. http: //www.kegel-mediendesign.de/XmpUtil/
16. Ling Liu, Calton Pu, and Wei Han. XWRAP: An XML-enabled wrapper construction system for web information sources. In *Internation Conference on Data Engineering (ICDE)*, pages 611–621, 2000.
17. Ling Liu, Calton Pu, and Wei Han. An XML-enabled data extraction toolkit for web sources. *Information Systems*, 26(8): 563–583, 2001.
18. Mustafa Jarrar and Robert Meersman. Formal Ontology Engineering in the DOGMA Approach. In *On the Move to Meaningful Internet Systems, 2002 - DOA/CoopIS/ODBASE 2002 Confederated International Conferences DOA, CoopIS and ODBASE 2002*, pages 1238–1254. Springer-Verlag, 2002.
19. N.W. Paton and O. Diaz. Active Database Systems. *ACM Computing Surveys*, 1(31): 63–103, 1999.
20. Yasu Technologies. Java rules engine, 2003. http://www.yasutech.com/products/quickrules/ index_SE.htm
21. Mike Uschold and Michael Grüninger. Ontologies: principles, methods, and applications. *Knowledge Engineering Review*, 11(2): 93–155, 1996.
22. World Wide Web Consortium (W3C). Owl web ontology language overview, 2003. http://www.w3.org/TR/owl-features/
23. E. James Whitehead and Meredith Wiggins. WEBDAV: IETF Standard for Collaborative Authoring on the Web. *IEEE Internet Computing*, 2(5): 34–40, 1998.

Integration of OWL Ontologies in MPEG-7 and TV-Anytime Compliant Semantic Indexing

Chrisa Tsinaraki, Panagiotis Polydoros, and Stavros Christodoulakis

Technical University of Crete, Laboratory of Distributed Multimedia Information Systems
and Applications (TUC/MUSIC), University Campus, 73100 Kounoupidiana, Crete, Greece
{chrisa,panpolyd,stavros}@ced.tuc.gr

Abstract. We describe a systematic methodology for extending the audiovisual content description standards (MPEG-7 and TV-Anytime) with domain-specific knowledge descriptions expressed in OWL. The domain-specific descriptions of the audiovisual content metadata are completely transparent to applications and tools that use MPEG-7 and TV-Anytime, allowing them to use the domain-specific ontologies without any software changes. We also present an interoperability mechanism between OWL and the audiovisual content description standards, which allows MPEG-7 and TV-Anytime descriptions and their domain-specific extensions to be described in OWL and vice versa. Thus, the methodology and the mechanisms presented here open up opportunities for reusing ontology tools and ontologies across a large number of applications (with or without audiovisual content) and across different professional and user communities. We present the details of the methodology and the implementation of the tools supporting it as well as its integration in a large framework for domain-specific indexing and retrieval of audiovisual content.

1 Introduction

During the last few years the provision of content services in specialized environments (e.g. digital libraries, web applications, digital TV applications, m-commerce, tourism, e-learning etc.) increases very rapidly. Emphasis is given in the provision of advanced personalized services, the final form of which is specified by the service provision context.

The success of such services imposes the support of advanced methods for the retrieval of audiovisual material, based on the material content. These methods may be used directly by the end-user requests (e.g. by queries for the retrieval of soccer games where a certain player scores) or transparently to him/her, by the services (s)he invokes (e.g. presentation of news items that are of user interest according to his/her preference profile).

Advanced audiovisual content retrieval methods require the existence of content-description metadata for the material. Several standards have been developed for the representation of metadata for audiovisual content description, among which the dominant ones are MPEG-7 [11] and TV-Anytime [12]. MPEG-7 provides in the Semantic Part of the MPEG-7 MDS [6] the complex data types needed for the full semantic description of audiovisual content as a set of *Description Schemes (DSs)*.

A. Persson and J. Stirna (Eds.): CAiSE 2004, LNCS 3084, pp. 398–413, 2004.
© Springer-Verlag Berlin Heidelberg 2004

TV-Anytime on the other hand provides only keyword-based capabilities for the semantic description of audiovisual content.

The major shortcoming of implementing systems based on one of the dominant standards [8] [7] [9] is that both MPEG-7 and TV-Anytime provide general-purpose structures for metadata representation, but not a concrete methodology for domain-specific extensions. Domain-specific knowledge however, could greatly increase the retrieval effectiveness of audiovisual content retrieval and it could also improve the user interaction with the system. In addition, there are no methodologies and tools currently which allow domain-specific ontologies defined in a general purpose ontology description language like OWL to be used with the audiovisual content description standards like MPEG-7 and TV-Anytime.

We have recently proposed the *DS-MIRF (Domain-Specific Multimedia Indexing, Retrieval and Filtering)* framework for the extension of MPEG-7 with domain-specific ontologies in a way that is transparent to applications that use MPEG-7 [14] [17]. This way retrieval effectiveness for multimedia content in specific application domains is enhanced. In addition, user interaction for query or profile specification is benefited from the use of the ontologies. This essentially provides a methodology for MPEG-7 to be used as an ontology specification language, for ontologies that are relevant to and can be expressed in MPEG-7.

There is however a major issue of interoperability with other ontology specification languages. Recently, OWL [3] has become the dominant standardization effort of the international research community in this area. This implies that in the future we will see many ontologies in specific knowledge domains expressed in OWL. It will be certainly easier for interoperability across applications (including audiovisual applications and applications that are not necessarily audiovisual) to have ontologies described in a standard ontology language. In such an environment it will be possible to extract (parts of) ontologies, join ontologies, map ontologies, import ontologies to different applications etc. It is of crucial importance therefore to be able to define MPEG-7 compatible ontologies in OWL and map them to MPEG-7 as well as vice versa, to transform ontologies expressed in MPEG-7 into ontologies expressed in OWL.

In this paper, we describe a methodology for the integration of OWL ontologies in the DS-MIRF framework that we have developed for the support of ontology-based semantic indexing and retrieval of audiovisual content, which follows the MPEG-7, and TV-Anytime standard specifications for metadata descriptions. Such methodologies have not been described in the literature so far.

An essential part of this methodology is to develop in OWL an ontology that fully captures the semantic metadata model defined in the Semantic Part of the MPEG-7 MDS. The need for an ontology that fully captures the MPEG-7 metadata model has been pointed out by several research groups [1] [13] [5]. Some important work in this direction has been carried out in [4] for the case of Resource Description Framework (RDF) [10], but it has some limitations: Classes corresponding to the MPEG-7 complex types have been defined, but not all of the (simple and complex) attributes of the classes are represented. In addition, typed relationships among the metadata items are not represented, although MPEG-7 provides complete support for typed relationships. Furthermore, this work has been based on RDF, which suffers form several limitations for representing ontologies, while the dominant standardization effort in ontology representation is now OWL.

The work described in this paper provides a systematic methodology for extending the multimedia content description standards with domain-specific knowledge descriptions expressed in OWL, and creates an interoperability mechanism between OWL and the dominant multimedia content description standards (MPEG-7 and TV-Anytime), thus opening up opportunities for reusing ontology tools and ontologies in a large number of applications and professional and user communities.

The rest of the paper is organized as follows: A brief overview of the DS-MIRF framework architecture focusing on the modules implementing OWL ontology integration is provided in section 2. The methodology of OWL ontology integration in the framework is discussed in section 3. The core ontology is described in section 4, while the methodology for domain-specific ontology definition is discussed in section 5. The transformation rules for the production of MPEG-7 and TV-Anytime compliant metadata from the RDF metadata structured according to the core ontology and the domain-specific ontologies are described in section 6. Conclusions and future work are discussed in section 7.

2   Overview of the DS-MIRF Framework

In this section we provide an overview of the architecture of the DS-MIRF framework that supports ontology-based semantic indexing and retrieval of audiovisual content, with emphasis in the framework modules where OWL ontology integration takes place. The framework architecture is depicted in Fig. 1.

As shown in Fig. 1, OWL ontologies are present during the Segmentation and Semantic Indexing process, when they are imported in the system in a systematic way. The use of the ontologies enhances the retrieval effectiveness but does not affect the software that uses MPEG-7 and TV-Anytime constructs only. This is achieved through the provision of appropriate search APIs and compatible semantic indexing for both standards. The major issue in our approach is the provision of end-user search interfaces based on both MPEG-7 and TV-Anytime standard specifications. This way, search and profiling software developed by third-parties that is compatible to MPEG-7 and TV-Anytime can still be used to access the audiovisual content. The major components of the framework architecture are:

- The *Segmentation & Semantic Indexing Tool*, used during the audiovisual content segmentation process, which also includes semantic indexing. Semantic indexing is carried out using the *Semantic Indexing Component* of the tool, which is responsible for the import of *domain-specific OWL ontologies* and *application-specific RDF metadata* (in both cases whenever needed), the definition of both application specific metadata and *instance description metadata*, and their storage in the system database. For example, in a soccer tournament application the application-specific metadata may be instances of the teams that participate in the tournament, instances of the team players, instances of the referees, coaches etc. These instances are reusable both in one game (e.g. they can be related with several events in the video program of the specific game), as well as across several games in the tournament. The *instance description metadata* describe in general which events of the real world take place in which parts of the video. The event types, the participants of the events, the time and the place that the events take place are described by the ontologies and the application-specific metadata. During the segmentation, MPEG-7 compliant semantic metadata as well as TV-Anytime metadata (keywords), which are validated against the ontologies and the application-specific metadata are produced (through the transformation of the RDF metadata formed according to the ontologies to metadata compliant to MPEG-7 and TV-Anytime) and used for the indexing of programs and segments. During querying or user profile formation, the specific queries or the user profile are validated against the ontologies and the application-specific metadata.

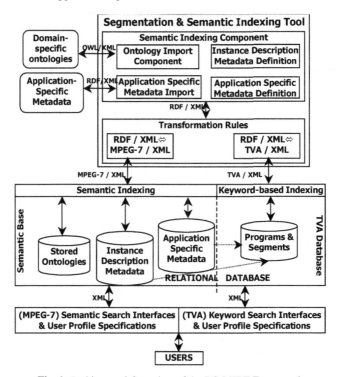

Fig. 1. Architectural Overview of the DS-MIRF Framework

- A relational database, where audiovisual segments and the metadata that describe them are stored. The relational database contains an *MPEG-7 compliant Semantic Base*, where the semantic metadata are stored and a *TV-Anytime compliant Database* where TV-Anytime metadata for audiovisual programs and segments are stored. References from the Semantic Base and the TV-Anytime database to the corresponding programs and/or segments are maintained.
- The appropriate interfaces, which permit the end users to pose both simple keyword-based queries (according to TV-Anytime) and more powerful, semantic queries (supported by MPEG-7). These interfaces are based on the existence of appropriate *query APIs (Application Programming Interfaces)*. The APIs supported validate their queries against the domain-specific ontologies and the application specific metadata before submitting the query.

3 OWL Ontology Integration Methodology

In this section we describe the methodology that we have developed for the integration of OWL ontologies with the MPEG-7 and TV-Anytime standards. This integration is a cornerstone of the DS-MIRF framework for the support of ontology-based semantic indexing and retrieval of audiovisual content.

In the DS-MIRF framework semantic indexing produces consistent MPEG-7 and TV-Anytime compliant semantic descriptions for the audiovisual content. The indexing process is guided by appropriate domain-specific ontologies, which permit more accurate description of the concepts of each application domain than the general-purpose concepts described by the standards themselves. In addition, ad-hoc domain-specific extensions of the standards are avoided. The domain-specific ontologies are based on the Semantic Part of the MPEG-7 MDS. Although it is possible to express the domain-specific ontologies using MPEG-7 syntax and structures [14] [17], interoperability issues make the use of the OWL ontology definition language more appealing, so the domain-specific ontologies in our framework are defined using the syntax of the OWL language. Thus, we have defined a core OWL ontology, which fully covers the Semantic Part of the MPEG-7 MDS, and then we define the domain-specific ontologies in OWL as extensions of the core ontology.

In the DS-MIRF framework we have adopted a two-layered model for multimedia metadata descriptions [15] [16]. The first layer is the metadata model defined in the Semantic Part of the MPEG-7 MDS, and the second layer is a set of domain-specific extensions of the first layer. The integration of OWL ontologies in the DS-MIRF framework provides a mechanism for capturing and extending the model for multimedia metadata descriptions using OWL ontologies and allows us to use these ontologies during semantic indexing and retrieval, remaining at the same time compatible with software which has been developed to work with the well-accepted standards of the audiovisual domain (TV-Anytime and MPEG-7).

The integration of OWL ontologies in the DS-MIRF framework utilizes three mechanisms:

a) A core OWL ontology, which fully covers the Semantic Part of the MPEG-7 MDS and captures the semantics of the first layer of the multimedia metadata model. We have decided to capture in the core ontology the MPEG-7 semantic metadata model, as it is more complete than the respective TV-Anytime model; in fact, the TV-Anytime model provides a subset of the semantic metadata representation facilities provided by the MPEG-7 model.

b) A methodology for the definition of domain-specific ontologies that extend the core ontology, in order to fully describe the concepts of specific application domains. The domain-specific ontologies defined using this methodology comprise the second layer of the multimedia metadata model.

c) Two sets of rules, used for the transformation of semantic metadata (formed according to the core ontology and its domain-specific extensions) to MPEG-7 and TV-Anytime compliant XML documents respectively. This way, interoperability with software developed to work with MPEG-7 and TV-Anytime is provided.

In the following sections we describe in more detail the above methodology and tools. The complete core ontology in OWL, as well as a complete example demonstrating the use of the methodology for domain-specific ontology definition in the domain of soccer games, are available at http://elikonas.ced.tuc.gr/ontologies/.

4   Core Ontology

Our approach for the integration of OWL ontologies in the framework for the support of ontology-based semantic indexing and retrieval of audiovisual content, utilizes an ontology that captures the model provided by the Semantic Part of the MPEG-7 MDS for the representation of semantic metadata for audiovisual content description. This ontology captures the semantics of the first layer of the two-layered model for semantic metadata used in the DS-MIRF framework. The second layer of the model encapsulates domain-specific knowledge, which extends the audiovisual content description standards so that they integrate transparently domain-specific ontologies. This ontology, referred to as the *Core Ontology* in the rest of the paper, has been implemented in OWL and is described in this section.

The model for the semantic description of audiovisual content provided in the Semantic part of the MPEG-7 MDS is comprised of complex data types defined, using the XML Schema Language syntax [2], in a set of Description Schemes (DSs) rooted in the SemanticBase DS. The more important among the description schemes together with the complex data types defined in them are listed below:

1. *SemanticBase DS:* The abstract type *SemanticBaseType* is defined here. SemanticBaseType is the base type extended by other description schemes according to the needs for the description of semantic entities of specific types. SemanticBaseType has a set of simple attributes (*id* for instance identification, *timeBase, timeUnit, mediaTimeBase* and *mediaTimeUnit* for timing support) and the following complex attributes:
   - *AbstractionLevel*, which represents the abstraction existing in the current semantic entity.
   - *Label*, corresponding to a term that describes in brief the semantic entity.
   - *Definition*, which is a textual annotation that describes the semantic entity.
   - *Property*, which is a term that associates a property with the semantic entity.
   - *Relation*, which relates the semantic entity with other semantic entities.
   - *MediaOccurrence*, which relates the semantic entity to specific media items (e.g. video segments, images etc.).
2. *SemanticBag DS* and *Semantic DS:* Description schemes used for the description of collections of semantic entities. *SemanticBagType* is an abstract type, defined in the SemanticBag DS, which extends SemanticBaseType, while *SemanticType* is defined in the Semantic DS. SemanticType is a concrete type, thus its instances are used for the representation of semantic entity collections.
3. *Object DS:* The *ObjectType* defined here extends SemanticBaseType and is used for the description of objects and object abstractions (e.g. a table).
4. *AgentObject DS:* The actors that appear in an audiovisual segment are related with the instances of the *AgentObjectType* type that extends the ObjectType. Actors in general are represented using the *AgentType*, an abstract type extending SemanticBaseType defined in the *Agent DS. PersonType, OrganizationType* and *PersonGroupType* extend AgentType, are defined respectively in the *Person DS*, the *Organization DS* and the *PersonGroup DS* and are used for the representation of persons (e.g. football players), organizations and groups of persons.

5. *Event DS:* The *EventType* defined here extends SemanticBaseType and is used for the description of events (e.g. a goal).
6. *SemanticState DS:* The *SemanticStateType* defined here extends SemanticBaseType and is used for the description of states described in an audiovisual segment and the parametric description of its features (e.g. the score in a soccer game before and after a goal).
7. *SemanticPlace DS:* The *SemanticPlaceType* defined here extends SemanticBaseType and is used for the description of places (e.g. Athens).
8. *SemanticTime DS:* The *SemanticTimeType* defined here extends *SemanticBaseType* and is used for the description of semantic time (e.g. Christmas).
9. *Concept DS:* The *ConceptType* defined here extends SemanticBaseType and is used for the description of concepts present in an audiovisual segment (e.g. co-operation).
10. *SemanticRelation DS:* The *SemanticRelationType* defined here extends SemanticBaseType and is used for the description of relationships among semantic entities. The relationships may be typed, as described in the SemanticRelation DS. In addition to the attributes inherited from SemanticBaseType, SemanticRelationType has the following attributes:
    –   *Source*, which is the id of the semantic entity that is the source of the relationship.
    –   *Target*, which is the id of the semantic entity that is the target of the relationship.
    –   *Argument*, which may be used as an alternate to source and target definition.
    –   *Strength*, which denotes the strength of the relationship.
    –   *Name*, which denotes the name of the relationship.
    –   *Arity*, which denotes the arity of the relationship.
    –   *Properties*, where the properties of the relationship are denoted.

For the representation of the Semantic part of MPEG-7 in OWL we developed the following methodology:

1. *MPEG-7 Simple Datatype Representation:* The simple datatypes needed are integrated in the core ontology, as OWL permits the integration in OWL ontologies of simple datatypes defined in the XML Schema Language [2].
2. *MPEG-7 Complex Type Representation:* MPEG-7 complex types correspond to OWL classes, which define groups of individuals that belong together because they share some properties. Thus, for every complex type defined in the MPEG-7 MDS a respective OWL class is defined.
    2.1. *Simple Attribute Representation:* The simple attributes of the complex type of the MPEG-7 MDS are represented as OWL datatype properties, which relate class instances to datatype instances (e.g. integer, string etc.). Thus, for every simple attribute of the complex type a datatype property is defined.
    2.2. *Complex Attribute Representation:* For the representation of the complex attributes of the complex type, OWL object properties are used, which relate class instances. For every complex attribute of the complex type the following actions are performed:
        2.2.1. An OWL class for the representation of the complex attribute instances is defined, if it does not already exist.

2.2.2. An OWL object property that relates the complex attribute instances with the appropriate complex type instances is defined.

2.3. *Constraints:* Constraints regarding value, cardinality and type for simple and complex attributes are expressed using the restriction mechanisms provided by OWL.

As an example, we show in Fig. 2 the definition of the OWL class "Organization-Type" (subclass of the "AgentType" that represents all the Agents), corresponding to the MDS complex type "OrganizationType". The "ElectronicAddress" object property, corresponding to the homonym complex attribute of the MDS "Organization-Type" type is also shown in Fig. 2.

```
<owl:Class rdf:ID="OrganizationType">
    <rdfs:subClassOf rdf:resource="#AgentType"/>
    <rdfs:subClassOf>
        <owl:Restriction>
            <owl:onProperty rdf:resource="#ElectronicAddress"/>
            <owl:maxCardinality
rdf:datatype="&xsd;nonNegativeInteger">1</owl:maxCardinality>
        </owl:Restriction>
    </rdfs:subClassOf>
</owl:Class>
<owl:ObjectProperty rdf:ID="ElectronicAddress">
    <rdfs:domain rdf:resource="#OrganizationType"/>
    <rdfs:range rdf:resource="#ElectronicAddressType"/>
</owl:ObjectProperty>
```

Fig. 2. OWL Definition of Organization

3. *MPEG-7 Relationship Representation:* Relationships between the OWL classes, which correspond to the complex MDS types, are represented by the instances of the "RelationBaseType" class and its subclasses. Every "RelationBaseType" instance is associated with a source and a target metadata item through the homonym object properties. A relationship is "attached" to a semantic entity through the "Relation" object property (corresponding to the "Relation" complex attribute of SemanticBaseType).

Relationships among semantic entities are represented by the instances of the "SemanticBaseRelationType" class (a "RelationBaseType" descendant) and the instances of its subclasses. The "SemanticBaseRelationType" subclasses, in addition to the other restrictions, have restrictions on the class that belongs their target and/or source. In Fig. 3 we show the definitions of the "RelationBaseType" class, its "source" datatype property and of the "ObjectObjectRelationType" class. The "ObjectObjectRelationType" class represents relationships between "ObjectType" instances and its source and target properties are restricted to have all their values from the "ObjectType" class instances.

The complete core ontology has been designed using the above rules but is not shown here due to space limitations. It is OWL-DL ontology, validated using the OWL species ontology validator[1] and is available at http://elikonas.ced.tuc.gr/ontologies/av_semantics.zip.

---

[1] The OWL species validator validates OWL ontologies and checks if an ontology conforms to one of the OWL species. It is available at http://phoebus.cs.man.ac.uk:9999/OWL/Validator

```
<owl:Class rdf:ID="RelationBaseType">
    <rdfs:subClassOf rdf:resource="#DSType"/>
</owl:Class>
<owl:DatatypeProperty rdf:ID="source">
    <rdfs:domain rdf:resource="#RelationBaseType"/>
    <rdfs:range rdf:resource="&xsd;anyURI"/>
    <rdf:type rdf:resource="&owl;FunctionalProperty"/>
</owl:DatatypeProperty>
<owl:Class rdf:ID="ObjectObjectRelationType">
    <rdfs:subClassOf rdf:resource="#SemanticBaseRelationType"/>
    <rdfs:subClassOf>
       <owl:Restriction>
         <owl:onProperty rdf:resource="#source"/>
         <owl:allValuesFrom rdf:resource="#ObjectType"/>
       </owl:Restriction>
    </rdfs:subClassOf>
    <rdfs:subClassOf>
       <owl:Restriction>
         <owl:onProperty rdf:resource="#target"/>
         <owl:allValuesFrom rdf:resource="#ObjectType"/>
       </owl:Restriction>
    </rdfs:subClassOf>
</owl:Class>
```

Fig. 3. OWL Definitions of RelationBaseType and ObjectObjectRelationType

5 Methodology for the Definition of Domain-Specific Ontologies

In this section we present the methodological steps for the definition of domain-specific ontologies and we make the definition process clear through a set of examples from different application domains.

As already mentioned in section 3, the domain-specific ontologies comprise the second layer of the semantic metadata model used in the DS-MIRF framework, with the first layer of the model encapsulated in the core ontology. Thus, the classes representing the domain-specific entities should be defined in a way that extends the core ontology. Having these in mind, the domain-specific ontologies are defined according to the following methodological steps:

1. Domain-specific entity types are represented by OWL classes defined to be subclasses of the appropriate core ontology classes. For example, in a football tournament application the "FootballTeam" subclass of the "OrganizationType" core ontology class, is used for the representation of football teams. As another example, in a Formula-1 championship application, the "Race" subclass of the "EventType" core ontology class will be used for race representation.

   1.1. Attributes (simple or complex) that cannot be covered by the existing properties of the superclass are represented as appropriate object or datatype properties in order to make use of domain-specific knowledge (e.g. the shirt number of a football player can be represented as an integer datatype property).

   1.2. On the attributes inherited from the parent class, some constraints may be applied using the restriction mechanism provided by OWL in order to make use of the domain knowledge and guide the indexers for the production of valid metadata (e.g. the "Place" property of the "EventType" class, that denotes the place where the event occurs, has to be restricted to Soccer Stadium values for football Match instances).

As an example, we show in Fig. 4 the definition of the "FootballTeam" class, a subclass of the "OrganizationType" core ontology class, which represents football teams.

```
<owl:Class rdf:ID="FootballTeam">
   <rdfs:subClassOf rdf:resource="#OrganizationType"/>
   <rdfs:subClassOf>
      <owl:Restriction>
         <owl:onProperty rdf:resource="#Kind"/>
         <owl:hasValue rdf:resource="#FootballTeamTerm"/>
      </owl:Restriction>
   </rdfs:subClassOf>
</owl:Class>
```

Fig. 4. OWL Definition of the FootballTeam class

2. Relationships with additional restrictions compared with the ones of the general relationships defined in the core ontology are usually needed (e.g. a Goal event may be related to player instances as goal agents). In these cases, the following actions are performed:

2.1. A subclass of "SemanticBaseRelationType" or of its appropriate subclass is defined and all the restrictions needed are set for the newly defined class.

2.2. An appropriate subproperty of the "Relation" property (inherited from the "SemanticBaseType" class) is defined in the domain of the classes capable of being sources of the relationship. We must note that OWL subproperties permit the implementation of property hierarchies: If an individual A is related to another individual B by property C, which is a subproperty of property D, then A is also related to B by D.

For example, supposing that we would like to express the restriction that only players may be the agents of a Goal event, the following should be done:

- Definition of the "hasAgentOfPlayerRelationType" class (subclass of the "Object-EventRelationType" that permits relating events with their agents). The "hasAgent-OfPlayerRelationType" class must be restricted to have the "PlayerObject" class as target and the "Goal" class as permitted source.
- Definition of the "hasAgentOfPlayerRelation" object property (subproperty of the "Relation" property), having the "Goal" class as domain and as permitted range the "hasAgentOfPlayerRelationType" class.

In order to test the above-described methodology, we have developed a complete OWL (DL) ontology for football games, available at
http://elikonas.ced.tuc.gr/ontologies/football.zip.

6 Transformation Rules

We describe in this section the transformation rules for the production of MPEG-7 and TV-Anytime compliant metadata from the RDF metadata structured according to the core ontology and the domain-specific ontologies and vice versa. The rules for the transformations to and from MPEG-7 are described in subsection 6.1, while the rules for the transformations to and from TV-Anytime are discussed in subsection 6.2.

6.1 Transformation to/from MPEG-7

In this subsection we describe the rules for transforming into MPEG-7 compliant metadata the RDF metadata structured according to the OWL core ontology and the domain-specific ontologies developed according to the methodology discussed above.

We have already mentioned that MPEG-7 provides all the constructs needed for the structured description of audiovisual content. These constructs are the complex types defined in the MPEG-7 Description Schemes using the syntax of XML Schema language, so MPEG-7 metadata descriptions are XML documents.

Since MPEG-7 does not provide direct support for domain-specific ontologies, we automatically translate the entities of the supported domain-specific ontologies into abstract MPEG-7 descriptions using the "AbstractionLevel" attribute of the "SemanticBaseType" in order to form abstraction hierarchies. "AbstractionLevel" is a complex attribute of type "AbstractionLevelType" and has only one attribute, "Dimension", of non-negative integer type. When "AbstractionLevel" is not present in a semantic description, the description refers to specific audiovisual material. When "AbstractionLevel" is present, abstraction exists in the description. When "AbstractionLevel.Dimension"=0, there exists a description of a semantic entity (e.g. the football player Kahn) that is related to every audiovisual segment where the entity appears. When "AbstractionLevel" has a non-zero "Dimension", it can specify classes for the description of abstract semantic entities. The bigger the value of "AbstractionLevel.Dimension", the more extended the abstraction in the description (e.g. Kahn, which has "AbstractionLevel.Dimension"=0, is an instance of the "Goalkeeper" class, which has "AbstractionLevel.Dimension"=1, while "Goalkeeper" is an instance of the "Player" class, which has "AbstractionLevel.Dimension"=2). The reason for using this methodology (instead for example from subtyping) is that we remain this way completely compatible to MPEG-7 so that all tools and applications that use MPEG-7 still work transparently with the produced MPEG-7 metadata.

The rules for the transformation of OWL domain-specific ontologies into MPEG-7 compliant documents containing abstract descriptions are the following:

1. Every OWL class is transformed into an appropriate instance of the MPEG-7 class corresponding to its nearest ancestor in the core ontology.
   1.1. The id of the instance is the OWL class name.
   1.2. The type of the instance is the type of the MPEG-7 class corresponding to its nearest ancestor in the core ontology.
   1.3. The "AbstractionLevel" of the instance is greater than or equal to 1.
2. For every instance representing an OWL class, the following relationships are generated for the representation of subclass/superclass relationships:
   2.1. A "specializationOf" relationship that relates the instance with the class or instance representing its direct superclass.
   2.2. A set of "generalizationOf" relationships relating the instance with the instances representing its subclasses.
3. For each of the OWL class properties having a specific value in the abstract instance, the following take place:
   3.1. If the property exists in its nearest ancestor in the core ontology, an instance of the corresponding MPEG-7 class attribute, having the desired value is generated.

3.2. If the property is a subproperty of a property of the class nearest ancestor in the core ontology, an instance of the attribute of the MPEG-7 class corresponding to the ancestor having the desired value is generated.

3.3. If none of the above holds, an MPEG-7 "TermUseType" instance, holding the information needed for the representation of the value and the type of the property is generated. The generated "TermUseType" instance is a "Property" complex attribute of the instance ("Property" is an attribute inherited from "SemanticBaseType").

According to the above rules, the MPEG-7 abstract instance generated for the FootballTeam class (see Fig. 4) is shown in Fig. 5.

```
<Organization id="FootballTeam" xsi:type="OrganizationType">
    <AbstractionLevel dimension="1"/>
    <Relation type="specializationOf" target="OrganizationType"
source="FootballTeam"/>
</Organization>
```

Fig. 5. MPEG-7 abstract description for the "FootballTeam" class

We must note here that OWL restrictions are not taken into account during the transformation process, as MPEG-7 does not support such restrictions for semantic entity instances (MPEG-7 supports restrictions at the schema level, in DS definition). For example, in the MPEG-7 description of the "FootballTeam" in **Fig. 5**, the restriction in "Kind" is not expressed. The restrictions are used during the semantic indexing process in order to enforce the indexers to define valid semantic metadata. This way, the produced MPEG-7 metadata are also valid.

Specific metadata descriptions are defined as specializations of the abstract entities, with "AbstractionLevel.Dimension=0", according to the following rules:

1. Every individual belonging to an OWL class defined in the core ontology is transformed into an appropriate instance of the corresponding MPEG-7 class.
   1.1. For each of the individual's properties an instance of the corresponding MPEG-7 class attribute, which has the desired value, is generated.
   1.2. The id of the instance is the individual's rdf:ID.
   1.3. The type of the instance is the type of the corresponding MPEG-7 class.
2. Every individual belonging to an OWL class defined in a domain-specific ontology is transformed into an appropriate instance of the MPEG-7 class corresponding to the class nearest ancestor in the core ontology.
   2.1. The id of the instance is the individual's rdf:ID.
   2.2. The type of the instance is the type of the MPEG-7 class corresponding to the nearest ancestor in the core ontology of the class of the individual.
   2.3. An "exampleOf" relation is generated, which relates the instance representing the individual with the instance representing the OWL class it belongs.
   2.4. For each of the individual's properties, the same actions with the ones performed for an OWL class are performed.

For example, using the above rules, the generated MPEG-7 compliant description for the RDF description of the "Real" football team individual (see Fig. 6) that has been defined according to the football ontology, is shown in Fig. 7.

```
<FootballTeam rdf:ID="Real">
   <Name>Real Madrid</Name>
      <hasKind rdf:resource="#FootballTeamTerm"/>
</FootballTeam>
<Term rdf:ID="FootballTeamTerm"/>
```

Fig. 6. Definition of the "Real" football team

The individual "Real" defined in Fig. 6 belongs to the FootballTeam OWL class (which is subclass of the "OrganizationType" core ontology class). The team name is "Real Madrid" and is related with the "FootballTeamTerm" individual through the "Kind" property.

```
<Organization id="Real" xsi:type="OrganizationType">
   <AbstractionLevel dimension="0"/>
   <Relation type="exampleOf" target="FootballTeam" source="Real"/>
   <Name>Real Madrid</Name>
   <Kind id="FootballTeamTerm" xsi:type="TermUseType"/>
</Organization>
```

Fig. 7. MPEG-7 compliant metadata for the "Real" football team

The inverse process, for the transformation of MPEG-7 compliant metadata containing abstract object descriptions to OWL ontologies and the transformation of non-abstract MPEG-7 compliant metadata to RDF metadata structured according to the OWL ontologies is possible and of significant importance, because working with MPEG-7 is common in the multimedia community. The limitation in this case is that a part of the domain knowledge (e.g. restrictions) cannot be expressed in MPEG-7, so the produced domain-specific OWL ontologies and the corresponding RDF metadata will be less expressive.

6.2   Transformation to/from TV-Anytime

In this subsection we discuss the rules for transforming the RDF metadata structured according to the OWL core ontology and the domain-specific ontologies into TV-Anytime compliant metadata.

As we have already mentioned, the only mechanism for the semantic description of audiovisual content provided by TV-Anytime is annotation based on keywords and keyword phrases. Thus, when translating RDF metadata defined using the OWL ontologies, we translate each metadata item to a set of keywords.

The following rules are applied, in order to obtain a TV-Anytime compliant keyword-based annotation from an RDF description structured according to the OWL core ontology and the domain-specific ontologies:
1. The name of the class to which an individual belongs, together with the rdf:ID of the individual, form a keyword phrase.
2. The name of each of the object properties of the individual is represented as a keyword.
   2.1. The individuals related to the described individual through the object property are used for the production of keywords and keyword phrases after the keyword containing the name of the object property.

3. A keyword phrase composed of the name and the value of every datatype property is produced.

3.1. A keyword phrase containing the value of the datatype property is produced.

In Fig. 8 we show the TV-Anytime compliant metadata produced for the "Real" football team defined in Fig. 6 according to the above rules.

```
<Keywords>
    <Keyword>FootballTeam Real</Keyword>
    <Keyword>Name Real Madrid</Keyword>
    <Keyword>Real Madrid</Keyword>
    <Keyword>Kind</Keyword>
    <Keyword>Term FootballTeamTerm</Keyword>
</Keywords>
```

Fig. 8. TV-Anytime compliant metadata for the "Real" football team

As expected, the TV-Anytime compliant annotation can be exploited in a less flexible and efficient way than the equivalent MPEG-7 compliant one, since keyword-based descriptions have less expressive power than structured metadata descriptions.

This also implies that even if OWL ontology and RDF metadata production from the TV-Anytime compliant metadata is possible, it will give as a result ontologies where much of the domain knowledge is not precisely captured and incomplete RDF metadata descriptions.

7 Conclusions – Future Work

In this paper we have presented the integration of OWL ontologies in the DS-MIRF framework for the support of ontology-based semantic indexing and retrieval of audiovisual content following the MPEG-7 and TV-Anytime standard specifications for metadata descriptions. In this framework, semantic indexing produces consistent MPEG-7 and TV-Anytime compliant semantic descriptions for the audiovisual content. The indexing process is guided by appropriate domain-specific ontologies, which are based on the Semantic Part of the MPEG-7 MDS and are defined using the syntax of the OWL language. We have also presented an interoperability methodology and tools for transforming audiovisual content descriptions in MPEG-7 and TV-Anytime together with the domain-specific extensions in OWL and vice-versa.

The methodology of OWL ontology integration and the interoperability methodology and tools have been based on (a) A core OWL ontology, which fully covers the Semantic Part of the MPEG-7 MDS (b) A methodology for the definition of domain-specific ontologies that extend the core ontology in order to fully describe the concepts of specific application domains (c) Two sets of rules, used for the transformation of semantic metadata (formed according to the core ontology and its domain-specific extensions) to MPEG-7 and TV-Anytime compliant XML documents respectively.

The DS-MIRF framework for domain-specific multimedia information retrieval and filtering that includes the interoperability methodologies and tools presented in this paper has been implemented in the Linux OS environment. MySQL was the platform selected for the relational database (that contains both the Semantic Base and the

TV-Anytime compliant database). XML data management in the relational database is carried out by a binder capable of fully representing XML documents as objects or objects as XML documents. The Segmentation & Semantic Indexing Tool (including the module responsible for the translation between OWL/RDF, MPEG-7 and TV-Anytime) has been implemented in java.swing.

Our future work in the domain of semantic description of audiovisual information includes:

- The extension of the core ontology, using the methodology discussed in section 3, in order to capture the other parts of the MPEG-7 metadata model (segmentation, user profiles, usage rights etc.).
- The deployment of the framework in order to provide automatic (or semi-automatic) abstractions of the audiovisual content, based on the domain-specific ontologies and the corresponding semantic information.

Acknowledgments

The work presented in this paper was partially funded in the scope of the DELOS II Network of Excellence in Digital Libraries (IST – Project Record Number 26059).

References

1. M.Doerr, J.Hunter, C.Lagoze, "Towards a Core Ontology for Information Integration", Journal of Digital Information, Volume 4 Issue 1, April 2003
2. D. Fallside, "XML Schema Part 0: Primer", W3C Recommendation, 2001, http://www.w3.org/TR/xmlschema-0/
3. D. Mc Guiness, F. van Harmelen, "OWL Web Ontology Language Overview", W3C Recommendation, 2004, http://www.w3.org/TR/owl-features/
4. J. Hunter, "Adding Multimedia to the Semantic Web - Building an MPEG-7 Ontology", in Proc. of International Semantic Web Working Symposium (SWWS), Stanford, July 30 - August 1, 2001
5. J. Hunter, "Enhancing the Semantic Interoperability of Multimedia through a Core Ontology", IEEE Transactions on Circuits and Systems for Video Technology, Special Issue on Conceptual and Dynamical Aspects of Multimedia Content Description, Feb 2003
6. ISO/IEC JTC 1/SC 29/WG 11/N3966, "Text of 15938-5 FCD Information Technology – Multimedia Content Description Interface – Part 5 Multimedia Description Schemes", Singapore, 2001
7. A. Jaimes, T. Echigo, M. Teraguchi, F. Satoh, "Learning Personalized Video Highlights from Detailed MPEG-7 Metadata", in Proc. of ICIP, Rochester, NY, USA, 2002
8. F. de Jong, T. Westerveld, "MUMIS: Multimedia Indexing and Searching", in Proc. of CBMI Workshop, Brescia, Italy, 2001, pp. 423-425
9. F. Kazasis, N. Moumoutzis, N. Pappas, "Informative Annex: Generic Architecture for handling TVA Metadata using relational database technologies", contribution TV-Anytime Forum/Metadata WG, 2nd Implementer's workshop, Geneva, 2002
10. G. Klyne, J. Caroll, "Resource Description Framework (RDF): Concepts and Abstract Syntax", W3C Recommendation, 2004, http://www.w3.org/TR/rdf-concepts/

11. MPEG Group, "MPEG-7 (Multimedia Content Description Interface)", http://www.chiariglione.org/mpeg/index.htm

12. TV-Anytime Forum, http://www.tv-anytime.org/

13. R. Troncy, "Integrating Structure and Semantics into Audio-visual Documents", in Proc. of 2nd International Semantic Web Conference (ISWC), 20-23 October 2003, Sanibel Island, Florida, USA

14. C. Tsinaraki, E. Fatourou, S. Christodoulakis, "An Ontology-Driven Framework for the Management of Semantic Metadata describing Audiovisual Information", in Proc. of CAiSE, Velden, Austria, 2003, pp 340-356

15. C. Tsinaraki, S. Papadomanolakis, S. Christodoulakis, "A Video Metadata Model supporting Personalization & Recommendation in Video-based Services", in Proc. of MDDE Workshop (in conjunction with RETIS), Lyon, France, 2001, pp. 104-109

16. C. Tsinaraki, S. Papadomanolakis, S. Christodoulakis, "Towards a two - layered Video Metadata Model", in Proc. of DEXA Workshop - DLib, Munich, Germany, 2001, pp 937-941

17. C. Tsinaraki, P. Polydoros, F. Kazasis, S. Christodoulakis, "Ontology-based Semantic Indexing for MPEG-7 and TV-Anytime Audiovisual Content", Special issue of Multimedia Tools and Applications Journal on Video Segmentation for Semantic Annotation and Transcoding, 2004

Adaptive Web-Based Courseware Development Using Metadata Standards and Ontologies

Lydia Silva Muñoz and José Palazzo Moreira de Oliveira

Federal University of Rio Grande do Sul - Instituto de Informática (II/UFRGS)
Caixa Postal 15.064, 91.501-970, Porto Alegre, RS, Brazil
{lydia,palazzo}@inf.ufrgs.br
http://www.inf.ufrgs.br

Abstract. Nowadays, the web enormously facilitates the information distribution and communication among teachers and students setting the stage for the development of Web-based courseware. In this context, adaptability is a key feature in order to obtain educational environments capable of giving the adequate instruction for the specific learning profile of each individual learner. Using the Web as the ubiquitous repository of educative content, standards for metadata to describe resources on the e-learning domain must be used in order to enable interoperability and reuse of learning content. To enable intelligent behavior in building complex learning objects "on demand" customized for an intended audience, ontologies can be used to represent the knowledge the system has on the domain to be taught and on the student profile. This paper briefly describes the main steps taken in developing an Adaptive Web Training Environment, delving into the definition of a new *application profile* of the Learning Object Metadata (LOM) standard and the Domain and Student Knowledge Models design and implementation as Web ontologies.

1 Introduction

To achieve adaptability in an educational hypermedia system, issues on modeling the student's profile, and the knowledge about the domain to be taught must be taken into account [1][2][3][4][5]. The student's profile provides the system with the knowledge about the student's learning goals, domain knowledge, background, cognitive learning style and hyperspace experience, while the knowledge about the domain to be taught lets the adaptive system "know" what is presented on a particular page or page fragment of the instructional material by means of metadata annotations describing it. Then, dynamic content sequence generation tailored to a student profile can be made using the knowledge the system has about the student profile and the system's learning domain. Metadata can be viewed as concise information containing the most significant attributes of an object. In our approach, the fundamental metadata describing the instructional material is partial generated automatically and stored in a web ontology. Ontologies are the description of the entities, relations and restrictions of a domain, expressed in a formal language to enable machine understanding. Tom Gru-

A. Persson and J. Stirna (Eds.): CAiSE 2004, LNCS 3084, pp. 414–428, 2004.

ber [8] has defined "an ontology is a formal, explicit specification of a shared concep-tualization". Additionally, ontologies to be used on the Web need to be supported by established web languages to facilitate interoperability and take advantage of existing tools. In order to make metadata understandable to the Web community, classification schemas defining vocabularies in an unambiguous way must be available on the Web forming *namespaces* [20], which give well understood semantics for the terms used in metadata descriptions. Interoperability and reuse of the learning content can be achieved by having metadata describing it in terms of an established standard meta-data model envisaged to describe e-learning content. An *application profile* [10][11] of a standard metadata model is a version of the standard tailored to the requirements of a particular application. This paper describes the main steps taken in creating the Adaptive Web Training Environment AdaptWeb [7], delving into the definition of a new application profile of the Learning Object Metadata (LOM) standard and the Domain and Student Knowledge Model design and implementation as Web ontologies. These ontologies are available at: http://www.inf.ufrgs.br/~tapejara/ Ontology/Generated/ AWOntology.daml and http://www.inf.ufrgs.br/~tapejara/ Ontology/Student.daml. The AdaptWeb is an in-progress research project supported by the CNPq, Brazilian Research Council, and presently in operation at the Federal University of Rio Grande do Sul. The remainder of this work is structured as follows: section 2 gives an overview of adaptive hypermedia systems, section 3 resumes the main steps taken in the development of the proposed environment, section 4 shows the constructed Knowledge Space model, section 5 explains how the metadata con-cerning the instructional content is generated, section 6 shows the constructed student model, section 7 briefly explains the adaptive content selection, section 8 shows the proposed system architecture and section 9 is a short conclusion.

2   Adaptive Hypermedia Systems

According to [4] an adaptive hypermedia system has two interconnected networks or "spaces": a network of elementary knowledge elements forming the *Knowledge Space* and a network of hypertext pages with educational material forming the *Hyper-space*. Links relating the Knowledge Space and the Hyperspace let the adaptive sys-tem "know" what is presented on a particular page of the educative content. As stated by authors in [5] the instructional contents' adaptation to the student's individual characteristics implies that the system must: (i) recognize the cognitive patterns of each student's learning and its pedagogical implications; (ii) know the training knowledge space being proposed, (iii) know the instructional material organization, and (iv) be able to dynamically generate the best suited selection and sequence for each student in a particular course stage.

In the AdaptWeb research project, the first such requisite is achieved by using a student model giving the system knowledge about the student's background, learning goals, domain knowledge, hyperspace experience and style of learning. For the sys-tem to know the training knowledge space being proposed and the instructional material organization, a machine understandable knowledge model of the domain to be taught was constructed, and the connections between this model and the instructional content were implemented. At the run-time, a teaching strategy to guide dynamic content sequence generation can make it possible to select the specific contents to be presented to the student using the knowledge the system has about the student profile and the system's learning domain.

3   General View

The main steps taken in the development of the AdaptWeb project are shown in figure 1. On the one hand, research was done concerning the different Cognitive Styles of Learning (CSL) students may have, which were described in [5][6]. Based on those CSL, a GUI interface was developed to enable the student himself to categorize his CSL, set his learning goals and characteristics of his work environment and the kind of course he wants to take. At run-time, the student model is updated taking into account the learning activities of the student. More details of the student model are given in section 6. On the other hand, to make an interoperable system, an application profile [10] [11] of the Learning Object Metadata (LOM) standard [9] suitable to the needs of the application educative context was developed, as explained in section 4. A Knowledge Space model based on such a standard application profile was built containing the knowledge the system has about the domain to be taught, as explained in section 4. This model was encoded as a web ontology. An authoring tool was implemented to facilitate the content creation, guiding the authoring process to relate educative content by semantic properties that define the hierarchical structure of the material to a given discipline, and the possible adaptation to pre-defined learning goals and general knowledge background of students. A model that follows a hierarchical approach resembling the structure of a textbook with chapters and sections is defined to structure the educative content. At authoring time the parts that compose a discipline are created and related. Then, learning objects representing topic explanations are related to exercises, examples and complementary material supporting the learning. Also, indications about the degree of difficulty and other characteristics of each learning object are declared. Adaptation to learning goals and knowledge background is made by defining at authoring time what the most adequate parts of the discipline material to be given to students with specific pre-defined learning goals and knowledge background are. For example, Computer Science, Engineering and Mathematics courses customizing the Numerical Methods discipline were defined to be directed to students who have a background knowledge determined by their graduation in such fields. The created instructional content is stored into the system Hyperspace taking advantage of the XML language facilities to represent hierarchical structures. The structure of the educational content is based on the existence of an XML file for each topic in the Knowledge Space Model. Each XML file representing a topic entails the HTML pages whose content is concerned with this topic. A special XML file is available for each discipline, relating the topic's hierarchical structure to the discipline, and the prerequisite relation among them. Since we have a structured

Hyperspace, it is possible automatically to connect the knowledge space with the hyperspace instances by making the semantics behind XML structures explicit, and inferring some metadata elements from others. A wrapper aware of the structure and the context of the hyperspace instances creation automatically generates the metadata describing what the Hyperspace instances contain in terms of the Knowledge Space, and how to use them. This wrapper is executed each time educative content is created. In order to recommend the use of any learning resource discovered on the web and considered suitable to support the explanation of a given topic, it is possible to augment the metadata by the ontology edition. Issues on metadata generation are better explained in section 5.

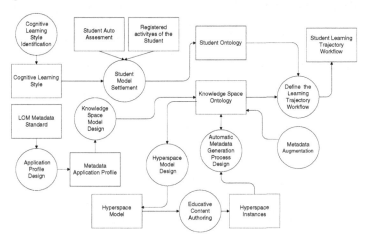

Fig. 1. Main steps in the AdaptWeb project development

Finally, a learning trajectory tailored to the student's profile as a workflow instance can be dynamically generated based on the metadata describing the educative content and the current student model. Also, navigation techniques as direct guidance and hiding links are used to adapt the content presentation to the student's hyperspace experience.

4   Knowledge Space Model

The AdaptWeb Knowledge Space Model describes the structure and semantics of the system learning content. Metadata based in the LOM standard is used. A formal web ontology provides the support so that the educative content composition to achieve adaptability is possible. Next subsections treat the use of standards in educational metadata on the web, which is the foundation of having a Knowledge Space Model that enables interoperability. Finally, the structure of the constructed model and the use of the LOM properties refinement mechanism to construct the AdaptWeb application profile are explained.

4.1 Metadata in the E-Learning Domain

Metadata can be viewed as information about the most relevant attributes of an object. It helps in the tasks of discovering, managing and using objects without the need to read, view or explore them directly. To make metadata understandable to the Web community, metadata schemas defining vocabularies in an unambiguous way must be available on the Web forming namespaces which give standard, well understood semantics for the terms used in metadata descriptions. One of the most common metadata schemas used to describe digital resources is the Dublin Core schema – DC [12], which defines the semantics of 15 properties intended to be used in descriptions of cross-disciplinary resources. For the educative domain the Learning Objects Metadata Standard – LOM [9] developed by the IEEE is used. LOM defines the semantics of more than 80 properties to describe metadata in a hierarchy given by the following categories: 1-General, 2-Lyfecycle, 3-Meta-Metadata, 4-Technical, 5-Educational, 6-Rights, 7-Relation, 8-Annotation and 9-Classification. Such a standard facilitates the search, evaluation, acquisition and use of learning objects by learners, instructors or automated agents. An application profile [10][11] is the combination of existing schemas into a package that is tailored to the functional requirements of a particular application while retaining interoperability with the original base schemas. Part of this adaptation may include the elaboration of local metadata elements that are important to given community or organization, but which are not expected to be important in a wider context. Several application profiles as ARIADNE [27], Heal-Health Education Assets Library [28], CanCore – Canadian Core Learning Resource Metadata [29], MERLOT [30] and SingCore [31] were developed in order to give more specific semantics to a subset of the LOM specification appropriate for the needs of particular learning contexts, and some crosswalks exist in order to provide mappings between them.

4.2 Application Profile Implementation

There are several possibilities to represent LOM metadata descriptions on the Web. One is to use an XML binding, i.e. the XML language [13] with a specific XML Schema [15] designed to validate documents with LOM descriptions of a certain Learning Object. Another alternative is the use of an RDF binding, i.e. use RDF [14][32] as the language to represent statements with assertions about the value of LOM properties to a given resource. RDF statements are triples with a subject indicating the resource being described, a property and a value for this property for the described resource (the property value is eventually another resource). We selected RDF to represent LOM descriptions since RDF offers a standard way to combine different vocabulary definitions supported by RDF Schemas [16], while XML documents have only the semantics resulting from their pre-defined tree structures. For example, we use the Creator property of the Dublin Core schema [12] to identify an Entity (eventually a person) who contributes to the creation of a learning object, and the property FN of the Vcard schema definition [18] to indicate the formal name of such an entity. We use the RDF binding described in [17] as the such an entity. We use the RDF binding described in [17] as the syntactical representation of the LOM standard. Table 1 shows the subset of LOM properties used as attributes describing each learning object, while the properties describing relations among the learning objects are treated in subsection 4.4. The corresponding abbreviations for namespaces used are vcard: http://www.w3.org/2001/vcard-rdf/3.0/, dc: http://purl.org/dc/elements/1.1/, dcterms: http://purl.org/dc/terms/, and lom-edu, lom-tech, lom-meta stand respectively for documents lom-educational, lom-technical and lom-metametadata in http://kmr.nada.kth.se/el/ims/schemas/.

Table 1. LOM properties used in the AdaptWeb application profile

LOM Property	RDF binding	Description
1.3- Language	dc:language using dcterms: RFC1766	Language used to communicate to the intended user.
1.4- Description	dc:description	Description of the content of the Learning Object.
1.5- Keyword	dc:subject with a literal value	A keyword describing a topic in the Learning Object.
2.3- Contribute	dc:creator and lom:Entity using Vcard:FN	Entity (people, organization) that contributed to the state of the Learning Object.
3.3- Metadata Schema	lom-meta: metadataScheme	The specification used to create the metadata instance.
4.3- Location	lom-tech:location	Location of the Learning Object.
4.4- Requirement	lom-tech:requirement	Technical capabilities necessary to use the Learning Object.
5.1- Interactivity Type	lom-edu: interactivityType	Predominant mode of learning of the Learning Object. Ex: expositive, interactive
5.2- Learning Resource Type	lom-edu: learningResourceType	Specific kind of Learning Object. Ex: Exercise, Example.
5.8- Difficulty	lom-edu:difficulty	How hard it is to work with the Learning Object. Ex: Easy, Difficult.

4.3 Knowledge Space Structure

Each piece of instructional content in the hyperspace is described in the Knowledge Space structure by metadata providing the information for find and reuse it. The Domain Knowledge Ontology implements the Knowledge space structure. It contains the knowledge describing the pieces of content in the hyperspace and the rules to correctly assemble them in order to compute complex learning objects adequate to the profile of each student. Follows is the description of its classes and relations. Figure 2 shows a graphical representation of the Domain Knowledge Ontology. The abbreviations for namespaces used are awo: http://www.inf.ufrgs.br/~tapejara/Ontology/ Generated/AWOntology.daml and daml: http://www.daml.org/2001/03/ daml+oil#.

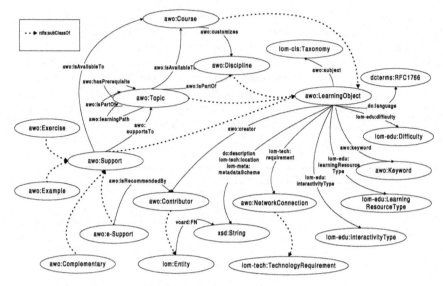

Fig. 2. Domain Knowledge ontology

Instances of class *awo:Topic* represent the explanation of some concept or idea, *topics* are considered to be part of the disciplines learning content. Generally, the explanation of a topic comes associated with some examples, exercises and complementary material supporting the topic study, which are represented in the classes *awo:Example*, *awo:Exercise*, *awo:Complementary* and *awo:e-Support*. Additionally, a topic may have sub-topics giving more specific and detailed explanations related by the *awo:isPartOf* relation, i.e. they are considered part of the explanation of the prime topic. The order in which the topics must be presented according to learning purposes is given by the *awo:learningPath* relation. The class *awo:Course* contains customizations of a discipline to be directed to students with common background knowledge and learning goals. In the case study used, we defined Computer Science, Engineering and Mathematics courses customizing the Numerical Methods discipline for students graduated on these fields.   The learning content of a course is composed of the discipline topics that are considered adequate for the intended audience of the course, i.e. the topics *available* for the course. The Exercises, Examples and Complementary material supporting a Topic explanation may or may not be available for a course even if the topic they support is available. Generally, the educative material is created in the system context, and an element of the class *awo:Contributor* is indicated as the author of the created learning object. On the other hand, a paper or some other kind of resource on the Web created out of the system environment may be considered adequate to complement the explanation of a given topic. When a Web resource is identified as holding this condition, a teacher places it as an element of the class *awo:e-Support* and   recommends it to be used by the *awo: isRecommendedBy* relation. He also cites the supported topic by the *awo:supportsTo* relation, indicates to which courses it will be available by the relation awo:isAvailableTo, and gives the fundamental metadata describing it. This recommendation of a resource to be used as a Learning Object is a kind of highly subjective metadata, which was indicated as very valuable [10] [19]. An element of class Taxonomy defined in http://kmr.nada.kth.se/ el/ims/schemas/lom-classification was created in order to give learning content classification by subject matter, available at http://www.inf.ufrgs.br/ ~tapejara/ Domain.daml. Learning objects are classified as having the dc:subject property pointing to an item in such a taxonomy.

4.4 Refinement of LOM Elements

Application profiles enable increasing semantic interoperability in one community, in a way that preserves full compatibility with the larger LOM context. The refinement of properties and classes of the LOM RDF binding specification [17] contributed to the application profile's definition. To begin with, Disciplines, Courses, Topics and Support material were declared as pertaining to classes that are subclasses of the *awo:LearningObject* class, which then inherit all their restrictions on properties values. To define a controlled vocabulary with a more specialized semantics, we defined the class *awo:NetworkConnection* as a sub class of *lom:TechnologyRequirement* containing all the valid elements to be used as values of the LOM property *lom-tech:requirement*. Similarly we have defined *awo:Contributor* as a subclass of *lom:Entity* whose instances are the teachers working in the educative content creation and recommendation. Figure 3 shows, among others, the property *dcterms:requires* refinement to the *awo:hasPrerequisite* relation standing for a learning object that is needed to correctly understand the current learning object. The *awo:hasPrerequisite* relation was also declared as transitive in the ontology code, and has an inverse relation *awo:*isPrerequisiteOf, both of which are useful to enable inference tasks. Any Web agent that can not understand our ontology specifications about the *awo:hasPrerequisite* relation, can still understand the more general property dcterms:requires, and interpret the *awo:hasPrerequisite* relation with the semantics of the known, more general property. Similarly other specializations were defined as shown in figure 3 and table 2. All the properties used in the AdaptWeb metadata repository are those proposed by the RDF binding [17] or refinements of them.

5 Metadata Generation

The AdaptWeb metadata repository is an ontology containing explicit, structural, contextual, and semantic metadata implementing the knowledge space model of the system. Such an ontology was encoded in DAML+OIL language [21] [22] [23] using the editor OilEd [24] to construct the model and the reasoner RACER [25] to check the model satisfiability. Metadata describing each piece of the learning content that populates the Hyperspace in terms of the knowledge space makes the necessary connection between the two spaces to let the system "know" what is presented on each piece of learning content and how is it related to each other. Such metadata is

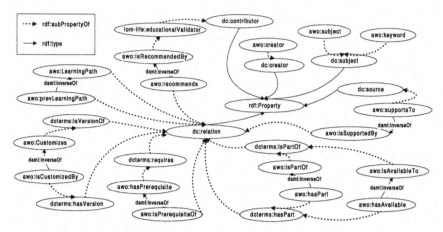

Fig. 3. Refinement of LOM properties

automatically generated. Each time new content is authored into the system, a PHP wrapper reads the XML files created by the authoring environment while being aware of their creation context (e.g. the metadata that can be inferred from the author information, like his or her language) and the structure and semantics of their content (i.e. the semantics inferable from the XML document tree structure and sequence of elements) generating RDF statements containing the metadata descriptions. Such metadata descriptions are Domain Knowledge ontology instances available at http://www.inf.ufrgs.br/~tapejara/Ontology/Generated/AWOntology.daml. At any time, the metadata repository, i.e. the ontology, can be augmented by human agents using the ontology editor OilEd [24], these augments can be over any existent element by editing comments or attribute values, and also by creating new RDF descriptions, for example pointing to resources discovered on the Web and considered valuable to complement some topic explanation. This is a way to enrich the educative content of the AdaptWeb system with resources not authored into it, but recommended to be used by identified contributors responsible for the quality of the educative content. These Web resources do not need to have previous metadata annotations describing them. The result of the enrichment by human agents is stored in http://www.inf.ufrgs.br/~tapejara/Ontology/Augmented/AWOntology.daml.

6   Student Model

The student model graphically depicted in figure 4 consists of the central class *st:Student* with properties characterizing the student profile. The property *st:has LearningStyle* indicates the student's cognitive style of learning (CSL) [5][6]. The property *st:hasLearningGoal* points to an element of *awo:Course* which customizes a discipline content directed to the background and objectives of a specific group of students, as defined in the Domain Knowledge ontology. The boolean property

Table 2. LOM properties refinement in the AdaptWeb application profile

Ontology Property	Refined Property	Ontology Property Description
awo: hasPrerequisite	dcterms: requires	A topic that must be taken previously to take the topic for which the property has been stated. Its domain and range are in class *awo:Topic*. It is transitive.
awo:isPartOf	dcterms: isPartOf	The whole of which the topic is part of. It is transitive. Its domain is in class *awo:Topic*. Is transitive.
awo: isAvailableTo	dcterms: isPartOf	To which courses a Topic or Support material is available. Its domain is in class *awo:LearningObject* and its range in *awo:Course*.
awo: customizes	dcterms:is VersionOf	A Discipline customization to certain general knowledge background and learning goals. Its domain is in class *awo:Course* and its range in *awo:Discipline*. It is functional.
awo: supportsTo	dc:source	Indicates that an educative material supports a Topic exposition. Its domain is in class *awo:Support* and its range in *awo:Topic*.
awo:is Recommended By	lom-life: educational Validator	The person responsible for recommendations to use an external learning object. Its domain is in class *awo:LearningObject* and its range in *awo:Contributor*.
awo: learningPath	dc:relation	The order the topics explaining an idea must be presented in according to learning purposes. Its domain and range are in class *awo:Topic*.
awo:creator	dc:creator	Entities that have created the learning object. Its domain is in class *awo:LearningObject* and its range in *awo:Contributor*.
awo:keyword	dc:subject	A keyword describing a topic in the Learning Object. Its domain is in class *awo:LearningObject* and its range in *awo:Keyword*.
awo:subject	dc:subject	A term within a taxonomy used to classify learning objects by subject matter. Its domain is in class *awo:LearningObject* and its range in *lom-cls:Taxonomy*.

st:wantsTutorial indicates if the student currently prefers to work in a tutored mode, according to his hyperspace experience. Using a simple overlay model, the student's knowledge on each topic of the Knowledge Model is indicated by the relation *st:hasKnowledgeOn,* i.e. if an instance of the relation *st:hasKnowledgeOn* exists relating the student to an instance of the class *awo:Topic,* then the system believes the student has knowledge about this topic. The property *awo:hasNetworkConnection* indicates the kind of Network Connection the student has declared in the current session. The property *st:locationLearningTrajectoryWF* indicates the URL where the current learning trajectory for the student is. The remaining classes in the model, which are the range of the described properties, are as follows: *awo:Course,* *awo:Topic* and *awo:NetworkConnection* all defined in the Knowledge Space Model; *xsd:String* and *xsd:Boolean* are defined in the XML Schema namespace [15];

and *st:CognitiveLearningStyle* is defined in the namespace of the Student Model: http://www.inf.ufrgs.br/~tapejara/Ontology/Student.daml, containing the four CLS identified in [5], i.e. (i) Analogue-Analytical; (ii) Concrete-Generic; (iii) Deductive-Evaluative and (iv) Relational-Synthetic. According to his CLS, a student may prefer to visit the examples about a topic, try to do the exercises, and then go on to the page containing the abstract explanation of the topic, while another student with a different CSL may prefer to read the abstract explanation of the topic content first. From this we can observe that the tutorial workflow path proposed by the system for each student will be strongly influenced by his CLS. The student model was implemented as an ontology encoded in DAML+OIL language [21] [22] [23] using the editor OilEd [26] to construct the model and the reasoner RACER [25] to check the model satisfiability. Its instances are created or updated automatically at the beginning of each session with the information the student gives about himself and also by the result of the continuous analysis of the student's activities [5].

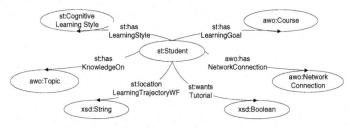

Fig. 4. Student Model

7 Adaptive Content Selection

Since ontology relations can be viewed as binary predicates in first order logic and class membership as unary predicates, we can use first order logic to represent statements about ontology elements. As an example scenario to show the adaptive content selection, we can assume a student *Stud1* graduated in Computer Science, with a dial-up network connection that intends to take a Numerical Methods course, then `learningGoal(Stud1, Computer Science)` is stated in the ontology because at authoring time it was indicated that *ComputerScience* is a course of Numerical Methods discipline customized to Computer Science students, and *learningGoal* is an ontology property relating students with learning goals. Also `networkConnection(Stud1, "dial-up")` is stated indicating the kind of connection that the student currently has. To begin with, it is necessary to determine what the first content to be offered to the student is. The educative content related to topics x available for course *Computer Science* with no prerequisites that also begin a learning path, are the learning objects the student is able to take at this stage. The following is computed.

```
hasAvailable(Computer Science,x) ∧
¬∃y(hasPrerequisite(x,y)) ∧ ¬∃z(learningPath(z,x))
```

Also, the student's Cognitive Style of Learning (CLS) is taken into account to define the first element among those selected above to give to the student. The existence of the following assertions indicating that the student has the CLS "Analogue-Analytical", and the order the students with CLS "Analogue-Analytical" usually prefer the educative material is assumed.

```
hasLearningStyle(Stud1, "Analogue-Analytical");
first(Analogue-Analytical,z) → Example(z);
second(Analogue-Analytical,t) → Topic(t)
```

The sentences above indicate that students with CLS Analogue-Analytical prefer to take a simple example prior to taking the theoretical exposition of a new topic. According to what is stated above, it will be concluded that the first learning object to offer the student must be an example s of Topic x whose degree of difficulty is *easy*. Additionally it must be a version suitable to the speed of the student network connection. Then, the following must hold:

```
isSupportedBy(x,s)  ∧ Example(s) ∧
requirement(s,"dial-up") ∧ difficulty(s,"Easy")
```

It can be observed that the inverses of relations *isAvailableTo* and *supportsTo* were used to compute the educative content available for the course and the support material available for a given topic respectively.

8 System Architecture

The proposed system architecture is depicted in figure 5. At the content creation time, the *Authoring* module provides a methodology and an editing tool to create new educative content. During the authoring process, the author can consult the Domain Knowledge ontology to be aware of pre-existing learning objects to eventually reuse them. Each time new content is created, the *Automatic Metadata Generation* wrapper generates its basic metadata according to what was explained in section 5, and store it in the Domain Knowledge ontology. At any time the *Metadata Augmentation* module can enable the Domain Knowledge ontology augmentation by human agents through the use of the editor OilEd [24]. A possible use of this metadata augmentation feasibility is to create metadata descriptions pointing to resources discovered on the Web and recommended by a teacher as adequate to complement some topic explanation. The *Student Monitoring* agent continuously updates the *Student Model* according to the activities of the student. The *Adaptive Content Selection* agent defines a teaching strategy to guide dynamic content sequence generation. It selects the specific contents to be presented, creating a learning trajectory tailored to the student profile. The *Adaptive Presentation* module determines the presentation style according to the preferences stated in the student model using the strategy of disabling links if the student has chosen the tutorial mode for his navigational preferences and offers the search by keywords if he has decided to learn in a free navigational style.

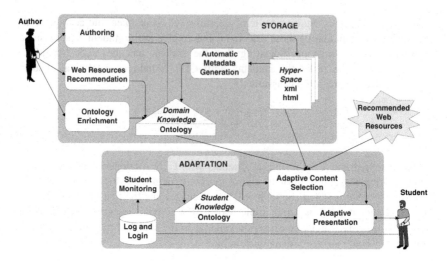

Fig. 5. System Architecture

9 Conclusions and Future Work

This paper describes the steps taken in the design and implementation of an in – progress project for adaptive content presentation of Web-based courses delving into the definition of an application profile of the Learning Object Metadata (LOM) standard [9] to represent the metadata of their educational content and the design and implementation of the student and domain model as Web ontology. The proposed solution is demonstrated with the application of the AdaptWeb system. A use case was implemented with the creation of the metadata concerning a Numerical Computation course, where specific and different contents of the same discipline are presented for students of three different programs (Mathematics, Engineering, or Computer Science). In the adaptive environment provided by the system, course contents are customized with different information complexity, sequence of contents access, example application, and supplementary material access. Authoring software is provided for syllabus generation, supported by XML standard files. The course content is adapted and presented to students, according to each student's program, current knowledge, and navigation preferences. An identified future work is to relate the top of each taxonomy used to classify learning objects by subject matter in the knowledge Space Model with the criteria of Discipline or Idea with a more general taxonomy existing on the Web, as the ACM Computer Classification system [33]. Additionally, future versions of the ontology will be encoded in OWL DL language [26].

References

1. Brusilovsky, P. Methods and Techniques of Adaptive Hypermedia. Adaptive Hypertext and Hypermedia. Kluwer Academic Publishers, pp. 1-43, 1998.
2. Brusilovsky, P. Adaptive and Intelligent Technologies for Web-based Education. In C. Rollinger and C. Peylo editors, Special Issue on Intelligent Systems and Teleteaching, Kunstliche Intelligenz, 4, 19-25, 1999.
3. Rousseau, F. Garcia-Macías, De Lima, J. Duda, A. User Adaptable Multimedia Presentations for the WWW. WWW1999, May 11-14, 1999, Toronto, Canada.
4. Brusilovsky, P. Developing Adaptive Educational Hypermedia Systems: From Design Models to Authoring Tools. in T. Murray, S. Blessing and S. Ainsworth (Eds.), Ablex, Norwood, 2002.
5. Souto, M. Nicolao, M. Viccari, R. Palazzo, J. Verdin, R. Beschoren, K. Madeira, M. Zanella, R. Web Adaptive Training System Based on Cognitive Student Style. IFIP World Computer Congress, 17th Edition, August 25-30, 2002, Montreal, Canada.
6. Souto, M. Verdin, R. Wainer, R. Madeira, M. Wapechowsky, M. Beschoren, K. Zanella, R. Correa, J. Vicari, R. Palazzo, J. Towards an Adaptive Web Training Environment Based on Cognitive Style of Learning: an Empirical Approach. AH 2002, 2002, Malaga, Spain.
7. Palazzo M. de Oliveira, J.; Silva Muñoz, L.; de Freitas, V. Marçal, V; Gasparini, I.; Abrahão Amaral, M. AdaptWeb: an Adaptive Web-based Courseware the 3rd Annual Ariadne Conference, 20-21 November 2003, Belgium.
8. Gruber, T. R. A translation approach to portable ontology specifications. Knowledge Acquisition, 5:199–220 1993.
9. Learning Technology Standards Committee of the IEEE. Draft Standard for Learning Object Metadata (LOM) IEEE 1484.12.1-2002.
10. Duval, E. Hodgins, W. Sutton, S. Weibel, S. Metadata Principles and Practicalities. D-Lib Magazine 8(4), 2002.
11. Heery, R. Patel, M. Application profiles: mixing and matching metadata schemas. September 2000, ARIADNE Issue 25.
12. The Dublin Core Metadata initiative. http://dublincore.org/
13. Bray, T. Paoli, J. Sperberg-McQueen, C. Maler, E. Extensible Markup Language (XML) 1.0 (Second Edition) W3C Recommendation, October 6, 2000.
14. Lassila, O. Swick, R. Resource Description Framework (RDF) model and syntax specification. W3C Recommendation, 1999.
15. Fallside, D. XML Schema Part 0: Primer W3C Recommendation, 2 May 2001.
16. Brickley, D. Guha, R. RDF Vocabulary Description Language 1.0: RDF Schema. W3C Working Draft 10 October 2003.
17. Nilsson, M. IEEE Learning Object Metadata RDF binding. May 2001. http://kmr.nada.kth.se/el/ims/metadata.html.
18. Vcard schema. http://www.w3.org/2001/vcard-rdf/3.0
19. Duval, E. Hodgins, W. A LOM Research Agenda. WWW2003, May 20-24, 2003, Budapest, Hungary.
20. Namespaces in XML, World Wide Web Consortium, 14-January 1999, Editors: Tim Bray, Dave Hollander and Andrew Layman. http://www.w3c.org/TR/REC-xml-names
21. Connolly, D. van Harmelen, F. Horrocks, I. McGuinness, D. Patel-Schneider, P. Stein, L. DAML+OIL (March 2001) Reference Description. W3C Note 18 December 2001.
22. Connolly, D. van Harmelen, F. Horrocks, I. McGuinness, D. Patel-Schneider, P. Stein, L. Annotated DAML+OIL Ontology Markup. W3C Note 18 December 2001.

23. Horrocks, I. DAML+OIL: a Description Logic for the Semantic Web. IEEE Data Engineering Bulletin 25(1): 4-9 (2002).
24. Bechhofer, S. OilEd 3.5 Manual. Information Management Group, Department of Computer Science, University of Manchester. http://www.cs.man.ac.uk/~horrocks/software
25. Haarslev, V.; Moller, R. RACER User's Guide and Reference Manual Version 1.7.7. September 17, 2003. http://www.fh-wedel.de/~mo/racer/index.html
26. Bechhofer, S. van Harmelen, F. Hendler, J. Horrocks, I. McGuinness, D. Patel-Schneider, P. Stein, L. OWL Web Ontology Language Reference. W3C Note 18 August 2003.
27. Ariadne. http://www.ariadne-eu.org
28. Heal. http://www.healcentral.org
29. Cancore. http://www.cancore.org.
30. Merlot. http://www.merlot.org
31. SingCore. http://www.ecc.org.sg/eLearn/ MetaData/SingCORE/index.jsp
32. NILSSON, Mikael. The semantic web: How RDF will change learning technology standards. CETIS, September 27, 2001 http://www.cetis.ac.uk/content/20010927172953.
33. The ACM Computing Classification System. http://www.acm.org/class/1998

Objects Meet Relations: On the Transparent Management of Persistent Objects

Luca Cabibbo

Dipartimento di Informatica e Automazione
Università degli studi Roma Tre
`cabibbo@dia.uniroma3.it`

Abstract. Many information systems store their objects in a relational database. If the object schema or the relational schema of an application can change often or in an independent way, it is useful to let a persistent framework manage the connection between objects and relations. M^2ORM^2 is a model for describing meet-in-the-middle mappings between objects and relations, to support the transparent management of object persistence by means of relational databases. This paper presents M^2ORM^2 and describes how operations on objects and links can be implemented as operations on the underlying relations. It also proposes necessary conditions for the correctness of M^2ORM^2 mappings.

1 Introduction

Many information systems are developed using relational and object-oriented technologies. Relational database management systems provide an effective and efficient management of persistent, shared and transactional data [6]. Object-oriented tools and methods include programming languages, modeling languages such as UML [3], development processes such as UP [8] and XP [2], as well as analysis and design methods [12]. In practice, it is common to develop object applications with a layered architecture, containing at least an application logic layer and a persistence layer. *Persistent classes* are classes in the application logic layer whose objects hold persistent data; they are made persistent by means of code that connect them, in a suitable way, to the persistence layer. In this paper, we assume that persistence of objects is implemented by a relational database.

Code in the persistence layer should change if either the structure of classes in the application logic layer or the relational database schema changes. If software is developed using an iterative process, such as UP or XP, those changes arise frequently. In this case, it is valuable to use a framework for the transparent management of object persistence [13, 14], rather than writing and maintaining such code directly. This way, the programmer manages persistent objects by means of standard API's, such as the ODMG ones [5], that is, the same way he would use objects in an object database. Persistence is transparent to the programmer, since he does not know actual implementation details.

Transparent persistence of objects is achieved mainly in two ways. In the *R/O mapping* approach (*Relation to Object mapping*, also called *reverse engineering*, implemented by, e.g., Torque [14]), persistent classes are automatically

A. Persson and J. Stirna (Eds.): CAiSE 2004, LNCS 3084, pp. 429–445, 2004.

generated from a relational database. The programmer populates the database by means of creations and modifications of objects from persistent classes. Then, persistent classes propagate such creations and modifications to the underlying database. In the *O/R mapping* approach (*Object to Relation mapping*, also called *forward engineering*, implemented by, e.g., OJB [13]), a database is automatically generated from the classes that should be made persistent, together with the code needed to propagate object persistence to the database. These two approaches can be unsatisfactory, however, since they do not allow the persistent classes and the relational database to be created or change in an independent way. The O/R mapping does not allow using a database shared among several applications, whereas the R/O mapping prevents the developer from applying object-oriented skills in implementing the application logic layer, such as using design patterns.

The *meet-in-the-middle* approach is a further way for the transparent management of object persistence. This approach allows developers to manage the cases in which the application logic and the database have been developed and evolve in an independent way, since it assumes that the persistent classes and the database are designed and implemented separately. In this case, the correspondences between persistent classes and the relational database should be given, possibly described in a declarative way. These correspondences describes a "meet in the middle" between the object schema and the relational schema, and are used by the persistence manager to let objects persist by means of the relational database. The meet-in-the-middle approach is very versatile, since modifications in persistent classes and/or in the relational database can be managed by simply redefining the correspondences. Unfortunately, existing systems support the meet-in-the-middle approach only in a limited way. Indeed, several object persistence managers are based on the O/R and R/O approaches. Furthermore, they manage only correspondences between similar structures (e.g., objects of a single class with tuples of a single relation). Some of them permit a meet between the object and database schemas, but only as a local tuning activity, after the schema translation from one model to the other.

This paper presents M^2ORM^2, a model to describe mappings (correspondences) between object schemas and relational schemas, to support the transparent management of object persistence based on the meet-in-the-middle approach. The goal of M^2ORM^2 is to generalize and extend the kinds of correspondences managed by currently available systems, thus allowing for more possibilities to meet schemas. Specifically, rather than considering only correspondences between single classes and single relations, as most systems do, in M^2ORM^2 it is possible to express complex correspondences between clusters of related classes (intuitively, each representing a single concept) and clusters of related relations. Furthermore, correspondences describing relationships between clusters can be expressed. With respect to other proposals, M^2ORM^2 takes into consideration specific details of the object and relational data models, together with the way in which objects and links are manipulated, to identify as many ways to meet schemas as possible.

M^2ORM^2 has been already introduced, in an informal way, in a previous paper by the same author [4]. There: (i) M^2ORM^2 has been presented in an informal way; (ii) the semantics of M^2ORM^2 has just been outlined only by means of a few examples; and (iii) the problem of identifying conditions for the correctness of M^2ORM^2 mappings has been just stated. The main contributions of this paper are: (i) the formalization of M^2ORM^2; (ii) a description of how operations on objects and links are realized as operations on the underlying relations; and (iii) the presentation of a number of necessary conditions for the correctness of M^2ORM^2 mappings.

For a comparison of M^2ORM^2 with the literature and a number of available systems for the transparent management of object persistence (e.g. [9–11, 13, 14]), we refer the reader to [4]. There, we have shown that M^2ORM^2 generalizes and extends the kinds of correspondences managed by various proposals and systems.

The paper is organized as follows. Section 2 proposes terminology and notation used to describe objects and relations. Section 3 presents M^2ORM^2, to describe mappings between schemas, together with an example. Section 4 presents the semantics of M^2ORM^2 mappings, by describing how operations on objects and links can be implemented as operations on an underlying relational database. Section 5 identifies a number of necessary conditions for the correctness of M^2ORM^2 mappings. Finally, in Sect. 6 we draw some conclusions.

2   Object Schemas and Relational Schemas

This section presents briefly the data models (an object model and the relational model) and the terminology used in this paper.

The *object model* we consider is a non-nested semantic data model (with structural features, but without behavioral ones). We have in mind a Java-like object model, formalized as a simplified version of the ODMG model [5] and of UML [3].

At the schema level, a *class* describes a set of *objects* having the same structural properties. Each class has a set of *attributes* associated with it. In this paper we make the simplifying hypothesis that all class attributes are of a same simple type, e.g., strings. An *association* describes a binary relation between a pair of classes. An *object schema* is a set of classes and associations among such classes. Figure 1 shows a sample object schema. (For simplicity, in this paper we do not consider generalization/specialization relationships among classes, although M^2ORM^2 is able to manage them.)

At the instance level, a class is a set of *objects*. Each object has an associated *oid*, an unique identifier for referencing the object. The *state* of an object is given by the set of values that its attributes hold in a certain moment. An association is a set of *links*; each link describes a relationship between a pair of objects.

This paper takes into consideration the following integrity constraints. Class attributes can have null value; an attribute whose value cannot be null is said to be *non null*. A *class with key* is a class in which an object can be identified

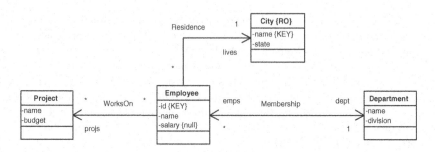

Fig. 1. An object schema

on the basis of the value of some of its attributes, called the *key attributes* of the class. Key attributes should be non null. A *read-only class* is a class from which it is not permitted to create new persistent objects and to modify or delete already existing objects. In an application, read-only classes are useful to access information generated by other applications. In Fig. 1, key attributes are denoted by constraint {*KEY*} and attributes that can be null by constraint {*null*}; constraint {*RO*} denotes read-only classes. For associations we consider multiplicity and navigability constraints. A *role* is an end of an association, that is, an occurrence of a class involved in the association. Roles have name, navigability, and multiplicity.

In the *relational model* [6], at the schema level a *relation* describes a set of tuples. A relation schema is a set of *attributes*. We assume that all relation attributes are of a simple type, e.g., strings. A *relational schema* is a set of relations. At the instance level, a relation is a set of *tuples* over the attributes of the relation.

We consider the following integrity constraints. Attributes can be or not be *non null*. Each relation has a *key*. A *key attribute* is an attribute that belongs to a key; key attributes should be non null. Sometimes relations are identified by means of *artificial keys* (or *surrogates*), rather than by means of *natural keys* (that is, keys based on attributes having a natural semantics). In a relation with artificial key, the insertion of a new tuple involves the generation of a new artificial key; the DBMS is usually responsible of this generation. For *referential constraint* (or *foreign key*) we mean a non-empty set of attributes of a relation used to reference tuples of another relation. Figure 2 shows a sample relational schema. Attribute forming natural keys are denoted by constraint {*NK*} and those forming artificial keys by constraint {*AK*}. Referential constraints are denoted by arrows and implemented by means of attributes marked with constraint {*FK*}. Constraint {*null*} denotes attributes that can be null.

We assume that programmers manage object schemas only in a programmatic way. In practice, objects and links are manipulated by means of *CRUD* operations (*Create, Read, Update, Delete*), which allow the programmer to create persistent objects, read persistent objects (that is, performing a unique search of an object based on its key), as well as to modify and delete objects per-

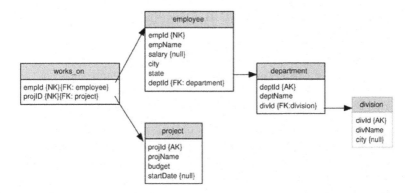

Fig. 2. A relational schema

sistently. Navigation, formation, breaking, and modification of persistent links between objects are also possible. Reading is meaningful only for classes with key. Creation, modification, and deletion is not meaningful for read-only classes. In correspondence to such programmatic manipulations of an object schema, a meet-in-the-middle-based object persistence manager should translate CRUD operations on objects and links into operations over an underlying relational database. This translation should happen in an automatic way, on the basis of a suitable mapping between the object schema and the relational schema, as described in the next sections.

3   A Model for Object/Relational Schema Mappings

In this section we formally present M^2ORM^2, a model for describing mappings among object schemas and relational schemas. M^2ORM^2 is an acronym for *Meet-in-the-Middle Object/Relational Mapping Model*. The goal of M^2ORM^2 is to support the transparent management of relationally persistent objects based on the meet-in-the-middle approach.

Let S_r and S_o be a relational schema and an object schema, respectively. We assume that such schemas have been independently developed. In particular, both of them can be partially denormalized: the relational schema for efficiency reasons and the object schema to contain "coarse grain" objects.

A mapping $\mathcal{M}_{\mathbf{S}_r,\mathbf{S}_o}$ between $\mathbf{S}_r$ and $\mathbf{S}_o$ is a multi-graph $(\mathcal{N}, \mathcal{A})$, where $\mathcal{N}$ is a set of *nodes* and $\mathcal{A}$ is a set of *arcs* between them. Each node describes a correspondence between a group of classes and a group of relations. Each arc describes a relationship between the elements represented by a pair of nodes. Intuitively, using the Entity-Relationship terminology [1], each node represents an entity (which can be denormalized in one of the schemas) and each arc represents a binary relationship between two entities[1].

---

[1] In M^2ORM^2, an arc can also represent a generalization/specialization relationship between two entities. However, we ignore this aspect in this paper.

Each node $N \in \mathcal{N}$ is a triple $(\mathbf{C}, \mathbf{R}, \alpha)$, where:

- $\mathbf{C}$ is a *class cluster* (or *c-cluster*), that is, a non-empty tuple $\langle C_1, \ldots, C_n \rangle$ of classes and a set of associations among such classes[2];
- $\mathbf{R}$ is a *relation cluster* (or *r-cluster*), that is, a non-empty tuple $\langle R_1, \ldots, R_m \rangle$ of relations, together with referential constraints among them;
- α is a set of *attribute correspondences* (defined next) between $\mathbf{C}$ and $\mathbf{R}$.

In a c-cluster $\mathbf{C}$, one of the classes should be selected as the *primary class* of the c-cluster. The other classes of the c-cluster are *secondary* classes. The associations of the node should be, directly or indirectly, of type one-to-one or many-to-one from the primary class to secondary classes. Intuitively, such associations should relate, by means of navigable roles, each object of the primary class with at most an object from each of the secondary classes.

Similarly, in an r-cluster $\mathbf{R}$, one of the relations should be selected as the *primary relation* of the r-cluster. The other relations of the r-cluster, called *secondary*, should be referenced, directly or indirectly, from the primary relation of the r-cluster. Intuitively, each tuple of the primary relation should be associated with at most a tuple in each of the secondary relations through the referential constraints of the r-cluster.

In a node $N = (\mathbf{C}, \mathbf{R}, \alpha)$, the correspondence among elements in $\mathbf{C}$ and elements in $\mathbf{R}$ is also specified by the set α of attribute correspondences. An *attribute correspondence* is a pair $(C_i.a, R_j.b)$, where C_i is a class in $\mathbf{C}$, a is an attribute of C_i, R_j is a relation in $\mathbf{R}$, and b is an attribute of R_j.

In $\mathrm{M}^2\mathrm{ORM}^2$, there are three kinds of nodes, to let a class correspond with a relation, a class with many relations, and many classes with a relation. Currently, the model does not permit that multiple classes correspond with multiple relations; however, correspondences of this kind can be usually represented by means of arcs.

Figure 3 shows, in a graphical way, a $\mathrm{M}^2\mathrm{ORM}^2$ mapping between the schemas of Fig. 1 and 2. It is based on three nodes: a node N_P, describing the correspondence between class *Project* and relation *project*; a node N_E, describing the correspondence between classes *Employee* and *City* and relation *employee*; and a node N_D, describing the correspondence between class *Department* and relations *department* and *division*.

More specifically, node $N_P = (\mathbf{C}_P, \mathbf{R}_P, \alpha_P)$ describes the correspondence between a class (*Project*) and a relation (*project*). The c-cluster $\mathbf{C}_P$ includes just the class *Project*, and the r-cluster $\mathbf{R}_P$ includes just the relation *project*. It is clear that both the class and the relation are primary in the node. The correspondence between them is based on the attribute correspondences *(Project.name, project.projName)* and *(Project.budget, project.budget)*; these are depicted as dotted lines in Fig. 3. Node N_P describes a total correspondence between a

---

[2] More precisely, each element of a c-cluster is associated with a class in the object schema, i.e., it is an occurrence of a class. Therefore, it is possible that a class takes part to more c-clusters, or that it takes part more than once in a same c-cluster. A similar consideration applies to r-clusters, that will be introduced shortly.

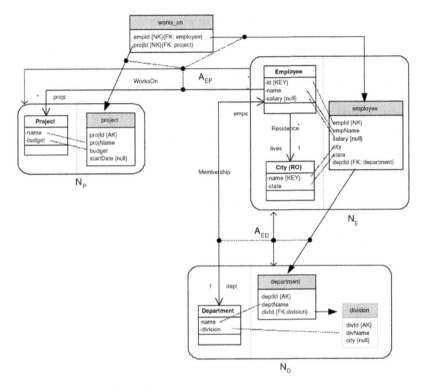

Fig. 3. A M^{2}ORM^2 mapping between the schemas of Fig. 1 and 2

class and a relation: each object of the class is represented by means of a tuple of the relation.

As a more complex case, node $N_E = (\mathbf{C}_E, \mathbf{R}_E, \alpha_E)$ describes the correspondence between two classes (*Employee* and *City*) and a relation (*employee*). The primary class of the node is *Employee*. It is linked to the secondary class *City* through the navigable role *lives* of the association *Residence*. In this case, the c-cluster $\mathbf{C}_E$ includes both the classes and the association. Intuitively, each object of the primary class *Employee* can be associated (by means of the association *Residence*) with an object of the secondary class *City*. Each tuple of the relation *employee* represents an *Employee* object together with the *City* object related to it, and also the link of type *Residence* between these two objects. In this node, the attribute correspondences include the correspondence between the key attributes of the primary class and of the primary relation *(Employee.id, employee.empId)* as well as *(Employee.name, employee.empName)*, *(Employee.salary, employee.salary)*, *(City.name, employee.city)*, and *(City.state, employee.state)*.

Furthermore, node N_D describes the correspondence between a class (*Department*) and two relations (*department* and *division*). The primary relation is *department*. Intuitively, each *Department* object is represented by a tuple of *department* and a tuple of *division*, related by means of a referential constraint. The correspondence is based on the attribute correspondences *(Department.name, department.deptName)* and *(Department.division, division.divName)*. The latter correspondence is meaningful with respect to the referential constraint between the primary relation *department* and the secondary relation *division* of the r-cluster. Indeed, this node represents in the mapping the two relations together with the referential constraint between them.

A M^2ORM^2 mapping can also contain arcs. Intuitively, arcs represent correspondences and elements which cannot be represented by means of nodes; specifically, further associations, referential constraints, and some further relations. Each arc describes a relationship between two nodes, and can be of type *one-to-one*, *one-to-many*, or *many-to-many*.

Each arc $A \in \mathcal{A}$ is a tuple (N_1, N_2, γ, ρ), where:

- N_1 and N_2 are the nodes connected by the arc;
- γ is a *class correspondence* (defined next), which describes the correspondence between the primary classes of the nodes N_1 and N_2 connected by the arc;
- ρ is a *relation correspondence* (defined next), which describes the correspondence between the primary relations of the nodes N_1 and N_2 connected by the arc.

A *class correspondence* is based on the navigable roles of an association between the classes. In practice, at the programming level, roles are implemented by means of reference variables (for to-one navigability) and/or variables of collection types (for to-many navigability). If an association is unidirectional, then a single role is involved; otherwise, if it is bidirectional, there are two roles involved. A *relation correspondence* is based on the attributes that implement the relationship between the two relations by means of referential constraints; further relations can be involved. An arc groups a class correspondence and a relation correspondence, representing a one-to-one, one-to-many, or a many-to-many binary relationship between the instances represented by a pair of nodes.

For example, the mapping shown in Fig. 3 contains two arcs: an arc A_{ED} for the one-to-many association between *Employee* and *Department* and an arc A_{EP} for the many-to-many association between *Employee* and *Project*.

Arc $A_{ED} = (N_E, N_D, \gamma_{ED}, \rho_{ED})$ is of type one-to-many, and connects the nodes N_E and N_D to describe a one-to-many relationship between employees and departments. The class correspondence γ_{ED} is the pair *[Employee.dept, Department.emps]* between the classes *Employee* and *Department*, whereas the relation correspondence ρ_{ED} is the attribute *[employee.deptId]*, implementing a referential constraint between the relations *employee* and *department*. Intuitively, this arc lets the association *Membership* between *Employee* and *Department* correspond with the referential constraint between *employee* and *department*.

Arc A_{EP} between nodes N_E and N_P describes a many-to-many relationship between employees and projects. This arc is based on the (unidirectional) class correspondence *[Employee.projs]* between *Employee* and *Project* together with the relation correspondence *[works_on.empId, works_on.projId]* between *employee* and *projects*. In practice, this arc lets the association *WorksOn* between *Employee* and *Project* correspond with the referential constraints between *employee* and *project* stored in the tuples of the relation *works_on*.

4   Management of Operations

In the previous section, M^2ORM^2 has been used as a syntactical tool to represent mappings. This section provides the semantics of M^2ORM^2 mappings, by explaining how CRUD operations on an object schema can be implemented as operations on a relational schema, with respect to a M^2ORM^2 mapping between the two schemas.

We consider sequences of CRUD operations on objects and links that, globally, transforms a valid instance of the object schema into another valid instance, that is, in which all the integrity constraints imposed by the object schema are satisfied. It is important to note that not every mapping is correct, that is, it is possible that some operation cannot be translated in a correct way. This happens, for example, if an integrity constraint over the relational schema is violated. Correctness of mappings will be discussed in Sect. 5.

We describe the management of operations with respect to the various kinds of nodes and arcs we can have in a M^2ORM^2 mapping.

4.1   Operations on Nodes

Node Mapping a Class to a Relation. We first consider the simplest case, that is, a node N mapping a single class (say, C_1) to a single relation (say, R_1) by means of a set α of attribute correspondences. An example is node N_P. In this case, each object of the primary class C_1 is *represented by* a tuple of the primary relation R_1.

The *creation* of a new object o_1 of the class C_1 is implemented by the insertion of a new tuple t_1 in R_1, computed as follows:

- the attributes of t_1 involved in the attribute correspondences α take their value from the corresponding attributes of o_1, that is, $t_1.b = o_1.a$ if $(C_1.a, R_1.b) \in \alpha$;
- if R_1 has an artificial key, then a new key for t_1 is generated by the system;
- the other attributes of t_1 defaults to *null*.

If the class C_1 has a key, then the *reading* of an object from C_1 by means of a value k for its key is implemented by a query searching for a single tuple t_1 in R_1. The selection condition of the query equates the attributes of the key of R_1 with the corresponding values in k. If there is already an object in memory representing this tuple, then such object is returned. Otherwise, a new object o_1 of the class C_1 is created in memory; the value for the attributes of o_1 are computed as follows:

– the attributes of o_1 involved in the set α of attribute correspondences take their value from the corresponding attributes of t_1, that is, $o_1.a = t_1.b$ if $(C_1.a, R_1.b) \in \alpha$;
– the other attributes of o_1 defaults to *null*.

The *update* of a non-key attribute a of an object o_1 of the class C_1 is implemented as follows, with respect to the tuple t_1 that represents o_1 in R_1:

– if the attribute a is *transient*, that is, if a is not involved in the attribute correspondences, then t_1 is not changed;
– otherwise, if the attribute a is involved in the attribute correspondences, the attributes that correspond to a are modified in the tuple t_1.

The *deletion* of an object o_1 of the class C_1 is implemented as the deletion of the tuple t_1 that represents o_1 in R_1.

Node Mapping Many Classes to a Relation. We now consider the case of a node mapping two or more classes (say, $\langle C_1, \ldots, C_n \rangle$), together with a number of associations among them, to a single relation (say, R_1), on the basis of a set α of attribute correspondences. We assume that C_1 is the primary class of the node. In such a node, each object o_1 of the primary class C_1 identifies, by means of the associations in the node, at most an object in each secondary class of the node; let us call $o_2, \ldots, o_n$ these objects, where each object o_i belongs to class C_i. In this case, the tuple of objects $\langle o_1, \ldots, o_n \rangle$ is *represented by* a single tuple t_1 of the relation R_1. An example is node N_E; each tuple of the relation *employee* represents an object o_e of *Employee* and, possibly, an object o_c of *City* and a link of type *Residence* from o_e to o_c.

More specifically, the associations in the node should have, directly or indirectly, multiplicity 1 (one, mandatory) or 0..1 (one, optional) from the primary class to secondary classes. We denote by *mandatory*(C, N) the set of classes that can be reached, directly or indirectly, from a class C by means of the navigable roles of the associations in the node N that have multiplicity 1 (not 0..1). Furthermore, given an object o, we denote by *reachable*(o, N) the set of objects that can be effectively reached, directly or indirectly, from the object o by means of the navigable roles of the associations in the node N; we assume that $o \in reachable(o, N)$ as well.

The *creation* of a new object o_1 in the primary class C_1, linked to the already existing objects *reachable*(o_1, N), is implemented by the insertion of a new tuple t_1 in R_1, computed as follows:

– the attributes of t_1 involved in the set α of attribute correspondences take their value from the corresponding attributes of *reachable*(o_1, N), that is, if $(C_i.a, R_1.b) \in \alpha$ and there is an object o_i of the class C_i in *reachable*(o_1, N), then $t_1.b = o_i.a$;
– if R_1 has an artificial key, then a new key for t_1 is generated by the system;
– the other attributes of t_1 defaults to *null*.

The creation of new objects in secondary classes of the node does not require the modification of the relation R_1. Indeed, these new objects are considered *transient*, at least until they will not be connected to an object of the primary class of the node. This possibility will be considered later, in the context of operations on links.

If the primary class C_1 has a key, then the *reading* of an object from C_1 by means of a value k for its key is implemented by a query searching for a single tuple t_1 in R_1, as in the case for a node mapping a class to a relation. The selection condition of the query equates the attributes of the key of R_1 with the corresponding values from k. If we retrieve a tuple t_1, then it represents an object o_1 of class C_1 together with the set *reachable*(o_1, N) of objects reachable from o_1. Then, if they do not already exists in memory, we should create such objects in memory, together with the links implied among them. Objects for the classes in *mandatory*(C_1, N) are always created. Objects in other classes participating to the node are created only if the corresponding attributes in t_1 are not null.

More specifically, if there are no objects in memory representing the various parts of the tuple t_1, then the following new objects are created in memory, together with the value for their attributes:

- a new object o_i in a class C_i in *mandatory*(C_1, N); the attributes of o_i involved in the attribute correspondences α take their value from the corresponding attributes of t_1, that is, $o_i.a = t_1.b$ if $(C_i.a, R_1.b) \in \alpha$; the other attributes of o_i defaults to *null*;
- a new object o_j in a class C_j that does not belong to *mandatory*(C_1, N), if all the non null attributes of C_j in the attribute correspondences α have a non null value in the corresponding attributes of t_1; in this case, such attributes take their value from the corresponding attributes of t_1, that is, $o_j.a = t_1.b$ if $(C_j.a, R_1.b) \in \alpha$; the other attributes of o_j defaults to *null*.

Furthermore, links for the associations in the node are formed in memory among the objects involved in this operation.

Let $o_1, \ldots, o_n$ be a tuple of objects represented by a tuple t_1 in R_1, as described by this node. Then, the *update* of a non-key attribute a of an object o_i of a class C_i that can be reached from an object o_1 is managed by modifying, if it is the case, the attributes corresponding to a of the tuple t_1 that represents the object o_1 and the associated objects $o_2, \ldots, o_n$, as follows:

- if the attribute a is transient (that is, is not involved in the attribute correspondences), then the tuple t_1 is not modified;
- otherwise, if the attribute a is involved in the attribute correspondences, the attributes that correspond to a are modified in the tuple t_1.

Let $o_1, \ldots, o_n$ be a tuple of objects represented by a tuple t_1 in R_1, as described by this node. The *deletion* of the object o_1 of the primary class C_1 is implemented as the deletion of the tuple t_1 that represents o_1 in R_1. Note that some of the objects $o_2, \ldots, o_n$ may become transient.

The modification of links of associations involved in the node should be considered as well. For example, the formation of a new link outgoing from an object

o_i of a class C_i involved in the node, whose type is an association involved in the node, may increase the number of objects reachable from o_i and, transitively, those reachable from an object o_1 of the primary class C_1 of the node. In this case, the tuple t_1 representing o_1 should be modified accordingly (by modifying null attributes to the new values owned by the new reachable objects). Conversely, if a link outgoing from o_i is broken, the number of objects reachable for o_1 may decrease. In this case, the tuple t_1 representing o_1 should be modified accordingly (by modifying to null attributes representing objects that are no more reachable). In practice, the tuple t_1 representing o_1 should be modified as the object o_1 would have been created after the link formation/modification/breaking.

Node Mapping a Class to Many Relations. We now consider the case of a node mapping a class (say, C_1) to two or more relations (say, $\langle R_1, \ldots, R_m \rangle$), together with referential constraints among them, on the basis of a set α of attribute correspondences. We assume that R_1 is the primary relation of the node. In such a node, each tuple t_1 of the primary relation R_1 identifies, by means of the referential constraints in the node, at most a tuple in each secondary relation of the node; let us call $t_2, \ldots, t_M$ these tuples, where each tuple t_i belongs to the relation R_i. In this case, the tuple of tuples $\langle t_1, \ldots, t_m \rangle$ *represents* an object o_1 of the class C_1. An example is node N_D; each object of the class *Department* is represented by a tuple t_{dept} of the relation *department* and, possibly, a tuple t_{div} of the relation *division*, where the tuple t_{dept} references the tuple t_{div}.

More specifically, the node contains referential constraints that, directly or indirectly, reference the secondary relations from the primary relations. A referential constraint is mandatory if the attribute implementing it cannot be null, but is optional if such attribute can be null. We denote by $mandatory(R, N)$ the set of relations that can be reached, directly or indirectly, from a relation R by means of the mandatory referential constraints in the node N. Furthermore, given a tuple t, we denote by $reachable(t, N)$ the set of tuples that can be effectively reached, directly or indirectly, from the tuple t by means of referential constraints in the node N; we assume that $t \in reachable(t, N)$ as well.

The *creation* of a new object o_1 in the class C_1 is implemented by the insertion of the tuples $t_1, \ldots, t_m$ in the relations $R_1, \ldots, R_m$, as follows:

- a tuple t_i in a relation R_i in $mandatory(R_1, N)$; the attributes of t_i involved in the attribute correspondences α take their value from the corresponding attributes of o_1, that is, $t_i.b = o_1.a$ if $(C_1.a, R_i.b) \in \alpha$; if R_i has an artificial key, then a new key for t_i is generated by the system;
- a tuple t_j in a relation R_j that does not belong to $mandatory(R_1, N)$, if all the non null attributes of R_j in the attribute correspondences α of the node have a non null value in the corresponding attributes of o_1; in this case, such attributes take their value from the corresponding attributes of o_1, that is, $t_j.b = o_1.a$ if $(C_1.a, R_j.b) \in \alpha$; if R_j has an artificial key, then a new key for t_j is generated by the system;
- if a tuple t_i should reference a tuple t_h of a secondary relation R_h by means of an attribute b, then $t_i.b$ equals the key of the tuple t_h;
- the other attributes of the tuples defaults to *null*.

If the primary class C_1 has a key, then the *reading* of an object from C_1 by means of a value k for its key is implemented by a query searching for a single tuple t_1 in the primary relation R_1, as in the case for a node mapping a class to a relation. The selection condition of the query equates the attributes of the key of R_1 with the corresponding values from k. Then, the retrieval of a tuple t_1 in R_1 is followed by the lookup of the tuples in the secondary relations that are reachable from t_1, so that all the tuples $reachable(t_1, N)$ representing an object of the class C_1 are retrieved. If there is no object in memory representing these tuples, then a new objects o_1 of the class C_1 is created in memory; the value for the attributes of o_1 are computed as follows:

- the attributes of o_1 involved in the attribute correspondences α take their value from the corresponding attributes of the tuples in $reachable(t_1, N)$, that is, $o_1.a = t_i.b$ if $(C_1.a, R_i.b) \in \alpha$;
- the other attributes of o_1 defaults to *null*.

Let o_1 be an object of the class C_1 represented by the tuples $t_1, \ldots, t_m$, as described by this node. Then, the *update* of a non-key attribute a of the object o_1 is managed as follows:

- if the attribute a is not involved in the attribute correspondences (i.e, it is transient), then no tuple is not modified;
- if the attribute a is involved in the attribute correspondences and is related to attributes of the primary relation R_1, then the attributes that correspond to a are modified in the tuple t_1;
- otherwise, if the attribute a is involved in the attribute correspondences and is related to attributes of a secondary relation R_i, then a new set of tuples is computed, as for the creation of a new object, to represent the object o_1, and, if it is the case, such tuples are added to the secondary relations of the node and the tuple t_1 is modified accordingly.

Let o_1 be an object of the class C_1 represented by the tuples $t_1, \ldots, t_m$, as described by this node. The *deletion* of the object o_1 is implemented as the deletion of the tuple t_1 that represents o_1 in the primary relation R_1. Note that the other tuples $t_2, \ldots, t_m$ may become useless; in such a case, they can be deleted as well.

4.2   Operations on Arcs

Arcs are used to represent binary relationships between nodes. In the object schema, each arc represents one or both the roles of an association between the primary classes of the two nodes. In the relation schema, each arc represents one or two referential constraints between the primary relations of the two nodes. The referential constraints may be either embedded in the relations that are already involved in the nodes or they may involve a different relation.

Suppose that A_{xy} is an arc from a node N_x to a node N_y, representing the roles r_y and r_x of an association a_{xy} from the primary class C_x of N_x to the primary class C_y of N_y (r_x references an object of the class C_y and r_y references an object of the class C_x).

Arc Embedded in Already Involved Relations. If arc A_{xy} is embedded in already involved relations, then the two roles r_x and r_y of the association correspond to two attributes (say, b_x and b_y) of the primary relations R_x of N_x and R_y of N_y, each of which references the primary relation of the other node.

The *creation* of a new link of the association a_{xy} from an object o_x of the class C_x to an object o_y of the class C_y is managed as follows:

- if the multiplicity of r_x is 0..1, then the attribute b_y of the tuple t_y of the relation R_y that represents o_y takes its value from the key of the tuple t_x of the relation R_x that represents o_x;
- if the multiplicity of r_y is 0..1, then the attribute b_x of the tuple t_x of the relation R_x that represents o_x takes its value from the key of the tuple t_y of the relation R_y that represents o_y.

The *breaking* of a link of the association a_{xy} from an object o_x of the class C_x to an object o_y of the class C_y is managed as follows:

- if the multiplicity of r_x is 0..1, then the attribute b_y of the tuple t_y of the relation R_y that represents o_y becomes null;
- if the multiplicity of r_y is 0..1, then the attribute b_x of the tuple t_x of the relation R_x that represents o_x becomes null.

The *modification* of a link of the association a_{xy} starting from an object o_x of the class C_x, from the object o_y to the object o'_y of the class C_y is managed as follows:

- if the multiplicity of r_x is 0..1, then the attribute b_y of the tuple t_y of the relation R_y that represents o_y becomes null;
- if the multiplicity of r_y is 0..1, then the attribute b_x of the tuple t_x of the relation R_x that represents o_x takes its value from the key of the tuple t'_y of the relation R_y that represents o'_y.

Arc Represented by a Different Relation. If arc A_{xy} is represented by a relation different from the primary relations of the nodes, then the two roles of the association correspond to two attributes (say, b_x and b_y) of a different relation (say, R_{xy}); these attributes reference the primary relations R_y and R_x of the two nodes N_y and N_x, respectively.

The *creation* of a new link of the association a_{xy} from an object o_x of the class C_x to an object o_y of the class C_y is managed as the insertion of a tuple t_{xy} in the relation R_{xy}, computed as follows:

- the attribute b_x of the tuple t_{xy} takes its value from the key of the tuple t_y of the relation R_y that represents o_y;
- the attribute b_y of the tuple t_{xy} takes its value from the key of the tuple t_x of the relation R_x that represents o_x;
- the other attributes of the tuple t_{xy} defaults to *null*.

The *breaking* of a link of the association a_{xy} from an object o_x of the class C_x to an object o_y of the class C_y is managed as the deletion of the tuple t_{xy} that represents the link between the two objects.

The *modification* of a link of the association a_{xy} starting from an object o_x of the class C_x, from the object o_y to the object o'_y of the class C_y is managed as the modification of the tuple t_{xy} in the relation R_{xy} that represents the link between o_x and o_y, as follows:

- the attribute b_x of the tuple t_{xy} takes its value from the key of the tuple t'_y of the relation R_y that represents o'_y.

5   Correctness of Mappings

It turns out that not every mapping that can be described using M^2ORM^2 is correct. Intuitively, a M^2ORM^2 mapping is *correct* if it supports, in an effective way, the management of CRUD operations on objects and links by means of the underlying relational schema. Otherwise, a mapping is *incorrect* if operations on objects and links can give rise to anomalies. There are various kinds of anomalies, but only two main causes for them: (i) incorrect correspondences between elements and (ii) incorrect representation of integrity constraints.

We now present a number of conditions for the correctness of a M^2ORM^2 mapping. These conditions are *necessary*: they should hold whenever the corresponding operations have to be managed on the basis of the mapping. The need for these conditions can be verified by means of counter examples and by referring to the semantics of M^2ORM^2 described in Sect. 4.

In what follows, consider a node $N = (\mathbf{C}, \mathbf{R}, \alpha)$, where $\mathbf{C} = \langle C_1, \ldots, C_n \rangle$, $\mathbf{R} = \langle R_1, \ldots, R_m \rangle$, C_1 is the primary class of the node, and R_1 is the primary relation of the node.

To implement the creation of a new object in the primary class C_1 of the node correctly, the following conditions are necessary:

[**C1**] If the primary relation R_1 of the node has a natural key, then it corresponds to the key of the primary class C_1 of the node; if R_1 has an artificial key, then it is not involved in the attribute correspondence α.

[**C2**] There are no two attributes of the classes in the node corresponding to a same attribute of a relation R_i in the node.

[**C3**] If an attribute of a relation R_i that is the primary relation of the node or that belongs to *mandatory*(R_1, N) (where R_1 is the primary relation of the node) cannot be null, then either it is the artificial key of R_i, or it is a reference to another relation $R_j \in mandatory(R_1, N)$, or it is involved in an attribute correspondence in α and corresponds to an attribute of a class C_j of the node that cannot be null, where C_j is the primary class of the node or belongs to *mandatory*(C_1, N) (where C_1 is the primary class of the node).

[**C4**] Each secondary relation R_i of the node has an artificial key, which is not involved in the attribute correspondence α.

Condition [C1] ensures that the key of the primary relation R_1 of the node has a unique value. Condition [C2] ensures that each attribute of a relation R_i in the node has at most one value. Condition [C3] ensures that each non null attribute of a mandatory relation R_i in the node has a non null value.

To implement the reading of an object of the primary class of the node C_1 correctly, the following conditions are necessary:

[R1] The primary relation R_1 of the node has a natural key, and the attribute correspondences let it correspond to the key of the primary class C_1.

[R2] There are no two attributes of the relations in the node corresponding to a same attribute of a class C_i in the node.

[R3] If an attribute of a class C_i that is the primary class of the node or that belongs to $mandatory(C_1, N)$ (where C_1 is the primary class of the node) cannot be null, then it is involved in an attribute correspondence in α and corresponds to an attribute of a relation R_j that cannot be null, where R_j is the primary relation of the node or belongs to $mandatory(R_1, N)$ (where R_1 is the primary relation of the node).

Condition [R1] ensures that at most one tuple is retrieved from the primary relation R_1. Condition [R2] ensures that each attribute of a class C_i in the node has at most one value. Condition [R3] ensures that each non null attribute of a mandatory class C_i in the node has a non null value.

We now consider the update of a non transient attribute a of a class C_i of the node; we suppose that the attribute a of the primary class C_1 is related to an attribute b of a relation R_i of the node by the attribute correspondences α. We have the following necessary conditions:

[U1] Attribute b is not part of the key of the primary relation R_1 of the node.

[U2] If R_i is the primary class of the node or it belongs to $mandatory(R_1, N)$ (where R_1 is the primary class of the node) and b cannot be null, then a cannot be null as well.

[U3] There cannot be another attribute a' of a class C_j in the node related to b by the attribute correspondences α.

If the node N is of type one class/many relations, then the conditions for the creation of a new object ([C1], [C2], [C3], and [C4]) are also required.

Condition [U1] avoids that the primary key of a relation is changed. Condition [U2] deals with null values. Condition [U3] prevents side effects on the attributes of the objects.

To implement the deletion of an object of the primary class C_1 of the node, no additional necessary conditions are required. Indeed, if the object has been created or read, it can also be safely deleted.

Necessary conditions for a correct management of the modification of a link of an association involved in a node are the same for the creation of a new object of the primary class of the node.

Before concluding the section, it is worth noting that, in practice (that is, for eventually implementing a persistence manager based on M^2ORM^2) *sufficient conditions* should be fixed as well, to manage mappings in an effective way. Current systems suffer from several limitations, since the conditions they are based on are very restrictive. One of the main goal of this research is to identify conditions that are as permissive as possible — permissive with respect to significance of mappings. Please note that we do not state sufficient conditions in this paper.

6 Discussion

In this paper we have presented M^2ORM^2, a model to describe correspondences between object schemas and relational schemas. The goal of M^2ORM^2 is supporting the transparent management of object persistence based on the meet-in-the-middle approach.

As future work, we plan to implement a Java framework for the management of persistent objects based on M^2ORM^2. To this end, a number of object-oriented techniques should be used, e.g., those in [7].

From a theoretical perspective, we plan to study several extensions to the model, e.g., the management of generalization/specialization hierarchies, transient classes and attributes, and of further integrity constraints. We also plan to study in a more precise way the correctness of M^2ORM^2 mappings, and specifically to state sufficient conditions that are as permissive as possible.

References

1. C. Batini, S. Ceri, and S.B. Navathe. *Conceptual Database Design, an Entity-Relationship Approach.* Benjamin-Cummings, 1992.
2. K. Beck. *EXtreme Programming EXplained: Embrace Change.* Addison-Wesley, 1999.
3. G. Booch, J. Rumbaugh, and I. Jacobson. *The Unified Modeling Language User Guide.* Addison-Wesley, 1999.
4. L. Cabibbo and R. Porcelli. M^2ORM^2: A Model for the Transparent Management of Relationally Persistent Objects. In *International Workshop on Database Programming Languages (DBPL)*, pages 166–178, 2003.
5. R.G.G. Cattell et al. *The Object Data Standard: ODMG 3.0.* Morgan Kaufmann, 2000.
6. R. Elmasri and S.B. Navathe. *Fundamentals of Database Systems.* Addison Wesley, 2003.
7. M. Fowler. *Patterns of Enterprise Application Architecture.* Addison Wesley, 2003.
8. I. Jacobson, G. Booch, and J. Rumbaugh. *The Unified Software Development Process.* Addison-Wesley, 1999.
9. Java Data Objects. http://www.jdocentral.com
10. JDX. http://www.softwaretree.com/
11. JRELAY. http://www.objectindustries.com/
12. C. Larman. *Applying UML and Patterns. An introduction to object-oriented analysis and design and the Unified Process.* Prentice Hall PTR, 2002.
13. ObJect relational Bridge. http://db.apache.org/ojb/
14. Torque. http://db.apache.org/torque/

The $\mathcal{GMD}$ Data Model and Algebra
for Multidimensional Information*

Enrico Franconi[1] and Anand Kamble[1,2]

[1] Faculty of Computer Science, Free University of Bozen-Bolzano, Italy
franconi@inf.unibz.it, anand.kamble@unibz.it
[2] Department of Computer Science, University of Manchester, UK

Abstract. In this paper we introduce $\mathcal{GMD}$, an abstract but rich data model for representing multidimensional information, equipped with logic-based semantics and seamlessly integrated with a fully compositional algebra also equipped with logic-based semantics. The aim of this work is to propose an homogeneous approach to formally represent all the aspects of multidimensional data, as proposed by the various data models presented in the literature.

1 Introduction

In this paper we introduce a novel data model for multidimensional information, $\mathcal{GMD}$, generalising the $\mathcal{MD}$ data model first proposed in [Cabibbo and Torlone, 1998]. A preliminary introduction to the $\mathcal{GMD}$ data model discussing only the core representational abilities but not the algebra nor the extended features can be found in [Franconi and Kamble, 2003]. The aim of this work is not to propose yet another data model, but to find a very general *logic-based formalism* encompassing the main features of all the proposals for a logical data model in the data warehouse field, as for example summarised in [Vassiliadis and Sellis, 1999]. Our proposal is compatible with all these proposals, making therefore possible a formal comparison of the different expressivities of the models in the literature. The $\mathcal{GMD}$ data model provides a very precise and, we believe, very elegant and uniform way to model multidimensional information. It turns out that most of the proposals in the literature make many hidden assumptions which may harm the understanding of the advantages or disadvantages of the proposal itself. An embedding in our model would make all these assumptions explicit. For lack of space, in the last section of this paper we only briefly suggest the encodings. So far, we have considered, together with the classical basic star and snowflake ER-based models and multidimensional cubes, the logical data models introduced in [Cabibbo and Torlone, 1998, Golfarelli *et al.*, 1998, Agrawal *et al.*, 1997, Gray *et al.*, 1996, Vassiliadis, 1998, Vassiliadis and Skiadopoulos, 2000, Franconi and Sattler, 1999, Gyssens and Lakshmanan, 1997, Tsois *et al.*, 2001, Abello *et al.*, 2001].

* This work has been partially supported by the EU projects Sewasie, KnowledgeWeb, and Interop.

A. Persson and J. Stirna (Eds.): CAiSE 2004, LNCS 3084, pp. 446–462, 2004.

$\mathcal{GMD}$ is completely defined using a logic-based model theoretic approach. We start introducing the notion of data warehouse signature, which has a data warehouse state as its model theoretic counterpart in the semantics. The data model is able to speak in a well founded manner of facts, dimensions, levels, level hierarchies, level attributes, measures, domains. We then introduce the data warehouse schema, which is nothing else than a collection of compositional *fact definitions* (i.e., axioms on the structure of the cubes), which restricts (i.e., constrains) the set of legal data warehouse states associated to the schema. By systematically defining how the various operators used in a fact definition compositionally constrain the legal data warehouse states, we give a formal logic-based account of the $\mathcal{GMD}$ data model. We introduce the aggregation (roll-up) operator with compound aggregation functions, the derivation of attributes, the slice and the multislice operators, the join, union, intersection, and difference operators.

2   The $\mathcal{GMD}$ Logical Data Model

We introduce in this Section the $\mathcal{GMD}$ logical data model. A data warehouse signature gives the building blocks for a data warehouse, but is does not provide any cube definition yet. A data warehouse schema basically introduces the structures of the cubes that will populate the warehouse, together with the types allowed for the components of the structures. Moreover, a schema may contain the definition of complex cubes obtained by composing other cubes through algebraic operations,. The operations that we will introduce are the typical basic OLAP operation.

Definition 1 ($\mathcal{GMD}$ Signature). *A $\mathcal{GMD}$ signature is a tuple* $< \mathcal{F}, \mathcal{D}, \mathcal{L}, \mathcal{M}, \mathcal{V}, \mathcal{A} >$, *where*

- $\mathcal{F}$ *is a finite set of **fact names** (like SALES, PURCHASES)*
- $\mathcal{D}$ *is a finite set of **dimension names** (like Date, Product)*
- $\mathcal{L}$ *is a finite set of **level names** (like year, month; brand, category),*
  *each one associated to a finite set of **level elements** (like 2003, 2004; heineken, drink); level elements are also called **dimension values***
- $\mathcal{A}$ *is a finite set of **level attribute names** (like is-leap, country-of-origin)*
- $\mathcal{M}$ *is a finite set of **measure names** (like Price, UnitSales)*
- $\mathcal{V}$ *is a finite set of **domain names** (like String, Integer, Boolean),*
  *each one associated to a finite set of **domain values**; domain values are also called **measure values***

Having just defined $\mathcal{GMD}$ signatures, we introduce now their semantics through a well founded model theory. We first define the notion of a data warehouse state, namely a collection of cells with their dimensions and measures, in agreement with the signature.

Definition 2 (Data Warehouse State). *A* data warehouse state *over the* $\mathcal{GMD}$ *signature* $< \mathcal{F}, \mathcal{D}, \mathcal{L}, \mathcal{M}, \mathcal{V}, \mathcal{A} >$ *is a tuple* $I = < \Delta, \Lambda, \Gamma, \cdot^I >$, *where*

- Δ *is a non-empty finite set of* **individual facts** (elements in Δ are the object identifiers for the *cells* in a multidimensional cube);
- Λ *is a finite set of* **level elements;**
- Γ *is a finite set of* **domain values;**
- $\cdot^I$ *is a function (the* interpretation function*) such that*

$$
\begin{array}{ll}
F^I \subseteq \Delta & \textit{for each } F \in \mathcal{F}, \textit{ where } F^I \textit{ is disjoint from any other } E^I \textit{ in } \mathcal{F} \\
L^I \subseteq \Lambda & \textit{for each } L \in \mathcal{L}, \textit{ where } L^I \textit{ is disjoint from any other } H^I \textit{ in } \mathcal{L} \\
V^I \subseteq \Gamma & \textit{for each } V \in \mathcal{V}, \textit{ where } V^I \textit{ is disjoint from any other } W^I \textit{ in } \mathcal{V} \\
D^I : \Delta \longrightarrow \Lambda & \textit{for each } D \in \mathcal{D} \\
M^I : \Delta \longrightarrow \Gamma & \textit{for each } M \in \mathcal{M} \\
(A_i^L)^I : L \longrightarrow \Gamma & \textit{for each } L \in \mathcal{L} \quad \textit{and } A_i^L \in \mathcal{A} \textit{ for some } i
\end{array}
$$

The interpretation functions defines a specific data warehouse state given a $\mathcal{GMD}$ signature. It associates to a fact name a set of cells (individual facts), which are meant to form a cube. To each cell corresponds a level element for some dimension name: the sequence of these level elements is meant to be the "coordinate" of the cell. Moreover, to each cell corresponds a value for some measure name.

Up to this stage, no cube definition is considered yet. That is, there is still no schema associated to the signature. Therefore, the dimensions and the measures associated to cells are still completely arbitrary. We now introduce the notion of $\mathcal{GMD}$ schema, which may contain various types of constraints and definitions. The simplest one is the definition of a basic fact, which is a cube whose dimensions and measures are well defined.

Definition 3 ($\mathcal{GMD}$ Schema: Fact Definitions). *A $\mathcal{GMD}$ schema includes a finite set of* fact *definitions of the form*

$$
F \doteq E \{D_1 \mid_{L_1}, \ldots, D_n \mid_{L_n}\} : \{M_1 \mid_{V_1}, \ldots, M_m \mid_{V_m}\},
$$

where $E, F \in \mathcal{F}, D_i \in \mathcal{D}, L_i \in \mathcal{L}, M_j \in \mathcal{M}, V_j \in \mathcal{V}.$

We call the fact name F a defined fact. *We say that F is based on E; that the fact F has the listed dimensions each one restricted to the corresponding level; and that the fact F has the listed measures each one restricted to the corresponding domain.. A fact name not appearing at the left hand side of a definition is called an* undefined fact. *We will generally call fact either a defined fact or an undefined fact. A fact based on an undefined fact is called* basic *fact. A fact based on a defined fact is called* aggregated *fact. A fact is* dimensionless *if $n = 0$; it is* measureless *if $m = 0$. The orderings in a defined fact among dimensions and among measures are irrelevant.*

We have here introduced the building block of a $\mathcal{GMD}$ schema: the fact definition. A basic fact corresponds to the base data of any data warehouse: it is the cube structure that contains all the data on which any other cube will be built upon. In the following example, BASIC-SALES is a basic fact, including base data about sale transactions, organised by date, product, and store (which are the dimensions of the fact) which are respectively restricted to the levels day, product, and store, and with unit sales and sale price as measures:

BASIC-SALES $\doteq$
   SALES $\{\text{Date}|_{\text{day}}, \text{Product}|_{\text{product}}, \text{Store}|_{\text{store}}\}$:
      $\{\text{UnitSales}|_{\text{int}}, \text{SalePrice}|_{\text{int}}, \text{UnitCost}|_{\text{int}}\}$

Level attribute names are properties associated to levels; for example:

product $\doteq$ $\{\text{prodname}|_{\text{string}}, \text{prodnum}|_{\text{int}}, \text{prodsize}|_{\text{int}}, \text{prodweight}|_{\text{int}}\}$

In the following, in order to give a semantics to fact definitions, we will introduce the notion of *legal* data warehouse state, which is the data warehouse state which conforms to the constraints imposed by the cube definitions. In general, a data warehouse state will be called legal for a given $\mathcal{GMD}$ schema if it is a data warehouse state in the signature of the $\mathcal{GMD}$ schema and it satisfies the additional conditions found in the $\mathcal{GMD}$ schema. In this case, we want that the data warehouse state satisfies the cube conditions as defined in the schema.

Please note that in the following we will omit the $\cdot^I$ interpretation function applied to some symbol whenever this is non ambiguous.

Definition 4 (Legal Data Warehouse State: The Cube Conditions). *A data warehouse state* $I = <\Delta, \Lambda, \Gamma, \cdot^I>$ *over the signature* $<\mathcal{F}, \mathcal{D}, \mathcal{L}, \mathcal{M}, \mathcal{V}, \mathcal{A}>$ *is legal with respect to a* $\mathcal{GMD}$ *schema if for each fact* $F \doteq E\{D_1|_{L_1}, \ldots, D_n|_{L_n}\} : \{M_1|_{V_1}, \ldots, M_m|_{V_m}\}$ *in the schema:*

1. *the function associated to a dimension which does not appear in a fact is undefined for its cells:*

   $\forall f.\ F(f) \to f \notin \mathbf{dom}(D)$

   for each $D \in \mathcal{D}$ *such that* $D \neq D_i$ *for each* $i \leq n$, *where* $\mathbf{dom}(D)$ *is the domain of the function* D

2. *each cell of a fact has a unique set of dimension values at the appropriate level:*

   $\forall f.\ F(f) \to \exists l_1, \ldots, l_n.\ D_1(f) = l_1 \wedge L_1(l_1) \wedge \ldots \wedge D_n(f) = l_n \wedge L_n(l_n)$

3. *a set of dimension values identifies a unique cell within a fact:*

   $\forall f, f', l_1, \ldots, l_n.\ F(f) \wedge F(f') \wedge$
      $D_1(f) = l_1 \wedge D_1(f') = l_1 \wedge \ldots \wedge D_n(f) = l_n \wedge D_n(f') = l_n \to$
      $f = f'$

4. *the function associated to a measure which does not appear in a fact is undefined for its cells:*

   $\forall f.\ F(f) \to f \notin \mathbf{dom}(M)$

   for each $M \in \mathcal{M}$ *such that* $M \neq M_i$ *for each* $i \leq n$

5. *each cell of a fact has a unique set of measures:*

$$\forall f.\ F(f) \rightarrow \exists m_1, \ldots, m_m.$$
$$M_1(f) = m_1 \wedge V_1(m_1) \wedge \ldots \wedge M_m(f) = m_m \wedge V_m(m_m)$$

Condition 1 states that the level elements associated to a cell of a fact should correspond only to the dimensions declared in the fact definition of the schema. That is, a cell has only the declared dimensions in any legal data warehouse state. Condition 2 states that the level elements associated to a cell of a fact are unique for each dimension declared for the fact in the schema. So, a cell has a unique dimension value for each declared dimension in any legal data warehouse state. Condition 3 states that a sequence of level elements associated to a cell of a fact are associated only to that cell. Therefore, the sequence of dimension values can really be seen as an identifying *coordinate* for the cell. In other words, these conditions enforce the legal data warehouse state to really model a cube according the specification given in the schema. Condition 4 states that the measure values associated to a cell of a fact in a legal data warehouse state should correspond only to the measures explicitly declared in the fact definition of the schema. Condition 5 states that the measure values associated to a cell of a fact are unique for each measure explicitly declared for the fact in the schema. So, a cell has a unique measure value for each declared measure in any legal data warehouse state.

3   Aggregated Cubes

We now introduce the first algebraic component in a $\mathcal{GMD}$ schema: the definition of aggregated cubes. An aggregated cube is based on another defined cube if in the schema it is defined how the measures of the aggregated cube can be computed from the measures of the cube it is based on. Moreover, it is possible to aggregate a cube by changing the levels of the involved dimensions.

Definition 5 ($\mathcal{GMD}$ Schema: Aggregated Facts). *A $\mathcal{GMD}$ schema may also include:*

- *a finite set of* measure definitions *of the form*

$$N \doteq f(g(M_1, \ldots, M_k))$$

  where $N, M_1, \ldots, M_k \in \mathcal{M}$, f is an aggregation function $f : \mathcal{B}(V) \longrightarrow W$ for some $V, W \in \mathcal{V}$, and g is a function (called attribute function*) $g : V_1 \times \ldots \times V_k \longrightarrow V$ for some $V_1, \ldots, V_k, V \in \mathcal{V}$. $\mathcal{B}(V)$ is the finite set of all bags obtainable from domain values in V whose cardinality is bound by some finite integer Ω.*
- *a partial order $(\mathcal{L}, \leq)$ on the levels in $\mathcal{L}$.*
  We call $\ll$ the immediate predecessor relation on $\mathcal{L}$ induced by $\leq$.

– a finite set of roll-up partial functions between level elements

$$\rho_{L_i,L_j} : L_i \longrightarrow L_j$$

for each L_i, L_j such that $L_i \ll L_j$, and $(\rho_{L_i,L_{i_1}} \circ \rho_{L_{i_1},L_{i_2}} \circ \cdots \circ \rho_{L_{i_{n-1}},L_{i_n}} \circ \rho_{L_{i_n},L_j}) = (\rho_{L_i,L_{k_1}} \circ \rho_{L_{k_1},L_{k_2}} \circ \cdots \circ \rho_{L_{k_{n-1}},L_{k_n}} \circ \rho_{L_{k_n},L_j})$ for any two paths in the partial order between any two level elements L_i and L_j.
We call $\rho^*_{L_i,L_j}$ the reflexive transitive closure of the roll-up functions inductively defined as follows:

$$\rho^*_{L_i,L_i} = \mathsf{id}$$
$$\rho^*_{L_i,L_j} = \rho_{L_i,L_k} \circ \rho^*_{L_k,L_j} \qquad \text{for some } k \text{ such that } L_i \ll L_k$$

– a finite set of level attribute names definitions:

$$L \doteq \{A_1 \,|\, V_1, \ldots, A_n \,|\, V_n\}$$

where $L \in \mathcal{L}$, $A_i \in \mathcal{A}$ and $V_i \in \mathcal{V}$ for each i, $1 \leq i \leq n$.

Levels and facts are subject to additional syntactical well-foundedness conditions:

– The connected components of $(\mathcal{L}, \leq)$ must have a unique least element each, which is called basic level.
– For each undefined fact there can be at most one basic fact based on it (this allows us to disregard undefined facts, which are in one-to-one correspondence with basic facts).
– Each aggregated fact must be congruent with the defined fact it is based on, i.e., for each aggregated fact G and for the defined fact F it is based on such that

$$F \doteq E \{D_1 \,|\, L_1, \ldots, D_n \,|\, L_n\} : \{M_1 \,|\, V_1, \ldots, M_m \,|\, V_m\}$$
$$G \doteq F \{D_1 \,|\, R_1, \ldots, D_p \,|\, R_p\} : \{N_1 \,|\, W_1, \ldots, N_q \,|\, W_q\}$$

the following must hold (for some reordering on the dimensions):

• the dimensions in the aggregated fact G are among the dimensions of the fact F it is based on:

$$p \leq n$$

• the level of a dimension in the aggregated fact G is above the level of the corresponding dimension in the fact F it is based on:

$$L_i \leq R_i \quad \text{for each } i \leq p$$

• each measure N_i in the aggregated fact G is computed via an aggregation function from some measure of the defined fact F it is based on:
$N_i \doteq \mathsf{f}_i(\mathbf{g}_i(M_{j_i(1)}, \ldots, M_{j_i(k_i)}))$
for each $i \leq q$ and for some $k_i \leq m$, where j_i is a permutation function
Moreover the range and the domain of the aggregation functions f_i and the attribute functions $\mathbf{g}_i$ should be in agreement each other and with the domains specified in the aggregated fact G and in the fact F it is based on. If $\mathbf{g}_i$ is the identity function then it can be omitted. For measureless facts, the aggregated measure may only have the form $N_i \doteq \mathsf{count}(\star)$.

Measure definitions are used to compute values of measures in an aggregated fact from values of the fact it is based on. For example:

Total-UnitSales $\doteq$ sum(UnitSales)
Total-Profit $\doteq$ sum(SalePrice - UnitCost)

The partial order defines the taxonomy of levels. For example: day $\ll$ month $\ll$ quarter and day $\ll$ week; product $\ll$ type $\ll$ category. When in a schema various hierarchically organised levels are introduced for a dimension, it is also necessary to introduce a roll-up function for them. A roll-up function defines how elements of one level map to elements of a superior level. Since we just require for the roll-up function to be a partial order, it is possible to have elements of a level which roll-up to an upper level, while other elements may skip that upper level to be mapped to a superior one. For example, $\rho_{\text{day,month}}(1/1/01) = \text{Jan-01}$, $\rho_{\text{day,month}}(2/1/01) = \text{Jan-01}, \ldots \rho_{\text{quarter,year}}(\text{Qtr1-01}) = 2001$, $\rho_{\text{quarter,year}}(\text{Qtr2-}01) = 2001, \ldots$

The basic level contains the finest grained level elements, on top of which all the facts are identified. For example, store $\ll$ city $\ll$ country; store is a basic level.

In the definition above, a precise characterisation of an aggregated fact is given: its dimensions should be among the dimensions of the fact it is based on, its levels should be generalised from the corresponding ones in the fact it is based on, and its measures should be all computed from the fact it is based on. For example, given the basic fact BASIC-SALES:

BASIC-SALES $\doteq$
    SALES $\{\text{Date}|_{\text{day}}, \text{Product}|_{\text{product}}, \text{Store}|_{\text{store}}\}$:
        $\{\text{UnitSales}|_{\text{int}}, \text{SalePrice}|_{\text{int}}, \text{UnitCost}|_{\text{int}}\}$

the following SALES-BY-MONTH-AND-TYPE is an aggregated fact computed from the BASIC-SALES fact:

SALES-BY-MONTH-AND-TYPE $\doteq$
    BASIC-SALES $\{\text{Date}|_{\text{month}}, \text{Product}|_{\text{type}}\}$:
        $\{\text{Total-UnitSales}|_{\text{int}}, \text{Avg-SalePrice}|_{\text{real}}, \text{Total-Profit}|_{\text{int}}\}$

with the following aggregated measures:

Total-UnitSales $\doteq$ sum(UnitSales)
Avg-SalePrice $\doteq$ average(SalePrice)
Total-Profit $\doteq$ sum(SalePrice - UnitCost)

Consider now as an example the measureless fact:

STUD-ENROL $\doteq$ ENROL $\{\text{Date}|_{\text{year}}, \text{Student}|_{\text{student}}, \text{Course}|_{\text{course}}\}$

The number of student per year is obtained as follows:

ENROL-BY-YEAR $\doteq$ STUD-ENROL $\{\text{Date}|_{\text{year}}\}$: $\{\text{No\_of\_student}|_{\text{int}}\}$

No_of_students $\doteq$ count($\star$)

Again, a data warehouse state is legal for a given $\mathcal{GMD}$ schema if it is a data warehouse state in the signature of the $\mathcal{GMD}$ schema and it satisfies the additional conditions found in the $\mathcal{GMD}$ schema. In this case, we want that the data warehouse state satisfies the additional *aggregated* cube definitions as defined in the schema.

Definition 6 (Legal Data Warehouse State: Aggregated Cubes). *A data warehouse state $I = <\ \Delta, \Lambda, \Gamma, \cdot^I\ >$ over the $\mathcal{GMD}$ signature $< \mathcal{F}, \mathcal{D}, \mathcal{L}, \mathcal{M}, \mathcal{V}, \mathcal{A} >$ is legal with respect to a $\mathcal{GMD}$ schema if, in addition to the conditions stated in Definition 4, (a) the cardinality of Δ is smaller than Ω, (b) for each level attribute name definition $L \doteq \{A_1 \mid_{V_1}, \ldots, A_n \mid_{V_n}\}$, the interpretation of level attribute names $(A_i^L)^I = L \longrightarrow \Gamma$ is in agreement with the domains specified in the definition itself, and (c) for each aggregated fact and for the defined fact it is based on in the schema:*

$$F \doteq E \{D_1 \mid_{L_1}, \ldots, D_n \mid_{L_n}\} : \{M_1 \mid_{V_1}, \ldots, M_m \mid_{V_m}\}$$
$$G \doteq F \{D_1 \mid_{R_1}, \ldots, D_p \mid_{R_p}\} : \{N_1 \mid_{W_1}, \ldots, N_q \mid_{W_q}\}$$
$$N_i \doteq \mathsf{f}_i(\mathsf{g}_i(M_{j_i(1)}, \ldots, M_{j_i(k)}) \ \textit{for each } i \leq q \ \textit{and for some } k \leq m, \ \textit{where } j \ \textit{is a}$$

permutation function

each aggregated measure function actually computes the aggregation of the values in the corresponding measure of the fact the aggregation is based on:

$$\forall g, v. \ N_i(g) = v \leftrightarrow \exists r_1, \ldots, r_p. \ G(g) \wedge D_1(g) = r_1 \wedge \ldots \wedge D_p(g) = r_p \wedge$$
$$v = \mathsf{f}_i(\{\!\mid \mathsf{g}_i(M_{j_i(1)}(f), \ldots, M_{j_i(k)}(f)) \mid$$
$$\exists l_1, \ldots, l_p. \ F(f) \wedge$$
$$D_1(f) = l_1 \wedge \ldots \wedge D_p(f) = l_p \wedge$$
$$\rho^*_{L_1, R_1}(l_1) = r_1 \wedge \ldots \wedge \rho^*_{L_p, R_p}(l_p) = r_p \mid\!\})$$

for each $i \leq q$, where $\{\!\mid \cdot \mid\!\}$ denotes a bag.

The legal data warehouse condition expressed above guarantees that if a fact is the aggregation of another fact, then in a legal data warehouse state the measures associated to the cells of the aggregated cube should be actually computed by applying the aggregation function to the measures of the corresponding cells in the original cube. The correspondence between a cell in the aggregated cube and a set of cells in the original cube is found by looking how their coordinates – which are level elements – are mapped through the roll-up function dimension by dimension.

To sum up, a legal data warehouse state for a $\mathcal{GMD}$ schema is a bunch of multidimensional cubes, whose cells carry measure values. Each cube conforms to the fact definition given in the $\mathcal{GMD}$ schema, i.e., the coordinates are in agreement with the dimensions and the levels specified, and the measures are of the correct type. If a cube is the aggregation of another cube, in a legal data warehouse state it is enforced that the measures of the aggregated cubes are correctly computed from the measures of the original cube.

4   Example

The following $\mathcal{GMD}$ schema summarises the examples shown in the previous Sections:

- Signature:
  - $\mathcal{F} = \{$SALES, BASIC-SALES, SALES-BY-MONTH-AND-TYPE, PURCHASES$\}$
  - $\mathcal{M} = \{$UnitSales, Price, Total-UnitSales, Avg-Price$\}$
  - $\mathcal{D} = \{$Date, Product, Store$\}$
  - $\mathcal{L} = \{$day, week, month, quarter, year, product, type, category, brand, store, city, country$\}$
    day $= \{1/1/01, 2/1/01, \ldots, 1/1/02, 2/1/02, \ldots\}$
    month $= \{$Jan-01, Feb-01, $\ldots$, Jan-02, Feb-02, $\ldots\}$
    quarter $= \{$Qtr1-01, Qtr2-01, $\ldots$, Qtr1-02, Qtr2-02, $\ldots\}$
    year $= \{2001, 2002\}$
    $\ldots$
  - $\mathcal{V} = \{$int, real, string$\}$
  - $\mathcal{A} = \{$dayname, prodname, prodsize, prodweight, storenum$\}$
- Partial order over levels:
  - day $\ll$ month $\ll$ quarter $\ll$ year, day $\ll$ week; **day** is a basic level
  - product $\ll$ type $\ll$ category, product $\ll$ brand; **product** is a basic level
  - store $\ll$ city $\ll$ country; **store** is a basic level
- Roll-up functions:
  $\rho_{\mathrm{day,month}}(1/1/01) = $ Jan-01, $\rho_{\mathrm{day,month}}(2/1/01) = $ Jan-01, $\ldots$
  $\rho_{\mathrm{month,quarter}}($Jan-01$) = $ Qtr1-01, $\rho_{\mathrm{month,quarter}}($Feb-01$) = $ Qtr1-01, $\ldots$
  $\rho_{\mathrm{quarter,year}}($Qtr1-01$) = 2001$, $\rho_{\mathrm{quarter,year}}($Qtr2-01$) = 2001$, $\ldots$
  $\rho^*_{\mathrm{day,year}}(1/1/01) = 2001$, $\rho^*_{\mathrm{day,year}}(2/1/01) = 2001$, $\ldots$
  $\ldots$
- Level Attribute names:
  day $\doteq \{$dayname$|_{\mathrm{string}}$, daynum$|_{\mathrm{int}}\}$
  product $\doteq \{$prodname$|_{\mathrm{string}}$, prodnum$|_{\mathrm{int}}$, prodsize$|_{\mathrm{int}}$, prodweight$|_{\mathrm{int}}\}$
  store $\doteq \{$storename$|_{\mathrm{string}}$, storenum$|_{\mathrm{int}}$, address$|_{\mathrm{string}}\}$
- Facts:
  BASIC-SALES $\doteq$
    SALES $\{$Date$|_{\mathrm{day}}$, Product$|_{\mathrm{product}}$, Store$|_{\mathrm{store}}\}$: $\{$UnitSales$|_{\mathrm{int}}$, SalePrice$|_{\mathrm{int}}\}$
  SALES-BY-MONTH-AND-TYPE $\doteq$
    BASIC-SALES $\{$Date$|_{\mathrm{month}}$, Product$|_{\mathrm{type}}\}$: $\{$Total-UnitSales$|_{\mathrm{int}}$, Avg-SalePrice$|_{\mathrm{real}}\}$
- Measures:
  Total-UnitSales $\doteq$ **sum**(UnitSales)
  Avg-SalePrice $\doteq$ **average**(SalePrice)

A possible legal data warehouse state for (part of) the previous example $\mathcal{GMD}$ schema is shown in the following.

BASIC-SALES$^I = \{s_1, s_2, s_3, s_4, s_5, s_6, s_7\}$
SALES-BY-MONTH-AND-TYPE$^I = \{g_1, g_2, g_3, g_4, g_5, g_6\}$

Date(s_1) = 1/1/01	Product(s_1) = Organic-milk-1l	Store(s_1) = Fair-trade-central
Date(s_2) = 7/1/01	Product(s_2) = Organic-yogh-125g	Store(s_2) = Fair-trade-central
Date(s_3) = 7/1/01	Product(s_3) = Organic-milk-1l	Store(s_3) = Ali-grocery
Date(s_4) = 10/2/01	Product(s_4) = Organic-milk-1l	Store(s_4) = Barbacan-store
Date(s_5) = 28/2/01	Product(s_5) = Organic-beer-6pack	Store(s_5) = Fair-trade-central
Date(s_6) = 2/3/01	Product(s_6) = Organic-milk-1l	Store(s_6) = Fair-trade-central
Date(s_7) = 12/3/01	Product(s_7) = Organic-beer-6pack	Store(s_7) = Ali-grocery

UnitSales(s_1) = 100	EuroSalePrice(s_1) = 71,00
UnitSales(s_2) = 500	EuroSalePrice(s_2) = 250,00
UnitSales(s_3) = 230	EuroSalePrice(s_3) = 138,00
UnitSales(s_4) = 300	EuroSalePrice(s_4) = 210,00
UnitSales(s_5) = 210	EuroSalePrice(s_5) = 420,00
UnitSales(s_6) = 150	EuroSalePrice(s_6) = 105,00
UnitSales(s_7) = 100	EuroSalePrice(s_7) = 200,00

Date(g_1) = Jan-01   Product(g_1) = Dairy
Date(g_2) = Feb-01   Product(g_2) = Dairy
Date(g_3) = Jan-01   Product(g_3) = Drink
Date(g_4) = Feb-01   Product(g_4) = Drink
Date(g_5) = Mar-01   Product(g_5) = Dairy
Date(g_6) = Mar-01   Product(g_6) = Drink

Total-UnitSales(g_1) = 830   Avg-EuroSalePrice(g_1) = 153,00
Total-UnitSales(g_2) = 300   Avg-EuroSalePrice(g_2) = 210,00
Total-UnitSales(g_3) = 0   Avg-EuroSalePrice(g_3) = 0,00
Total-UnitSales(g_4) = 210   Avg-EuroSalePrice(g_4) = 420,00
Total-UnitSales(g_5) = 150   Avg-EuroSalePrice(g_5) = 105,00
Total-UnitSales(g_6) = 100   Avg-EuroSalePrice(g_6) = 200,00

daynum(day) = 1   prodweight(product) = 100gm   storenum(store) = S101

5 $\mathcal{GMD}$ Full Algebra

On top the data model described so far, we now introduced a full cube algebra, which has the very desirable property of being compositional (any new cube is always introduced by means of an additional definition in the schema, possibly making use of other cube definitions), and of being equipped with a formal semantics (in the sense that a logic based definition of *legal* data warehouse state is given for all valid algebraic constructs). We introduce the operator to add derived measures to cubes, the operator to create slices and multislices to cubes, the join operator between two cubes, and finally the union, the intersection, and the difference operators between pairs of cubes.

We start by defining the *derived measure* operator: a new cube G can be computed from a cube F by just adding a measure whose value can be computed from the other measures of F.

Definition 7 (Derived Measures). *A $\mathcal{GMD}$ schema may also include definitions of the kind:*

$$F \doteq E\ \{D_1\ |_{L_1}, \ldots, D_n\ |_{L_n}\} : \{M_1\ |_{V_1}, \ldots, M_m\ |_{V_m}\}$$
$$G \doteq F + \{N\ |_V\}$$
$$N \doteq \mathbf{g}(M_{j(1)}, \ldots, M_{j(k)})$$

where $k \leq m$, and $\mathbf{g}$ is a function $\mathbf{g} : V_1 \times \ldots \times V_k \longrightarrow V$ for some $V_1, \ldots, V_k, V \in \mathcal{V}$ in agreement with the various domain constraints.

A data warehouse state $I = <\Delta, \Lambda, \Gamma, \cdot^I>$ over the $\mathcal{GMD}$ signature $<\mathcal{F}, \mathcal{D}, \mathcal{L}, \mathcal{M}, \mathcal{V}, \mathcal{A}>$ is legal with respect to a $\mathcal{GMD}$ schema if, in addition to the conditions to be satisfied by the other parts of the schema, the following holds:

$$\forall f, g, l_1, \ldots, l_n, v_1, \ldots, v_m.\ (F(f)\ \land D_1(f) = l_1 \land \ldots \land D_n(f) = l_n\ \land$$
$$M_1(f) = v_1 \land \ldots \land M_m(f) = v_m)$$
$$\leftrightarrow$$
$$(G(g) \land D_1(g) = l_1 \land \ldots \land D_n(g) = l_n\ \land$$
$$M_1(g) = v_1 \land \ldots \land M_m(g) = v_m \land$$
$$N(g) = \mathbf{g}(M_{j(1)}(f), \ldots, M_{j(k)}(f)))$$

Moreover, the fact G should satisfy the cube conditions as specified in Definition 4 with respect to the same dimension, levels and measures as for fact F with the additional measure N.

As an example we could have as part of the schema:

DERIVED-SALES $\doteq$ SALES + {Profit$|_{\text{int}}$}
Profit $\doteq$ SalePrice - UnitCost

Two selection operators are also available in the full $\mathcal{GMD}$ algebra. The slice operation simply selects the cells of a cube corresponding to specific values for some dimension, resulting in a cube which contains a subset of the cells of the original one and fewer dimensions. The multislice allows for the selection of ranges of values for a dimension, so that the resulting cube will contain a subset of the cells of the original one but retains the selected dimension.

Definition 8 (Slice/Multislice). *A $\mathcal{GMD}$ schema may also include definitions of the kind:*

(slice)
$$F \doteq E\{D_1|_{L_1}, \ldots, D_n|_{L_n}\} : \{M_1|_{V_1}, \ldots, M_m|_{V_m}\}$$
$$G \doteq F[D_{i+1}|_{l_{i+1}}, \ldots, D_n|_{l_n}]$$
where $1 \le i \le n$ and l_j is level element of a level L_j for each j, $i \le j \le n$.

(multislice)
$$F \doteq E\{D_1|_{L_1}, \ldots, D_n|_{L_n}\} : \{M_1|_{V_1}, \ldots, M_m|_{V_m}\}$$
$$G \doteq F[D_{i+1}|_{X_{i+1}}, \ldots, D_n|_{X_n}]$$
where $1 \le i \le n$ and $X_j \subseteq L_j$ for $i \le j \le n$.
A data warehouse state $I = <\Delta, \Lambda, \Gamma, \cdot^I>$ over the $\mathcal{GMD}$ signature $< \mathcal{F}, \mathcal{D}, \mathcal{L}, \mathcal{M}, \mathcal{V}, \mathcal{A} >$ is legal with respect to a $\mathcal{GMD}$ schema if, in addition to the conditions to be satisfied by the other parts of the schema, the following holds:

(slice)
$$\forall f, g, l_1, \ldots, l_i, v_1, \ldots, v_m.\ (G(g) \wedge D_1(g) = l_1 \wedge \ldots \wedge D_i(g) = l_i \wedge$$
$$M_1(g) = v_1 \wedge \ldots \wedge M_m(g) = v_m) \leftrightarrow$$
$$(F(f) \wedge D_1(f) = l_1 \wedge \ldots \wedge D_i(f) = l_i \wedge$$
$$D_{i+1}(f) = l_{i+1} \wedge \ldots \wedge D_n(f) = l_n \wedge$$
$$M_1(f) = v_1 \wedge \ldots \wedge M_m(f) = v_m)$$

Moreover, the fact G should satisfy the cube conditions as specified in Definition 4 with respect to the same dimension, levels and measures as for fact F less the dimensions $D_{i+1}, \ldots, D_n$.

(multislice)
$$\forall f, g, l_1, \ldots, l_i, l_{i+1} \in X_{i+1}, \ldots, l_n \in X_n, v_1, \ldots, v_m.$$
$$(G(g) \wedge D_1(g) = l_1 \wedge \ldots \wedge D_i(g) = l_i \wedge$$
$$D_{i+1}(g) = l_{i+1} \wedge \ldots \wedge D_n(g) = l_n \wedge$$
$$M_1(g) = v_1 \wedge \ldots \wedge M_m(g) = v_m) \leftrightarrow$$
$$(F(f) \wedge D_1(f) = l_1 \wedge \ldots \wedge D_i(f) = l_i \wedge$$
$$D_{i+1}(f) = l_{i+1} \wedge \ldots \wedge D_n(f) = l_n \wedge$$
$$M_1(f) = v_1 \wedge \ldots \wedge M_m(f) = v_m)$$

Moreover, the fact G should satisfy the cube conditions as specified in Definition 4 with respect to the same dimension, levels and measures as for fact F but for the dimensions $D_{i+1}, \ldots, D_n$ the levels being $X_{i+1}, \ldots, X_n$.

As an example we could have as part of the schema:

SALES-BY-TYPE-IN-JAN'02 $\doteq$
    SALES-BY-MONTH-AND-TYPE [Date$|_{jan'02}$]
SALES-BY-MONTH-AND-TYPE-IN-1ST-QTR'02 $\doteq$
    SALES-BY-MONTH-AND-TYPE [Date$|_{\{jan'02,feb'02,mar'02\}}$]

The $\mathcal{GMD}$ algebra includes a join operation defined only between cubes sharing the same dimensions and the same levels. We argue that a more general join operation is meaningless in a cube algebra, since it may leads to cubes whose measures are no more consistent.

Definition 9 (Join). *A $\mathcal{GMD}$ schema may also include definitions of the kind:*

$F \doteq E\text{-}1 \, \{D_1 \,|_{L_1}, \ldots, D_n \,|_{L_n}\} : \{M_1 \,|_{V_1}, \ldots, M_m \,|_{V_m}\}$
$G \doteq E\text{-}2 \, \{D_1 \,|_{L_1}, \ldots, D_n \,|_{L_n}\} : \{N_1 \,|_{W_1}, \ldots, N_q \,|_{W_q}\}$
$H \doteq F \bowtie G$

A data warehouse state $I = \; < \Delta, \Lambda, \Gamma, \cdot^I >$ over the $\mathcal{GMD}$ signature $< \mathcal{F}, \mathcal{D}, \mathcal{L}, \mathcal{M}, \mathcal{V}, \mathcal{A} >$ is legal with respect to a $\mathcal{GMD}$ schema if, in addition to the conditions to be satisfied by the other parts of the schema, the following holds:

$\forall f, g, h, l_1, \ldots, l_n, v_1, \ldots, v_m, w_1, \ldots, w_q.$
$\quad (H(h) \wedge D_1(h) = l_1 \wedge \ldots \wedge D_n(h) = l_n \; \wedge$
$\quad M_1(h) = v_1 \wedge \ldots \wedge M_m(h) = v_m \; \wedge$
$\quad N_1(h) = w_1 \wedge \ldots \wedge N_q(h) = w_q) \; \leftrightarrow$
$\qquad (F(f) \; \wedge D_1(f) = l_1 \wedge \ldots \wedge D_n(f) = l_n \; \wedge$
$\qquad M_1(f) = v_1 \wedge \ldots \wedge M_m(f) = v_m \; \wedge$
$\qquad G(g) \; \wedge D_1(g) = l_1 \wedge \ldots \wedge D_n(g) = l_n \; \wedge$
$\qquad N_1(g) = w_1 \wedge \ldots \wedge N_q(g) = w_q)$

Moreover, the fact H should satisfy the cube conditions as specified in Definition 4 with respect to the same dimension, levels as for the facts F, G and the union of the measures of F, G.

As an example we could have as part of the schema:

SALES-BY-MONTH-AND-TYPE $\doteq$
    BASIC-SALES $\{Date|_{month}, Product \,|_{product}, Store \,|_{store}\}$:
$\{Total\text{-}Sale\text{-}Price \,|_{real}\}$
PURCHASES-BY-MONTH-AND-TYPE $\doteq$
    BASIC-PURCHASES $\{Date|_{month}, Product \,|_{product}, Store \,|_{store}\}$:
$\{Total\text{-}Cost \,|_{real}\}$
SALES&PURCHASES-BY-MONTH-AND-TYPE $\doteq$
    SALES-BY-MONTH-AND-TYPE $\bowtie$ PURCHASES-BY-MONTH-AND-TYPE

Finally, we introduce briefly the union, intersection, and difference operators. In order to be compatible for these operators, two facts should have the same dimensions, levels, and measures; we do not allow a general union operator like the one proposed in [Gray *et al.*, 1996], but it can be shown how the algebra proposed by Gray can be reconstructed using the $\mathcal{GMD}$ algebra.

Definition 10 (Union, Intersection, Difference). *A $\mathcal{GMD}$ schema may also include definitions of the kind:*

$$F \doteq E\text{-}1 \{D_1 \mid_{L_1}, \ldots, D_n \mid_{L_n}\} : \{M_1 \mid_{V_1}, \ldots, M_m \mid_{V_m}\}$$
$$G \doteq E\text{-}2 \{D_1 \mid_{L_1}, \ldots, D_n \mid_{L_n}\} : \{M_1 \mid_{V_1}, \ldots, M_m \mid_{V_m}\}$$
$$H \doteq F \otimes G$$

where $\otimes$ is one of $\{\bigcup, \bigcap, \backslash\}$.

A data warehouse state $I = \; <\Delta, \Lambda, \Gamma, \cdot^I>$ over the $\mathcal{GMD}$ signature $< \mathcal{F}, \mathcal{D}, \mathcal{L}, \mathcal{M}, \mathcal{V}, \mathcal{A} >$ is legal with respect to a $\mathcal{GMD}$ schema if, in addition to the conditions to be satisfied by the other parts of the schema, the following holds:

$$\forall f, g, h, l_1, \ldots, l_n, v_1, \ldots, v_m.$$
$$(H(h) \wedge D_1(h) = l_1 \wedge \ldots \wedge D_n(h) = l_n \wedge$$
$$M_1(h) = v_1 \wedge \ldots \wedge M_m(h) = v_m) \leftrightarrow$$
$$(\; (F(f) \; \wedge D_1(f) = l_1 \wedge \ldots \wedge D_n(f) = l_n \wedge$$
$$M_1(f) = v_1 \wedge \ldots \wedge M_m(f) = v_m)$$
$$\oplus$$
$$(G(g) \; \wedge D_1(g) = l_1 \wedge \ldots \wedge D_n(g) = l_n \wedge$$
$$M_1(g) = v_1 \wedge \ldots \wedge M_m(g) = v_m) \;)$$

where $\oplus$ is "$\vee$" in the case of union, *is "$\wedge$" in the case of* intersection, *is "$\wedge \neg$" in the case of* difference. *Moreover, the fact H should satisfy the cube conditions as specified in Definition 4 with respect to the same dimension, levels, and measures as for the facts F, G.*

6   Related Work

As we were mentioning in the introduction, one outcome of the formal definition of the $\mathcal{GMD}$ data model is in the full encoding of many data warehouse logical data models as $\mathcal{GMD}$ schemas. We are able in this way to give an homogeneous semantics (in terms of legal data warehouse states) to the logical model and the algebras proposed in all these different approaches. The star and the snowflake schemas, Gray's cube, Agrawal's and Vassiliadis' models, $\mathcal{MD}$ and other multidimensional conceptual data models can be captured uniformly by $\mathcal{GMD}$. In this way it is possible to formally understand the real differences in expressivity of the various models.

The classical relational based *star model* comprises a single fact table at the centre and multiple dimension tables around connected to it. The fact table consists of a set of dimension attributes forming the primary key and several measure non-key numeric attributes. Each dimension attribute is also foreign key to a dimension table. Each dimension table consists of attributes including a primary key and several non-key attributes, and it represents the properties of elements of a single level for the dimension. The star model does not explicitly provide the support for dimension hierarchies. In the *snowflake model* the dimension hierarchy is explicitly represented by normalising the dimension tables, while in the *fact constellation model* multiple fact tables may share dimension tables. It can be easily seen how the star, the snowflake, and the fact constellation models can be encoded into corresponding $\mathcal{GMD}$ schemas, in a way that the legal data warehouse states identified by the encoded $\mathcal{GMD}$ schema are the same possible instantiations of the original schema.

The other classical data model for multidimensional data is the *cube model*, which contains n-dimensional arrays where each dimension is associated to a hierarchy of levels of consolidated data. The data is represented by means of matrices whose indexes range over natural numbers. This structure has an obvious mapping into the $\mathcal{GMD}$ data model.

The $\mathcal{MD}$ data model was introduced by [Cabibbo and Torlone, 1998] as a first proposal of a homogeneous logical data model for multidimensional data. The central element of an $\mathcal{MD}$ schema is a *f-table* representing factual multidimensional data. A *f-table* is the abstract logical representation of a multidimensional cube, and it is a function associating symbolic coordinates (one per involved dimension) to measures. Dimensions are organised into hierarchies of levels according to the various granularity of basic data. A $\mathcal{MD}$ dimension consists of a finite set of levels with partial ordering on these levels. Within a dimension, levels are related through roll-up functions. Levels can have level descriptions that provide information about the levels. It is possible to encode a $\mathcal{MD}$ schema into an equivalent $\mathcal{GMD}$ schema. However, $\mathcal{GMD}$ is richer than $\mathcal{MD}$. First, in $\mathcal{GMD}$ each set of connected levels is rooted through a basic level – the unique least level in the dimension hierarchy, and there is partial order among the levels (a notion stressed by, e.g., [Vassiliadis, 1998]); whereas in $\mathcal{MD}$ a uniqueness of a least element (level) has not been considered in the partial ordering of levels. Then, in $\mathcal{MD}$, the join of fact tables is like a join of relational tables; the join contains non-common dimensions apart from the common ones. An instance of the resulting fact table (join) may be erroneous for an f-table entry; whereas in $\mathcal{GMD}$, a join is possible only between the cubes sharing same dimensions and levels, and the join takes place only on common dimension values so that the each cell is consistent with respect to the measure values. Moreover, $\mathcal{GMD}$, supports correct aggregations (summarisations) irrespective of the path chosen for the rolling up thanks to the application of transitive reflexive roll-up functions, and an aggregated fact can be computed from another aggregated fact. Finally, the $\mathcal{GMD}$ model includes in its core definition all the algebraic operators, which are consistently and, most importantly, compositionally defined over the basic notion of cube.

In [Agrawal *et al.*, 1997], a logical data model has been proposed based on the notion of multidimensional cube, together with an algebraic query language over it. The model is characterised by a symmetric treatment for dimensions and measures. The most notable difference with $\mathcal{GMD}$ is the lack of compositionality in the basic definitions of the model and in the algebraic operators. The dimension hierarchies are implemented using a special query language operator whereas level hierarchies are part of the core $\mathcal{GMD}$ model. The algebra is grounded on operators dealing with *destruction* and *restriction* of dimensions, general join of cubes, and merge among levels within a cube. For example, the aggregation is defined as the join of two cubes with a subsequent merge. It can be shown that the algebra of cubes of [Agrawal *et al.*, 1997] can be encoded in $\mathcal{GMD}$.

The cube operator introduced in [Gray *et al.*, 1996] expands a relational table by aggregating over all possible combinations of the attributes of the relation. A cube operator is an n-dimensional generalisation of the SQL GROUP BY operator. For n attributes in the select-list, it results in 2^n group-by computations. The data cube operator builds a table containing all these values. The $\mathcal{GMD}$ data model can not represent directly a cube generated by means of the cube operator, since it is impossible to directly represent in the same fact table data at different levels for the same dimension; this is captured in Gray's cube with the special aggregated level element all. We propose a possible encoding of the cube operator in $\mathcal{GMD}$ which goes around this problem. The idea is based on extending the set of level element names with the special constant all for each level, and then building the complete cube by means of a sequence of aggregations and unions. It should be noted, however, that the introduction of the special constant all may affect the consistency of the aggregated cubes in general, and so it should be used only in the special case of generating the completed cube, which itself shouldn't be used anymore for further aggregations (like in Gray's approach).

[Vassiliadis and Skiadopoulos, 2000], propose a logical model equipped with a lattice of dimension levels, so that the values of each dimension level can be grouped into a single all special value. It is emphasised that a cube is always a view over an underlying data set – which corresponds to the $\mathcal{GMD}$ basic level. Cubes (views) are computed over a base cube which holds the most detailed data. Aggregation is carried out with a special operator called *navigate* always defined from the base data, while in $\mathcal{GMD}$ it is possible to aggregate already aggregated data. It is possible to show that the composition of aggregations in $\mathcal{GMD}$ down to the basic level corresponds to the navigation as proposed by [Vassiliadis and Skiadopoulos, 2000].

In [Golfarelli *et al.*, 1998], a multidimensional data model called *Dimensional Fact Model* (DFM) has been introduced. DFM is a graphical model, independent on the logical (multidimensional/relational) model, but substantially based on the star model. DFM is a quasi-tree (weakly connected) of attributes, whose root is a fact. A fact is represented by a box at the centre of the diagram associated with a fact name and its multiple measures; the dimension attributes are linked to the fact and are represented by circles. Non-dimensional attributes are leaf nodes linked to the fact. Subtrees rooted in dimensions represent the hierarchy of levels for the dimension. The hierarchies are constrained by x-to-one (i.e., many-to-one, etc) relationships between nodes (representing the levels). Each n-tuple of values taken from the domains of n dimensions of a fact defines an elemental cell called a primary fact instance where one unit of information for the data warehouse can be represented. Aggregation at different levels of abstraction (e.g. roll-up) is called a secondary fact instance which aggregates the set of primary fact instances. A query language is also provided for computing fact instances (primary and secondary) with n-dimensions and selections (using boolean predicates). DFM can easily be encoded in all its aspects as a $\mathcal{GMD}$ schema.

The most important aspect of DFM is that it is associated with a very powerful data warehouse design methodology and many supporting tools are available for it. Since it is possible to encode in $\mathcal{GMD}$ various steps of the data warehouse design methodology, it becomes possible to support those stages of the methodology by means of some automated tool which can be proved correct with respect to the $\mathcal{GMD}$ semantics. Our main line of research for the future is to extend and adapt the powerful data warehouse design methodologies proposed by [Golfarelli et al., 1998] to the full $\mathcal{GMD}$ data model. We will do this in the spirit of the work done in [Franconi and Sattler, 1999].

[Lehner et al., 1998] introduce a generalised multidimensional normal form (GMNF) which ensures the summarisability but restricts the roll-up function between the hierarchical levels to be total (similar to [Hutardo et al., 1999]), whereas in $\mathcal{GMD}$ the relationship between hierarchical levels is a more general partial roll-up function. [Jagadish et al., 1999] model hierarchies in a relational way by using SQL, overcoming the limitations on modelling hierarchies in the snowflake schema. In this way there is a reduction in the number of joins that are required to join the level hierarchies (dimension tables) while querying the snowflake schema. Also in this case the roll-up functions are considered total.

7 Conclusions

In this paper we have introduced the $\mathcal{GMD}$ data model and algebra, an abstract but rich data model for representing multidimensional information, equipped with logic-based semantics and seamlessly integrated with a fully compositional algebra also equipped with logic-based semantics. The aim of this work is to propose an homogeneous approach to formally represent all the aspects of multidimensional data, as proposed by the various data models presented in the literature. We hinted how actually $\mathcal{GMD}$ captures these various proposals. Starting with the $\mathcal{GMD}$ data model, our current research work is to adapt the conceptual data warehouse methodologies appeared in the literature – in the spirit of [Golfarelli et al., 1998, Franconi and Sattler, 1999].

References

[Abello et al., 2001] A. Abello, J. Samos, and F. Saltor. Understanding analysis dimensions in a multidimensional object-oriented model. In *Proc. of the International Workshop on Design and Management of Data Warehouses (DMDW'2001),Interlaken, Switzerland*, pages 4-1-4-9, 2001.

[Agrawal et al., 1997] R. Agrawal, A. Gupta, and S. Sarawagi. Modeling multidimensional databases. In *Proc. of ICDE-97*, 1997.

[Cabibbo and Torlone, 1998] Luca Cabibbo and Riccardo Torlone. A logical approach to multidimensional databases. In *Proc. of EDBT-98*, 1998.

[Franconi and Kamble, 2003] Enrico Franconi and Anand S. Kamble. The $\mathcal{GMD}$ data model for multidimensional information. In *Proc. 5th International Conference on Data Warehousing and Knowledge Discovery*, pages 55–65, 2003.

[Franconi and Sattler, 1999] E. Franconi and U. Sattler. A data warehouse conceptual data model for multidimensional aggregation. In *Proc. of the Workshop on Design and Management of Data Warehouses (DMDW-99)*, 1999.

[Golfarelli et al., 1998] M. Golfarelli, D. Maio, and S. Rizzi. The dimensional fact model: a conceptual model for data warehouses. *IJCIS*, 7(2-3):215–247, 1998.

[Gray et al., 1996] J. Gray, A. Bosworth, A. Layman, and H. Pirahesh. Data cube: a relational aggregation operator generalizing group-by, cross-tabs and subtotals. In *Proc. of ICDE-96*, 1996.

[Gyssens and Lakshmanan, 1997] M. Gyssens and L.V.S. Lakshmanan. A foundation for multi-dimensional databases. In *Proc. of VLDB-97*, pages 106–115, 1997.

[Hutardo et al., 1999] Carlos Hutardo, Alberto Mendelzon, and A. Vaisman. Maintaining data cube under dimension updates. In *Proc. 15th IEEE-ICDE International Conference*, 1999.

[Jagadish et al., 1999] H.V. Jagadish, Laks V.S. Lakshmanan, and Divesh Srivastava. What can hierarchies do for data warehouses? In *Proc. 25th International Conference on Very Large Databases (VLDB)*, pages 530–541, 1999.

[Lehner et al., 1998] W. Lehner, H. Albrecht, and H. Wedekind. Normal forms for multidimensional databases. In *Proc. 10th International Conference on Scientific and Statistical Database Management (SSDBM)*, pages 63–73, 1998.

[Tsois et al., 2001] A. Tsois, N. Karayiannidis, and T. Sellis. MAC: Conceptual data modelling for OLAP. In *Proc. of the International Workshop on Design and Management of Warehouses (DMDW-2001)*, pages 5-1-5-13, 2001.

[Vassiliadis and Sellis, 1999] P. Vassiliadis and T. Sellis. A survey of logical models for OLAP databases. In *SIGMOD Record*, volume 28, pages 64–69, December 1999.

[Vassiliadis and Skiadopoulos, 2000] P. Vassiliadis and S. Skiadopoulos. Modelling and optimisation issues for multidimensional databases. In *Proc. of CAiSE-2000*, pages 482–497, 2000.

[Vassiliadis, 1998] P. Vassiliadis. Modeling multidimensional databases, cubes and cube operations. In *Proc. of the 10th SSDBM Conference*, Capri, Italy, July 1998.

Towards a Framework for Model Migration

Werner Esswein, Andreas Gehlert, and Grit Seiffert

University of Technology Dresden, Dresden, 01069, Germany
{esswein,gehlert}@wise.wiwi.tu-dresden.de
grit.seiffert@mailbox.tu-dresden.de
Phone: ++49 351 463 36304, Fax: ++49 351 463 37203

Abstract. Model migration is needed to transform a model from one modelling language to another to reuse these models and thus, to reduce the costs of building new models. This topic has received much attention mainly because of the OMG's MDA initiative. However, these approaches are tailored to transform design models. In this paper, we argue that this approach cannot be applied to the field of domain modelling. Therefore, we propose a theoretical framework for model migration, which extends the existing approaches adding a role and a process model to satisfy the requirements of model migrations in a material problem domain.

Keywords: model migration, domain modelling, modelling method

1   Introduction

Modelling is an important technique to gather insights into specific problem domains. Models are created by specific – mostly visual – modelling languages. These modelling languages are suited to analyse a specific aspect and/or view of a problem domain (see [1], p. 401, [2], p. 22f). Thus, different modelling languages have been created using different concepts suited for these views and aspects. The number of modelling languages has further been increased by the method engineering discipline (see [3], [2] and [4]), which aims to propose modelling languages especially suitable for a specific project. Because of conceptual discrepancies interchanging of models between different modelling languages is non trivial.

One of the prerequisites for reusing models is, that the modelling language of the original model is the same as the language used for a specific project at hand. If this is not the case, the original model has to be transformed into the new modelling language. If the modelling languages involved in such a transformation have different concepts (not only a different graphical representation), this process is called model *migration*[1].

Many solutions to the migration problem have been presented ranging from an ad hoc comparison of meta models for a specific purpose (see [6], p. 58) to complete methodologies for model migration (see [6], [5][2]). These approaches are

---

[1] This process is also known as model transformation (see [5], p. 2-7).
[2] For an overview of the approaches in the MDA field, see [7].

A. Persson and J. Stirna (Eds.): CAiSE 2004, LNCS 3084, pp. 463–476, 2004.

tailored for migrating design models only. Design models regard a mathematical or formal domain. However, in a material problem domain a complete model migration has to respect syntactic, semantic and especially pragmatic aspects of models (see subsection 2.1). Current approaches to model migration do not account for the pragmatic aspects in a material problem domain.

Therefore, we propose in section 2 of this paper a theoretical framework for model migration, which extends the existing approaches to satisfy the requirements of a model migration in a material problem domain. This framework consists of a role model (subsection 2.2), a process model and an – interchangeable – meta model based migration approach (section 3). Furthermore, we provide an example demonstrating the application of the framework (subsection 3.3). The paper finishes with a summary of the results and states the remaining problems.

2 Theoretical Foundations of Model Migration

A *model* is characterised by three properties. First, models are representations of (natural or artificial) originals (problem domain). Second, not the complete problem domain is represented in such a model but only the relevant parts of it. Third, each model has a pragmatic relativization, which means it is only valid for a special purpose, at a certain time and for a special (group of) user(s) (see [8], p. 131ff).

In this paper we use the term model to refer to *domain models* as visual models for the purpose of information system development in its broadest sence. The problem domain is – in contrast to implementation models for instance – a material not mathematical or logical domain (see subsection 2.1 for that differentiation).

Any model serves as a problem definition. Problems are per definition not well-structured, highly subjective and individual and thus, not objectively well formed (see [9], p. 2). Consequently, domain modelling is always concerned with structuring the real world not with merely mapping it. Domain models which fulfil this definition are for example ER models (see [10]), EPC models (see [11]) and UML models (see [12], p. 3-34ff).

2.1 Semantics and Pragmatics in Models

After the clarification what we understand by the term model, we analyse the elements to which semantics and pragmatics in models are assigned. These elements are of special interest for reusing and migrating models (see [6], p. 23f; [13]).

The modelling language communicates important pars of the semantics of the model. In general, three aspects of languages are important. First, the *syntax* describes the language expressions and their lawful combinations, second, the *semantics* maps these expressions to a semantic domain (see [14]) and third, the *pragmatics* describes the meaning of an expression for the individual who uses it.

Two stances of semantics must be separated. First, semantics understood as rules for automated interpretation as it is used implicitly in the MDA approach and, second, semantics as interpretation of real world constructs and their representation in language artifacts (see [13]). The later terminology is used in the field of domain modelling.

Consequently, domain models always represent concepts of real world entities. This conceptualisation and interpretation of the real world cannot be formalised because it is determined in a social process (see [15], p. 127).

As stated before, a model is always represented by a specific modelling language. Furthermore, it is constructed using an implicit or explicit process model. The models of the modelling language and the process model are called *meta models* (MM). To distinguish between these meta models we name them meta model of the modelling language[3] (MM_L) describing the syntax of M and meta process model (MM_P) describing the modelling process of M. Both meta models form a modelling method (see [3], p. 11). Figure 1 summarises these aspects.

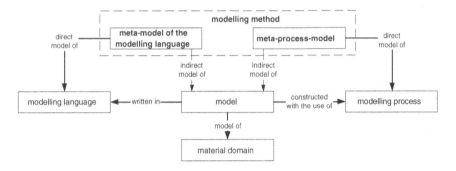

Fig. 1. The role of meta models (according to [16], p. 958, figure 2)

To specify the semantics of a model the modelling language and the modelling process must be highlighted. The semantics of a model element, $sem(E)$, is primarily described with the help of the concepts of both meta models $(C_{MM_L}$ and $C_{MM_P})$. This aspect is called *abstract semantics* $(sem(E_a) = sem(C_{MM_L}) \cup sem(C_{MM_P}))$. For example, an entity type order has semantics because it was modelled as entity type. Thus, it is seen as a concept of the real world and not a relation between concepts in the real world (see [10], p. 11f). Furthermore, semantics is added because this entity type was created within a concrete modelling process.

Additionally, each model element adds a specific meaning, which we refer to as *concrete semantics* $(sem(E_c))$. For example, the entity type order itself carries a meaning (e. g. customer-order). Consequently, the semantics of a model element can be defined as union of the abstract and concrete semantics of this element $(sem(E) = sem(E_c) \cup sem(C_{MM_L}) \cup sem(C_{MM_P}))$.

In line with recent research in the field of visual modelling, the layout of modelling graphs can also communicate semantics (see [13], [17]). For instance,

---

[3] Often referred to as meta model of the abstract syntax (see [14], p. 5).

a grouping of processes could indicate that they belong to each other. According to the method engineering discipline we regard this aspect to belong to the modelling language and is thus described in its meta model MM_L (see [1], p. 405). So, the semantics communicated by the layout of the graph is included in $sem(C_{MM_L})$.

Individuals interpret the semantics of a model in different ways. This is the pragmatic aspect of a model. So, individuals assign a concrete pragmatics to any model element $(prag(E_c))$.

Moreover, the same can be said about the modelling methods and their description MM_L and MM_P. Individuals form their own interpretation of the meta model's concepts C_{MM_L}, C_{MM_P} ($prag(C_{MM_L})$ and $prag(C_{MM_P})$). The pragmatics of any model element can now be described as $prag(E) = prag(E_c) \cup prag(C_{MM_L}) \cup prag(C_{MM_P})$.

These pragmatic aspects are assigned to a model by the model creators during the interactive modelling process. Because the pragmatics is manifested in the relation between the language expressions and the individuals who use them, it is not explicit in any model[4].

Models are used as an instrument for solving problems in different domains. Therefore, these models are usually created by domain experts rather than modelling experts. These domain experts may implement their knowledge in different ways in models because of their potential inexperience in modelling. Consequently, the pragmatic aspect of models needs to be addressed to migrate domain models.

In contrast, meta models are used for describing models. They are created by modelling experts only. Thus, the differences in the interpretation of different meta models will be minimal. Therefore, the pragmatic aspect of meta models will be neglected at this point.

To sum up the analysis so far: The information assigned to a model has not only semantic but particularly pragmatic aspects. These pragmatic aspects are not explicit in any model. Therefore, models are interpreted differently by different individuals. Consequently, we need to develop an organisational framework to examine under which circumstances reuse and migration of domain models is feasible. This will be the focus of the next subsection.

2.2   The Role Model

To take the pragmatic aspects of models into acount we must further analyse the roles involved in the modelling and the model migration process. The subsequent argumentation is summarised in figure 2.

---

[4] Important prerequisites to reduce the pragmatic influence in models are a rigorous definition of the modelling method, the suitability of this method for the problem and the rigorous use of this method. Many approaches have been developed to fulfil these requirements such as the Guidelines of Modelling (see [18]) and the use of ontologies (see [19] as one example). However, since pragmatics describes the usage of language expressions by individuals, each modeller will assign pragmatic aspects to models. Therefore, it will not be possible to completely rule out these pragmatic aspects.

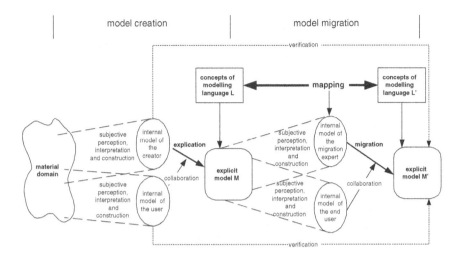

Fig. 2. Different roles in the modelling and migration process (see [20], p. 61)

To create a model at least two roles must be separated. On the one hand there is the creator of the model and on the other hand there is the one who uses the model to solve a specific problem. Both roles can be implemented by groups of different individuals or by a single person only.

During the modelling process people involved create automatically an internal model of the problem domain and explicate this model (external model) step by step in interaction with all other individuals. The process ends if everybody has reached a consensus about the internal and external models. Consequently, at the end each individual involved in this modelling process has the same understanding not only of the semantics but particularly of the pragmatics of the resulting model.

If the model M is to be transformed from its modelling language L to the modelling language L', two new roles – the migration expert and the end-user – are needed. The migration expert takes M as input and creates automatically an internal model of it. With the help of the modelling languages L and L' and the end user he or she creates the model M'.

If the migration expert did not carry the role of the user or the creator of the model M, a transformation of all information into the new modelling language is not possible, because of the implicit pragmatics. Consequently, a verification of the resulting model M' by its users or creators is necessary. This insight leads us to the initial migration process (see figure 3).

This process takes a model M created in a modelling language L as input and produces a model M' of a modelling language L' ($L \neq L'$) as output. We expect the resulting model M' to have the following properties:

Fig. 3. Initial process model

1. M' is syntactically correct against L',
2. M' has the same semantics as M and
3. M' has the same pragmatics as M for the creator, user, migration expert and the end-user.

Additionally, the *information loss* – the information lost because of the semantic weakness of the destination language – and the *information deficit* – the information added to the source model because of the semantic richness of the destination language – must be determined explicitly.

To enhance the effectiveness of the migration process the migration expert should work independently from the creator and user of the initial model M. Furthermore, the process should be automated as far as possible.

In the next subsection we show how the transformation process itself can be unfolded.

2.3   Migration Costs

To analyse the transformation process in detail we first concentrate on different techniques for model migration. Second, we analyse the costs of these techniques. Third, we develop our own framework on that basis.

There are two different ways for migrating a model M created with a modelling language L to a model M' in a modelling language L'.

1. The migration can be founded on the model M only. This means that the language descriptions MM_L and $MM_{L'}$ are not used for the transformation.
2. The migration can also be done by using the meta models. That means the migration expert must determine the concepts of MM_L used in M and must create a mapping of these concepts to $MM_{L'}$. After this mapping the concrete model elements of M can be transformed.

The first approach describes a remodelling of the problem domain but disregards the semantics of the meta model concepts. Therefore, we follow the second approach.

To analyse this approach in further detail the costs of the transformation process must be considered. The converter that implements this transformation determines these costs. This converter has three responsibilities:

1. Mapping of the concepts C_{MM_L} to $C_{MM_{L'}}$.
2. Transformation of all instances of the concepts C_{MM_L} into their counterparts $\left(I_{C_{MM_L}}\ \text{to}\ I_{C_{MM_{L'}}}\right)$.

3. Determination of the information loss and the information deficit for each mapping.
4. Layout of the visual model M'.

Let the costs for creating the converter be K_c, the costs of the transformation itself K_t and the costs for the information loss during the conversion be K_i [5]. The overall costs of a transformation K_o calculates as $K_o = K_t + K_i + K_c/n$, where n is the number of models converted by the converter K.

The transformation process must not be completed in one single step. There are at least three possibilities to complete this operation (see figure 4 and [22]).

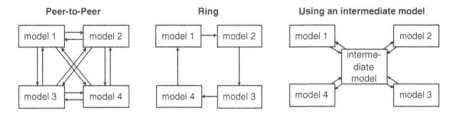

Fig. 4. Possibilities of converting a model (see [21], p. 5 figure 2.1; [22])

1. *Peer to peer migration*: This means, that models are translated directly from M to M' using a single converter for each pair of modelling languages. For this concrete mapping the transformation costs and costs of information loss are low. Since each converter works only for a pair of languages the costs of the converters are high (low n). Consequently, this strategy works for a small number of languages.
2. *Ring migration*: The model is transformed in a ring structure from M over $M_{i1}, M_{i2}, ..., M_{in}$ to M' in this case. The costs of this transformation are rather high, since up to $l - 1$ transformations are needed (where l is the number of languages). K_i is also high because the errors made during one transformation are added up. The costs of the converter are rather low, because only two converters are needed for each modelling language and it can be reused very often. The ring transformation can be used for a medium amount of languages.
3. *Migration with an intermediate model*: With this strategy a model is translated into an intermediate language L_i first and second transformed to the language L'. This involves two transformation steps. Thus, the transformation costs are higher than in the peer to peer approach while the information

---

[5] The information loss, which stems from the different semantics of the corresponding concepts of the two modelling languages is not important for this cost aspect since it is inherent to the migration process. Relevant for the transformation costs is the information loss that occurs because of the nature of the transformation process itself.

loss is low. Only l converters are needed for l languages so that the converters can often be reused (high n). The creation of the intermediate modelling language L_i is expensive, since it must cover all concepts of the modelling languages involved. So K_c/n is moderate. This approach is suited for a high number of modelling languages.

Generally, we follow the peer to peer migration. This allows on the one hand low costs for the model migration, but on the other hand requires a high number of converters. To reduce the number of converters, we use an intermediate meta-model, which provides a mapping between the concepts C_{MM_L} and $C_{MM_{L'}}$. With this mapping the model can be transformed directly from L to L' (see figure 5 for the unfolded process).

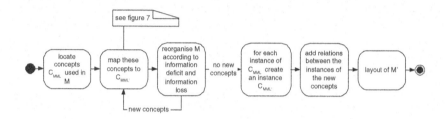

Fig. 5. Process model for the transformation process

The process starts with the determination of all meta model concepts C_{MM_L} in M. Second, these concepts can be mapped to the language L' (1:n mapping). This step reveals the information loss and deficit of this mapping. Third, because of this information deficit or loss the migration expert might decide to remodel M. Fourth, according to the mapping of the meta model concepts all instances of these concepts $I_{C_{MM_L}}$ in the model M are transformed to instances $I_{C_{MM_{L'}}}$ of the language L'. For each instance $I_{C_{MM_L}}$ the migration expert chooses the appropriate concept $C_{MM_{L'}}$ and creates an instance $I_{C_{MM_{L'}}}$. At this point of the transformation the information deficit and loss is known for the entire model. Fifth, the relations between the instances $I_{C_{MM_{L'}}}$ can be added. Lastly, M' can be laid out graphically.

As stated above the process cannot be completed automatically and always involves a human to address the pragmatic needs. Only the mapping of the language concepts C_{MM_L} and $C_{MM_{L'}}$ as well as the creation of the instances of $C_{MM_{L'}}$ can be automated. The migration expert must especially handle the information loss and must gain additional information to satisfy the information deficit. Additionally, the layout of the resulting diagram must be done manually[6].

---

[6] Automatic layout of diagrams is a mathematically difficult task. The main problem of laying out modelling graphs is to respect the specific graphical constraints defined in the modelling languages. Furthermore, modelling graphs contain a high number of vertexes, which make the layout process mathematically expensive (see [23]).

In the next section we present a meta model based migration approach including an intermediate meta model used to fulfil the step of mapping the language concepts to each other as well as to determine the information deficit and loss.

3   The Meta-model Based Migration Approach

3.1   The Intermediate Meta-model

The intermediate model is constructed for the purpose of the migration of models. Consequently, the concepts of different modelling languages that are viewed as semantically equivalent (for this purpose) must be related to each other.

For the sake of brevity we provide the intermediate model only for the modelling languages ERM (see [10]) and for simple UML class diagrams (see [12], p. 3-34ff). We use a UML class diagram for the description of the meta model itself.

The UML notation is extended by a special inheritance concept with the stereotype $<< eInheritance >>$. The graphical representation is a closed, filled arrow. All subclasses connected with this relation have the same meaning and are viewed as semantically equivalent and thus can be related to each other without information loss or deficit.

For the mapping of the concepts of the modelling languages the intermediate meta model is divided into two parts. First, the core meta model describes the core concepts needed to associate concepts of different modelling languages to each other. The core part is, second, extended by the concepts of the modelling languages involved using the $<< eInheritance >>$ relation. A stereotype with the name of the modelling technique is assigned to these concepts. Figure 6 shows the intermediate meta model.

We use the inheritance hierarchy to distinguish between general and specific concepts. The information deficit and loss can be determined by two factors. First, it is defined by additional attributes of the subclasses and second, by additional association and their specific counterparts aggregation and composition. This specification is summarised using the UML inheritance discriminator (see [12], p. 2-39).

The intermediate core meta model is the first part of the converter that maps the concepts of the modelling languages. The second part of the converter is the assignment of concrete language concepts to this core model. Third, we must describe how the actual mapping is derived from this meta model and how the information loss and deficit can be determined. These issues are discussed in the next subsection.

3.2   Process Model

After the concepts C_{MM_L} in M are determined (see figure 5) they can be located in the intermediate model by the algorithm depicted in figure 7.

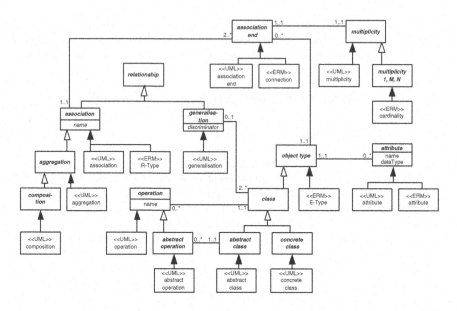

Fig. 6. The intermediate meta model

With this approach the destination concepts with no information loss and deficit result first. After this all special concepts (information deficit) are determined. If there is no result until this step, general concepts are found (information loss) and the whole process is repeated for these general concepts (information loss and deficit).

To illustrate the application of the complete framework an example is provided in the next subsection.

3.3 Application of the Meta-model Approach

Figure 8(a) shows the initial model, which is to be migrated to an ERM schema.

The first analysis step is to determine the UML concepts used in the initial model and to map these concepts to ERM concepts using the intermediate model. Table 1 shows the results of this step including the analysis of the information loss and deficit.

Because of this mapping the migration expert might decide to resolve the inheritance relation between **BusinessPartner**, **Customer** and **Supplier** (see figure 8(b)).

In this example there is already a 1:1 mapping between the UML and ERM concepts. So, the next step in the process model can be omitted and all instances $I_{C_{MM_L'}}$ can be created. After this step the migration expert lays out the model M' presented in figure 9. Finally, the user or creator of M verifies the resulting model.

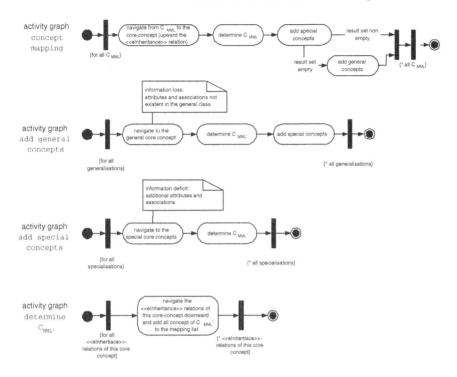

Fig. 7. Process to map the concepts of the language L to L' using the intermediate meta model

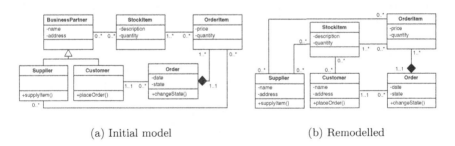

(a) Initial model   (b) Remodelled

Fig. 8. Model to be migrated

4   Summary

We have shown in this paper that the migration of models of a material problem domain needs to address the syntactic, semantic and pragmatic aspects of these models. Furthermore, we have provided a framework for this purpose. It consists of a role model, a process model and an – interchangeable – meta model based migration approach.

Table 1. Mapping of the UML concepts to ERM concepts

UML concept	ERM concept	information loss	information deficit
concrete class	E-type	operations	none
abstract class	E-type	abstract operations; operations	none
operation	-	complete	none
attribute	attribute	none	none
generalisation	association	relation to class	relation to association end, name
composition	association	dependency	none
multiplicity	cardinality	none	type of cardinality

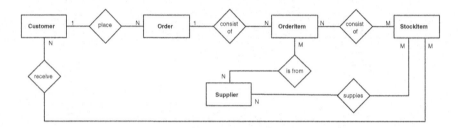

Fig. 9. Resulting Model

The role model of the migration process describes at least four roles, the modeller, the user (of the initial model M), the migration expert and the end-user (of the resulting model M'). In a material problem domain a complete migration of the model with its full semantic and pragmatic meaning is only feasible iff the migration expert is either the modeller itself (e. g. during the system development process) or the user of M or if the later verifies the resulting model. In all other cases there is a loss of information.

The process model consists of three core activities. First, the migration expert analysis the model M forming an internal model of it. Second, this model is transformed to the destination language L' using the mapping of the meta model concepts C_{MM_L} and $C_{MM_{L'}}$. The migration expert handels the information loss and deficit during this phase. Finally, the resulting model M' is verified by the creator or the user of M. Only this chain of activities ensures that the resulting model contains the same semantic and pragmatic information as the initial model M.

In this study the model migration framework was examined focusing on the aspect of modelling languages. Further research must concentrate on the aspect of modelling languages including the scientific findings of the semiotics. Additionally, we must incorporate the meta model of the modelling process into the framework, because it may lead to different models. Therefore, it may has an impact on the model migration.

References

1. Hofstede, A., Verhoef, T.: On the feasibility of situational method engineering. Information Systems **22** (1997) 401–422
2. Nuseibeh, B. A.: A multi-perspective framework for method integration. PhD thesis, University of London, Department of Computing (1994)
3. Harmsen, A. F.: Situational method engineering. Master's thesis, University of Twente (1997)
4. Brinkkemper, S., Saeki, M., Harmsen, F.: Assembly techniques for method engineering. Number 1413 in Lecture Notes of Computer Science, Springer (1998) 381–400
5. OMG: MDA guide version 1.0.1. Document Number: omg/2003-06-01, http://www.omg.org/docs/omg/03-06-01.pdf, Download: 19.02.2003 (2003)
6. Sprinkle, J.M.: Metamodel driven model migration. PhD thesis, Graduate School of Vanderbilt University, Nashville, Tennessee (2003)
7. Czarnecki, K., Helsen, S.: Classification of model transformation approaches. In: OOPSLA 2003, 2nd OOPSLA Workshop on Generative Techniques in the constext of the Model Driven Architecture http://www.softmetaware.com/oopsla2003/czarnecki.pdf, Download: 27.02.2004 (2003)
8. Stachowiak, H.: General model theory. Springer, Vienna (1973) – in German
9. Dresbach, S.: Modeling by construction: A new methodology for constructing models for decision support. http://www.winfors.uni-koeln.de/pub/wp_mbc.htm, Download: 25.11.2003 Working Paper 5, Chair for Business, Information Science and Operations Research, University of Cologne, Germany (1995)
10. Chen, P. P. S.: The entity relationship model – toward a unified view of data. ACM Transactions on Database Systems **1** (1976)
11. Keller, G., Nüttgens, M., Scheer, A. W.: Semantic process modelling on the basis of event-driven process chains (EPC). http://www.iwi.uni-sb.de/Download/iwihefte/heft89.pdf, Download: 27.02.2004, Technical Report 89, Publications of the Institute of business and computing, University of Saarland (1992) – In German
12. OMG: OMG unified modeling language specification: Version 1.5. Document Number: formal/03-03-01, http://www.omg.org/cgi-bin/apps/doc?formal/03-03-01.pdf, Download: 27.02.2004 (2003)
13. Guizzardi, G., Pires, L. F., van Sinderen, M. J.: On the role of domain ontologies in the design of domain-specific visual modeling languages. http://www.cis.uab.edu/info/OOPSLA-DSVL2/Papers/Guizzardi.pdf, Download: 06.11.2003 In: OOPSLA 2002 Second Workshop on Domain Specific Visual Languages, November 4, 2002, Seattle, WA, USA (2002)
14. Harel, D., Rumpe, B.: Modeling languages: Syntax, semantics and all that stuff, part I: The basic stuff. http://wisdomarchive.wisdom.weizmann.ac.il/archive/00000071/01/00-16.ps, Download: 22.11.2003 Technical report msc00-16, Weizmann Institute Of Science (2000)
15. Schefe, P.: Software engineering and epistemology. Informatik Spektrum **22** (1999) 122–135 – In German
16. Greiffenberg, S.: Methods as theories in the business and informations science discipline. In: Proceedings of the 6th international conference of business and information science, Physica (2003) 947–967 – In German

17. Gurr, C.A.: Effective diagrammatic communication: Syntactic, semantic and pragmatic issues. Journal of Visual Languages and Computing **10** (1999) 317–342
18. Becker, J., Rosemann, M., von Uthmann, C.: Guidelines of business process modeling. Volume 1806 of Lecture Notes in Computer Science, Springer (2000) 30–49
19. Weber, R.: Ontological foundations of information systems. Coopers & Lybrand (1997)
20. Schütte, R.: Guidelines of reference modelling: construction of configurable and adaptable models. Gabler (1998) – In German
21. Su, S.Y.W., Fang, S.C., Lam, H.: An object-oriented rule-based approach to data model and schema translation.
    http://citeseer.nj.nec.com/ su93objectoriented.html,
    Download: 10.10.1993, Technical Report TR-92-015, Database Systems Research and Development Center, University of Florida, USA (1992)
22. Wüstner, E., Hotzel, T., Buxmann, P.: Converting business documents: A classification of problems and solutions using xml/xslt. In: Proceedings of the 4th International Workshop on Advanced Issues of E-Commerce and Web-based Systems (WECWIS2002) (2002)
23. Jünger, M., Mutzel, P.: Automatic layout of diagrams. OR News (2001) 5–12 – In German

OLAP Hierarchies: A Conceptual Perspective*

Elzbieta Malinowski** and Esteban Zimányi

Department of Informatics CP 165/15
Université Libre de Bruxelles, 50 av. F.D. Roosevelt
1050 Brussels, Belgium
{emalinow,ezimanyi}@ulb.ac.be

Abstract. OLAP (On-Line Analytical Processing) tools support the decision-making process by giving users the possibility to dynamically analyze high volumes of historical data using operations such as roll-up and drill-down. These operations need well-defined hierarchies in order to prepare automatic calculations. However, many kinds of complex hierarchies arising in real-world situations are not addressed by current OLAP implementations. Based on an analysis of real-world applications and scientific works related to multidimensional modeling, this paper presents a conceptual classification of hierarchies and proposes graphical notations for them based on the ER model. A conceptual representation of hierarchies allows the designer to properly represent users' requirements in multidimensional modeling and offers a common vision of these hierarchies for conceptual modeling and OLAP tools implementers.

1 Introduction

Decision-making users increasingly rely on Data Warehouses (DWs) as an important platform for data analysis. DW architecture and tools provide the access to historical data with the aim of supporting the strategic decisions of organizations.

The structure of a DW is usually represented using the star/snowflake schema, also called multidimensional schema, consisting of fact tables, dimension tables, and hierarchies [9].

A *fact table* represents the subject orientation and the focus of analysis. It typically contains *measures* that are attributes representing the specific elements of analysis, such as quantity sold, sales. A *dimension table* includes attributes allowing the user to explore the measures from different perspectives of analysis. These attributes are called *dimension levels*[1] [5, 6, 7]. The dimension levels may form a hierarchy, such as City – State – Country, allowing the user to see detailed as well as generalized data. Further, a dimension may also have descriptive attributes called *property attributes*[2][8] that are not used in hierarchy, such as Store number, E-mail address, etc.

---

* This work was funded by a scholarship of the Cooperation Department of the Université Libre de Bruxelles.
** Currently on leave from the Universidad de Costa Rica.
[1] Other names, such as *dimension attributes* [5] or *category attributes* [15] are also used.
[2] They also are called *non-dimension attributes* [5].

A. Persson and J. Stirna (Eds.): CAiSE 2004, LNCS 3084, pp. 477–491, 2004.
© Springer-Verlag Berlin Heidelberg 2004

Property attributes are orthogonal to dimension levels and they complement each other [2].

On-Line Analytical Processing (OLAP) tools allow decision-making users to dynamically manipulate the data contained in a DW. OLAP tools use hierarchies for allowing both a general and a detailed view of data using operations such as drill-down and roll-up.

Although OLAP tools have been successfully used in decision-support systems for many years, they can only manage a limited number of hierarchies comparing to those existing in real-world applications. Usually, OLAP tools only cope with hierarchies that ensure summarizability or that can be transformed so that summarizability conditions hold [10, 11]. Summarizability refers to the correct aggregation of measures in a higher hierarchy level taking into account existing aggregations in a lower hierarchy level.

In this paper, we adopt a conceptual approach and propose an extension of the ER model for representing hierarchies appearing in real-world applications as well as a categorization of such hierarchies. The benefits of using conceptual models in database design have been acknowledged for several decades; however, the domain of conceptual design for multidimensional modeling is still at a research stage. As stated in [17], the analysis of achievements in data warehouse research showed the little interest of the research community in conceptual multidimensional modeling. The proposed conceptual models do not cope with the different kinds of hierarchies existing in real-world applications. Some of these models formally define and offer special notations for commonly-known hierarchies. In many cases, these notations can be extended to manage other kinds of hierarchies proposed in this work. However, there is a lack of a general classification of hierarchies, including their characteristics at the schema and at the instance levels. This situation leads to repeated research efforts in "rediscovering" hierarchies and providing solutions for managing them.

Presenting the different kinds of hierarchies in a systematic way will help OLAP tools implementers to focus on implementation issues, e.g., they can enhance the system performance materializing the aggregated measures of common hierarchy levels or ensure meaningful combination of hierarchies. Further, a DW is in continuous development, coping with new analysis requirements and incorporating new structures. Therefore, a conceptual representation of the hierarchies facilitates this evolution and mitigates the possible technology changes. Furthermore, conceptual hierarchies establish a better communication bridge between decision-making users and designer/implementer.

This paper is organized as follows. Section 2 proposes different kinds of hierarchies including their notations. Section 3 refers to works related to representing hierarchies in different multidimensional models, and Section 4 gives conclusions and future perspectives.

2   Hierarchies and Their Categorization

We define a hierarchy as follows. A *hierarchy* is a set of binary relationships between dimension levels. A dimension level participating in a hierarchy is called *hierarchical level* or in short *level*. The sequence of these levels is called a *hierarchical path* or in short *path*. The number of levels forming a path is called the *path length*. The first level of a hierarchical path is called *leaf* and the last is called *root*. The root represents the most generalized view of data. Given two consecutive levels of a hierarchy, the higher level is called *parent* and the lower level is called *child*. Every instance of a level is called *member*. The *cardinality* indicates the minimum and maximum numbers of members in one level that can be related to a member of another level.

Even though in some works the root of a hierarchy is represented using a level called ALL, we consider that its inclusion in a conceptual graphical representation can be ambiguous or meaningless for decision-making users.

Hierarchies are usually presented using a *flat table*, as shown in Figure 1 a), or using a normalized structure called *snowflake scheme*, as shown in Figure 1 b) [9].

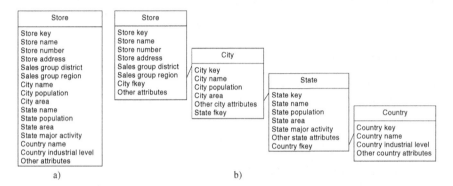

Fig. 1. Flat table (a) and snowflake (b) representations of hierarchies.

Instead of representing hierarchies at a logical level, we propose to adopt a conceptual perspective and use the ER-like graphical notations shown in Figure 2. Some of these notations are inspired from [18, 19, 20].

A fact relationship represents an n-ary relationship among several dimensions; it can contain attributes called *measures* describing this relationship. Since the roles of a fact relationship always have (0,N) cardinality, we omit such cardinalities to simplify the model.

On the other hand, the relationship linking the levels of a hierarchy is a usual binary relationship and can be represented with the same symbol as the fact relationship. However, since such relationships are only used for traversing from one level to the next one, we propose to represent hierarchies using the graphical notation of Figure 2 c). Notice that if a hierarchy level has specific property attributes, they can be included without ambiguity (Figure 2 c). This enriches the expression power of the model and gives more clarity by grouping the property attributes into their corresponding levels.

Hierarchies can express different structures according to the criteria used for analysis, for example, geographical location, organizational structure, etc. We propose to represent these criteria in the model using a special symbol (Figure 2 e) linking the dimension to be analyzed (leaf level) with the hierarchy. Making this criterion explicit is important since, as will be shown in Section 2.4, the same dimension (e.g., an employee) can be analyzed according to several criteria (e.g., home location and work location), possibly sharing the same hierarchy levels.

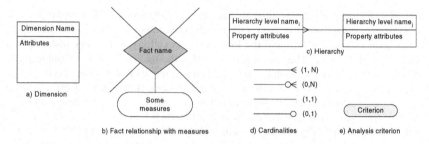

Fig. 2. Notations for multidimensional model: (a) dimension, (b) fact relathiship, (c) hierarchy, (d) cardinalities, and (e) analysis criterion.

2.1 Simple Hierarchies

Simple hierarchies are those hierarchies where the relationship between their members can be represented as a tree. Further, these hierarchies use only one criterion for analysis. Simple hierarchies can be further categorized into symmetric, asymmetric, and generalized hierarchies.

Figure 3 shows the symmetric hierarchy from Figure 1 b) using the proposed notations. A *symmetric hierarchy*[3] has at the schema level only one path where all levels are mandatory (Figure 3 a). At the instance level the members form a tree where all the branches have the same length (Figure 3 b). As implied by the cardinalities, all parent members must have at least one child member and a child member cannot belong to more than one parent member. In commercial systems, this kind of hierarchies is commonly represented at the logical level using a star/snowflake schema.

Another type of simple hierarchy is called an *asymmetric hierarchy*[4] [9]. Such hierarchies have only one path at the schema level (Figure 4 a) but, as implied by the cardinalities, some lower levels of the hierarchy are not mandatory. Thus, at the instance level the members represent a non-balanced tree (Figure 4 b), i.e., the branches of the tree have different lengths since some parent members will not have associated child members. As for symmetric hierarchies, the cardinalities imply that every child member may belong to at most one parent member.

Figure 4 a) shows a hierarchy where a bank consists of several branches: some of them have agencies with ATM, some only agencies, and small branches do not have any organizational divisions. Figure 4 b) illustrates some instances of this hierarchy. As shown in the figure, cardinalities clearly indicate the levels that may be leaves for some branches of the tree, as it is the case for Branch, since it can be related to zero or more Agencies.

Asymmetrical hierarchies are not easy to manage at the implementation level. A typical solution either transforms an asymmetrical hierarchy into a symmetrical one, introducing placeholders for the shorter branches of the tree [13, 15], or uses the representation of the parent-child relationships existing between the hierarchy members [13, 14].

---

[3] Such hierarchies are also called *homogenous* [7], *balanced* [13], or *level-based* [14].
[4] Several terms are used: *non-balanced* [13], *non-onto* [15].

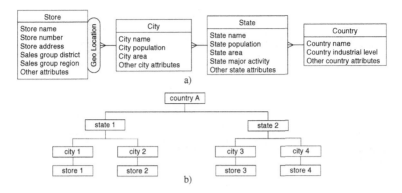

Fig. 3. A symmetric hierarchy (a) model and (b) example of instances.

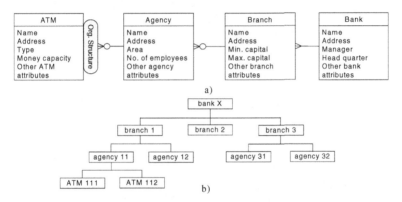

Fig. 4. An asymmetric hierarchy: (a) schema and (b) examples of instances.

Other kinds of hierarchies existing in real-world applications have been explored in the literature, although no commercial system cope with them. Sometimes a dimension includes subtypes that can be represented by the generalization/specialization relationship [1, 12]. Moreover, the specialized subtypes can include their own hierarchy. Figure 5 shows an example where the Customer dimension can be specialized into Company and Person, each of them having its own hierarchy: the hierarchy for the subtype Company consists on the levels Company Type-Sector-Branch-Area while the hierarchy for the Person subtype is formed by the levels Profession Name-Category-Branch-Area. Both subtypes include common levels for Branch and Area.

While both hierarchies can be represented independently repeating the common levels, the complexity of the schema reduces if it is possible to represent shared levels characterized by the same granularity of aggregation. Also, to ensure adequate measure aggregations, the distinction between specific and common hierarchy levels should be clearly represented in the model [6, 7]. However, existing multidimensional conceptual models do not offer this distinction. This work proposes the graphical notation shown in Figure 6 where the common and specific hierarchy levels are represented. We call such hierarchies generalized.

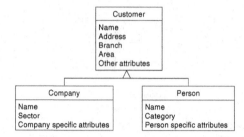

Fig. 5. Specialization of Customer into Company and Person with common and specific hierarchy levels.

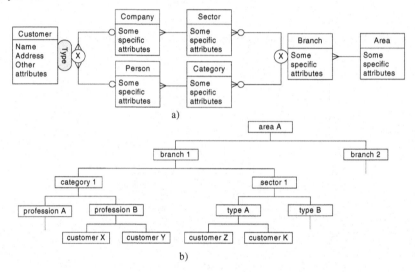

Fig.6. A generalized hierarchy for a sales company: (a) schema and (b) examples of instances.

At the schema level a *generalized hierarchy* can contain multiple exclusive paths sharing some levels. All these paths represent one hierarchy and account for the same analysis criterion. At the instance level each member of the hierarchy can belong to only one of the paths. We propose to include the symbol Ⓧ to indicate that paths are exclusive. Such a notation is equivalent to the {xor} annotation used in UML [3].

Currently, it is not possible to manage generalized hierarchies in commercial tools. If the members differ in hierarchy structure, the common solution is to treat each of the subtypes as a separate dimension with its own hierarchy. This solution has the disadvantages of not allowing to analyze the data according to common hierarchy levels and makes the structure more complex.

Generalized hierarchies include a special case commonly referred as *non-covering hierarchies* [13, 15]. An example of this kind of hierarchy is illustrated in Figure 7 representing a company that has offices in different countries; however, the geographical division in these countries is different, e.g., skipping the division into counties for some countries.

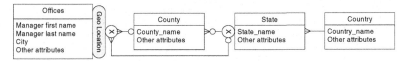

Fig. 7. A non-covering hierarchy.

Thus, a non-covering hierarchy is a special case of a generalized hierarchy with the additional restrictions that at the schema level (1) the root and the leaves are the same for all paths and (2) only one (or several) intermediate level(s) can be skipped without including additional levels.

A logical-level implementation for generalized hierarchies will either (1) ignore the specific levels and use only the common levels for roll-up and drill-down operations, or (2) take into account the existing hierarchy levels for every hierarchy member. Some proposals of logical-level solutions for this kind of hierarchy have been already described [2, 5, 10] and used in commercial systems [13]. For example, Microsoft Analysis Services [13] allows the definition and manipulation of non-covering hierarchies called *ragged hierarchies*. They can be represented in a flat table or in a parent-child structure. It is possible to display such hierarchies in different ways using the dimension properties *Hide Member If* and *Visible*.

2.2 Non-strict Hierarchies

For the simple hierarchies presented before we assumed that each link between a parent and child levels has one-to-many cardinalities, i.e., a child member is related to at most one parent member and a parent member may be related to several child members. However, a many-to-many cardinality between parent and child levels is very common in real-life applications: e.g., an employee working in several departments, a diagnosis belonging to several diagnosis groups [15], a week that may belong to two consecutive months, etc.

We call a hierarchy *non-strict* if at the schema level it has at least one many-to-many cardinality; it is called *strict* if all cardinalities are one-to-many. The fact that a hierarchy is strict or not is orthogonal to its type. Thus, the different kinds of hierarchies already presented can be either strict or non-strict.

Figure 8 a) shows a symmetric non-strict hierarchy where employees may work in several sections. Since at the instance level, a child member may have more than one parent member, the members of the hierarchy form a graph (Figure 8 b).

There are several possibilities to manage this kind of hierarchy at the logical level. For example, using a *bridge table* [9], transforming the non-strict hierarchy into a strict hierarchy [15], or changing the model into the dimensional normal form proposed by [10].

2.3 Multiple Hierarchies

Multiple hierarchies represent the situation where at the schema level there are several non-exclusive simple hierarchies sharing some levels. However, all these hierar-

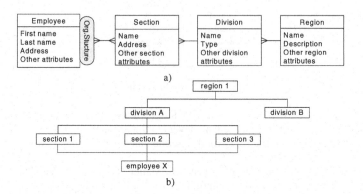

Fig. 8. A symmetric non-strict hierarchy: (a) model and (b) example of instances.

chies account for the same analysis criterion[5]. At the instance level such hierarchies form a graph since a child member can be associated with more than one parent member belonging to different levels. The nodes at which the parallel hierarchies split and join are called, respectively, *splitting level* and *joining level*.

Multiple hierarchies can be inclusive and alternative. In a *multiple inclusive hierarchy* all members of the splitting level participate simultaneously in parent levels belonging to different hierarchies. Thus, when traversing the hierarchy (e.g., during roll-up operation), the measure presented in a fact relationship must be distributed between several hierarchies. We use the symbol $\oplus$ to represent the requirement of measure distribution.

An example of a multiple hierarchy is presented in Figure 9 where sport club' activities are classified into association and recreation programs. Here, both hierarchies are simple and share the level of Regional Committee. They represent the same analysis criterion of sport activity type. Currently, multiple inclusive hierarchies are not considered in OLAP tools.

In *multiple alternative* hierarchies it is not semantically correct to simultaneously traverse the different composing hierarchies. The user must choose one of the alternative hierarchies for analysis. An example is given in Figure 10 where the Time dimension includes two hierarchies corresponding to calendar periods: Month-Quarter-Year and Week-Year. As can be seen in the example it is meaningless to combine both hierarchies.

Multiple alternative hierarchies can be implemented in commercial tools, for example in Microsoft Analysis Services [13]. However, meaningless intersections may appear since there are no restrictions for simultaneously combining the simple hierarchies composing a multiple hierarchy.

Notice that even though generalized and multiple hierarchies share some levels and use only one analysis criterion, they can be easily distinguished from each other.

---

[5] As we will see in Section 2.4, hierarchies with multiple paths accounting for different criteria are called parallel hierarchies.

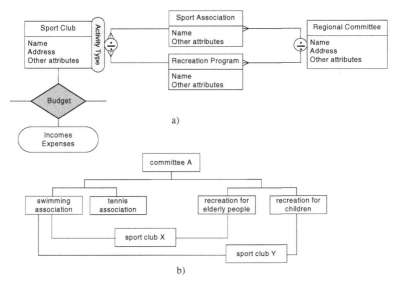

a)

b)

Fig. 9. Example of a multiple inclusive hierarchy: (a) model and (b) instances.

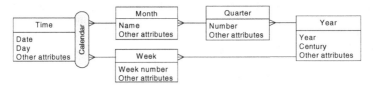

Fig. 10. A multiple alternative hierarchy.

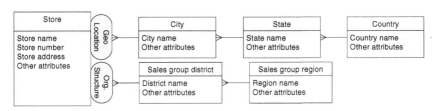

Fig. 11. Parallel independent hierarchies associated to one dimension.

2.4 Parallel Hierarchies

Parallel hierarchies arise when a dimension has associated several hierarchies accounting for different analysis criteria. These hierarchies can be composed of different kinds of hierarchies presented before. Such hierarchies can be independent or dependent.

In a *parallel independent hierarchy,* the different hierarchies do not share levels, i.e., they represent non-overlapping sets of hierarchies. An example is given in Figure 11.

In contrast, *parallel dependent hierarchies*, have different hierarchies sharing some levels. An example is given in Figure 12. It represents an international company that sells products and analyzes the achievements of their employees. The dimension Sales Employee contains two hierarchies: one symmetric that represents the sales organization structure and other one, non-covering, that represents the geographic division of the address of the sales employee. Both hierarchies share the common levels of State and Country.

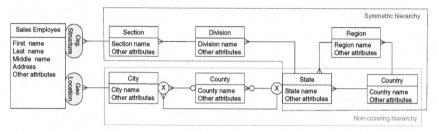

Fig. 12. Parallel dependent hierarchies including symmetric and non-covering hierarchies.

Notice that both multiple and parallel dependent hierarchies share some level(s). However, the main distinction between them is that parallel dependent hierarchies account for different analysis criteria. Thus, the user can use them independently during the analysis process. Moreover, for multiple alternative hierarchies as well as for parallel dependent hierarchies the fact that the shared level(s) are explicitly represented is important since, at the implementation level, the aggregated measures for these levels can be reused. For example, Microsoft OLAP Server [13] already adopted this solution for their multiple alternative hierarchies.

2.5 Metamodel

This section summarizes the proposed classification of hierarchies using the metamodel of Figure 13.

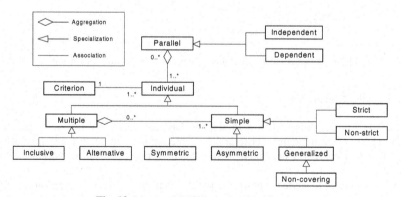

Fig. 13. Metamodel of hierarchy classification.

Parallel hierarchies can be specialized into independent and dependent hierarchies. A parallel hierarchy is an aggregation of individual hierarchies. Each individual hierarchy is associated with one analysis criterion, while the same criterion can be used for many individual hierarchies. An individual hierarchy can be simple or multiple.

Simple hierarchies are divided into symmetric, asymmetric, and generalized hierarchies. Also, generalized hierarchies include the special case of non-covering hierarchies. Moreover, for each of these simple hierarchies, another specialization can be applied, making them strict or non-strict. Multiple hierarchies are composed of one or more simple hierarchies. Additionally, multiple hierarchies can be specialized into inclusive and alternative.

3   Related Work

Table 1 compares conceptual multidimensional models that, at the best of our knowledge, cope with hierarchies. We use four symbols for their comparison: blank space indicates no reference to the hierarchy exists, ± a definition of the hierarchy is presented, □ the hierarchy can be represented in the model, and √ a definition and a graphical representation are given. In case that a different name for a hierarchy is proposed, it is included in the table. All the models include explicitly or implicitly the strict and parallel independent hierarchies. On the other hand, none of the models refer to multiple inclusive hierarchies. Thus, we omit them in Table 1. However, none of the models take into account different analysis criteria applied for hierarchies; in consequence, the multiple alternative and parallel dependent hierarchies cannot be distinguished.

Pedersen et al. [15] presents different types of hierarchies appearing in a healthcare application. They distinguish some of the hierarchies presented in this work as can be seen in Table 1. Other kinds of hierarchies (such as generalized and parallel) are not considered in his work.

Hüsemann et al. [8] adopt a conceptual model approach based on functional dependencies and a multidimensional normal form [10] to ensure correctness of schemas. Their model represents two kinds of hierarchies: symmetric and what they called multiple. The latter category is further divided into optional and alternative hierarchies corresponding to, respectively, generalized and multiple alternative hierarchies.

Golfarelli et al. [5] propose a conceptual model called DFM based on directed, acyclic, and weakly-connected graphs. This graphical model allows to represent symmetric and parallel independent hierarchies. The model is also able to represent other hierarchies (Table 1) although it is difficult to distinguish them.

Tryfona et al. [19] propose the StarER model, an extension of the ER model. They refer to different kinds of hierarchies based on Pedersen's work and showed that their graphical model is able to represent hierarchies as shown in Table 1. Since they do not refer to generalized hierarchies as discussed in this paper, their model does not make the difference between this and multiple hierarchies.

Sapia et al. [18] develop an extension of the ER model called ME/R model. With respect to hierarchy modeling, they allow to represent only symmetric and multiple alternative hierarchies or parallel dependent. Similarly to the previous model, ME/R can be extended to manage some of the hierarchies presented in this work (Table 1).

Table 1. Comparison of the models with different kinds of hierarchies.

Hierarchy /Model	Symmetric	Asymmetric	Generalized	Non-covering	Non-strict	Multiple alternative or Parallel dependent
[15]	Onto ±	Non-onto ±		Non-covering ±	Non-strict ±	Multiple ±
[8]	Simple √		Multiple Optional √	±		Multiple alternative √
[5]	√		□	□		√
[19]	√	□			Non-strict √	Multiple √
[18]	√					√
[16]	Classification ±	Aggregation[6] ±	Aggregation[6], Multiple[6] ±	Aggregation[6] ±		Multiple[6] Multiplicity ±
[6]	Strictly homogenous ±	Homogenous ±	Heterogeneous ±	Heterogeneous ±		Heterogeneous ±
[1]	√		□		√	√
[12]	√		Specialization □	√	√	Multiple, Alternative √
[20]	√			√	±	□

Purabbas et al. [16] define a classification hierarchy that corresponds to symmetric hierarchies. Their definition of aggregation hierarchies includes asymmetric, generalized, and non-covering hierarchies without making clear distinction between them. They do not allow the existence of non-strict hierarchies. Moreover, their definition of multiple hierarchies can be applied to generalized, multiple alternative, and parallel dependent hierarchies.

Hurtado et al. [6, 7] define homogenous and heterogeneous hierarchies. The former include symmetric and asymmetric hierarchies. The latter can be used for generalized, non-covering, and multiple alternative or parallel dependent hierarchies. They extended the notion of summarizability to heterogeneous hierarchies by including constraints that can be applied for the logical-level implementation of the hierarchies proposed in this paper. They do not focus on conceptual modeling and a graphical representation of them.

Abelló et al. [1] proposed a conceptual multidimensional model called YAM^2 based on UML. According to hierarchies, their model allows to include symmetric, non-strict, and multiple alternative hierarchies using the part-whole relationship.

Luján-Mora et al. [12] represent hierarchies using the UML model. They consider hierarchies as specified in Table 1. They distinguish a categorizing dimension based on the specialization/generalization relationship. Using this representation, they do not focus on hierarchies that include common and specific levels as proposed in this work for generalized hierarchy.

---

[6] No distinction can be made for different kinds of hierarchies.

Tsois et al. [20] propose the MAC model, which is used for modeling OLAP scenarios. Regarding to hierarchy specification, even if they refer informally to some of hierarchies proposed by this work; they do not propose a graphical representation for them.

Current commercial OLAP products do not allow conceptual modeling of different kinds of hierarchies. They usually represent multidimensional model limited to star or snowflake view of data without distinguishing different kinds of hierarchies. Further, ADAPT (Application Design for Analytical Processing Technologies) [4] even though introduces new features for multidimensional modeling such as dimension scope, dimension context, it does not include different kinds of hierarchies limiting the graphical representation to hierarchies commonly-used in OLAP tools. These implementation-level tools allow to manage symmetric and parallel hierarchies, some of them extends their product functionalities and include asymmetric, and non-covering hierarchies [13, 14].

4 Conclusions

Nowadays many organizations use data warehouses to support the decision-making process. Data warehouses are defined using a multidimensional model that includes measures, dimensions, and hierarchies. OLAP tools allow interactively querying and reporting a multidimensional database using operations such as drill-down and roll-up. OLAP tools exploit the defined hierarchies in order to automatically aggregate the measures to be analyzed. However, although many kinds of hierarchies can be found in real-world applications, current OLAP tools manage only a limited number of them.

Therefore, designers must apply different "tricks" at the implementation level to transform some hierarchy types into simple ones. Moreover, there is not a common classification and representation of the different kinds of hierarchies. Thus, when the user requires complex multidimensional analysis including several kinds of hierarchies, this situation is difficult to model and therefore it is not clear how to implement it.

In this paper, we took a conceptual approach and studied in a systematic way the different kinds of hierarchies referring them to a common multidimensional model. We also proposed a graphical notation for representing such hierarchies in conceptual models.

We distinguished simple and multiple hierarchies. The latter are composed of one or more simple hierarchies accounting for the same analysis criterion and include the inclusive and alternative hierarchies. This distinction is important since simple hierarchies generate tree structures for instances whereas multiple hierarchies generate acyclic graph structures. Moreover, simple hierarchies include further types: symmetrical, asymmetrical, generalized, and non-covering hierarchies. We also analyzed the case where the usual one-to-many cardinality linking a child level to a parent level in the hierarchy is relaxed to many-to-many leading to non-strict hierarchies. Finally, we discussed the situation where several hierarchies accounting for different analysis criteria may be attached to the same dimension. Depending on whether they share or not common levels, we called them parallel dependent and parallel independent hierarchies, respectively.

The proposed hierarchy classification will help designers to build conceptual models of multidimensional databases used in decision-support systems. This will give decision-making users a better understanding of the data to be analyzed, and provide a better vehicle for studying how to implement such hierarchies using current OLAP tools. Moreover, the proposed notation allows a clear distinction of each type of hierarchy taking into account their differences at the schema as well as at the instance levels. Most of the existing conceptual multidimensional models do not distinguish between the different kinds of hierarchies proposed in this paper, although some of these models can be extended to take into account the proposed hierarchy classification. Further, the proposed hierarchy classification provides OLAP tool implementers the requirements needed by business users for extending the functionality offered by current OLAP tools.

The present work belongs to a larger project aiming at developing a conceptual methodology for data warehouses. We are currently developed mappings for transforming the different kinds of hierarchies into relational model. This logical level also includes the analysis of summarizability as well as dimensional and multidimensional normal forms. We are also working on the inclusion of spatial and temporal features into the model.

References

1. Aballó A., Samos J., Saltor F. YAM^2 (Yet Another Multidimensional Model): An extension of UML. In *Proc. of the Int. Database Engineering and Application Symposium*, pp. 172-181, 2002.
2. Bauer A., Hümmer W., Lehner W. An Alternative Relational OLAP Modeling Approach. In *Proc. of the 2nd Int. Conf. on Data Warehousing and Knowledge Discovery*, pp. 189-198, 2000.
3. Booch G., Jacobson I., Rumbaugh J. *The Unified Modeling Language: User Guide*. Addison-Wesley, 1998.
4. Bulos D., Forsman S. Getting Started with ADAPT™ OLAP Database Design. *White Paper*. http://www.symcorp.com/download/ADAPT%20white%20paper.pdf, 1998.
5. Golfarelli M., Rizzi S. A Methodological Framework for Data Warehouse Design. In *Proc. of the 1st ACM Int. Workshop on Data Warehousing and OLAP*, pp. 3-9, 1998.
6. Hurtado C., Mendelzon A. Reasoning about Summarizabiliy in Heterogeneous Multidimensional Schemas. In *Proc. of the 8th Int. Conf. on Database Theory*, pp. 375-389, 2001.
7. Hurtado C., Mendelzon A. OLAP Dimension Contraints. In *Proc. of the 21st ACM Int. Conf. on Management of Data and Symposium on Principle of Databases Systems*, pp. 169-179, 2002.
8. Hüsemann B., Lechtenbörger J., Vossen G. Conceptual Data Warehouse Design. In *Proc. of the Int. Workshop on Design and Management of Data Warehouses*, p. 6, 2000.
9. Kimball R., Ross M., Merz R. *The Data Warehouse Toolkit: The Complete Guide to Dimensional Modeling*. John Wiley & Sons, 2002.
10. Lehner, W., Albrecht J., Wedekind H. Normal Forms for Multidimensional Databases. In *Proc. of the 10th Int. Conf. on Scientific and Statistical Database Management*, pp. 63-72, 1998.
11. Lenz H. and Shoshani A. Summarizability in OLAP and Statistical Databases. In *Proc. of the 9th Int. Conf. on Scientific and Statistical Database Management*, pp. 132-143, 1997.

12. Luján-Mora S., Trujillo J., Song I. Multidimensional Modeling with UML Package Diagrams. In *Proc. of the 21ˢᵗ Int. Conf. on Conceptual Modeling,* pp. 199-213, 2002.
13. Microsoft Corporation. *SQL Server 2000. Books Online.* (Updated – Service Pack 3). http://www.microsoft.com/sql/techinfo/productdoc/2000/books.asp, 2003.
14. Oracle Company. Oracle 9i OLAP User's Guide, http://otn.oracle.com/products/bi/pdf/ Userguide.pdf, 2002.
15. Pedersen T., Jensen Ch., Dyreson C. A foundation for Capturing and Querying Complex Multidimensional Data. *Information Systems,* 26(5): 383-423, 2001.
16. Pourabbas E., Rafanelli M. Characterization of Hierarchies and Some Operators in OLAP Environment. In *Proc. of the 2ⁿᵈ ACM Int. Workshop on Data Warehousing and OLAP,* pp. 54-59, 1999.
17. Rizzi S. Open Problems in Data Warehousing: 8 Years Later. In *Proc. of the 5ᵗʰ Int. Workshop on Design and Management of Data Warehouses,* http://sunsite.informatik.rwth-aachen.de/ Publications/CEUR-WS/Vol-77/keynote.pdf, 2003.
18. Sapia C., Blaschka M., Höfling G., Dinter B. Extending the E/R Model for Multidimensional Paradigms. In *Proc. of the 17ᵗʰ ER Int. Workshop,* pp. 105-116, 1998.
19. Tryfona N., Busborg F., Borch J. StarER: A Conceptual Model for Data Warehouse Design. In *Proc. of the 2ⁿᵈ ACM Int. Workshop on Data Warehousing and OLAP,* pp. 3-8, 1999.
20. Tsois A., Karayannidis N., Sellis T. MAC: Conceptual Data Modeling for OLAP. In *Proc. of the Int. Workshop on Design and Management of Data Warehouses,* p. 5, 2001.

Analysing Slices of Data Warehouses to Detect Structural Modifications

Johann Eder[1], Christian Koncilia[1], and Dieter Mitsche[2]

[1] University of Klagenfurt
Dep. of Informatics-Systems
{eder,koncilia}@isys.uni-klu.ac.at
[2] Swiss Federal Institute of Technology in Zurich (ETHZ)
Institute of Theoretical Computer Science
dmitsche@inf.ethz.ch

Abstract. Data Warehouses provide sophisticated tools for analyzing complex data online, in particular by aggregating data along dimensions spanned by master data. Changes to these master data is a frequent threat to the correctness of OLAP results, in particular for multi- period data analysis, trend calculations, etc. As dimension data might change in underlying data sources without notifying the data warehouse we are exploring the application of data mining techniques for detecting such changes and contribute to avoiding incorrect results of OLAP queries.

1 Introduction

A data warehouse is an integrated, usually materialized view over several data sources, e.g., data that comes from On-Line Transaction Processing systems, from spreadsheets, from the world wide web or from other sources. Data Warehouses are building blocks for many information systems, in particular systems supporting decision making, controlling, revision, customer relationship management (CRM), etc.[WB97, HLV00]. The most popular architectures are multidimensional data warehouses (data cubes) where facts (transaction data) are "indexed" by several dimensions representing a hierarchical organization of master data.

In this paper, we will address the problem of how to detect changes in these dimensions. To the best of our knowledge only [EKM03] focuses on this problem. Whereas the approach presented in [EKM03] was very much trimmed to cope with the important question of performance in data warehouses and focuses on identifying only simple types of structural changes, we will present a second approach in this paper that analyzes the data in more detail to get a better quality of the detected structural changes. Furthermore, we will provide some experiments and a comparison of both approaches.

Although data warehouses are typically deployed to analyse data from a longer time period than transactional databases, they are not well prepared for changes in the structure of the dimension data. This surprising observation originates in the (implicit) assumption that the dimensions of data warehouses

A. Persson and J. Stirna (Eds.): CAiSE 2004, LNCS 3084, pp. 492–505, 2004.

ought to be orthogonal, which, in the case of the dimension time means that all other dimensions ought to be time-invariant.

When analysts place their queries they have to know which dimension data changed. If the analyst wants analyze the population of European countries along the last 20 years, he or she has to be aware of the reunification of Germany, the separation of Slovenia, Croatia, etc. Although in this example the structural changes are obvious there are also hidden changes. For instance, when data that stems from the web is being analyzed the sources might change in a way that effects the structures in the data warehouse but without any notification about the changes.

In this paper we address the following important issue: how can such structural changes be recognized, even if the sources do not notify the data warehouse about the changes. This defensive strategy, of course, can only be an aid to avoid some problems, it is not a replacement for adequate means for managing knowledge about changes. Nevertheless, in several practical situations we trace erroneous results of OLAP queries back to structural changes not known by the analysts and the data warehouse operators. Erroneous in the sense that the resulting data did not correctly represent the state of affairs in the real world.

As means for detecting such changes we propose the use of data mining techniques. In a nutshell, the problem can be described as a multidimensional outlier detection problem. We will discuss two different approaches to solve this problem.

The problem is related to the effects of structural changes in data warehouses and approaches to overcome the problems they cause were subject of several projects [Yan01, BSH99, Vai01, CS99] including our own efforts [EK01, EKM02] to build a temporal data warehouse structure with means to transform data between structural versions such that OLAP tools work on data cleaned of the effects of structural changes.

The remainder of this paper is organized as follows: in section 2 we will discuss the different types of structural changes in data warehouse dimensions. In section 3 we will briefly overview different data mining techniques for automatic detection of structural changes is issued. In section 4 we will discuss two different approaches in depth. In section 5 we will present the results of different experiments we conducted. Finally, we conclude in section 6.

2   Types of Structural Changes

A multidimensional view on data consists of a set of measures arranged by different dimensions [OLA97]. Hence, a cube can also be seen as an n-dimensional array. Measures are numerical values that are referenced by a vector $\nu = (DM_1, DM_2, ..., DM_n)$ where DM_i is a member belonging to dimension D_i [Kur99].

Typical examples of dimensions frequently found in multidimensional databases are *Time*, *Facts* or *Products*. The structure of each dimension is defined by a set of categories. For instance, the dimension *Time* could consist of the categories *Year*, *Quarter* and *Month* that are in the hierarchical relation $Year \rightarrow Quarter \rightarrow Month$ ($A \rightarrow B$ means that B rolls-up to A).

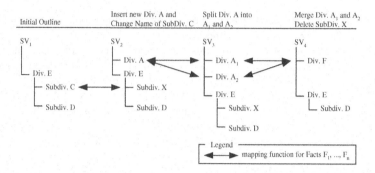

Fig. 1. An example of structural changes

Each category consists of a set of dimension members. Dimension members define the instances of a data warehouse schema. For instance, *January, February* and *March* are dimension members assigned to the category *Month*.

We will now briefly discuss different types of structural changes. Furthermore, we will argue why some of these structural changes do not need to be detected automatically.

In [EK01] we showed how the basic operations INSERT, UPDATE and DELETE have to be adopted for a temporal data warehouse. With respect to dimension members these basic operations may be combined to represent the following complex operations:

i.) SPLIT: One dimension member M splits into n dimension members, M_1, ..., M_n.

For instance, Figure 1 shows a split operation between the structure versions SV_2 and SV_3 where a division *"Div.A"* splits up into two divisions *"Div.A_1"* and *"Div.A_2"*.

ii.) MERGE: n dimension members $M_1, ..., M_n$ are merged together into one dimension member M.

A merge is the opposite to a split, i.e. a split in one direction of time is always a merge in the opposite direction of time. Consider, for the example given above, that these modifications occur at the timepoint T. For each analysis that requires measures from a timepoint before T for the structure version which is valid at timepoint T we would call these modifications "a split". For each analysis that requires measures from timepoint T for a structure version valid before timepoint T these modifications would be called "a merge".

iii.) CHANGE: An attribute of a dimension member changes, for example, if the product number or the name of a department changes. Such a modification can be carried out by using the update operation defined above.

With respect to dimension members representing facts, CHANGE could mean that the way how to compute measures changes (for example, the way how to compute the unemployment rate changed in Austria because they joined the European Union in 1995) or that the unit of facts changes (for instance, from Austrian Schillings to EURO).

iv.) MOVE: A dimension member moves from one parent to another, i.e., we modify the hierarchical position of a dimension member.

v.) NEW-MEMBER: A new dimension member is inserted.

vi.) DELETE-MEMBER: A dimension member is deleted.

For two of these operations, namely NEW-MEMBER and DELETE-MEM-BER, there is no need to use data mining techniques to automatically detect these modifications. When loading data from data sources for a dimension member which is new in the data source but does not exist in the warehouse yet, the NEW-MEMBER operation is detected automatically by the ETL-Tool (extraction, transformation and loading tool). On the other hand, the ETL-Tool automatically detects when no fact values are available in the data source for deleted dimension members.

3   Data Mining Techniques

In this section a short overview of different data mining techniques for automatic detection of structural changes is issued.

The simplest method for detecting structural changes is the calculation of deviation matrices. Absolute and relative differences between consecutive values, and differences in the shares of each dimension member between two chronons can be easily computed - the runtime of this approach is clearly linear in the number of analyzed values. Since this method is very fast, it should be used as a first sieve.

A second approach whose runtime complexity is in the same order as the calculation of traditional deviation matrices is the attempt to model a given data set with a stepwise constant differential equation (perhaps with a simple functional equation). This model, however, only makes sense if there exists some rudimentary, basic knowledge about factors that could have caused the development of certain members (but not exact knowledge, since in this case no data mining would have to be done anymore). After having solved the equation (for solution techniques of stepwise differential equations refer to [Dia00]), the relative and absolute differences between the predicted value and the actual value can be considered to detect structural changes.

Other techniques that can be used for detecting structural changes are mostly techniques that are also used for time-series analysis:

- *autoregression* - a significantly high absolute and relative difference between a dimension member's actual value and its predicted value is an indicator for a structural change of that dimension member. Several models to predict data may be used (for instance, the *AutoRegression Moving Average* (p,q)-model or the *AutoRegression Integrated Moving Average*(p,d,q)-model).
- *autocorrelation* - the usage of this method is similar to the method of autoregression. The results of this method, however, can be easily visualized with the help of correlograms.

- *crosscorrelation* and *regression* - these methods can be used to detect significant dependencies between two different members. Especially a very low correlation coefficient (a very inaccurate prediction with a simple regression model, respectively) could lead to the roots of a structural change.
- *discrete fourier transform (DFT)*, *discrete cosine transform (DCT)*, different types of *discrete wavelet transforms* - the maximum difference (scaled by mean of the vector) as well as the overall difference (scaled by mean and length of the vector) of the coefficients of the transforms of two dimension members can be used to detect structural changes.
- *singular value decomposition (SVD)* - unusually high differences in singular values can be used for detecting changes in the measure dimension when analyzing the whole data matrix. If single dimension members are compared, the differences of the eigenvalues of the covariance matrices of the dimension members (= *principal component analysis*) can be used in the same way.

In this paper, due to lack of space no detailed explanation of these methods is given, for details refer to [Atk89] (fourier transform), [Vid99] (wavelet transforms), [BD02] (autoregression and -correlation), [Hol02] (SVD and principal component analysis), [Wei85] (linear regression and crosscorrelation).

4   Different Data Mining Approaches

In this section different ways of treating the fact that the data are referenced over a set of n dimensions are presented. Since in data warehouses there is usually a multidimensional view on the data, the techniques shown in the previous section have to be applied carefully. If all structure dimensions are considered simultaneously and a structural change occurred in one structure dimension, it is impossible to detect the dimension that was responsible for this change. Two approaches to solve this problem are presented: the first one analyzes matrices that result from grouping all values along one dimension whereas the second one analyzes matrices where in all but one structure dimensions a special dimension member is fixed. Finally, a short comparison of the efficiency and runtime complexity of the two approaches is given.

Before the start of one of the two approaches, the whole data matrix should be checked for changes in the measure dimension: differences of the sums of all absolute values of two consecutive chronons are calculated. Under the assumption, that the number of chronons C is very small compared to the number of dimension members in structure dimensions, this step can be neglected for the analysis of overall runtime complexity (only $O(C)$ values have to be analyzed). If the differences between two consecutive chronons are substantially bigger than those between other chronons, then this is an indicator for a change in the measure dimension. Changes at this level that are detected must be either corrected or eliminated - otherwise the results in both of the following approaches will be biased by these errors; if one change (e.g. a change in the calculation of the formula) is detected and the data are corrected (e.g. then all values are noted in the same currency), it is recommended to repeat this difference calculation

- maybe further changes in the measure dimension can be detected. If no further change in the measure dimension can be recognized, then one of the two following approaches may proceed.

4.1 Approach 1: Grouping along One Dimension

This approach consists of different steps of analyzing the data and is therefore best explained by the following enumeration:

1.) In the first step of this approach the data are grouped by one structure dimension. The deviation matrices that were described in section 3 can be applied here to detect dimension members that were affected by structural changes.

2.) If the data grouped by one structure dimension can be adequately modelled with a stepwise constant differential equation (or a simple functional equation) then also the deviation matrices that calculate the absolute and relative difference between the model-estimated value and the actual value should be used.

3.) In each structure dimension where one dimension member is known that definitely remained unchanged throughout all chronons (fairly stable so that it can be considered as a dimension member with an average development, mostly a dimension member with rather big absolute values), other data mining techniques such as autocorrelation, autoregression, discrete fourier transform, discrete wavelet transform, principal component analysis, cross-correlation and linear regression can be used to compare this 'average' dimension member with any other dimension member detected in steps 1 and 2. If one of the methods shows big differences between the average dimension member and the previously detected dimension member, then this is an indicator for a structural change of the latter one. Hence, these methods on the one hand are used to make the selection of detected dimension members smaller, on the other hand they are also used to 'prove' the results of the previous steps. However, all these methods should not be applied to a dimension member that is lacking values, whose data are too volatile or whose values are often zero. If no 'average' dimension member is known, the dimension members that were detected in previous steps can also be compared with the sum of the absolute values of all dimension members. In any case, it is for performance reasons recommended to use the method of autocorrelation at first; among all wavelet transforms the Haar method is the fastest.

4.) If in steps 1, 2 and 3 no (or not all) structural changes are detected and one still assumes structural changes, then the values are grouped by $i+1$ structure dimensions, where i ($i = 1 \ldots n - 1$, n = number of structure dimensions) is the number of structure dimensions that were used for grouping values in the current step. Again, steps 1, 2 and 3 can be applied.

To make the idea of this approach clear, one small example is given. If you consider the data given in table 1, the whole data set seems to be very volatile

Table 1. Structural changes in a data warehouse with four structure dimensions

SD_1	SD_2	SD_3	SD_4	$year_1$	$year_2$	$year_3$	$year_4$
SD_{11}	SD_{21}	SD_{31}	SD_{41}	100	20	60	18
SD_{11}	SD_{21}	SD_{31}	SD_{42}	200	40	80	122
SD_{11}	SD_{21}	SD_{32}	SD_{41}	300	60	20	6
SD_{11}	SD_{21}	SD_{32}	SD_{42}	400	80	40	54
SD_{11}	SD_{22}	SD_{31}	SD_{41}	500	500	700	210
SD_{11}	SD_{22}	SD_{31}	SD_{42}	600	600	800	1290
SD_{11}	SD_{22}	SD_{32}	SD_{41}	700	700	500	150
SD_{11}	SD_{22}	SD_{32}	SD_{42}	800	800	600	950
SD_{12}	SD_{21}	SD_{31}	SD_{41}	900	180	220	66
SD_{12}	SD_{21}	SD_{31}	SD_{42}	1000	200	240	394
SD_{12}	SD_{21}	SD_{32}	SD_{41}	1100	220	180	54
SD_{12}	SD_{21}	SD_{32}	SD_{42}	1200	240	200	326
SD_{12}	SD_{22}	SD_{31}	SD_{41}	1300	1300	1500	450
SD_{12}	SD_{22}	SD_{31}	SD_{42}	1400	1400	1600	2650
SD_{12}	SD_{22}	SD_{32}	SD_{41}	1500	1500	1300	390
SD_{12}	SD_{22}	SD_{32}	SD_{42}	1600	1600	1400	2310

SD=structure dimension, SD_{ij}=j-th dimension member in structure dimension i

at first sight (especially between $year_3$ and $year_4$). Since no changes in the measure dimension can be detected, the approach may proceed by grouping all values along one structure dimension. On the resulting view the differences of shares of dimension members are calculated (this deviation matrix was chosen because it shows the outliers most clearly in this case) - the results are presented in table 2; it is clearly pointed out that there are strong indicators for a structural change in structure dimension SD_2 between $year_1$ and $year_2$, for a structural change in structure dimension SD_3 between $year_2$ and $year_3$ and for a structural change in structure dimension SD_4 between $year_3$ and $year_4$ (in this example with just two dimension members per structure dimension the changes in the one member have to be counted up in the other - it is therefore not known whether between $year_1$ and $year_2$ dimension member SD_{21} or SD_{22} changed. In real-world data warehouses with many more dimension members, however, it usually is clear which dimension member changed). Here, due to lack of space steps 2 and 3 are omitted; if one assumes further structural changes, the detected structural changes have to be corrected, and the above deviation matrix can be calculated once again. In this case, however, all differences of all dimension members between all years are zero - all dimension members stay unchanged throughout the four years. Hence, a further analysis of combined structural changes is useless.

4.2   Approach 2: Fixing $n-1$ Dimension Members

The previous approach might detect many examples in his first step, but not all of them. This approach therefore does not group values along one dimension,

Table 2. Detection of changes in the structure dimension

$\Delta(\%)$	$year_{12}$	$year_{23}$	$year_{34}$
SD_{11}	3.19%	0%	0%
SD_{12}	-3.19%	0%	0%
SD_{21}	**-27.22%**	0%	0%
SD_{22}	**27.22%**	0%	0%
SD_{31}	0.8%	**10.17%**	0%
SD_{32}	-0.8%	**-10.17%**	0%
SD_{41}	0.4%	0%	**-33.22%**
SD_{42}	-0.4%	0%	**33.22%**

SD=structure dimension, SD_{ij}=j-th dimension member in structure dimension i,
$\Delta(\%)$=change in share of a dimension member between two consecutive years,
$year_{mn}$=comparison of shares of different dimension members between year m and year n

Table 3. A small data warehouse with a structural change

SD_1	SD_2	$year_1$	$year_2$	$year_3$	$year_4$
SD_{11}	SD_{21}	200	190	200	205
SD_{11}	SD_{22}	150	155	165	160
SD_{11}	SD_{23}	30	29	**49**	48
SD_{11}	SD_{24}	200	220	215	205
SD_{12}	SD_{21}	200	190	200	205
SD_{12}	SD_{22}	150	155	165	160
SD_{12}	SD_{23}	30	29	**49**	48
SD_{12}	SD_{24}	200	220	215	205
SD_{13}	SD_{21}	200	190	200	205
SD_{13}	SD_{22}	150	155	165	160
SD_{13}	SD_{23}	30	29	**9**	9
SD_{13}	SD_{24}	200	220	215	205
SD_{14}	SD_{21}	200	190	200	205
SD_{14}	SD_{22}	150	155	165	160
SD_{14}	SD_{23}	30	29	**9**	9
SD_{14}	SD_{24}	200	220	215	205

SD_{ij}=j-th dimension member in structure dimension i

but it fixes $n-1$ dimension members and analyzes the remaining n-th structure dimension on the matrices addressed by those fixed dimension members.

Consider the following example with two dimensions SD_1 with four dimension members $SD_{11}, \ldots, SD_{14}$ and SD_2 with four dimension members $SD_{21}, \ldots, SD_{24}$. Their values for four consecutive years for a certain measure are shown in table 3. As boldly pointed out, there has been a structural change in four of the sixteen combinations of dimension members in $year_3$ (marked in bold).

When grouping the values along one structure dimension (as suggested in the previous section), the change cannot be recognized anymore, as table 4 shows.

Table 4. Values of the small data warehouse grouped along one dimension

SD	$year_1$	$year_2$	$year_3$	$year_4$
SD_{11}	580	594	629	618
SD_{12}	580	594	629	618
SD_{13}	580	594	589	579
SD_{14}	580	594	589	579
SD_{21}	800	760	800	820
SD_{22}	600	620	660	640
SD_{23}	120	116	116	118
SD_{24}	800	880	860	820

$SD_{ij}=j$-th dimension member in structure dimension i

Any data mining technique attempting to find the real change in this matrix will not work.

The solution of this approach to cope with this problem is different from the previous one: in all but one structure dimensions one dimension member is fixed; this combination of fixed dimension members leads to a simple 2-dimensional matrix with the time dimension on the x-axis and the only dimension that was excluded on the y-axis. In other words, instead of aggregating all values along one dimension (as shown in the previous section), the data matrix is cut into different slices that are analyzed separately. On this data matrix a simple deviation matrix with relative differences is computed (more sophisticated techniques should not be applied since this might cause a very poor performance): let $data(i,j)$ denote the value of the original 2-dimensional matrix, and let $d(i,j)$ denote the value of the resulting deviation matrix in row i and column j (the value of the i-th dimension member of the excluded dimension between chronons j and $j+1$), then $d(i,j)$ is computed as follows:

$$d(i,j) = \begin{cases} \Delta(i,j)/max(i,j), & \text{if } \Delta(i,j)/max(i,j) \leq 0, \\ 1, & else, \end{cases}$$

where $\Delta(i,j) := abs(data(i,j) - data(i,j-1))$, and
$max(i,j) := max(abs(data(i,j)), abs(data(i,j-1))), \forall i = 1, \ldots, n, \forall j = 2, \ldots, m$.
Using this normalization $d(i,j)$ can be interpreted as the probability that a structural change of the i-th dimension member of the dimension on the y-axis has occurred between chronon j and $j+1$. All these 'probabilities' over all possible matrices with the same dimension on the y-axis are summed and divided through the number of possible matrices (since not necessarily all possible combinations of dimension members of different dimensions have to have values in the data warehouse it is recommended to use a counter of occurrences when implementing this approach) - in this way a robust estimate for the probability is computed. Hence, the final result of this approach is a probability matrix P for each structure dimension, where $P_k(i,j)$ indicates the probability of a structural change of the i-th dimension member in structure dimension k between chronon j and $j+1$.

Table 5. Values of structure dimension SD_2 on slice $SD_1 = SD_{11}$ (same result on slice $SD_1 = SD_{12}$)

$SD_1 = SD_{11}$	$year_1$	$year_2$	$year_3$	$year_4$
SD_{21}	200	190	200	205
SD_{22}	150	155	165	160
SD_{23}	30	29	49	48
SD_{24}	200	220	215	205

$SD_{ij}=j$-th dimension member in structure dimension i

Table 6. Values of structure dimension SD_2 on slice $SD_1 = SD_{11}$ (same result on slice $SD_1 = SD_{12}$)

$SD_1 = SD_{13}$	$year_1$	$year_2$	$year_3$	$year_4$
SD_{21}	200	190	200	205
SD_{22}	150	155	165	160
SD_{23}	30	29	9	9
SD_{24}	200	220	215	205

$SD_{ij}=j$-th dimension member in structure dimension i

Table 7. Probabilities of a structural change in structure dimension SD_2 on slice $SD_1 = SD_{11}$ (same result on slice $SD_1 = SD_{12}$)

$SD_1 = SD_{11}$	$year_{12}$	$year_{23}$	$year_{34}$
SD_{21}	0.05	0.05	0.024
SD_{22}	0.032	0.06	0.03
SD_{23}	0.033	0.408	0.02
SD_{24}	0.09	0.022	0.047

$SD_{ij}=j$-th dimension member in structure dimension i,
$year_{ij}=$difference between $year_i$ and $year_j$

The effectiveness of this approach is illustrated at the data given in table 3. In tables 5 and 6 all possible slices for dimension SD_2 are presented, and in tables 7 and 8 the corresponding deviation matrices are presented. Similarly, all four matrices for dimension SD_1 are computed (matrices not shown here). The final probability matrices for structure dimension SD_1 and SD_2 are presented in tables 9 and 10, respectively. If the probability threshold for a structural change is 10%, then the detected structural changes are all values in tables 9 and 10 that are marked in bold typeface.

As can be seen from the probability matrices, there is a relatively high probability (0.549, see table 10) of a structural change of dimension member SD_{23} between $year_2$ and $year_3$; this change even affected the values of all dimension members in structure dimension SD_1 (see table 9): the values of all dimension members between $year_2$ and $year_3$ are higher than the threshold of 10%. In such a case it is useful to increase the threshold to detect the real source of the

Table 8. Probabilities of a structural change in structure dimension SD_2 on slice $SD_1 = SD_{13}$ (same result on slice $SD_1 = SD_{14}$)

$SD_1 = SD_{13}$	$year_{12}$	$year_{23}$	$year_{34}$
SD_{21}	0.05	0.05	0.024
SD_{22}	0.032	0.06	0.03
SD_{23}	0.033	0.69	0
SD_{24}	0.09	0.022	0.047

SD_{ij}=j-th dimension member in structure dimension i,
$year_{ij}$=difference between $year_i$ and $year_j$

Table 9. Probability matrix P for structure dimension SD_1

P	$year_{12}$	$year_{23}$	$year_{34}$
SD_{11}	0.052	**0.135**	0.03
SD_{12}	0.052	**0.135**	0.03
SD_{13}	0.052	**0.206**	0.025
SD_{14}	0.052	**0.206**	0.025

SD_{ij}=j-th dimension member in structure dimension i,
$year_{ij}$=difference between $year_i$ and $year_j$

Table 10. Probability matrix P for structure dimension SD_2

P	$year_{12}$	$year_{23}$	$year_{34}$
SD_{21}	0.05	0.05	0.024
SD_{22}	0.032	0.06	0.03
SD_{23}	0.033	**0.549**	0.01
SD_{24}	0.09	0.022	0.047

SD_{ij}=j-th dimension member in structure dimension i,
$year_{ij}$=difference between $year_i$ and $year_j$

structural change. However, in real data warehouses, there are usually more than four dimension members in a structure dimension - if in the previous example there were 100 dimension members in structure dimension, then the change of dimension member SD_{23} would only have an insignificant effect on the probability matrix of structure dimension SD_1; in any case, it is important to find the right threshold for the method.

4.3   Comparison of the Two Approaches

When comparing the two different approaches shown in section 4.1 and 4.2 the differences become clear: whereas the first approach is very much trimmed to cope with the important question of performance in data warehouses and focuses on identifying only simple types of structural changes, the second approach analyzes the data in more detail to get a better quality of the detected structural changes. More formally, if D_i denotes the number of dimension members in dimension i, $i = 1, \ldots, n$ (ordered in such a way that $D_1 \geq D_2 \geq \ldots \geq D_n$), then in the first step (which is often the only step when choosing this approach) of the first approach only $O(D_1)$ values have to be analyzed, in the i-th step $O(D_1^i)$ (it is again assumed that the number of chronons C is small compared to D_1, therefore it is neglected in the complexity order). In the second approach for each structure dimension $O(D_1 * D_2 * \ldots * D_{n-1})$ matrices have to be computed, since all possible combinations of dimension members in $n - 1$ structure dimensions can address a matrix. This is valid for all n structure dimensions, but since only one structure dimension is analyzed at once, the overall runtime complexity is also $O(D_1 * D_2 * \ldots * D_{n-1})$ (again under the assumption that C is very small compared to D_i, i=1,…,n). The second approach tries to use the fact that the results of the analysis are not immediately necessary for daily business but are part of long-term strategic planning - therefore it should not cause troubles if the analysis might last for a couple of days.

5 Experiments

Both approaches were tested on different data sets. The running times of the different approaches as well as precision and recall of both approaches are listed in table 11 below.

All running times were measured on a Pentium III 866 MhZ processor with 128 MB SDRAM. In all examples three structure dimensions and one time dimension with the same number of dimension members in each dimension were used, and 4-5 structural changes in certain dimension members were hidden.

As can be seen from table 11, two things are most remarkable: on the one hand the running time of the 'grouping' approach is far lower than the running time of the 'fixing' approach, on the other hand the 'grouping' approach does not detect structural changes when they appear in dimension members with small absolute values - their contribution to the overall sum of all dimension members is vanishingly small; hence these changes remain undetected (in the third data set all changes were designed to happen in such dimension members - and precision and recall are very bad - 0 %!).

Table 11. Running times, precision and recall for both approaches on test data sets

#d. mem	file size	$time(G)$	$time(F)$	$Precision(G)$	$Recall(G)$	$Precision(F)$	$Recall(F)$
20	1.44 MB	0.11	12.85	100%	100%	100%	100%
35	8.52 MB	0.11	68.66	100%	80%	100%	80%
35	11.1 MB	0.11	67.77	0%	0%	100%	100%
60	136 MB	0.99	1'521.3	100%	100%	100%	100%

G='Grouping' data along one structure dimension, F='Fixing' $n-1$ structure dimensions; running times for both approaches are measured in seconds; differences in file sizes between second and third data set are due to different data types (integer vs. real) - megabytes represent file sizes of simple textfiles; # d. mem = number of dimension members in each of the three structure dimensions and in the time dimension

6   Conclusion

In the previous sections two different approaches for detecting changes in data warehouses were proposed; we showed that both approaches can detect structural changes in data warehouses - whereas the 'grouping' approach is faster, an application of the 'fixing' approach may yield better results. In our opinion the 'grouping' approach should be chosen if and only if the results are so urgent that the fixing approach is infeasible due to its high runtime complexity.

As a conclusion it can be said that in principle, the methods work well, but further work remains to be done in these areas:

- The thresholds for detecting structural changes in the different methods were so far just found by experience and 'trial and error'. Here more sophisticated methods (probably based on sub-sampling the data) for automatic, data-adapted fine-tuning of the thresholds still need to be investigated.
- The performance of the 'fixing' approach may become too bad in huge real-world data warehouses - sophisticated sub-sampling methods might hold the key for dealing with this important issue.

References

[Atk89]   K. E. Atkinson. *An Introduction to Numerical Analysis*. John Wiley, New York, USA, 1989.

[BD02]   P. J. Brockwell and R. A. Davis. *Introduction to Time Series Forecasting*. Springer Verlag, New York, USA, 2002.

[BSH99]   M. Blaschka, C. Sapia, and G. Höfling. On Schema Evolution in Multidimensional Databases. In *Proceedings of the DaWak99 Conference*, Florence, Italy, 1999.

[CS99]   P. Chamoni and S. Stock. Temporal Structures in Data Warehousing. In *Proceedings of the 1st International Conference on Data Warehousing and Knowledge Discovery (DaWaK'99)*, pages 353–358, Florence, Italy, 1999.

[Dia00]   F. Diacu. *An Introduction to Differential Equations - Order and Chaos*. W. H. Freeman, New York, USA, 2000.

[EK01]   J. Eder and C. Koncilia. Changes of Dimension Data in Temporal Data Warehouses. In *Proceedings of 3rd International Conference on Data Warehousing and Knowledge Discovery (DaWaK'01)*, Munich, Germany, 2001. Springer Verlag (LNCS 2114).

[EKM02]   J. Eder, C. Koncilia, and T. Morzy. The COMET Metamodel for Temporal Data Warehouses. In *Proceedings of the 14th International Conference on Advanced Information Systems Engineering (CAISE'02)*, Toronto, Canada, 2002. Springer Verlag (LNCS 2348).

[EKM03]   J. Eder, C. Koncilia, and D. Mitsche. Automatic Detection of Structural Changes in Data Warehouses. In *Proceedings of the 5th International Conference on Data Warehousing and Knowledge Discovery (DaWaK 2003)*, Prague, 2003. Springer Verlag (LNCS 2737).

[HLV00]   B. Hüsemann, J. Lechtenbörger, and G. Vossen. Conceptual Data Warehouse Design. In *Proceedings of the International Workshop on Design and Management of Data Warehouses (DMDW 2000)*, Stockholm, 2000.

[Hol02]   J. Hollmen. Principal component analysis, 2002.
            URL: http://www.cis.hut.fi/~jhollmen/dippa/node30.html
[Kur99]   A. Kurz. *Data Warehousing - Enabling Technology*. MITP-Verlag, Bonn, 1
            edition, 1999.
[Mad03]   S. Madnick. Oh, so That Is What You Meant! The Interplay of Data Quality
            and Data Semantics. In *Proceedings of the 22nd International Conference on
            Conceptual Modeling (ER 2003)*, Chicago, IL, USA, 2003. Springer Verlag
            (LNCS 2813).
[OLA97]   OLAP Council. *The OLAP Council: OLAP and OLAP Server Definitions*.
            OLAP Council, 1997.
            URL: http://www.olapcouncil.org/research/glossaryly.htm
[Vai01]   A. Vaisman. Updates, *View Maintenance and Time Management in Multi-
            dimensional Databases*. Universidad de Buenos Aires, 2001. Ph.D. Thesis.
[Vid99]   B. Vidakovic. *Statistical Modeling by Wavelets*. John Wiley, New York, USA,
            1999.
[WB97]   M. Wu and A. Buchmann. Research Issues in Data Warehousing. In *Daten-
            banksysteme in Büro, Technik und Wissenschaft (BTW'97) GI-Fachtagung*,
            Ulm, Germany, 1997.
[Wei85]   S. Weisberg. *Applied Linear Regression*. John Wiley, New York, USA, 1985.
[Yan01]   J. Yang. *Temporal Data Warehousing*. Stanford University, June 2001. Ph.D.
            Thesis.

Empirical Validation of Metrics
for Conceptual Models of Data Warehouses

Manuel Serrano[1], Coral Calero[1], Juan Trujillo[2],
Sergio Luján-Mora[2], and Mario Piattini[1]

[1] Alarcos Research Group, Escuela Superior de Informática
University of Castilla – La Mancha
Paseo de la Universidad, 4, 13071 Ciudad Real
{Manuel.Serrano,Coral.Calero,Mario.Piattini}@uclm.es
[2] Dept. de Lenguajes y Sistemas Informáticos
Universidad de Alicante
Apto. Correos 99. E-03080
{jtrujillo,slujan}@dlsi.ua.es

Abstract. Data warehouses (DW), based on the multidimensional modeling, provide companies with huge historical information for the decision making process. As these DW's are crucial for companies in making decisions, their quality is absolutely critical. One of the main issues that influences their quality lays on the models (conceptual, logical and physical) we use to design them. In the last years, there have been several approaches to design DW's from the conceptual, logical and physical perspectives. However, from our point of view, there is a lack of more objective indicators (metrics) to guide the designer in accomplishing an outstanding model that allows us to guarantee the quality of these DW's. In this paper, we present a set of metrics to measure the quality of conceptual models for DW's. We have validated them through an empirical experiment performed by expert designers in DW's. Our experiment showed us that several of the proposed metrics seems to be practical indicators of the quality of conceptual models for DW's.

Keywords: Data warehouse quality, data warehouse metrics

1 Introduction

Data warehouses, which have become the most important trend in business information technology, provide relevant and precise historical information enabling the improvement of strategic decisions [14]. A lack of quality can have disastrous consequences from both a technical and organizational points of view: loss of clients, important financial losses or discontent amongst employees [8]. Therefore, it is absolutely crucial for an organization to guarantee the quality of the information contained in these DW's from the early stages of a DW project.

The information quality of a data warehouse is determined by (i) the quality of the system itself and (ii) the quality of the data presentation (see figure 1). In fact, it is important not only that the data of the data warehouse correctly reflects the real world, but also that the data are correctly interpreted. Regarding data warehouse quality, three aspects must be considered: the quality of the DBMS (Database Manage-

A. Persson and J. Stirna (Eds.): CAiSE 2004, LNCS 3084, pp. 506–520, 2004.
© Springer-Verlag Berlin Heidelberg 2004

ment System) that supports it, the quality of the data models[1] used in their design (conceptual, logical and physical) and the quality of the data themselves contained in the data warehouse. In this paper, we will focus on the quality of the data models, and more concretely, on the quality of conceptual models.

Regarding logical and physical models, some approaches and methodologies have been lately proposed - see [1] and [25] for a detailed classification of conceptual, logical and physical models). Even more, several recommendations exist in order to create a "good" dimensional data model - the well-known and universal star schema by [15] or [12]. However, from our point of view, we claim that design guidelines or subjective quality criteria are not enough to guarantee the quality of a "dimensional" model for DW's.

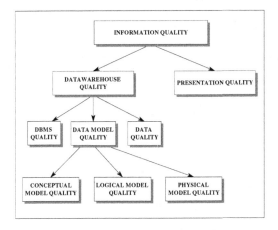

Fig. 1. Quality of the information and the data warehouse

Following this consideration, in the last years, we have been working in assuring the quality of logical models for DW's and have proposed and validated both formally [6] and empirically [20][21] several metrics that enable the evaluation of the complexity of star models (dimensional models) at the logical level.

Although conceptual modelling has not been a first priority in real world data warehouse projects, several approaches have been lately presented to represent the data warehouse information from a conceptual perspective. Some approaches propose a new notation [5][11], others use extended E/R models [19][23][7] and finally others use the UML class model [1][24][17]. Due to space constraints, we refer the reader to [1] for a detailed comparison and discussion about most of these models.

However, even using these approaches, to guarantee the quality of data warehouse conceptual models is a difficult task, with the exception of the model proposed by Jarke et al. [14], which is described in more depth in Vassiladis' Ph.D. thesis [25]. Nevertheless, even this model does not propose metrics that allow us to replace the intuitive notions of "quality" regarding the conceptual model of the data warehouse

---

[1] The term "model" refers to a modelling technique, language or model itself (eg. The E/R model) and "schema" refers to the result of applying this technique to a specific Universe of Discourse.

with formal and quantitative measures that reduce subjectivity and bias in evaluation, and guide the designer in his work. Recently, two proposals about data warehouse conceptual model metrics have appeared: [21] have proposed different metrics for model maintainability and Si-Saïd and Prat [22] have proposed some metrics for measuring multidimensional schemas analysability and simplicity. However, none of the metrics proposed so far has been empirically validated, and therefore, have not proven their practical utility. It is well known that empirical validation is crucial for the success of any software measurement project as it helps us to confirm and understand the implications of the measurement of the products [9][16]. Thus, in this work we show a first empirical validation of the metrics proposed by [21].

The proposed metrics have been defined for guaranteeing the quality of data warehouse conceptual models, focusing on the complexity of the models, which is one of the most important factors regarding the quality in data warehouses. In defining the metrics, we have used the extension of the UML (Unified Modeling Language) presented in [24][17]. This is an object-oriented conceptual approach for data warehouses that easily represents main data warehouse properties at the conceptual level.

The remain of the paper is structured as follows: Section 2 summarizes the conceptual model for DW's, based on the UML, which we will use as the framework to define our metrics. Section 3 defines the metrics for data warehouse conceptual models we will use in our study. Section 4 describes the empirical validation we have performed with the proposed metrics. Finally, Section 5 draws conclusions and introduces future investigation arising from this work.

2   Object – Oriented Conceptual Modelling with UML for Data Warehouses

In this section, we outline our approach[2] to data warehouse conceptual modelling, based on the UML. This approach has been specified by means of a UML profile[3] that contains the necessary stereotypes in order to carry out conceptual modelling successfully [17]. The main features of multidimensional modelling considered are the relationships "many-to-many" between the facts and one specific dimension, degenerated dimensions, multiple classification and alternative path hierarchies, and the non strict and complete hierarchies. In this approach, the structural properties of multidimensional modelling are represented by means of a UML class diagram in which the information is clearly organized into facts and dimensions.

Facts and dimensions are represented by means of fact classes and dimension classes respectively. Fact classes are defined as composite classes in shared aggregation relationships of n dimension classes. The minimum cardinality in the role of the dimension classes is 1 to indicate that all the facts must always be related to all the dimensions. The relations "many-to-many" between a fact and a specific dimension are specified by means of the cardinality 1...* in the role of the corresponding dimen-

---

[2] We refer the reader to (Trujillo et al., 2001; Luján-Mora et al. 2002) for a complete description of our approach.

[3] A *profile* is a set of improvements that extend an existing UML type of diagram for a different use. These improvements are specified by means of the extendibility mechanisms provided by UML (stereotypes, properties and restrictions) in order to be able to adapt it to a new method or model.

sion class. In our example in figure 2, we can see how the Sales fact class has a many-to-many relationship with the product dimension.

A fact is composed of measures or fact attributes. By default, all measures in the fact class are considered to be additive. For non-additive measures, additive rules are defined as constrains and are included in the fact class. Furthermore, derived measures can also be explicitly represented (indicated by /) and their derivation rules are placed between braces near the fact class.

Our approach also allows the definition of identifying attributes in the fact class (stereotype OID). In this way "degenerated dimensions" can be considered [15], thereby representing other fact features in addition to the measures for analysis. For example, we could store the ticket number (ticket_number) as degenerated dimensions, as reflected in figure 2.

With respect to dimensions, each level of a classification hierarchy is specified by a base class. An association of base classes specifies the relationship between two levels of a classification hierarchy. The only prerequisite is that these classes must define a Directed Acyclic Graph (DAG) rooted in the dimension class (DAG restriction is defined in the stereotype Dimension). The DAG structure can represent both multiple and alternative path hierarchies. Every base class must also contain an identifying attribute (OID) and a descriptor attribute[4] (D). These attributes are necessary for an automatic generation process into commercial OLAP tools, as these tools store this information on their metadata.

Due to the flexibility of UML, we can also consider non-strict hierarchies (an object at a hierarchy's lower level belongs to more than one higher-level object) and complete hierarchies (all members belong to one higher-class object and that object consists of those members only). These characteristics are specified by means of the cardinality of the roles of the associations and defining the constraint {completeness} in the target associated class role respectively. See Store dimension in figure 2 for an example of all kinds of classification hierarchies. Lastly, the categorization of dimensions is considered by means of the generalization / specialization relationships of UML.

3 Metrics for Data Warehouse Conceptual Models

A metric definition should always be based on clear measurement goals. Metrics should be defined following organisation's needs that are related to external quality attributes. We must firstly specify the goals of the metrics we plan to create to follow our organization's needs, and we then state the derived hypotheses. In our particular context, the main goal is "Defining a set of metrics to assess and control the quality of conceptual data warehouse schemas".

As [4] said, the structural properties (such as structural complexity) of a schema have an impact on its cognitive complexity (see figure 3). By cognitive complexity we mean the mental burden of the persons who have to deal with the artefact (e.g. developers, testers, maintainers and final users). High cognitive complexity leads an artefact to reduce their understandability and this conduce undesirable external quality attributes, such as decreased maintainability - a characteristic of quality; ISO 9126 [13].

---

[4] A descriptor attribute will be used as the default label in the data analysis in OLAP tools.

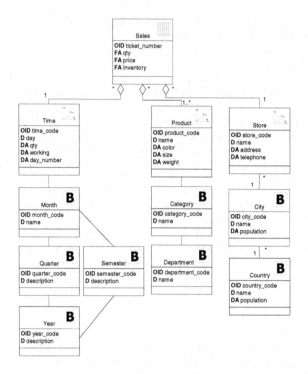

Fig. 2. Example of an Object Oriented data warehouse conceptual model using UML

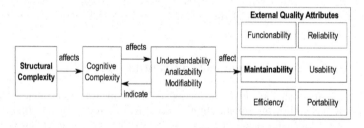

Fig. 3. Relationship between structural properties, cognitive complexity, understandability and external quality attributes, based on [4]

Therefore, we can state our hypothesis as: "Our metrics (defined for capturing the structural complexity of a data warehouse conceptual schema) can be used for controlling and assessing the quality of a data warehouse (through its maintainability)".

Taking into account the metrics defined for data warehouses at a logical level [20] and the metrics defined for UML class diagrams [10], we can propose an initial set of metrics for the model described in the previous section. When drawing up the proposal of metrics for data warehouse models, we must take into account 3 different levels: class, star and diagram.

In table 1 metrics for the class level are shown.

Table 1. Class scope metrics

Metric	Description
NA(C)	Number of FA (fact attributes), D (descriptor attributes) or DA (dimensional attributes) of the class C
NR(C)	Number of relationships (of any type) of the class C

The following table (see table 2) details the metrics proposed for the star level, one of the main elements of a data warehouse, composed of a fact class together with all the dimensional classes and associated base classes.

Table 2. Star scope metrics

Metric	Description
NDC(S)	Number of dimensional classes of the star S (equal to the number of aggregation relations)
NBC(S)	Number of base classes of the star S
NC (S)	Total number of classes of the star S $NC(S) = NDC(S) + NBC(S) + 1$
RBC(S)	Ratio of base classes. Number of base classes per dimensional class of the star S
NAFC(S)	Number of FA attributes of the fact class of the star S
NADC(S)	Number of D and DA attributes of the dimensional classes of the star S
NABC(S)	Number of D and DA attributes of the base classes of the star S
NA(S)	Total number of FA, D and DA attributes of the star S. $NA(S) = NAFC(S) + NADC (S) + NABC(S)$
NH(S)	Number of hierarchy relationships of the star S
DHP(S)	Maximum depth of the hierarchy relationships of the star S.
RSA(S)	Ratio of attributes of the star S. Number of attributes FA divided by the number of D and DA attributes.

Finally, in table 3, we present metrics at the diagram level of a complete data warehouse which may contain one or more stars.

Tables 4, 5 and 6 summarize the values for the defined metrics, regarding the example presented in the previous Section (figure 2). As the example has only one star, in table 6 only those values of the metrics that are different at the star and model levels are shown.

Table 3. Diagram scope metrics

Metric	Description
NFC	Number of Fact classes
NDC	Number of dimensional classes
NBC	Number of base classes
NC	Total number of classes $NC = NFC + NDC + NBC$
RBC	Ratio of base classes. Number of base classes per dimensional class
NSDC	Number of dimensional classes shared by more than one star
NAFC	Number of FA attributes of the fact classes
NADC	Number of D and DA attributes of the dimensional Tables.
NASDC	Number of D and DA attributes of the shared dimensional classes.
NA	Number of FA, D and DA attributes
NH	Number of hierarchies
DHP	Maximum depth of the hierarchical relationships
RDC	Ratio of dimensional classes. Number of dimensional classes per fact class.
RSA	Ratio of attributes. Number of FA attributes divided by the number of D and DA attributes.

Table 4. Class level metrics values

CLASS	NA	NR
Sales	3	3
Time	4	2
Product	4	2
Store	3	2
Month	1	3
Quarter	1	2
Semester	1	2
Year	1	2
Category	1	2
Department	1	1
City	2	2
Country	2	1

Table 5. Star level metrics values

Metric	Value
NDC(S)	3
NBC(S)	8
NC (S)	12
RBC	8/3
NAFC(S)	3
NADC(S)	11
NABC(S)	10
NA(S)	24
NH(S)	3
DHP(S)	3
RSA(S)	3/21

Table 6. Model level metrics values

Metric	Value
NFC	1
NSDC	0
NASDC	0
RDC	3

4 Empirical Validation

In this section, we will present our empirical validation for the metrics defined in the previous section. In doing this, we must firstly define the experimental settings (including the main goal of our experiment, the subjects that participated in the experiment, the main hypothesis under which we will run our experiment, the independent and dependent variables to be used in our model, the experimental design, the experiment running, material used and the subjects that performed the experiment). After that we discuss about the collected data validation. Finally, we analyse and interpret the results to find out if they follow the formulated hypothesis or not.

4.1 Experimental Settings

Experiment Goal Definition

The goal definition of the experiment using the GQM approximation [2] can be summarized as:

> *To analyze* the metrics for data warehouse conceptual models
> *for the purpose* of evaluating if they can be used as useful mechanisms
> *with respect of* the data warehouse maintainability
> from the designer's *point of view*
> *in the context of* practitioners

Subjects

Seventeen practitioners participated in the experiment (see table 7). The subjects work at a Spanish software consultancy that specially works on information systems development. The subjects were thirteen men and three women (one of the subjects did not give us this information), with an average age of 27.59 years. Respect to the experience of the subjects, they have an average experience of 3.65 years on computers, 2.41 years on databases, but they have little knowledge working with UML (only 0.53 years on average).

Table 7. Subjects of the experiment

Subject#	Sex	Age	Computers	Databases	UML
1	M	24	3	1	0
2	M	23	5	4	0
3	M	27	5	4	1
4	M	30	2	0	0
5	M	28	8	4	4
6	M	25	5	3	3
7	M	34	6	4	1
8	M	23	1	1	0
9	M	32	4	3	0
10	M	30	1	0	0
11	-	35	6	5	0
12	F	27	2	1	0
13	M	29	4	3	0
14	F	22	1	1	0
15	M	24	4	2	0
16	F	26	2	2	0
17	M	30	3	3	0
Mean		27,59	3,65	2,41	0,53
Minimun		22	1	0	0
Maximun		35	8	5	4
Std_Dev.		3,91	2,03	1,54	1,18

Hypotheses Formulation

The hypotheses of our experiment are:

Null hypothesis, H_0: There is no a statistically significant correlation between metrics and the maintainability of the schemas.

Alternative hypothesis, H_1: There is a statistically significant correlation between metrics and the maintainability of the schemas.

Alternative hypothesis H_1 is stated to determine if there is any kind of interaction between the metrics and the maintainability of a data warehouse schema, based on the fact that the metrics are defined in an attempt to acquire all the characteristics of a conceptual data warehouse model.

Variables in the Study

Independent Variables. The independent variables are the variables for which the effects should be evaluated. In our experiment these variables correspond to the metrics being researched. Table 8 presents the values for each metric in each schema.

Dependent Variables. The maintainability of the tests was measured as the time each subject used to perform the tasks of each experimental test. The experimental tasks consisted in two different tasks, the former involves understanding the models by counting the number of classes that must be visited to access to a concrete information. The latter one involves the modification of the models to fit new design requirements. On correcting the tests we found that all the subjects answered correctly and we were therefore able to work with the results of the ten subjects.

Regarding time, it is necessary to point out that for each schema we separately record the understanding time (including understanding the model and the answering time to the first type of questions) and the modification time that includes the time spent in performing the second type of tasks.

Table 8. Values of the metrics for the schemas used in the experiment

	NDC	NBC	NC	RBC	NAFC	NADC	NABC	NA	NH	DHP	RSA
S01	6	16	23	2,67	1	7	9	17	6	4	0,06
S02	5	19	25	3,8	1	11	20	32	9	4	0,03
S03	2	5	8	2,5	4	4	6	14	3	2	0,4
S04	4	17	22	4,25	4	6	17	27	9	3	0,17
S05	3	21	25	7	4	8	24	36	7	4	0,13
S06	5	13	19	2,6	3	0	31	34	5	4	0,1
S07	3	6	10	2	3	7	2	12	5	2	0,33
S08	4	5	10	1,25	3	13	5	21	2	3	0,17
S09	3	5	9	1,67	2	12	5	19	2	3	0,12
S10	2	4	7	2	1	7	2	10	3	2	0,11

Material Design and Experiment Running

Ten conceptual data warehouse models were used for performing the experiment. Although the domain of the schemas was different, we tried to select representative examples of real world cases in such a way that the results obtained were due to the difficulty of the schema and not to the complexity of the domain problem. We tried to have schemas with different metrics values (see table 8).

We selected a within-subject design experiment (i.e. all the tests had to be solved by each of the subjects). The documentation, for each design, included a data warehouse schema and a questions/answers form. The questions/answers form included the tasks that had to be performed and a space for the answers. For each design, the subjects had to analyse the schema, answer some questions about the design and perform some modifications on it.

Before starting the experiment, we explained to the subjects the kind of exercises that they had to perform, the material that they would be given, what kind of answers they had to provide and how they had to record the time spent solving the problems. We also explained to them that before studying each schema they had to annotate the start time (hour, minutes and seconds), then they could look at the design until they were able to answer the given question. Once the answer to the question was written, they had to annotate the final time (again in hour, minutes and seconds). Then they had to repeat the process with the modifications of the schema.

Tests were performed in distinct order by different subjects for avoiding learning and fatigue effects. The way we ordered the tests was using a randomisation function. To obtain the results of the experiment we used the number of seconds needed for each task on each schema by each subject.

4.2   Collected Data Validation

After marking the test, we obtained all the times for each schema and subject (tables 9 and 10). We notice that subject 11 did not answer to the understanding tasks of schema 7 and that subjects 2 and 10 did not answer to the modification tasks on schemas 8 and 9 respectively. The times for these subjects in these exercises were considered as null values.

We decided to study the outliers before working with the average data. In order to find the outliers we made a box plot (figures 4 and 5) with the collected data (table 9 and 10). Observing these box plots (figures 4 and 5) we can observe that there are several outliers (shown in table 11 and 13). The outliers values were eliminated from the collected data. The eliminated values are shown in tables 9 and 10 in italic font. The descriptive statistics of the final set of data can be found in tables 14 and 16. Then, we performed the analysis with this data.

Table 9. Collected data from the experiment (Understanding time)

Subject#	S01	S02	S03	S04	S05	S06	S07	S08	S09	S10
1	60	60	30	75	128	60	35	30	96	45
2	60	89	35	120	55	85	55	75	45	48
3	45	110	30	50	45	105	40	45	70	40
4	60	30	60	90	60	60	30	60	*300*	*150*
5	65	50	30	62	50	60	30	45	40	15
6	80	55	30	*240*	82	85	80	45	27	27
7	125	75	30	*270*	70	60	60	50	45	80
8	70	64	70	180	90	90	45	45	50	30
9	65	60	50	85	100	60	65	45	65	30
10	105	82	51	89	90	48	35	101	36	38
11	60	300	120	120	120	60	-	60	180	60
12	34	55	65	115	81	111	41	72	63	54
13	45	39	48	100	48	48	75	26	70	42
14	*140*	*310*	105	90	115	*210*	105	115	*185*	*220*
15	30	12	25	34	32	43	32	28	32	18
16	90	125	90	80	90	*174*	60	110	120	110
17	57	80	30	120	150	100	82	70	38	40

Table 10. Collected data from the experiment (Modification time)

Subject#	S01	S02	S03	S04	S05	S06	S07	S08	S09	S10
1	109	65	45	58	55	60	57	91	75	70
2	150	90	63	80	130	70	140	-	50	238
3	115	145	65	120	125	255	105	155	145	75
4	120	120	50	85	110	180	90	50	120	300
5	240	200	45	95	100	135	65	185	130	120
6	180	190	*250*	160	95	185	180	150	80	119
7	270	91	25	*355*	115	205	205	135	120	95
8	180	240	120	175	180	95	125	145	130	135
9	110	155	90	105	100	210	300	55	130	190
10	111	138	72	70	74	100	395	92	-	220
11	60	300	120	120	180	300	60	60	180	60
12	169	174	66	140	112	208	126	168	203	216
13	116	47	40	208	87	93	223	85	150	50
14	90	260	110	155	*270*	330	210	160	40	265
15	127	115	72	110	85	107	117	92	77	104
16	115	178	90	180	120	223	150	180	120	160
17	207	273	192	*330*	227	165	60	78	140	110

Validity of Results

As we know, different threats to the validity of the results of an experiment exist. In this section we will discuss threats to construct internal, external and conclusion validity.

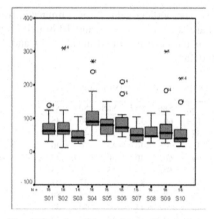

Table 11. Outliers

Schema	Subject Outliers
S01	14
S02	14
S03	
S04	6, 7
S05	
S06	14, 16
S07	
S08	
S09	4, 14
S10	4, 14

Fig. 4. Box plot of the understanding time.

Table 12. Descriptive statistics of the understanding time

	S01	S02	S03	S04	S05	S06	S07	S08	S09	S10
Average	65,69	80,38	52,88	94,00	82,71	71,67	54,38	60,12	65,13	45,13
Minimum	30	12	25	34	32	43	30	26	27	15
Maximum	125	300	120	180	150	111	105	115	180	110
Deviation	24,79	65,04	28,90	35,01	32,78	22,22	22,36	27,36	40,55	24,31

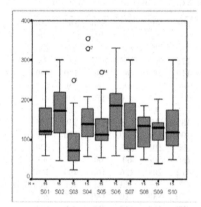

Table 13. Outliers

Schema	Subject Outliers
S01	
S02	
S03	6
S04	7, 17
S05	14
S06	
S07	
S08	
S09	
S10	

Fig. 5. Box plot of the modification time.

Table 14. Descriptive statistics of the modification time

	S01	S02	S03	S04	S05	S06	S07	S08	S09	S10
Average	145,24	163,59	79,06	124,07	118,44	171,82	153,41	117,56	118,13	148,65
Minimum	60	47	25	58	55	60	57	50	40	50
Maximum	270	300	192	208	227	330	395	185	203	300
Deviation	55,37	73,90	41,35	44,29	43,97	79,39	91,95	46,71	44,30	76,38

Construct Validity. The construct validity is the degree to which the independent and the dependent variables are accurately measured by the measurement instruments used in the study. The dependent variables we use are understanding and modification times, i.e., the time each subject spent performing these tasks, so we consider these variables constructively valid. The construct validity of the measures used for the independent variables is guaranteed by the Distance framework [18] used for their theoretical validation.

Internal Validity. The internal validity is the degree to which conclusions can be drawn about the causal effect of independent variables on the dependent variables. The following issues should be considered:

- **Differences among subjects.** Within-subject experiments reduce variability among subjects.
- **Differences among schemas.** The domain of the schemas were different and this could influence the results obtained in some way.
- **Precision in the time values.** The subjects were responsible for recording the start and finish times of each test. We believe this method is more effective than having a supervisor who records the time of each subject. However, we are aware that the subject could introduce some imprecision.
- **Learning effects.** Using a randomisation function, tests were ordered and given in a distinct order for different subjects. So, each subject answered the tests in the given order. In doing this, we tried to minimize learning effects.
- **Fatigue effects.** The average time for completing the experiment was 33 minutes varying from a minimum of approximately 16 minutes and a maximum of about 61 minutes. With this range of times we believe that fatigue effects hardly exist at all. Also, the different order of the tests helped to avoid these fatigue effects.
- **Persistence effects.** In our case, persistence effects are not present because the subjects had never participated in a similar experiment.
- **Subject motivation.** Subjects were volunteers and they were convinced that the exercises they were doing were useful. The subjects wanted to participate in the experiment and to contribute to this field. Therefore, we believe that subjects were motivated at doing the experiment.
- **Plagiarism and influence among subjects.** In order to avoid these effects a supervisor was present during the experiment. Subjects were informed they should not talk to each other or share answers with other subjects.

External Validity. The external validity is the degree to which the results of the research can be generalised to the population under study and to other research settings. The greater the external validity, the more the results of an empirical study can be generalised to actual software engineering practice. Two threats to validity have been identified which limit the ability to apply any such generalisation:

- **Materials and tasks used.** We tried to use schemas and operations representative of real world cases in the experiments, although more experiments with larger and more complex schemas are necessary.
- **Subjects.** Although this experiment was run by practitioners, we are aware that the number of subjects (17) could be insufficient for generalise the results. More experiments with practitioners and professionals must be carried out in order to be able to generalise the results.

Conclusion Validity. The conclusion validity defines the extent to which conclusions are statistically valid. The only issue that could affect the statistical validity of this study is the size of the sample data (17 values), which perhaps is not enough for both parametric and non-parametric statistic tests [3]. We will try to obtain bigger sample data through more experimentation.

4.3 Analysis and Interpretation

We used the data collected in order to test the hypotheses formulated previously. As we were not able to assure that the data we collected followed a common statistical distribution (mainly because we had a very small group of subjects), we decided to apply a non-parametric correlational analysis, avoiding assumptions about the data normality. In this way, we made a correlation statistical analysis using the Spearman's Rho statistic and we used a level of significance $\alpha = 0.05$

Table 15 shows the results obtained for the correlation between each of the metrics and the time each subject used (on each schema) to perform the task of understanding. Table 16 shows the same data for the modification tasks.

Table 15. Results of the experiment (understanding time)

Metric	NDC	NBC	NC	RBC	NAFC	NADC	NABC	NA	NH	DHP	RSA
Correlation	0,601	0,890	0,860	0,772	0,258	0,006	0,805	0,855	0,755	0,764	-0,285
Significance	0,066	0,001	0,001	0,009	0,472	0,987	0,005	0,002	0,012	0,010	0,425

Table 16. Results of the experiment (modification time)

Metric	NDC	NBC	NC	RBC	NAFC	NADC	NABC	NA	NH	DHP	RSA
Correlation	0,452	0,313	0,329	0,267	-0,459	-0,288	0,262	0,139	0,479	0,334	-0,588
Significance	0,190	0,379	0,353	0,455	0,182	0,419	0,464	0,701	0,162	0,346	0,074

Analysing both tables, we can conclude that there exists a high correlation between the understanding time used (understandability of the schemas) and the metrics NBC, NC, RBC, NABC, NA, NH and DHP (the value of significance is lower than $\alpha = 0.05$). The other metrics do not seem to be correlated with the time. On the other hand, there is not correlation at all, between the modification time and the metrics.

In considering these results, it seems that understandability is closer related to metrics that capture in some sense the "complexity" of the schemas. This complexity is captured by the number of classes of the schemas (size of the schema) and the number of hierarchy relationships in the stars. The modification time is not related to the metrics, perhaps because the modification tasks could be solved focusing only on a small part of the schema.

5 Conclusions and Future Research

Data warehouses play a key role in the decision making process of companies, and therefore, assuring their quality is absolutely critical for this process. One way to achieve this quality objective is to assure the quality of the models (conceptual, logical and physical) used in designing them and one way of assuring the quality is using metrics.

In this paper we have focused on the empirical validation of the metrics proposed for conceptual data warehouse models as quality indicators, presenting the first experiment we have accomplished. As a result of this first experiment it seems that there exist correlation between several of the metrics and the understandability of the conceptual data warehouse models.

We are currently involved on the empirical validation of the proposed metrics process. As a result of this process the proposed metrics will be accepted, discarded or refined. When the process will finish, we will we have a set of metrics that could be used as quality indicators. These metrics could be used by the designers on their task. For example using the provided metrics they could choose among different design alternatives semantically equivalents the most maintainable one. It would also be advisable to study the influence of the different analysis dimensions on the cognitive complexity of an object-oriented model; as well as the repercussion of using packages in the conceptual modelling of complex and extensive data warehousess in order to simplify their design.

Acknowledgements

This research is part of the CALIPO project, supported by Dirección General de Investigación of the Ministerio de Ciencia y Tecnologia (TIC2003-07804-C05-03). This research is also part of the MESSENGER project, supported by Consejeria de Ciencia y Tecnologia de la Junta de Comunidades de Castilla-La Mancha (PCC-03-003-1).

We would like to thank all the people in Cronos Iberica who kindly volunteered to take part in the experiment.

References

1. Abelló, A., Samos, J. and Saltor, F. YAM2 (Yet Another Multidimensional Model): An extension of UML. *International Database Engineering & Applications Symposium (IDEAS'02)* July, pp. 172-181. (2002).
2. Basili V. and Weiss D. A Methodology for Collecting Valid Software Engineering Data, *IEEE Transactions on Software Engineering* 10, 728-738 (1984).
3. Briand L., El Emam K., Morasca S. Theoretical and empirical validation of software product measures. *Technical Report ISERN-95-03*, International Software Engineering Research Network. (1995).
4. Briand. L., J. Wüst, H. Lounis A Comprehensive Investigation of Quality Factors in Object-Oriented Designs: an Industrial Case Study. *21st Int'l Conf. Software Engineering*, Los Angeles, 345-354 (1999).
5. Cabbibo, L. and Torlone, R. A logical approach to multidimensional databases. *Sixth International Conference on Extending Database Technology (EDBT'98)*, Valencia. Spain *Lecture Notes in Computer Science 1377*, Springer-Verlag, pp 183-197. (1998).
6. Calero, C., Piattini, M., Pascual, C. and Serrano, M.A. Towards Data Warehouse Quality Metrics, *Workshop on Design and Management of Data Warehouses (DMDW'01)* (2001).

7. Cavero, J.M., Piattini, M., Marcos, E., and Sánchez, A. A Methodology for Data warehouse Design: Conceptual Modeling. *12th International Conference of the Information Resources Management Association* (IRMA2001), Toronto, Ontario, Canada. (2001).
8. English, L. *Information Quality Improvement: Principles, Methods and Management, Seminar*, 5th Ed., Brentwood, TN: Information Impact International, Inc. (1996).
9. Fenton, N. and Pfleeger, S. *Software Metrics: A Rigorous Approach*, Chapman & Hall. London, 2nd. edition. (1997).
10. Genero, M., Olivas, J., Piattini, M. and Romero, F. Using metrics to predict OO information systems maintainability. *Proc. of 13th International Conference on Advanced Information Systems Engineering (CAiSE'01)*. Lecture Notes in Computer Science 2068, 388-401. (2001).
11. Golfarelli, M., Maio, D. and Rizzi, S. The Dimensional Fact Model: A Conceptual Model for Data Warehouses. International Journal of Cooperative Information Systems (IJCIS), 1998, vol. 7, 2-3, pp. 215-247. (1998).
12. Inmon, W.H. Building the Data Warehouse, third edition, John Wiley and Sons, USA. (2003).
13. ISO International Standard ISO/IEC 9126. Information technology – Software product evaluation. ISO, Geneve. (2001).
14. Jarke, M., Lenzerini, M., Vassiliou, Y. and Vassiliadis, P. *Fundamentals of Data Warehouses*, Ed. Springer. (2000).
15. Kimball, R. and Ross, M. The Data Warehouse Toolkit, second edition, John Wiley & Sons. (2002).
16. Kitchenham, B., Pflegger, S., Pickard, L., Jones, P., Hoaglin, D., El-Emam, K. and Rosenberg, J. Preliminary Guidelines for Empirical Research in Software Engineering. *IEEE Transactions of Software Engineering* 28(8) 721-734. (2002).
17. Luján-Mora, S., Trujillo, J. and Song, I-Y. Extending UML for Multidimensional Modeling. *5th International Conference on the Unified Modeling Language* (UML 2002), LNCS 2460, 290-304. (2002).
18. Poels G. and Dedene G. Distance-based Software Measurement: Necessary and Sufficient Properties for Software Measures. *Information and Software Technology*, 42(1), 35-46. (2000).
19. Sapia, C., Blaschka, M., Höfling, G. and Dinter, B. Extending the E/R Model for the Multidimensional Paradigm. *ER Workshops 1998*, Singapore, Lecture Notes in Computer Science (LNCS), vol. 1552, pp. 105-116. (1998).
20. Serrano, M., Calero, C. and Piattini, M. Validating metrics for data warehouses. *IEE Proceedings SOFTWARE*, Vol. 149, 5, 161-166 . (2002).
21. Serrano, M., Calero, C. and Piattini, M. Experimental validation of multidimensional data models metrics, *Proc of the Hawaii International Conference on System Sciences* (HICSS'36), IEEE Computer Society (2003).
22. Si-Saïd, S. and Prat, N. Multidimensional Schemas Quality : Assessing and Balancing Analyzability and Simplicity. ER 2003 Workshops. Jeusfeld, M.A. and Pastor, O. (eds.), LNCS 2814, 140-151. (2003).
23. Tryfona, N., Busborg, F. and Christiansen, G.B. starER: A Conceptual Model for Data Warehouse Design. *Proceedings of the ACM Second International Workshop on Data Warehousing and OLAP (DOLAP'99)*, Kansas City, USA, pp. 3-8. (1999).
24. Trujillo, J., Palomar, M., Gómez, J. and Song, I-Y. Designing Data Warehouses with OO Conceptual Models. *IEEE Computer*, Special issue on Data Warehouses, 34 (12), 66 - 75. (2001).
25. Vassiliadis, P. *Data Warehouse Modeling and Quality Issues*. Ph.D. Thesis. National Technical University of Athens. (2000).

Goal-Driven Analysis of Process Model Validity

Pnina Soffer[1] and Yair Wand[1,2]

[1] Haifa University, Carmel Mountain, Haifa 31905, Israel
{wand,spnina}@mis.hevra.haifa.ac.il
[2] The University of British Columbia, Vancouver, Canada
yair.wand@commerce.ubc.ca

Abstract. Business process modeling and design, which has attracted much attention in recent years, emphasizes mainly graphical representation, usually without an underlying theory. The lack of a theoretical foundation causes several important issues to remain intuition- rather than theory -based. In particular, many process-modeling methods, being semi-formal, lack a mechanism for verifying the "correctness" of a process in terms of completeness, consistency, and feasibility. The paper proposes a generic theory-based process modeling (GPM) framework and criteria for validity evaluation of process models. The framework, which is based on Bunge's ontology, is formal and notation-independent. Validity is defined as the possibility of the process to achieve its goal. The paper discusses and characterizes causes for process invalidity and suggests ways to avoid these situations. The concepts of the framework and their usefulness for evaluating the validity of process models are demonstrated by applying them to a process taken from the Supply-Chain Operations Reference-model (SCOR).

1 Introduction

Business process modeling and design has attracted much attention in recent years in the context of integrated information systems and Business Process Reengineering.

Numerous methods for process modeling and representation have been proposed (e.g., Business Modeling Language (BML) [9], Event-driven Process Chains (EPC) [15]), addressing different aspects of processes, such as activity sequencing, resource allocation, and organizational responsibility for execution.

Process goals are included in many definitions of business processes (e.g., "a business process is a set of partially ordered activities aimed at reaching a goal" [7]). However, as opposed to process structure, the notion of goal has received relatively little attention in the literature. There are two main outcomes of this situation. First, goals are often viewed as external concepts, not integrated with process models. Second, most process modeling methods focus on graphical representation, usually without an underlying theory. The lack of a theoretical foundation causes several important issues to remain intuition- rather than theory -based. In particular, most process-modeling methods lack a mechanism for verifying the "correctness" of a process model in terms of completeness, consistency, and feasibility. An exception is some workflow-related process models, which use formalisms (e.g Petri-nets) and apply

A. Persson and J. Stirna (Eds.): CAiSE 2004, LNCS 3084, pp. 521–535, 2004.
© Springer-Verlag Berlin Heidelberg 2004

verification mechanisms [20, 21]. However, verification of workflow models addresses a limited set of aspects of the process, mainly activity sequencing.

This paper proposes a Generic Process Model (GPM), which is a theory-based, formal and notation-independent process modeling framework. The framework provides clear-cut criteria for evaluating model validity based on the integration of goals into process models.

We start by presenting the theoretical framework, then develop validity criteria and demonstrate their application to a process taken from the Supply Chain Operations Reference-model (SCOR) [16].

2   Generic Process Model Framework

In this section we present a theoretical framework for process modeling based on Bunge's ontology [3, 4], as adapted for information systems modeling (e.g., [14, 22]) and for modeling business process concepts [17, 18].

According to the ontological framework, the world is made of *things* that possess *properties*. Properties can be *intrinsic* (e.g. height) to things or *mutual* to several things (e.g. a person works for a company). Things can compose to form a *composite* thing that has *emergent* properties, namely, properties not possessed by the individuals composing it. Properties (intrinsic or mutual) are perceived by humans in terms of *attributes*, which can be represented as functions on time. The *state* of a thing is the set of values of all its attribute functions (also termed state variables). When properties of things change, these changes are manifested as state changes or *events*. State changes can happen either due to internal transformations in things (self action of a thing) or due to *interactions* among things. Not all states are possible, and not all state changes can occur. The rules governing possible states and state changes are termed *state laws* and *transition laws*, respectively.

In addition to the basic ontological concepts we define some more concepts to provide a formal basis for expressing process-related concepts in ontological terms.

Domain: Part of the world changes of which we want to model.

In ontological terms, a domain includes a set of things and their interactions. By defining a process over a domain we set the *scope* of the process and provide a clear distinction between what would be considered *external events*, which are outside of the process' control, and *internal events* that may occur while processes are enacted and are governed by the processes in the domain.

State: A set of time-dependent attributes (state variables) that provide sufficient information about the domain for the purpose of modeling.

Note, the state of the domain is determined by the states of the things included in it. However, due to interactions, emergent state variables of composite things or of the domain might exist. As well, we view states as being discrete, meaning that any change is from one state to another at a certain moment in time.

Sub-domain: Part of the domain that can be represented by a (fixed in time) subset of the set of state variables.

A state can be *projected* on a sub-domain by considering the sub-set of state variables describing the sub-domain. This subset defines the state of the sub-domain. Hence on "state" means a state of a domain or any sub-domain. A sub-domain may set the scope of a sub-process (part of the process occurring in the sub-domain), similarly to the way a domain sets the scope of a process.

States can be classified as being *stable* or *unstable*. The motivation to this distinction is that later on we will view the execution of a process as a sequence of unstable states that terminates when a stable state is reached.

Stable State: A state that can only change as a result of an action of something outside the (sub)domain.

Unstable state: A state of the (sub)domain that must change.

Whether a state is stable or unstable and how an unstable state might change is defined in terms of the *laws* that govern the states of the domain and their transitions:

A Law: A function from the set of states S into itself.

A Transition law: A function on the set of possible unstable states S_u into the set of states S.

Implied in this definition is that the transition law is fully deterministic. However, our process model allows for uncertainty in how the process will progress when enacted. This is because we allow for external events to affect the state of the domain while the process is in progress. Consequently, state variables that affect the law might change in ways not controlled in the process.

A transition law can be extended to all states as follows: for an unstable state the law is the transition law, otherwise it maps the state into itself. Hence on we will refer to the extended laws as domain laws (designated by L).

For modeling processes we will be interested in sequences of unstable states that terminate on stable states. It is not guaranteed that a domain law will always lead to a stable state. We therefore need a condition under which every process will terminate (i.e. the domain will reach a stable state).

Stability Condition: A domain will always achieve a stable state if for every $s \in S_u$ there exists n such that $L^n(s) = L^{n+1}(s)$.

The stability condition means that a stationary point exists for every sequence of unstable states. The sequence of unstable states, transforming by law until a stable state is reached is the basic mechanism of a process:

A Process: A sequence of unstable states leading to a stable state.

This definition of a process does not mention the origin of the initial unstable state. In particular, it can be the outcome of an interaction between the domain and a thing outside the domain when the domain is in a stable state. Furthermore, the definition does not mention the process goal explicitly. However, it implicitly assumes that the stability condition holds and a stable state can be reached.

Our purpose is to add the notion of goal to the formal model of a process. The formalization below establishes and operationalizes a process goal integrated into a process model. Note that by "goal" we relate to an operational goal of the process only, as opposed to business goals of the organization. Business goals, which may serve as "soft-goals" in process design, are discussed in [18].

Definition 1: Assume the set of state variables defining a domain is $s=<x_1,...,x_n>$.

Let $S=\{s \mid s$ lawful$\}$ be the set of possible domain states. Let $S_{st} \subseteq S$ be the subset of domain stable states. Then a *Goal* (G) is a set of stable states $G \subseteq S_{st}$.

We now relate the notion of a goal to a process:

Definition 2: A goal G will be said to be a *process goal* if every execution of the process terminates in G.

Definition 2 is technical in the sense that it does not provide any meaningful understanding of how a process is designed to always end in a specific subset of states. We need to operationalize the concept of goal so it can be related to the actual design of a process leading to it.

Definition 3: A *criterion function* is a function on the set of states C: S $\rightarrow$ D, where D is a certain domain (of values).

A criterion function maps the values of state variables into a domain where a decision can be made on whether the process achieved its purpose or not. Examples for criterion functions are the average of certain state variable values or their distance from a target value. Often, the mapping is on a subset of state variables that are considered relevant for deciding whether the process has reached its "goal". The domain mapped into is then a sub-domain of the process domain. For example, in a manufacturing process a criterion function can map the entire set of state variables into a sub-domain specified by two Boolean state variables sufficient for determining process termination: "Production is completed" and "Product quality is approved".

Definition 4: A *condition* is a logical expression E made of simple expressions of the
form: R::= C rel g,
         where   rel$\in$ {'>', '=', '<'}, where C a criterion and g is a value from the
         same domain as C, combined by 'AND', 'OR', 'NOT' and precedences indicated by '( )'.
We can now operationalize the definition of a goal as: G ={s | E(C(s)) is 'true'}.

Considering the manufacturing process discussed above, its goal set is
{s| (Production is completed='true') AND (Product quality is approved='true')}.

Having defined and operationalized the goal of a process, we can now apply a set of concepts to formalize a process model.

Definition 5: A *process model* is a quadruple M_p = <S,L,I,G> where:
         S is a set of states
         L is a law defined on S
         I is a subset of unstable states in S: the set of possible initial states
         G is a subset of stable states in S: the goal set
This definition does not seem to address many elements that are usually included in process models, such as ordered activities, pre and post conditions, resources, and actors. Nevertheless, we shall now show how the concepts used in the definition relate to those common process modeling concepts, by viewing a law as a mapping from a condition over a criterion function to a condition over a criterion function.

Ordered activities are state transitions caused by transformations defined by the law. *Triggering events* (or pre-conditions) are the conditions that define the set of initial states I of the entire process and sub-processes. *Post-conditions* are the conditions that define the goal sets for the process and sub-processes. *Actors and resources* are things in the ontological model. Our process model represents actors as things that take actions in response to their state changes and resources as things that take no further actions.

In summary, modelling the states that change by law from a set of initial states to a set of stable states is sufficient for addressing most of process model elements.

Note, definition 5 implies that a set of ordered activities is not a process unless it leads to a defined goal. Consequently, if L does not satisfy the stability condition a process cannot be defined.

3 Validity of Process Models

This section uses the GPM theoretical framework to develop conditions for identifying validity and completeness in a process model. Different sources of invalidity are indicated so that actions to remedy the invalidity can be suggested.

As discussed in Section 2, a process is aimed at attaining a goal, which is a set of stable states that satisfy a condition over a criterion function. Such a set can, potentially, be attained in many different ways or *paths*.

Definition 6: a *process path* is a set of states $<s_1,...s_n>$ such that: $s_i \neq s_j$, $s_1 \in I$, and $s_{k+1}=L(s_k)$ for every $k \in \{1,n-1\}$.

Note, definition 6 does not relate to the process goal. Accordingly, process path might be unsuccessful by leading to a stable state which is not in the process goal set.

Definition 7: a *successful process path* is a path such that $s_n \in G$.

We base the evaluation of a process model on whether its goal is reachable or not. For this purpose, we define and discuss the reachability of states in the goal set.

Definition 8: A goal state $s \in G$ will be termed *reachable* if there is one (successful) process path such that $s_n = s$.

If the goal set of a process includes unreachable states it either means these states are redundant in the goal definition and the goal set can be redefined, or that some other process paths should be designed and successfully reach these states. However, we do not consider the existence of redundant goal states as model invalidity.

Definition 9: A process model will be called a *valid model* iff there exists at least one successful process path.

Three notes are in order. First, definition 9 relates to validity of a process with respect to a given goal. Second, the definition does not address the "validity" of the goal itself in terms of what the process is intended to accomplish. The result of a "faulty" goal definition may be a "valid" process model that does not provide all the outputs required from it (typically, by other processes). For example, assume at the end of a production process the identity of the worker is needed for computing salaries. Yet, providing this identity is not necessarily defined as part of the production process goal criterion function ("complete product"). Hence, the production process can be considered valid with respect to its goal set even if it does not provide the information required by other processes.

On a more general note - completeness of goal definition should be evaluated in relation to a set of processes. We do not discuss goal completeness here.

Third, a path might exist, yet not guaranteed to complete. The reason is that some events that bring about state changes might be considered external to the (sub) domain on which the process is defined. Since external events are not under the control of the process, the process might reach a stable state not in the goal that is not guaranteed to change further. For example, the domain of replenishment might include suppliers. However, for the replenishment process in the company, suppliers' behavior is external. Therefore order delivery is not an internal event of the process sub-domain. The process is not "guaranteed" to complete and might "hang" waiting for delivery.

Based on the above, we distinguish three types of situations when a process model is invalid, namely, it is not guaranteed to reach its goal. These types are (1) Incompleteness in the process definition. (2) Inconsistency between the law and the goal definition. (3) Dependency of the process on external events, where the process is "waiting" for an external event.

In what follows, we will discuss these situations and suggest remedies for the reasons the process model is not valid.

Incompleteness in the Process Definition: The domain and law definition determines which state variables are addressed by the model. Specifically, the domain law is defined in terms of a mapping between two conditions over criterion functions. It may be that a certain combination of state variable values obtained in a given step (according to the definition of the domain law), does not appear in the law definition for the following steps. As a result, the following step cannot be "fired".

Definition 10: A process definition is considered *complete* iff the domain law is defined for every combination of state variable values that may be reached from the initial process states via state transitions defined by the law.

Incompleteness in the process definition can relate to internal events or to external events. In the case of internal events not completely defined, it may be that steps 1..j of a process path lead to states defined by $C_1(x_1,..x_{n-1})$, while the initial state of step j+1 is defined by $C_2(x_1,..x_n)$. The law for the current value of x_n might not be defined. Consider, for example, a production-to-order process, in which production should be triggered by the acceptance of a customer order. Suppose that when an order is received not all details needed for production are provided. The law might not specify how to proceed. The problem can be solved simply by correcting the law (as defined for the order acceptance step) so that all the necessary details will be provided.

In the case of external events not completely defined, some state variables obtain values by external events and become known during the process (a formal definition of this situation appears in [18]). In words, the value of state variables that are determined by an external event is subject to uncertainty until it is *realized* during the process. Possibly, not all the potential results of the external event are taken into account by the law. Hence, the process might reach a state for which L is undefined.

As an example, consider a process of periodical car maintenance, which includes examining the state of various systems in the car (e.g., the braking system). If failure is detected it will be fixed, while otherwise no action is taken. The damage to be detected reflects an external event which has already occurred by the time the car is in the garage. It only becomes known during the maintenance process. The law defined for the maintenance process must consider all the possible states in the state space. This will in turn specify various possible process paths depending on the findings.

Inconsistency between the Law and the Process Definition: It is possible that as the process begins progressing, it reaches a state from which it cannot proceed further to reach a goal state. Two possibilities exit. First, the law keeps causing transitions without reaching a stable state. If the state space is finite, this would imply the process has entered an "infinite loop", meaning the law does not satisfy the stability condition. Second, it is possible the process has reached a stable state not in the goal for which there is no external event that can change it to an unstable state. For either case, this implies there is no continuous path from the start state to a goal state. In other words, the goal is inconsistent with the law. In practice, this situation can be recognized by detecting state variable values in the goal that can not be set properly by the law.

If the goal is derived from organizational needs, it should not be changed. Hence, the process model can be made consistent only by correcting the law definition.

Process continuance Depends on an External Event: An external event may be the trigger for a step in the process, in which case the process is in a stable state "waiting" for the external event to occur, with no guarantee that it will eventually occur.

Definition 11: A process path will be termed *non-continuous* iff it includes a stable state $s_j \notin G$.

Based on this definition, the only way for a non-continuous path to lead to the goal is if an external event occurs changing the stable state to unstable.

Definition 12: A process will be termed *non-continuous* iff all its paths are non-continuous.

A non-continuous process is technically invalid. However, it is common that a process will be waiting for external events (we do not want to proscribe this, as it would limit what is a useful process model). For example, handling a manuscript submitted for publication involves sending it to reviewers. Once the manuscript is sent to the reviewers the process is in a stable state, and is reactivated by the arrival of the reviews. However, this might take an indefinite period of time. In fact, theoretically there is no guarantee that all the reviews will arrive at all.

Assuring the process reaches its goal would require the following corrections:

(1) Add to the Law L a specification that will include some measure of time in the criterion function, and a condition specifying values in which the combination of the time variable and other state variables makes the state unstable. The time can be "absolute" or "waiting" time.

(2) The unstable state should be mapped to (a) connect to a process path, (b) end on a new stable state that can be affected by external events or be considered a new goal.

(3) Add the stable state of (2b) to the Goal set.

It can be shown that these corrections are all necessary and together sufficient. The idea is as follows: given the process might be halted on a stable state not in the goal set, the only way it can be reactivated is via an external event. In theory, this could be an event of any source. However, this might again raise the same possibility of failed external event. Thus, we must include a type of external event that by definition will always change the state. This must be time, as the passage of time is external to all processes in the world. In organizational practice one might conceive of other necessary events that would happen, however, they all will be somehow tied to time.

When defining a state that becomes unstable as a result of the time event, a new process path must be defined and connected to it. The new process path may include a *monitoring* activity, aimed at verifying that the expected external event will indeed occur. The monitoring activity itself might have to be tied to time.

In addition (or alternatively), the new process path may lead to an "exception" state, where a process terminates with some special actions reflecting a failure somewhere. The condition for reaching the exception state can be based on the time variable, on the number of repetitions of the monitoring activity (which in itself reflects time), or on a combination of both.

We distinguish between two types of stable states reached as a result of monitoring. First, the stable state is an exception and should be added to the goal set of the process, implying that the process terminates when its original objective is achieved or when failure in achieving this objective is evident. Second, the new stable state could be such that is more likely to be changed by an external event. For example, notify a supervisor of the problem, and wait for response.

Consider again the example of the manuscript handling process. In order to make it valid we need to specify time in which to inquire about the status of the review, or time periods for repeating this inquiry. We should also specify a path for failing to get a review, in which decision can be made based only on the reviews that have arrived.

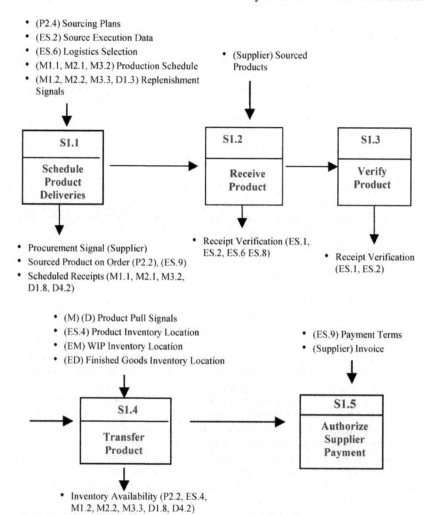

Fig. 1. SCOR S1 process of sourcing stocked products

4 Application to the SCOR Model

In this section we demonstrate our approach by applying it to a process taken from the Supply Chain Operations Reference-model (SCOR) [16].

The SCOR model is a reference model of supply chain management processes, developed and endorsed by the Supply Chain Council as a cross-industry standard. While primarily targeted for industrial use, the SCOR model has been used in quite a number of research works (e.g., [1, 8, 19]) as a comprehensive body of common and accepted supply chain business processes.

SCOR contains three levels of process details. The top level includes five basic processes: Plan, Source, Make, Deliver, and Return. The second level defines categories for each of the five basic processes, according to different logistic categories (e.g. make to stock). The third level decomposes each process category into elements, to be further decomposed into activities in practical implementation. The SCOR model specifies inputs and outputs of each of these elements, and provides metrics and "best practices" associated with each process category and element.

We demonstrate our approach using the SCOR process Source Stocked Products, denoted as S1, presented in Figure 1 (taken from SCOR directly). The inputs and outputs in the figure refer to other SCOR processes they relate to (e.g., P2.4, etc.).

4.1 Expressing the SCOR Process

The S1 process includes five steps (or sub-processes). We may apply our set of concepts to the entire process or to each of its steps, as shown in Table 1.

With respect to the entire process, I is the set of states where all the inputs to the first step exist. Specifically, the instability of the states is caused by the *replenishment Signals* given. Therefore, this is the external event that triggers the process. The Law is not completely and explicitly specified. Rather, it is manifested by the state transformation caused by each of the process steps. Table 1 specifies the conditions that define I and G for each step. The law is defined by the mapping from I states to G states. In the transformation from Figure 1 to Table 1 we applied domain knowledge to specify the exact condition values (e.g., *Sourcing plans* = In process), which were not provided in the SCOR model. The goal of the entire process is not specified in the SCOR model at all, but is implicitly understood as the set of states where supplier payment is completed. Considering each step, it is a sub-process defined over a sub-domain. Its goal states, while clearly not stable in terms of the entire domain, are stable in terms of the specific sub-domain. For example, consider the step *S1.2 Receive Product*, whose output is *Receipt Verification* (obviously with respect to quantity rather than quality). The goal of this step includes all the states where the quantity received is verified. It is clearly not a stable state in terms of the entire process, since the quality of the product is not yet verified. However, it is a stable state in terms of a sub-domain, which may include a person whose job is to unload goods and verify that the content of the shipment delivered. This person has completed his job once the quantity received is verified.

Table 1. SCOR process representation

Step	I condition	G condition
S1.1	(*Sourcing plans* = Open) AND (*Source Execution Data* = Defined) AND (*Logistics Selection* = Defined) AND (*Production Schedule* = Defined) AND (*Replenishment signals* = Given) AND (*Sourced products* = Not Ordered)	(*Sourcing plans* = In process) AND (*Replenishment signals* = Closed) AND (*Procurement signal* = Sent to supplier) AND (*Sourced products* = On Order) AND (*Scheduled Receipts* = Date, quantity)
S1.2	*Sourced products* = Arrived	*Sourced products* = Quantity verified
S1.3	*Sourced products* = Quantity verified	*Sourced products* = Quality verified
S1.4	(*Sourced products* = Quality verified) AND (*Pull signal* = Given) AND [(*Inventory location* = Defined) OR (*WIP location* = Defined) OR (*Finished goods location* = Defined)]	(*Sourced products* = Transferred) AND (*Pull signal* = Closed) AND [(*Inventory* = location, quantity) OR (*WIP* = location, quantity) OR (*Finished goods* = location, quantity)]
S1.5	(*Sourced products* = Transferred) AND (*Payment Terms* = Defined) AND (*Invoice* = Received)	(*Sourced products* = Paid) AND (*Invoice* = Paid)

4.2 Validity Analysis

Table 2 is a basis for analyzing the process model validity. The table addresses the state variables whose state is transformed by each step of the process and specifies the source from which each variable receives its initial and final value. The table also indicates whether a state variable constitutes (possibly in combination with other state variables) the external event that triggers the sub-process by putting the sub-domain in an unstable state. The sources of the initial values of the state variables can be external events or some other steps in the process. The source of the goal values of the state variables is the law, possibly on the basis of external events whose outcome is realized in the process (denoted in the table as By Law | external).

Note, the table specifies for each step only the *goal defining* state variables [18], i.e., state variables that are part of the goal criterion function of the specific step.

Analysis tables such as Table 2 can indicate the three cases of invalidity discussed:

(1) Incompleteness of process definition can be identified by tracking:
   (a) State variable whose initial value depends on a previous step of the process, where the required value is not specified as part of the goal condition of that step. Then a pre-condition might not be satisfied and a step cannot be fired. In our example the changes in *Sourced Products*, that progress from step to step, are specified correctly.
   (b) State variables whose goal value depends on external events (By law | external), where the law is not specified for all their possible values. In our example there are two such cases, namely steps S1.2 and S1.3. In both cases not all possible results are considered, as it is possible that the quantity will not be verified (S1.2) or quality will not be approved (S1.3). Hence, these are two cases of incomplete specification.
(2) Goal-law inconsistency can be identified by detecting loops in the process – when the initial value of state variables is obtained in the goal state of a step

that is not previous to the current one. Loops can also be the result of repeating external events. Such possibility can be identified if the initial state of a step depends on an external event only, without considering the value of goal-defining state variables (that changes once the step is performed). Once a loop is detected there must be a state variable whose value serves as a guaranteed termination condition (repetition counter, time, etc.). Otherwise the stability condition is violated. In our example the process does not include loops.

(3) Dependency on external events can be identified by state variables, which constitute triggering events for steps (other than the first step of the process), and whose initial value is of an external source. These could indicate that the process is non-continuous. In our example there are three such cases, in steps S1.2, S1.4, and S1.5. In all these three cases the occurrence of the external triggering events is not guaranteed and is not monitored.

In summary, Table 2 indicates that the process model is invalid, since it includes two cases of incomplete law specification with respect to state variables whose value is realized in the process, and three cases of unmonitored non-continuity.

Table 2. Sources of state variable values

Process step	State variable	Source of initial value	Triggering event	Source of goal value
S1.1	*Sourcing plans*	External	No	By Law
	Replenishment signals	External	Yes	By Law
	Procurement Signal		No	By Law
	Sourced Products		No	By Law
	Scheduled Receipts		No	By Law
S1.2	*Sourced Products*	External	Yes	By Law | External
S1.3	*Sourced Products*	S1.2	Yes	By Law | External
S1.4	*Pull Signals*	External	Yes	By Law
	Sourced Products	S1.3	Yes	By Law
	Inventory	External	No	By Law
	WIP	External	No	By Law
	Finished goods	External	No	By Law
S1.5	*Sourced Products*	S1.3	Yes	By law
	Supplier invoice	External	Yes	By law

4.3 Modifying the Process Model to Achieve Validity

In this section we suggest example corrective actions to achieve validity of the S1 process. Clearly, different solutions may be suggested, depending on the procedures of the specific organization. Table 3 summarizes the modified process model. The possible values of the realized state variables are specified and mapped to relevant goal states in S1.2 and S1.3. In S1.3 the case of unapproved quality will terminate the process, when the sourced products are to be returned to the supplier by another process and a re-planning signal is given. This state should be added to the goal of S1.

Table 3. Modifications to Process S1

Step	I condition	Realized value of state variables	G condition	Explanation
S1.1	See Table 1			
S1.2m	*(Time passed = t$_i$) AND (i≤n) AND (Sourced products = Order Opened)*		*[(Arrival Control = OK) OR (Arrival Control = Exception)] AND (i = i +1).*	*i* is a counter. Begin monitoring if t$_i$ time has passed.
S1.2e	*(i > n) OR (Arrival Control = Exception)*		*(Sourced products = Order closed) AND (Re-planning signal = given).*	If monitoring time ended (*i > n*) or exception is recognized by inquiry – process ends
S1.2	*Sourced products = Arrived*	*Actual quantity = Stated Quantity*	*(Sourced products = Quantity verified)*	
		Actual quantity ≠ Stated Quantity	*(Sourced products = Quantity verified) AND (Claim to supplier = to be sent)*	
S1.3	*Sourced products = Quantity verified*	*Quality = meets specification*	*Sourced products = Quality verified*	
		Quality ≠ meets specification	*(Sourced products = to be returned) AND (Re-planning signal = given)*	
S1.4m	*Pull signal ≠ Given*		*Pull Control = OK*	Monitoring by an immediate notification
S1.4	See Table 1			
S1.5m	*(Time condition = t) AND (Invoice ≠ Received)*		*Invoice Control = OK*	Monitoring by notification when waiting time = t
S1.5	See Table 1			

The non-continuous parts need, as discussed in Section 3, to be monitored. The monitoring procedure may vary, depending on the level of uncertainty related to the external event and on the criticality of continuance to the organization. In the case of S1.2, waiting for goods to arrive from the supplier involves a relatively high level of uncertainty and is indeed critical. Hence we proposed a time-dependent control, which repeats itself in time intervals of t_i, where i is the number of repetitions. The exception path will be taken based on the number of monitoring repetitions or on the inquiry response, and its goal state should be added to the goal set of the entire process, S1. The monitoring activity is denoted in Table 3 as S1.2m, and the exception, which terminates the process, is marked S1.2e.

The two other cases of discontinuity in the process (S1.4, S1.5) seem less critical or likely to occur. Hence, the monitoring suggested (S1.4m, S1.5m) is less tight as it includes no repetitions, and a possible exception is not considered.

This demonstrates how the proposed model can be used as the basis for design decisions and the type of considerations that may guide the process' designer.

5   Related Work

Related work includes the areas of goal-driven process models and process model verification. Attempts to incorporate goals into process modeling include [12], who suggest an informal approach in which goals provide a basis for process definition. Business process modeling is addressed by [10] using the Enterprise Knowledge Development (EKD) framework, which entails a goal model among other views, and sets the understanding of goals as a basis for business process identification.

A formally defined set of concepts, incorporating goals and processes, is provided in [11], whose model is based on mathematical systems theory. Their approach to process modeling is state-oriented, viewing a process as a subset of trajectories in some state space, and a process goal as a set of conditions defining a surface in the state space. This set of concepts is extended in [2] and used for defining a process pattern, allowing the design of generic processes that can be specialized for specific situations. This model bears much similarity to our model. However, the distinction of external events is not explicitly made there.

Verification of process models is mainly associated with workflow control models. Workflow model verification is notation-specific, defined often for Petri-nets [20, 21], and sometimes for other languages, e.g., UML Activity diagrams [6].

Basically there are two approaches to the verification. In one, the model is converted into formal specifications that can be analyzed by existing formal model checkers (e.g., SPIN, that also served for verifying UML statecharts [5, 13]) or dedicated model checkers [6]. The other approach is based structural properties of the model (e.g., soundness) [20, 21]. Note, our validity criteria are not structural only, addressing semantics as well via the values of the state variables in the model.

Our process model is less restrictive than the soundness property required in workflow models. For example, in sound workflow models only one termination place is allowed, in contrast to our goal set.

Note, workflow models represent the behavior of the workflow management system (WFMS) only and not its environment. Specifically, workflow processes are usually non-continuous, since the WFMS has to wait for human actions to be reported to it. Hence, workflow models generally assume the environment behaves fairly [21]. In addition, as opposed to workflow verification methods, our approach is conceptual rather than technical. It explores the sources of invalidity and provides remedy to specific cases. Finally, it is independent of any specific notation.

6   Concluding Discussion

The GPM, proposed in this paper, is a theory-based model of a process. This model is utilized for defining validity of a process model and identifying causes for invalidity. Understanding these causes can lead to suggestions for correcting invalid models.

The suggested process model is goal-driven, basing the notion of validity on goal reachability. A process goal is not an obscure notion, but a set of stable states defined by a condition. Hence, goal reachability can be systematically verified.

The verification criteria, though systematic, are conceptual rather than technical. They provide an understanding of the sources of invalidity, so the insight gained will assist the modeler in designing valid process models from the beginning. Alternatively, they provide guidance for modifying the model and make it a valid one.

The suggested process model is generic and notation-independent. It employs a small number of constructs to express many aspects addressed by various process modeling languages. Consequently, models in these languages can be mapped to our generic model and their validity evaluated regardless of the specific notation.

Furthermore, applying the suggested model as an infrastructure to models created in any modeling language can help to structure the modeling process, by presenting a set of questions to the modeler. As an example, assume a process is modeled using Petri nets. Normally the modeler would be occupied with transitions (activities) and firing sequence. Using our model as infrastructure, the modeler will also have to understand the process goal (a condition over a criterion function) and define the places in the model in terms of state variables.

The application of the GPM framework is not limited to validity evaluation. Currently we are extending it to other aspects of process modeling, such as process decomposition, process specialization, and process model reuse.

References

1. Arns, M., Fischer, M., Kemper, P., and Tepper, C. (2002), "Supply Chain Modelling and its Analytical Evaluation", Journal of the Operational Research Society, Vol. 53, pp. 885-894.
2. Bider, I., Johannesson, P., Perjons, E. (2002), "Goal-Oriented Patterns for Business Processes", Position paper for Workshop on Goal-Oriented Business Process Modeling (GBPM'02).
3. Bunge. M., *Treatise on Basic Philosophy: Vol. 3, Ontology I: The Furniture of the World.* Reidel, Boston, 1977.
4. Bunge. M., *Treatise on Basic Philosophy: Vol. 4, Ontology II: A World of Systems*, Reidel, Boston, 1979.
5. Eshuis, R., Jansen, D. N., and Weiringa, R. (2002), "Requirements-Level Semantics and model Checking of Object-Oriented Statecharts", *Requirements Engineering*, 7, pp. 243-263.
6. Eshuis, r., and Weiringa, R. (2002), "Verification Support for Workflow Design with UML Activity Graphs", *Proceedings of the 24th International Conference on Software Engineering (ICSE)*, ACM Press NY USA, pp. 166-176.
7. Hammer, M. and Champy, J. (1994), *Reengineering the Corporation – A manifesto for Business Revolution*, Nicholas Brealey Publishing, London.
8. Humphreys, P. K., Lai, M. K., and Sculli, D. (2001), "An Inter-organizational Information System for Supply Chain Management", International Journal of Production Economics, Vol. 70 No. 3, pp. 245-55.
9. Johannesson, P. and Perjons, E., 2001, "Design Principles for Process Modeling in Enterprise Application Integration", *Information Systems* 26 pp. 165-184.
10. Kavakli, V., and Loucopoulos, P. (1998), "Goal-Driven Business Process analysis Application in Electricity Deregulation", in Pernici, B. and Thanos, C. (ed.), Advanced Information Systems Engineering (CAiSE'98), LNCS 1413, Springer-Verlag Berlin, pp. 305-324.

11. Khomyakov M., and Bider, I. (2000), "Achieving Workflow Flexibility through Taming the Chaos" OOIS 2000 - 6th international conference on object oriented information systems. Springer-Verlag Berlin, pp. 85-92.
12. Kueng, P., and Kawalek, P. (1997), "Goal-based Business Process Models: Creation and Evaluation", BPMJ, Vol. 3 No.1, pp. 17-38.
13. Latella, D., Majzik, I., and Massink, M. (1999), Automatic Verification of a Behavioural Subset of UML Statechart Diagrams Using the Spin Model-checker, *Formal Aspects of Computing*, 11, pp. 637-664.
14. Paulson, D. and Wand, Y., (1992) "An Automated Approach to Information Systems Decomposition", IEEE Transactions on Software Engineering, Vol. 18 No. 3, pp. 174-189.
15. Scheer, A. W., 1999, *ARIS – Business Process Frameworks*, Springer, Berlin.
16. SCOR Reference model, Supply chain council. www.supply-chain.org.
17. Soffer, P., Golany, B., Dori, D., and Wand, Y. (2001) "Modeling Off-the-Shelf Information Systems Requirements: An Ontological Approach", Requirements Engineering, Vol. 6, pp.183-199.
18. Soffer, P., and Wand, Y., 2003, "On the Notion of Soft Goals in Business Process Modeling", *Business Process Management Journal* (to appear).
19. Stephens S. (2001), "Supply Chain Operations Reference Model Version 5.0: a New Tool to Improve Supply Chain Efficiency and Achieve Best Practice", Information Systems Frontiers, Vol. 3 No. 4, pp. 471-476.
20. Van der Aalst, W. M. P. (1997), "Verification of Workflow Nets", *Application and Theory of Petri Nets*, LNCS 1248, Springer-Verlag, Berlin, pp. 407-426.
21. Van der Aalst, W. M. P. And Ter Hofstede, A. H. M., 2000, "Verfication of Workflow Task Structure: A Petri-net-based Approach", *Information Systems* 25(1), pp. 43-69.
22. Wand, Y. and. Weber, R (1990), "An Ontological Model of an Information System", IEEE Trans. on Software Engineering, Vol. 16, No. 11, pp. 1282-1292.

Data Warehouse Methodology:
A Process Driven Approach

Claus Kaldeich and Jorge Oliveira e Sá

Universidade do Minho, Escola de Engenharia
Departamento de Sistemas de Informação, Campus de Azurém
4800-058 Guimarães, Portugal
{cka,jos}@dsi.uminho.pt

Abstract. The current methods of the development and implementation of a Data Warehouse don't consider the integration with the organizational-processes and their respective data. In addition to these current methods, based on demand-driven, data-driven and goal-driven, we will introduce in this paper a new approach to DW development and implementation. This proposal will be based on the integration of organizational processes and their data, denote by: Integrated-Process-Driven (IPD. The principles of this approach are founded on the relation-ships between business-processes and Entity-Relationship-Models (ERM), the Relational Database (RDB) data models. These relationships are originated in the Architecture of Integrated Information Systems (ARIS) methodology. IPD will use the information extracted from the data-driven, on the one side, to match (or define) the AS-IS business processes model. On the other hand, IPD will use the information returned from the demand-driven (required by the DW users) to define the TO-BE business process model based also on the AS-IS model. IPD will integrate the new data models, originated in the TO-BE business processes model, with the DW requirements. The aim of IPD is to define (or to redefine) the organizational processes which will supply the DW with data. The added-value of this approach will be the integration of the previous methods (demand-driven and data-driven) with organizational processes that will treat these sets of informations to be used by the DW. Our approach is also a trigger for business processes reengineering and optimization. Finally, the goal-driven will verify if the IPD achieves the business goals.

1 Introduction

Data Warehouse (DW) systems became an essential component of decision support systems in organizations. DW systems offer access to integrated and historic data from heterogeneous sources to support managers in their planning and decision-making activities. The DW does not create value to an organization; value comes from the use of his data and, of course, the improvement of decision-making activity is the result from the existence of better information available in the DW. The greatest potential benefits of the DW occur when it is used to redesign business processes and to support strategic business objectives [21], [10], but these are also the most difficult benefits to achieve, due to the amount of top management support, commitment, and involvement and the amount of organizational change required.

A. Persson and J. Stirna (Eds.): CAiSE 2004, LNCS 3084, pp. 536–549, 2004.
© Springer-Verlag Berlin Heidelberg 2004

Building a DW is a very challenging issue and once compared to software engineering it reveals quite a young discipline that does not yet offer well-established strategies and techniques for the development process. Current DW development methods can fall within three basic groups: data-driven, goal-driven and demand-driven. The current methods of the development and implementation of a DW don't consider the organizational processes integration with their respective data. In this paper we will introduce a new approach to DW development and implementation. This proposal will be based on the integration of organizational processes and their data: Integrated-Process-Driven (IPD). IPD will use the information requirements from the analysis of the operational (corporate) data model (ERM) [3] and relevant transactions – the data-driven approach, on one side, to match (or define) the AS-IS business process model. On other hand, IPD will use the information requirements from the end user requirements – the demand-driven approach to define the TO-BE business process model based also on the AS-IS model. IPD will integrate the new data models, coming from the TO-BE business process model, with the DW requirements. The aim of the IPD, is to define (or redefine) the organizational processes which will supply the DW data.

In section 2, three approaches to DW development methods are discussed: data-driven, goal-driven and demand-driven. In section 3, the IPD approach is described. In section 4, the relation between processes, functions and data, based on ARIS are presented and discussed. In section 5, a simple example is showed. This paper concludes with section 6, which presents our final comments and future research.

2   Three Approaches to DW Development Methods

Although it seems to be obvious that matching information requirements of future DW users with available information supply is the central issue of DW development, only few approaches seem to address this issue specifically. Based on whether information demand or information supply is guiding the matching process, demand-driven approaches and data-driven approaches can be differentiated. A special type of demand-driven approach is to derive information requirements by analyzing business processes by increasing detail and transforming relevant data structures of business processes into data structures of the DW. This approach is named goal-driven. All three approaches are described in detail:

- Data-Driven (or supply-driven) approach: the DW development strategy is based on the analysis of organisational data models and relevant transactions [9]; this is completely different from the development of classical systems, which have a requirement-driven development life cycle. The requirements are the last thing to be considered in the decision support development life cycle; they are understood after the DW has been populated with data and results of queries have been analysed by users. This approach ignores the needs of DW users a priori. Organizational goals and user requirements are not reflected at all [7], [8]. However, this approach risks to waste resources by handling many unneeded information structures. Moreover, it may not be possible to motivate end users sufficiently to participate in the project once they are not used to work with large data models developed for and by specialists [4].

- Goal-Driven approach: the first stage of this approach is the process's derivation which determines the goals and services the organization provides to its customers. Then, the business process is analysed to highlight the customer's relations and their transactions with the process under study. In a third step, sequences of transactions are transformed into sequences of existing dependencies that refer to information systems. The last step identifies measures and dimensions needed to design the DW [1], [16]. For decision processes, however, a detailed business process analysis is not feasible because the respective tasks are often unique and unstructured or, what is even more important, because decision makers/knowledge workers often refuse to disclose their processes in detail.
- Demand-Driven (or user-driven) approach: this approach assumes that the organization goal is the same for everyone and the entire organization will therefore be pursuing the same direction. It is proposed to set up a first prototype based on the needs of the business. Business people define goals and gather, prioritise as well as define business questions supporting these goals. Afterwards the business questions are prioritised and the most important business questions are defined, to identify data elements terms, including the definition of hierarchies [22].

These approaches are aimed to determine information requirements of DW users. End users alone are able to define the business goals of the DW systems correctly. So, end users should be able to specify information requirements by themselves. However, end users are not capable to specify objectively unsatisfied information requirements, once: their view is subjective by definition, they cannot have sufficient knowledge of all available information sources, and they only use a specific business unit's interpretation of data. Moreover, end users can often not imagine which new information the DW system could supply [2], [4].

To minimize this it is possible to use a catalogue for conducting user interviews in order to collect end user requirements, or by interviewing different user groups in order to get a complete understanding of the business [18].

As described above all approaches have positive and negative aspects, but our objective is to merge "all" positive aspects to a new approach - IPD – Integration Process Driven.

3   IPD Approach

This approach will be based on the integration of organizational processes: Integrated-Process-Driven (IPD). The principles of this approach are based on the relationships between organizational-processes and Entity-Relationship-Models (ERM) (data models) see figure 1. These relationships come from the Architecture of Integrated Information Systems (ARIS) [19], [20].

IPD will use the information extracted from the data-driven, on one side, to match (or define) the AS-IS organizational process model. On the other hand, IPD will use the information returned from the demand-driven (required by the DW users) to define the TO-BE organizational process model based also on the AS-IS model. IPD will integrate the new data models, originated in the TO-BE organizational process model, with the DW requirements. The aim of the IPD, is to define (or to redefine) the organizational processes which will supply the DW data. The added-value of this

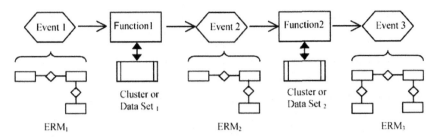

Fig. 1. Event (driven) – Process Chain

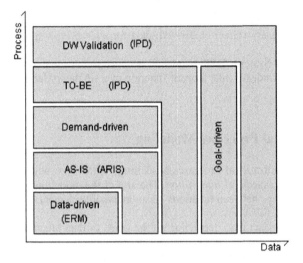

Fig. 2. IPD model

approach will be the integration of the previous methods (demand-driven and data-driven) with organizational processes that will deal with these sets of information's to be used by the DW. Our approach is also a trigger for organizational processes optimization. Finally, the goal-driven will verify if the IPD achieve the business goals, see figure 2.

The relationship between organizational-processes and the respective data sets are trivial. But, not so trivial are the relationships between 'combinations' or 'transformations' from data into sequences of processes (later we will determine this 'combinations' or 'transformations' by *congruencies* of data [13]). These sequences of processes can be parallel, synchronous, asynchronous and so on. Data can be 'derived' from a data set 'transformed' by a process or process-sequences. Data can be the result of *congruencies* of data extracted from different data sets coming from different sources through complex sequences of processes.

In this sense, it is easy to see that a DW can be defined, developed and implemented by different ways to achieve several goals.

Whenever we talk about *data-integration* or *process-integration* along with organizational-processes must be considered the *integration* defined by the *Enterprise Resource Planning* (: ERP) (as an Integrated Information System).

Different grades of data-integration can be achieved in an ERP. For example, the printout of an invoice in an ERP can generate data only for:

1. the Sales-Department: data for the update of accumulated invoice amount/client or accumulated invoice amount /period) or for,
2. the Accounting-Department: data for the update of valued-added-tax accounting/period.

But, the grade of data-integration can be higher and the printout of an invoice in an ERP can generate data also for:

3. treasury: all necessary (direct or derived) data for a Cash-Flow-Simulation until a date-line, and
4. Decision-Support-System (DSS): up to all necessary data for the update of some micro-economics indexes, like a profit-function of a single product/set of products and so on.

4 Organizational Processes Modeling

Concerning to Organizational-Processes-Modelling (OPM), we will use the ARIS[1] regarding important aspects of *integration*. The aim of the modelling with ARIS will define the relationships between functions (as an indivisible element of a process) and respective data [19].

Remarkable is the fact that, depending on the grade of data-integration in an Integrated Information Systems, e.g. an ERP can have multiples processes-chains (interactive, automatics or batch) to increase the data-set, beginning on 'basic' data (like the data from a new invoice) until derived-data (like accumulated invoice amounts up until to the cash ratio) [20].

As well important as the multiples processes-chains is the fact that an ERP can have over thousands of processes-chains and thousands upon thousands transactions which access a Database System to create, update or delete data. Basically, all these data are coming from the organizational-processes and will feed the DW and the DSS.

To support the IPD scope it will be necessary to define some algebraic structures. These structures are connected to the definition of Congruence and Tolerance Relations for Relational Models (in sense of Database Systems) [11],[12], [13], [14]. The aim of these definitions is to apply some algebraic formalism to describe the integration between organizational-processes and data models (ERM). These relations will be used, also, to justify by formalism in the transition from the AS-IS to TO-BE organizational-processes models. The IPD will underline the integration between organizational-processes, data models (ERM).

---

[1] © IDS-Scheer, Saarbrücken, Germany.

4.1 Definition: Relational Database (RDB)

A Relational Database, $RDB := (FL, I, IC)$, is defined as:
1. $FL := (S, W)$ is a formal language, where:

    1.1. S is a set of symbols, and

    1.2. W is a set of words defined by elements of S.

2. I is a *interpretation* of FL.

3. IC is a set of formulas of FL, with will define the Integrity Constraints of the RDB: $IC := \{\delta_i \mid \delta_i : \forall \varepsilon_j \rightarrow \psi_k; \, i,j,k \in \{1,...,n\}, j \neq k; \, \delta,\varepsilon,\psi \in W\}$ ■

4.2 Definition: The Relation R of a RDB

A relation $R := (Sch_R, D_R, FD_R, T_R)$, is defines as:
1. $Sch_R := \{at_1,..., at_n\}$, is a set of attributes of R.

2. D_R is the set of Domains of the dos attributes of R:
    $D_R = D_{at_1} \cup ... \cup D_{at_n}$.

3. FD_R is the set of functional dependencies of R:
    $FD_R \subseteq \{F_1 \rightarrow F_2 \mid F_1, F_2 \subseteq Sch_R; F_1 \neq F_2\}$. ■

4.3 Definition: *Function-Data* Relation (fdr)

Given a function f_i, which is defined as a set of instructions[2] that process a data set. The *function-data* relation is defined as:
1. Let be the structure: $fdr' := (f_i, \{d_{i_1},...,d_{i_n}\})$

    1.1. Where f_i is a function, and

    1.2. the set of data processed by f_i is: $\{d_{i_1},..., d_{i_n}\}$

2. Applying the Decomposition Rule[3] on fdr' :
    $f_i \rightarrow \{d_{i_1},...,d_{i_n}\}) \Rightarrow f_i \rightarrow d_{i_1}, f_i \rightarrow d_{i_2}, ... , f_i \rightarrow d_{i_n}$.

3. The *function-data* relation for the function f_i, is defined as:
    $fdr_{f_i} := (f_i \rightarrow d_{i_k}), k \in \{1,...,n\}$.

4. In this sense is easy to define the *function-data classes* of a family of functions, will be: $fdr_{f_{i,n}} := \biguplus_{k=i}^{n} fdr_{f_k}$. ■

---

[2] Concern about instructions of a formal language, for example: C++.
[3] Analogous to the *decomposition rule* of the Relational Theory, applied to the Functional Dependencies.

Based on the definitions 0 and 0, some questions emerge:

1. Which following relations can be defined based on these relations to achieve the proposed goal?

2. How these above mentioned new relations complement the definitions 0 and 0?

Strictly speaking these questions derive from some simples ideas:

The definition of FD_R are included in a definition of a relation R (definition 0), which describe the set of functional dependencies of R, where a set of data-attributes, represented by F_1 implies an other set of data-attributes, namely $F_2 : F_1 \rightarrow F_2$; why not to define a relation based on the relation fdr (definition 0) to link functions (obtained from organizational-processes) through the related data to a further extended set of data (describe by the Entity-Relationship-Models)? (Further can considered other relationships between data-attributes or data.)

The AS-IS model, represented by a set of EPC's, will define the executions orders of the functions into a process (and processes sequences). The over mentioned functions orders will define the order of the respectively data processing.

Each element of the demand-driven data set can be defined as a semantic conclusion from the data-driven data set (also denoted by 'basic data') and an additional data set coming from the TO-BE organizational-processes model and integrated by the IPD.

Integrated by the IPD, for the demand-driven data set can be defined:

i. *The set of functions which will process these data, they executions orders (based on the AS-IS model and the TO-BE model (represented trough new EPC's)).*

ii. *The matching of all processes and respective data with the goal-driven: the validation of the TO-BE model generated by the IPD to support the DW-model.*

4.4 Definition: *Dependency-Data* Relation *(ddr)*

The *ddr* is defined as:

1. Given FD_R , like in the definition 0 .

2. Give $F_1 := \{at_p,..., at_j\}$ and $F_2 := \{at_{j+1} ,...., at_n\}$ then:

3. $F_1 \rightarrow F_2 \approx (at_1 \wedge ... \wedge at_j) \rightarrow (at_{j+1} \wedge ... \wedge at_n) \approx \{(at_1 \rightarrow at_{j+1}), (at_1 \rightarrow at_{j+2}),...,$
   $(at_1 \rightarrow at_n), (at_2 \rightarrow at_{j+1}), (at_2 \rightarrow at_{j+2}),..., (at_2 \rightarrow at_n), ... \}$.
   Expressed as binary relation:
   $\{(at_p, at_{j+1}), (at_p, at_{j+2}),..., (at_p, at_n), (at_2, at_{j+1}), (at_2, at_{j+2}),..., (at_2, at_n), ...\}$.

4. Now, let $e_j \in Dat_i$, $j \in \{1,...,m\}$, $i \in \{1,...,n\}$; be the extensions of the attributes $at_1 ,...., at_n$. Let I be a Interpretation of $F_1 \rightarrow F_2$, then:
   $I (F_1 \rightarrow F_2) \subseteq \{ \{(e_1 , e_{j+1}), (e_1 , e_{j+2}),..., (e_1 , e_n), (e_2 , e_{j+1}), (e_2 , e_{j+2}),..., (e_2 , e_n), ...\}$.
   In this way the relation *rdd* is defined as:

$ddr \subseteq I\,(F_1 \rightarrow F_2\,) \subseteq \{(e_1, e_{j+1}\,), (e_1, e_{j+2}\,),..., (e_1, e_n\,), (e_2, e_{j+1}\,), (e_2, e_{j+2}\,),...,$
$(e_2, e_n\,), ...\}$.

■

Based on the definitions above, is possible increase the semantics of the *integration* concept.

4.5 Definition: *Auxiliary* Relation *(auxr)*

Given the function-data relation: $fdrf_i := (\,f_i\,, d_j\,),..., (\,f_i\,, d_n\,))$ and dependency-data relation: $ddr := \{(e_1, e_k\,), (e_1, e_{k+1}\,),..., (e_1, e_n\,), (e_2, e_k\,), (e_2, e_{k+1}\,),...,(e_2, e_n\,), ...\}$.
The *auxr* for the function f_i will be defined as follow:

1. $auxrf_i := \{(\,f_i\,, e_k\,) \mid \forall\,(\,f_i\,, d_j\,)\,\forall\,(e_m, e_k\,) : d_j = e_m \Rightarrow (\,f_i\,, e_k\,), i, j, k, m \in \{1,...,n\}.$
    This rule will be denoting by *functional-transitivity rule*.

■

In this way a *functional transitivity* can be establish between a function f_i and extended set of tuples of related data.
In order to extend our definitions to allow the 'construction' of factors of processes or data it is possible to define other relations based on the above ones. The factors will allow the definition of 'equivalence classes' of data, based on one or more functions or one or more function based on a set of data. So, we can increase the scope of the data set related to a function and reciprocal.

4.6 Definition: *Functional-Transitive* Relation *(ftr)*

Given the relations $fdrf_i$ and $auxrf_i$, defined for the function f_i , the *functiona-transitive* relation for the function f_i is defined as: $ftrf_i := fdrf_i \cup auxrf_i$.

■

4.7 Definition: Factorization of a *Functional-Transitive Relation* by a Function

Given a *functional-transitive relation* defined on a function $f_i : ftrf_i$, a set of all data concerning to f_i is defined as:
1. $ftrf_{i/f_i} := \{d_j \mid d_j \in \{d_1,..., d_n\} \lor d_j = e_k\,, j, k \in \{1,..., n\}\}$. (So far, trivial).

2. For the functions f_i and f_j is possible to define:
    $ftrf_i, f_{j/\{f_i, f_j\}} := \{d_k \mid (f_i, d_k\,) \in ftrf_i \lor (f_j, d_k\,) \in ftrf_j\}$.

3. $ftrf_i, f_{j/f_j} := \{d_k \mid (f_i, d_k\,) \in ftrf_i \land (f_j, d_k\,) \in ftrf_j\}$.

Now, the sets of data linked to a function or to functions are defined. In principle, this definition is trivial as far as natural derivation of the earliest definitions.   ■

Important Remarks:
In addition to all sets and structures defined upon to now, we can emphasize:

1. Let the *demand-driven data* set be denoted by: $ddd := \{d_r, d_{r+1},..., d_s\}$.

2. Further, let the semantic conclusion of the elements of *ddd*, be denoted as:
    $\{d_j,..., d_h\} \models d_i$ for each $d_i \in ddd$ ($i \in \{r, r+1,..., s\}$).

3. Based on the AS-IS organizational-processes model the ordered set of the functions can define a process: $P_l := \{f_1, f_2,..., f_n\}$. (If P_l has parallel sub-processes then, we will have, for example, $P_l := \{\{f_1,..., f_k\}, \{f_2,..., f_m\},...\}$. But this is not the aim of this paper, therefore, we assume the processes as linear sequences of functions.).

4.8 Definition: Factorization of a *Functional-Transitive Relation* by a Set of Data.

Given a functional-transitive relation ftr_F defined on a set of functions $F := \{f_1, f_2, , f_k\}$, the set $ddd := \{d_r, d_{r+1},..., d_s\}$. Then, for each $d_i \in ddd$ and $\{d_j,..., d_h\}$ d_i is valid, then $ftrF_{/\{d_j, d_n\}} := \{f_j \mid f_j \in F \wedge (f_j, d_m) \in ftrF, m \in \models \{j,...,n\}\}$ is the set of the functions which provide data for d_i . ∎

In the sense of the IPD, the sets defined by Definition 0 will be the bases for the TO-BE models (the new EPC and respective data) integrated with the *Demand-Driven* data set.

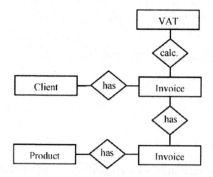

Fig. 3. Invoice system example

5 Example

In this example we will describe an invoice system. This system has an initial ERM (data-driven approach), see figure 3.

This ERM has 5 entities, containing the following data:
- Client entity – d_1 : client code; d_2 : client name; d_3 : client address; d_4 : city; d_5 : phone; d_6 : fax; d_7 : tax number; d_8 : total invoice in period.
- Invoice entity - d_{10} : invoice number; d_1 : client code; d_2 : client name; d_3 : client address; d_4 : city; d_7 : tax number; d_{30} : invoice total.

- Invoice-line entity - d_{10} : invoice number; d_{20} : product code; d_{21} :product net value; d_{22} : product VAT code; d_{23} : calculated VAT value (based in d_{21}); d_{24} : product total value.
- Product entity - d_{20} : product code; d_{41} : product description; d_{21} : product net value; d_{43} : stock quantity; d_{23} : calculated VAT value (based in d_{21}).
- VAT - d_{20} : product code; d_{21} : product net value; d_{22} : product VAT code; d_{23} : product VAT code (based in d_{21}); d_{24} : product total value.

This system has 5 functions: f_1 verification of client data; f_2 create invoice head; f_3 VAT (Value Add Tax) calculation; f_4 verification of product data to invoice-line; and f_5 invoice print.

Assume f_1 as function to verify and load the client data. This function manipulates the following data:

1. d_1 : client code.
2. d_2 : client name.
3. d_3 : client address.
4. d_4 : city.
5. d_5 : phone.
6. d_6 :fax.
7. d_7 : tax number.
8. d_8 : total invoice in period.

Assume f_2 as function to create and process an invoice head. This function manipulates the following data:

9. d_{10} : invoice number
10. d_1 : client code.
11. d_2 : client name.
12. d_3 : client address.
13. d_4 : city.
14. d_7 : tax number.

Assume f_3 as function to calculate VAT. This function manipulates the following data:

15. d_{20} : product code.
16. d_{21} : product net value.
17. d_{22} : product VAT code.
18. d_{23} : calculated VAT value. (based in d_{21}).
19. d_{24} : product total value.

Assume f_4 as function to verify and load the product data to the invoice-line. This function manipulates the following data:

20. d_{10} : invoice number
21. d_{20} : product code.
22. d_{41} : product description.
23. d_{21} : product net value.
24. d_{43} : stock quantity.
25. d_{22} : product VAT code.
26. d_{21} : product net value.
27. d_{22} : product VAT code.
28. d_{23} : calculated VAT value (based in d_{21}).
29. d_{24} : product total value.
30. d_{30} : invoice total.

Assume f_5 as function to print the invoice. This function manipulates the following data:

31. d_{10} : invoice number
32. d_1 : client code.
33. d_2 : client name.
34. d_3 : client address.
35. d_4 : city.
36. d_7 : tax number.
37. d_{20} : product code.
38. d_{41} : product description.
39. d_{21} : product net value.
40. d_{22} : product VAT code.
41. d_{23} : calculated VAT value (based in d_{21}).
42. d_{24} : product total value.
43. d_{30} : invoice total.

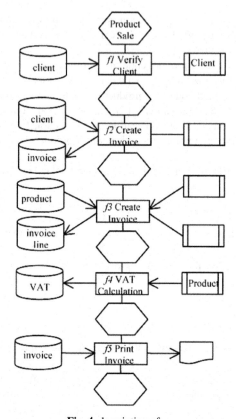

Fig. 4. description of p_1

Based on these 5 functions, we can describe the process p_1 (sale a product) which is a sequence of f_1, f_2, f_3, f_4, and f_5, see figure 4.

The aim of the next step is gather user requirements (demand-driven approach). As result of this step we will obtain two user-requirements: compare sales information by region; and the accumulation of invoices by client and product, see figure 5. Region can be obtained through the zip code data, which is included in the data d_3 : client address. So we include two functions $f6$ and $f7$, the order of this functions .

Now we can achieve a final ERM changed by IPD, see figure 6.

As demonstrated, the differences between the initial and final ERM (see figure 3 and 6) are obtained from a process p_1 with a sequence of functions [f_1,f_2,f_3,f_4,f_5] and two additional functions added by IPD $f6$ and $f7$. These differences are justified through a very well defined sequence of processes – the EPC. Thus, it was started for describing the initial ERM (data-driven approach) where we obtain the AS-IS model. Its integration with the processes was demonstrated through the model EPC of the ARIS. Based on the requirements of the DW end-users (demand-driven approach) we have the TO-BE model, shaped, one more time, through model EPC of the ARIS. The differences between the TO-BE and AS-IS models, would have to be verified by the

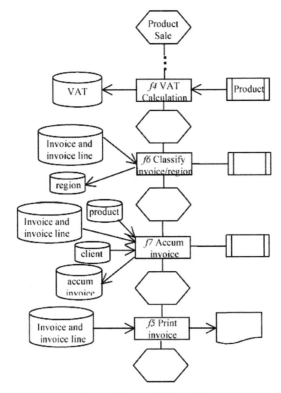

Fig. 5. EPC modified by IPD

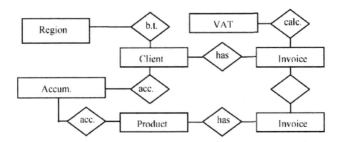

Fig. 6. ERM modified by IPD

existing goals of business (goal-driven approach) but, for the dimension of the example, it is not justified.

We have a new model ERM (figure 6). This model facilitates the design of a DW system (and respective operations to load data, usually named ETL - Extraction, Transforming and Loading) once this model include more data than the original model and, by regarding our example, more data is available to supply the needs expressed by Demand-Driven end-users. It's important to understand that IPD, described above, can be repeated for diverse times - iterations, so the model ERM final could be the ERM initial for a similar process.

6 Conclusion

With the presented proposal we can include the organizational-processes in a DW system methodology. Since organizational-processes generate data to the DW system, these organizational processes will have to suffer a "re-engineering process", in order to satisfy the demand-driven approach. The data-driven approach only supplies part of these information's; the missing part of information would not have any relation with the organizational processes. Our proposal aims to put an end to this lack of relation between the new information and the organizational processes to get a new model of data (ERM), as well as new models of organizational processes [15].

With this approach the fundamentals of the DW methodologies have a more integrated component with the organizational processes. The IPD will enrich the DW theory with a more rigorously requirements gathering to design the DW.

In terms of research based on IPD approach, we intend to get the data model (ERM) of the DW system. By further research, we will want to framework this approach into new definitions of information systems and integrated information systems, as well as the definition of relations of congruence for the IPD to define an order, sequence of data transformations in organizational processes, with the aim to define a high degree of information integration.

References

1. Boehnlein, M., Ulbrich vom Ende, A.: *Business Process Oriented Development of Data Warehouse Structures*, In: Proceedings of Data Warehousing, Physica Verlag (2000)
2. Connelly, R. A., R. McNeill and R.P. Mosimann: *The Multidimensional Manager*, Ottawa: Cognos Inc (1999)
3. Elmasri, R.; Navathe, S. B.: *Fundamentals of Database Systems*, 3ª ed., Addison-Wesley, Massachusetts, EUA (2000)
4. Gardner, S.: *Building the Data Warehouse*, Communications of the ACM, vol. 41, no. 9, 52-60 (1998)
5. Gable, G.; Stewart, G.: *SAP R/3 Implementation Issues for Small to Medium Enterprises*, Information Systems Management Research Centre, Queensland University of Technology, Brisbane, Australia. (g.gable@qut.edu.au, g.stewart@qut.edu.au) (2000)
6. Gable, G.; Scott, J. E.; Davenport, T. D.: *Cooperative ERP Life-Cycle Knowledge Management*, Information Systems Management Research Centre, Queensland University of Technology, Brisbane, Australia. (g.gable@qut.edu.au) (2000)
7. Golfarelli, M.; Maio, D.; Rizzi, S.: *Conceptual Design of Data Warehouse from E/R Schemas*, Proceedings of the 3th Hawaii International Conference on System Sciences, Kona, Hawaii; EUA (1998)
8. Golfarelli, M.; Maio, D.; Rizzi, S.: *A methodological Approach for Data Warehouse Design*, Proceedings of the 1st International Workshop on Data Warehouse and OLAP (DOLAP'98), Washington DC; EUA (1998)

9. Immon, W. H.: *Building the Data Warehouse*; 2nd Ed., Wiley Computer Publishing, EUA (1996)

10. List, B.; Schiefer, J.; Tjoa A M.; Quirchmayr, G.: *Multidimensional Business Process Analysis with the Process Warehouse*, In: W. Abramowicz and J. Zurada (eds.): Knowledge Discovery for Business Information Systems, Kluwer Academic Publishers (2000)

11. Kaldeich, C.: *An algebraic approach to the Information Systems Integrated Theory: The binary relation (function, data)*. 13ª Jornadas Hispano-Lusas de Géstion Científica, Universidade de Santiago de Compostela, Lugo, Espanha, Fevereiro (in portuguese) (2003)

12. Kaldeich, C.: *A Mathematical Method for Refinement and Factorisation of Relational Databases*; International Conference on Information System Concepts - ISCO 3 (IFIP), Marburg, R.F.A. (1993)

13. Kaldeich, C.: *Congruence relations in relational databases: incomplete information*; The 2nd Workshop on Non-Standard Logic and Logical Aspects of Computer Science - NSL'95, Irkutsk, Russia (1995)

14. Kaldeich, C.: *Toleranz- und Kongruenzrelationen in Relationalen Datenbanken*; Ed. INFIX, Sankt Augustin, R.F.A (1996)

15. Kaldeich, C.; Sá, J.: *Data Warehouse to Support Assembled Cost Centres (diagonals)*, 7º Congresso Brasileiro de Custos, Universidade de Pernambuco, Recife, Brasil. (in Portuguese) (2000)

16. Kimball, R.: *The Data Warehouse Toolkit: Practical Techniques For Building Dimensional Data Warehouse*, John Wiley & Sons (1996)

17. Kirchmer, M.: *Business Process Oriented Implementation of Standard Software: How to Acthieve Competitive Advantage Quickly and Efficiently*, Berlin, Springer (1998)

18. Poe, V.: Building a Data Warehouse for Decision Support, Prentice Hall (1996)

19. Scheer, A.-W.: *Business Process Engineering. Reference Models for Industrial Enterprises*, 2ª ed., Springer-Verlag, Berlin (1994)

20. Scheer, A.-W.; Nüttgens, M.: *ARIS Architecture and Reference Models for Business Process Management*, in: van der Aalst, W.M.P.; Desel, J.; Oberweis, A.: Business Process Management - Models, Techniques, and Empirical Studies, LNCS 1806, Berlin et al., pp. 366-379 (2000)

21. Watson, H.; Haley, B.: *Managerial Considerations*, In Communications of the ACM, Vol.41, No. 9 (1998)

22. Westerman, P.: Data Warehousing using the Wal-Mart Model, Morgan Kaufmann (2001)

Interactive Models
for Supporting Networked Organisations

John Krogstie and Håvard D. Jørgensen

SINTEF Telecom and Informatics and IDI, NTNU
PO Box 124, Blindern
N-0314 Oslo, Norway
{jok,hdj}@sintef.no

Abstract. This paper presents a novel approach to the development and operation of dynamic networked organization. The approach is based on the idea of
using interactive models. Interactive models are visual models of enterprise aspects that can be viewed, traversed, analyzed, simulated, adapted and executed
by industrial users as part of their work. The approach was developed in the
EXTERNAL-project, where experiences from three case studies were used as a
basis for validation and further enhancement of the approach in follow-up projects. The main innovative contributions include an environment to support
concurrent modelling, meta-modelling, management and performance of work,
integrated support for planned and emergent processes, and customisable
model- and process-driven integration.

1 Introduction

The business environment is getting increasingly dynamic and complex. Co-operation
across traditional organizational boundaries is increasing, as outsourcing and electronic business is enabled by the Internet and other information systems. As a consequence of this, organisations are becoming less self-sufficient and increasingly dependent on business partners and other actors. When such co-operation moves beyond
the buying and selling of goods and well-defined services, there is a need for a flexible infrastructure that supports not only information exchange, but also knowledge
creation, evolution and sharing.

A dynamic networked organisation (DNO) is being developed more or less ad-hoc
to reach a certain goal based on the resources of several co-operating enterprises.
Such networks consist of independent partners, unlike top-down virtual enterprises
where the main partner lays down the rules for coordination, e.g. in outsourcing. The
partners often come from different countries, using different languages and having
different cultural background. They aim to harvest knowledge from the DNO to be
reused in their traditional organization, and in other DNO's.

The approach and working environments to enable this must allow dynamic, concurrent execution, modelling, and meta-modelling in distributed teams. This demands
a new approach to enterprise integration and system engineering, which will be described in this paper. We first present the concept of interactive models. We then
outline the EXTERNAL IST-project [3], and the 3 layers of infrastructure that this

A. Persson and J. Stirna (Eds.): CAiSE 2004, LNCS 3084, pp. 550–563, 2004.
© Springer-Verlag Berlin Heidelberg 2004

project provides to support this thinking. Major aspects of the infrastructure are presented, and a case study shows the feasibility and usefulness of the approach. Finally we briefly position interactive models in context with related work, and point out directions for further research.

2 Interactive Models and the EXTERNAL Project

An interactive model is a visual externalization of enterprise aspects that can be viewed, traversed, analyzed, simulated, adapted and executed by users [16]. What does it mean that the model is interactive? First of all, the visual model must be available to the users of the underlying information system at runtime. Second, the model must influence the behaviour of the computerised support system. Third, the model must be dynamic, users must be supported in changing the model to fit their local reality, enabling tailoring of the system's behaviour. Users thus manipulate and utilise interactive models as part of their day-to-day work.

2.1 The Interactive Model Approach

Utilisation of interactive models implies that modelling, meta-modelling and work can be performed in parallel. To support this in practice is dependent on a rich, generic infrastructure. Being able to support collaborative work and managing knowledge will decide the quality of the solution. The usage and value of the approach also depend on the competence and knowledge of the teams involved.

2.2 Concurrent Meta-modeling, Modeling, Work Management and Performance

One of the cornerstones of the approach is to integrate learning and knowledge management into everyday work and management *practice*. This is supported through supporting concurrent definition of extensions of modelling language (meta-modelling), modelling and planning of the work, model-driven management, coordination, and performance of work. There is thus a direct link from knowledge management activities to work performance, as depicted in Fig.1.

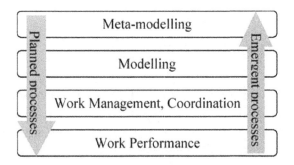

Fig. 1. Concurrent meta-modelling, modelling and work performance

2.3 Planned vs. Emergent Processes

Most process support systems target planned processes, where generic models of work are applied to several instances of projects. Models are constructed prior to work performance, and not expected to change much during performance. A number of case studies have demonstrated the limitations of this approach. It often leads to models that do not accurately depict the way work is actually performed [18], and models that bias a management perspective at the expense of work performance [21]. Such models can cause constraining more than facilitating tool support, and are poor resources for process improvement. Consequently, our approach also supports *emergent* processes [8], processes that are represented by evolving models, where local changes are allowed and supported. All real work processes have aspects and parts that are best described as emergent, but also aspects and parts that can be thoroughly planned in advance. It is thus necessary to integrate the support for both kinds of processes if we are to provide an infrastructure for knowledge-based networked organisations.

2.4 Process and Model Integration

Models and processes are the core means of integration in the approach, both vertically and within each layer in Fig. 1. Meta-models define the language for modelling, and models define the work processes to be performed and managed. For emergent processes, modelling may be intertwined in the performance and management of work, bringing local knowledge into more detailed and accurate plans. By developing and sharing models of their joint enterprise, participants in a networked organization construct shared understanding at the levels of work and management, but also the language and models for their internal communication.

Process integration is an important aspect of reflection in the approach. Through modelling and management, the primary work is articulated, controlled and coordinated. But modelling and management are themselves work activities, thus models of how we perform the processes of modelling, project planning, follow-up and coordination are defined. These models customize and guide the modellers and managers through their work just like the primary models support those performing that actual work of the networked organizations. In the approach work and knowledge management is thus supported just like other work activities.

3 Overview of the Infrastructure Layers

The infrastructure to support networked organisations developed in EXTERNAL can be described as consisting of three layers [10, 12]. These layers are identified as:

- Layer 1, the *information and communication technology* (ICT) layer: – defining and describing the execution platform, software architectures, tools, software components, connectivity and communication.

- Layer 2, the *knowledge representation* layer: - defining and describing constructs and mechanisms for modelling.
- Layer 3, the *work performance and management* layer; - modelling and implementing customer solutions, generating work environments as personalized and context-sensitive user interfaces available through portals, and performing work.

3.1 The ICT Layer

The ICT-infrastructure is an integration of the enterprise and process modelling tools brought into the EXTERNAL project by the partners:

- METIS [15], a general purpose enterprise modelling and visualization tool,
- XCHIPS [6], a cooperative hypermedia tool integrated with process support and synchronous collaboration,
- SimVision (previously Vite) [14], a project simulator used to analyze resource allocation, highlighting potential sources of delay and backlogs.
- WORKWARE [7, 8], a web-based emergent workflow management system with to-do-lists, document sharing, process enactment and awareness mechanisms.
- FrameSolutions [9], a commercially available framework for building automated workflow applications.

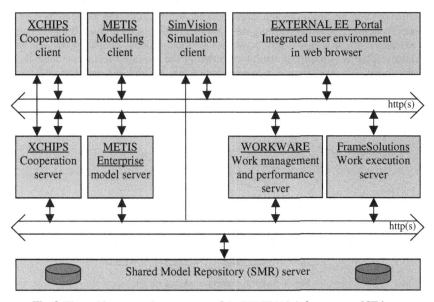

Fig. 2. The architecture and components of the EXTENAL infrastructure, ICT layer

Fig. 2 depicts the technical infrastructure. The architecture has 3-tiers, clients, application servers, and data servers. The implementation is web-based, utilizing HTTP both for control and data integration, and exchanging data with XML format. The integration work has proceeded in three steps.

1. Data-centred integration: based on a common EXTERNAL XML DTD, XML importing/exporting utilities are implemented in each of the enterprise tools for data exchange between the tools or between an XML repository and the tools.
2. Control-centred integration: this is done by using the APIs provided by the tools and the repository to be integrated. With the APIs, the tools can call each other and access the shared repository. Some of the APIs may have parameters for denoting content objects and the implementation of them requires the data-centred integration capability as developed in step one.
3. Worktop-based integration: this is a service-based integration at the user-interface level which makes use of both data-centred integration and control-centred integration methods to access shared models, information objects, and to invoke individual tools.

3.2 The Knowledge Representation Layer

The knowledge representation layer defines how models, meta-models and meta-data are represented, used and managed. A version of Action Port Modeling (APM) [1, 8] constitutes the core of EXTERNAL's modelling language (EEML). The kernel concepts are shown in Fig. 3 as a simplified logical meta-model of EEML. The process logic is mainly expressed through nested structures of *tasks* and *decision points*. The sequencing of the tasks is expressed by the *flow* relation. *Roles* are used to connect resources of various kinds (people, organisations, information, and tools) to the tasks. Hence, modelling the networked organisation in EEML results in models that capture an extensive set of relationships between the organisations, people, processes and resources. This is particularly useful considering the dynamic nature of networked organisations. For new partners joining the network, the rich enterprise models provide a valuable source of knowledge on how to "behave" in the network.

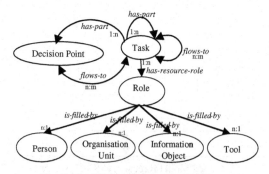

Fig. 3. Simplified meta-model of EEML

Moreover, the interactive nature of the models, meaning that the users are free to refine them during execution, increases their potential as sources of experience and knowledge. As such they *document* details on how the work was actually done, not only how it was once planned.

The notation of the main concepts within the language is illustrated in Fig. 4 which consist of a conceptual meta-model of EEML. In addition to the core concepts of tasks, decision points (including milestones) roles and resources, it illustrates support of goal modeling and competency modeling.

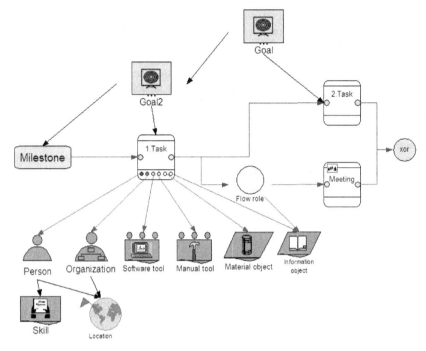

Fig. 4. Conceptual meta-model of EEML

From a knowledge management perspective, process models are carriers of process knowledge; knowledge of how to do things. But through the possibility in EEML of attaching information resources to the tasks at any level, such a model also imposes a structure upon the set of information resources relevant for the work described by the process model. That way, the process models themselves form the basis for information management.

3.3   The Work Performance and Management Layer

Users access their solutions through project portals. A project portal for a networked organisation must have support for methodology adaptation and for communication, co-ordination and collaboration in teams. Project work management, reporting and other services must be offered, and finally project work must be performed with possibilities for repetition, providing security and privacy to knowledge workers.

In the EXTERNAL infrastructure, the web-based portal registers and qualifies users, and invokes other tools through WORKWARE. The modelled tasks are also executed through the invocation of tools and applications from the web based user environment comprised of the portal and WORKWARE. WORKWARE sets up the context for each task, giving access to the knowledge and resources needed to perform the task. The actual work performance is done by invoking appropriate services. The task performers may access desktop tools, organisational information systems, web services, or automated processes (in FrameSolutions) through this user environment.

User environments are generated dynamically based on the definition of tasks using EEML. Forms and components for interacting with different model objects are selected and composed based on user interface policies. These policies are also modelled objects. This enables user interface customization and personalization.

The dynamically generated work management interface (lowest level) includes services for work performance, but also for process modelling and meta-modelling. The *worktop* is the main component in this interface. Each task has its own worktop. In addition to the services for performing and managing the task, it contains links to all knowledge in the process models that is relevant for the task. Since the worktop is dynamically generated, subject to personal preferences, the skill levels of task performers can be taken into account, e.g. to provide more detailed guidelines for people who have not previously worked on such tasks. Similarly, customized worktops for project management can support the project management team. The contents may include an overview of the project, adopted management principles, applicable methodologies, project work-break-down structure, results, plans and tasks, technologies and resources, status reporting and calculations.

4   Case Study: Project Planning and Performance

In the EXTERNAL project, a number of case studies have been used to explore the feasibility and usefulness of the approach and the current infrastructure [3, 17] including research projects and industrial cases from a network of small and medium sized IT companies, and from business consulting. In this work, the situated knowledge we can capture from user experiences, methodologies, and models, is complemented by a formal evaluation [17].

4.1   Joint Project Planning (JPL)

Project planning is a knowledge-intensive task, which utilizes the process modelling tools for work performance. The first implementation of this case included the *plan* (a process model) as well as the *planning process* (meta-process), but not the operation of the plans once they were completed. Both the plan and the planning process were modelled in EEML. In advance, it was expected that the need for coordination between different work package plans would require the real-time collaborative modelling services of XCHIPS. Consequently, this tool was selected as the main worktop for this task. XCHIPS support more focused collaboration than the web-based portal environment provided through WORKWARE. When two people work on the same task, they immediately see the effects of each others' actions. The interface provides real-time awareness of who is currently working in the process, in addition to showing the current status of the tasks by colour coding as in METIS and WORKWARE. The use case report contains an example of how these features were utilized for defining a template [5]:

Once the joint planning process model was finished, one designer created a work package model template [in] the METIS modelling environment and made the template available by using the shared repository [...] Subsequently, she put a link to the template into the JPL process model. Now, another designer used that template to create a sample work package model for WP 4, by using modelling services. This model was reviewed by the first designer and improved during a number of iterations. The final example model was made available in the shared repository and linked to from the JPL process model.

This mixture of largely asynchronous work and some synchronous discussions was greatly facilitated by the shared repository, collaboration, and modelling services.

The template produced here is a typical example of a process model. It includes a basic structure for objects, with separate folders for tasks, inputs, outputs, organizations and people, as well as a project document archive. Many elements, e.g. parts of the archive and the organizational structure, are shared among the different work packages. The organization of the models into folders facilitated such sharing and reuse. The inputs to one work package (WP) in many cases are the outputs of another. At the same time, the separation of responsibility among WP managers is reflected in the granularity of the process models, with each WP articulated in its own model. The poor support for relationships between model files is currently a major limitation of the EXTERNAL infrastructure. At the same time the modularization of models in this case simplified the modeling work for the WP managers.

This example shows how (meta) process support can facilitate knowledge management tasks. XCHIPS was also used for enacting the meta-process of defining new projects in this version of the EXTERNAL infrastructure, invoking METIS to let users define the first plan of the project and then forwarding it to WORKWARE for enactment.

4.2 Action Lists for Emergent Processes

The first implementation in the JPL case presented above took a *planned process* perspective, where managers were responsible for planning the work inside their work package. These plans, however, seldom are detailed enough to cover all the tasks that are to be performed. Consequently, the EXTERNAL project also had a web-based action list on the project web server. This solution had a number of limitations, typical for publish-oriented web solutions:

- Only the project manager could change the list,
- The actions lacked context, and were sometimes hard to understand for the persons responsible,
- The actions were not explicitly connected to project plans (the process models),
- The action descriptions contained no links to a work area or documents and tools that could be used for performing the actions,
- Although the list could be sorted on different attributes and filtered according to certain criteria, it was not possibly to add user-defined lists.

The action lists were consequently not actively used by many of the project participants. When the EXTERNAL infrastructure became available, it was thus decided to use that instead. WORKWARE has a central role in this application, managing the actions as EEML tasks. It took only two hours of work to customize a WORKWARE server for action lists. In this solution engineering process, worklists were defined that organize actions according to these criteria:

- Status, e.g. most lists contain only ready-to-be-performed and/or ongoing tasks,
- Delay,
- Work packages,
- Teams that have shared responsibility for distributing, scheduling and coordinating interrelated tasks across work packages,
- Persons, separating the actions which the current user is responsible for from the ones where she is just a participant,
- Follow-up lists, containing all tasks that the current user is customer of. Lack of follow-up from other people than the project manager, was reported as a major problem with the previous system.

The increased access to edit actions should make the lists more up to date. Although the structure for the actions was not connected to a full project plan, at least the work packages provided some increased context for the work. Explicit assignment of follow-up responsibility and the ability to look in the event log to see who created the action, made each item easier to understand. The old, static action lists contained 288 actions after two and a half years of operation, while WORKWARE contained 131 after just two months, even though it was installed during the summer holidays. This, as well as feedback given in meetings, indicates that the users experienced the second application as a substantial improvement.

This case demonstrates how quickly and easily interactive models can be customized to a particular usage need by defining an overall process model, a menu structure, and some specialized worklists and web services. After people started to use the application, further customization was made based on usage experiences. The case also shows how bottom-up, emergent process articulation can complement top-down planning.

4.3 Proposal Writing for an International Project

A final aspect to be illustrated here in relation to this case is the use within proposal writing for a follow-up project, involving also a number of additional partners. The process used as an outset was the methodology for planning, developing, deploying, running, and decommissioning networked organisations developed in the EXTERNAL project itself. The methodology was represented as a generic model EEML-model to be specialised as an interactive model on individual projects.

An overall plan was developed in METIS. The model is a specialisation of the proposal writing part of the generic EXTERNAL methodology. The plans were transferred to Workware, where a more detailed work-breakdown structure was developed and tasks where allocated to specific persons (see Fig. 5), acting as a support environment. The task with an id-number in the list on the left is taken from the generic model, whereas the more detailed levels are specific for this task.

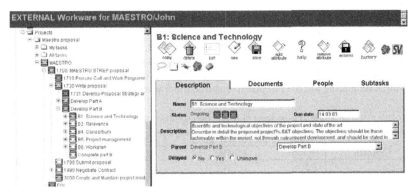

Fig. 5. Generated work environment for the proposal task

4.4   Evaluation

The experiences from the EXTERNAL cases were subject to a formal evaluation [13, 17]. An independent researcher who had not participated in the project performed the evaluation. He followed a quasi-experimental strategy measuring how participants of the separate case studies perceived their working environment, before and after EXTERNAL was implemented. A quasi-experiment resembles a classical experiment in the social sciences, since specific attitudes of a group of people are measured before and after the group is given a stimulus believed to impact on these attitudes. However, in a classical experiment the attitudes of a control group (that is not given the stimulus) are compared to the group that is subject to the stimulus. In addition, both the experimental group and the control group are selected by randomisation. Our evaluation did not encompass a control group and the respondents were not selected by randomisation, hence it is a quasi-experiment.

In order to provide the best possible basis for judgement, measurements were performed by way of a structured questionnaire submitted to all case-study participants before and after the implementation of the EXTERNAL infrastructure supporting their work in the case-study. In addition, semi-structured interviews have been conducted with selected participants on all case studies. The use of interviews was performed to provide more depth and to unveil areas of improvement.

To measure the impact of EXTERNAL, we identified a set of statements indicating various attitudes towards working in networked organisations (indicators). In the surveys, 16 participants were asked to state (along a six-level scale) the extent to which they agreed, or disagreed, to the statements. To assess whether EXTERNAL have brought about changes in the way the participants perceived their work environment, a selection of these statements were evaluated both before and immediately after the implementation. The remaining statements were aimed specifically at investigating the quality of EXTERNAL and were for this reason evaluated only after the implementation.   In the following section we present some main results from the survey questionnaire together with interview data. Due to space limitations, we only present parts of the results.

A literature survey led us to highlight technical viability, cost effectiveness, functionality and impact on business processes, as key dimensions for this evaluation. The following criteria were regarded as critical enablers for these objectives: Ease of use, easy access to tools, effective communication, learning, and trust. A number of statements were used as indicators for each of these criteria, and users were asked to rate to which degree they agreed to the statements as outlined above. Agreement signifies required qualities. Table 1 gives a high-level summary with the results from the questionnaires indicating the overall positive shifts in opinion among the users.

Table 1. Summary of evaluation results (average scores)

Criteria	Number of people who agree		Number of people who disagree	
	Before	After	Before	After
Access	2,8	9,3	13	5,6
Usability	Not asked	8,7	not asked	6,6
Communication	6	12	10	4
Learning	2,4	8,8	13	7
Trust	8	12,8	8	3

Although the tendency is clear, there are also a number of limitations related to these results, including the potential for bias, and lack of control group. Still, a number of lessons can be learned especially from the supporting interviews. For instance, customisation was the area within usability that had the lowest score, but the respondents were polarised on this issue, with most people saying that they "agree a little" that tailoring is easy, while a number of people "strongly disagreed". This may reflect the fact that the customisation services, e.g. of WORKWARE, had not been made easily available to all participants. Also, no specialized customization user interface existed, other than general modelling and editing of policy data objects. Feelings were also mixed regarding simplicity and ease of use, but here the interviews uncovered that while web-based tools were rated high, other tools were not. This was part of the motivation for the later trials with action lists, and also for using the web based interfaces as front end in the second version of the infrastructure. Within communication and coordination, statements concerning overview of tasks and feedback to information showed the greatest improvements, while real-time communication seemed not to meet all expectations.

For the planning case in particular, results were mixed. Some of the respondents felt quality and effectiveness had improved, while others claimed the opposite. A clear majority however felt that the accuracy of the plans had improved. When asked what the most important problem was in planning, half of the respondent originally thought lack of joint planning. After having tried the tools, however, all but one chose "identify dangerous delays" [5]. This indicates that the tools did indeed solve some of the collaboration problems. The action lists were conceived as the next step, putting the plans into action, so it was evident than problems related to planning support were largely solved.

5 Related Work

The EXTERNAL infrastructure combines a number of mechanisms that use interactive models for customizing and tailoring the information systems.

With respect to supporting dynamically networked organizations, most B2B E-business frameworks including ebXML and BPML [20] focus on information exchange and business transactions. They lack support for the dynamic and knowledge-intensive parts of inter-organizational processes.

Enterprise ontologies have been proposed as a way of solving the communication problems arising from different interpretative frameworks in different organizations [4]. This approach is based on conventional notions of model interpretation, i.e. the Turing paradigm, where the interpretation and activation of models are fully automated. The more powerful interaction machine paradigm [7, 22, 23], allows users to influence model interpretation. The main characteristic of an interaction machine is that it can pose questions to human actors during its computation. The problem solving process is thus no longer just a user providing input to the machine, which then processes the request and provides an answer (output), it is a multi-step conversation between the user and the machine, each being able to take the initiative. Interactive models support ongoing modelling, model interpretation and activation also by the end-users, following the interaction paradigm.

Another main aspect in the approach is that the modelling languages can be updated as part of the development. This is similar to a domain specific modelling (DSM) approach [11]. However, most work within DSM is geared towards supporting technical design rather than the development and customisation of business solutions.

Workflow management systems have also been proposed as a solution for inter-organizational collaboration [2, 19]. Approaches such as ServiceFlow [24] points to the need for flexible solutions, although not taking a model-based approach. The focus of EXTERNAL on knowledge intensive processes requires a degree of flexibility not enabled by conventional production workflow systems [7, 8].

Another popular solution for cross-enterprise integration is middleware frameworks like OMG's CORBA. The recent shift in the focus of OMG to modeling (MDA and UML), standardisation of meta-object integration (MOF), business objects and workflow management indicate an interest in model-driven enterprise integration also from the more technical side. That these software engineering approaches are transferable to interactive modelling has not been shown.

6 Conclusions and Further Work

Interactive models allow enterprises and networked organisations to control and customize their IT infrastructure through visual modelling of work processes. In an integrated knowledge management framework, concurrent meta-modelling, modelling, management and work performance become interwoven, supporting both planned and emergent work tasks. The EXTERNAL infrastructure has been used in three case studies, and parts of it are also used in other commercial and research projects. It has been found adequate for building the models for use in the project, and for supporting a wide range of tasks. This demonstrates the power and possibilities of the approach in finding solutions to the industrial challenges mentioned in the introduction.

We are currently pursuing extensions and improvements to the infrastructure in a number of areas mentioned in this paper. Model harvesting and reuse mechanisms, supporting process knowledge management, are among the most challenging components to design. Further experimentation with the infrastructure in other business domains is also planned. In particular, we will seek closer integration with existing enterprise information system in order to provide a full project environment for business users.

References

1. Carlsen, S. *Action Port Model: A Mixed Paradigm Conceptual Workflow Modeling Language*, Third IFCIS Conference on Cooperative Information Systems (CoopIS'98), New York, 1998.
2. Casati, F. and Shan, M. C. *Dynamic and Adaptive Composition of e-Services*, Information Systems Journal, vol. 26, no. 3, 2001.
3. EXTERNAL *EXTERNAL - Extended Enterprise Resources, Networks And Learning*, EU Project, IST-1999-10091, *New Methods of Work and Electronic Commerce, Dynamic Networked Organisations*. Partners: DNV, GMD-IPSI, Zeus E.E.I.G., METIS, SINTEF Telecom and Informatics, 2000-2002.
4. Fox, M. S. and Gruninger, M. *On Ontologies and Enterprise Modelling*, International Conference on Enterprise Integration Modelling Technology 97, 1997.
5. Haake, J., Ohren, O. and Krogstie, J. *EXTERNAL WP4 - D13. Prototype: Use case - External Project*, The External Project - IST 1999-10091 4-00-D-2002-01-0, 2002.
6. Haake, J. M. and Wang, W. *Flexible Support for Business Processes: Extending Cooperative Hypermedia with Process Support*, GROUP '97, Phoenix, Arizona USA, 1997.
7. Jørgensen, H. D. *Interaction as a Framework for Flexible Workflow Modelling*, Proceedings of GROUP'01, Boulder, USA, 2001.
8. Jørgensen, H. D. *Interactive Process Models*, PhD-thesis, NTNU, Trondheim, Norway, 2004 ISBN 82-471-6203-2.
9. Kallåk, B. H., Pettersen, T. B. and Ressem, J. E. *Object-Oriented Workflow Management: Intelligence, Flexibility, and Real Support for Business Processes*, OOPSLA Workshop on Implementation and Application of Object-Oriented Workflow Management Systems, Vancouver, Canada, 1998.
10. Karlsen, D., Lillehagen, F., Tinella, S., Krogstie, J., Jørgensen, H. D., Johnsen, S. G., Wang, W., Rubart, J. and Lie, F. T. *EXTERNAL D3 - EE Infrastructure*, Deliverable from the The EXTERNAL Project - IST 1999-10091, Lysaker, Norway 2001.
11. Kelly, S. and Pohjonen, R. *Domain Specific Modelling for Cross-platform Product Families*, ER Workshop on Conceptual Modelling Approaches to Mobile Information Systems Development, Tampere, Finland, 2002.
12. Krogstie, J. et al. *EXTERNAL D6 - EE Methodology*, Deliverable from the EXTERNAL Project - IST 1999-10091, Oslo, Norway, 2002.
13. Krogstie, J., Hildrum, J., Chrysostalis, M. and Hestvik, R. *Enterprise Methodology Evaluation Report*, The EXTERNAL Consortium D19, 9-92-S-2002-01-4, 2002.
14. Kuntz, J. C., Christiansen, T. R., Cohen, G. P., Jin, Y. and Levitt, R. E. *The Virtual Design Team: A Computational Simulation Model of Project Organizations*, Communications of the ACM, vol. 41, no. 11, 1998.
15. Lillehagen, F. *Visual Extended Enterprise Engineering Embedding Knowledge Management, Systems Engineering and Work Execution*, IEMC '99, IFIP International Enterprise Modelling Conference, Verdal, Norway, 1999.
16. Lillehagen, F., Dehli, E., Fjeld, L., Krogstie, J. and Jørgensen, H. D. *Active Knowledge Models as a Basis for an Infrastructure for Virtual Enterprises*, PRO-VE'02, 3rd IFIP Working Conference on Infrastructures for Virtual Enterprises, Sesimbra, Portugal, 2002.

17. Lillehagen, F., Krogstie, J., Jørgensen, H. D. and Hildrum, J. *Active Knowledge Models for Supporting eWork and eBusiness*, ICE'2002 - 8th International Conference on Concurrent Enterprising, Rome, Italy, 2002.

18. Orr, J. *Talking about Machines*. Ithaca, New York: Cornell University Press, ILR Press, 1996.

19. Reichert, M., Bauer, T. and Dadam, P. *Enterprise-Wide and Cross-Enterprise Workflow-Management: Challenges and Research Issues for Adaptive Workflows*, Enterprise-wide and Cross-enterprise Workflow Management, Paderborn, Germany,, 1999.

20. Shim, S. S. Y., Pendyala, V. S., Sundaram, M. and Gao, J. Z. *Business-to-Business E-Commerce Frameworks*, IEEE Computer, vol. 33, no. 10, 2000.

21. Suchman, L. *Plans and Situated Actions*. New York: Cambridge University Press, 1987.

22. Wegner, P. *Why interaction is more powerful than algorithms*, Communications of the ACM, vol. 40, no. 5, 1997.

23. Wegner, P. and Goldin, D. *Interaction as a Framework for Modeling*, in *Conceptual Modeling. Current Issues and Future Directions, LNCS 1565*, P. P. Chen, J. Akoka, H. Kangassalo, and B. Thalheim, Eds. Berlin, Germany: Springer, 1999.

24. Wetzel, I. and Klischewski, R. (2002) Serviceflow beyond Workflow? Concepts and Architectures for Supporting Interorganizational Service Processes. In Pidduck, A. B., Mylopoulos, J. Woo, C. C. and Ozsu, M. T. (Eds.) Proceeding s from CAiSE'14, Toronto, Canada.

Cooperation of Processes
through Message Level Agreement

Jelena Zdravkovic[1,2] and Paul Johanesson[2]

[1] Department of Computer Science, University of Gävle
Kungsbäcksvägen 47, 80 277 Gävle, Sweden
[2] Department of Computer and Systems Sciences
Stockholm University and Royal Institute of Technology
Forum 100, SE-164 40 Kista, Sweden
{jzc,pajo}@dsv.su.se

Abstract. E-Business is constantly growing as organizations are trying to integrate electronically in order to automate exchange of information and services. To construct inter-organizational processes, the involved enterprises must agree on ways how to invoke process services on the business partner's system. A problem is that existing processes are so diverse in protocols, activity and message forms that it is impossible to start collaboration without comprehensive adaptations. In this paper, we propose a framework for interoperation of processes, which is based on requirements for equivalence of document exchanges. We argue that this level of equivalence is sufficient to enable existing enterprise processes to collaborate without internal redesign. The proposed framework is aimed to facilitate process collaboration by using a mediator layer to perform necessary adaptations, while minimizing requirements for process similarity.

1 Introduction

Since the Internet revolution, enterprises have opened their core functions to customers, business partners and financial institutions. The rapidly growing interest in e-business has emphasized the need for tools able to support automated collaboration among enterprise processes. In the context of business-to-business (B2B) collaboration, workflow management systems are often used as a base technology to integrate back-end application services as a set of enterprise process activities. Collaboration requires that enterprises, willing to do business with each other, agree on ways how to invoke process services on a business partner's system and how to exchange data. Even processes sharing a common business context are often highly diverse in activity and message structures as well as incompatible in business protocols. Therefore, it is typically not possible to start collaboration without comprehensive adaptations.

Numerous recent studies have addressed the problem of B2B integration across enterprises. Many authors follow the concept of *public-to-private* processes [1], [2], [3]. A public process represents external behavior of an enterprise (private) process. It

A. Persson and J. Stirna (Eds.): CAiSE 2004, LNCS 3084, pp. 564–579, 2004.

defines a form of message exchange with another party, with a predefined ontology, protocol and format of the message exchange. When defining public processes, enterprises may either mutually agree on their own B2B protocol, or they may follow a B2B interaction standard. RosettaNet [4] and ebXML [5] are examples of such standards. With any of the approaches, matching between the processes must be achieved. Some works suggest flexible matching by following the concept of workflow inheritance. In [2], a private process is compatible with the public process if it inherits the exchange sequence from the public process and extends it with enterprise internal behavior, by following a set of rules. Conversely, in [6], customization of a public process in the context of message formats and business signals is seen as a way to match it with the private process. Recently, a number of proposals for service-based B2B integration have been proposed. Following them, a private process should be adapted to expose its public behavior as a set of structured services. Thus, business partners may collaborate if their process services are compatible [7] and orchestrated in a compatible way [8], [9].

A common assumption in these works is that in the concept of matching two processes, a service (transaction) in one process must be compatible with a corresponding service in the other process. As an example, this means that if an enterprise sends a purchase order and receives the confirmation as one single transaction, it cannot match with another enterprise that receives the order and sends the confirmation as two separate transactions. It also means that an enterprise sending document payment confirmation together with the delivery information as one message, cannot match with an enterprise that receives those documents as separate messages. These examples illustrate that services have to match on a one-to-one basis is a too strong requirement for process matching. In this paper, we introduce a process equivalence concept that allows for differences in transaction and document structures, as long as processes match semantically, i.e. in the communicated information and in the control flow of message exchanges. We argue that such processes may collaborate through a mediating layer that performs necessary adjustments of the processes. The contribution of the paper is to relax the requirements for matching between B2B processes, which facilitates integration of a larger number of enterprise processes without additional redesign.

The rest of the paper is structured as follows. In Section 2 we shortly describe rules and formalisms for modeling workflow processes with Petri nets. In Section 3 we propose our concept of equivalence for B2B processes. In section 4, we describe a mechanism for integration and collaboration of processes, based on the theory provided in the previous section. In Section 5 we discuss the approach on the public-to-private B2B model and apply it on a real collaboration case. In Section 6, we conclude the paper and discuss issues for further research.

2   Modeling Workflow Processes with Petri Nets

Standard process models define activities in a process and the flow of control between these. For the purpose of this work, we describe process models with Petri nets

[10]. Each activity of a process is translated into a transition in the resulting Petri net. In this paper, reverse coloring is used to indicate those transitions that correspond to activities. Process flow structures such as sequence, iteration, splits (AND and OR) and joins (AND and OR) are modeled as additional transitions, places and arcs [11], [12]. Some examples of these translations are shown in Figure 1:

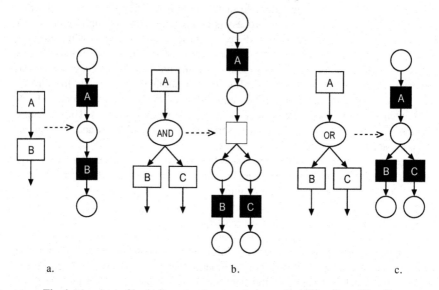

a.   b.   c.

Fig. 1. Mappings of basic flow structures: a. sequence, b. AND split, c. OR split.

Thus, in a Petri net some transitions correspond to activities, while other transitions are used to manage the control flow. Labels are used to identify transitions. Activity transitions are labeled uniquely, as shown in Figure 1 (transitions A, B and C). Every activity transition has an input place (p_i) and an output place (p_o). Places contain tokens. The distribution of tokens over places at some point of time, demarks a *state* of a process. In a workflow process, we require that two specific places exist – a *source*, with no incoming arcs, and a *sink*, with no outgoing arcs. Every place or a transition is on a path from the source place to the sink place. More formally, we define a workflow process as follows:

Definition 1. A *workflow process* is a labeled Petri net, $W =< P, T, F, L >$ where: P is a set of places, with two special places, the source p_{source} and the sink place p_{sink}, T is a set of transitions, F is a set of flow relations $F \subseteq (P \times T) \cup (T \times P)$, L is a set of transition labels as defined in Definition 3.

For a more detailed discussion on modeling workflow processes with Petri nets, the reader is referred to [11].

In a B2B context, the activities are *transactions*. A transaction consists of the sending and/or receiving of documents. From one actor's perspective, a transaction can be identified as sending a document, receiving a document, or having both these messages in a specified order.

Definition 2. In a workflow process, four *transaction types* are distinguished:
SR: Send a document and receive a document
S: Send a document
RS: Receive a document and send a document
R: Receive a document

This means that in the translation to Petri nets, each transition corresponding to an activity, is labeled for identifying the transaction. A label contains information on the transaction type and the document(s) being exchanged. As an example, a transition labeled with type *SR*, specifies a transaction containing the message that sends a document and the next one that receives a document. In most workflow languages, activities contain a field that designates the target party of the service, i.e. to whom a message is to be sent, or to be received from. We assume therefore, that those process activities that do not have the target role relevant to a B2B context, indicate internal behavior. Such activities are modeled as *silent* transitions, labeled as τ [13].

The activities relevant to a B2B interaction, i.e. transactions, are modeled as transitions and labeled as follows:

Definition 3. A non-silent *transition label* is a tuple $t = < Type, d_1, d_2 >$ where:
$Type \in \{S, R, SR, RS\}$,

d_1 and d_2 are documents.

A document may have an internal structure, i.e. a document may consist of smaller components. An example could be an order, which consists of an order header and a number of order lines. Another example is a document containing a rejection of a previous offer together with a counter offer. Formally, a document can be seen as a regular expression over base elements, where the base elements are the smallest components into which a document can be broken down. The form and content of the base elements depend on the ontology chosen for expressing business communication, and we will not make any specific assumptions about this but only assume that a set of base elements is given.

Definition 4. A *document* is a regular expression over a set of *base elements*. A *document* is *atomic* if it consists of exactly one *base element*.

3   Equivalence of Processes in a B2B Context

In this section we define our concept of equivalence for B2B processes. We first define equivalence notions for documents and transitions following their structures, as described in the previous section.

Definition 5. Two atomic documents d_1 and d_2 are *equivalent,* denoted $d_1 \, eq \, d_2$, if their base elements are the same. Equivalence of two documents is then defined recursively over the structure of documents.

Definition 6. Let t' and t'' be two transitions. t' and t'' are *equivalent,* denoted $t' \, eq \, t''$, if they have the same type, and if their documents are equivalent.

The internal structure of transactions and documents gives rise to additional difficulties when comparing B2B processes. The main difficulty is that a single transaction, with a complex structure, in one process may correspond to several transactions, with simpler structures, in another process. An example of such a situation is shown in Figure 2 below. In the example, as well as in the rest of the paper, we use an abbreviated form for transition labels, e.g. "Send Order" instead of $<S, \, Order,->$.

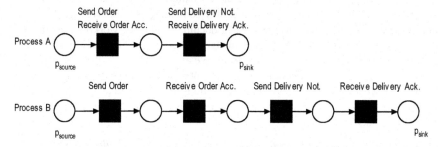

Fig. 2. Two processes with different transaction structures.

Both processes in the figure represent similar order processes, but they differ in the granularity of the transactions. In process A, the transactions are more complex and involve simultaneously sending and receiving of documents, while the transactions in process B are smaller with just one single sending or receiving in each transaction. Intuitively, the first transaction in A corresponds to the two first transactions in B, while the second one in A corresponds to the two last ones in B.

Another example is shown in Figure 3. In this case, there is a difference in the structure of the documents being sent. In process A, there is one transaction for sending the rejection of a previous offer and another transaction for sending a counter offer. In process B, on the other hand, these two transactions are collapsed into one with a more complex document stating the rejection as well as the counter offer.

In both examples above, the compared processes are syntactically quite dissimilar with a different number of transactions. Semantically, however, they are close to each other as they represent the same communicative intents between two agents. It would, therefore, be useful to have a process equivalence concept that allows for differences in transaction and document structures as long as these do not affect the control flow of message exchanges and the communicated information. In the following definitions, we introduce such an equivalence concept. A basic idea in the definitions is to initially transform the processes to be compared into a "normal form", where differences in transaction and document structure have been leveled out. The processes are then compared using the well-known concept of *bisimilarity* [14].

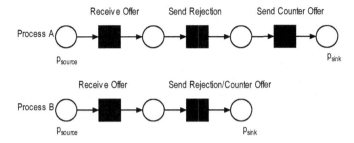

Fig. 3. Two processes with different document structures.

Definition 7. Let W be a workflow process. W' is the *transaction flattened version* of W if W' is obtained from W by repeatedly applying the following transformations until every transition of W is of type S or R:

i) If W contains a transition $t = <SR, d_1, d_2>$ with input place p_i and output place p_o, then t is replaced with two transitions in sequence, $t' = <S, d_1, ->$ with input place p_i and output place p_{new}, and $t'' = <R, -, d_2>$ with input place p_{new} and output place p_o.

ii) If W contains a transition $t = <RS, d_1, d_2>$ with input place p_i and output place p_o, then the transition t is replaced with two transitions in sequence, $t' = <R, -, d_2>$ with input place p_i and output place p_{new}, and $t'' = <S, d_1, ->$ with input place and p_{new} output place p_o.

Definition 8. Let W' be the transaction flattened version of a process W. W'' is the *document flattened version* of W' if W'' is obtained from W' by repeatedly applying the following transformations until every document in W is atomic:

i) If W contains a transition $t = <S, ab, ->$ with input place p_i and output place p_o, then t is replaced with two transitions in sequence $t' = <S, a, ->$ with input place p_i and output place p_{new}, and $t'' = <S, b, ->$ with input place p_{new} and output place p_o.

ii) If W contains a transition $t = <R, -, ab>$ with input place p_i and output place p_o, then t is replaced with two transitions in sequence $t' = <R, -, a>$ with input place p_i and output place p_{new}, and $t'' = <R, -, b>$ with input place p_{new} and output place p_o.

iii) If W contains a transition $t = <S, a^*, ->$ with input place p_i and output place p_o, then t is replaced with two transitions $t' = <S, a, ->$ with input place p_i and output place p_{new}, and $t'' = <S, \epsilon, ->$ with input place p_{new} and output place p_o.

iv) If W contains a transition $t = < R,-,a^* >$ with input place p_i and output place p_o, then t is replaced with two transitions $t = < R,-,a >$ with input place p_i and output place p_{new}, and $t'' = < R,-,\in >$ with input place p_{new} and output place p_o.

The process W'' is the document and transaction flattened version of the process W, or shorter, W'' is the *flattened version* of the W.

The flattened processes are to be compared for equivalence. Bisimilarity ([14], [16]) is a common equivalence concept used to compare the behavior of two labeled transition systems. Practically, bisimilar systems are those that may interchange in any environment without observing the difference in external behavior. By this concept, two Petri-Nets in similar states are equivalent if they are able to simulate any of each other actions (transitions). As we explained before, processes modeled with Petri-Nets have both internal (silent) and external (observable) behavior. Following this, the relation of *branching bisimilarity* is used to compare observable behavior of two Petri-Nets, as it allows abstracting from the internal behavior, i.e. silent transitions. A definition of branching bisimilar Petri-Nets may be found in [15]. Formally, we define the requirement for equivalence between two B2B processes as:

Definition 9. Let W and X be two processes and W', X' are their flattened versions. The processes W and X are *flat bisimilar* if W' and X' are *branching bisimilar*.

4   Integration and Collaboration of Processes in a B2B Context

It is unrealistic to expect that two enterprise processes could interact without adaptations. In the previous section, we have proposed an equivalence concept for B2B processes that relaxes requirements for similarities in activity structures. We stated that *flat bisimilar* processes are processes, which normalized around transaction and document structures, become *bisimilar*.

Our approach for process equivalence is realized through an integration model we name *process mediator*. It is used to compare processes for flat bisimilarity and if they match (integration phase), to bind them at runtime (collaboration phase). (Figure 4) shows the architecture of the process mediator in the form of a UML class diagram. The model consists of three packages: *process*, *integration* and *collaboration*.

The *process* package includes models of the original processes and their flattened counterparts. The *integration* package governs process flattening and equivalence comparison. Imported process definitions (from a private and a public process, for example) are first processed, as described in Section 2, to create transitions and document classes. The processes are then flattened (Definitions 7 and 8 in Section 3). The transitions are marked (indexed) to relate flat versions to their originals. The flattened processes are then compared for transition equivalence as described in Definitions 6 from Section 3. If all non-silent transitions can be pair-wise related, the processes are further checked for branching bisimilarity (a well known algorithm is provided in [16]); otherwise, a report on non-matching transitions is submitted. If the compared processes appear as branching bisimilar, it means they may collaborate without redesign. The *collaboration* package is used at runtime, to integrate the matched processes – for example, to map an enterprise process to a required public process. This means that a message originating from a transaction of the enterprise process is first transformed (normalized) according to the format specified in the flat process. It is then, based on the information on the transactions coupling, transformed (de-normalized) to the required transaction in the public process. As an illustration, a message originating from an *S* transaction from a private process, containing a non-atomic document is normalized to a number of messages belonging to *S* transactions containing atomic documents. Those messages are then de-normalized in the transaction(s) as required in the public process, and as such sent outside.

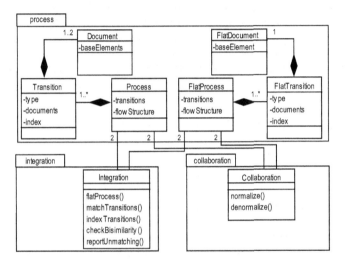

Fig. 4. Process Mediator architecture.

If processes fail matching during the integration phase, it means that they do not have all transitions equivalent and/or they cannot simulate each other transitions by the same protocol. Both non-equivalent transitions and non-similar process protocols provide information for involved business parties on the changes required in their processes. This will be illustrated in more detail in the example section.

The functions of the process mediator may be further extended to reflect the requirements for equivalence, according to specific characteristics of a B2B interaction model.

5   The Public-to-Private B2B Model

In this section we describe our approach for cooperation of processes on the public-to-private B2B interaction model. We discuss some specific aspects of the model, and accordingly, we extend the core concept of process integration, to relax further requirements for equivalence. We provide then an example of B2B interaction between two companies, using ebXML as the public framework.

5.1 Equivalence and Integration of Processes

B2B frameworks provide common process protocols that individual enterprise processes should conform to. Basically, a public process predefines the documents that have to be exchanged, their structures, and the flow protocol of the exchange. A public process protocol is role based, i.e. separate process protocols for each of the business parties may be extracted. To comply with this model, an existing private process must expose external behavior exactly as defined in the public process.

In Section 3 we have defined an equivalence concept for B2B processes, in general. We stated that equivalent processes, in their flattened versions, must be bismilar. In the public-to-private model, it is only required that the public process be simulated by a private process, and not conversely. This circumstance raises two relaxation aspects:

a. a private process containing transactions not related to any transaction in a given public process may still comply with that public process, if the additional transactions can be disregarded.
b. a private process having a different flow structure than a given public process, may still comply with that public process, if the public process flow structure can be simulated.

As explained in the Section 1, we investigate the minimal conditions for the compliance of B2B processes without requiring redesign of existing private processes. Following this, we consider that the first relaxation aspect allows for having additional (non-matched) transactions in a private process, whose executions can be disregarded in the collaboration context, as they are not required by the public process. This means that during the integration phase, such additional transactions are modeled as silent transitions, and during the collaboration phase, their execution is disregarded, since the process mediator inhibits their messages or because they are never invoked. Not every additional transaction, however, may be disregarded. In the following we discuss under what circumstances additional transactions can be disregarded, depending on flow structures and transaction types.

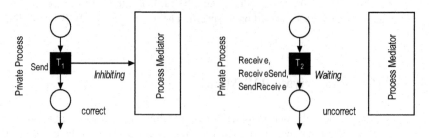

Fig. 5. Disregarding different transaction types in a sequential flow structure.

In a sequential flow structure (or iterative, parallel), an additional transaction of type S (Send) (Figure 5) in the private process, may be disregarded from a collaboration, since the process mediator can simply inhibit such a sent message without any consequences for the collaboration. Conversely, any transaction of types R, RS or SR cannot be disregarded, since the private process would then wait infinitely for a "receive" message from the process mediator. In an alternative (implicit OR) flow structure (Figure 6), transactions of type R or RS may be disregarded, as long as there is at least one matched transaction among the alternatives. This is because the opposite B2B side private process initiates such transactions, and consequently, it will never invoke such an additional transaction. In such flow structure it would be impossible to disregard a transaction of type S or SR, since the decision on initiating a transaction is ruled by the private process. In such a situation, the private process could initiate an additional transaction, which cannot be handled by the other side.

Fig. 6. Disregarding different transaction types in alternative (implicit OR) flows. The process on the left side will wait for the other B2B side to invoke a matched transaction. The process on the right side, however, may invoke itself a non-matched transaction.

Formally, we define the described behavior as an extension of the core concept of process equivalence (Section 3):

Definition 10. Let W be a private process. Let t be a transition from W that has no the equivalent transition in the public process. The transition t may be labeled *silent* if:

i) transition t belongs to a sequence, parallel or iterative flow structure, and it has transaction type S.

ii) transition t belongs to an alternative flow structure with at least one matched transition, and it has transaction type R or RS.

The proposed extension is realized in the process mediator (Figure 4), by adding the operation for finding additional transitions in the private process that may be marked as silent, in the integration class (findAdditional()), and adding an operation for inhibiting (inhibitSilent()), in the collaboration class.

As stated by the second relaxation aspect for the B2B model discussed here, it is required for a private process to expose the same external behavior as that defined by a public process, but not the opposite. This leads to a conclusion that it is enough for a private process to be *branching similar* to the public process. Similarity [14] is a weaker equivalence notion than bisimilarity, as it requires only one process to be able to simulate every action from another process. Therefore, for the public-to-private B2B model, the requirement for process equivalence (Definition 9, Section 3) may be redefined as follows:

Definition 11. Let W be a private process and X be the public processes, and W', X' are their flattened versions. The process W is *flat similar* to the process X, if the process W' is *branching similar* to the process X', after zero or more transitions from the process W' are labeled as silent.

This relaxation is important as it allows a private process having a different flow structure than a given public process, as long as it may simulate the required protocol. This means that a private process with partially ordered transactions may simulate a public process with totally ordered transactions. As an example, Figure 7 shows how a private process having a parallel flow structure may comply with a public process with a sequential flow structure:

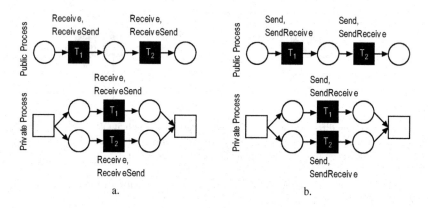

Fig. 7. Parallel flow structures are *similar* to sequential.

Both private processes in Figure 7 are equivalent to the given public processes, as they may simulate any transition in the public processes. In situation 7a., the private process is a "passive" actor, waiting for the other collaboration party to initiate a transaction, as defined by the public process. In situation 7b., in the private process, transaction T_1 may be initiated before T_2. In such a situation, the process mediator holds the message from T_1 until the message from transaction T_2 arrives.

The described equivalence relaxation is realized in the process mediator (Figure 4), by adding the operation for checking on branching similarity (checkSimilarity()) in the integration class, and adding the operation for holding transactions (hold()), in the collaboration class.

In this section, we have proposed the extensions of our core concept for process equivalence and integration, regarding the public-to-private B2B model. The extensions are related to the concepts and techniques for hiding (traversing) and blocking (removing) transitions in workflow inheritance, proposed by van der Aalst in [15]. Our approach differs as we distinguish characteristics of transactions behavior, originating from the different transaction types. Additionally, we consider only transformations that would allow for relaxations of the requirements for process equivalence, without requiring changes in the process description (such as removing a transaction).

Following the rules for process matching given in the previous section relaxed with the outlined concepts, we illustrate our approach for identifying equivalence or possible incompatibilities in the business logic of collaboration partners, on a small but realistic example.

5.2   The Scenario of a B2B Interaction

For the example, we consider a "request for order" case. DailyNews (company A) needs a provider of clip-art images to put them in its newspapers. By matching the correct business context in an ebXML registry [5], DailyNews finds ImageWorks (company B) as a potential partner. The companies then agree on the protocol of the interaction by defining (or reusing) an ebXML Business Process Specification Schema (BPSS, [5]). The protocol says that the customer (company A) should first send a clip-art order to the provider (company B). Based on the order, the company B sends the invoice. Company A then sends the payment and receives the confirmation for the reception. Finally, company B sends information on a web address from where company A may download the requested images. The role-based public protocols are illustrated in Figure 8, together with the private processes as existing today in DailyNews and ImageWorks, respectively:

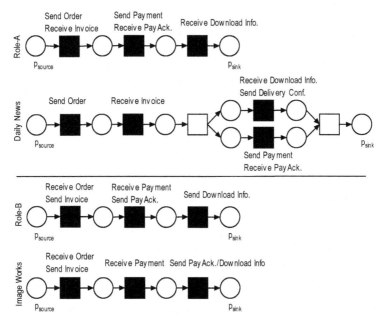

Fig. 8. The role-A (public) process vs. the DailyNews private process and the role-B vs. the ImageWorks private process.

On a first view, the processes representing the customer behavior (the role-A and DailyNews processes) in the clip-art ordering are different. In the role-A process, the order sending and invoice receiving are viewed as a single transaction, as opposite to the private process where these messages are in separated transactions. Then, the role-A process requires payment to be sent before image downloading, while the DailyNews process is designed in a way to allow more flexible, i.e. parallel flow of these activities. Finally, upon receiving the information for the download, the Daily-News process sends the confirmation for the reception, but the public process does not require that.

After the two processes are flattened as explained in Section 3, the following structures are obtained (Figure 9):

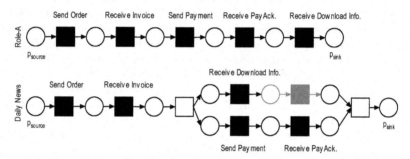

Fig. 9. The flattened versions of the processes role-A and DailyNews.

By the rules explained in the previous section, the transition "Send Delivery Confirmation" may be disregarded (by inhibiting) and accordingly, labeled as silent. The rest of activity transitions are equivalent. The flattened DailyNews process satisfies Definition 11 (Section 5.1), i.e. the process is branching similar with the process role-A, as it may "simulate" every step in that process.

If for example, the DailyNews process would not have the "Send Payment" transaction, then in the public process this transaction could not be matched and the information on the missing transaction in the private process would be reported. As another example, if the DailyNews process would have the "Send Payment" transaction, but sequentially ordered after "Receive Download Information", the processes would have all transactions matched, but a fail on branching similarity would be reported as the private process is not able to simulate transitions in the order required by the public process.

Comparing the role-B and the ImageWorks processes (Figure 8), we may observe that in the private process, receiving the payment and sending the payment acknowledge are not the parts of a single transaction, as in the public process.

In addition, by the ImageWorks protocol, the payments acknowledge is sent all together with the download information, as a single document. When the two processes are flattened, the structures as shown in Figure 10 are obtained. As it may be observed from the figure, after flattening transactions and documents, the processes become equivalent as required by Definition 9, i.e. the processes are even bisimilar.

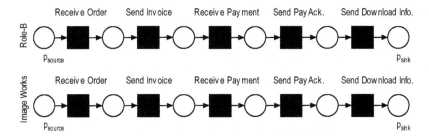

Fig. 10. The flattened versions of the processes role-B and ImageWorks.

As by the concept of flat equivalence both private processes match with the required public protocols, they may collaborate in the given B2B context. The private processes will be integrated through the process mediator tool. After the collaboration starts, the process mediator on the DailyNews side will, according to the explanation in Section 4, transform (de-normalize) messages "Send Order" and "Receive Invoice" from the transactions in the private process, to a single transaction, as required by the public protocol. Afterwards, the mediator will split (normalize) the private process transaction "Receive Download Information, Send Delivery Confirmation", according to the specification in the public protocol, and in addition, will inhibit the later message ("Send Delivery Confirmation") since it is marked as silent. During the collaboration, the mediator on the ImageWorks side will, upon receiving the message about the payment, from the transaction "Receive Payment, Send Payment Acknowledge", normalize it to belong to a separate transaction "Receive Payment", as required by the private process. The next transaction message from the private process, "Send Payment Acknowledge/Download Info", will be de-normalized around document structure and accordingly split into two transactions.

6   Conclusion and Future Work

In this work we have proposed a concept for compatibility of processes through message level agreement. We modeled processes with the Petri nets as this was sufficient for our purposes, but some other approach could be applied in the same way (such as π-calculus).

Our interest was focused to the B2B context, where we have assumed it is sufficient for processes to have compatible external behavior, exposed through communicated documents and the control flow of their exchange. That assumption led us to an equivalence concept that would allow for differences in transaction and document structures of processes, as long as the processes would comply with required external behavior. Equivalent processes, when flattened out around transaction and document structures, are branching bisimilar. We have argued, therefore, that such processes could collaborate through a layer (the process mediator), which would perform necessary transformations to present processes as similar to each other. The transformations concern flattening (normalization) and de-normalization of documents as well as synchronization of transactions to comply with process definitions of partners sides. We have shown on the public-to-private B2B model example that the concept for equivalence between B2B processes may be further relaxed, as it is sufficient for a private process to comply with the public process, but not conversely. Thereafter, in such a model, the private process is allowed to have transactions not required by the public protocol, which could be disregarded at collaboration time. The model also allows for some differences in flow structures of the processes, as it is enough for the private process to be able to simulate actions from the public process.

In the study, we examined requirements for interoperability between processes on the level of core business semantics and conversation flow. In the future work it is our intention to implement the concept of the mediating layer (the process mediator), and also, to go further and extend the model to support coordination of nested processes and transactions.

References

1. Bussler, C.: The Application of Workflow Technology in Semantic B2B Integration. In: Distributed and Parallel Databases, Vol. 12. Kluwer Academic Publishers (2002) 163–191
2. Aalst, W. M. P. van der, Weske, M.: The P2P Approach to Interorganizational Workflows. In: Proceedings of the 13th International Conference on Advanced Information Systems Engineering (CAiSE'01), Lecture Notes in Computer Science, Vol. 2068. Springer-Verlag, Berlin (2001) 140-156
3. Sayal M., Casati F., Dayal U., Shan, M.-C.: Integrating Workflow Management Systems with Business-to-Business Interaction Standards. Proceedings of 18th International Conference on Data Engineering (ICDE 2002). IEEE Computer Society (2002) 287-296
4. RosettaNet. www.rosettanet.org
5. ebXML. www.ebxml.org
6. Bussler, C.: Public Process Inheritance for Business-to-Business Integration. In: Proceedings of Workshop on Technologies for E-Services (TES 2002), Lecture Notes in Computer Science, Vol. 2444. Springer-Verlag, Berlin (2002) 19-28
7. Mecella M., Pernici B., Craca P.: Compatibility of e-Services in a Cooperative Multi-platform Environment. In: Proc. of Workshop on Technologies for E-Services (TES 2001), Lecture Notes in Computer Science, Vol. 2193. Springer-Verlag, Berlin (2001) 44-57
8. Mecella M., Pernici B.: Designing Wrapper Components for e-Services in Integrating Heterogeneous Systems. In: VLDB Journal, Vol.10. Springer-Verlag, Berlin (2001) 2-15
9. Piccinelli G., Emmerich W., Zirpins C., Schütt K.: Web Service Interfaces for Interorganisational Business Processes - An Infrastructure for Automated Reconciliation. In: 6th International Enterprise Distributed Object Computing Conference (EDOC 2002). IEEE Computer Society (2002), 285-292
10. Aalst, W. M. P. van der, Hee, K. van, Houben, G. J.: Modeling and Analysing Workflow Using a Petri Net Approach. In: Proceedings 2nd Workshop on Computer-Supported Cooperative Work, Petri nets and related formalisms, (1994) 31-55
11. Aalst, W. M. P. van der: The Application of Petri Nets to Workflow Management. In: The Journal of Circuits, Systems and Computers, Vol. 8(1). (1998), 21-66

12. Kiepuszewski B., Hofstede1, A.H.M. ter, Aalst W.M.P. van der: Fundamentals of Control Flow in Workflows. In: QUT Technical report, FIT-TR-2002-03, Queensland University of Technology, Brisbane, (2002)
13. Aalst, W. M. P. van der: Inheritance of Interorganizational Workflows to Enable Business-to-Business E-commerce. Electronic Commerce Research, Vol. 2(3). (2002), 195-231
14. Glabbeek R.J. van, Weijland W.P.: Branching Time and Abstraction in Bisimulation Semantics (extended abstract). In: Information Processing 89: Proceedings of the IFIP 11th. World Computer Congress. G.X. Ritter. Elsevier Science Publishers B.V., North-Holland (1989) 613-618.
15. Aalst, W. M. P. van der, Basten, T.: Inheritance in Workflows. An Approach to Tackling Problems Related to Change. In: Theoretical Computer Science, Vol. 270. (2002) 125-203
16. Groote J. F., Vaandrager F.: An Efficient Algorithm for Branching Bisimulation and Stuttering Equivalence. In: Proceedings 17th ICALP. Lecture Notes in Computer Science Vol. 443. Springer-Verlag, (1990) 626-638

CoDoc: Multi-mode Collaboration over Documents

Claudia-Lavinia Ignat and Moira C. Norrie

Institute for Information Systems, ETH Zurich
CH-8092 Zurich, Switzerland
{ignat,norrie}@inf.ethz.ch

Abstract. In software engineering as well as in any engineering domain, a way of customizing the collaborative work to various modes of collaboration, i.e. synchronous and asynchronous, and the possibility of alternating these modes along the phases of a project is required. Our goal is to develop a universal information platform that can support collaboration in a range of application domains, the basic sharing unit being the document. Since not all user groups have the same conventions and not all tasks have the same requirements, this implies that it should be possible to customize the collaborative environment at the level of both communities and individual tasks. In this paper we present the consistency maintenance models underlying the synchronous and asynchronous modes of collaboration. We highlight the importance of choosing a general structured model of the document and particularly analyze the multi-mode collaboration for two main representative types of documents: textual and graphical.

1 Introduction

Within the CSCW field, collaborative editing systems have been developed to support a group of people editing documents collaboratively over a computer network. The collaboration between users can be synchronous or asynchronous.

Synchronous collaboration means that members of the group work at the same time on the same documents and modifications are seen in real-time by the other members of the group. We have developed a real-time collaborative text editor [7] and a real-time collaborative graphical editor [8].

Asynchronous collaboration means that members of the group modify the copies of the documents in isolation, working in parallel and afterwards synchronizing their copies to reestablish a common view of the data. Version control systems are asynchronous systems used in group environments and merging plays a key role for achieving convergence in such systems.

In software engineering as well as in any engineering domain, the reduction of the product life cycle, i.e. fewer months between releases, together with the increase in the product complexity and the size of the team, requires a means of customizing the collaborative work to various modes of collaboration, i.e. synchronous and asynchronous, and the possibility of alternating these modes along the phases of a project.

A. Persson and J. Stirna (Eds.): CAiSE 2004, LNCS 3084, pp. 580–594, 2004.

Our goal is to develop a universal information platform that can support collaboration in a range of application domains such as engineering design (CAD or CAAD) and collaborative writing (news agency, authoring of scientific papers or scientific annotations), the basic unit for collaboration being the document. Since not all user groups have the same conventions and not all tasks have the same requirements, this implies that it should be possible to customize the collaborative editor at the level of both communities and individual tasks.

In this paper we present the synchronous and asynchronous modes of collaboration for two main classes of documents, namely, textual and graphical. We describe how the real-time collaborative systems that we have developed can be extended to support also asynchronous functionality. In this way we can customize the collaborative editor and be able to support collaboration in a range of application domains. Choosing a general structured model offers a set of enhanced features such as increased efficiency and improvements in the semantics for both modes of collaboration. Moreover, the general model of the document allows a general consistency model to be found for multi-mode collaboration. An integrated system supporting both synchronous and asynchronous collaboration is needed in practice because these two modes of communication can be alternatively used in developing a project at different stages and under different circumstances.

The *real-time* feature is needed when the users in the team want to frequently interact to achieve a common goal. For example, before a paper deadline when there is time pressure for the authors of the paper, the real-time feature is very helpful. Suppose the two authors of the paper agreed that one of them, the one that is a native english speaker, will go through the whole paper and check the english, while the second author is adding some new sections. The first author can go through the whole document and correct the english and then go on to revise the content and correct the english of the sections written in the meanwhile by the second author and distinguished by a different colour. Another application of real-time collaboration is in the case of editing computerized cooperative music notation both in orchestras and music schools, where the musicians may perform changes simultaneously on the same music score [1]. The cooperative distributed editor of music may be seen as a particular case of a collaborative graphical editor.

The *non-real-time* feature is required if the users do not want to coordinate interactively with each other. An application of this mode of collaboration is when users prefer working in their private workspaces, performing modifications and only afterwards publishing their work to the other members of the group. For example, co-authors of a book that collaboratively write different chapters will merge their work only after finishing a first draft. Another relevant example that requires the need of asynchronous communication is the following one: two users concurrently modelling a huge XML database have a basic DTD and want to work on enhancing the DTD, each one on some specific parts. In the meantime they fill in data into the XML document conforming to the DTD and use XSLT to produce transformations on the XML. In this example, uncoupled editing is desired: During their individual work, the two programmers need to repeatedly edit the DTD, fill in data into the XML and test the transformations, this fact requiring that the DTD is kept in separately consistent states. Also, the asynchronous mode of communication is useful in the case that a real-time collaboration cannot be performed for some period of time due to some temporary failures but can operate again afterwards. For instance, consider the case of a teleconference where the users share a common whiteboard that is interrupted by a communication failure. It should be possible that the members work in isolation on their local copies of the whiteboard during the failure, but be able to merge their work when the communications are restored.

The paper is structured as follows. In the first section we describe the main features of the real-time editing systems that we have developed by highlighting the principles we have used for maintaining consistency in the case of both text and graphical documents. In section 3 we go on to describe the asynchronous mode of collaboration, first giving an overview of the copy/modify/merge technique used in the asynchronous communication and then showing in detail how this paradigm can be implemented by applying the same basic principles as for real-time collaboration. In section 4 we compare our approach with some related work. Concluding remarks are presented in the last section.

2   Real-Time Collaborative Editing Systems

In this section we are going to briefly describe the algorithms for maintaining consistency that underly the functionality of the collaborative text and graphical editors which form the basis of our multi-mode collaborative system CoDoc.

A replicated architecture where users work on local copies of the shared documents and instructions are exchanged by message passing has been used in both cases of the text and graphical collaborative editors. Also, both systems are characterized by high concurrency, meaning that any number of users are able to concurrently edit any part of the shared document, as opposed to turn-taking and locking protocols.

We have chosen a hierarchical representation both for text and graphical documents. We model the text document as consisting of paragraphs, each paragraph consisting of sentences, each sentence consisting of words and each word consisting of letters. We also use a tree model for representing the scene of objects in the graphical document. Groups are represented as internal nodes, while simple objects are represented as leaves. A group can contain other groups or simple objects.

In the next subsections we describe in turn the techniques underlying the functionality of the collaborative text and graphical editors.

2.1   Real-Time Collaborative Text Editor

The operational transformation approach has been identified as an appropriate approach for maintaining consistency of the copies of shared documents in

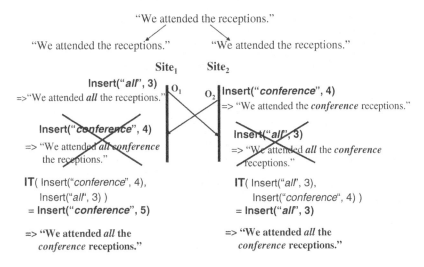

Fig. 1. Operation transformation example

real-time collaborative editing systems. It allows local operations to be executed immediately after their generation and remote operations need to be transformed against the other operations. The transformations are performed in such a manner that the intentions of the users are preserved and, at the end, the copies of the documents converge. Various operational transformation algorithms have been proposed: dOPT [5], adOPTed [14], GOT/GOTO [16], SOCT2, SOCT3 and SOCT4 [19].

Figure 1 illustrates a very simple example of the operation transformation mechanism. Suppose the shared document contains a single sentence *"We attended the receptions."* Two users, at $Site_1$ and $Site_2$, respectively, concurrently perform some operations on their local replicas of the document. $User_1$ performs operation O_1 of inserting the word *"all"* as the 3rd word into the sentence, in order to obtain *"We attended all the receptions."* Concurrently, $User_2$ performs operation O_2 of inserting the word *"conference"* as the 4th word into the sentence, in order to obtain *"We attended the conference receptions."* Let us analyse what happens at each site when the operation from the other site arrives. At $Site_1$, when operation O_2 arrives, if executed in its original form, the result would be *"We attended all conference the receptions."* which is not what the users intended. At $Site_2$, when operation O_1 arrives, if executed in its original form, the result, fortunately, would be a merge of the intentions of the two users, i.e. *"We attended all the conference receptions."* But, generally, executing the operations in their generation form at remote sites, will not ensure that the copies of the documents at $Site_1$ and $Site_2$ will converge. So, we see the need of transforming the operations when they arrive at a remote site.

The simplest form of operation transformation is the *Inclusion Transformation* - $IT(O_a, O_b)$, which transforms operation O_a against a concurrent operation O_b such that the impact of O_b is included in O_a.

In the previous example, at $Site_1$, when operation O_2 arrives, it needs to be transformed against operation O_1 to include the effect of this operation. Because the concurrent operation O_1 inserted a word before the word to be inserted by operation O_2, operation O_2 needs to adapt the position of insertion, i.e. increase its position by 1. In this way the transformed operation O_2 will become an insert operation of the word *"conference"* into position 5, the result being *"We attended all the conference receptions."*, satisfying the intentions of both users. At $Site_2$, in the same way, operation O_1 needs to be transformed against O_2 in order to include the effect of O_2. The position of insertion of O_1 does not need to be modified in this case because operation O_2 inserted a word to the right of the insertion position of O_1. Therefore, the transformed operation O_1 has the same form as the original operation O_1. We see that the result obtained at $Site_2$ respects the intentions of the two users and, moreover, the two replicas at the two sites converge.

Another form of operation transformation called *Exclusion Transformation* $ET(O_a, O_b)$ transforms O_a against an operation O_b that precedes O_a in causal order such that the impact of O_b is excluded from O_a.

Most real-time collaborative editors relying on existing operational transformation algorithms for consistency maintenance use a linear representation for the document, such as a sequence of characters in the case of text documents. All existing operational transformation algorithms keep a single history of operations already executed in order to compute the proper execution form of new operations. When a new remote operation is received, the whole history needs to be scanned and transformations need to be performed, even though different users might work on completely different sections of the document and do not interfere with each other. Keeping the history of all operations in a single buffer decreases the efficiency.

In [7] we proposed a consistency maintenance algorithm called treeOPT relying on a tree representation of documents. The hierarchical representation of a document is a generalisation of the linear representation and, in this way, our algorithm can be seen as extending the existing operational transformation algorithms. An important advantage of the algorithm is related to its improved efficiency. In our representation of the document, the history of operations is not kept in a single buffer, but rather distributed throughout the whole tree, and, when a new operation is transformed, only the history distributed on a single path of the tree will be spanned. Moreover, when working on medium or large documents, operations will be localized in the areas currently being modified by each individual user and these may often be non-overlapping. In these cases, almost no transformations are needed, and therefore the response times and notification times are very good. Another important advantage is the possibility of performing, not only operations on characters, but also on other semantic units (words, sentences and paragraphs). The transformation functions used in the operational transformation mechanism are kept simple as in the case of character-wise transformations, not having the complexity of string-wise transformations. An insertion or a deletion of a whole paragraph can be done in a single operation. Therefore, the efficiency is further increased, because there are fewer operations to be transformed, and fewer to be transformed against. Moreover, the data is sent using larger chunks, thus the network communication is more efficient. Our approach also adds flexibility in using the editor, the users being able to select the level of granularity at which they prefer to work.

The algorithm applies the same basic mechanisms as existing operational transformation algorithms recursively over the different document levels (paragraph, sentence, word and character) and it can use any of the operational transformation algorithms relying on linear representation such as dOPT [5], adOPTed [14], GOT/GOTO [16], SOCT2, SOCT3 and SOCT4 [19] (see [6]).

2.2   Real-Time Collaborative Graphical Editor

In the object-based collaborative graphical editor developed in our group, the shared objects subject to concurrent accesses are the graphic primitives such as lines, rectangles, circles and text boxes. The operations operating on these primitives are *create/delete, changeColor/changeBckColor, changePosition, changeSize, bringToFront/sendToBack, changeText* and *group/ungroup*.

In the case of conflicting operations, we have identified two types of conflict between the operations: real conflict and resolvable conflict.

Real conflicting operations are those conflicting operations for which a combined effect of their intentions cannot be established. A serialization order of execution of these operations cannot be obtained: executing one operation will prevent or completely mask the execution of the other operation. An example of real conflicting operations are two concurrent operations both targeting the same object and changing the colour of that object to different values.

The collaborative graphical editing system we have implemented is a customizable editor allowing groups of users to choose a policy for dealing with concurrency. Our system offers three policy modes in the case that a set of concurrent operations are conflicting: the null-effect based policy where none of the operations in conflict are executed, the priority based policy when only the operation issued by the user with the highest priority wins the conflict and the multi-versioning policy when the effects of all operations are maintained. The last of these has still to be implemented.

In the case of the null-effect based policy for dealing with conflicts, none of the concurrent real conflicting operations will be executed. In the case of the priority based policy, given a set of concurrent real conflicting operations, only the operation with the highest priority will be executed, the other operations being cancelled.

Resolvable conflicting operations are those conflicting operations for which a combined effect of their intentions can be obtained by serializing those operations. Consequently, ordering relations can be defined between any two concurrent operations. Any two resolvable conflicting operations can be defined as being in right order or in reverse order.

Although the model used for representing the text and, respectively, the graphical document is hierarchical and the same consistency model (causality preservation, convergence and intention preservation) has been applied to both text and graphical domains, the techniques used for achieving consistency are different. For maintaining consistency in the case of the object-based graphical documents, a serialization mechanism has been applied rather than the operation transformation principle as in the case of the text editor. In what follows we will give an explanation of this difference. As we have seen, the text document has been modelled as a set of paragraphs, each paragraph as a set of sentences and so on. Each semantic unit (paragraph, sentence, word, character) can be uniquely identified by its position in the sequence of the children elements of its parent. In order to achieve consistency, the insertion and deletion operations on these elements may shift the positions of the elements in the sequence of the children elements of their parent for adapting to the effect of concurrent operations. In the case of graphical documents, the objects are not organized into sequences and identified by their position in the sequence. Rather, they are identified by unique identifiers which are immutable. So, there is no need to adapt the identifiers due to the concurrent operations. Graphical objects in the case of graphical documents have associated attributes which are subject to concurrent operations. The elements in the tree model of the text document have no associated attributes. In the case that we want to associate different fonts and styles to elements of the text document, we could represent those elements using object identifiers and attach attributes such as font size to the elements.

3   Asynchronous Collaborative Editing Systems

In this section, we first describe briefly the copy/modify/merge paradigm supported by configuration management tools. Afterwards, we investigate how each of the steps of this paradigm can be implemented using the same basic mechanisms as for real-time collaboration.

3.1   Copy/Modify/Merge Techniques

All configuration management tools support the Copy/Modify/Merge technique. This technique consists basically of three operations applied on a shared repository storing multiversioned objects: checkout, commit and update.

A *checkout* operation creates a local working copy of an object from the repository.

A *commit* operation creates in the repository a new version of the corresponding object by validating the modifications done on the local copy of the object. The condition of performing this operation is that the repository does not contain a more recent version of the object to be committed than the local copy of the object.

An *update* operation performs the merging of the local copy of the object with the last version of that object stored in the repository.

In Fig. 2 a scenario is illustrated in order to show the functionality of the Copy/Modify/Merge paradigm. $User_1$ and $User_2$ checkout the document from the repository and create local copies in their private workspaces (operations 1 and 2, respectively). $User_1$ modifies the document (operation 3) and afterwards commits the changes (operation 4). $User_2$ modifies in parallel with $User_1$ the local copy of the document (operation 5). Afterwards, $User_2$ attempts to commit his changes (operation 6). But, at this stage, $User_2$ is not up-to-date and therefore cannot commit his changes on the document. $User_2$ needs to synchronize his version with the last version, so he downloads the last version of the document from the repository (operation 7). A merge algorithm will be performed in order to merge the changes performed in parallel by $User_1$ and $User_2$ (operation 8). Afterwards, $User_2$ can commit his changes to the repository (operation 9).

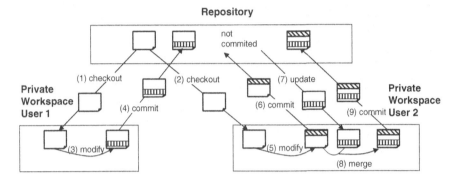

Fig. 2. Copy/Modify/Merge paradigm

Two different ways of performing the merging operations have been devised: state-based merging and operation-based merging.

State-based merging [2, 17] uses only information about the states of the documents and no information about the evolution of one state into another. In the merging process the two states of the document are compared and a delta is generated (the most well-known algorithm used is diff3 [11]). Afterwards, this delta is applied on one of the states of the document to generate the document state representing the result of merging.

Operation-based merging [10, 15] keeps the information about the evolution of one state of the document into another in a buffer containing the operations performed between the two states of the document. The merging is done by executing the operations performed on a copy of the document onto the other copy of the document to be merged.

In what follows we analyze the problems that arise at the committing stage when a user commits a copy from the private workspace into the repository and at the updating stage when the copy from the private workspace is updated by a version from the repository.

3.2   Committing Stage

In the case that a user wants to commit the working copy into the repository, he sends a request to the repository server. In the case that the process of another concurrent committing request is under current development, the request is queued in a waiting list. Otherwise, in the case that the base version (the last updated version from the repository) in the private workspace is not the same as the last version in the repository, the repository sends to the site a negative answer that the site needs to update its working copy before committing. In the case that the base version from the working space is the same as the last version in the repository, the site will receive a positive answer. Afterwards, the site sends to the repository the log of operations representing the delta between the last version in the repository and the current copy from the workspace and increases the base version number. Upon receiving the list of operations, the repository executes sequentially the operations from the log and updates the number of the latest version.

3.3   Updating Stage

Merging at the updating stage is more difficult to achieve than the merging at the committing stage. Updates made on a committed working copy by another user cannot be simply reapplied in the private working space, because they were generated in another context. In the updating stage, a set of conflicts among operations occurs.

Our aim is to find a unifying approach for collaborative text and graphical editors working in both synchronous and asynchronous modes.

In the case of the real-time collaborative text editor application, the semantics are somehow already incorporated in the way of resolving the conflicts. Always there is a way of combining the individual intentions of the users to obtain a group intention (although this does not completely satisfy the individual intentions). For example, consider a shared document consisting of the sentence: *"He has discovered that we do not like his company."* Suppose two users concurrently edit the copies of this document, the first one inserting the word *"finally"* in order to obtain *"He has finally discovered that we do not like his company."* and the second one deleting *"He has discovered that"* in order to obtain *"we do not like his company."* After performing both operations the result will be *"finally we do not like his company."* which is not what either of the users expected. However, the use of different colours provides awareness of concurrent changes made by other users and the users can further edit the result.

As we have already seen, in the case of the real conflicting operations for the graphical editor, the individual intentions of the users cannot be respected. For instance, consider the case of two users concurrently moving the same object to different positions. The only way of respecting the intentions of the two users is by creating versions of the object, which might not be the preferred solution. As alternative solutions, the collaborative graphical editor offers a null-effect based policy, i.e. none of the two operations will be executed, or the priority based policy where the operation of the user that has the highest priority is executed.

Our solution for dealing with conflicts in a flexible way is to allow the possibility to specify, both for the text and graphical editor, a set of rules that define the conflicts as well as a function showing if there is a conflict between any two operations in a certain context. The conflicts can therefore be defined specifically for any application domain. In this way, we make a distinction between the syntactic and semantic consistency. *Syntactic consistency* means to reconcile the divergent copies by using either operational transformation or a serialization mechanism. It ensures that all sites have the same view, even if that view has no meaning in the context of the application. On the other hand, *semantic consistency* is defined specifically for an application, in our approach being modelled by the set of rules that specify the conflicts. For resolving the conflicts, either an automatic solution can be provided or human intervention can be required. Different merge policies in the context of various collaborative activities have been analysed in [13].

In Fig. 3, we have sketched the updating stage of the merging. In the repository, the difference between version V_{n+1} and version V_n is represented by the sequence of operations $DL = [O_{d1}, O_{d2}, ..., O_{dm}]$. In the private workspace of a site, after the checkout of version V_n from the repository, the local copy of the document W_0 has been updated by the sequence of operations $LL = [O_{l1}, O_{l2}, ..., O_{lk}]$ to the local copy W_k. Afterwards, the local copy W_k needs to be updated with the version V_{n+1} from the repository. So, a merge between the sequence of operations from list DL and the operations from LL will be performed in order to obtain the local copy W_{k+1}. Afterwards a commit can be performed to the repository. But, in order to perform a commit, the difference between the local copy in the private workspace (W_{k+1}) and the last updated version from the repository (V_{n+1}) should be computed.

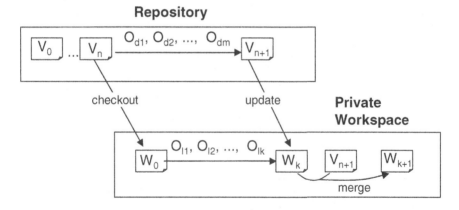

Fig. 3. The updating stage of the Copy/Modify/Merge paradigm

From the list DL of operations, not all of them will be re-executed in the private workspace because some of these operations may be semantically in conflict with some of the operations in the list LL.

A nonconflicting operation needs to be integrated into the log LL of operations in the same way a remote operation is integrated into the history buffer of a site in the case of the real-time mode of communication, as described in [7].

In the case that some conflicting operations precede a nonconflicting operation O, O needs to be transformed before its integration into LL. The transformation consists of excluding from O the effect of the conflicting operations (by applying the exclusion transformation) because the context of definition of O changed. The new form of O can then be integrated into the list LL.

In order to compute the difference between the local copy in the private workspace (W_{k+1}) and the last updated version from the repository (V_{n+1}), the operations in LL need to be transformed according to the sequence of operations from DL that have been re-executed in the private workspace. Moreover, the fact that some operations from DL have been in conflict with some of the operations in LL and could not be executed in the private workspace needs to be included into the delta as their inverse in order to cancel the effect of those operations. For instance, the inverse of the operation of inserting the word *"love"* in paragraph 2, sentence 3, as the 4th word, *InsertWord(2,3,4, "love")*, is *DeleteWord(2,3,4, "love")*.

Let us give an example to illustrate the asynchronous communication. Suppose the repository contains as version V_0 the document consisting of only one paragraph with one sentence: *"He enjoy going to cinemas."* Suppose two operations concurrently inserting the same character in the same position in the document are conflicting. Further, suppose two users check out version V_0 from the repository into their private workspaces and have as first version in their private workspace $W_{10} = V_0$ and $W_{20} = V_0$ respectively. The first user performs operations O_{11} and O_{12}, where $O_{11}=InsertSentence("He loves movies.", 1,1)$ and $O_{12}=InsertCharacter("s", 1,2,2,6)$. Operation O_{11} inserts the sentence *"He loves movies."* in the first paragraph as the first sentence, in order to obtain the version $W_{11}=$ *"He loves movies. He enjoy going to cinemas."* Operation O_{12} inserts the character *"s"* in paragraph 1, sentence 2, word 2, as the last character (position 6) in order to obtain the version $W_{12}=$ *"He loves movies. He enjoys going to cinemas."* The second user performs the operations O_{21} and O_{22}, $O_{21}=InsertCharacter("s", 1,1,2,6)$ and $O_{22}=DeleteCharacter(1,1,5,7)$. Operation O_{21} inserts character *"s"* to correct the spelling of the word *"enjoy"* in order to obtain $W_{21}=$ *"He enjoys going to cinemas."* Operation O_{22} deletes the last character from the word *"cinemas"* in order to obtain $W_{21}=$ *"He enjoys going to cinema."*

Suppose that, after performing these operations, both users try to commit, but $User_1$ gets access to the repository first, while $User_2$'s request will be queued. After the commit operation of $User_1$, the last version in the repository will be $V_1=$ *"He loves movies. He enjoys going to cinemas."* and the list DL_{01} representing the difference between V_1 and V_0 in the repository will be $[O_{11}, O_{12}]$.

When $User_2$ gets access to the repository he will receive a message to update the local copy. At this moment, a merge between the list of operations DL_{01} and the local list $[O_{21}, O_{22}]$ is performed, i.e. according to the semantic rules, O_{11} and O_{12} will be integrated into the local list. There is no semantic conflict between O_{11} and either of the operations O_{21} and O_{22}. Moreover, neither of the operations O_{21} and O_{22} are operations of sentence insertion, so, according to the treeOPT algorithm, the execution form of O_{11} is the same as its original form, i.e. $O'_{11} = InsertSentence(\text{"He loves movies."}, 1,1)$. Operation O_{12} will not be executed because O_{12} and O_{21} are conflicting operations. As a result of merging, the current state of the document is: *"He loves movies. He enjoys going to cinema."* In order to compute the difference DL_{21} between the current copy of the document of $User_2$ and version V_1 in the repository, the operations in the local list $[O_{21}, O_{22}]$ need to be transformed according to the nonconflicting operations from DL_{01}, i.e. operation O_{11}. Because O_{11} inserts a sentence before the target sentence of operations O_{21} and O_{22}, operations O_{21} and O_{22}, will have their execution form: $O'_{21} = InsertCharacter(\text{"s"}, 1,2,2,6)$ and $O'_{22} = DeleteCharacter(1,2,5,7)$. Since O_{12} was a conflicting operation, $DL_{21} = [inverse(O_{12}), O'_{21}, O'_{22}]$.

When $User_1$ will update the local workspace, the operations in DL_{21} need to be executed in their form, because no other concurrent operations have been executed in the local workspace of $User_1$ since the creation of version V_1. So, the local copy of the document will be *"He loves movies. He enjoys going to cinema."*

We can see that, for the collaborative text editor, the same principle of operation transformation for integrating an operation into a log containing concurrent operations applies both for asynchronous communication as well as for real-time communication. As in the case of the real-time mode of communication, also in the case of the asynchronous mode of collaboration, a set of improvements can be obtained because of the way of structuring the document. Only a few transformations need to be performed when integrating an operation into a log as described above, because the operations in the log are distributed throughout the tree model of the document. Only those histories that are distributed along a certain path in the tree are spanned and not the whole log as in the case of a linear model of the document. For example, two operations inserting words in two different paragraphs will not need to be transformed because they do not interfere with each other. Moreover, the function for testing if two operations are conflicting can be expressed more easily using the semantic units used for structuring the documents (paragraphs, sentences, words, characters) than in the case of a linear representation of the document. For example, rules interdicting the concurrent insertion of two different words into the same sentence could be very easily expressed and checked.

The same extension from the synchronous to the asynchronous mode of communication can be achieved in the case of the graphical editor. In the case of the updating stage of the asynchronous communication, and more specifically in the case of merging, instead of using the operational transformation approach as in the case of the text document, the serialization approach together with the undo/redo scheme can be used in the same way it was used for real-time communication. The set of conflicting operations can be expressed in the function for defining the semantic conflicts between the operations. For integrating an operation into a log containing other concurrent operations, an undo/redo scheme is performed taking into account a set of serialization rules as explained in [8].

4   Related Work

We have already presented the advantages of our approach that uses a hierarchical structure over the other approaches that use a linear structure for the representation of the document.

In the case of the asynchronous communication, we have adopted the same merging mechanism as in FORCE [15]. It is best suited to our requirements since it uses operation-based merging and semantic rules for resolving conflicts. However, in [15], the approach is described only for the linear representation of text documents. The hierarchical representation that we have adopted in our approach yields a set of advantages such as an increased efficiency and improvements in the semantics. Moreover, we have described the synchronous/ asynchronous modes of communication, not only for the case of text documents, but also for graphical documents. Our goal is to build a general information platform supporting multi-mode collaboration over general types of documents. So far, we have considered text and graphical documents as representative for our research.

Other research works looked at the tree representation of documents in the case of the collaborative editing. In [18] an XML diff algorithm has been proposed. The approach uses a state-based merging involving a complex mechanism to compute the difference between the two tree structures representing the initial and the final document, respectively. This difference is represented as a set of operations that transforms the initial document into the final one. Our approach is operation-based, the operations being kept in a history buffer during the editing process, and therefore the comparison of tree structures is unnecessary.

The dARB algorithm [9] uses a tree structure for representing the document and an arbitration scheme for resolving the conflicts in the case of the real-time collaboration. The arbitration scheme decides to keep the intentions of only one user in the case that some users perform concurrent operations that access the same node in the tree. The arbitration is done according to priorities assigned to operation types. For instance, the operations to create/delete words are assigned a greater priority than the operations that modify a character in the word. There are cases when one site wins the arbitration and it needs to send, not only the state of the vertex itself, but maybe also the state of the parent or grandparent of the vertex. For example, if one user performs a split of a sentence, while another user concurrently performs some modification in the original sentence, the user performing the split will win the arbitration and need to send to all other users the state of the whole paragraph that contains the sentence. By allowing the customization of specifying the conflicts for various application domains, our approach is more general than the one defined in [9] that considers any concurrent operations performed on a vertex of a tree to be conflicting. By using operational transformation, we try to accommodate the intentions of all the users and we do not need the retransmission of whole sentences, paragraphs or, indeed, the whole document in order to maintain the same tree structure of the document at all sites.

In [3], the operational transformation was applied to documents written in dialects of SGML such as XML and HTML. However, the approach was applied only for the real-time communication of these types of documents.

In [12], the authors proposed the use of the operational transformation approach for defining a general algorithm for synchronizing a file system and file contents. The main difference between our approach and the one in [12] is that, in our approach, semantic conflicts among operations can be defined specifically for any application domain, while the synchronizer proposed in [12] automatically finds a solution in the case of conflict.

5   Concluding Remarks

Rather than adopting a single solution for supporting collaboration, we propose a customizable approach that can be adapted for various application domains and can offer a set of solutions for the different stages of the development of a common task. In this paper, we have described the solutions that we offer, both in terms of the types of documents that form the basic unit of collaboration, i.e. textual and graphical, and also in terms of the modes of collaboration, i.e. synchronous and asynchronous. We have shown how the algorithms necessary for supporting the asynchronous functionality extend the consistency maintenance algorithms that we previously developed for real-time collaboration.

We use a general structured model of the document that offers a set of enhanced features such as increased efficiency and improvements in the semantics and allows a general consistency model to be found for multi-mode collaboration.

We plan to evaluate our system according to some suggestions given in [4], mainly by performing user studies for testing the functionality of our systems and by measuring performance.

References

1. Bellini, P., Nesi, P., Spinu, M.B.: Cooperative visual manipulation of music notation. ACM Trans. on CHI, vol.9, no.3, Sept 2002, pp.194-237.
2. Berliner, B.: CVS II: Parallelizing software development. Proceedings of USENIX, Washington D.C., 1990.
3. Davis, A.H., Sun, C.: Generalizing operational transformation to the Standard General Markup Language. Proc. of CSCW, 2002, pp. 58-67.
4. Dewan, P.: An integrated approach to designing and evaluating collaborative applications and infrastructures. CSCW, no. 10, 2001, pp. 75-111.
5. Ellis, C.A., Gibbs, S.J.: Concurrency control in groupware systems. Proc. of the ACM SIGMOD Conf. on Management of Data, May 1989, pp. 399-407.
6. Ignat, C.L., Norrie, M.C.: Tree-based model algorithm for maintaining consistency in real-time collaborative editing systems. The 4th Intl. Workshop on Collaborative Editing, CSCW, New Orleans, USA, Nov. 2002.

7. Ignat, C.L., Norrie, M.C.: Customizable collaborative editor relying on treeOPT algorithm. Proc. of the 8th ECSCW, Helsinki, Finland, Sept. 2003, pp. 315-334.
8. Ignat, C.L., Norrie, M.C.: Grouping/ungrouping in graphical collaborative editing systems. IEEE Distributed Systems online, The 5th Intl. Workshop on Collaborative Editing, 8th ECSCW, Helsinki, Finland, Sept. 2003.
9. Ionescu, M., Marsic, I.: Tree-based concurrency control in distributed groupware. CSCW: The Journal of Collaborative Computing, vol. 12, no. 3, 2003.
10. Lippe, E., van Oosterom, N.: Operation-based merging. Proc. of the 5th ACM SIGSOFT Symposium on Software development environments, 1992, pp. 78-87.
11. Miller, W., Myers, E.W.: A file comparison program. Software - Practice and Experience, 15(1), 1990, pp. 1025-1040.
12. Molli, P., Oster, G., Skaf-Molli, H., and Imine, A.: Using the transformational approach to build a safe and generic data synchronizer, Group 2003 Conf., Nov. 2003.
13. Munson, J.P., Dewan, P.: A flexible object merging framework. Proc. of the ACM Conf. on CSCW, 1994, pp 231-242.
14. Ressel, M., Nitsche-Ruhland, D., Gunzenbauser, R.: An integrating, transformation-oriented approach to concurrency control and undo in group editors. Proc. of the ACM Conf. on CSCW, Nov. 1996, pp. 288-297.
15. Shen, H., Sun, C.: Flexible merging for asynchronous collaborative systems. Proc. of CoopIS/DOA/ODBASE 2002, pp. 304-321.
16. Sun, C., Ellis, C.: Operational transformation in real-time group editors: Issues, algorithms, and achievements. Proc. of the ACM Conf. on CSCW, Seattle, Nov. 1998, pp. 59-68.
17. Tichy, W.F.: RCS- A system for version control. Software - Practice and Experience, 15(7), Jul. 1985, pp. 637-654.
18. Torii, O., Kimura, T., Segawa, J.: The consistency control system of XML documents. Symposium on Applications and the Internet, Jan. 2003.
19. Vidot, N., Cart, M., Ferrié, J., Suleiman, M.: Copies convergence in a distributed real-time collaborative environment. Proc. of the ACM Conf. on CSCW, Philadelphia, USA, Dec. 2000, pp.171-180.

Author Index

Lecture Notes in Computer Science

For information about Vols. 1–2976

please contact your bookseller or Springer-Verlag